HISTORY OF THE COMMUNIST PARTY
OF THE UNITED STATES

BY THE SAME AUTHOR:

Outline Political History of the Americas

The Twilight of World Capitalism

American Trade Unionism: Principles and Organization, Strategy and Tactics

Pages from a Worker's Life

HISTORY
OF THE
COMMUNIST PARTY
OF THE
UNITED STATES

By William Z. Foster

INTERNATIONAL PUBLISHERS, NEW YORK

COPYRIGHT, 1952, BY
INTERNATIONAL PUBLISHERS CO., INC.

PRINTED IN THE UNITED STATES OF AMERICA

CONTENTS

PREFACE   13

1. **EARLY AMERICAN CLASS STRUGGLES (1793-1848)**   16
   Jeffersonian Democracy, 16 ... The Beginnings of the Trade Union Movement, 18 ... Labor's First Steps Toward Independent Political Action, 20 ... Ideology of the Early Labor Movement, 21 ... Utopian Socialism, 22

2. **PIONEER MARXISTS IN THE UNITED STATES (1848-1860)**   26
   German Marxist Immigrants, 27 ... Weydemeyer, Pioneer of American Socialism, 28 ... The Proletarian League, 29 ... Formation of the Communist Club, 31 ... Laying the Theoretical Foundations of Marxism in the U.S., 32

3. **MARXISTS IN THE STRUGGLE AGAINST SLAVERY (1848-1865)**
   The Abolitionist Movement, 37 ... The Role of the Marxists, 38 ... The Maturing of the Crisis, 40 ... The Election of Abraham Lincoln, 41 ... The Civil War, 43 ... The Negro People and the Working Class in the War, 45 ... Role and Strategy of the Marxists in the War Period, 47

4. **THE INTERNATIONAL WORKINGMEN'S ASSOCIATION (1864-1876)**   50
   From Revolution to Counter-Revolution, 50 ... The Marxists and the National Labor Union, 53 ... The N.L.U. and the Negro Question, 54 ... The N. L. U. and the First International, 56 ... The Decline of the National Labor Union, 56 ... The Marxists and the Lassalleans, 58 ... Dissolution of the First International, 60

5. **THE SOCIALIST LABOR PARTY (1876-1890)**   62
   The S.L.P. and the Great Railroad Strike, 63 ... Workers' and Farmers'

Political Struggles, 64 . . . The Anarcho-Syndicalist Movement, 66 . . . The Knights of Labor, 68 . . . The American Federation of Labor, 69 . . . The National Eight-Hour Fight, 71 . . . The Henry George Campaign, 73 . . . The Status of the S.L.P. in 1890, 74

6. **THE S.L.P.: DE LEONISM AND DECLINE (1890-1900)** 77

   Fierce Labor Struggles, 78 . . . The Role of De Leon, 79 . . . The S.L.P. and the Trade Unions, 82 . . . The Socialist Trades and Labor Alliance, 84 . . . Labor Party and Populist Movement, 85 . . . The S.L.P. and the Negro, 86 . . . The Decline of the Socialist Labor Party, 88 . . . The Split in the S.L.P., 89

7. **THE SOCIALIST PARTY (1900-1905)** 91

   Corruption of the A.F. of L. Leadership, 92 . . . Formation of the Socialist Party, 94 . . . The Socialist Party Program, 95 . . . The Employers' Open-Shop Offensive, 97 . . . Socialist Party Activity, 98 . . . The Formation of the I.W.W., 100 . . . The Status of the Party, 101 . . . The Party's Chauvinist Negro Policy, 103 . . . Opportunist Influence of the Second International, 105

8. **THE HEYDAY OF THE SOCIALIST PARTY (1905-1914)** 107

   The Conditions of the Workers, 108 . . . The Fight of the Trade Unions, 109 . . . The Struggle of the I.W.W., 110 . . . Growth of the Socialist Party, 112 . . . Renaissance of the Negro Liberation Movement, 114 . . . Formation of the Syndicalist League, 117 . . . The New Freedom and the Square Deal, 118 . . . Lefts Versus Rights in the Party, 119 . . . The S.P. Split in 1912, 122 . . . The Status of the Left Wing, 123

9. **WORLD WAR I: SOCIAL-DEMOCRATIC BETRAYAL (1914-1918)** 127

   The Great Social-Democratic Betrayal, 128 . . . The U.S. During the Early Years of the War, 130 . . . The U.S. Joins the War, 132 . . . The Socialists and the War, 134 . . . The I.W.W. and the War, 136 . . . The I.T.U.E.L., 137 . . . Government Terror Against the Left, 140

10. **THE RUSSIAN REVOLUTION (1917-1919)** 143

    U.S. Intervention, 144 . . . The Social-Democrats Betray the Revolution, 145 . . . Impact of the Revolution on the American Labor Movement, 147 . . . The Teachings of Marxism-Leninism, 148 . . . Marxism-Leninism and the American Marxists, 151

11. THE SPLIT IN THE SOCIALIST PARTY (1919) — 157
   The Long Internal Struggle, 157 . . . The Immediate Causes of the 1919 Split, 158 . . . The Relationship of Party Forces, 160 . . . The Developing Struggle, 161 . . . Hillquit's "Pink Terror," 163 . . . The National Left-Wing Conference, 164 . . . The Left Wing Manifesto, 166 . . . The Decline of the Socialist Party, 169

12. THE FORMATION OF THE COMMUNIST PARTY (1919-1921) — 171
   The Two Communist Conventions, 171 . . . The Communist Programs, 172 . . . The Palmer Raids, 174 . . . Formation of the United Communist Party, 177 . . . The Role of the Communist International, 178 . . . Party Unity Achieved, 180 . . . Concentrating the Communist Forces, 182

13. THE WORKERS PARTY (1921) — 186
   The American Labor Alliance, 187 . . . The Workers Council, 188 . . . Formation of the Workers Party, 189 . . . The Workers Party Program, 191 . . . The Party Asserts Its Democratic Rights, 194

14. THE COMMUNISTS AND THE CAPITALIST OFFENSIVE (1919-1923) — 196
   The First Blow Falls Upon the Left, 198 . . . The Drive Against the Trade Unions, 198 . . . Misleaders of Labor, 201 . . . The Communist Party Breaks Its Isolation, 202 . . . Early Activities of the T.U.E.L., 203 . . . Mass Campaigns of the T.U.E.L., 205 . . . The A.F. of L. Convention of 1923, 207 . . . Defense of Class War Prisoners, 208

15. THE COMMUNISTS AND THE LaFOLLETTE MOVEMENT (1922-1924) — 211
   The Developing LaFollette Movement, 213 . . . The Workers Party and the Farmer-Labor Party, 215 . . . The Federated Farmer Labor Party Convention, 216 . . . The Farmer-Labor Party, 217 . . . Tactical Mistakes of the Workers Party, 219 . . . Factionalism in the Workers Party, 221 . . . The Death of Lenin, 223

16. TOWARD NEGRO-WHITE LABOR SOLIDARITY (1919-1924) — 225
   The Garvey Movement, 226 . . . Attempts to Divide Negro and White Workers, 228 . . . Growing Unity Between Negro and White Workers, 230 . . . The Communists and Negro-White Co-operation, 232 . . . A New Stage in the Negro People's Movement, 234

17. **A.F. OF L. CLASS COLLABORATION DURING THE COOLIDGE "PROSPERITY" (1923-1929)** 236

The Speed-Up, or "Rationalization," Drive, 237 ... The Unions as Speed-Up Agencies of the Bosses, 239 ... Ford Versus Marx, 240 ... "The Higher Strategy of Labor," 242 ... Degeneration of the Labor Bureaucracy, 243 ... The Bill of Reckoning, 245

18. **COMMUNIST CLASS STRUGGLE POLICIES (1923-1929)** 247

The Expulsion Policy, 248 ... Hard-Fought Textile Strikes, 250 ... The Needle Trades Strikes, 252 ... The Struggle in the Mining Industry, 255 ... Formation of the T.U.U.L., 257 ... International Labor Unity, 259

19. **BUILDING THE PARTY OF THE NEW TYPE (1919-1929)** 260

Party Work Among Women and the Youth, 263 ... The Death of Ruthenberg, 264 ... The Sixth World Congress of the Comintern, 265 ... The Negro Question as a National Question, 266 ... The American Negro Labor Congress, 268 ... The Expulsion of the Trotskyites, 269 ... Lovestone and Exceptionalism, 270 ... The Unification of the Party, 274

20. **THE COMMUNIST PARTY AND THE GREAT ECONOMIC CRISIS (1929-1933)** 276

Marxists Anticipate the Crisis and Gird for the Storm, 277 ... Hoover's Starvation Policies, 279 ... A.F. of L. and S.P. Political Bankruptcy, 280 ... The Communists Lead the Mass Struggle: March 6th, 281 ... Unemployed Councils and Hunger Marches, 282 ... The Fight Against Wage Cuts, 284 ... The Penetration of the South, 285 ... The Farmers' Revolt, 288 ... The National "Bonus March," 289 ... The Presidential Elections of 1932, 290 ... The Status of the Party and the Y.C.L., 291

21. **EARLY STRUGGLES UNDER THE NEW DEAL (1933-1936)** 293

Why Not Fascism in the U.S.?, 295 ... The National Industrial Recovery Act, 296 ... Beginning of the Mass Struggle, 297 ... The Big Strike Movement of 1934-36, 298 ... The San Francisco General Strike, 300 ... The T.U.U.L. Merges with the A.F. of L., 303 ... The Formation of the C.I.O., 304 ... The Growing Communist Party, 307

22. **THE BROAD DEMOCRATIC STRUGGLE (1933-1936)** — 308

The National Negro Congress, 308 . . . The American Youth Congress, 309 . . . The Women's Movement, 312 . . . The "Panacea" Mass Movements, 314 . . . The Cultural Upsurge, 317 . . . The Seventh Comintern Congress and the Roosevelt Coalition, 320 . . . The Communist Party and the Nation, 323

23. **ROOSEVELT AND WALL STREET (1933-1936)** — 325

Wall Street's Attack Upon the New Deal, 326 . . . The American Liberty League, 327 . . . Roosevelt Fights Back, 328 . . . The Elections of 1936, 330 . . . Labor in the Elections, 332 . . . The Political Line of the Communist Party, 334 . . . Browder and American Democratic Traditions, 336

24. **THE COMMUNISTS IN THE BUILDING OF THE C.I.O. (1936-1940)** — 340

The A.F. of L. Leaders Sabotage the Campaign, 342 . . . Labor's Solidarity Overcomes All Obstacles, 343 . . . The Role of the Communist Party, 345 . . . The Communists in the Steel Industry, 349 . . . The Communists in the Auto Industry, 351 . . . The Communists and Progressives in Other Industries, 353

25. **THE GOOD NEIGHBOR POLICY (1933-1941)** — 356

The Yankee Record of Exploitation and Tyranny, 357 . . . American Imperialism Gets a "New Look," 359 . . . The Stunted Economy of Latin America, 360 . . . The Exploited and Famished Peoples of Latin America, 362 . . . The Latin American Peoples Fight Against Fascism, 363 . . . The Communist Party and Latin America, 365

26. **THE FIGHT AGAINST FASCISM AND WAR (1935-1939)** — 368

The Soviets for Collective Security, 369 . . . The People's Front, 370 . . . The Spanish Civil War, 371 . . . Munich and War, 373 . . . The U.S. and the War, 375 . . . The American People—Anti-Fascist and Anti-War, 377 . . . The Elections of 1938, 379 . . . The Growth of the Communist Party, 380

27. **WORLD WAR II: THE EARLY WAR PHASES (1939-1941)** — 383

The "Phony" War, 384 . . . American Reactions to the War, 386 . . The Communist Position on the War, 387 . . . Roosevelt Heads Toward War,

389 ... The 1940 Elections, 390 ... Persecution of the Party, 391 ... The America First Committee, 393 ... Hitler Marches Toward Disaster, 394

28. WORLD WAR II: THE PEOPLE'S ANTI-FASCIST WAR (1941-1945) — 396

The Great German Offensive, 397 ... The Japanese Attack Upon Pearl Harbor, 398 ... The Soviets March to Victory, 398 ... The Question of the Western Front, 400 ... The War Against Japan, 402 ... An Estimate of World War II, 404

29. THE COMMUNISTS IN THE WAR (1941-1945) — 408

The Battle for Production, 410 ... The Fight for the Second Front, 412 ... The Fair Employment Practices Commission, 413 ... The Dissolution of the Communist International, 414 ... Opportunist Conception of National Unity, 415 ... Browder's Plan for Organized Capitalism, 417 ... Browder's Opportunism and the Chinese Revolution, 419 ... The Party and the Masses, 420

30. THE COMMUNIST POLITICAL ASSOCIATION (1944-1945) — 422

The Essence of Browder's Opportunism, 425 ... How Browder's Revisionism Originated, 427 ... Foster Opposes Browder's Line, 428 ... Dissolution of the Communist Party, 430 ... Effects Upon Mass Work, 432 ... Growing Opposition in the C.P.A., 433 ... The Duclos Article, 434 ... The Emergency Convention, 435 ... The Expulsion of Browder, 437

31. THE REVOLUTIONARY AFTERMATH OF THE WAR (1945-1951) — 439

The Advance of the Soviet Union, 439 ... The Rise of the European People's Democracies, 441 ... The People's Revolution in China, 442 ... The Advance of the American Negro People, 444 ... The World Federation of Trade Unions, 446 ... World Organizations of Women and Youth, 447 ... The Post-War Upsurge Among Cultural Workers, 448 ... The Growth of the Communist Parties, 449 ... The Capitalist and Socialist Worlds, 451

32. AMERICAN IMPERIALISM DRIVES FOR WORLD MASTERY (1948-1951) — 452

American Capitalist Hegemony, 452 ... Forces Behind Wall Street's War Drive, 454 ... The Peace Will of the Peoples, 457 ... The U.S. Pushes

Toward War, 459 ... The Trend Toward Fascism, 463 ... Building a Police State in the U.S., 465

33. **THE COMMUNIST PARTY AND THE "COLD WAR" (1945-1951)** 469

    The Nine-Party Communist Conference, 470 ... The 1948 Elections, 471 ... The Party and the Korean War, 473 ... Anti-War Activities of the Party, 474 .. The Communists and the Negro People, 476 ... The Formation of the Labor Youth League, 479 ... The Communists and the Republic of Israel, 479 ... The Question of Keynesism, 481 ... The Party Meets the Test, 484

34. **AMERICAN IMPERIALISM HOBBLES THE TRADE UNION MOVEMENT (1945-1951)** 485

    The Taft-Hartley Law, 487 ... Labor and the Marshall Plan, 489 ... The Split in the C.I.O., 491 ... The A.F. of L.-C.I.O. Attack Upon the C.T.A.L., 495 ... The Attempt to Wreck the W.F.T.U., 496 ... The Crisis of the American Labor Movement, 500 ... The Independent Unions, 503

35. **PERSECUTION OF THE COMMUNIST PARTY (1945-1951)** 506

    The Sharpening Attack Against the Left, 506 ... The Indictment of the Communist Party, 509 ... A Political Persecution, 510 ... The Government's Case, 511 ... The Party Fights Back, 514 ... The Supreme Court Sustains the Frame-Up, 516 ... Multiplying Raids and Persecutions, 518 ... The McCarran Act, 519 ... The Situation of the Communist Party, 521

36. **VICTORY AHEAD FOR THE PEOPLE** 524

    What If War Comes?, 526 ... A Suicidal War for Capitalism, 528 ... The Decay of World Capitalism, 530 ... The U.S. and the General Crisis, 533 ... Bourgeois Culture and the Crisis, 535 ... Socialism, the Basic Answer, 537

37. **THE AMERICAN WORKING CLASS AND SOCIALISM** 541

    Factors Retarding the Ideological Development of the Workers, 542 ... Factors Making for Class Consciousness, 544 ... The Impoverishment of the Workers, 545 ... The Workers Will Turn to Socialism, 547 ... The American Road to Socialism, 549 ... Lessons of Communist World Experience, 557

38. **THE PARTY OF THE WORKING CLASS AND THE NATION**   560

The Communist Party as Working Class Leader, 560 ... The Communist Party and the Negro People, 562 ... The Communist Party and Other Democratic Strata, 563 ... The Communist Party, the Party of the Nation, 564 ... Socialism in the National Interest, 566 ... The Party's Immediate Demands, 567 ... The Progress of the Communist Party, 570

APPENDIX   573

INDEX   575

Acknowledgments

The author wishes to thank all those who helped in the preparation of this history of the Communist Party. Their cooperation covered a wide range of work—extensive research in many fields, the writing of various studies, and the reading and correcting of the manuscript and proofs. Of especially great value were the large number of penetrating criticisms and constructive proposals made by these co-workers, without which this history could not have been written.

William Z. Foster

1. Early American Class Struggles (1793-1848)

The history of the Communist Party of the United States is the history of the vanguard party of the American working class. It is the story and analysis of the origin, growth, and development of a working class political party of a new type, called into existence by the epoch of imperialism, the last stage of capitalism, and by the emergence of a new social system—Socialism. It is the record of a Party which through its entire existence of more than three decades has loyally fought for the best interests of the American working class and its allies—the Negro people, the toiling farmers, the city middle classes—who are the great majority of the American people. It is the life of a Party destined to lead the American working class and its allies to victory over the monopoly warmongers and fascists, to a people's democracy and socialism.

The life story of the Communist Party is also the history of Marxism for a century in the United States. The C.P.U.S.A. is the inheritor and continuer of the many American Marxist parties and organizations which preceded it during this long period. It incorporates in itself the lessons of generations of political struggle by the working class; of the world experience of the First, Second, and Third Internationals; of the writings of the great Socialist theoreticians, Marx, Engels, Lenin, Stalin; and of the great revolutions in Russia, China, and Central and Eastern Europe. It is also the continuation and culmination of American scientific, democratic, and artistic culture, embracing and carrying forward all that is sound and constructive in the works of Franklin, Jefferson, Douglass, Lincoln, Morgan, Edison, Twain, Dreiser, and a host of American thinkers, writers, and creators.

The Party history is the record of the American class struggle, of which it is a vital part. It is the story, in general, of the growth of the working class; the abolition of slavery and emancipation of the Negro people; the building of the trade union and farmer movements; the numberless strikes and political struggles of the toiling masses; and the growing political alliance of workers, Negroes, farmers, and intellectuals. The Party is the crystallization of the best in all these rich democratic and revolutionary traditions of the people; it is the embodiment of the toilers' aspirations for freedom and a better life.

The story of the Communist Party is also necessarily the history, in outline, of American capitalism. It is the account and analysis of the revolutionary liberation from British domination and establishment of the Republic, the expansion of the national frontiers, the development of industry and agriculture, the armed overthrow of the southern slavocracy, the recurring economic crises, the brutal exploitation of the workers, the poles of wealth and poverty, the growth of monopoly and development of imperialism, the savage robbery of the colonial peoples, the great world wars, the barbarities of fascism, the bid of American imperialism for world domination, the fight of the people for world peace, the general crisis of capitalism, and the development of the world class struggle, under expanding Marxist-Leninist leadership, toward socialism.

JEFFERSONIAN DEMOCRACY

The American Revolution of 1776, which Lenin called one of the "great, really liberating, really revolutionary wars,"[1] began the history of the modern capitalist United States. It was fought by a coalition of merchants, planters, small farmers, and white and Negro toilers. It was led chiefly by the merchant capitalists, with the democratic masses doing the decisive fighting. The Revolution, by establishing American national independence, shattered the restrictions placed upon the colonial productive forces by England; it freed the national market and opened the way for a speedy growth of trade and industry; it at least partially broke down the feudal system of land tenure; and it brought limited political rights to the small farmers and also to the workers, who were mostly artisans, but it did not destroy Negro chattel slavery. And for the embattled Indian peoples the Revolution produced only a still more vigorous effort to strip them of their lands and to destroy them.

The Revolution also had far-reaching international repercussions. It helped inspire the people of France to get rid of their feudal tyrants; it stimulated the peoples of Latin America to free themselves from the yoke of Spain and Portugal; and it was an energizing force in the world wherever the bourgeoisie, supported by the democratic masses, were fighting against feudalism. The Revolution was helped to success by the assistance given the rebelling colonies by France, Spain, and Holland, as well as by revolutionary struggles taking place currently in Ireland and England.

The Revolution was fought under the broad generalizations of the Declaration of Independence, written by Thomas Jefferson, which called for national independence and freedom for all men. It declared the right

[1] V. I. Lenin, *A Letter to American Workers*, p. 9, N. Y., 1934.

of revolution and the dominance of the secular over the religious in government. But these principles meant very different things to the several classes that carried through the Revolution. To the merchants they signified their rise to dominant power and an unrestricted opportunity to exploit the rest of the population. To the planters they implied the continuation and extension of their slave system. To the farmers they meant free access to the broad public lands. To the workers they promised universal suffrage, more democratic liberties, and a greater share in the wealth of the new land. And to the oppressed Negroes they brought a new hope of freedom from the misery and sufferings of chattel bondage.

The Constitution, as originally formulated in 1787, and as adopted in the face of powerful opposition, consisted primarily of the rules and relationships agreed upon by the ruling class for the management of the society which they controlled. The Bill of Rights, the first ten amendments of the Constitution, providing for freedom of speech, press, and assembly, religious liberty, trial by jury, and other popular democratic liberties, was written into the Constitution in 1791 under heavy mass pressure.[1]

Great as were the accomplishments of the Revolution, it nevertheless left unsolved many bourgeois-democratic tasks. These unfinished tasks constituted a serious hindrance to the nation's fullest development. The struggle to solve these questions in a progressive direction made up the main content of United States history for the next three-quarters of a century. Among the more basic of these tasks were the abolition of slavery, the opening up of the broad western lands to settlement, and the deepening and extension of the democratic rights of the people. The main post-revolutionary fight of the toiling masses, in the face of fierce reactionary opposition, was aimed chiefly at preserving and extending their democratic rights won in the Revolution.

It was a great post-revolutionary political rally of these democratic forces that brought Jefferson to the presidency in 1800. Coming to power on a program of wresting the government from the hands of the privileged few, Jefferson sought to create a democracy based primarily upon the small farmers, but excluding the Negroes. From this fact many have drawn the erroneous conclusion that his policies were a brake on American industrial development. Actually, however, by the abolition of slavery in the North, the opening up of public lands, the battle against British "dumping" in America, and the extension of the popular franchise, all during Jefferson's period, the growth of the country's economy was greatly facilitated.

[1] Herbert M. Morais, *The Struggle for American Freedom*, pp. 254-57, N. Y., 1944.

The extraordinary rapidity of the United States' economic advance in the decades following the victorious revolution was to be ascribed to a combination of several favorable factors, including the presence of vast natural resources, the relative absence of feudal economic and political remnants, the shortage of labor power, the constant flow of immigrants, and the tremendous extent of territory under one government. Another, most decisive factor was the immense stretch of new land awaiting capitalist development, the opening up of which played a vital part for decades in the economic and political growth of the country. It absorbed a vast amount of capital; it largely shaped the workers' ideology and also the progress and forms of the labor movement; and it was a main bone of contention between the rival, struggling classes of industrialists and planters. As Lenin, a close student of American agriculture, noted, "That peculiar feature of the United States . . . the availability of unoccupied free land" explains "the extremely wide and rapid development of capitalism in the United States."[1]

THE BEGINNINGS OF THE TRADE UNION MOVEMENT

The swiftness of the industrial growth of the United States was matched by that of the working class. In pre-revolutionary days the stable part of the free working class was largely made up of skilled craftsmen—ship-builders, building mechanics, tailors, shoemakers, bakers, and so on—who inherited much of the European guild system, with its relations of masters and journeymen. The shift of the center of production from home to mill, however, and the development of the factory system, especially after the war of 1812, revolutionized the status of American labor. The development of the national market enabled the budding capitalists, with their expanding factories and large crews of workers, soon to replace the master craftsmen employing only a few mechanics at the bench. The new capitalists resorted to the most ruthless exploitation of the workers, which included huge numbers of women and children, and they displaced skilled labor by machinery.

The conditions of the workers in this period were abominable. The hours of labor extended from sun-up to sun-down—13 to 16 hours per day. Wages were often no more than a dollar a day for men, and far less for women and children. In the shops the workers were subjected to the worst boss tyranny. Health conditions were unspeakable, and safety precautions totally absent. The workers also had no protection whatever against the hazards of unemployment, accidents, sickness, and old age. When they could not pay their way, they were thrown

[1] V. I. Lenin, *Capitalism and Agriculture in the United States*, p. 40. N. Y., 1946.

into debtors' prisons—as late as 1833 there were 75,000 workers in these monstrous jails. Irish immigrants and free Negro workers were employed building turnpikes and canals, and they died like flies in the swamps.

The workers were faced with the alternatives of going west, of submitting to the harsh conditions of this work, or of fighting back. Inasmuch as the great bulk could not afford the expense of going west and taking up land, they stood and fought the exploiters. Mostly their struggles, at first, were in the shape of blind, spontaneous strikes. But soon they learned, particularly the skilled workers, that in order to fight effectively they needed organization. The trade union movement began to take shape, and strikes multiplied. But the employers struck back viciously, using the old English common law, which branded as "conspiracies" all "combinations" (organizations) to improve wages and other conditions of work.

Before the 1819 economic crisis there were already many unions in various trades and cities. During that industrial crash these early unions collapsed, but no sooner had industrial conditions begun to improve again when the workers, with ever-greater energy and clearer understanding, resumed the building of their unions. The next decade saw very important strikes of the new-born labor movement.

The unions, in this early period, began to extend into many new occupations and to combine into city-wide federations. By 1836 such union centers existed in 13 of the major seaboard cities. The unskilled were also being increasingly drawn into the movement. A high point in the rising labor movement was reached in 1833-37, when 173 strikes were recorded—chiefly for better wages and the shorter workday. During these years, in March 1834, the National Trades Union, the workers' first attempt at a general labor federation, was organized. It lasted three years.[1]

The panic of 1837 again wiped out most of the trade unions, yet the great struggles of the 20's and 30's had produced lasting results. In addition to the 10-hour day gains, imprisonment for debt was abolished, a mechanics' lien law passed, a common school system set up in the North, and property qualifications for voting as yet only by whites in the North were practically eliminated.

[1] Philip S. Foner, *History of the Labor Movement in the United States*, pp. 97-120, N. Y., 1947.

LABOR'S FIRST STEPS TOWARD INDEPENDENT POLITICAL ACTION

The workers of young America, oppressed by ruthless exploiters, had been quick to learn the value of trade unionism, and the most advanced among them also saw early the necessity for political action on class lines. They realized that it was not enough that they had the voting franchise; they had to organize to use it effectively.

Bourgeois historians have coined the theory that the American workers historically have resorted alternately to economic or political action, as they lost faith in one form and turned to the other. The facts show, however, as indicated by these early American experiences, that the same working class upsurge that produced great economic struggles, also found its expression in various forms of political activity. Thus, the city of Philadelphia, the first to build a labor union, to organize a central labor body, and to call a general strike, was also the starting place for the first labor party in the United States.

The call for a political party issued by the Philadelphia labor unions in 1828 declared that "The mechanics and working men of the city and county of Philadelphia are determined to take the management of their own interests, as a class, in their own immediate keeping."[1] The New York Workingmen's Party was launched a year later, and during the years 1828-34, some 61 local labor parties were established, with 50 labor newspapers. These local parties, despite ferocious attacks from the employers, made many gains such as the 10-hour day on public works, the free public schools, and limitations on the labor of women and children. The workers dovetailed this political struggle with the economic battles of the trade unions. But within a few years the local parties had passed out of existence.[2]

Although these local labor parties did not develop into a permanent national organization, they nevertheless prepared the ground for the next phase of the political struggles on a national scale—the farmer-labor alliance that formed around Andrew Jackson during the 1830's. Labor, although still weak, was particularly attracted to support Jackson, the frontiersman president, because of his vigorous attacks upon the United States Bank, the darling project of the budding capitalists of the time. This movement in support of Jackson was the beginning of labor's organized functioning in the support of bourgeois political parties, a pol-

---

[1] *Mechanics' Free Press*, Philadelphia, Aug. 16, 1828, cited by Foner, *History of the Labor Movement in the U.S.*, p. 127.
[2] Foner, *History of the Labor Movement in the U.S.*, pp. 121-42.

icy which was to become of decisive importance in later decades.

The disappearance of the early labor-party movement was to be ascribed to various reasons. The local parties were torn by internal dissension, cultivated by outside politicians, who sought either to lead them back to the bourgeois parties or else to destroy them. They were undermined also by political confusion, engendered by various schemes and panaceas of utopian reformers. They were subjected, too, to extreme attacks from the reactionaries on moral and religious grounds. Besides, the major bourgeois parties, largely for purposes of demagogy, took over much of their program. Underlying all these weaknesses, however, was the basic fact that the continued existence of the frontier made possible the persistence of Jeffersonian illusions and prejudices which prevented the development of a stable working class and the establishment of an independent class political movement.

IDEOLOGY OF THE EARLY LABOR MOVEMENT

The American labor movement entered the industrial era with a Jeffersonian ideology inherited from the agrarian and colonial past. The mass of workers who took part in the struggles of the 1820's and 30's of the immature working class, could not and did not raise the question of the overthrow of the existing social order. Their fight, instead, was directed toward realizing the promises of 1776, as expressed in the Declaration of Independence. They held tenaciously to the concept of a government representing the interests of all the people. They saw the solution of their problems, not in changing the existing order, but in improving and democratizing it.

The workers predominantly held the Jeffersonian theory of democracy. This was largely the adaptation to American conditions of John Locke's conceptions of "natural rights" and "equalitarianism." These ideas, seized upon by the revolutionary bourgeoisie in its struggle against feudalism, had become the dominant ideology of the Revolution and as such were absorbed by the workers. The great influence of the Declaration of Independence upon working class thinking during the pre-Civil War decades was evidenced by the repetition of its language and form in many union constitutions and statements.

But the bitter capitalist exploitation soon began to give a different class content to the outlook of the working class. The workers' demand for equality was no longer limited to formal equality at the ballot box; it was also directed against economic inequality and exploitation. Crude but penetrating attacks upon the capitalist system began to be formulated in proletarian circles.

"We are prepared to maintain," said the *Mechanics' Free Press* of Philadelphia, "that all who toil have a natural and inalienable right to reap the fruits of their own industry, and that they who labor . . . are the authors of every comfort, convenience, and luxury."[1] The Workingmen's Political Association of Penn Township, Pennsylvania, declared that "There appears to exist two distinct classes, rich and poor, the oppressors and the oppressed, those that live by their own labor and those that live by the labor of others."[2] The *Workingmen's Advocate* of New York demanded a revolution which would leave behind it no trace of the government responsible for the workers' hardships.[3] And Thomas Skidmore, one of the most famous radicals of the times, proposed a co-operative society which would "compel all men, without exception, to labor as much as others must labor for the same amount of enjoyment, or in default thereof, to be deprived of such enjoyment altogether."[4] The land reform theory of George Henry Evans fell under this general head. Many poets and writers—Thoreau, Whittier, Emerson, and others—expressed similar radical ideas.

These anti-capitalist expressions represented a groping of the masses for a program of working class emancipation. But they lacked a scientific foundation and a firm set of working principles. It was the historical role of Marxism to give the needed clarity and purpose to this early proletarian theoretical revolt and to raise it to the level of scientific socialism.

UTOPIAN SOCIALISM

The crisis of 1837, and the twelve long years of depression that followed it, profoundly influenced the thinking of labor and the progressive intellectuals. In their search for a way out of the bitter evils which encompassed them, many advanced beyond the limits of capitalism proper. In the face of the reduced standards of the workers, the sufferings of the unemployed, and the general paralysis of industry, they concluded that what was needed was a new social system which would end the exploitation and oppression of the many by the few. Lacking a scientific analysis of the laws of capitalist society, however, they had no recourse but to devise or support various ingeniously concocted plans for new

---

[1] *Mechanics' Free Press*, Oct. 25, 1828.
[2] *Mechanics' Free Press*, June 5, 1830, cited by John R. Commons and associates, *History of Labor in the United States*, Vol. 1, p. 193, N. Y., 1918.
[3] *The Working Man's Advocate*, Oct. 31, 1829, cited by Commons, *History of Labor in the U.S.*, Vol. 1, p. 238.
[4] Thomas Skidmore, *The Rights of Man to Property*, p. 6, N. Y., 1829.

social orders. Thus was initiated an era of utopian experiments.

While these utopian schemes originated mainly in Europe, they were most extensively developed in the United States. At least 200 such projects were undertaken within a few years. American soil was particularly inviting for them. There was ample land to be had cheaply; the people were burdened with few feudal political restrictions; and the masses, near in experience to the great Revolution, were readily inclined to try social change and experimentation.

Indeed, America, long before this time, had already had considerable experience with co-operative regimes. The Indian tribes all over the western hemisphere had been organized on a primitive communal basis.[1] Also the colonies in both Virginia and Massachusetts, during their early critical years, practiced some sharing in common of the general production.[2] And from 1776 on numerous European religious societies, on a primitive communal basis—Shakers, Rappites, Zoarites, Ebenezers, Bethelites, Perfectionists, etc.—took root in the United States and expanded widely. But the three utopian schemes most important in the pre-Civil War era were those of Robert Owen, a Scotsman, and Charles Fourier and Etienne Cabet, both Frenchmen.[3]

Owen, a humanitarian industrialist, planning to found a society in which all the workers would own the means of production and where there would be no exploitation, came to the United States in 1824 and established co-operative colonies in New Harmony, Indiana, and also in a few other places. At first these enterprises attracted wide attention, but by 1828 they had all perished. Owen was invited to speak to Congress. In 1845 he called an international Socialist convention in New York, but it amounted to very little.

The Fourierist utopians made even more of a stir than the Owenites. Differing from Owen, who abolished private property rights, Fourier preserved individual ownership. Unlike Owen also, Fourier considered industry an unmitigated evil and relied upon an agrarian, handicraft economy. The Fourierists, with the support of such prominent figures as Albert Brisbane, Horace Greeley, James Russell Lowell, Nathaniel Hawthorne, Margaret Fuller, and Henry Thoreau, during the 1840's set up some forty "Phalanxes," or colonies. The most famous of these was Brook Farm, near Boston. By 1850, however, the movement had virtually disappeared.

The Cabet, or Icarian movement established its first agrarian colony in Texas, in 1848. Various others were soon set up in Missouri and Iowa.

1 Lewis H. Morgan, *Ancient Society*, Chicago, 1907.
2 Richard T. Ely, *The Labor Movement in America*, pp. 7-8, Boston, 1886.
3 Charles Nordhoff, *The Communist Societies of the United States*, N. Y., 1875.

Some of these co-operative ventures lingered on in skeleton form until as late as the 1890's.

During this same general period Wilhelm Weitling, a German immigrant worker, tried, with but little success, to establish a utopian-conceived labor exchange bank, from which the workers would receive certificates to the full value of their product. It was Weitling's idea that this scheme would gradually replace capitalist production; but it soon went the way of all such enterprises.

In the 1840's and 1850's a big movement also developed toward producers' and consumers' co-operatives, which the numerous utopians advanced as a social cure-all. Many of the great crop of land reformers of the period were also filled with grandiose conceptions of fundamental social change, largely of a utopian character. Even as late as the 1890's traces of this agrarian utopianism were still to be observed, as for example, in the Debs colonization schemes (see page 94).

The many utopian colonies and movements which sprang up in the pre-Civil War period eventually died out because they were not based upon the realities of material conditions or upon an understanding of society and its laws of growth and decay. They were constructed according to arbitrary plans, emanating from wishful thinking. These little island colonies were artificial creations and could not survive in the midst of the broad capitalist sea, which inevitably engulfed them one and all. They proved, among other things, that it is impossible "to build the new society within the shell of the old." The more definitely utopian schemes, with the exception of Weitling's, never greatly attracted the workers, who turned to more practical projects, such as trade unionism and political action. They were mostly anti-slavery, but they had few Negro members. The supporters of the various utopias consisted chiefly of white farmers and city middle class elements.

The great European utopian leaders, with their artificially constructed social regimes and ignorance of the leading role of the workers, could not lay the foundations of a solid Socialist movement. Nevertheless, they performed a very useful service for the workers by their sharp condemnations of capitalist exploitation. As Marx and Engels pointed out, they were definitely the forerunners of scientific socialism. And as Engels said: "German theoretical socialism will never forget that it rests upon the shoulders of St. Simon, Fourier, and Owen, the three who, in spite of their fantastic notions and utopianism, belonged to the most significant heads of all time, and whose genius anticipated numerous things, the correctness of which can now be proved in a scientific way."[1]

[1] Frederick Engels, *The Peasant War in Germany*, p. 28, N. Y., 1926.

This, briefly, was the course of the class struggle in this country before the rise of Marxism. The workers were with increasing vigor combating their exploiters economically, politically, and ideologically, but in this fight, because of the youth of capitalism, the working class still lacked the class consciousness, energizing force, and clear direction, which finally was to manifest itself in the Communist Party.

2. Pioneer Marxists in the United States (1848-1860)

The foundation of scientific socialism dates from the publication of *The Communist Manifesto* in 1848 by Karl Marx and Frederick Engels.[1] These two great scientists were the first to explain that socialism, contrary to the ideas of the utopians, was not the invention of dreamers, but the inevitable outcome of the workings of modern capitalist society. They discovered the laws of capitalist development and proved that the growth of capitalist society, with the class struggle going on within it, must inevitably lead to the downfall of capitalism, to the victory of the working class, to the dictatorship of the proletariat and socialism. They taught that the proletariat was the grave digger of capitalism and that its victory would rid humanity of all exploitation.

The doctrines of scientific socialism were introduced into the United States during the decade preceding the Civil War. The objective conditions had become ripe for them. Industry was growing rapidly and despite the restrictive power of the slavocracy, American capitalism had already reached fourth place among the industrial nations of the world. During this decade the volume of manufactured goods doubled, railroad mileage increased from 9,000 to 31,000, annual coal production (50,000 tons in the 1830's) reached 14 million in 1850, and a tremendous advance took place in the concentration and centralization of capital. The discovery of gold in California had given a big stimulus to general capitalist development. The working class had also become numerically stronger, and class relations were sharpening. Immigrants, mostly skilled workers and farm hands, were pouring into the country at double the rate of the preceding decade, and already about one-third of the population was depending upon manufacturing for its livelihood.

[1] During these early decades, revolutionary Socialists called themselves Communists. As Marx pointed out, this was because the utopians and opportunists had discredited the name of Socialist. During the period of the Second International, however, from 1889 to 1914, when opportunists and revolutionaries found themselves within one organization, the terms Socialist and Social-Democrat again came into general use. After the Russian Revolution, for the same reasons that had originally moved Marx to adopt the term Communist, the Bolsheviks ceased calling themselves Social-Democrats and resumed the designation of Communists. The name Communist is also more accurate scientifically.

Marxism took root in the United States after the working class had already experienced two deep economic crises. The workers had long undergone severe exploitation at the hands of the employers, they had built many trade unions and local labor parties, waged innumerable hard-fought strikes and political campaigns, and won various important concessions in sharp class struggle. As we have seen, the most developed thinkers among them had already begun to attack the capitalist system as such and to seek a way of escape from its evils. The acceptance of Marxist socialism by these advanced sections of the working class was, therefore, the logical climax of the whole course of social development in the United States since the Revolutionary War. It was further stimulated by the current revolutionary events in Europe—the Chartist movement in England and the revolutionary struggles in France, Germany, and Ireland—with all of which the awakening American working class felt a vivid and direct kinship.

The traditional charge by employers that Marxist socialism, because it originated in Europe, is therefore alien to the United States, is typically stupid. As well assert the same of the alphabet, the multiplication table, the law of gravity, and a host of other scientific principles and discoveries, all of which also developed outside of the United States. "Marxism is no more alien to the United States because of the historically conditioned German origin of its founders, or the Russian origin of Lenin and Stalin, than is the American Declaration of Independence because of the British origin of John Locke, and the French origin of the Encyclopedists."[1]

GERMAN MARXIST IMMIGRANTS

Marxist thought, based on the generalized experiences of the toiling masses of all countries and worked into a science on European soil, was transmitted to the American working class by the stream of political immigrants, mainly German, who came to this country following the defeat of the European revolutions of 1848. During the 1830's about 2,000 German immigrants arrived yearly, but after 1848 this stream became a torrent of over 200,000 annually throughout the 1850's. There were also large numbers of Irish immigrants, and Italian and French as well (the latter particularly after the Franco-Prussian war and the defeat of the Commune in 1871); but it was the Germans who remained the most decisive force in developing Marxist thought in the United States throughout most of the rest of the nineteenth century. They were the earliest forerunners of the modern Communist Party.

---

[1] V. J. Jerome in *The Communist*, Sept. 1939, p. 836.

The Germans settled chiefly in such main industrial centers as New York, Chicago, Philadelphia, St. Louis, Milwaukee, and Cincinnati. Many entered industry as skilled mechanics and soon began to exert a strong influence on the development of the trade union movement. While most of them considered themselves Socialists and revolutionaries, they brought along with them a wide variety of political ideas, and they reflected the many ideological divisions that existed in their homeland. Their primary preoccupation was with events in the old country, but many of the Germans, in the early 1840's, began to be drawn into American political affairs.

In 1845 a group of Germans formed the Social Reform Association, as part of the National Reform Association. The principal figure in this movement was Hermann Kriege, once a co-worker with Marx, who later swallowed the doctrines of George Henry Evans, a labor editor who had become a land reformer. Kriege was probably the first radical exponent of "American exceptionalism." In substance he was already generating the notion that there existed in the United States a capitalist system fundamentally different from that of Europe, and he developed the theory that because of the great mass of free land, the American workers need not follow the revolutionary course of their European brothers. He declared that if the 1,400,000,000 acres of United States lands were distributed to the poor, "an end will be put to poverty in America at one stroke."[1] Marx castigated Kriege for this opportunism and riddled his agrarian illusions.

Another important figure among the early circles of German immigrant workers was Wilhelm Weitling. After an earlier visit, he returned to the United States in 1849. Weitling was one of the first revolutionary leaders to come from the ranks of the workers. He took a position midway between utopian and scientific socialism. His plan for a "labor exchange bank," previously indicated, attracted much working class support, and for the next decade it proved to be a confusing element in the developing Marxist movement.

WEYDEMEYER, PIONEER OF AMERICAN SOCIALISM

Joseph Weydemeyer, born in Germany, an artillery officer who had participated in the Revolution of 1848, was the best-informed Marxist early to immigrate to the United States.[2] More than any other, he contributed toward laying the foundations of scientific socialism in the new world. Arriving in 1851, Weydemeyer stood out as the leader among the

[1] Cited by V. I. Lenin, *Selected Works*, Vol. 12, p. 299, N. Y., 1943.
[2] Karl Obermann, *Joseph Weydemeyer: Pioneer of American Socialism*, N. Y., 1947.

American Marxists, which then included such men as F. A. Sorge, Adolph Douai, August Willich, Robert Rosa, Fritz Jacobi, and Siegfried Meyer, most of whom had known and worked with Marx personally in Germany. Sorge, like Weydemeyer, was a well-developed Marxist. Marx and Engels long carried on a voluminous correspondence with him.[1]

Weydemeyer and his co-Marxists found the Socialist movement in the United States in confusion. There were the disintegrating effects of Weitling's labor exchange bank scheme; Kriege was advocating his agrarian panacea; Willich and Gottfried Kinkel were seeking to transform the movement simply into a campaign to advance the revolution in Germany; and there were various groups of utopians and anarchists.

Of all the groupings only the German Sports Society, the *Turnverein*, organized in 1850, had a relatively sound program. Founded upon advanced socialist ideas, this body opposed conspiratorial groups and proposed instead a broad democratic movement rooted among the masses. While these Marxists supported the free soil and other reform movements, they warned that these were not the path to socialism and they emphasized that the emancipation of the working class could only be achieved in struggle led by the proletariat against the capitalist class.

Weydemeyer, a close co-worker of Marx and Engels and well-grounded in Marxist theory, was singularly qualified to undertake the task of clarifying the ideology of the budding American Socialist movement. He was an extremely capable and energetic organizer, and he had spent three years in underground work in Germany, where in the face of the fierce Prussian terror, he had continued to spread the works of Marx and Engels. A gifted polemist, Weydemeyer ably defended Marxism against many distortions. He possessed the ability to apply Marxist principles to American conditions. He avoided the errors of the utopians, of the radical agrarians, and also those of the "exceptionalists," who believed that the workings of American bourgeois democracy on the land question would solve the problems of the working class. Marx considered Weydemeyer as "one of our best men," and had agreed to his going to the United States only because of the growing importance of America in the world labor movement.

THE PROLETARIAN LEAGUE

The Proletarian League, founded in New York in June 1852, was the first definitely Marxist organization on American soil. It was composed of seventeen of the most advanced Marxists in New York City, at the initiative of Weydemeyer and Sorge. The rising tide of labor struggle

[1] See Karl Marx and Frederick Engels, *Letters to Americans*, N. Y., 1952.

and organization, and the rapidly developing strike movement in the United States, together with the foundation by Marx of the German Workers Society in Europe, gave the immediate impetus to the formation of the pioneer Proletarian League.

In starting the League, and in the ensuing work of that organization, the Marxists, then called Communists, based themselves upon the newly-published *Communist Manifesto*. This historic document, which still serves as a guide for the world's Socialist movement, furnished a clear and basic program for the young and still very weak American movement. Marx and Engels, who always paid very close attention to developments in the United States, were prompt in seeing to it that copies of the great *Manifesto* were sent to Weydemeyer and his co-workers.

The Communist Manifesto, among its many fundamental political lessons, teaches that "the emancipation of the working class must be the act of the working class itself";[1] that "every class struggle is a political struggle";[2] that the building of a political party of the most advanced section of the workers is fundamental to the success of the Socialist movement; that the proletariat, in its struggles, must make alliances with other progressive forces in society; that the Marxists have no interests separate and apart from those of the proletariat as a whole; that Communists must fight for the immediate as well as the ultimate interests of the working class; and that socialism can be established only through the abolition of the capitalist system.

Die Revolution, the first American Marxist paper, founded in 1852 and edited by Weydemeyer, popularized this basic program. In the first of the only two issues of the paper there appeared, years before it was published in Europe, Marx's classic historical work, *The Eighteenth Brumaire of Louis Bonaparte*. During the following year this original Marxist journal was succeeded by another, *Die Reform*, also with Weydemeyer as its guiding spirit. This paper, finally a daily, became the leading labor journal in the United States.

As consistent Marxists, the League members did not live in an ivory tower. Together with centering major attention upon theoretical clarification, they also, in the spirit of *The Communist Manifesto*, participated actively in the struggles of the working class. In all this work Sorge played a role second only to that of Weydemeyer, and thenceforth, for over a generation, he was to be a tower of strength in the political movements of the American working class.

In line with their general policy of supporting the workers' struggle,

---

[1] Karl Marx and Frederick Engels, *The Communist Manifesto*, p. 6, N. Y., 1948 (Preface to the English edition of 1888).
[2] Marx and Engels, *The Communist Manifesto*, p. 18.

the Marxists, small though they were in number, issued in March 1853 a call through the trade unions of German-speaking workers for the formation of one large workers' union. Consequently, over 800 workers gathered in Mechanics' Hall, New York, and launched the American Labor Union. The platform of this organization, avoiding the utopianism of Weitling and the "ultra-revolutionary fantasies" of Willich and Kinkel, adopted a short program of immediate demands. This first American Marxist program of immediate demands had the weakness of not being specific and also of ignoring the basic issue of slavery. The organization was composed almost exclusively of German workers. It was a sort of labor party, with affiliated trade unions and ward branches. Its life span was short.

While stressing the united political action of all workers, the American Labor Union directed its energies to the organization of new workers in each craft. Its program called for the immediate naturalization of all immigrants, passage of federal labor laws, removal of burdensome taxes, and the limitation of the working day to 10 hours. It gave active support to the many strikes of the period. And upon its initiative, representatives of 40 trades with 2,000 members launched the General Trade Union of New York City.

The impact of these movements made itself felt among the English-speaking workers in other cities. Through the efforts of two leading Marxists, Sam Briggs and Adolph Cluss, the Workingmen's National Association was set up in the city of Washington in April 1853. The organization, however, died during the same year. The American Labor Union was reorganized in 1857 as the General Workers' League, but it, too, died out by 1860.[1]

FORMATION OF THE COMMUNIST CLUB

The severe economic crisis that struck the country in the autumn of 1857 sharply changed the character of the workers' struggles. Although it hit the native workers hard, causing them much suffering, it was the newly-arrived immigrants who felt the brunt of the depression. The major struggles of the period were waged by the unemployed, and they developed into battles of unprecedented scope and sharpness.

In the forefront of these struggles stood the Marxists who, though few in number, were able to give the workers clear-sighted and militant leadership. Big demonstrations of the unemployed, led by the Communists, took place in New York, Philadelphia, Chicago, Newark, and elsewhere. They demanded relief and denounced the ruling class and

[1] Foner, *History of the Labor Movement in the U.S.*, pp. 232-33.

its system that created starvation amid plenty. So outstanding was the role of the Marxists in this period that all important struggles of the time were labeled "Communist revolts" and attempts at revolution.

To better co-ordinate their activities the Marxists reorganized their forces, forming the Communist Club in New York on October 25, 1858. Friedrich Kamm was elected chairman and Fritz Jacobi secretary, although Sorge was the real leader of the organization. A Communist Club resolution proclaimed as the aims of the Communists: "We recognize no distinction as to nationality or race, caste, or status, color, or sex; our goal is but reconciliation of all human interests, freedom, and happiness for mankind, and the realization and unification of a world republic."[1]

The Communist Club of New York, exercising national leadership, began to establish communication with similar but smaller groups springing up in other major centers, notably Chicago, Milwaukee, and Cincinnati. With many leading Marxists, including Weydemeyer, who had moved to the Middle West, the center of the movement also soon shifted to Chicago, where the *Arbeiter Verein* (Workers' Club) was coming forward as the most effective socialist organization of the period.

Developments abroad and the growing movement for international solidarity occupied much of the attention of the Marxists in the United States. The formation of an international committee in London in 1856 to commemorate the great French revolution, stimulated these trends. Consequently, an American Central Committee of the International Association was set up, with contacts in many cities. One of its first and most successful undertakings was a mass meeting to commemorate the historic June days of the 1848 Revolution in France. Another event, in April 1858, was a big torchlight parade in honor of Felice Orsini, the Italian patriot who had attempted the assassination of Napoleon III. All of these activities brought the German Marxists into contact with other working class forces, and consequently helped to prepare the groundwork for the International Workingmen's Association, founded in 1864 and later known as the First International.

LAYING THE THEORETICAL FOUNDATIONS OF MARXISM IN THE UNITED STATES

The early Marxists were confronted with the task of developing the ideological, tactical, and organizational bases for Marxism in America. As yet, however, this movement was not united ideologically, nor was it organized into a national party. This meant that first of all the Marx-

[1] Obermann, *Joseph Weydemeyer*, p. 96.

ists themselves had to master the teachings of Marx and Engels. This implied, furthermore, acquiring the ability to apply the principles of Marxism to the specific conditions in this country. They also had to lay the foundations of a national Marxist political party. All this called for the most persistent struggle to free the minds of the workers from the many Jeffersonian, bourgeois agrarian illusions which persisted with particular stubbornness among them.

The needs for ideological clarification and political organization were freshly stressed when, with the easing of the economic crisis of 1857, various petty-bourgeois conceptions began to make themselves increasingly felt afresh in the thinking of the workers. These were also reflected in growing confusion and friction in the Marxist movement. Thus, some of the leaders did not push the fight against slavery, although claiming to be true disciples of Marx; also various utopian sects reappeared, and Weitling's harmful notions sprang up again in new garb.

In undertaking their great tasks of ideological and organizational development, the early Marxists were favored by the fact that in the decade before the Civil War many of the fundamental problems of Marxist theory—its philosophy, political economy, and revolutionary tactics—had been developed by Marx and Engels. In addition to the famous *Manifesto,* they had also completed such basic works as *Wage-Labor and Capital, Ludwig Feuerbach, The Eighteenth Brumaire,* and *The Peasant War in Germany.* The American movement also had the tremendous advantage of close personal contact with Marx and Engels, who both carefully observed and advised on its development.

The great problem of the Marxists in the United States, of course, was to apply Marxist principles to specific American conditions. Here the early Marxists were faced with many objective and subjective difficulties. These difficulties, in their essence, continued constantly to reappear in new forms and under new conditions, and they have persisted in many ways down to the present day.

Already in the 1850's the Marxists noticed a seeming contradiction between the great militancy and fighting capacity of the American working class, and the slowness with which the workers developed a class-conscious outlook toward politics and society. They noted the contradiction between the highly advanced development of American capitalism and the subjective backwardness of the labor movement. Some of the German immigrants tried to explain this on the basis of a supposed innate political inferiority of the American working class, while others concluded that Marxism had no validity in the new, democratic United States.

Combating such illusions, the early Marxist leaders pointed out the destructive effects upon labor of slavery in the South. They pointed out further that the existence of the free land in the West, by absorbing masses from the East, hindered the development of class consciousness and of a stable working class, and that the current petty-bourgeois Jeffersonian ideas among the workers stemmed from the Revolution of which the bourgeoisie were the ideological leaders, and also from the whole history of the country. They also gave a Marxist explanation of the recurrent economic crises, which deeply perplexed the workers and the whole American people.

So powerful were the current bourgeois illusions and disintegrating influences among the workers that Engels, in 1892, wrote as follows to Hermann Schlueter: "Up to 1848 one could only speak of the permanent native working class as an exception; the small beginnings of it in the cities in the East always had still the hope of becoming farmers or bourgeois."[1]

The pioneer Marxists, Weydemeyer, Sorge, and the others—greatly aided by the many new books, articles, letters, and the personal advice of Marx and Engels, fought on two ideological fronts—against the "lefts," who believed that political activity was futile and that Socialism was to be brought about by conspiratorial action and by directing themselves exclusively to supporting revolutionary movements in Germany; and also against the rights, who toyed with agrarian panaceas, sought to tie the workers to corrupt bourgeois politicians, and denied the role of Marxism in the United States.

The Marxists especially attacked the budding theories of "American exceptionalism," advocated by those who, like Kriege, sought to liquidate Marxism by arguing that communism was to be achieved in the United States by a different route from that in Europe—through agrarian reform. Of great help in this struggle were the current writings of Marx and Engels. They pointed out that the establishment of a bourgeois democracy, such as existed in the United States, did not abolish but greatly intensified all the inherent contradictions, and that the forces making for the speedier development of American capitalism were also producing more clear-cut class divisions and sharpening all class relations. They pointed out that the "land of opportunity" was also the classical land of economic crises, unemployment, and of the sharpest extremes between the wealth of the few and the poverty of the great masses.

One of the difficulties peculiar to early Marxism was that its founders, nearly all German immigrants, were striving to introduce their Socialist ideas into a labor movement speaking a different language and having

[1] Karl Marx and Frederick Engels, *Selected Correspondence*, p. 496, N. Y., 1942.

a background and traditions which they little understood. Many of these immigrants also thought that their own stay in America was only temporary, until victory was won in Germany. These circumstances provided fertile ground for sectarian tendencies, which manifested themselves in strong trends among the Socialist-minded German workers to stay apart by themselves and to consider the American workers as politically immature. This sectarianism was a very serious obstacle to the bringing of Socialist ideas to the masses of native workers, and for a full generation Engels thundered against it.

The early Marxists carried on a great deal of propaganda on the need of the workers to act politically in their own interests. They stressed the importance of the workers fighting the employers on all levels; they exposed the fallacy of separating the political from the economic struggles; they showed that every economic struggle, such as the 10-hour day fight, when the working class fought as a class against the ruling class, was a political struggle.

The developed Marxists of the decade just prior to the Civil War were only a handful; yet, for all their weakness, they made tremendous contributions to the young American labor movement. They were pioneer builders of the trade unions; they fought in the front line of every struggle of the workers; they helped break down the barriers between native and immigrant workers; along with native Abolitionists, they were militant fighters against Negro slavery; they helped to build up a solid and influential labor press; and above all, they created the first core of organized Marxists in America, and they spread far and wide the writings of Marx and Engels. The extent of the general influence of the pioneer Marxists may be gauged from the fact that many young trade unions of the period, in their preambles, used *The Communist Manifesto* as their guide.

For all their relative sensitivity to the position of the white workers, the Negroes, the immigrants, and other oppressed sections of the population, the pioneer Marxists did not, however, become aware of the significance of the struggle of the Indian tribes, who during these years were being viciously robbed and butchered by the ruthless white invaders of their lands. Indeed, in the whole period from Jefferson right down to our own day, the long series of workers' trade unions and political parties have almost completely ignored the plight and sufferings of the abused and heroic Indian peoples. The story of labor's relations with the Indians is practically a blank.

3. The Marxists in the Struggle Against Slavery (1848-1865)

The United States Constitution, drawn up after the Revolutionary War and implying the continuation of Negro slavery, was a compromise between the rival classes of southern planters and northern merchants and industrialists. But it established no stability between these classes, and they were soon thereafter at each other's throats. The plantation system and slavery spread rapidly in the South after the invention of the 1795. In the North the power of the industrialists grew rapidly with cotton gin in 1793 and the development of sugar cane production in the expansion of the factory system and the settlement of the West. The interests of the two systems were incompatible and the clash between them sharpened continuously.

Developing relentlessly over the basic, related questions of control of the newly-organized territories and of the federal government, this struggle was finally to culminate in the great second revolution of 1861-65. As the vast new territories acquired by the Louisiana Purchase of 1803, by the seizure of Florida in 1819, and by the Oregon accession and the Mexican War of 1846, were carved up into states and brought into the Union, the bitter political rivals grabbed them off alternately as free or slave states. Thus, a very precarious balance was maintained.

The northern industrialists vigorously opposed the extensive infiltration of the slave system into the West and Southwest, even threatening secession from the Union. They contested the Louisiana Purchase, and bitterly condemned the unjust Mexican War, in which the United States took half of Mexico's territory (the present states of Texas, California, Arizona, Nevada, Utah, New Mexico, Colorado, and part of Wyoming). Lincoln denounced this predatory war, and opposition to it was intense in the young labor movement.[1] On the other hand, the industrialists were eager to seize Oregon, and they never ceased plotting against the territorial integrity of Canada, as these were non-slavery areas.

Despite all its expansion, the slave system, however, could not possibly keep pace in strength with the great strides of industry in the North. By 1860, 75 percent of the nation's production was in the North, and the same area also held $11 billion of the national wealth as against five

[1] Foner, *History of the Labor Movement in the U.S.*, pp. 277-79.

billion held by the South. To redress the balance of power shifting rapidly against them, the southern planters embarked upon a militant offensive to consolidate their own power. In the face of this drive the northern industrialists at first retreated. Their ranks were split, as many bankers, shippers, and textile manufacturers were tied up economically with the South; they were confused as to how to handle the complex slavery issue; and they feared the growing power of the working class.

During the 1850's the planters, through the Democratic Party, controlled both houses of Congress, the presidency, and seven of the nine Supreme Court judges. They used their power with arrogance. They passed the Fugitive Slave Act, repealed the Missouri Compromise by adopting the pro-slavery Kansas-Nebraska Act, slashed the tariff laws, adopted the infamous Dred Scott decision, vetoed the homestead bill, and declared slavery to be legal in all the territories. Marx raised the real issue when he spoke of the fact that twenty million free men in the North were being subordinated to 300,000 southern slaveholders.[1] Class tensions mounted and the country moved relentlessly toward the great Civil War.

THE ABOLITIONIST MOVEMENT

It was the leaders and fighters of the Abolitionist movement, in their relentless opposition to slavery, who most fully expressed the historic interests of the as yet hesitant bourgeoisie, and of the whole people. Men and women like Frederick Douglass, Wendell Philips, William Lloyd Garrison, Susan B. Anthony, Elizabeth Cady Stanton, John Brown, and Elijah P. Lovejoy prodded and stirred the conscience of the nation. They fought to destroy slavery, built the underground railway, and aggressively combated the fugitive slave laws. With few exceptions they based their fight for Negro emancipation mainly upon ethical and humanitarian grounds.

The most powerful force fighting for abolition, however, was the four million Negro slaves in the South. For generations, and especially since the turn of the century, the recurring slave revolts, violent protests against the horrible conditions of slavery, shook the very foundations of the slavocracy. Despite the most ferocious suppression, the Negroes sabotaged the field work, burned plantations, killed planters, and organized many insurrections. These struggles grew more intense as the Civil War approached. The South became a veritable armed camp, with

---

[1] Karl Marx and Frederick Engels, *The Civil War in the United States*, p. 71, N. Y., 1937.

the planters making desperate efforts to stamp out the growing revolt of their slaves. Imperishable are the names of Harriet Tubman, Sojourner Truth, Denmark Vesey, Nat Turner, and the many other brave Negro fighters in this heroic struggle for liberty.

The northern white workers also played a vital part in the great struggle. The existence of slavery in the South was a drag on these workers' living conditions and the growth of their trade unions in the North. Marx made this basic fact clear in his famous statement that "Labor cannot emancipate itself in the white skin when in the black it is branded."[1] Retarding factors to the northern workers' understanding of the slavery issue, however, were the anti-labor union tendencies among middle class Abolitionists and the pressure in the workers' ranks of opportunist leaders. Such men as George Henry Evans, the land reformer, for example, argued that the emancipation of the slaves prior to the abolition of wage slavery would be contrary to the interests of the workers, as it would confront the latter with the competition of a great mass of cheap labor. Once organized labor sensed, however, that the abolition of slavery was the precondition for its own further advance it was ready to join in the great immediate task of destroying the block that stood in the path of its development and that of the nation. With this realization, during the late 1850's, labor became the inveterate enemy of slavery, and it became a foundation force in the great coalition of capitalists, workers, Negroes, and farmers that carried through and won the Civil War.

THE ROLE OF THE MARXISTS

From the beginning, under the general advice of Karl Marx, the Marxists in the United States took the most consistent and clear-sighted position within the labor movement in fighting for the outright abolition of slavery. The strong leadership of the present-day Communist Party among the Negro people has deep roots in the fight of these Marxist pioneers. They saw in the defeat of the slavocracy the precondition for consolidating the nation's productive forces, for the expansion of democracy, and for the creation of a numerous, independent, and homogeneous proletariat advancing its own interests. They also saw in the emancipation of the Negroes a great cause of human freedom. They realized that in order to clear the decks for the next historic advance, the working class must join with other anti-slavery forces and do its ut-

[1] Karl Marx, *Capital*, Vol. 1, p. 287, N. Y., 1947.

most in carrying through the immediate, democratic, revolutionary task of ending slavery and the slave system.

The contribution of the early Marxists to the Abolitionist movement was out of all proportion to their small numbers. They were very active in the terror-ridden South. Outstanding here was the work of Adolph Douai, who had been a close co-worker of Karl Marx in Europe. In 1852, Douai settled in Texas where, at the time, it was said that one-fifth of the white population was made up of 48'ers from Europe. In San Antonio Douai published an Abolitionist paper, until he was finally compelled to leave in peril of his life. Important work was also done in Alabama under the leadership of the immigrant Marxist, Hermann Meyer, who was likewise forced to flee.

In the North the anti-slavery Marxists were particularly active, notably the Communist Club of Cleveland. A conference in 1851 declared in favor of using all means which were adapted to abolishing slavery, an institution which they called repugnant to the principles of true democracy. In St. Louis and other centers where the German immigrants were numerous, the Marxists carried on intense anti-slavery activities. They developed these activities especially after the passage in 1854 of the Kansas-Nebraska Act, which broke down the barriers against slavery in the Middle West. A few days after this bill reached Congress the Chicago Socialists, led by George Schneider, a veteran of 1848 in Germany and editor of the Illinois *State Gazette*, initiated a campaign which culminated in a large public demonstration.

On October 16, 1859, the heroic Abolitionist, John Brown, and his twenty-one followers, Negroes and whites, electrified the country by seizing Harper's Ferry in a desperate but ill-fated attempt to develop an armed rising of the Negro slaves of the South. The Marxists hailed Brown's courageous action, and they organized supporting mass meetings in numerous cities. The Cincinnati Social Workingmen's Association, led by Socialists, declared that "The act of John Brown has powerfully contributed to bringing out the hidden conscience of the majority of the people."[1] Ten of Brown's men were killed in the struggle and he himself was later hanged.

Joseph Weydemeyer, the Marxist leader, considered that all these developments signalized the beginnings of a new political awakening of the American labor movement. Along with Marx, however, he had to combat the sectarian views, held by Weitling, Kriege, and others, that Marxists should limit themselves to questions of the conditions of the workers and the struggle against capital, and that labor should avoid

---

[1] *Cincinnati Communist*, Dec. 5, 1859.

"contamination" with political activities. Some sectarians even branded participation in the anti-slavery movement as a "betrayal" of the special interests of the working class.

In all his activities Weydemeyer contended for the position that the fight against slavery was central in the work of Marxists in that period. He strove to involve the trade unions in the great struggle. He showed that without a solution of the slavery question no basic working class problem could be solved. He linked the workers' immediate demands with the fundamental issue of Negro emancipation. In this fight the American Workers' League, under Marxist influence, played an important role in winning the workers and organized labor for the abolition struggle. Thus, in 1854, after the passage of the infamous Kansas-Nebraska Act, the League held a big mass meeting which declared that the German-American workers of New York "have, do now, and shall, continue to protest most emphatically against both white and black slavery and brand as a traitor against the people and their welfare everyone who shall lend it his support."[1]

THE MATURING OF THE CRISIS

Following the "Nebraska infamy" of 1854, events moved rapidly toward the decisive struggle. The arrogant actions of the planters, who controlled the government, aroused and sharpened the opposition in the North and West. The old political parties began to disintegrate, and the Republican Party was formed in February 1854. Alvin E. Bovay, former secretary-treasurer of the National Industrial Congress and a prominent leader in New York labor circles, brought together at Ripon, Wisconsin, a group of liberals, reformers, farmers, and labor leaders— all of whom were disgusted with the policies of the Whig and Democratic parties. This group decided "to forget previous political names and organizations, and to band together" to oppose the extension of slavery.[2] Their program also supported those who were fighting for free land.

The response of the northern industrialists to the new party was immediate and favorable. Most of them saw in it the instrument with which to wrest political control from the slave-owners and to advance their own program; protective tariffs, subsidies to railroads, absorption of the national resources, national banking system, etc. The mercantile and banking interests, however, tied financially to the cotton interests of the slave-owners in the South, largely condemned the new party.

[1] Hermann Schlueter, *Lincoln, Labor, and Slavery*, p. 76, N. Y., 1913.
[2] Elizabeth Lawson, *Lincoln's Third Party*, p. 26, N. Y., 1948.

The initial response of the workers to the Republican Party was varied. While many broke their traditional ties with the Democratic Party, others hesitated to join the same party with the industrialists. Among the northern and western farmers the new party, however, got wide acceptance from the outset.

The Marxists, basing themselves on the Marxist teachings (*The Communist Manifesto*) of fighting "with the bourgeoisie whenever it acts in a revolutionary way,"[1] unhesitatingly supported the Republican Party and called upon labor to do likewise. *Die Soziale Republik,* organ of the Chicago *Arbeiterbund,* then the foremost Marxist group in the country, stated this policy. Although the Marxists were firm advocates of full emancipation of the Negroes, they held that they could best advance the anti-slavery cause by uniting with other social groups upon the basis of the widely accepted program of opposition to the further extension of slavery. This tactic was, in fact, a transition to a later, more advanced revolutionary struggle.

In the elections of 1856 the Republicans especially strove to win the support of the workers. The Marxists took a very active part in the campaign. For example, in February 1856, they helped to initiate a conference in Decatur, Illinois, of 25 newspaper editors, including the German-American press, to organize the anti-Nebraska Act forces for participation in the election campaign. Abraham Lincoln was present at this gathering and he ardently supported the resolution which it passed. This resolution was also adopted at the 1856 Philadelphia convention which nominated John C. Fremont for President. Fremont polled 1,341,264 votes, or one-third of the total vote cast. In consequence the Democratic Party was split, the Whig Party was practically destroyed, and the Republican Party emerged as a major party.

THE ELECTION OF ABRAHAM LINCOLN

The election in 1860 was the hardest fought in the history of the United States up to that time. The Republican Party made an all-out and successful effort to win the decisive support of the great masses of farmers, workers, immigrants, and free Negroes, who were all part of the great new coalition under the leadership of the northern bourgeoisie. Philip S. Foner states that "It is not an exaggeration to say that the Republican Party fought its way to victory in the campaign of 1860 as the party of free labor."[2]

---

[1] Marx and Engels, *The Communist Manifesto*, p. 43.
[2] Foner, *History of the Labor Movement in the U.S.*, p. 293.

Lincoln was a very popular candidate among the toiling masses. He was known to be an enemy of slavery; his many pro-labor expressions had won him a wide following among the workers; his advocacy of the Homestead bill had secured him backing among the farmers of the North and West; and his fight against bigoted native "know-nothingism" had entrenched him generally among the foreign-born. He faced three opposing presidential candidates—Stephen A. Douglas, John C. Breckinridge, and John Bell—representing the three-way split in the Democratic Party, and all supporting slavery in one way or another. Lincoln stood on a platform of "containing slavery" to its existing areas. There was no candidate pledged for outright abolition.

In the bitterly fought election the slavocrats, who also had many contacts and supporters in the North, denounced Lincoln with every slander that their fertile minds could concoct. The redbaiters of the time shouted against "Black Republicanism" and "Red Republicanism." Pro-slavery employers and newspapers tried to intimidate the workers by threatening them with discharge, by menacing them with a prospect of economic crisis, and by warning them that Negro emancipation would create a flood of cheap labor which would ruin wage rates. At the same time, the reactionaries tried to split the young Republican Party by cultivating "know-nothing" anti-foreign movements inside its ranks.

The Marxists were very active in this vital election struggle. The clarity of their anti-slavery stand and their militant spirit made up for their still very small numbers. Their key positions in many trade unions enabled them to be a real factor in mobilizing the workers behind Lincoln's candidacy. To this end they spared no effort, holding election meetings of workers in many parts of the North and East. Undoubtedly, the labor vote swung the election for Lincoln, and for this the Marxists were entitled to no small share of the credit.

The Marxists were energetic in winning the decisive foreign-born masses to support Lincoln. In 1860 the foreign-born made up 47.62 percent of the population of New York, 50 percent of Chicago and Pittsburgh, and 59.66 percent of St. Louis, with other cities in proportion. The Germans, by far the largest immigrant group in the country, were a powerful force in Missouri, Iowa, Minnesota, Illinois, Wisconsin, Ohio, Michigan, Indiana, Maryland, Pennsylvania, New York, New Jersey, and Connecticut. They heavily backed Lincoln. "Of the 87 German language newspapers, 69 were for Lincoln."[1]

The Marxists were especially effective in creating pro-Lincoln sentiment among the German-American masses. This was graphically demonstrated at the significant *Deutsches Haus* conference held in Chicago in

[1] Lawson, *Lincoln's Third Party*, p. 41

May 1860, two days before the opening of the nominating convention of the Republican Party. This national conference represented all sections of German-American life. The Marxists Weydemeyer and Douai, who led the working class forces at the conference, were of decisive importance in shaping the meeting's action. Douai, selected as head of the resolutions committee, wrote for the conference a series of resolutions demanding that "they be applied in a sense most hostile to slavery."[1] These resolutions largely furnished the basis for the election platform of the Republican Party.

The fierce campaign of 1860 concluded with the election of Lincoln. The final tabulation showed: Lincoln, 1,857,710; Douglas, 1,291,574; Breckinridge, 850,082; Bell, 646,124.

THE CIVIL WAR

In the face of Lincoln's victory, the oligarchy of southern planters acted like any other ruling class suffering a decisive democratic defeat, by taking up arms to hold on to and extend their power at any cost. Acting swiftly and disregarding the will for peace of their people, seven southern states seceded, setting up the Confederate States of America, with Jefferson Davis as president. All of this was done before Lincoln was inaugurated on March 4, 1861, while the planters' stooge president, James Buchanan, was still in office. Eventually the Confederacy contained eleven states. The seceders opened fire on Fort Sumter on April 12, 1861, thus beginning the war. The conquest aims of the rebellious South were boundless. "What the slaveholders, therefore, call the South," said Marx, "embraces more than three-quarters of the territory hitherto comprised by the Union."[2] The second American revolution had passed from the constitutional stage into that of military action.

The North, ill-prepared, met with indecision the swift offensive of the southern planters. This weakness reflected the prevailing divisions in the ranks of the bourgeoisie. Among these were the Copperhead bankers and merchants, who strove for a negotiated peace on the slavocracy's terms. Then there were the Radical Republicans, representative of the rising industrial capitalists, whose most revolutionary spokesman was Thaddeus Stevens and who insisted upon a military offensive to crush the rebellion, with the freeing and arming of the slaves. And finally there was the vacilating middle class, largely represented by Lincoln's hesitant course.

[1] V. J. Jerome in *The Communist*, Sept. 1939, p. 839.
[2] Marx and Engels, *The Civil War in the U.S.*, p. 71.

The leaders of the government sought evasive formulas, instead of taking energetic steps to win the war. Lincoln, ready for any compromise short of disunion, proclaimed the slogan, "Save the Union," at a time when the situation demanded clearly also the revolutionary slogan of "full and complete emancipation of the slaves." Stevens, bolder and clearer-sighted, declared that "The Constitution is now silent and only the laws of war obtain." On the question of the slaves, Stevens stated that "Those who now furnish the means of war but are the natural enemies of the slaveholders must be made our allies."[1] This position was strongly supported by the Negro masses, whose leading spokesman, Frederick Douglass, declared, "From the first, I reproached the North that they fought the rebels with only one hand, when they might effectively strike with two—that they fought with their soft white hand, while they kept their black iron hand chained and helpless behind them—that they fought the effect, while they protected the cause, and that the Union cause would never prosper till the war assumed an anti-slavery attitude, and the Negro was enlisted on the loyal side."[2]

While Lincoln carried on his defensive leadership the military fortunes of the North continued to sink. Events combined, however, to change the conduct of the war from an attempt to suppress the slaveowners' rebellion into a revolutionary struggle to liquidate the slave power. These main forces were, the increasing power of the northern bourgeoisie through the rapid growth of industry and the railroads; the lessons learned from the bitter defeats in the early part of the war; and the tremendous pressure exerted by the farmers, the Negro masses, and the white workers—especially the foreign-born—for an aggressive policy in the war.

Hence, on September 22, 1862, after about 18 months of unsuccessful war, President Lincoln issued the Emancipation Proclamation, proclaiming that after January 1st persons held as slaves in areas in rebellion "shall be then, thenceforward, and forever free." In August 1862, the enlistment of free Negroes into the armed forces had been authorized.[3] Lincoln removed the sabotaging General McClellan in March 1862 from his post as head of the Union forces, and generally adopted a more aggressive policy. The liberation of the slaves, with its blow to the slave economy and the addition of almost 200,000 Negro soldiers to the northern armies, proved to be of decisive importance. From the beginning of 1863 the slave power was clearly doomed. But it took two more

---

[1] Elizabeth Lawson, *Thaddeus Stevens*, p. 16, N. Y., 1942.
[2] Philip S. Foner, ed., *Frederick Douglass: Selections From His Writings*, p. 63, N. Y., 1945.
[3] Herbert Aptheker, *To Be Free: Studies in American Negro History*, p. 71, N. Y., 1948.

years of bitter warfare until the South admitted defeat, with Lee's surrender to Grant at Appomattox Court House, Virginia, on April 9, 1865. At the cost of half a million soldiers dead and a million more permanently crippled, the reactionary planters had been driven from political power and their slaves freed.

The Civil War constituted a bourgeois-democratic revolution. The capitalists of the North broke the dominant political power of the big southern landowners and seized power for themselves; the slave system, which had become economically a brake upon the development of capitalism, was shattered; four million slaves were formally freed; and the tempo of industrialization and the growth of the working class were enormously speeded up all over the country.

THE NEGRO PEOPLE AND THE WORKING CLASS IN THE WAR

In this long and bloody war the oppressed Negro people displayed boundless heroism. In many ways they sabotaged the war efforts of the South; they captured Confederate steamers and brought them into northern ports; and they were the major source of military intelligence for the North. In the plantation areas the slaves' spirit of rebellion was so pronounced that the South was compelled to divert a large section of its armed forces to the task of keeping them suppressed.

The heroism and abandon with which the newly-freed slaves fought in the Union armies amazed the white soldiers and officers. Characteristic of many similar reports was the statement of Colonel Thomas Wentworth Higginson: "It would have been madness to attempt with the bravest white troops what [I] successfully accomplished with black ones."[1] The action of the almost legendary Negro woman, Harriet Tubman, who led many forays deep into the South to free slaves, was bravery in its supremest sense. And when Lincoln was urged in 1864 to give up the use of Negro troops, he replied: "Take from us and give to the enemy the hundred and thirty, forty, or fifty thousand colored persons now serving us as soldiers, seamen, and laborers, and we cannot longer maintain the contest."[2]

Together with the approximately 200,000 Negro fighters in the northern army and navy, there were also about 250,000 more employed in various capacities with the armed forces. Aptheker quotes government figures estimating that over 36,000 Negro soldiers died during the

[1] Cited by Foner, *History of the Labor Movement in the U.S.*, p. 319.
[2] Carl Sandburg, *Abraham Lincoln: The War Years*, Vol. 3, p. 210, N. Y., 1939.

war. He states that "the mortality rate among the United States Colored Troops in the Civil War was thirty-five percent greater than that among other troops, notwithstanding the fact that the former were not enrolled until some eighteen months after the fighting began."[1] Of the enlisted personnel of the northern navy, about one-fourth were Negroes, and of these Aptheker estimates approximately 3,200 died of disease and in battle. These gallant fighting services were recompensed at first by paying the Negro soldiers at lower rates than the white soldiers.

Organized labor also played a large and heroic part in the Civil War. The outbreak of the war found the great mass of the workers backing the war as a struggle to stop the further extension of slavery. Only a small section supported the advanced stand of the Marxists, who demanded abolition. A small minority of workers, the most backward elements in the big commercial centers of Boston and New York, were strongly under the anti-war influence of the Copperheads. There was also a small but influential group that opposed all wars on pacifist grounds. All through the war the workers suffered the most ruthless exploitation from the profiteering capitalists. Price gouging was rampant, and the capitalists brazenly used every means to cheat the government and to enrich themselves.

The call for volunteers received a tremendous response from the workers. Overnight, regiments were organized in various crafts. Foreign-born workers responded with great enthusiasm. Among the labor contingents to enlist were the DeKalb regiment of German clerks, the Polish League, and a company of Irish laborers. One of the first regiments to move in the defense of Washington was organized by the noted labor leader, William Sylvis, who only a few months before had voted against Lincoln. It has been estimated that about fifty percent of the industrial workers enlisted. T. V. Powderly, head of the Knights of Labor, was not far wrong when he declared years later that in the Civil War, "the great bulk of the army was made up of working men."[2]

At the start of the war, the labor movement was in a weakened condition, not yet having fully recovered from the ravages of the 1857 economic crisis. In the main, organized labor followed the bourgeoisie led by Lincoln, without as yet entering the struggle as a class having its own political organization and full consciousness of its specific aims. There was an actual basis for this course, inasmuch as the interests of the workers, in the fight against slavery, coincided with those of the northern industrialists. As the war progressed, labor's line strengthened and

1 Aptheker, *To Be Free*, p. 78.
2 Terence V. Powderly, *Thirty Years of Labor*, p. 58, Columbus, Ohio, 1889.

the workers became a powerful force pressing for the freedom of the slaves and for a revolutionary prosecution of the war.

ROLE AND STRATEGY OF THE MARXISTS IN THE WAR PERIOD

The war record of the Marxists, predecessors of the Communist Party of today, was one of the most inspiring chapters in the annals of the Civil War. Their response to Lincoln's call for volunteers set a good example for the entire nation. Within a few days the New York Turners, Marxist-led, organized a whole regiment; the Missouri Turners put three regiments in the field; the Communist clubs and German Workers' Leagues sent over half their members into the armed forces. The Marxists fought valorously on many battlefields.

Joseph Weydemeyer, formerly an artillery officer in the German army, recruited an entire regiment, rose to the position of colonel, and was assigned by Lincoln as commander of the highly strategic area of St. Louis. August Willich, who became a brigadier general, Robert Rosa, a major, and Fritz Jacobi, a lieutenant who was killed at Fredericksburg, were all members of the New York Communist Club. There were many other Marxists at the front.

The American Marxists, taught by Marx and Engels, had a more profound understanding of the nature of the war than any other group in the nation. They realized that a defeat for the Union forces would mean the end of the most advanced bourgeois-democratic republic and a retrogression to semi-feudal conditions. Victory for the North, they knew, would greatly advance democracy. They understood the war as a basic conflict of two opposed systems, which could only be resolved by revolutionary measures.

Hence, from the very beginning, the Marxists raised the decisive slogans of emancipation of the slaves, arming of the freedmen, confiscation of the planters' estates, and distribution of the land among the landless Negro and white masses. They understood, too, the Marxist policy of co-operation with the bourgeoisie when it was fighting for progressive ends. During the war they tended to strengthen the position of the working class and its Negro and farmer allies and practically, if not consciously, to make them the leading force in the war coalition. They fought against pacifism and against Copperhead influences within and without labor's ranks. A major service of the Marxists was in helping to defeat the aspirations of Fremont to get the Republican nomination away from Lincoln in 1864. Marx urged the working class to make the outcome of the Civil War count in the long run for the workers as much as the outcome of the War for Independence had counted for the bourgeoisie. This, however, the weak forces of the workers were unable to do. Nevertheless, their relative clarity of political line and their tireless spirit made the Marxists a political force far out of proportion to their still very small numbers.

During the Civil War Karl Marx himself played a vitally important part, his genius displaying great brilliance. Marx's many writings in the New York *Daily Tribune* and elsewhere constituted an outstanding demonstration of the power of revolutionary theory in interpreting developments, in seeing their inherent connections, and in understanding the direction in which the classes were moving. From the inception of the conflict and through every one of its crucial stages, Karl Marx, incomparably deeper than any other person, grasped the basic significance of events and projected the necessary line of policy and action. Lenin considered this "a model example" of how the creators of the *Communist Manifesto* defined the tasks of the proletariat in application to the different stages of the struggle.

Far better than the northern bourgeois leaders, Marx clearly understood that here was a conflict between "two opposing social systems" which must be fought out to "the victory of one or the other system." He blasted those who believed that it was just a big quarrel over states rights which could be smoothed over; he criticized the bourgeois leaders of the North for "abasing" themselves before the southern slave power, and he pressed Lincoln again and again to take decisive action. From the outbreak of hostilities Marx urged the North to wage the struggle in a revolutionary manner, as the only possible way to win the victory. He demanded that Lincoln raise the "full-throated cry of emancipation of slavery"; he called for the arming of the Negro slaves, and he pointed out the tremendous psychological effects that would be produced by the formation of even a single regiment of Negro soldiers. In the most discouraging times of the war Marx never despaired of the North's ultimate victory. His and Engels' proposals for military strategy were no less sound than their penetrating political analysis. Marx clearly gave the theoretical lead to the northern democratic forces in the Civil War.[1]

Marx, as the leader of the First International, exerted a powerful influence in mobilizing the workers of England and the Continent in support of the northern cause. With his position as correspondent to the important *Die Presse* of Vienna, Marx was also able to influence general European opinion regarding the decisive events in America. He upheld the Union cause in his inaugural address to the International and in three major official political documents addressed by that organization,

[1] Marx and Engels, *The Civil War in the U.S.*

in less than a year, to President Lincoln, President Johnson, and the National Labor Union.

The British ruling class, despite all their pretended opposition to slavery, wanted nothing better than to intervene in the war on the side of the Confederacy. If they were prevented from doing this, it was primarily due to the militant anti-slavery attitude of the British working class, who hearkened to the advice of Marx and developed a powerful anti-slavery movement. As Marx said, "It was not the wisdom of the ruling classes, but the heroic resistance to their criminal folly by the working classes of England that saved the west of Europe from plunging headlong into an infamous crusade for the perpetuation and propagation of slavery on the other side of the Atlantic."[1]

History records few such effective demonstrations of international labor solidarity. Lincoln himself recognized this when, addressing the Manchester textile workers who were starving because of the cotton blockade, he characterized their support as "an instance of sublime Christian heroism which has not been surpassed in any age in any country."[2] Lincoln also thanked the First International for its assistance, and the United States Senate, on March 2, 1863, joined in tribute to the British workers. The international support of labor was a real factor in bringing to a successful conclusion this "world historic, progressive and revolutionary war," as Lenin called it.

[1] Karl Marx, Inaugural Address, Sept. 28, 1864, in *Founding of the First International*, p. 38, N. Y., 1937.
[2] Sandburg, *Abraham Lincoln: The War Years*, Vol. 2, p. 24.

4. The International Workingmen's Association
(1864-1876)

The International Workingmen's Association was founded in London on September 28, 1864. Its leading organizer and political leader was Karl Marx. The I.W.A. was formed during a period of rising political struggle in Europe and the United States. It was the first international organization of the rapidly growing trade union and socialist movements of the period, the first great realization of Marx's famous slogan, "Workingmen of all countries, unite!" The I.W.A. was committed to a program of the complete emancipation of the working class. Engels described it as "an association of workingmen embracing the most progressive countries of Europe and America, and concretely demonstrating the international character of the socialist movement to the workingmen themselves as well as to the capitalists and governments."[1]

The Marxists began to build the I.W.A. in the United States shortly after the Civil War, in 1867. Section No. 1, formed in 1869, was an amalgamation of the German General Workers Union and the Communist Club of New York. The combined group was called the Social Party of New York. Toward the end of 1870 two additional sections, French and Bohemian, were set up. These first three sections established the North American Federation of the I.W.A., with F. A. Sorge as corresponding secretary of the Central Committee. By 1872, the I.W.A. had 30 sections, with a membership of over 5,000, distributed in many parts of the country.

FROM REVOLUTION TO COUNTER-REVOLUTION

The I.W.A., a most important stage in the development of American Marxism, for the first time provided at least a loose national center for the groups of Marxists, and began to function during a most crucial era of American history. With the defeat of the slave-owners in the Civil War, the revolution had completed but its first phase, the freeing of the slaves. It was now necessary to confiscate the planters' estates, to give

[1] Cited by Morris Hillquit, *History of Socialism in the United States*, p. 178, N. Y., 1903.

land to the Negro ex-slaves, and also to prevent the return to power of the defeated slavocracy.¹ These were the revolutionary tasks of the Reconstruction period.

The bourgeoisie was split over these basic questions. The left, or Radical Republicans, led by Stevens, called for a democratic reconstruction of the South; whereas the right forces, grouped around President Johnson (after Lincoln's assassination on April 14, 1865) wanted to halt the revolution and to restore the landowners to power in the South.

In December 1865, the Stevens forces, who controlled Congress, succeeded in rejecting Johnson's reactionary reconstruction program, and they also passed the Thirteenth Amendment, abolishing slavery throughout the United States. During 1866, after scoring a victory in the hard-fought elections of that year, they enacted the Civil Rights Bill, the Freedmen's Bureau Bill, and the Fourteenth Amendment, providing for equal rights of Negroes and whites. In 1867, they also put through the Reconstruction Acts. The sum total of these measures was to give the Negro people a minimum of freedom, but not the land which they so basically needed.

The Negro freedmen, with strong revolutionary initiative and consciousness, organized people's conventions, engaged actively in political action, elected many high Negro officials in local and state governments, and in various places fought arms in hand for the all-important land. Together with their white allies, they played an important part in many of the reconstruction period state governments in the South and they wrote a large amount of advanced and progressive legislation. They gave a brilliant demonstration of their political capacity. There were two Negro U.S. Senators, H. R. Revels and Blanche K. Bruce, both of Mississippi, between 1870 and 1881. Fourteen Negroes were members of the House during the same general period. There were also Negro lieutenant-governors in Louisiana, South Carolina, and Mississippi, as well as large numbers of Negro state and local officials in many southern states.

Karl Marx, with his great revolutionary knowledge and experience, understood the need of consolidating the victory won during the Civil War and he anticipated the danger of counter-revolution. In the famous September 1865 "Address to the People of the United States" of the General Council of the I.W.A., Marx warned the American people to "Declare your fellow citizens from this day forth free and equal, without any reserve. If you refuse them citizens' rights while you exact from them citizens' duties, you will sooner or later face a new struggle which will once more drench your country in blood."² This was the general line

---
1 James S. Allen, *Reconstruction, the Battle for Democracy*, p. 31, N. Y., 1937.
2 Schlueter, *Lincoln, Labor, and Slavery*, p. 200.

of the I.W.A. forces in the United States, but the American Marxists did not fully understand how to make the fight against the counter-revolution.

The working class, supported by the farmers and Negroes, was the only class that could have carried through the bourgeois-democratic revolution of 1861-65 to completion in the Reconstruction period. But it was much too immature politically to accomplish this huge task. Preoccupied as it was with its urgent economic problems and afflicted with petty-bourgeois illusions, labor did not yet understand its true role as leader of all the oppressed. It could not, therefore, rally its natural allies—the working farmers, and Negro people—against the growing reaction of northern industrialists and southern planters. Consequently, the counter-revolution triumphed in the South.

The northern bourgeoisie had accomplished its major purposes by the Civil War. It smashed the national political control of the planters; it held the country intact; it removed the principal barriers to rapid capitalist development; it won complete control of the government. This was what it sought. With northern capital grown enormously stronger during the war and no longer fearing its old-time enemy, the planters, the bourgeoisie sought to make the latter its obedient allies, and it had no interest whatever in creating a body of free Negro farmers in the South. It wanted instead to put a halt to the revolution. Hence, during the presidency of Andrew Johnson, the northern capitalists, after defeating the Stevens Radicals, arrived at a tacit agreement with the planters whereby, with Ku Klux Klan violence, the latter were able to repress the Negro people and to force them down into the system of peonage in which they still live. This was a characteristic example of how the ruling, exploiting class, faced by a revolutionary situation, has resorted to terrorism and illegal counter-revolutionary violence.

Stimulated by the requirements of the war and released from the restraints of the slavocracy, industrial development, especially in the North, advanced at an unprecedented pace during the next decades. Heavy industry and the railroads recorded a very rapid expansion. The concentration of industries and the growth of corporations were among the significant features of the times. The bourgeoisie hastened to use its new political power to plunder the public domain and the public treasury. Thus the Civil War set off roaring decades of expansion and speculation, and a wild orgy of graft and corruption. It was the "Gilded Age." The swift development of capitalism also caused a rapid realignment of class forces, and the sharpening of all class antagonisms.

THE MARXISTS AND THE NATIONAL LABOR UNION

The broad expansion of capitalism, the increase in the number of industrial workers, and the intensification of labor exploitation during the Civil War decade also brought about a rapid growth in the trade union movement. Thus, in 1863 there were 79 local unions in 20 crafts, and a year later the figure had jumped up to 270 locals in 53 crafts. With the end of the war the tempo of growth became still faster. The need for a general national organization of labor grew acute. After an ineffectual effort with the Industrial Assembly of America in 1864, success came with the setting up of the National Labor Union in Baltimore on August 26, 1866. Joseph Weydemeyer, the Marxist leader, who contributed greatly to its founding, died of cholera in St. Louis on the day the N.L.U. convention began.

Marxist influence was definitely a factor in this great stride forward of the working class, but the N.L.U. was not a Marxist organization. In all the industrial centers the socialists were active trade union builders, and they had a number of delegates at the Baltimore convention. William H. Sylvis[1] of the Molders Union and leader of the National Labor Union, although not a Marxist, was a friend of Weydemeyer and Sorge and also a supporter of the I.W.A. He had a great talent for organization and was the first real national trade union leader. William J. Jessup, head of the New York Carpenters, was in direct communication with the General Council of the I.W.A. A. C. Cameron, editor of the *Workingman's Advocate,* reprinted in full all the addresses of the I.W.A. General Council, as well as many articles by Marx, Wilhelm Liebknecht, and Sorge. Ira Steward, noted eight-hour day leader, read parts of *Capital* and was profoundly impressed by it. Even Samuel Gompers, then a young member of the labor movement and a friend of Sorge, was affected by the I.W.A. He said: "I became interested in the International, for its principles appealed to me as solid and practical." Of this time Gompers declared: "Unquestionably, in these early days of the 'seventies the International dominated the labor movement in New York City."[2]

The N.L.U. during its six years of existence led important struggles and developed much correct basic labor policy. One of its main activities was campaigning for the eight-hour day. As a result of these efforts, Congress, on June 25, 1868, passed a law according the eight-hour day to laborers, mechanics, and all other workers in Federal employ.[3]

---

[1] Charlotte Todes, *William H. Sylvis and the National Labor Union,* N. Y., 1942.
[2] Samuel Gompers, *Seventy Years of Life and Labor,* Vol. 1, pp. 60, 85, N. Y., 1925.
[3] Foner, *History of the Labor Movement in the U.S.,* p. 377.

The N.L.U. was also active in defending the unemployed. And it was the first trade union movement in the world to advocate equal pay for women and men doing equal work. Kate Mullaney, an outstanding union fighter, was appointed by Sylvis in 1868 as assistant secretary and organizer of women.[1] The N.L.U. also campaigned against child labor and for the organization of the unorganized in all crafts and industries.

The founders of the N.L.U. understood the need for independent political action. This led to the formation of the Labor Reform Party in 1871. The N.L.U. and the Labor Reform Party, however, fell into the hands of opportunists and reformers, who finally ran both of them into the ground. This trend was hastened by the sudden death of Sylvis in July 1869.

The Marxists took an active part in all N.L.U. activities. They were militant builders of the trade unions and advocates of independent political action. They participated in all the strikes and other struggles of the period. They helped to organize the historic eight-hour day parade in New York in 1871. In this parade a large I.W.A. contingent marched with the 20,000 workers, carrying through the streets of the city for the first time a red banner inscribed with the slogan, "Workingmen of all countries, unite!" As the I.W.A. section entered the City Hall plaza, it was greeted with lusty cheers from the 5,000 assembled, who shouted, "*Vive la Commune.*" The Marxists were also a leading factor in the great Tompkins Square, New York, demonstration of the unemployed in 1874.

During this period of activity one of the big achievements of the I.W.A. was to secure the affiliation of the United Irish Workers, a group of Irish laborers. They were led by J. P. McDonnell, an able Marxist, a Fenian, and co-worker of Marx in the First International congresses. McDonnell, a capable and active trade unionist, was very effective in organizing the unorganized. For many years he was the editor of the *Labor Standard,* the leading trade union journal of the period. Gompers called him "the Nestor of trade union editors."

THE N.L.U. AND THE NEGRO QUESTION

During these years the question of Negro labor was a burning issue for the labor movement. The bosses were systematically playing the white workers against the newly-freed Negro workers, and were trying to use Negro workers to keep down the wages of all workers—even as strikebreakers. The more advanced leaders of the N.L.U., especially the Marx-

[1] Todes, *William H. Sylvis,* p. 84.

ists, had some conception of the necessity of Negro and white labor solidarity and of the N.L.U. undertaking the organization of the freedmen. But, despite Sylvis, Richard Trevellick, and others, nothing much was done about it. Strong Jim Crow practices existed in many of the unions, and consequently the body of Negro workers were not organized nor their interests protected.

As a result, the Negro workers launched their own organization. In December 1869, after failure of the N.L.U. to give the Negro workers consideration at its convention a few months earlier, they called together a convention of 156 delegates, mostly from the South, and organized the National Colored Labor Union, with Isaac Myers as president. Trevellick was present, representing the N.L.U. The convention elected five delegates to attend the next convention of the N.L.U. The N.C.L.U. also set up, as headquarters, the National Bureau of Labor in Washington. Its paper was the *New National Era*.[1]

"In February, 1870, the Bureau issued a prospectus containing the chief demands of the Negro people; it called for a legislative body to fight for legislation which would gain equality before the law for Negroes; it proposed an educational campaign to overcome the opposition of white mechanics to Negroes in the trades; it recommended cooperatives and homesteads to the Negro people."[2]

Relations between the N.L.U. and N.C.L.U. became strained over a number of questions. They reached the breaking point on the formation of the National Land Reform Party. That this first great effort to establish unity between Negro and white workers failed was to be ascribed chiefly to the short-sighted policies of the white leaders of the N.L.U. They never understood the burning problems of the Negro people during the reconstruction period, some of them holding ideas pretty much akin to those of President Johnson. The N.C.L.U. soon disappeared under the fierce pressure of the mounting reaction in the South.

The Marxists, both within and without the N.L.U., were active on the Negro question, primarily in a trade union sense. They demanded the repeal of all laws discriminating against Negroes. Section No. 1 of the I.W.A. set up a special committee to organize Negro workers into trade unions. Consequently, the Negro people looked upon the Socialists as trustworthy friends to whom they could turn for co-operation. In the big New York eight-hour day parade Negro union groups participated with the I.W.A. contingent. And in the parade against the execution of the Communards a company of Negro militia, the Skidmore guards, marched under the banner of the First International.

[1] Charles H. Wesley, *Negro Labor in the United States*, p. 174, N. Y., 1927.
[2] Foner, *History of the Labor Movement in the U.S.*, p. 405.

THE N.L.U. AND THE FIRST INTERNATIONAL

From its beginning, the National Labor Union had a strong international spirit. This was largely due to German Marxist and English Chartist influences within its ranks. It maintained friendly relations with the International Workingmen's Association. Marx was highly gratified at the founding of the new national labor center in the United States. The question of affiliation to the I.W.A. occupied a prominent place at all N.L.U. conventions. Sylvis especially appreciated the importance of the international solidarity of the workers.

At the 1867 convention of the N.L.U. President W. J. Jessup moved to affiliate with the I.W.A., with the backing of Sylvis. The convention did not vote for affiliation, however, but it did agree to send Richard F. Trevellick to the next I.W.A. congress. Lack of funds, however, prevented his going. Good co-operative relations always existed between the two organizations, Karl Marx paying special attention to the promising N.L.U. Finally, late in 1869, A. C. Cameron attended the I.W.A. congress at Basle, as the representative of the N.L.U. There he presented several proposals, providing for co-operation between European and American labor to regulate immigration and to prevent the shipping of scabs to break strikes in the United States. The 1870 convention of the N.L.U., while not actually voting affiliation to the I.W.A., nevertheless adopted a resolution which endorsed the principles of the International Workingmen's Association and expressed the intention of affiliating with it "at no distant date."[1]

The death of Sylvis in 1869 was a heavy blow to the growing international labor solidarity. Commons says, "Had it not been for this loss of its leader, the alliance of the National Labor Union with the International, judging from Sylvis' correspondence, would have been speedily brought about."[2] The General Council of the I.W.A. sent a letter to the N.L.U., signed by Karl Marx, mourning the loss of Sylvis. It said that his death, by removing "a loyal, persevering, and indefatigable worker in the good cause from among you, has filled us with great grief and sorrow."

THE DECLINE OF THE NATIONAL LABOR UNION

The N.L.U. reached its high point, with an estimated 600,000 members, in 1869. After that date it began to decline, and its decay was rapid. At its 1871 convention there were only 22 delegates, and these mostly

[1] Todes, *William H. Sylvis*, p. 90.
[2] Commons, *History of Labor in the U.S.*, Vol. 2, p. 132.

agrarian reformers. The American Section of the I.W.A., which was affiliated, quit in discontent at the way the organization was being run. The 1872 convention brought forth only seven delegates, old-time leaders. This was the end of the N.L.U. Attempts were made to call conventions to revive it, in 1873 and 1874 at Columbus and Rochester, but these efforts were fruitless, the organization being dead beyond recall.

Numerous reasons combined to bring about the end of the once-promising National Labor Union. Among these was the fact that the organization was not definitely a trade union body. From the outset it was composed of "trade unions, workers' associations, and eight-hour leagues," and in the end it had been invaded by numerous preachers, editors, lawyers, and other careerists, who cultivated petty-bourgeois illusions among the workers. Moreover, the organization was poorly financed, and it was too decentralized. It had no dues system, nor any paid, continuous leadership. Its main activity was the holding of national conventions, with the follow-up work being done by its affiliated organizations. Last and most important of its weaknesses, the organization, under the influence of Lassalleans, finally deprecated trade union action and turned its major attention to the currency question and to other petty-bourgeois reformist political activities. This alienated the trade unions, which quit the organization, and it fell a prey to all sorts of non-working class elements. As early as 1870, Sorge wrote a letter to Karl Marx in which he clearly foresaw the course of events: "The National Labor Union, which had such brilliant prospects in the beginning of its career, was poisoned by Greenbackism and is slowly but surely dying."[1] The influence of the Marxists upon the N.L.U. was much too limited to counteract these disintegrating influences.

The National Labor Union, despite its short six years of life, played an important part in the development of the American labor movement. It was the successor of the National Trades Union of the 1830's and the predecessor of the Knights of Labor and the American Federation of Labor. It was a pioneer in the organization of Negro workers, in the defense of the rights of women and all other workers, in the organization of independent political action, and in the development of the international solidarity of the working class. The traditions of struggle that Sylvis and his co-workers left behind them will long be an inspiration to the forces of American labor. They are vivid in the Communist Party of today.

[1] Cited by Foner, *History of the Labor Movement in the U.S.*, p. 429.

THE MARXISTS AND THE LASSALLEANS

During the period of the International Workingmen's Association a major ideological struggle of the Marxists was directed against Lassalleanism. Ferdinand Lassalle in 1863 organized the General Association of German Workers in Germany, the program of which was to win universal suffrage and then to use the workers' votes to secure state credits for producers' co-operatives. This Lassalle saw as the road to socialism.[1] He considered as futile the trade union struggle of the workers for better economic conditions. This rejection he based upon his theory of "the iron law of wages," which assumed that the average wages of workers, always down to minimum levels, could not be raised by economic action. Hence trade unionism was useless.

The German immigrants brought Lassalle's ideas with them, and these gained considerable currency among the German workers in the United States. In this country, where the workers already had the vote, apparently all that remained for them to do was to use their ballots to gain control of the government and then to apply Lassalle's scheme of state-financed co-operatives. Whereupon, the workers' problems would be solved. This theory led to extremely pernicious results in practice. It meant the weakening of the everyday struggles of the workers and the Negro people; it led to neglect and isolation from the trade unions; it tended to reduce the workers' struggle to opportunist political activity. Lassalleanism was largely responsible for the fatal lessening of the basic trade union economic functions of the National Labor Union, where it exerted great influence. Seeing the unions breaking up during the big economic crisis of 1873 and in the lost strikes of the period, many workers lost faith in trade unionism and gave ear to the Lassallean illusions.

From the first appearance of Lassalleanism the Marxists, led by Sorge, took issue actively with its theory and practice, showing it to be false and injurious. Of great help to the American Marxists in this struggle was Marx's celebrated polemic against Weston in England, which was published, after Marx's death, under the title, *Value, Price and Profit*. In this pamphlet Marx proved conclusively that whereas the trend of capitalism is to bring about the relative and absolute impoverishment of the workers, the latter, by resolute economic and political action, can nevertheless secure a larger share of the value which they create. Marx demonstrated that while it was possible to abolish exploitation only by abolishing capitalism, the workers can successfully resist the efforts

[1] Thomas Kirkup, *History of Socialism*, p. 108, London, 1920.

of the capitalists to force them down to a bare subsistence level.

The fight between the Marxists and Lassalleans raged with special sharpness for several years during the 1870's in all the journals and branches of the I.W.A., and it was also reflected in the trade unions. In this struggle the Marxists stood four-square for strong trade unions and for active economic struggle. They also contended that the workers should put up candidates in elections only when they had solid trade union backing. Good theory and the stern realities of life fought on the side of the Marxists. The workers, faced with hard necessity, continued to build their unions and to strike, and the opportunistic political campaigns of the Lassalleans suffered one defeat after another. The Lassalleans fought a losing battle. Gompers, at that time a radical young trade unionist, sided with the Marxists in this historic struggle.

During the course of the controversy, in 1874, the Lassalleans organized the Labor Party in Illinois and the Social-Democratic Party of North America in the East. They had their own journal, the *Vorbote*. Most active in these Lassallean developments were Karl Klinge and Adolph Strasser, the cigarmaker, who later played a prominent part with Gompers in the formation of the American Federation of Labor. The Marxists gradually won a large measure of control over the Lassallean journals and organizations and eventually gave them a Marxist program.

Besides this fight against the right, against the Lassalleans, the American Marxists, with the active advice of Marx and Engels, also conducted a struggle against the deep-seated and persistent left sectarianism within the I.W.A. Among the current manifestations of this disease were tendencies among the German socialist workers to neglect to learn the English language and the American customs, to isolate themselves from the broad American masses and their daily struggles, to launch trade unions solely of German workers and dual to existing labor organizations, and generally to fail to apply Marxist principles concretely to American conditions. Some years later Engels, dealing with the still persisting sectarianism in the United States, stated: "The Germans have not understood how to use their theory as a lever which could set the American masses in motion; they do not understand the theory themselves for the most part and treat it in a doctrinaire and dogmatic way, as something which has got to be learned off by heart but which will then supply all needs without more ado. To them it is a *credo* and not a guide to action."[1] Marx was equally outspoken in his criticism of this doctrinaire and sectarian weakness in the United States.

[1] Marx and Engels, *Selected Correspondence*, pp. 449-50.

DISSOLUTION OF THE FIRST INTERNATIONAL

The years of the International Workingmen's Association were full of storm and struggle. Organized reaction in Europe, frightened at the revolutionary implications of the International, waged ruthless war against it. This was particularly true after the defeat of the historic Paris Commune in 1871. The I.W.A. was outlawed in France and other countries. But more effective in bringing the First International to an end were profound internal ideological weaknesses. To correct these, numerous theoretical and practical battles were waged by the Marxists to establish Marxism as the predominant working class ideology. They fought against the opportunist trade union leaders in England, against the Proudhonists in France, against the Lassalleans in Germany, and against the Bakuninists on a general scale. The fight against the Bakuninists was the most severe.

Michael Bakunin, a Russian anarchist, led a determined struggle to wrest the leadership of the world's workers away from the Marxists. In 1868, he organized the so-called Black International, with a program of anti-political, putschist violence, and he demanded affiliation with the I.W.A. Refused by the General Council, Bakunin carried the fight into the 1869 Congress of the I.W.A. at Basle, Switzerland. Marx won the day, with a substantial majority. In the ensuing split Bakunin was able to carry with him important French, Spanish, and Belgian organizations. The struggle grew very bitter, and at its 1872 congress the I.W.A., in view of the unfavorable internal and external situation, decided to move its headquarters to New York. F. A. Sorge was chosen as secretary.

The difficulties which beset the First International on a world scale also, with variations, afflicted its American section. The I.W.A. in the United States, in view of the political immaturity of the working class and the socialist movement, was undermined by all sorts of reformists, pure and simple trade unionists, Lassalleans, and Bakuninist anarchists. The I.W.A., after shifting its headquarters to the United States, continued for four more years. But, on July 15, 1876, at its Philadelphia convention, which was attended almost exclusively by American delegates, the First International formally dissolved itself. Thirteen years would pass before a new international would take the place of the I.W.A.; but in the United States, as we shall see later, the dissolution was but a prelude to a new upward swing of Marxism.

During its twelve years of existence the International Workingmen's Association in the United States contributed much to the development of the socialist movement. At the beginning it found a few scattered groups of Marxists with an uncertain ideology. It greatly strengthened their Marxist understanding, and it did much to unite them as a national grouping. In short, it laid the ideological and organizational foundations of the structure which has finally become the modern Communist Party. On an international scale, the I.W.A. did immense work in giving the workers a revolutionary outlook and in building their mass trade unions and political parties. The First International raised the world's labor movement out of its former muddle of utopian societies and half socialist sects and gave it a scientific Marxist groundwork. In the words of Lenin, "It laid the foundation of the international organization of the workers in order to prepare their revolutionary onslaught on capital . . . the foundation of their international proletarian struggle for socialism."[1]

[1] Lenin, *Selected Works*, Vol. 10, pp. 30-31.

5. The Socialist Labor Party
(1876-1890)

For a quarter of a century, from the dissolution of the International Workingmen's Association in 1876 to the foundation of the Socialist Party in 1900, the Socialist Labor Party was the standard bearer of Marxism in the United States. This marked the next big stage in the pre-history of the Communist Party. The decades of the S.L.P. were a period of intense industrialization, of growing monopoly capitalism and imperialism, of sharpening class struggles, of many of the greatest strikes in our national history, of big farmer movements, and of the gradual consolidation of Marxism into an organized force in the United States.

The need for a Marxist party being imperative, the socialist forces proceeded to reorganize one in Philadelphia, July 19-22, 1876, just a few days after the old I.W.A. was dissolved in that same city. The new body was the Workingmen's Party of America, the following year to be named the Socialist Labor Party. It was based primarily upon a fusion of the Marxist elements of the I.W.A., headed by F. A. Sorge and Otto Weydemeyer, son of Joseph Weydemeyer, and of the Lassallean forces of the Illinois Labor Party and the Social-Democratic Party, led by Adolph Strasser, A. Gabriel, and P. J. McGuire. All told, there were about 3,000 members represented. The Philadelphia founding convention had been preceded by a unity conference in Pittsburgh three months earlier.

The Lassalleans at the convention succeeded in securing a majority of the national committee of the new Party, and they also elected one of their number, Philip Van Patten, to the post of national secretary. In the shaping of policy, however, the influence of the Marxists was predominant. The Party demanded the nationalization of railroads, telegraphs, and all means of transportation, and it called for "all industrial enterprises to be placed under the control of the government as fast as practicable and operated by free co-operative trade unions for the good of the whole people."[1] The Declaration of Principles was taken from the general statutes of the I.W.A., and in the vital matters of trade unionism and political action, the Party's program unequivocally took the position of the old International.[2] That is, the new Party would energetically

[1] *The Socialist*, July 29, 1876.
[2] Commons, *History of Labor in the U.S.*, Vol. 2, p. 270.

support trade unionism and would base its parliamentary activity upon substantial trade union backing. A program of immediate demands was also adopted, and the Party headquarters was established in Chicago. J. P. McDonnell became editor of the Party's English organ, *The Labor Standard,* and Douai was made assistant editor of all Party publications.

Organizational, if not ideological, unity was thus established. The conflicting Marxist and Lassallean groups went right on with their disputes in the new organization. Lassallean opportunism, although as such a declining force during the next decade, was soon to graduate into its lineal political descendant, pseudo-Marxist right opportunism.

THE S.L.P. AND THE GREAT RAILROAD STRIKE

The economic crisis of 1873 was one of the severest in American history. The employers, taking advantage of the huge unemployment, slashed wages on all sides. The workers desperately replied with a series of bitter strikes, such as this country had never before experienced. These strikes were mainly spontaneous, most of the unions having fallen to pieces during the economic crisis. In 1874-75, there were broad, hard-fought strikes in the textile and mining industries. The "long strike" of 1875 in the anthracite coal region of Pennsylvania culminated in the hanging of ten Irish workers and the imprisonment of twenty-four others, as "Molly Maguires." They were falsely charged with murder, arson, and other violence against the mine owners. This was another of the many shameful labor frame-up cases that have disfigured American history.

The most important strike of this period, however, was the big railroad strike of 1877. This reached the intensity of virtual civil war. Beginning in Martinsburg, West Virginia, on July 17, 1877, all crafts, Negro and white, struck against a deep wage slash. Like a prairie fire the spontaneous strike spread over many railroads, from coast to coast. The existing weak railroad brotherhoods, led by conservatives, were but a small factor. For the first time the United States found itself in the grip of a national strike.

The government proceeded ruthlessly to break the strike. The big railroad centers were flooded with militia and federal troops. About 100,000 soldiers were under arms.[1] In many places the soldiers fraternized with the strikers; in others they fired upon the crowds, and in some places the militant strikers drove them out. Many scores were killed. Finally, the desperate strike was crushed. The workers learned at bitter cost the need for strong unions and organized political action. This near-

[1] Justus Ebert, *American Industrial Evolution*, p. 60, N. Y., 1907.

civil war deeply shook all sections of the population throughout the land.

The Workingmen's Party was very active in this great strike, as in all others of the period. The Party executive urged the workers and the public to support the strike; it raised the eight-hour demand and called for nationalization of the railroads. In Chicago, a socialist stronghold, the Party organized an effective general strike. "Chicago is in possession of the Communists," shrieked the newspapers. Albert R. Parsons was then one of the most active Party leaders in Chicago. The leadership of the socialists in St. Louis was also equally outstanding, and it made the strike very effective. "This is a labor revolution," cried the local paper, *The Republican.* For a week the Party-led strike committee was in virtual possession of St. Louis.[1] Finally, the strike was crushed by troops and the wholesale arrest of the strikers' leaders. Activities were carried on by the Party in other strike centers.

For the Workingmen's Party all this was a new and tremendous experience in leading huge masses in struggle. It was a powerful blow against the sectarian barriers that were separating the Party from the workers. Marx and Engels hailed the great mass struggle. In its 1877 convention the Party changed its name to the Socialistic Labor Party of North America. The Party grew rapidly; by 1879 it had 10,000 members in 25 states, and between 1876 and 1878, 24 papers were established.

During this critical period, in 1877, there was published in the United States the famous scientific work, *Ancient Society,* by Lewis Henry Morgan. It was primarily a study of the social organization of the Iroquois Indians and perhaps the most important book ever written in the Western Hemisphere. Engels declared that "it is one of the few epoch-making books of our times." Morgan was not a Socialist, but Engels said of him that "in his own way [he] discovered afresh in America the materialist conception of history discovered by Marx forty years ago."[2]

WORKERS' AND FARMERS' POLITICAL STRUGGLES

Following the big strikes of 1877, the workers, outraged by the brutal suppression methods of the government, took a sharp turn toward political action. Labor parties sprang up in many cities and states. In the meantime, the farmers, under the pressure of the severe economic crisis, also embarked upon political activity. They created the Greenback Party, whose cure-all panacea was the issuance of paper-money green-

[1] Hillquit, *History of Socialism in the U.S.*, p. 233.
[2] Frederick Engels, *The Origin of the Family, Private Property, and the State,* p. 5, N. Y., 1942 (Preface to 1884 edition).

backs, hopefully to pay off the farmers' mortgages, to liquidate the national debt, and to finance a general prosperity. In the 1876 elections the workers' parties refused to support the Greenback Party, because it had no labor demands in its program.

By 1878, however, there had developed a farmer-labor alliance, the National Greenback-Labor Party. This party, which by then included in its program minimum labor demands, scored considerable success in the elections of that year, polling its high vote of 1,050,000 and sending 15 members to Congress. The capitalist press shouted that the Communist revolution was at hand. But it was an uneasy alliance of workers and farmers. Labor's forces resented the domination of the party by businessmen and big farmers, and they also reacted against the minor stress that was placed upon the workers' demands. Disintegration of the party, therefore, set in; so that in the 1880 presidential elections its candidate, General Weaver, got only 300,000 votes. The Greenback-Labor Party was already far along the road to oblivion.

The Marxists generally took a position of participating in these important political struggles. They actively supported the building of the local and state workingmen's parties, and they also endorsed the general plan of a worker-farmer political alliance. They raised demands, too, for the Negro workers. However, they had opposed supporting the Greenback Party in the 1876 elections on the sound ground that it did not defend the workers' interests. In the 1878 elections considerable socialist support was given to the Greenback-Labor Party candidates, and in 1880 a national endorsement of that party's candidates was extended by the Socialist Labor Party.

In the carrying out of this general line there was gross opportunism. The Lassalleans, headed by Van Patten and other middle class intellectuals, controlled the Party. Taking advantage of the heavy defeats suffered by the trade unions during the economic crisis and misinterpreting the swing of the workers toward political action, they held that the trade unions had proved themselves to be worthless and that thenceforth the Party should devote itself exclusively to parliamentary political action. They elaborated upon this opportunism by making impermissible compromises with the Greenbackers and by surrendering to Denis Kearney of the Pacific Coast, with his reactionary slogan, "The Chinese must go." They also watered down the S.L.P. program until it called for the abolition of capitalism by a step-at-a-time process. The Lassalleans, here and in Germany, were gradually dropping Lassalle's original utopian demand for state-financed producers' co-operatives, and were being transformed into the characteristic right-wing Social-Democrats, who were to wreak such havoc with the whole world's labor movement for many decades.

The crass opportunism of the S.L.P. right-wing leadership antagonized Sorge, Parsons, Schilling, McDonnell, and other Marxists and trade unionists in the Party. The latter elements, in particular, insisted that the Party should combine economic with political action. The Party conventions from 1877 to 1881 were torn with quarrels over this issue. The factional split widened, minor secession movements developed, membership declined, papers succumbed, and the Party sank into an internal crisis. Meanwhile, a new danger appeared on the horizon —anarcho-syndicalism. During the next few years, this was to threaten the very life of the Socialist Labor Party.

THE ANARCHO-SYNDICALIST MOVEMENT

Anarcho-syndicalism originated from a number of causes. Among these were the following: (a) the extreme violence with which the government repressed strikes generated among workers the idea of "meeting force with force"; (b) the robbing of workers' election candidates of votes tended to discredit working class political action altogether; (c) the fact that millions of immigrant workers had no votes also operated against organized political action; (d) the opportunist policies of the reformist leadership of the S.L.P. disgusted and repelled militant workers; (e) the influence of petty-bourgeois radicals upon the working class, and (f) the injection of European anarchist ideas gave a specific ideological content to the movement.

As early as 1875, to defend themselves, German workers in Chicago formed an armed group. This tendency spread rapidly, as a result of the government violence in the big 1877 strikes. In 1878, the S.L.P. national executive condemned the trend and ordered its advocates to leave the Party. In October 1881, the supporters of "direct action," led principally by Albert R. Parsons[1] and August Spies, met in Chicago and organized the Revolutionary Socialist Labor Party. This movement, however, did not take on a definitely anarchist complexion until after the arrival of Johann Most, a German anarchist, in 1882. Most found willing hearers, and in October 1883, a joint convention of anarchists and members of the Revolutionary Socialist Labor Party was held.

This convention formed the International Working People's Association.[2] Its program proposed "the destruction of the existing class gov-

---

[1] Parsons was nominated as the S.L.P. candidate for president in 1879, but did not accept because he was too young. See Lucy E. Parsons, *Life of Albert R. Parsons*, p. 22, Chicago, 1889.

[2] Not to be confused with the International Workingmen's Association. See Chapter 4.

ernment by all means, *i.e.*, by energetic, implacable, revolutionary, and international action," and the establishment of a system of industry based on "the free exchange of equivalent products between the production organizations."[1] The program condemned the ballot as a device designed by the capitalists to fool the workers. The Chicago group, more syndicalist than anarchist, inserted the clause that "the International recognizes in the trade union the embryonic group of the future society." Behind this movement was the anarchist anti-Marxist conception that socialism could be brought about by the desperate action of a small minority of the working class, impelling the masses into action.

The opportunist-led S.L.P. shriveled in the face of the strong drive of the anarcho-syndicalists. By 1883 the S.L.P. membership had dwindled to but 1,500, whereas that of the International went up to about 7,000. Also, the latter's several journals were flourishing. In April 1883, after six years as S.L.P. national secretary, Van Patten suddenly disappeared, turning up later as a government job-holder. Shortly afterward attempts were made by prominent S.L.P. members to fuse that organization with the anarcho-syndicalist group; but to no avail, the latter replying that the S.L.P. members should join their organization individually. From then on it was an open struggle between the two parties.

The anarcho-syndicalist International met shipwreck in May 1886, at Chicago. The militants of that organization were taking a leading part in the A.F. of L. trade unions' big agitation for the national eight-hour general strike movement, which climaxed on May first. At the McCormick Harvester plant six striking workers were killed by the police. The anarcho-syndicalists called a mass meeting of protest in the Haymarket on May 4th, with Parsons, Spies, and Fielden as the principal speakers. Some unknown person threw a bomb, killing seven police and four workers and wounding many more. In the wild hysteria following this event, Parsons, Fischer, Lingg, Fielden, Schwab, Spies, Engel, and Neebe were arrested. After a criminally unfair trial, another on the growing list of labor frame-ups, they were all convicted. Neebe, Schwab, and Fielden were given long prison terms; Lingg committed suicide while awaiting trial; and Parsons, Spies, Fischer and Engel were hanged on November 11, 1887. Governor John Altgeld, six years later, released the four remaining in prison and proclaimed their innocence.

The Haymarket Affair was a heavy blow especially to the International group, and after a futile effort in 1887 to amalgamate with the S.L.P. it dissolved. The substance of the Haymarket outrage was an attempt by the employers to destroy the young trade union movement.

1 Hillquit, *History of Socialism in the U.S.*, p. 238.

THE KNIGHTS OF LABOR

With the revival of industry, beginning in 1879, trade unionism, weakened in the long economic crisis, again spread with great rapidity. To meet the fierce exploitation by the employers, the workers had to have organization. Local trades councils and labor assemblies grew in many cities, and small craft unions also began to take shape. The Socialists, while only a small minority in the membership and leadership of the unions, were very active in all this work. The S.L.P. *Bulletin,* in September 1880, declared that the formation of the central bodies "has been accomplished mainly by the efforts of Socialists who influence and in some places control these assemblies, and are respected in all of them."[1]

A serious attempt to organize the labor movement upon a national scale was made through the International Labor Union, formed early in 1878. This center developed out of the joint efforts of such Socialists as Sorge, McDonnell, and Otto Weydemeyer, and also of the noted eight-hour day advocates, Ira Steward and G. E. McNeill. The I.L.U. laid heavy stress upon the eight-hour day, and advocated the ultimate emancipation of the working class. The organization finally developed, however, chiefly as a union of textile workers. It conducted a number of strikes, but was formally dissolved in 1887. More successful was the next big effort, the Knights of Labor.

The Noble Order of the Knights of Labor was organized in Philadelphia in December 1869, by Uriah S. Stephens and a handful of workers. It was at first limited to garment workers, but in 1871 it expanded to other trades. With the decline of the National Labor Union, the Knights of Labor grew and by 1877 it had 15 district or state assemblies. Like various other labor unions of the period, the K. of L. was a secret organization with an elaborate ritual. It held its first general assembly, or national convention, in Reading, Pennsylvania, in 1878, when it became an open body. The Order grew rapidly in the aftermath of the great 1877 strikes and under the effects of reviving industry. In 1883, the K. of L. had 52,000 members; in 1885, 111,000; and in 1886, its peak, about 700,000. Stephens was its Grand Master Workman until 1879, when he was succeeded by T. V. Powderly, who served until 1893, at which time he was replaced by J. R. Sovereign.

The K. of L. contained trends of Marxism, Lassalleanism, and "pure and simple" trade unionism. Its program set as its goal the Lassallean objective, "to establish co-operative institutions such as will tend to supersede the wage system by the introduction of a co-operative in-

[1] Cited by Foner, *History of the Labor Movement in the U.S.,* p. 498.

dustrial system." It proposed a legislative program which included labor, currency, and land reforms, and also government ownership of the railroads and telegraphs, as well as national control of banking. The Marxist influence was to be seen chiefly in the many militant strikes of the K. of L. The Order considered craft unionism too narrow in spirit and scope, and it aimed at a broad organization of the whole working class. Its motto was "An injury to one is the concern of all." The K. of L. accepted workers of all crafts into its local mixed assemblies. It had many Negro workers in its ranks and about 10 percent of its members were women. Professionals and small businessmen were also admitted, to the extent of 25 percent of the local membership.

Although its conservative leadership, heavily influenced by Lassallean and outright bourgeois conceptions, deprecated strikes, even sinking to the level of actual strikebreaking, the K. of L. made its greatest progress as a result of economic struggles. During 1884-85 the organization was especially effective in a number of big strikes of telegraphers, miners, lumbermen, and railroaders. Harassed masses of workers turned hopefully to the new organization, and the employers viewed it with the gravest alarm. The K. of L. swiftly became a powerful force in the industrial struggle. It also was active politically, participating generally in the broad labor and farmer political movements of its era.

The period of the rise of the K. of L. was one of internal crisis within the S.L.P.—what with the crippling effects of the right-wing leadership, the continuing pest of sectarianism, and the severe struggle of the Party against the anarcho-syndicalists. Nevertheless, the Party did exercise a considerable influence in the K. of L. from its earliest period as an open organization, particularly in the local assemblies, in various cities where German immigrant workers were in force.

THE AMERICAN FEDERATION OF LABOR

As the Knights of Labor developed, a new, rival union movement, eventually to become the A.F. of L., also began to take shape. This was based upon the national craft unions, which could find no satisfactory place in the K. of L. These organizations, some of which antedated the Civil War, objected to the mixed form of the K. of L., to its autocratic centralized leadership, to its chief concern with other than direct trade union questions, and to its neglect of their specific craft interests. Hence, gathering in Pittsburgh, on November 15, 1881, six national craft unions —painters, carpenters, molders, glass workers, cigar makers, and iron, steel, and tin workers—were the prime movers in setting up an organization more to their liking, the Federation of Organized Trades and Labor Unions of the United States and Canada.

Marxist influence was manifest but not dominant in this new movement. Samuel Gompers, a Jewish immigrant cigar maker born in London, who was its leading spirit, had long been associated with Marxist circles; indeed, he had probably belonged to the I.W.A., but later found it expedient to deny the fact. Gompers said that he had studied German so as to be able to read Marx's *Das Kapital.* Adolph Strasser, Ferdinand Laurrell, and P. J. McGuire, close Gompers associates, had been members of the S.L.P. There were eight S.L.P. members present among the 107 delegates at the founding convention. Marxist conceptions also stood out in the new body's preamble, still in effect in the A.F. of L. today. This signalizes "a struggle between capital and labor, which must grow in intensity from year to year." The constitution, which granted a high measure of autonomy to the national unions, was copied almost verbatim from that of the British Trades Union Congress and its Parliamentary Committee.[1]

The general trade union programs of the K. of L. and the new Federation were similar, but there were also important differences. "The Knights demanded government ownership of the systems of transportation and communication, but the new Federation did not. Nor did the Federation accept the monetary program of the Knights of Labor, indicating that it definitely regarded the industrial capitalist rather than the banker as the chief enemy of the wage-earners, and—unlike the Knights—had pretty nearly rid itself of the belief in financial panaceas. It is also significant that the Federation made no reference to producers or consumers co-operatives, and failed to recommend compulsory arbitration which the Knights supported."[2] The new Federation was evidently geared to limiting itself to concessions under capitalism, rather than aiming at the abolition of the existing regime of wage slavery.

It was clear soon after its foundation that the new labor center, basing itself upon the skilled workers, was little concerned with the welfare of the masses of semi-skilled and unskilled. The A.F. of L. aimed chiefly at organizing the developing labor aristocracy, a policy which dovetailed with the employer policy of corrupting the skilled workers at the expense of the unskilled. An anti-Negro bias was also to be observed in the affiliated A.F. of L. unions, reflecting the employers' policy of discriminating against these workers. These were long steps

[1] Lewis L. Lorwin, *The American Federation of Labor,* p. 13, Washington, 1933.
[2] Foner, *History of the Labor Movement in the U.S.,* pp. 523-24.

backward from the National Labor Union and the Knights of Labor. The K. of L. at its height, with some 700,000 members, had about 60,000 Negroes in its ranks, a figure not reached by the A.F. of L. for about fifty years, when it counted, however, a total of some three million members.

At first the new Federation was not considered as an enemy of the Knights of Labor—thus, at its first convention, 47 of the 107 delegates came from K. of L. organizations. Potential antagonisms sharpened, however, and soon the two labor centers were at loggerheads. Efforts were made, especially by the A.F. of L. leaders in the early years, to harmonize and unite the two bodies, but these came to naught and the rivals fought it out, to the eventual disappearance of the Knights.

For its first five years the Federation stagnated along, with only about 50,000 members. After its initial year Gompers was its president. At the Federation's second convention, in 1882, only 19 delegates attended. Nor were the three succeeding annual conventions any more promising. The attention of the workers, dazzled by the successful strikes of the K. of L., was focused on that organization. But the great events of 1886 were soon radically to change the whole labor union situation.

THE NATIONAL EIGHT-HOUR FIGHT

The developing class struggle after the Civil War reached a new height of militancy in the great fight for the eight-hour day in 1886. The agitation for this measure had been on the increase ever since the end of the war. Its foundation was the intensified exploitation to which the workers were being subjected. Marx called the eight-hour movement "the first fruit of the Civil War . . . that ran with the seven leagued boots . . . from the Atlantic to the Pacific."[1]

The Federation leaders, who were far more militant then than now, seized upon the shorter-hours issue. "Hovering on the brink of death, the Federation turned to the heroic measure of a universal strike which had been suggested a decade before by the Industrial Brotherhood. At its convention in Chicago in 1884 a resolution was adopted to the effect that from and after May 1, 1886, eight hours shall constitute a day's work."[2] The Federation put its forces behind the movement, but Powderly, the head of the Knights of Labor, a rank conservative, made the fatal mistake of opposing the strike.

The general strike centered in Chicago, where the Parsons-Schilling

[1] Marx, *Capital*, Vol. 1, p. 287.
[2] Lorwin, *The American Federation of Labor*, p. 19.

forces headed the Central Labor Union. Nationally, it was highly successful, some 350,000 workers, including large numbers of K. of L. members, going on strike. The eight-hour day was established in many sections, particularly in the building trades. And more important, despite the Haymarket outrage committed by the bosses (described earlier), a tremendous wave of trade union organization was set on its way. This laid the basis for the modern trade union movement.

Out of this movement was born historic International May Day, which, however, the A.F. of L., its creator, has never seen fit to celebrate, although A.F. of L. unions participated in May Day celebrations for many years. May first was adopted as the day of celebration of world labor at the International Socialist Congress in Paris, France, in July 1889. Since then, tens of millions of workers have marched on that day in every city of the world, in anticipation of the final victory of the working class.[1]

The 1886 strike virtually decided that the Federation and not the K. of L. would be the national trade union center. At its December 1886 convention in Columbus, the original Federation, now with some 316,469 members, and growing rapidly, reorganized itself and adopted its new name of the American Federation of Labor. Although the K. of L. gained heavily in numbers as a result of the great 1886 struggle, it had definitely lost the leadership of labor and soon thereafter began to decline in strength. By 1890 it had only 200,000 members and was no longer the decisive labor factor.

In the struggle for leadership the A.F. of L. had a number of advantages over the K. of L. The craft form of organization, based on the key role of the skilled workers in this period, was superior to the hodgepodge mixed assemblies of the K. of L. Its decentralized form was also more effective than the paralyzing overcentralization of the K. of L. The A.F. of L.'s policy of confining its membership strictly to workers likewise gave it a big advantage over the K. of L., which took in large numbers of farmers, professionals, and small businessmen. Its strike policy, too, was a big improvement over the no-strike attitude of Powderly and his fellow bureaucrats. The rejection of current money nostrums and other social panaceas that infested the K. of L. also helped the A.F. of L., and so did the opposition to the K. of L.'s adventurous petty-bourgeois political policies.

Despite these advantages, which compared favorably with the Knights of Labor, the A.F. of L. program contained a whole series of weaknesses which were to manifest themselves with deadly effect in the com-

[1] For a fuller account, see Alexander Trachtenberg, *History of May Day*, N. Y., 1947.

ing decades. The A.F. of L.'s gradual rejection of a Socialist perspective implied its eventual outright acceptance of capitalism and a slave role for the working class. Its concentration upon the skilled workers finally developed into direct betrayal of the unskilled and the foreign-born masses. Its obvious white chauvinism was a callous sell-out of the Negro people from the start. Its opposition to independent political action grew into a surrender to the fatal two-party system of the capitalists. Its general program, which through the years became a real adaptation of the labor movement to the profit interests of the powerful and arrogant monopolists, finally resulted in the wholesale corruption of the labor aristocracy, in the growth of a monstrous system of inter-union scabbing, and eventually in the creation of the most corrupt and reactionary labor leadership the world had ever known.

In the early years of the A.F. of L. the non-Marxist leadership of the unions, not yet solidly organized as a dominating clique, reflected some of the militancy of the rank and file under the latter's pressure. But with the development of American imperialism, particularly from 1890 on, they soon fell into the role allotted to them by the employers, as "labor lieutenants of capital," basing themselves upon the skilled at the expense of the unskilled. They proceeded to build up the notorious Gompers machine, which ever since has been such a barrier to working class progress. They were able to do this because of the whole complex of specifically American factors, related to the rapid growth of American industry, which had resulted in relatively high living standards for the workers as compared to those in other countries, and which were operating to prevent a rapid radicalization of the American working class.

THE HENRY GEORGE CAMPAIGN

The great eight-hour struggle naturally had important political repercussions for the workers. As the 1886 fall elections approached, the workers organized labor parties in a number of cities. The Socialists were active in all these parties, which played a considerable role in the local elections. But by far the most important of such independent movements was the 1886 campaign of Henry George for mayor of New York City.

Henry George, because of his notable book on the single tax, *Progress and Poverty,* published in 1879 and selling eventually up to several million copies, had gained a wide popularity among the toiling masses. George considered the people's woes as originating basically from the private monopolization of the land, and his main social remedy was to tax this monopoly out of existence. This was the single tax. George failed to note, however, as Engels and the S.L.P. leaders sharply pointed out, that the main cause of the workers' poverty and the antagonism of classes was the capitalists' ownership of all the social means of production and that, therefore, the final solution, as the Socialists proposed, could only be had through the collective ownership by society of all these means of production. George did not understand the capitalist class as the basic enemy of the working class and the people. In his election platform, however, he included demands for government ownership of the telegraph and railroads, as well as some minor labor planks.

Henry George was nominated by the local trade union movement in New York. The S.L.P. also endorsed his candidacy as a struggle of labor against capital, "not because of his single tax theory, but in spite of it." While basically criticizing the single tax, Engels, who paid close attention to American labor developments, agreed that the Socialists should offer Henry George qualified support. The main thing, he said, was that the masses of workers were taking important first steps in independent political action.

The bitterly contested local campaign resulted in votes as follows: Abram S. Hewitt, 90,456; Henry George, 67,930; Theodore Roosevelt, 60,474.[1] The George forces claimed with justification that they had been counted out. Following the New York elections, the Socialists and the George forces split over the question of program, and the single tax movement, torn with dissension, soon petered out.

THE STATUS OF THE S.L.P. IN 1890

In the aftermath of the tremendous class struggles, beginning with the big national railroad strike of 1877, which climaxed in the eight-hour fight of 1886, the S.L.P., although still weakened by internal confusion and dissension, began to grow. At its seventh convention, in 1889, the Party claimed to have 70 sections, as against 32 at its convention of two years before. The Party press was also looking up. The Party, however, was far from having developed a solid Marxist program and leadership. As yet, those who could actually be called Marxists were very few. Consequently, the Party, while abiding by its ultimate goal of socialism and using the writings of Marx and Engels as its guide, was wafted hither and yon by the pressures of the current class struggle. Still torn with division, the Party had, in its fourteen years of life so far, developed various ideological deviations, most of which were to plague the Socialist movement for years to come.

[1] Nathan Fine, *Labor and Farmer Parties in the United States*, p. 43. N. Y., 1928.

THE SOCIALIST LABOR PARTY

There were the "rights," who had dominated the Party's leadership since its foundation in 1876. They underestimated the importance of trade unionism, made opportunistic deals with Greenbackers and other movements, yielded to Chinese exclusionist sentiment, catered to the skilled workers, and generally played down the leading role of the Party. Then there were the sectarian "lefts," who wanted to cast aside the ballot as a delusion, refused to participate in broad labor and farmer movements, toyed with dual unionism, and satisfied themselves with mere propaganda of revolutionary slogans. There were also the "direct actionists," anarcho-syndicalists who, as we have just seen, had nearly wrecked the Party. And finally, on the part of all these groupings, there was a deep misunderstanding and neglect of the vital Negro question.

Marx, and especially Engels, gave direct advice to the American Socialist movement during the seventies and eighties, fighting against all the characteristic deviations.[1] These two great leaders sought tirelessly to break the isolation of the Socialists from the broad masses, urging their active participation in all the elementary movements of the working class and its allies—in the trade unions, the labor parties, and the farmer movements. But the great Marx died in 1883, and Engels followed him a dozen years later in 1895. Thus the young American proletariat lost its two most brilliant and devoted teachers and leaders.

One of the most serious handicaps of the S.L.P. during this whole period was its almost exclusive German composition. The publication of Lawrence Grönlund's *Cooperative Commonwealth* in 1884, and Edward Bellamy's famous *Looking Backward* in 1888, helped to popularize Socialist and semi-Socialist ideas among the American masses, but Justus Ebert could still say, "The Socialist Labor Party of the eighties was a German party and its official language was German. The American element was largely incidental."[2] And Lawrence Grönlund also said that in 1880 one could count the native-born Socialists on one hand.

Engels spoke of the "German-American Socialist Labor Party," and he fought to improve its isolated situation. In a letter to Florence Kelley Wischnewetsky, he said of the S.L.P.: "This Party is called on to play a very important part in the movement. But in order to do so they will have to doff every remnant of their foreign garb. They will have to become out and out American. They cannot expect the Americans

---

[1] Most of Frederick Engels' writings on the American question are to be found in the preface to the American edition of his book, *The Condition of the Working Class in England in 1844* (N. Y., 1887), and in many letters to Florence Kelley Wischnewetsky, Sorge, and others. See Karl Marx and Frederick Engels, *Letters to Americans*, New York, 1952.

[2] Ebert, *American Industrial Evolution*, pp. 66-67.

to come to them; they, the minority, and the immigrants, must go to the Americans who are the vast majority and the natives. *And to do that, they must above all things learn English.*"[1]

In 1889, the internal dissensions within the S.L.P. reached a breaking point. The opposition to the opportunist leadership, according to Ebert, turned around three major points: "First . . . its compromising political policy; second, its stronger pure and simple trade union tendencies; third, its German spirit and forms."[2] The revolt was led by the New York *Volkszeitung* (Schewitsch-Jonas group), founded in 1878 as a German daily paper. The Busche-Rosenberg official leaders of the Party, a hangover from the old opportunist Van Patten group, were deposed and the Schewitsch-Jonas faction elected instead. This led to a split, and in consequence for a while there were two S.L.P.'s. The Rosenberg group, the minority faction, got the worst of the struggle. It lingered along weakly, calling itself the Social Democratic Federation, until finally it fused in 1897 with Debs' Social Democracy. Lucien Sanial wrote the new program of the S.L.P. The split strengthened the Marxist elements in the Party. The S.L.P. of today dates its foundation from this period.

In the following year, 1890, an event of major importance to the S.L.P. and the labor movement took place. This was the entrance of Daniel De Leon into the Party. De Leon, born in 1852 on the island of Curaçoa off the coast of Venezuela, was a professor of international law at Columbia University, and had supported Henry George in the 1886 campaign. Brilliant, energetic, and ruthless, De Leon immediately became a power in the S.L.P. In 1891 he secured the post as editor of the *Weekly People* (later a daily) which he held from then on. For the next thirty years, long after his death in 1914, De Leon's writings were to exert a profound influence not only upon the S.L.P., but upon the whole left wing, right down to the formation of the Communist Party in 1919, and even beyond.

[1] Engels, Preface to the American edition of *The Condition of the Working Class in England in 1844*, p. v. See Marx and Engels, *Letters to Americans*, Appendix.
[2] Ebert, *American Industrial Evolution*, p. 66.

6. The S.L.P: De Leonism and Decline (1890-1900)

During the period from the mid-eighties to the end of the century, American industrial development proceeded at an unheard-of pace. "The United States," wrote Lenin in 1913, "is unequaled in the rapidity of development (of capitalism at the end of the 19th and the beginning of the twentieth century)."[1] In these years the United States leaped from fourth to first place as an industrial nation, leaving England, "the workshop of the world," far behind. Kuszynski says that the United States, in 1894, was turning out, in value of manufactures, over twice as much as England.[2]

Meanwhile, as American industry expanded it also became monopolized. In 1901, J. Moody listed a total of 440 large industrial, financial, and franchise trusts, with a total capital of over $20 billion.[3] United States Steel, Standard Oil, and many other great trusts in railroad, sugar, coal, etc., date from this period. Morgan, Rockefeller, Kuhn, Loeb, and others were already huge concerns by the end of the century. A great financial oligarchy, ruthlessly ruling the country, had grown up. This was a time of the fiercest competition, and particularly during the economic crises of 1885 and 1893 the big capitalist beasts devoured thousands of the smaller ones. The middle classes were being ground down, nor could the Sherman anti-trust law of 1890 save them. The workers were barbarously exploited and slaughtered in the industries.

The United States had become a powerful imperialist country. With its home market now assured, monopoly reached out for foreign conquests. The arrogant Wall Street monopolists, dominating the industries and the government, transformed the Monroe Doctrine into an instrument for the subjugation and exploitation of Latin America. By 1893, they had also virtually annexed the Hawaiian islands, on the route of conquest across the Pacific. In 1898, under the pretext of freeing Cuba, they provoked a war with Spain, with the result that the Philippines, Guam, Puerto Rico, and Cuba fell into the hands of the United States. Flushed with imperialist ambition, Senator Lodge declared, "The

---

1 Lenin, *Capitalism and Agriculture in the U. S.*, p. 9.
2 Jurgen Kuczynski, *Labor Conditions in the United States*, p. 71, London, 1943.
3 J. Moody, *The Truth about the Trusts*, p. 477, N. Y., 1904.

American people and the economic forces which underlie all are carrying us forward to the economic supremacy of the world."[1]

FIERCE LABOR STRUGGLES

The 1890's were a period of great labor struggles, exceeding in intensity and scope even those of the two previous decades. The working class, more and more employed in large enterprises, had grown very greatly in size. The arrogant capitalists, resolved to strip their wage slaves of every trade union defense and to subject them to the most intense exploitation humanly possible, met with extreme violence all resistance on the part of the workers to their imperious will. But they encountered a working class rapidly growing in numbers, understanding, and organization, and the hardest-fought strikes in our nation's history developed.

One of the most desperate of these was the great Homestead, Pennsylvania, strike of July 1892. The strike was directed against the Carnegie Steel Company by the Amalgamated Association of Iron, Steel and Tin Workers, to prevent an announced wage cut. The company brought in 300 Pinkerton detective-gunmen to break the strike, but the armed workers drove them out and occupied the plants. Finally, however, the strike was broken, and a mortal blow was dealt to trade unionism throughout the trustified steel industry.

In the metal-mining country of the Rocky Mountain states, at the same time, there developed a whole series of strikes, in Colorado, Idaho, and Montana. These reached the pitch of actual civil war, with armed encounters between strikers and troops. Many were killed on each side. These historic strikes, led by Bill Haywood, Vincent St. John, and other radicals, laid the basis for the famous Western Federation of Miners.

In this decade many important strikes also took place on the railroads. They culminated in the historic strike, beginning in May 1894, of the American Railway Union. This organization, which was industrial in form and a rival of the conservative railroad craft unions, was headed by Eugene V. Debs, who was not yet a Socialist. The strike began in the Pullman shops in Chicago against a wage reduction. It developed into a general strike on the railroads, with more than 100,000 workers out and many western roads tied up. The big strike was finally broken by the company's and government's use of scabs, troops, court injunctions, and the wholesale arrest of the strike leaders, including Debs.

Another big strike of this period was that of the coal miners, beginning in May 1893. Some 125,000 struck. The strike was broken; neverthe-

[1] Henry Cabot Lodge, Speech, Jan. 7, 1901.

less the United Mine Workers virtually established itself as a solid union during this strike. Still another important workers' movement was the march of the unemployed to Washington in the hard times of 1894, led by General Jacob S. Coxey, a well-to-do businessman. In the final decade of the century the Knights of Labor faded out and the American Federation of Labor became the dominant organization, slowly increasing its membership to 548,321 in 1900.

THE ROLE OF DE LEON

The S.L.P. bore heavy political responsibilities of leadership in the 1890's, faced as it was by rapidly developing American monopoly capitalism and by the intensely sharpening class struggle. If the Party was to function effectively and to grow it had to serve as the vanguard of the whole labor movement. This required that it should not only educate the workers regarding the final goal of socialism, but, imperatively, that it also give them practical leadership in all their daily struggles. But this mass guidance the S.L.P., under the leadership of Daniel De Leon, proved quite unable to provide.

De Leon made strong pretensions of being a Marxist, but until the day of his death in May 1914, he never succeeded in really becoming one. De Leon formally accepted such basic Marxist concepts as historical materialism, Marxist economics, and the class struggle. He also circulated the Marxist classics, knew the importance of industrial unionism, and was an advocate of a strong, centralized party. And above all, De Leon was a relentless fighter against right opportunism, his attacks against the right-wing Social-Democrats and against the reactionary leadership of the trade unions being classics of polemics. Nevertheless, De Leon's position was fundamentally revisionist, as he rewrote Marx in many important essentials. His general outlook was a mixture of "left" sectarianism and syndicalism. He was essentially a left petty-bourgeois radical.

De Leon, for example, had a non-Marxist, syndicalist conception of the future socialist society. Marx, in *The Communist Manifesto,* pointed out the necessity of the dictatorship of the proletariat, which, as we see in the Soviet Union and the People's Democracies of Eastern Europe, implies the establishment of a workers' government in the interim period of socialism, between capitalism and communism. The function of this government is to act as an organ to repress the defeated, counter-revolutionary capitalist class, to build the new society, and to defend the country from foreign imperialist attacks. But De Leon never realized these facts. Departing radically from Marxist thinking, he early developed the syndicalist theory, borrowed mainly from the earlier anarcho-syndicalists,[1] that the industrial unions would be the basis of the future society. This industrial organization, according to De Leon, would not be a state, with coercive powers, but simply an administrative apparatus.

In this respect De Leon's conceptions were in basic harmony with those of the I.W.W. syndicalists from 1905 on. De Leon said, "Industrial Unionism is the Socialist Republic in the making, and the goal once reached, the Industrial Union is the Socialist Republic in operation."[2] He subscribed to the I.W.W. preamble, which declared that "By organizing industrially we are forming the structure of the new society within the shell of the old." And he definitely declared, "Where the General Executive Board of the Industrial Workers of the World will sit there will sit the nation's capital."[3]

After the Russian Revolution the S.L.P. leaders claimed that De Leon, with his concept of an industrial republic, had forecast the Soviet system, and that Lenin had congratulated him for so doing. But this was nonsense. De Leon's ideas of the structure of Socialist society were rooted in anarchist and left sectarian, not Marxist, sources. Significantly, De Leon's present-day followers, who rigidly cling to his ideas, have repudiated the whole organization of the Soviets.

De Leon also diverged widely from Marxism in his conception of how the revolution was to be brought about in the United States. He saw this in the sense of the workers taking over society in the face of a virtually unresisting capitalist class. It is a fact, of course, that Marx, long before, had made an exception of England and the United States in his generalization that the resistance of the capitalists to social progress would necessarily make the Socialist revolution violent in character. In this respect he said that "if, for example the working class in England and the United States should win a majority in Parliament, in Congress, it could legally abolish those laws and institutions which obstruct its development."[4] Marx qualified this with an "if"—that is, if the capitalists did not resist the legal transfer of power. Lenin later showed that the advance of imperialism in these two countries, by creating a big army and state bureaucracy, had changed this. The workers, true to their democratic instincts, would seek to make a peaceful transition from capitalism to socialism, but they would have to face and defeat the capitalists' attempts to block them by violence.

[1] See the program of the anarcho-syndicalist International Working People's Association in Chapter 3.
[2] Daniel De Leon, *Industrial Unionism*, p. 48, N. Y., 1947.
[3] Daniel De Leon, *Socialist Reconstruction of Society*, p. 47, N. Y., 1947 (speech delivered July 10, 1905).
[4] Cited by William Z. Foster, *In Defense of the Communist Party and Its Leaders*, p. 22, N. Y., 1949.

De Leon, however, ignored these political changes in the United States and their consequences upon the ultimate fight for socialism. He elaborated his opportunist idea that the Party would peacefully win a majority at the polls and then, the Party's political function finished, it would at once dissolve; whereupon, the industrial unions would "take and hold" the industries, "locking out the capitalists." In the unlikely event that the latter would violently resist, the industrial unions, although simply an administrative apparatus, would take care of them.[1]

De Leon had little conception of the leading role of the Party. His whole stress was upon the industrial unions before, during, and after the revolution. In his thinking they played the decisive role at all stages. Nor did he have any conception of Party democracy and discipline. He ruthlessly expelled all those who in any jot or tittle diverged from his dogmatism.

De Leon likewise deviated widely from Marxism on a whole series of vital questions of strategy and tactics. He had no conception of the farmers, middle class, and Negro people as natural allies of the working class. He rejected the labor party on principle, made no effort whatever to rally the Negro masses, withdrew from all farmer movements, and sneered at the fight of the middle classes against the trusts.

De Leon also had an almost solicitous regard for trusts as a basically progressive development. He stated, "We say, even if the Trust could be smashed, we would not smash it, because by smashing it, we would throw civilization back."[2] This schematic attitude sufficed to cut the S.L.P. off from the mass struggle, healthy but not always skillfully waged, against the advance of ruthless monopoly capital. This wrong attitude toward the trusts also prevailed in the Socialist Party for many years, the latter dovetailing it with the slogan, "Let the Nation Own the Trusts."

Such sectarian trends sharply isolated the S.L.P. from all the elementary popular mass movements of the working people. To make this isolation doubly sure, De Leon also condemned on principle the fight for all immediate demands, which he characterized as "banana peels under the feet of the workers." Starting out with an acceptance of Henry George's wholly opportunistic program, De Leon wound up by rejecting partial demands altogether. Eventually he slashed the program of the S.L.P. to but one single demand, "the unconditional surrender of the capitalist class."

The trend of De Leonism was to reduce the Party to an isolated, sectarian, dogmatic body, propagating socialism in the abstract, as the S.L.P. continues to do to this very day. In 1891, when De Leon took the helm

---

[1] De Leon, *Socialist Reconstruction of Society*.
[2] De Leon-Berry, *Debate on Solution of the Trust Problem*, N. Y., 1913.

of the party, there were no Marxists able to challenge effectively his sectarian vagaries. Marx was dead, Engels was to die before De Leon got well going, the aged Sorge was no longer active, McDonnell had long since given up the work in the S.L.P., and the other Marxists, such as Sanial and Vogt, quickly fell under the spell of De Leon's brilliance. The tragedy of it all was that De Leonite thinking came to dominate the whole left wing for many years. Indeed, it was not until the advent of the stern realities of the Russian Revolution, the arrival in America of the profound Marxist writings of Lenin, and the formation of the Communist Party, a generation later, that the ideological influence of De Leon was finally broken.

THE S.L.P. AND THE TRADE UNIONS

By the 1890's the big capitalists of the United States had definitely launched upon a policy of hamstringing the fighting capacity of the working class by cultivating a labor aristocracy of better-paid, native-born, skilled workers. This they did at the expense of the unskilled and Negro workers. With the many advantages enjoyed by capitalism in this country, the capitalists had the financial reserves to carry out this policy of labor corruption to an extent far beyond anything ever achieved by the employers of Great Britain or any other capitalist country. The opportunist leaders of the A.F. of L. went right along with this general plan, with their bitter anti-socialism, class-collaborationism, opposition to a labor party, craft unionism, exclusion of Negroes and unskilled, and strike betrayals.

De Leon militantly attacked this official corruption, assailing the Gompers bureaucrats as "labor lieutenants of the capitalist class."[1] But the general conclusion he drew from his analysis was wrong: namely, that the Socialists should withdraw from the old, conservative-led trade unions and devote themselves to building a professedly socialist labor movement. The effect of this policy was to leave the old unions in the hands of the reactionaries and to isolate the Socialists from these basic economic organizations of the working class. De Leon heaped his greatest scorn upon those who advocated the improvement of the conservative unions by "boring from within."

De Leon's dualist line went directly counter to the advice of Engels, who definitely favored working within the old unions. Already in 1887, warning against such isolating tendencies as De Leon's, Engels declared: "I think that all our practice has shown that it is possible to work along

[1] Daniel De Leon, *Two Pages from Roman History*, N. Y., 1903.

with the general movement of the working class at every one of its stages without giving up or hiding our own distinct position, and even organization, and I am afraid that if the German-Americans choose a different line they will commit a great mistake."[1]

The De Leon leadership in 1890 split with the A. F. of L. over the well-known "Sanial case." The S.L.P., with only a vague idea of the dividing line between Party and trade union, had its "American Section" affiliate with the independent Central Labor Federation of New York, which the Socialists led. Hence, when this body applied to the A.F. of L. for a charter, its delegate, Lucien Sanial, was rejected by Gompers on the grounds that the A.F. of L. did not accept the affiliation of political parties. After a bitter fight, the 1890 A.F. of L. convention in Detroit sustained Gompers' contention by a vote of 1699 to 535. Both Engels and Sorge later declared that Gompers was formally right in this issue, but De Leon seized upon the quarrel to drive a deep wedge between the S.L.P. and the A.F. of L. and to reduce greatly the socialist work done in that organization. The New York Central Labor Federation remained independent.

De Leon next turned his attention to the Knights of Labor, then definitely on the decline. He joined Mixed Assembly 1563 and had himself elected a delegate from this local to District Assembly No. 49 of New York, which the Socialists controlled. From this body De Leon was sent as a delegate to the 1893 General Assembly of the K. of L. There the Socialist delegates were chiefly responsible for defeating the reactionary Powderly and for electing J. R. Sovereign as Master Workman in his stead. Sovereign promised to make Lucien Sanial editor of the Order's *Journal,* but he later backed down on this agreement. Relations between Sovereign and the S.L.P. leaders therefore grew very strained; so that at the 1895 General Assembly of the K. of L. in Washington De Leon was refused a seat as a delegate.[2]

This experience finally sickened De Leon with work inside the old unions in general. Henceforth, he was as violently opposed to participation in the K. of L. as he was to work within the A.F. of L. Consequently, he had the Socialists, including District No. 49, also withdraw from the K. of L., as he had done from the A.F. of L. Then he proceeded to organize a new Socialist labor movement, one after his own liking, the Socialist Trades and Labor Alliance.[3] Significantly, Debs, with similar sectarian reasoning, had preceded De Leon by two years by founding the

1 Marx and Engels, *Letters to Americans.*
2 Anthony Bimba, *History of the American Working Class,* p. 200, N. Y., 1927.
3 Ella Reeve Bloor was a member of the General Executive Board of the S.T.L.A. See her book, *We Are Many,* p. 55, N. Y., 1940.

industrial union, the A.R.U., in competition with all the railroad craft unions.

THE SOCIALIST TRADES AND LABOR ALLIANCE

The S.T.L.A. was organized by De Leon without formal consultation with the party. He simply called a conference of the heads of the independent New York Central Labor Federation, the United Hebrew Trades, the Newark Central Labor Federation, and the seceded District Assembly No. 49, decided on a new organization, and launched the S.T.L.A. on December 13, 1895, at a mass meeting in Cooper Union. De Leon assured the doubting S.L.P. national executive committee that the S.T.L.A. would not be a rival to the A.F. of L., but would confine itself to organizing the unorganized. Experience quickly proved otherwise, however, and soon the new organization was in death grips with the old unions. Opposition to the S.T.L.A. began to mount also among S.L.P. trade unionists, but De Leon nevertheless managed to have the new organization endorsed at the Party's 1896 convention in New York, by a vote of 71 to 6.

In 1898 the S.T.L.A. claimed, excessively, to have 15,000 members. In reality it stagnated, incapable of growth. An auxiliary of the S.L.P., committed to support S.L.P. candidates in elections, and generally tied to De Leon's dogmas, the new general union could not attract the masses. It conducted a few minor strikes, and that was all. Ten years after its foundation, the S.T.L.A., in 1905, fused with other left-wing unions in forming the Industrial Workers of the World. At this convention De Leon claimed to represent 1,500 members in the S.T.L.A., but even this was an exaggerated figure. Meanwhile, the A.F. of L., which De Leon had long ago pronounced "deader than dead," continued to grow, expanding from 260,000 in 1895 to 1,480,000 in 1905.

One of the chief results of the S.T.L.A. was to create what turned out to be a fatal schism between the Party's trade unionists and the De Leon leadership. The dual organization, by pulling many militants out of the A.F. of L. unions, greatly weakened the Socialist forces in these bodies, and also their participation in the big strikes of the period. In the 1893 A.F. of L. convention in Chicago, the Socialist delegation, led by Thomas J. Morgan, had succeeded in getting through a twelve-point resolution including "the collective ownership by the people of all means of production and distribution." The latter plank was later defeated in a referendum. In the 1894 convention, the Socialists succeeded in defeating Gompers and electing as president for the ensuing year the conservative John McBride of the Miners Union. At this same convention the Socialists also had a resolution on the Negro question adopted, stating: "The A.F. of L. does not draw the color line, nor do its affiliates . . . a union that does cannot be admitted into affiliation with this body." In these formative years of the A.F. of L. a correct Marxist policy could have changed very considerably in a progressive direction the future history of that organization. But such dual unionism as that of the S.T.L.A., which in various forms was to plague the Marxists for twenty-five years after 1895, effectively crippled the left wing in the trade unions and facilitated the consolidation of the reactionary Gompers leadership.

LABOR PARTY AND POPULIST MOVEMENT

Traditionally, the Marxists in the United States, whatever their mistakes in applying this policy, had followed the basically correct line of participating in the many mass labor and farmer parties set up by the workers during more than two generations of class struggle. But De Leon proceeded to make ducks and drakes of this policy and to separate the Marxists from these mass political activities, even as he had largely cut them off from the mass trade unions. He declared against the labor party in principle, and condemned the farmer movement out of hand, plumping for direct support of the sectarian S.L.P. politically under all circumstances.

This narrow line was directly contrary to the one carefully promulgated over many years by Engels. Thus, in connection with the big political movements of the 1880's, the latter wrote that "A million or two of workingmen's votes next November for a *bona fide* workingmen's party is worth infinitely more at present than a hundred thousand votes for a doctrinally perfect platform." And again, he said, "The first great step of importance for every country newly entering into the movement is always the organization of the workers as an independent political party, no matter how, so long as it is a distinct workers' party."[1]

De Leon also had a narrow policy regarding the farmers. During the 1890's the farmers' grievances came to a head in the Populist movement.[2] This struggle grew out of capitalist pressure against the farmers, in the shape of usurious mortgages, gouging freight rates, excessive prices for what the farmers had to buy, and minimum prices for what they had to sell. Droughts and hard times helped to fill the farmers' cup of misery to overflowing.

The farmers' movement had roots running far back through a long

[1] Marx and Engels, *Selected Correspondence*, pp. 454, 450.
[2] Anna Rochester, *The Populist Movement in the United States*, N. Y., 1943.

series of struggles of the Grangers, Greenbackers, and other agrarian organizations. The People's Party was organized in St. Louis, on February 22, 1892. Its program called for government ownership of the telegraphs and railroads, government reclamation of the land, and a number of minor labor demands. In the 1892 elections the Populist party's candidate, General Weaver, polled 1,027,329 votes. In 1894, a crisis year, the party's vote went up to 1,523,979. In 1896, however, following an ill-fated fusion with the Democratic Party behind William Jennings Bryan, the vote fell to but 200,000, and the People's Party was dead. It had been led to destruction by opportunists.

Organized labor did not fully support this big farmers' Populist movement. This was a major reason why it collapsed. In its 1892 and 1896 conventions the United Mine Workers and the declining Knights of Labor were represented, but the Gompers group, already committed to the two-party system, kept the American Federation of Labor from participating. Under De Leon's prodding, the Socialist Labor Party, at its convention in July 1893, sharply condemned the People's Party as "antagonistic to the interests and aims of the proletariat."[1] In 1892 the S.L.P. nominated, for the first time, its own presidential candidates, Simon Wing, a small manufacturer, and Charles Matchett, an electrician. The ticket polled 21,534 votes in six eastern states. The Party also put up candidates in 1896—Matchett and M. Maguire—who got 36,534 votes.

De Leon's isolationist policy toward the spontaneous political movements of the workers and farmers did infinite harm to the Party as well as to these mass movements. It remained the dominant policy not only of the Socialist Labor Party, but also of the Socialist Party, for a full thirty years, down to the 1920's.

THE S.L.P. AND THE NEGRO

One of the greatest weaknesses throughout the history of the Socialist Labor Party was its incorrect position on the Negro question. It is a fact that ever since the Civil War, and even before it, the Marxists fought resolutely to include the Negro workers in the trade unions and to defend their economic interests. But they did not understand the Negro question as a developing national question, and they did not work out a full program of demands for the Negro people. Nor did they realize the true significance of the broad political demands raised by the Negro people themselves. This misunderstanding was particularly a handicap to the Negro masses during the reconstruction period after

[1] Fine, *Labor and Farmer Parties in the U.S.*, p. 155.

the Civil War, when the urgent need for working class support was most vital in their fight for land and freedom.

De Leon did nothing to clear up the weakness and confusion of the Marxists on the Negro question. On the contrary, he intensified it. After the Civil War the newly-emancipated Negro people, under heavy economic and political pressures, began to develop toward becoming a nation. This development has continued down to our years.[1] De Leon, who claimed to be the leading Marxist theoretician in this country, had no inkling whatever of this basic development, even in its most elementary aspects. In fact, he virtually ignored the burning Negro question altogether. His writings are almost bare of references to the struggles and hardships of the Negro people, although the news dispatches of the times were full of reports of barbarous lynchings of Negroes, and the Negro people were being outrageously discriminated against politically, economically, and socially all over the country. Behind such gross neglect, as in the case of many later Socialist and trade union leaders, lurked the corroding disease of white chauvinism.

White chauvinism, the bourgeois ideology of white supremacy, is based upon the false notion that Negroes are inferior beings to whites. It is systematic discrimination and persecution directed against the Negro people economically, politically, socially. Although completely disproved innumerable times scientifically and in the real life of our people, it still persists. This is because the planters and industrialists, finding that it enables them to force lower living standards upon the Negro people, assiduously cultivate it. Originally the plantation owners' ideological justification for slavery, white chauvinism still infects in varying degrees all the strata of the white population, including large sections of the working class.

What little De Leon did write on the Negro question was incorrect. He reduced it all only to a class issue. The Negro constitutes, he said, "a special division in the ranks of labor. . . . In no economic respect is he different from his fellow wage slaves of other races; yet by reason of his race, which long was identified with serfdom, the rays of the Social Question reached his mind, through such broken prisms that they are refracted into all the colors of the rainbow, preventing him from appreciating the white light of the question."[2]

The only program that De Leon had for the bitterly persecuted Negro people was eventual socialism. He saw no need to raise immediate demands to relieve the barbarous persecution to which they were being subjected. This basically incorrect attitude, as formulated by De Leon,

[1] See Harry Haywood, *Negro Liberation*, N. Y., 1948.
[2] Cited by Eric Hass, *Socialism*, p. 19, N. Y., n.d.

became for many years the settled Socialist theoretical and practical approach to the Negro question, not only by "rights," but also largely by "lefts." It was not until after the advent of the Communist Party, a generation later, that the immense importance of the struggle of the Negro people to the Socialist movement in general was fully realized, that its nature as a national question came to be understood, and that correct Marxist policies were formulated to meet it.

THE DECLINE OF THE SOCIALIST LABOR PARTY

In 1900, after twenty-four years of existence, the S.L.P. had not more than five or six thousand members, in twenty-six states.[1] The Party's national vote had advanced to 82,204. The great preponderance of the membership was foreign-born—German, Jewish, Scandinavian, Polish, etc. The party was largely isolated from the mass organizations and struggles of the toiling masses. Obviously, this was not the picture of a prospering vanguard party of the working class.

Undoubtedly, adverse objective conditions were in large part responsible for the S.L.P.'s failure to grow—a question discussed in Chapter 37. Even with the most correct of policies, under the circumstances of the time, it would have been difficult to build a strong Marxist party in a capitalist country such as the United States. Nevertheless, there were far greater opportunities for increasing the Party's numbers and influence than the S.L.P. was able to realize. This failure was largely due to De Leon's grave sectarian political errors. His withdrawal from the conservative trade unions, his anti-labor-party, anti-Negro, and anti-farmer-movement policies, and his abandonment of all immediate demands, all of which became the Party line, had particularly disastrous consequences for the Party during the big economic and political struggles of the 1890's.

That the S.L.P. under De Leon was unable to unite and give leadership to the Marxists of the country was also graphically demonstrated by the growth, during De Leon's period, of a whole series of Socialist and near-Socialist tendencies outside the control of the official De Leon leadership. Among these were the Debs movement in the Middle West, the radical Socialist group of Haywood and others among the miners of the Rocky Mountain states, the left and radical elements in the disintegrating Populist movement, and the crystallization of an opposition group within the S.L.P. itself.

The S.L.P. under De Leon's sectarian, dogmatic leadership, was also

[1] Fine, *Labor and Farmer Parties in the U.S.*, p. 180.

quite incapable of learning from its mistakes. Consequently, it could not reorient itself to draw into its ranks the new Socialist forces, nor meet the new and pressing problems being thrust upon it by developing American imperialism. In short, it had exhausted its role as the Socialist party of the American proletariat. Hence it began to disintegrate and to split, in the first stage of being overwhelmed by the new Socialist forces and of being supplanted by a new organization, the Socialist Party.

THE SPLIT IN THE S.L.P.

The split movement began over the question of the S.T.L.A., but it soon involved the whole sectarian, authoritarian regime of De Leon. Almost immediately after the founding of the new general union, the trade unionists in the party had begun to line up against it. De Leon tried to stifle the growing discontent with a policy of repressions and expulsions. In December 1898, however, the *Volkszeitung*, taking an opposition stand, made so bold as to criticize openly the party policy. This brought about a sharp factional battle between the De Leonites and the dissidents. Among the *Volkszeitung* movement's leaders was Morris Hillquit. Born in Riga, in 1870, Hillquit had come to America when he was fifteen years old and worked at shirtmaking and other trades. At one time he was secretary of the United Hebrew Trades. He acquired a degree in law in 1893. As a member of the S.L.P., Hillquit took an active part in the anti-De Leon struggle.

The bitter Party fight came to a climax on July 10, 1899, when Section New York, which by a decision of the convention of 1896 had the authority to elect the national executive committee and the national secretary of the S.L.P., voted to remove the officials then in office and elected a new set. Thus, Henry L. Slobodin became the national secretary, in place of Henry Kuhn. De Leon refused to recognize this action, denouncing the rebels as "Kangaroos." A physical struggle ensued for possession of the Party's buildings, newspapers, and funds. Both groups claimed to be the Socialist Labor Party and each published its own *The People*. Eventually the courts ruled that the De Leon faction had the legal right to use the Party name.[1]

In the meantime, the seceding group, still calling itself the S.L.P., held a convention in Rochester on January 1, 1900. Present were 59 delegates, representing about half of the Party's membership. The convention promptly condemned the S.T.L.A., drafted a new platform, enacted a new set of by-laws for governing the Party, and put up

---

1 Hillquit, *History of Socialism in the U.S.*, p. 327; Harry Kuhn, ed., *Daniel De Leon, a Symposium*, p. 22, N. Y., 1919.

presidential candidates for the coming elections, Job Harriman and Max Hayes. The convention also adopted a resolution proposing fusion with the Social-Democratic Party, of which Debs and Victor Berger were the leaders.

The split was irretrievably disastrous to the old S.L.P. Its membership fell off to about one-half, and its candidates in the 1900 elections, James T. Maloney and Valentine Remmel, polled only 34,191 votes, or less than half the Party's vote in 1898. De Leon, no longer facing any opposition at the 1900 convention, promptly cut out "the tapeworm of immediate demands" from the Party's platform and left it with but one plank—a demand for the revolution. The S.L.P. convention also adopted a resolution prohibiting its members, on pain of expulsion, from becoming officers in old-line trade unions. The S.L.P., having lost the leadership of the Marxist movement in the United States, was now fully on the way to becoming the tiny, dry-as-dust, backward-looking, reactionary sect that it is today. De Leonism in the S.L.P. had arrived at its logical goal. But unfortunately De Leon's sectarian influence was long to linger in left-wing circles in the United States.

7. The Socialist Party (1900-1905)

At its foundation in 1900-01 the Socialist Party, which was eventually to give birth to the Communist Party, confronted a powerful and triumphant capitalist system in the United States. From 1860 to 1900, the value of manufactured products had leaped up from $1,885,825,000 to $11,406,927,000; the amount of capital invested rose from $1,000,856,000 to $8,975,256,000; the number of workers in industry increased from 1,310,000 to 4,713,000 and 14,000,000 immigrants had poured into the country. The population grew during these four decades from 31,443,321 to 75,994,575. The United States had been transformed from a predominantly agricultural country into the leading industrial nation in the world. Its tempo of development was to go right on through the period we are here discussing.

American capitalism, at the turn of the century, had definitely entered the stage of imperialism, as scientifically defined by Lenin. Its industries had acquired a high degree of monopoly; its financial system had become dominated by a few large banks; its big industrialists and bankers had fused into an oligarchy of finance capital which dominated the state; it was already a decisive factor in dividing up the world's markets; and it had, in the Spanish-American War, begun its grab for its imperialistic share of the world's territories. The agrarian country of Jefferson, Jackson, and Lincoln had become the monopolist, imperialist land of the Morgans and the Rockefellers.[1]

The big capitalists, in forging their way ahead to solid class domination of the United States, had slugged the workers, farmers, and middle classes in many hard-fought political battles since the Civil War, as we have seen, and they controlled the government from stem to gudgeon. In 1900, under the leadership of Bryan, the Democratic candidate, and with their main slogan directed against American imperialism, the farmers and small business elements made another bid for power. But to no avail. The Republican candidate of Wall Street, William McKinley, won handily. And when the new president was assassinated in Buffalo, on September 6, 1901, by Leon F. Czolgosz, an anarchist, he was succeeded by the ultra-jingoist and imperialist, Theodore Roosevelt.

[1] Anna Rochester, *Rulers of America*, N. Y., 1936.

CORRUPTION OF THE A. F. OF L. LEADERSHIP

Toward the workers the arrogant employers followed a two-phased policy of repression; on the one hand, violently combating every attempt at labor organization and struggle, and on the other hand, making minor wage concessions to the skilled workers in order to use them as a means to paralyze the struggles and to keep down the wages of the mass of the working class. The many bloody strikes of this general period and the extreme corruption of the A.F. of L. leaders were eloquent testimonials to the vigor with which the employers followed this labor-crushing policy.

By 1900 the top A.F. of L. leadership, ardent supporters of capitalism, had become thoroughly corrupted, politically and personally. They had accepted as their basis the employer policy, which became more and more marked as the imperialist era developed, of bribing the skilled workers at the expense of the semi-skilled and unskilled. They were indeed what De Leon called them, "labor lieutenants of the capitalists." The A.F. of L. leaders, in line with this policy, clung to their antique craft union system of having a dozen or more unions in each given industry, although the rise of the trusts and intense specialization of labor had rendered craft unionism obsolete. They fought desperately against every left-wing suggestion of industrial unionism, whether in the shape of new organizations or by the transformation of the old craft unions. Scores of lost strikes, in which habitually some of the unions would remain at work while the rest were striking, testified to the complete inadequacy of the craft form of organization and indicated the urgent need of the workers for industrial unionism. If the unions managed to register some growth during this period it was in spite of the policies of their reactionary leaders and because of the desperate need of the workers to defend their living standards. The Socialists militantly urged the foreign-born to unionize.

Especially did the labor bureaucrats of the A.F. of L. and Railroad Brotherhoods, loyal to the basic interests of the bosses, stand guard against independent political action by the workers. In 1895 the A.F. of L. convention decided "that party politics, whether they be Democratic, Republican, Socialistic, Populistic, Prohibitionist, or any other, would have no place in the convention of the American Federation of Labor."[1] This policy, the Gompersites interpreted by making rabid attacks against the Socialist Party and by a solid resistance against all attempts to form a labor party. They developed a sort of "economism,"

---

1 *Proceedings of the 1895 Convention, American Federation of Labor*, p. 79.

American brand, having practically no labor political program whatever. At the same time they were venal agents of the capitalist parties. With their slogan of "reward your friends and punish your enemies," they kept the workers locked in the two-party system. All of which worked measureless harm to the political interests of the working class.

Another keystone of A.F. of L. policy was to prevent the organization of the unskilled masses, especially the Negro workers, by keeping them out of the unions through high initiation fees, "male white" clauses, apprenticeship regulations, refusal to organize the basic industries, and various other devices. As for the Negro people as a whole, they were abandoned completely to the mercies of the employers, the plantation owners, and white supremacists generally.

The essence of Gompersite policy was class collaboration, which meant class subordination of the workers to the capitalists. During the period from 1900 to World War I this policy was symbolized as well as organized by the National Civic Federation. The N.C.F. was established in Chicago in 1893, supposedly "to bring about better relations between labor and capital." In 1900, under the guidance of Ralph M. Easley, it was broadened out onto a national scale. "Employers, labor, and the public were separately represented on the leading committees of the Civic Federation. Senator Mark Hanna was Chairman, Gompers was Vice-Chairman, and among the representatives of the "public" were "August Belmont, Grover Cleveland, and President Charles W. Eliot."[1] John Mitchell, head of the Miners Union, and many other labor leaders also became members. The Civic Federation set out to stifle every semblance of radicalism and life in the labor movement.

The establishment of the Civic Federation, with the help of the Gompers leadership, was one phase of the employers' offensive against the working class, which took on added virulence after 1900. The other phase of the offensive was a big drive of many big employers' associations to establish the "open shop," or more properly speaking, the anti-union shop. This union-smashing drive was backed up by the courts, which annulled one labor law after another and confronted every important body of strikers with drastic injunctions. The immediate impulse for all this capitalist reaction came from the fact that the unions, despite the Gompers misleadership, were in a period of rapid growth, which carried them from 300,000 in 1898 to 1,676,200 in 1904.

It was in the middle of this general situation of expanding capitalism and labor misleadership that the Socialist Party came into being in 1900-01. Its predecessor, the Socialist Labor Party, under the leadership

[1] Selig Perlman and Philip Taft, *History of Labor in the United States*, Vol. 4, p. 48, N. Y., 1935.

of De Leon, had signally failed to meet the new problems placed before the workers by the rise of imperialism. The main political fight of the most advanced sections of the workers, thenceforth for almost twenty years, was to be organized through the new Socialist Party. The foundation of the S.P. was another stage in the evolution of American Marxism, which was finally to produce the Communist Party.

FORMATION OF THE SOCIALIST PARTY

As we have already remarked, the seceding Hillquit faction of the S.L.P., at its January 1900 convention in Rochester, sent a proposal to the Social-Democratic Party convention, proposing the fusion of the two groups. Eugene V. Debs, leader of this party, was born in 1855. A railroad worker for many years, he was formerly active in Democratic and Populist politics. He became interested in socialism, under the tutelage of Victor L. Berger, while he was serving six months in the Woodstock, Illinois, jail as a result of the American Railway Union strike of 1894. It was some time, however, before he was ready to take a definite stand for socialism. At the 1896 convention of the People's Party, 412 of the 1,300 delegates gave written pledges to Debs for his candidacy against that of Bryan.[1] The latter was nominated, however, and Debs supported him in the election. In January, 1897, Debs declared himself a Socialist.

In June 1897, at Chicago, the American Railway Union, now only a skeleton organization, dissolved itself into the Social Democracy of America, with Debs at the head. This party had a confused program, its principal aim being an impractical plan of colonization. The idea was to capture some western state at the polls and then to launch socialism within that area. This utopian scheme, however, soon bred an opposition inside the party, especially from the more socialistic elements. At the organization's first convention in June 1898 in Chicago, therefore, a split developed, the seceding minority creating a new body, the Social-Democratic Party of America. This party, with a radical labor program, and with Theodore Debs, Eugene's brother, as national secretary, scored some local election successes in Massachusetts. At its first national convention, on March 6, 1900, it had an estimated membership of 5,000.

The S.D.P. convention delegates responded favorably to the proposals of the Hillquit group for amalgamation. Debs and others of the party leaders, however, were a bit shy. After complicated maneuverings by both sides, the two organizations finally agreed to put up a joint ticket in the 1900 presidential election. The candidates chosen were Debs of

[1] *Social-Democratic Handbook*, p. 54.

the S.D.P. and Job Harriman of the S.L.P. seceders. The ticket polled 97,730 votes, or triple the vote secured by the old S.L.P. in the election.

Unity between the two organizations, however, was not yet achieved. The leaders of both factions jockeyed for position, while the membership pressed for unification. Finally, on July 29, 1901, a joint convention assembled in Indianapolis. The total membership represented by all groups numbered approximately 10,000. Of the 125 delegates, 70 came from the Hillquit group, 47 from the Debs group, and 8 from smaller groups. It was the largest and most representative gathering of American Socialists ever held up to that time. In addition to the Debs and Hillquit factions, there were representatives from the more or less independent Socialist groups of western metal miners, from the left wing of the disintegrating agrarian People's Party, and from grouplets of Christian Socialists. Three-fourths of the delegates were native-born. For the first time, there were Negro delegates (three) at a Socialist convention.

The convention formally united the Socialist movement. It adopted a constitution, worked out a platform, named the new organization the Socialist Party of America, established national headquarters in St. Louis, and elected Leon Greenbaum, a relatively unknown figure, as national secretary. Debs was the outstanding mass personality at the convention, with Hillquit and Berger the real political leaders.

THE SOCIALIST PARTY PROGRAM

The unity convention was pretty well agreed on the general aim of the Party which was broadly stated as "conquering the powers of government and using them for the purpose of transforming the present system of private ownership of the means of production and distribution into collective ownership by the entire people."[1] On specific issues, however, sharp divisions prevailed. Strong De Leonist influence was present; nevertheless, the Hillquit-Berger forces wrote the bulk of the program.

The S.P. convention, like that of the S.L.P. in the previous year, displayed little understanding of the general question of imperialism, notwithstanding the fact that Bryan, the Democratic candidate, made this, confusedly, the central issue of the campaign. Both Debs and De Leon had opposed the Spanish-American war, and the A.F. of L. in its 1898 convention adopted a sharp resolution condemning the seizure of the Philippines and combating imperialism in general.[2] But neither Debs

---

[1] Hillquit, *History of Socialism in the U.S.*, p. 349.
[2] American Federation of Labor, *History, Encyclopedia, Reference Book*, p. 243, Washington, D. C., 1919.

nor De Leon had a grasp upon the basic significance of imperialism. De Leon (and pretty much Debs also) looked upon imperialism as simply "expansionism," as merely a quantitative growth of capitalism. The trusts, they both considered as a basically progressive development, about which nothing could or should be done in an opposition way. Said De Leon, "The issue of imperialism, which seems to be a political question, is only an economic question, being based upon and part of the economic question, expansion." Thus, De Leon mechanically accepted the development of imperialism, even as he did the growth of the trusts.[1] In both respects, his fatalistic attitude tended to cut the party off from those masses, who wanted to fight both the trusts and imperialism generally.

In November 1898, an Anti-Imperialist League was founded in Chicago.[2] Eventually it had some 500,000 members. It was essentially middle class, with leaders such as U.S. Senators Hoar and Pettigrew, Carl Schurz, Mark Twain, Finley Peter Dunne, and the big steel magnate, Andrew Carnegie. Samuel Gompers was a vice-president of the organization, and Debs displayed some interest in it. There was a strong pro-Philippines independence sentiment among the Negro people, and this found widespread expression in the Negro press of the time. Generally the tendency of the Socialists in the 1900 campaign was to reply to Bryan's and other attacks upon American imperialism by intensifying their anti-capitalist agitation, without grasping the special tasks thrust upon them by the rise of imperialism. Not the fight against imperialist policies, but the fight to destroy capitalism itself, is the issue, cried the De Leonites. Both Socialist parties in their current platforms completely misunderstood, underestimated, and ignored the entire question of imperialism.

A sharp debate occurred in the unity convention over the question of immediate demands. The "impossibilists," the incipient left wing, reflecting De Leon influence, insisted that all such demands should be kept out of the Party's program, and that the Party should confine itself to making propaganda for socialism. The "possibilists," however, beat down this argument, and by a vote of 5,358 to 1,325 the convention decided to support a policy of partial demands. The party's platform, therefore, in addition to demands for public ownership of public utilities and the means of transportation and communication, included demands also for reduced hours and increased wages, social insurance, equal civil and political rights for men and women, and the initiative, referendum, and recall.

The convention stated only generally its principles on the trade union question. It declared that both economic and political action were nec-

1 *The Weekly People*, Sept. 22, 1900.
2 Henry Steele Commager, *Documents of American History*, p. 19, N. Y., 1949.

essary to bring about socialism, and it also took the position that "the formation of every trade union, no matter how small or how conservative it may be, will strengthen the power of the wage working class." No mention was made in the Party's program, however, of the vital issue of industrial unionism.

De Leonite influence was strong so far as the Party's attitude toward farmers was concerned. But the convention could not come to a decision on what to do about the matter, so the whole question was postponed until the next convention. Also, no demands were made for Negro rights —a resolution was adopted, however, inviting Negro workers to join the Party. This was the only resolution on the Negro question passed by the Party for many years, in fact up to the time of World War I.

The unity convention in Indianapolis revealed the political immaturity of the founders of the Socialist Party, by compounding many De Leonite weaknesses and by displaying various reformist tendencies. The "unity" on the trade union question did not resolve existing basic differences on the matter, what with Hillquit leaning toward collaboration with Gompers, while Debs' tendency was toward dual unionism. In the main, the convention failed to hammer out sound political policies and tactics firmly grounded in Marxist principles. Nevertheless, the founding of the Socialist Party, by bringing the socialist movement into contact with broad masses, was a progressive development. It broke with the De Leonite sectarianism which was strangling the advanced working class movement. But the Socialist Party could not be the "party of the new type," as later defined by Lenin, as it finally failed to meet the demands of the imperialist era into which it was born.

THE EMPLOYERS' OPEN-SHOP OFFENSIVE

Meanwhile, led by the National Association of Manufacturers, the attack of the employers against the trade unions and the living standards of the workers went on ferociously. In 1901, 62,000 steel workers, striking against the U.S. Steel Corporation, were defeated and unionism was practically wiped out in the trust mills. During the same year the National Metal Trades smashed a national strike of 58,000 machinists, knocking the union out of most of their big plants. From 1901 to 1904 a whole series of strikes and semi-civil wars raged in the Rocky Mountain mining regions, led and largely won by the militant Western Federation of Miners, headed by such fighters as Bill Haywood and Vincent St. John. In 1902 the anthracite miners of Pennsylvania, organized in the United Mine Workers and led by the conservative John Mitchell, waged a long and mostly unsuccessful strike.[1] And in 1905 the Chicago teamsters lost a strike of 5,000 men; casualties—20 killed, 400 injured, 500 arrested.

All these strikes were savagely fought by the employers, with every known strikebreaking weapon—troops, injunctions, scabs, gunmen, and all the rest. The A.F. of L. leadership, deeply corrupted by the employers, met the onslaught by laying every obstacle in the way of the workers' solidarity and militancy. The general result of the anti-strike drive was to weaken the craft unions gravely in the basic industries. Nevertheless, the unions managed to grow—from a total of 868,500 in 1900 to 2,022,000 in 1905—mostly in the building trades and the lighter, not yet trustified, industries.

The arrogant employers also pushed their drive against the workers in the political field. N.A.M. agents in 1902 defeated the eight-hour and anti-injunction bills before Congress. They also knocked out many local and congressional election candidates who showed sympathy toward labor. In 1903 there began, also, the celebrated Danbury Hatters' Case, which was eventually to outlaw sympathy strikes, boycotts, and the union label. Divided and misled, organized labor's political influence, nationally and in the various states, was down almost to the vanishing point.

SOCIALIST PARTY ACTIVITY

The Socialists, at least partially freed from the fetters of De Leon's crippling sectarianism, plunged into this maelstrom of class struggle; that is, the worker Socialists, the growing left wing, did. They were active in all the strikes and union-organizing campaigns of the period. Consequently, they became influential in many local unions, city labor councils, and international unions. They also carried their struggle into the A.F. of L. conventions, where the bureaucratic union leaders were a definite section of the employers' strikebreaking forces. In these years the Socialist militants fought for independent political action, industrial unionism, the organization of the unorganized, a more effective strike strategy. They ran Socialist candidates against the Gompers machine.

In the A.F. of L. convention of 1902 in New Orleans the Socialist group introduced a resolution, calling upon the A.F. of L. to "advise the working people to organize their economic and political power to secure for labor the full equivalent of its toil and the overthrow of the

[1] During this big strike the notorious President Baer of the coal-carrying Philadelphia and Reading Railroad declared that industrial relations would be regulated by "the Christian men to whom God in his infinite wisdom, has given control of the property interests of the country." (*The Independent*, Aug. 28, 1902.)

wage system." After a prolonged and heated debate, the Gompersites defeated the resolution by the narrow margin of 4,899 to 4,171.[1] Among the unions which supported the Socialists' resolution were such important organizations as the miners, carpenters, and brewery workers. A similar political resolution, together with one on industrial unionism, were brought up in the 1903 convention, but both were beaten by a large margin.

The Gompersites violently resisted every effort of the Marxists to improve and modernize the craft unions. Their denunciations of socialism were as violent as those of the capitalists. Gompers himself, who only a few years before had freely expressed his sympathy for the First International, set the pace in this redbaiting. At the 1903 convention of the A.F. of L. he delivered himself of his well-known denunciation of the Socialists: "Economically you are unsound; socially you are wrong; and industrially you are an impossibility."[2] This feud between the A.F. of L. leadership and the Socialists, which dated back to De Leon in the early 1890's, was to rage with greater or less intensity until the end of World War I.

Many petty-bourgeois intellectuals in the S.P. looked askance at the struggle against the corrupt and reactionary A.F. of L. leadership. They figured that it interfered with their vote-getting activities. Their reformism, in fact, was the same in substance as that of the A.F. of L. bureaucracy, arising out of the corruption of the labor aristocracy by imperialism. Gompers' bitter fight against socialism was directed basically against the left wing, the sequel showing that he had no real quarrel with the middle class intellectuals.

Already Hillquit and his fellow opportunists were developing their policy of "neutrality" toward the trade unions. A correct Marxist policy signified working in the unions in order to strengthen them, to defend the rights of the workers, and to develop their class consciousness in the direction of socialism. The opportunist "neutrality" policy, on the contrary, meant no struggle; that is, allowing the workers to be influenced by the ideas of the bourgeoisie and dropping all fight against the corrupt Gompers misleaders. Consequently, with the latter line in mind, at the 1904 convention of the A.F. of L., no general Socialist resolution was introduced. Max Hayes, a printer and prominent Socialist unionist, declared "that the Socialists had come to realize that socialism would win not by passing resolutions, but by agitation."[3]

[1] Lorwin, *The American Federation of Labor*, p. 74.
[2] *Proceedings of the 1903 Convention, American Federation of Labor.*
[3] Lorwin, *The American Federation of Labor*, p. 74.

THE FORMATION OF THE I.W.W.

The Industrial Workers of the World was founded in Chicago, on June 27, 1905.[1] Present at the convention were 203 delegates, representing an estimated 142,991 members, of whom about 50,000 actually joined the new organization. There were 16 local and national A.F. of L. unions in attendance, but the main constituent bodies were the Western Federation of Miners (27,000), American Labor Union (16,750), United Metal Workers (3,000), United Brotherhood of Railway Employees (2,087), and the Socialist Trades and Labor Alliance (1,450). C. O. Sherman of the United Metal Workers was selected general president.

The purpose of the new organization was to re-establish the labor movement on a new, Socialist basis. Its form was the industrial union; its method was militant struggle in both the economic and political fields, and its goal was the abolition of the capitalist system.

The I.W.W. was left-wing dual unionism. It was a militant answer of the workers to the stupidities and treacheries of Gompersite trade unionism—with its major concentration upon the skilled and betrayal of the unskilled; its craft unionism and union scabbing in an industry that had become highly trustified, where the skilled craftsmen played less and less a role and where worker solidarity had become imperative; its overpaid and financially crooked officials; its vicious practices of class collaboration; its corrupt alliances with the Republican and Democratic parties; and its worshiping at the shrine of the capitalist system. The fundamental mistake of dual unionism, however, was that by withdrawing the most advanced elements of the trade unions into ineffective competitive unions, the basic mass unions in the A. F. of L. were left in the virtually uncontested control of the corrupt Gompers machine.

The I.W.W. at its inception was a Socialist union, the creation of the left wing of the S.P. All its chief founders called themselves Marxists. Debs, De Leon and Haywood,[2] the three outstanding left-wingers of the period, "shook hands over the bloody chasm" of past quarrels in setting up the organization. The anarchists and other "direct actionists" were but a negligible factor at the initial stage.

The immediate impulse for forming the I.W.W. came from the metal miners of the West. The Western Federation of Miners, born in fierce struggle, had been organized in 1893 in Butte. Receiving no support from the A.F. of L., however, this union became independent. In May, 1898, it established the Western Labor Union, the aim of which

---

[1] Paul F. Brissenden, *The Industrial Workers of the World*, N. Y., 1920.
[2] For biographies of these three men see Ray Ginger, *The Bending Cross*, Harry Kuhn, ed., *Daniel De Leon, a Symposium*, and *Bill Haywood's Book*, an autobiography.

was to organize generally the workers of the Rocky Mountain areas. In 1902, the W.L.U. reorganized itself into the American Labor Union, with the idea of one day superseding the whole A.F. of L. It was a national dual union. The A.L.U. had a Socialist leadership, and both Haywood and Debs were active in its formation. It was in following out this general line of independent Socialist unionism that the A.L.U. leaders three years later took the initiative in forming the I.W.W. De Leonist dual-unionist thinking predominated in the whole development.

The establishment of the I.W.W. brought about the first real crystallization of the left wing nationally within the Socialist Party, of those forces which, under new circumstances and with a sounder program, were to produce the Communist Party. The S.P. right-wing leadership condemned the I.W.W. vigorously, as they had rejected the A.L.U., on the grounds that it compromised the position of the Socialist forces in the trade unions. Between right and left the struggle sharpened over the basic question of trade unionism, with the I.W.W. in the center of the fight. This quarrel was fated to become more and more intense as the spectacular history of the I.W.W. developed during the next few years.

THE STATUS OF THE PARTY

Immediately upon its formation in 1901, the Socialist Party began to flourish. At its second convention, in May 1904, it had 184 delegates, representing 1,200 locals in 35 states. The Party's dues-paying membership had doubled since 1901, now being 20,768. The Party press was also growing rapidly, amounting at this period to several dailies in German and other non-English languages, 20 English weeklies, and seven monthlies. The Socialist workers were active in all strikes and organizing campaigns; they vigorously attacked Gompersism, and they carried on a militant anti-capitalist campaign. The Party's trade union influence in consequence was rapidly on the rise, and its success in the 1904 national elections was significant. The S.P.'s candidates, Eugene V. Debs and Ben Hanford, polled 409,230 votes, or about a 350 percent increase over the vote in 1900.

Despite all this vigor and progress, however, the Party was already beginning to feel the effects of numerous negative influences which were to undermine it and to prevent it from becoming the vanguard party of the working class. For one thing, the Party was already attracting a large and motley array of doctors, lawyers, dentists, preachers, small businessmen, and other reformers and opportunists. These elements, the radical wing of the city middle class, then being crushed by the advancing trusts, hoped to make use of the proletarian membership and following of the Party for their own ends, and they descended upon the Socialist Party in force. By concentrating upon innumerable opportunist partial demands and by damping down all militant struggle and revolutionary propaganda, they were transforming the Party into a vehicle for middle class reform. Closely allied with the reformists of the Second International, these elements fought against the Party basing itself upon the industrial proletariat and developing an anti-capitalist program. Already by 1905, the petty-bourgeois elements were busily consolidating their hold upon the Party, a control which was to last throughout the life of the organization.

The opportunist intellectuals were able to seize the leadership of the Socialist Party because the working class left wing of the Party, afflicted with sectarianism, lacked an effective program. Moreover, the bulk of the working class members, who were foreign-born, had big language difficulties, and were split into more or less isolated national groups (eventually the "language federations"), lacked the unity necessary to cope with the highly vocal middle class opportunists. Not until World War I and the Russian Revolution, as we shall see, did the proletarian left wing of the Party develop the program and solidarity necessary for it to become dominant in the Socialist Party.

A specific grave weakness of the Socialist Party, largely a reaction against the former experience with the stifling overcentralization of the De Leonite regime in the S.L.P., was the extremely decentralized form of the Party. Each state organization in the Party did pretty much as it pleased, with little or no direction from the national center (except when it wanted to curb the left wing). National Party discipline was almost at zero. The Socialist press, privately owned, was also in chaos. The various papers propagated their own particular ideas of socialism and Party policy. These ideas were many, various, conflicting, and often bizarre, ranging all the way from Christian socialism to leftist "impossibilism." There was no established body of Socialist thought, developed and defended by the Party as such. This confused and undisciplined programmatic set-up provided a perfect situation wherein the opportunists could peddle their wares, and they made the most of it.

From the beginning the S.P. leadership displayed a deep lack of appreciation of the role of Marxist theory. They were afflicted with so-called American practicality, devoting themselves almost exclusively to immediate tasks, combined with an abstract propagation of socialism. They and the Party as a whole paid little attention to the theoretical and tactical struggles going on in the European parties.

Another serious shortcoming of the party, also in evidence at the outset, was its sectarian attitude toward the labor party movement, local outcroppings of which were frequent. The National Executive Committee stated, on January 12, 1903, that "Any alliance, direct or indirect, with such [labor] parties is dangerous to the political integrity and the very existence of the Socialist Party."[1] The Party leadership definitely considered the labor party a rival. This anti-labor party policy, a mixture of De Leonism and a right sectarian attempt to apply European Social-Democratic policies artificially in the United States, was to continue in force in the S.P. for many years, until after World War I, and the appearance of the Communist Party upon the scene. Such a policy of abstention set up a high barrier between the S.P. and the spontaneous political movements of the masses, and it contributed much to the Party's eventual isolation and failure.

Dual unionism was a further weakness of the Party. This trend was already strongly marked at the time of the Party's foundation, as we have seen in the formation of the American Labor Union and the I.W.W. Dual unionism was particularly a disease of the left wing, one of the worst hang-overs of De Leonism. Indeed, for a quarter of a century, from the launching of the American Railway Union by Debs in 1893 until Lenin's blistering attacks upon dual unionism in 1920,[2] the left wing was hamstrung by the leftist notion that a new trade union movement could be established, in rivalry to the existing mass unions and on the basis of ideally constructed, Socialist unions.

THE PARTY'S CHAUVINIST NEGRO POLICY

Throughout its entire existence the Socialist Party has had a chauvinist line on the Negro question. It has not only failed grievously to come to the assistance of the Negro people, harassed by lynching, Jim Crow, and a host of other discriminations and persecutions, but it has always completely misunderstood the theoretical nature of the question. Traditionally, it has been S.P. policy to ignore the national character of the Negro question and to present it all only as a class matter. The S.P.'s sole answer to the oppressed Negro people was that they should vote the Socialist ticket and hope for socialism. The S.P. could not see the Negro people as allies of the working class because of its opportunist-sectarian policies toward the Negro masses; neither could it understand the nature of the oppression of the Negro people because its leaders were blinded by the white chauvinist ideology of the ruling class.

[1] *International Socialist Review*, Feb. 1903.
[2] V. I. Lenin, *"Left Wing" Communism, an Infantile Disorder*, N. Y., 1934.

This policy, to ignore the special status of the Negro people as an oppressed people and to treat the matter only as a class question, which was also De Leon's policy, was already manifest in the founding convention of the Socialist Party in 1901. The resolution on the Negro question adopted by that convention proclaimed "that we declare to the Negro worker the identity of his interests and struggles with the interests and struggles of all workers of all lands, without regard to race or color or sectional lines—that the only line of division which exists in fact is that between the producers and the owners of the world—between capitalism and labor."[1] This policy, to consider the Negro people as proletarians (whereas about 85 percent of them worked on the land, mostly as sharecroppers), and to reduce their whole immediate problem primarily to one of trade unionism, was the policy of the Party for many years, with but slight variations.

The left wing of the Party also did not rise very much above this narrow right-wing sectarian conception of the Negro question. While condemning lynching and insisting upon the admission of Negro workers to the industries and unions, the left did not work out special demands to meet the Negro people's most burning problems. Thus, when proposals were made in the Party in 1903 to develop a Negro program, Debs opposed them, arguing: "We have nothing special to offer the Negro, and we cannot make separate appeals to all the races. The Socialist Party is the Party of the whole working class regardless of color."[2] Debs said also, on the Negro question, "Social equality . . . forsooth . . . is pure fraud and serves to mask the real issue, which is not *social* equality, but *economic freedom*."[3] And, "The Socialist platform has not a word in reference to social equality."[4]

Behind the failure of the Socialist Party from its outset to take up the Negro people's special grievances and to penetrate the South lay a very obvious white chauvinism, particularly among the petty-bourgeois leadership within the Party. This often found open and brutal expression in the Party press. Thus, Victor Berger, in the *Social Democratic Herald*, in May 1902, stated that "There can be no doubt that the Negroes and mulattoes constitute a lower race."[5] And William Noyes, writing as a "friend" of the Negro, had an article in the *International Socialist Review*, reeking with outrageous and unquotable anti-Negro slander, repeating every slave-owner insult and belittlement of this oppressed people. And nobody in the *Review* challenged his chauvinism.

1 Alexander Trachtenberg, ed., *American Labor Year Book*, p. 125, N. Y., 1916.
2 Ray Ginger, *The Bending Cross*, p. 260, New Brunswick, N. J., 1949.
3 Eugene V. Debs in the *International Socialist Review*, Nov. 1903.
4 Eugene V. Debs in the *International Socialist Review*, Jan. 1904.
5 Ginger, *The Bending Cross*, p. 259.

Today, not even the most blatant white supremacist in the Deep South would dare to say publicly what Noyes, as a matter of course, wrote in 1901 openly in the Socialist press.[1] The fact that the constant expressions of white chauvinism on the part of the S.P. leaders did not provoke a bitter condemnation from the left showed that the Marxists in the Party were themselves by no means clear about this deadly political disease. With such false policies and attitudes prevailing, small wonder then that the Negro members of the Socialist Party were few and far between and that the Party's influence was negligible among the Negro masses.

OPPORTUNIST INFLUENCE OF THE SECOND INTERNATIONAL

Another detrimental influence upon the young Socialist Party, and one that was to continue to injure it from then on, was the opportunistic pressure of the Second International. During the period of the First International (1864-1876) and for a decade thereafter, the American Marxists had the inestimable advantage of the direct advice of Marx and Engels. But with the development of the policy of the Second International into more and more of an opportunist position, after that body's foundation in 1889, the former revolutionary international leadership came to a sudden halt. The Marxists in the United States were cut off from the left forces in Europe and exposed to a full stream of revisionist poison. Although, at the turn of the century, there grew up in Russia a great Socialist genius—Lenin—comparable to Karl Marx, the American Marxists down to World War I knew practically nothing about him and his writings, or of the growth of Bolshevism in tsarist Russia. Even the Russian Revolution of 1905, filtered as it was through the interpretations of the opportunistic leaders of the Second International, impressed few major lessons upon the American Socialist Party.

The Second International, with its parties, unions, co-operatives, and parliamentary groups growing rapidly in the 1890's, early developed reformist illusions to the effect that it was therefore in the process of establishing socialism step by step in various countries.[2] Its leaders came to believe that Marx, with his perspective of a militant struggle for socialism, had become outmoded and obsolete. This right opportunism was an outgrowth of the developing imperialist stage of capitalism, with its markedly increased bribery and corruption of the labor aristocracy upon which the Social-Democratic leadership mainly based itself.

This revisionism took strong root and the most outstanding spokes-

[1] *International Socialist Review*, Dec. 1901
[2] Joseph Stalin, *Foundations of Leninism*, p. 20, N. Y., 1939.

man of the trend was Eduard Bernstein, in Germany.[1] In 1899 he expressed his revisionist doctrines in his book, published in the United States under the title *Evolutionary Socialism*. Bernstein rejected the Marxist theories of surplus value, concentration of capital, the progressive pauperization of the working class, the class struggle, and the materialist conception of history, and he ridiculed the social revolution as the "ultimate goal." In this period, Bebel and Kautsky in Germany, as well as Lenin, Plekhanov, and others in Russia and on an international scale, waged energetic war upon Bernsteinism. Nevertheless it eventually became the predominant philosophy of the opportunist leaders of the Second International, with disastrous results to the working class movement in many countries.

This reformist poison the Second International steadily pumped into the veins of the young American Socialist Party. Victor Berger, from the early 1900's, openly supported Bernsteinian revisionism through his paper in Milwaukee and in the Party councils. Scores of other middle class Socialist Party leaders in the United States took a similar position. Thus they sapped the very foundations of Marxism in the Party. As in the Social-Democratic Party of Germany and in the general leadership of the Second International, Bernsteinism, with specific national adaptations, became, as early as 1905, the predominant philosophy of the ruling group of intellectuals in the Socialist Party of America. Hillquit himself, however, was a centrist, a follower of Kautsky, who, as the sequel showed, was only a disguised brand of Bernsteinist.

[1] V. I. Lenin and Joseph Stalin, *Marxism and Revisionism*, N. Y., 1946.

8. The Heyday of the Socialist Party (1905-1914)

The decade prior to the beginning of the first World War was a time of rapid growth and trustification of American industry, and also of imperialist expansionism. In the United States, as Lenin pointed out, the period of "imperialism, in particular, the era of finance capital, the era of gigantic capitalist monopolies, the era of the transformation of simple trust-capitalism into state-trust capitalism, shows an unprecedented strengthening of the state and an unheard of development of the bureaucratic and military apparatus."[1]

Following up its victory in the Spanish-American War, American imperialism turned its chief attention to the conquest of Latin America, particularly the Caribbean area. American investments soared and American armed forces intervened directly in the life of many of the countries—Venezuela, Honduras, Haiti, Guatemala, Nicaragua, the Dominican Republic, and others. Cuba and Puerto Rico were held in colonial bondage. American aggression was one of the major factors that caused the Mexican Revolution, which began in 1910. Yankee imperialism was systematically pushing the older British imperialism aside in the Caribbean. But the biggest conquest for Wall Street during the period was the seizure of Panama and the building of the Panama Canal.

The capitalists in the United States were busily grabbing the wealth of the country and its industries. In 1914, according to the report of an official government commission, "forty-four families have yearly incomes of $1,000,000 or more, and less than two million of the people . . . own 20 percent more of the nation's wealth than all the other 90 millions. The rich two percent own 60 percent of the wealth, the middle class 33 percent own 35 percent, and the poor 65 percent own but five percent."[2] The wholesale capitalist robbery of the people was enforced through a complete control of the government and through elaborate systems of espionage and gunmen in the company towns of the basic industries.

1 V. I. Lenin, *State and Revolution*, p. 29, N. Y., 1932.
2 *Final Report of the Commission on Industrial Relations*, Washington, D. C., 1915.

THE CONDITIONS OF THE WORKERS

While generally the skilled workers of these times had considerably higher wages than those prevailing in other countries, the masses of the unskilled, unorganized, foreign-born workers, who made up the great majority of the workers in nearly all the trustified industries, were forced down to a bare subsistence level. The noted report of the Commission on Industrial Relations[1] pointed out: "It is certain that at least one-third and possibly one-half of the families of wage earners employed in manufacturing and mining earn in the course of the year less than enough to support them in anything like a comfortable and decent condition" (p. 10). And, "No better proof of the miserable condition of the mass of American workers need be sought than the fact that in recent years laborers in large numbers have come to this country only from Russia, Italy, Austria-Hungary, and the backward and impoverished nations of southern and eastern Europe" (p. 3). And, "Have the workers secured a fair share of the enormous increase in wealth which has taken place in this country, during the period, as a result largely of their labors? The answer is emphatically—No!" (p. 8).

On the eve of World War I women worked for about 30 percent less than men, child labor was a great national evil, and the Negro toilers, barred from many industries and trade unions, were by far the worst off of all. Owing to the employers' boundless greed, the industries were also literal slaughter-houses for the workers, the Commission on Industrial Relations stating, "Approximately 35,000 persons were killed last year in American industry, and at least half of these deaths were preventable" (p. 46). The Commission suggested that the situation might be improved if the capitalists were held criminally responsible for such needless deaths. Working hours ranged up to twelve per day, seven days per week (steel, railroads, etc.), with relatively few workers having the eight-hour day (coal mining, building, printing, etc.). In many localities, the immigrant workers' "homes" were mere bunkhouses, each working shift taking its turn in bed. The workers had little or no financial protection from industrial accidents. Nor was there any trace of insurance protection against old age and sickness. The workers were also fully exposed to the terrors of joblessness through economic crises.

The government, in all its branches, actively sustained this brutal exploitation. "The workers," says the Commission's report, "have an almost universal conviction that they, both as individuals and as a class, are denied justice in the enactment, adjudication, and administra-

[1] This Commission, headed by Frank P. Walsh, was created by an act of Congress, Aug. 23, 1912, and was appointed by President Wilson.

tion of law" (p. 38). And, "It is quite clear that the fourteenth amendment not only has failed to operate to protect personal rights but has operated almost wholly for the protection of the property rights of corporations" (p. 56).

THE FIGHT OF THE TRADE UNIONS

The pre-World War I period that we are dealing with was one of an intense offensive against labor and the people by the greedy and arrogant monopolists. It was also a time of intensive counter-offensive by the working class against intolerable working and living conditions, a period of fierce strikes and of rapid growth of the workers' economic and political organizations.

During these years the A.F. of L. and railroad unions, despite the Gompersite theories of class collaboration, conducted many bitterly fought struggles. These were precipitated by the militant fighting spirit of the workers. The strikes were intensified by the economic crises of 1907 and 1913. Among the more important of the current strikes were those of the "shirtwaist" girls in New York in 1909 and the cloakmakers in New York and the men's clothing workers in Chicago in 1910, the national Harriman railroad strike in 1911, the desperate fight to organize the West Virginia coal miners in 1913, the Calumet copper mine strike of the same year, and the murderous Colorado coal strike of 1914. In all these strikes, the left wing was active. Everywhere the employers used the utmost violence. During the Calumet copper strike a company gunman shouted "Fire!" in a hall crowded with strikers' children, and 73 were crushed to death in the panic. The employers continued, too, to harpoon the unions in the political field, notably in the famous Danbury Hatters and Buck Stove and Range anti-boycott injunction cases. The first case led to a fine of $232,000 against the workers, and the latter case brought about the indictment, but not jailing, of Gompers, Morrison, and Mitchell, the top A.F. of L. leaders.

The politically and personally corrupt Gompersite leaders met this employers' onslaught in their usual spirit of retreat and surrender. Basing themselves principally upon the skilled workers and upon collaboration with employers, they rejected every proposal to establish industrial unionism; they voted down repeated moves for a labor party; and they broke their own strikes with the outrageous system of "union scabbing"—that is, part of the unions in a given industry working while the rest were striking. Their one feeble reply to the onslaught of capital was, in 1907, the outlining of what was called "Labor's Bill of Grievances." This series of timid legislative proposals finally resulted, in 1914, in the passage of the Clayton Act, which was supposed to shield organized labor from the Sherman anti-trust law, but did not. If during this period the membership of the A.F. of L. advanced from 1,676,200 in 1904 to 2,020,671 in 1914, this was due very largely to the efforts of the rank-and-file Socialists in the trade unions and to the effects of the big I.W.W. strikes, but not to the work of the overpaid and corrupt A.F. of L. leadership.

Two famous labor cases developed during this stormy decade. The first was the arrest, in February 1906, of Moyer, Haywood, and Pettibone, national officers of the Western Federation of Miners, who were charged with the bomb-killing of Governor Frank Steunenberg of Idaho in December 1905. After a bitter court fight which attracted national attention, this notorious frame-up was defeated and the three defendants were triumphantly acquitted. The second big labor case was that of the two McNamara brothers, James and John (and eventually Matt Schmidt and David Kaplan). The McNamaras were arrested in April 1911, and charged with dynamiting the *Los Angeles Times* building during a fierce struggle between the National Erectors Association and the Structural Iron Workers Union. The two brothers, after being betrayed into pleading guilty, served long terms in California penitentiaries. James B. McNamara died in prison after being there 29 years. Several years before he died this indomitable fighter became a Communist.

Regarding the aggressions of American imperialism in Latin America, the A.F. of L. leaders, who in 1898 had vigorously opposed the seizure of the Philippines and "expansion" generally, had radically changed their position. They were now imperialistically minded themselves. Identifying their interests with those of the capitalists, they condoned Wall Street's infringement upon the sovereignty of the peoples to the south. In particular their pro-imperialist meddling in the Mexican Revolution during these years was a deterrent to that great movement. The S.P. and the I.W.W., however, took more of a militant position against Wall Street's interventions and particularly in support of the Mexican Revolution.

THE STRUGGLE OF THE I.W.W.

The I.W.W. played a most important part during these immediate pre-war, pre-Communist Party years. At its foundation in June 1905, the organization was largely Socialist, but shortly thereafter it began to develop an anarcho-syndicalist, anti-political orientation. Already at the 1907 convention an unsuccessful attempt was made to strike out the endorsement of political action from the I.W.W. preamble. In the 1908 convention the "direct actionists," mostly floating workers from the West, who were led by Vincent St. John and William L. Trautmann, were in control, and they deleted altogether the hated "political clause." Thenceforth, the organization was to place its reliance upon the general strike, sabotage, and other methods of "direct action." More and more it took an anti-Marxist position in ensuing years. This move of the I.W.W. into syndicalism alienated the political Socialists. The W.F. of M. quit the I.W.W. during the first year, Debs withdrew shortly afterward, and the break with De Leon came in 1908. De Leon later organized the Workers International Industrial Union, which was similar to the old S.T.L.A.

The turn of the I.W.W. to syndicalism was to be explained by a number of factors, including (a) the disfranchised condition of many millions of foreign-born workers[1]; (b) the workers' disgust at the opportunist political policies of the A. F. of L. and S.P. leaders; (c) the current widespread corruption in American political life; (d) the influx of consciously anarchist elements. As we have seen, roughly similar forces had combined to produce anarcho-syndicalism in Parsons' Chicago movement of the 1880's. A further important element in creating I.W.W. syndicalism was the long-continued influence of De Leonism itself. De Leon in his theorizing constantly played down the role of the Party and exaggerated that of the industrial unions before, during, and after the revolution. St. John and the other anti-parliamentarians and "direct actionists" of the I.W.W., by eliminating the Party altogether from their program, simply carried De Leon's ideas to their logical conclusion. Notwithstanding all his eventual denunciations of the I.W.W., De Leon was in truth the ideological father of anarcho-syndicalism in the United States.

The I.W.W. during this pre-war decade conducted many important and hard-fought strikes—at Goldfield, McKees Rocks, Lawrence, Akron, Paterson, New Bedford, Chicago, Little Falls, and in various parts of Louisiana, Minnesota, California, and Washington. These strikes were mostly among metal miners, lumber workers, textile workers, farm workers, and construction workers—largely foreign-born. The I.W.W. also led many courageous local fights for the right to speak on the streets to the workers—in Spokane, San Diego, Denver, Kansas City, Sioux City, Omaha, and elsewhere. During these fights many hundreds of members were slugged and jailed by vigilante-police gangs.[2] The I.W.W. became the very symbol of indomitable, fighting proletarian spirit.

[1] From 1905 to 1914 inclusive, a vast host of 10,121,943 immigrants, mostly from southern and eastern Europe, poured into the United States.
[2] Vincent St. John, *The I.W.W.: Its History, Structure and Methods*, Chicago, 1919.

During this period I.W.W. militants were barbarously framed and prosecuted. Among the more outrageous of many such cases were those of Preston and Smith, Nevada, 1907, 25 and 10 years; Cline and Rangel, Texas, 1913, 25 years to life; Ford and Suhr, California, 1913, life imprisonment; and—most shocking of all—Joe Hill, celebrated I.W.W. song-writer, Utah, November 19, 1915, executed on a false murder charge.

The I.W.W. won, or half won, most of its bitterly contested struggles. Nevertheless, by 1914 it had organized only about 100,000 members. Already it was sharply displaying many of the internal weaknesses which were eventually to prove fatal to its growth and development. Among the more crucial of these weaknesses were its destructive head-on collision with the trade unions and the Socialist Party; its failure to cultivate the political struggle of the working class; its reckless use of the general strike; its incorrect handling of the religious question (the "No God, no master" slogan in Lawrence); its anarchistic decentralization, which prevented all solid organization; its identification with sabotage; its reliance upon spontaneity; and its sectarian insistence, among conservative workers, upon their acceptance of its syndicalist conception of the revolution.

GROWTH OF THE SOCIALIST PARTY

In all the strikes, free speech fights, labor cases, and political struggles of this period, the left-wing worker fighters of the Socialist Party were in the front line. The dominant intellectuals patronizingly called them the "Jimmy Higginses"[1] of the movement. That is, they did the work and the fighting, while the petty-bourgeois leadership got the credit and held the party's official posts. A good example of the militancy of the left-wing was the great fight it waged to save Moyer, Haywood, and Pettibone. For example, Dr. Herman Titus, long the outstanding left-wing leader on the Pacific coast, moved his paper, the Seattle *Socialist*, to Boise, Idaho, the trial center, and published it from there, making the great trial almost its sole subject. The *Appeal to Reason* also carried on a tremendous campaign for the accused. In his famous *Appeal* article, "Arise Ye Slaves," the fiery Debs declared: "If they attempt to murder Moyer, Haywood, and their brothers, a million revolutionists, at least, will meet them with guns."[2]

In consequence of its many activities in the sharp class struggle of the period, the Party grew rapidly in numbers and influence. By 1912,

[1] Ben Hanford originated this well-known characterization.
[2] Eugene V. Debs in the *Appeal to Reason*, March 10, 1906.

HEYDAY OF THE SOCIALIST PARTY

the high-water mark achieved by the S.P., the Party had some 120,000 members. Pennsylvania was the banner state, with 12,000. The party had a powerful base in the trade unions. There was also strong organization among the western farmers. In this same year Max Hayes of the Typographical Union ran for President of the A. F. of L. and received 5,073 convention votes as against Gompers' 11,974. At this time, supporting the S.P. were the following A. F. of L. unions: Brewery, Hat and Cap Makers, Ladies Garment Workers, Bakery, Fur, Machinists, Tailors, and Western Federation of Miners. There were also large Socialist contingents among the leadership of the Coal Miners, Flint Glass, Painters, Carpenters, Brick, Electrical, Printers, Cigarmakers, and other unions. The Socialists likewise led many local and state councils of the A. F. of L. and they were generally a rapidly growing force in the unions.

The S.P. was also expanding its activity into many new fields. In 1905 the Intercollegiate Socialist Society was formed; in 1906 the Rand School was established; and in 1913 the Young People's Socialist League was organized. Very special attention was also paid to winning over the preachers, the Christian Socialists being a strong force in the party. The party carried on some work among women. In 1908 a national women's commission was set up. The same year the Socialist women of the East Side in New York organized a suffrage demonstration on March 8th, a date which later on became International Women's Day. Neglect of women's historical struggle for the vote, and underestimation of women's work in general, however, characterized both the S.L.P. and S.P. There were, nevertheless, many outstanding women workers in the Socialist Party.

The Party had considerable election success. In 1910 Emil Seidel was elected mayor of Milwaukee, and six months later Victor Berger was elected as the first Socialist in Congress from the same district. The Party in this period elected 56 mayors in Ohio, Pennsylvania, New York, Montana, and New England, as well as 300 councilmen. In 1912 some 1,039 dues-paying Party members were holding elected offices. The presidential campaign of 1912, with Debs and Seidel as the candidates, resulted in a big advance for the Party—the vote, 897,011, being the highest polled by the Party up to that time.

The S.P. also built up a strong press. In 1912 the Party had 323 periodicals. Among these were five English and eight non-English dailies; 262 English and 36 non-English weeklies; and 10 English and two non-English monthlies. The most important of these papers were the *International Socialist Review*, with about 200,000 circulation; *Jewish Daily Forward*, 200,000; *National Rip Saw*, 200,000; *Wilshire's Magazine*, 270,000; and the *Appeal to Reason*, 500,000. The latter weekly, which then claimed the biggest circulation of any Socialist paper in the world, was owned by J. A. Wayland and edited by Fred D. Warren, with Debs a frequent contributor. It was a very aggressive organ, with a mixed policy of opportunist socialism, populism, and militant unionism. During 1912 it circulated 36,091,000 copies. It concentrated on large special editions. The big "Moyer-Haywood" and "Debs' Reply to Roosevelt" editions ran to three million copies each.[1] It took four solid mail trains of ten cars apiece to transport each of these immense issues. The *Appeal* had behind it a devoted, organized "army" of up to 80,000 workers and farmers.

During this general period an internal development took place in the S.P. which was destined to have a profound effect upon the Party's future. This was the organization of the national groups, or "language federations." The opportunist leaders of the Party, with eyes fastened upon the skilled workers and the middle classes, characteristically paid little or no attention to Party organization work among the many millions of voteless, non-English-speaking immigrants. As a result the Socialist workers among these groups themselves took up their own organization along national lines. Thus, successively, there developed national federations of Finns, 1907; Letts, 1908; South Slavs, 1911; Italians, 1911; Scandinavians, 1911; Hungarians, 1912; Bohemians, 1912; Germans, 1913; Poles, 1913; Jews, 1913; Slovaks, 1913; Ukrainians, 1915; Lithuanians, 1915; Russians, 1915.[2] These groups, largely unskilled workers in the basic industries, developed highly organized movements, with elaborate papers, co-operatives, and educational institutions. Gradually, the federations, at first independent, became affiliated to the S.P.— to begin with, loosely as national groups, but finally also as individual members and branches. Each language group had a translator-secretary in the S.P. headquarters. By 1912 the federations had added some 20,000 very important proletarian members to the S.P.

RENAISSANCE OF THE NEGRO LIBERATION MOVEMENT

The period 1905-14, among its many important developments, brought about a new resurgence of struggle by the Negro people, the most important since the crushing of the Negro people during the Reconstruction years following the Civil War. American monopoly capitalism, imperialism, with its generally accentuated reaction, was having catastrophic effects upon the persecuted and oppressed Negro people in the South. Among these reactionary consequences were the repeal of the

---

1 George Allen England, *The Story of the Appeal*, p. 277.
2 Fine, *Labor and Farmer Parties in the U.S.*, p. 325.

so-called Force Bills by Congress in 1894, the adoption all over the South of a whole series of Jim Crow laws relegating the Negro people to a position of semi-serfdom, the radical decline of land ownership in the South by Negroes, the rebirth of Ku Klux Klan terrorism, and the betrayal of the Populist movement in the South by such opportunists as Tom Watson and Ben Tillman. Particularly contemptible was the Jim Crow attitude of the southern white churches, which evidently looked forward to a "lily white" heaven. During 1888-1900, there was an average of 165 Negro lynchings yearly.[1] Bravely the Negro people fought against all this persecution.[2]

The greatly increased capitalist pressure upon the Negro people provoked sharp reactions from them. The first important expression of this was the organization of the Niagara movement in 1905. This movement was headed by the noted scholar, W. E. B. Du Bois, and it sounded a ringing note of militant struggle for the Negro masses. Previously, from the early nineties on, Booker T. Washington had been the most outstanding spokesman of the Negro people. Through his Tuskegee movement he maintained that the Negro masses' path to progress was through improvement of their economic position by cultivating their skills and developing a strong middle class. He combated all struggle for social equality as "extremest folly." Washington was quite popular among white reformers and philanthropists; Andrew Carnegie, for example, gave him $600,000 for Tuskegee Institute.

The Niagara movement collided head-on with Washington's economic, political, and social doctrines. It rejected his policy of retreat and submission. "We shall not be satisfied with less than full manhood rights," its leaders declared. They demanded an end to all discrimination and insisted upon social equality. The modern Negro liberation movement can be said to have started with the Niagara agitation, which greatly alarmed the bourgeoisie. In 1909 the National Association for the Advancement of Colored People was founded. This was an alliance of Negro middle class intellectuals and their white friends, mostly liberals and a few Socialists. Its line was to secure civil-rights justice in the courts and equal economic, trade union, and social opportunities. It fought against lynching and the poll tax. In 1910 the Niagara movement merged with the N.A.A.C.P. The National Urban League was established in 1911. A number of Socialist leaders helped to form these organizations.

The growing Negro liberation movement was, however, primarily the creation of the Negro middle class. The workers were not the vital factor in it that they were to become later. The organized Negro masses

[1] Haywood, *Negro Liberation*; W. E. B. DuBois, *Dusk of Dawn*, N. Y., 1940.
[2] Herbert Aptheker in *Jewish Life*, July 1950.

were also largely isolated from the general labor and Socialist movement. The A.F. of L. leadership, reeking with race prejudice, freely tolerated and encouraged unions with "lily-white" clauses in their constitutions. The Railroad Brotherhoods were even worse, all of them barring Negro workers from the unions and seeking to force them out of the railroad service. The I.W.W., however, took a much more advanced position, Haywood and the other leaders roundly condemning all manifestations of Jim Crow. The I.W.W. Brotherhood of Timber Workers, which conducted important strikes in the lumber industry of Louisiana during 1911-12, was composed about fifty percent of Negroes. Ben Fletcher, Philadelphia longshoreman, was the outstanding Negro leader in the I.W.W.

The S.P., under its petty-bourgeois leadership, virtually ignored the hardships and struggles of the Negro people. It held to the incorrect theory that the Negro was persecuted not because of his color, but only because he was a worker. The few Negroes who joined the Party in the South were placed in segregated locals. The Party conducted no campaign to halt the frightful campaign of lynching which was raging throughout the South.

This S.P. indifference to the oppression of the Negro people, as previously remarked, was largely due to white chauvinism, which is white supremacist Jim Crow. The extent to which this reactionary poison affected the S.P. middle class leadership was shockingly illustrated during the debate on Chinese exclusion at the S.P. national congress in 1910. The upshot of the discussion was that the Party, aligning itself with the corrupt A.F. of L. bureaucracy and in the face of strong opposition from Debs and other left-wingers, went on record with a weasel-worded resolution not to admit to this country Chinese and other Asian peoples who might "reduce" American living standards. Lenin sharply condemned this action, and even the opportunist Second International could not stomach it, publicly criticizing the American Socialist Party.

During this notorious debate, various right-wing leaders freely came forth with chauvinistic expressions, hardly to be outdone by the most rabid white supremacists. For example, the extreme right-winger, Ernest Untermann, who made the minority report at the convention, declared that "The question as to what race shall dominate the globe must be met as surely as the question as to what class shall dominate the world. We should neglect our duty to the coming generation of Aryan peoples if we did not do everything in our power, even today, to insure the final race victory of our own people."[1]

[1] William English Walling, *Progressivism and After*, p. 378, N. Y., 1914.

FORMATION OF THE SYNDICALIST LEAGUE

The Syndicalist League of North America was formed in March 1912, with William Z. Foster as national secretary and with headquarters in Chicago. The League was primarily a split-off from the I.W.W. Foster, after a year's study of the labor movement in France and Germany, during 1909-10, had become convinced that the I.W.W.'s policy of dual unionism was wrong. Returning to the United States, he pointed out that the effects of this dual unionism were to isolate the militants from the masses and to fortify the control of the Gompers bureaucracy in the old unions. He proposed that the I.W.W. should consolidate with the trade unions and devote itself to building the "militant minority" there in order to revolutionize these bodies. Frank Little was among those who agreed with Foster, but the I.W.W. as a whole would not hear of his policy. Foster, along with a few other militants, therefore, launched the new industrial organization.[1]

The League was not Marxist; it was syndicalist, modeled after the French Confederation of Labor. It advocated the general strike, industrial unionism, sabotage, anti-parliamentarism, anti-statism, anti-militarism, anti-clericalism, and an aggressive fighting policy. The S.L.N.A. had a distinct position of its own, however, in disputing the current syndicalist conception that the industrial unions would be the basis of the future society, taking the stand that labor unions were not producing bodies and that industry in the future would develop its own specific industrial organizations.[2]

The S.L.N.A. established about a dozen branches from Chicago westward, including a couple in western Canada. It carried on numerous strikes and organizing activities, and it produced four papers: *The Syndicalist*,[3] in Chicago; *The Toiler*, in Kansas City; *The Unionist*, in Omaha; and *The Internationalist*, in San Diego. Tom Mooney was a member of the organization, and he established a flourishing national section in the Molders Union.[4] Tom Mann of England, in 1913, made a highly successful national tour of the United States for the League.

The anarchist movement (Goldman-Berkman group), then almost completely decayed, tried to exploit the rising sentiment for French syndicalism. In *Mother Earth*, on September 30, 1912, Alexander Berkman and others published a call for the establishment of a syndicalist league, but nothing came of it.

[1] William Z. Foster, *From Bryan to Stalin*, p. 58 ff., N. Y., 1937.
[2] Earl C. Ford and William Z. Foster, *Syndicalism*, Chicago, 1913.
[3] The editor of this paper was Jay Fox, a veteran of the Haymarket affair.
[4] *International Socialist Review*, Dec. 1912.

The League petered out in 1914. Its death was primarily due to its incorrect syndicalist program. Its position against dual unionism was sound, but the left wing in the I.W.W. and S.P. was too deeply imbued with dual unionism to pay heed to the League's arguments for working within the old unions. Particularly so, as at this time the I.W.W. was carrying through a series of spectacular strikes. It is difficult to conceive now of how fervidly the left wing at that time believed in dual unionism. Bill Haywood said, "The 28,000 local unions of the A.F. of L. are 28,000 agencies of the capitalist class," and he added that he would rather cut off his right arm than belong to the A.F. of L. Vincent St. John declared that "The American Federation of Labor is not now and never can become a labor movement." De Leon stated that "The American Federation of Labor is neither American, nor a federation, nor of labor." Joe Ettor, Lawrence strike organizer, declared that it is "the first duty of every revolutionist to destroy the A.F. of L."[1] Debs poured out a constant denunciation of the old craft unions and glorification of the dual industrial unions, and early in 1914 he called (in vain) for the establishment of a new labor movement, based upon an amalgamation of the U.M.W.A., the W.F. of M., and a regenerated I.W.W.[2] With such deep-seated convictions on dual unionism saturating the entire left wing, there was no place for the S.L.N.A. policy of "boring-from-within" the old unions. The S.L.N.A.'s anti-politics was also a big factor against it.

THE NEW FREEDOM AND THE SQUARE DEAL

The big capitalists, greatly alarmed by the current growth of the trade unions, the I.W.W., and the Socialist Party during this period, in 1912 greatly elaborated their bourgeois reformism—in addition to their already extensive methods of breaking strikes, smashing unions, and generally fighting the advance of the working class. Thus was born in Democratic Party ranks the "New Freedom" of Woodrow Wilson, and in Republican circles the "Square Deal" of Theodore Roosevelt.

Wilson, with his anti-red demagogy, cried, "We are on the verge of a revolution," at the same time warning the people against the domination of the trusts. In general terms, he promised the people a new freedom, which, of course, failed to materialize. Roosevelt went even further than Wilson in his demagogy. With the steel trust behind him and sensing the need for a reform campaign, Roosevelt tried to get the Re-

[1] William Z. Foster, *The Bankruptcy of the American Labor Movement*, p. 47, N. Y., 1922.
[2] *International Socialist Review*, March 1914.

HEYDAY OF THE SOCIALIST PARTY

publican Party to write a few liberal planks into its platform. When he failed in this he seceded and launched the Progressive Party, with himself and Hiram Johnson as presidential candidates. This was the "Bull Moose," "Square Deal" ticket.

Roosevelt's program called for many reforms. He said, "We stand for the most advanced factory legislation. We will introduce state control over all the trusts, in order that there should be no poverty, in order that everyone shall receive decent wages. We will establish social and industrial justice; we bow and pay homage to all reforms; there is one reform and one only that we do not want and that is the expropriation of the capitalists."

In the three-cornered big-party fight Wilson won the election, with a million short of a majority; but with 435 electoral votes, against 88 for Roosevelt and 8 for Taft. The S.P., as we have seen, in spite of the double-barreled demagogy from the old party candidates, polled its largest vote up till then. The Progressive Party died after the campaign.

Lenin recognized the importance of the 1912 election, stating, "The significance of the election is an unusually clear and striking manifestation of bourgeois reformism as a means of struggle against socialism. . . . Roosevelt has been obviously hired by the clever billionaires to preach this fraud."[1] The extreme right-wing elements in the S.P., on the other hand, began to see in this bourgeois reformism a "progressive capitalism" and, thus, a step toward socialism. Walling, for example, stated that bourgeois reform leads to state capitalism, hailed its coming as a basic step forward, like the growth of the trusts. He said that "certainly the Socialist platform did not go any further than Roosevelt's unqualified phrase that 'the people' should control industry collectively."[2] Both the Socialists and the LaFollette progressives complained that Roosevelt stole their thunder. Organized labor stayed aside from the movement, seeing in it a sort of neo-Republican Party.

LEFTS VERSUS RIGHTS IN THE PARTY

From its very beginning the Socialist Party, as indicated earlier, was a prey to the numerous middle class intellectuals and businessmen. Increasingly, they descended upon it—lawyers, doctors, preachers, dentists, journalists, professors, small employers, and even a few priests. Such people as these were Hillquit, Berger, Harriman, Wilson, Unterman, Hoan, Wilshire, Wayland, Russell, Mills, Frank and William Bohn,

[1] V. I. Lenin, *Collected Works*, Vol. 16, pp. 190-91 (Fourth Russian edition).
[2] Walling, *Progressivism and After*, p. 171.

Simons, Ghent, and others. By 1908 there were 300 preachers in the Party, with other professional groups in proportion. There was also a substantial group of "millionaire Socialists"—Stokes, Walling, Lloyd, Patterson, Hunter, and company. These non-proletarian elements, plus certain conservative Socialist union leaders—Barnes, Johnston, Germer, Maurer, Walker, Schlesinger, and others—progressively fastened their grip upon the Party as the years went by. The national secretaries of the Party, from 1901 to 1914—Leon Greenbaum, W. Mailly, J. M. Barnes, and J. M. Work—functioned in harmony with the middle class leadership.

There is a proper and effective place in the Marxist Party for middle class intellectuals. They can help especially in its theoretical development. But this only upon the condition that they get rid of their petty-bourgeois illusions and identify themselves completely with the immediate and ultimate aims of the proletariat. Few of those in the S.P., however, did this; the bulk of them clung to their reformism and thus comprised the right wing of the Party. Their deleterious influence was not lessened by the fact that many of them, including Hillquit himself, had proletarian backgrounds.

On this general question, Lenin said, in speaking of the development of class consciousness among the workers: "This consciousness could only be brought from without. The history of all countries shows that the working class, exclusively by its own effort, is able to develop only trade union consciousness, *i.e.* it may realize the necessity for combining in unions, to fight against the employers and to strive to compel the government to pass necessary labor legislation, etc. The theory of socialism, however, grew out of the philosophic, historical, and economic theories that were elaborated by the educated representatives of the propertied classes, the intellectuals. The founders of modern Socialism, Marx and Engels, themselves belonged to the bourgeois intellectuals."[1]

As we have previously remarked, these right-wing elements generally tended toward Bernsteinism. Their whole attention was devoted to parliamentary opportunism. They proposed to buy out the industries, and to them municipal and government ownership under capitalism amounted to socialism. They were "post-office Socialists." Their whole tendency was to kill the proletarian fighting spirit of the membership and to transform the Party into one of middle class reform. Among the dominant petty-bourgeois intellectuals were a group of centrists—Hillquit, Stokes, Hunter, *et al.* Radical in words, the latter elements, when it came to a showdown, traditionally served as a fig-leaf to cover up the political nakedness of the right opportunists.

[1] V. I. Lenin, *What Is To Be Done?*, pp. 32-33, N. Y., 1929.

The S.P. intellectuals produced many books and pamphlets, but not one important Marxist work. The many books of Myers, Russell, and Sinclair, although full of valuable factual material, were only a little above the bourgeois-reformist muckraking of Steffens, Tarbell, and others of the period. Hillquit's and Boudin's writings were but academic Marxism, and those of Simons and Oneal presented an opportunist conception of American history. Ghent's *Benevolent Feudalism* was something of a contribution, but quite important among the S.P. writings was *The Iron Heel* by Jack London—a book which foresaw, in a sense, the eventual development of fascism.

The S.P., like the S.L.P. before it, had a sectarian attitude toward American bourgeois culture. Its leaders, despite the contrary policies of Marx and Engels (and later of Lenin and Stalin), systematically ignored or deprecated the work of this country's scientists, inventors, artists, novelists, and democratic thinkers. It was only after the advent of the Communist Party, under the teachings of Lenin, that a correct Marxist attitude toward bourgeois culture began to be developed.

From the outset of the S.P. the working class membership, who wanted to make the Party into a fighting, proletarian Party heading toward socialism, tended to conflict sharply with the opportunists who controlled the Party. This growing left wing was the direct forerunner of the Communist Party. Its struggles were not without considerable progressive influence upon the Party's policies, particularly in the earlier years. Numerous collisions between the right and left took place in various cities and states. The traditional handicap of the young left wing in these fights was its lack of a sound program, free of sectarianism.

The first crucial struggle developed in the state of Washington, coming to a split at the Everett convention, held in July 1909. The leader of the left was Dr. Herman F. Titus, editor of the Seattle *Socialist* and for many years an outstanding national left leader in the Party. The local leader of the right wing was Dr. E. J. Brown, a rank opportunist. Alfred Wagenknecht and William Z. Foster were both members of the local S.P. in Seattle during this significant fight. The immediate cause of the split was a fight over control of the convention; but the basic reason was a long-developing opposition generally among the left-wingers to petty-bourgeois domination of the S.P. The outcome was a split and then two Socialist parties in the state. The National Executive Committee recognized the right-wing forces in Washington, although the left clearly had a majority. Consequently the latter found themselves outside the Party, most of them, including Foster, never to return.

The expelled left wing, those who did not commit themselves entirely to the I.W.W., formed the Wage Workers Party, with Joseph S. Biscay as secretary. This Party, which perished shortly, was typically ultra-leftist. It laid particular stress upon the fact that it confined its membership solely to proletarians, specifically excluding lawyers, preachers, doctors, detectives, soldiers, policemen, and capitalists. It published but one issue of its journal, *The Wage Worker*, in September 1910, before it died. Dr. Titus, with a grim logic, abandoned his profession and became a proletarian. Foster and many other expelled members, upon the demise of the W.W.P., joined the I.W.W.

THE S.P. SPLIT IN 1912

The next big clash between left and right in the S.P. came at the Party's convention in May 1912, held in Indianapolis. This marked a new high stage in the development of the left wing, parent of the eventual Communist Party. The convention fight involved the whole line of the Party, including the perennial matter of petty-bourgeois leadership. The fight at the convention, however, boiled down to two basic questions—sabotage and industrial unionism. The right wing undoubtedly came to the convention determined to crush the left wing, which with the growth of the I.W.W. and the development of the "language federations," was threatening the control of the petty-bourgeois intellectuals, as well as their whole opportunist political policy. To this end, among their other preparations, they invited the opportunist German Social-Democrat, Karl Legien, to make a rabid anti-left speech at the convention.

The big struggle occurred over the question of sabotage. The I.W.W. and the left wing in the S.P., following the example of the French and Italian syndicalists, had been laying some stress upon sabotage as an important working class weapon. The right wing at the 1912 convention, with Hillquit in the chair, made its main attack upon this issue, proposing the following amendment to the constitution, the well-known Article II, Section 6: "Any member of the Party who opposes political action or advocates crime, sabotage, or other methods of violence as a weapon of the working class to aid in its emancipation, shall be expelled from membership in this Party." While the right wing concentrated its main assault upon sabotage, which should not have been defended by the left wing as a working class weapon in the daily class struggle, its main objective was to destroy the revolutionary perspective and militancy generally of the left wing of the Party. The rights, in this historic fight, were intensifying their drive to make the Party into simply an election machine with an opportunist program. This was the real meaning of the amendment and it was made quite clear in the discussions.

If most of the left wing voted against the amendment, this was primarily for the purpose of preserving the fighting spirit of the Party, then under attack from the right wing, rather than an endorsement of sabotage as a working class tactic. Marxists, on principle, condemn not only sabotage, but also syndicalism generally, as a destructive tendency in the class struggle. The previous S.P. convention of 1908, with but one dissenting vote, had rejected the use or advocacy of force and violence.

After a very bitter fight, the new clause was adopted by a vote of 190 to 91. The rights then pushed through a trade union resolution which evaded the burning issue of industrial unionism and virtually adopted a policy of neutality on trade union questions, a resolution for which the left wing mistakenly voted. The rights even tried to defeat Debs for the presidential nomination, but in this case they were frustrated. C. E. Ruthenberg, eventual chief founder of the Communist Party, was an active left-wing delegate at this convention.

After their victory at the convention, the rights carried the war to the lefts by filing fake charges against Bill Haywood, alleging that he had violated the amended constitution by advocating force and violence in a public speech. This false charge was rammed through by a national referendum, which the rights won by a vote of 22,000 to 11,000. Haywood was thus recalled from the National Committee, whereupon he quit the Party. Without any formal split, many thousands of Socialist workers soon followed Haywood's example.

The effects of the split provoked by the right wing were almost catastrophic for the Party. In May 1912, the party had numbered 150,000 members (although the average for the same year was 120,000), but in four months' time it had dropped by 40,000. The Party also immediately went into a financial crisis. By 1915 the Party's membership had tobogganed to 79,374, and in 1916 with Benson as the candidate and with Debs refusing to run, its national vote was but 585,113, a falling-off of over 300,000 since 1912. In its policies the Party moved rapidly toward the right. Thenceforth, for example, it put up no more candidates against Gompers at A.F. of L. conventions, and it soon dropped its practice of introducing resolutions there for industrial unionism. The Socialist Party's opportunist leaders were now well on the way to their eventual tight alliance with the Gompers reactionaries. The S.P. was never able to recover fully from the 1912 split.

THE STATUS OF THE LEFT WING

On the eve of World War I, the broad left wing, although greatly increased in strength over earlier years, was still lacking in developed leadership, solid organization, and a correct political line. There were three streams or segments in the growing left forces which were later to form the Communist Party. The major one was the left wing in the S.P.; then there were the Marxist forces in the I.W.W.; and finally, the militants of the Syndicalist League.

The real mass leader of the S.P. left wing during this crucial period was William D. Haywood. Born in Salt Lake City in 1869, Haywood was a fighting metal miner. He became secretary-treasurer of the Western Federation of Miners in 1901. His trial in 1907 gave him enormous prestige, and from then on he was the most dynamic figure on the left. He was a bold, dogged battler, although not a theoretician. He always recognized the workers' enemies—whether employers, capitalist politicians, labor fakers, or opportunist Socialists—and he fought them all relentlessly, with indomitable courage and without giving or asking quarter.

Eugene V. Debs, too, was of the left. He was a militant trade union fighter, a pioneer industrial unionist, a fiery and brilliant orator who boldly challenged capitalism and who did more than any other in his time to popularize socialism among the masses. He was an important forerunner of the Communist Party, despite the fact that, old and sick when the Party was formed, he did not grasp its significance and never joined it. A great weakness of Debs was his theoretical inadequacy. Also, while he courageously and tirelessly attacked the capitalists, he did not systematically attack their reflection in the Party—the right wing of the Party. He never attended Party conventions, nor did he accept any official Party posts until his final years. He never understood the basic anti-Socialist character of the Hillquits and Bergers. Haywood finally became a Communist, while Debs did not.

Two other men, eventually to become left wing leaders, began to function nationally in this period. These were Charles Emil Ruthenberg and William Z. Foster. Ruthenberg, a former carpenter, who joined the Party in 1909, was already a power in Ohio, and he played a big part in the ranks of the left at the S.P. 1912 convention. Foster, a railroad worker, had belonged to the Party from 1900 to the split in 1909, and was now busily organizing the left-wing forces within the old trade unions.

There were many outstanding women in this pre-war period, among them such well-known left wing S.P. fighters as Mary Marcy, Kate Sadler Greenhalgh, Rose Pastor Stokes, Anita Whitney, Margaret Prevey, Jeannette Pearl, and others. Especially to be mentioned are "Mother" Mary Jones, an early S.P. member and noted United Mine Workers organizer, who, when she died in 1930 at the age of 100, for almost three-fourths of a century had been in the forefront of all big strikes in every industry; Elizabeth Gurley Flynn, nationally-known I.W.W. speaker and leader, now a member of the National Committee of the Communist Party, who was very active in the I.W.W. all through its heroic period; and "Mother" Ella Reeve Bloor, who died August 10, 1951, at the age of 89, and who had been an active organizer in Socialist ranks since 1897.

The national left wing rallied principally, in an organizational sense, around the *International Socialist Review*. But it was by no means a clear-cut Marxist journal. This monthly paper, founded in 1901, was edited by A. M. Simons until 1908, when he resigned and the Bill Haywood-Charles H. Kerr-Mary Marcy group took over completely. Here and there in the localities, the left wing also had more or less control over local papers, such as *The Socialist* in Cleveland; and in 1914-15, *The New Review*, a left organ of middle class intellectuals, was published in New York.

The program of the developing left wing left much to be desired from a Marxist standpoint. As we have seen, the line of the I.W.W. and also that of the S.L.N.A. was purely syndicalist. The policies of the left forces in the S.P. were also very heavily tinctured with syndicalism and De Leonist "leftism." There was, however, a qualitative difference between the S.P. left wing and the syndicalists. The S.P. left wing based itself upon the writings of Marx and Engels, called itself Marxist, believed in a workers' political party, and carried on political action (although sectarian)—to all of which the syndicalists were diametrically opposed. The most authoritative statement of the S.P. left's program in this period was the pamphlet, *Industrial Socialism* (published by Charles H. Kerr Co. in 1911) by William D. Haywood and Frank Bohn. The latter was formerly national secretary of the S.L.P.

This pamphlet, while not specifically endorsing the I.W.W., presented much of the latter's program, except that it called also for some measure of political action. The political line was the familiar De Leon conception of the political party winning the powers of government in an election, whereupon the industrial unions would really take over. The program declared that "The labor union will become organized industrial society"; and, "Under socialism the government of the nation will be an industrial government, a shop government." This was De Leon's Industrial Republic all over again. The Haywood-Bohn conception was called "socialism in overalls." The pamphlet was full of the characteristic syndicalist-De Leonist underestimation of the Party, overestimation of the role of the industrial unions, misconceptions of the state, playing down of immediate demands, and indifference toward the urgent Negro question.

An important distinction must be made, however. The De Leonite S.L.P., even in its best years of 1890-1900, was not a fighting, but a propaganda organization, and it organized and led no important strikes or other mass struggles. In contrast, the I.W.W. and S.P. left wing fought the Gompers bureaucracy, agitated tirelessly for industrial unionism, were highly militant, and conducted some of the hardest-fought strikes and free speech fights in American history.

The broad left wing during this period, while it paid much lip service to Marxism, nevertheless carried out a revisionist line in a "leftist" sense. Had it studied the Marxist classics more carefully, had it but grasped the lessons of the great *Communist Manifesto,* not to mention the other Marxist classics and the innumerable writings of Marx, Engels, and Lenin on the American question, it could have avoided its gross theoretical errors. But this elementary task of putting the American left wing upon a truly Marxist path was to await the time when the writings of the great Lenin should come to the United States and the Communist Party be founded.

9. World War I: Social-Democratic Betrayal

(1914-1918)

The first World War was an inevitable consequence of the entry of capitalism into its imperialist stage. It was a ruthless clash among the big imperialist powers, each fighting for a greater share of the world, its resources, and its markets. They began a battle royal for mutual subjugation or extermination. This struggle, which had been previously fought by economic and political means, was now to be decided on the field of battle. The war grew out of the very nature of the capitalist system. Capitalism, based on greed and force, could find no other way than war for resolving the fundamental conflicts among the big powers.

The outbreak of the war expressed the working out of the law of the uneven development of capitalism, which was first stated by Lenin.[1] That is, instead of developing at an even pace, the rate of growth and state of development of all the capitalist countries varied widely in tempo and extent. This spasmodic, jerky course of capitalist growth inevitably threw the great powers into violent collision with each other, to battle out a redivision of the world according to their changed economic and political relationships.

After the turn of the century Great Britain, the pioneer imperialist landgrabber, held more foreign territory than Germany, France, Russia, Italy, and the United States combined. But she had already lost her industrial leadership of the world. As Perlo says, "Between 1899 and 1913 steel production in the United States and Germany increased threefold, while British steel production increased by little more than fifty percent, and British iron production declined. The former industrial leader of the world fell far behind its rivals."[2] Consequently, the rival imperialists were impelled to redivide the world in accordance with the new power relationships, and World War I resulted.

All the imperialist powers were war-guilty. Germany aimed at seizing colonies from Great Britain and France, and at grabbing the Ukraine, Poland, and the Baltic provinces from Russia; tsarist Russia fought for the dismemberment of Turkey and the acquisition of the Dardanelles; Britain strove to defeat its great rival, Germany, and also to take over Meso-

[1] Lenin, *Selected Works*, Vol. 5, p. 141.
[2] Victor Perlo, *American Imperialism*, p. 26, N. Y., 1951.

potamia and Palestine; the French wanted the Saar, Alsace, and Lorraine from Germany[1]; and the United States began to figure that with the weakening of its European rivals it could dominate the world.

The alliance, primarily, of Great Britain, France, and Russia (eventually involving the United States), fought against the alliance of Germany, Austria-Hungary, and Turkey. All the great powers of the world were finally involved. The war, in which 65,000,000 soldiers were engaged, started July 28, 1914, and lasted over four years, until November 11, 1918. It cost 10,000,000 soldiers dead, 21,000,000 wounded, innumerable civilian casualties, and it wasted $338 billion in wealth. In this typical capitalist wholesale butchery, the U.S.-British-French forces won the war and therewith the power to redivide the world to suit their imperialist greed.

World War I was an explosion of basic imperialist tensions. It evidenced the fact that the world capitalist system had begun to sink into general crisis. The system's internal contradictions had now become so deep-seated and destructive that their working out began to undermine and destroy the capitalist system itself. World War I, by costing capitalism the loss of one-sixth of the world's territory, Russia, to socialism, did irreparable harm to the world's capitalist system.

THE GREAT SOCIAL-DEMOCRATIC BETRAYAL

The Marxists had long foreseen the coming of the first World War. Engels predicted it as early as 1892, and Lenin had repeatedly signalized its approach, its causes, and its imperialist character. Even the right wing Social-Democrats recognized the looming war clouds upon the world horizon. Consequently, after 1900 the question of the growing war danger was repeatedly considered at the congresses of the Second International. These discussions climaxed at the Congress of Stuttgart, Germany, in 1907, in the adoption of an anti-war resolution containing the following key amendment, presented by Lenin, Rosa Luxemburg, and Martov, for the Russian and Polish delegations: "In case a war should, nevertheless, break out, the Socialists shall take measures to bring about its early termination and strive with all their power to use the economic and political crisis created by the war to arouse the masses politically and hasten the overthrow of capitalist class rule."[2] This resolution was adopted at the Copenhagen Congress of 1910 and unanimously endorsed at the Conference of Basle in 1912. American dele-

---

[1] *History of the Communist Party of the Soviet Union*, p. 161, N. Y., 1939.
[2] William English Walling, *The Socialists and the War*, p. 39, N. Y., 1915.

gates from the S.P. and S.L.P. attended these gatherings. Meanwhile, the syndicalist leaders in France, Italy, and elsewhere were also militantly declaring that they would checkmate and defeat the threatened capitalist war by declaring a general strike against it.

But when the war crisis actually came, the right-wing Social-Democratic leaders promptly and in general ignored the "unanimous" resolutions against war, which they had adopted tongue in cheek. These people, as history has since so abundantly proved, were not Socialists at all. At most, they were but believers in a fake "progressive capitalism," and their interests all dovetailed with those of the capitalists in their countries. So they shamelessly followed the latter into the war, blessing it as a defensive war, and making no resistance to it whatsoever. This was the logical climax to their whole reformist, opportunist line. The chief syndicalist leaders of Europe, despite all their previous fiery denunciations of war, mainly took the same chauvinist position.

The German Social-Democrats took the lead in this treason to the working class. Three days after Germany entered the war the Social-Democratic fraction in the Reichstag voted the government war credits with only the courageous Karl Liebknecht and a few others firmly standing by their anti-war pledges. Soon the conservative Social-Democratic leaders all over western Europe, the dominant Socialist group in each country, followed the lead of the German Social-Democrats, and lured and drove the masses into the slaughter on the pretext that they were fighting a defensive war. "The leaders of the Second International proved to be traitors, betrayers of the proletariat, and servitors of the bourgeoisie." The Second International was dead. "Actually it broke up into separate social-chauvinist parties which warred against each other."[1]

But the Russian Bolsheviks and small groups of left-wingers in various countries held fast. This, too, was the result of their entire history of Marxism and internationalism. The Russian Bolsheviks, who since 1903 had combated the right wing within the Social-Democratic Labor Party of their country until they split and formed their own party in 1912, further developed their international policies in fighting against the war. They resolutely combated the war in Russia, and they took steps to unite the international anti-war forces. Besides eventually having revolutionary consequences in Russia, these anti-war activities led to the holding of the important wartime conferences in Zimmerwald, in September 1915, and in Kienthal, in 1916 (both in Switzerland). At these conferences Lenin presented his famous slogan of transforming the imperialist war into civil war, for the establishment of socialism. Lenin was a great champion of peace, and his slogan would

[1] *History of the Communist Party of the Soviet Union*, p. 164.

not only have ended the current slaughter in World War I, but would have prevented the even greater butchery of World War II. Lenin's orientation for peace, was shown by a general appeal to all the warring countries to end World War I which was made upon the establishment of the Soviet government. The conferences in Switzerland, while not adopting Lenin's slogan, nevertheless represented significant first steps toward uniting the anti-war forces and toward the eventual establishment of the Third, or Communist International, to take the place of the defunct Second International.[1]

THE UNITED STATES DURING THE EARLY YEARS OF THE WAR

When the war broke out in Europe the policy of the American bourgeoisie was to play neutral, to watch its imperialist rivals kill each other off, and to furnish them the necessary munitions with which to do the job, meanwhile making huge profits in blood money from the terrible slaughter. At the time the war began the United States was in the midst of an economic crisis, but the flood of war orders soon had the industries humming busily again. Profits piled sky-high, the monopolies expanded and multiplied, and before the war ended there were 20,000 new millionaires in the United States.

From August 1914 to the end of 1918 the cost of living rose very rapidly with wage rates dragging, and the workers were in a very militant strike mood. But the A.F. of L. leaders, obedient as ever to the basic interests of the capitalists, re-echoed the latter's neutrality slogans and damped down the efforts of the more and more impoverished workers to organize and strike. Most of the 4,924 strikes that took place during 1915 and 1916 were spontaneous, the work of the rank and file themselves. A notable struggle was the national eight-hour movement of the four Railroad Brotherhoods in 1916, which culminated in the passage of the Adamson law, a substantial victory for the 350,000 workers involved. The I.W.W., unlike the A.F. of L., carried out an active strike policy, with strikes, among others, of 8,000 oil workers in Bayonne, 15,000 iron miners in Minnesota, and 6,000 steel workers in Youngstown.

The Socialist Party, in August 1914, adopted a resolution denouncing the "senseless conflict," expressing "its opposition to this and all other wars, waged upon any pretext whatsoever," and calling upon the United States, while carrying out a policy of strict neutrality, to use all its

---

[1] V. I. Lenin, *Collected Works*, Vol. 18 *The Imperialist War*, N. Y., 1930.

efforts to have the war ended as quickly as possible. It also demanded that the question of war should be referred to the people in a general referendum before the government could engage in hostilities. In December 1914, the party also proposed a whole program upon the basis of which the war should be settled.[1] This pacifist program, which did not discriminate between just and unjust wars, was supported in practice by a general agitation against war and against the campaign to bring the United States into the struggle. The left wing especially led a strong fight against conscription.[2]

The American S.P. leadership promptly exonerated the Social-Democrats in Europe of war guilt. In a statement on September 19, 1914, the National Executive Committee declared: "We do not presume to pass judgment upon the conduct of our brother parties in Europe. We realize that they are victims of the present vicious, industrial, political, and military system and that they did the best they could under the circumstances."[3]

The left wing of the S.P., while not yet clearly differentiating itself from the official pacifist policy of the Party, began to sharpen up its anti-war activity. In doing this it utilized principally the columns of the *International Socialist Review*. On November 26, 1916, the Socialist Propaganda League of America, an S.P. left-wing organization, with headquarters in Boston, issued a manifesto sharply repudiating the war and condemning the treason of the right opportunists of the Second International.[4] Lenin replied to this document, greeting its general line and expressing the desire "to combine our struggle with yours against the conciliators and for true internationalism."[5]

One of the outstanding events of the years just before the entry of the United States into the war, was the arrest in San Francisco of Tom Mooney and Warren K. Billings. They were charged with responsibility for the bomb explosion in the Preparedness Day Parade on July 22, 1916, which killed nine and wounded forty persons. In the prevailing war hysteria Mooney and Billings were shamefully framed up and sentenced to die, a sentence which later, under the pressure of the masses, including the revolutionary workers of Russia and other countries, was commuted to life imprisonment. The generation-long struggle of Mooney and Billings for freedom had begun.

---

1 Walling, *The Socialists and the War*, pp. 468-70.
2 See Alexander Trachtenberg, ed., *American Socialists and the War*, N. Y., 1917.
3 Bimba, *History of the American Working Class*, p. 257.
4 *International Socialist Review*, Feb. 1917.
5 Lenin, *Collected Works*, Vol. 18, p. 375.

THE UNITED STATES JOINS THE WAR

This country entered the war on April 6, 1917, three weeks after the world was startled by the bourgeois revolution in Russia, on March 14th. The reason why the United States went into the war was the fear on the part of the American bourgeoisie that the Anglo-French-Russian alliance would lose the struggle under the heavy blows of the German armies. The Wall Street monopolists, who could handle the declining British empire, feared the rise of a far more powerful German empire. The latter would have jeopardized their whole structure of foreign trade and investments. Hence, they plunged the United States into the war, eventually turning the tide against Germany.

Just five months before this, Woodrow Wilson got himself re-elected president with the hypocritical slogan, "He kept us out of war." This slogan was a pledge that the United States would continue to stay out; but as soon as Wall Street saw its vital interests threatened, it cynically trampled upon all such pacifist demagogy and flung the nation into the wholesale slaughter. In doing this the capitalists were quite unconcerned that the American people had repeatedly showed that they were opposed to going into the war. Monopolist America, as Wilson declared, was now out to "make the world safe for democracy."

In order to circumvent the peace will of the people, big capital needed to mobilize the support of the labor leaders for the war. This proved to be only a small chore, however. The Gompers clique, obedient servants of capitalism, were ready and eager for the task. Gompers, in the early stages of the war, called himself a pacifist; but keeping step with the war plans of the capitalists, he grew more and more belligerent, until finally he became the most rabid of warmongers. As the entry of the United States into the war approached, Gompers called a general trade union conference of the top officialdom, on March 12, 1917. This conference declared that "should our country be drawn into the maelstrom of the European conflict, we . . . offer our service . . . and call upon our fellow workers . . . devotedly and patriotically to give like service."[1] This gave the government the green light, and three weeks later it rushed the country into the war.

Gompers, however, faced a considerable opposition to his war treason in the ranks of organized labor. The United Mine Workers, Typographical Union, Ladies Garment Workers, Western Federation of Miners, and Journeymen Barbers refused to attend his pro-war conference. Besides, local unions, city central bodies, and state federations in many parts

---

[1] John Steuben, *Labor in Wartime*, p. 25, N. Y., 1940.

of the country were evidencing a strong anti-war spirit. But the Gompers machine, with the active help of the government, overrode this peace sentiment. One of the most effective means for doing this was the American Alliance for Labor and Democracy, organized on August 16, 1917, by the A.F. of L., jointly with pro-war renegades from the Socialist Party. The Alliance, acting virtually as a government agency, held meetings in many parts of the country, peddling the war slogans of the imperialists.

The Gompers machine promptly became part of American imperialism's war apparatus. Gompers himself was chairman of the Committee on Labor of the Advisory Commission of the Council of National Defense. Other officials occupied war posts of various kinds all over the country. Gompers remained a close co-worker of President Wilson all the way along, even at the peace conference of Versailles in 1919. The enemies of the workers hailed him as a great "labor statesman."

Gompers eventually wangled into the Versailles Treaty a watered-down version of his well-known dictum that "the labor of a human being is not a commodity or article of commerce." This sentence was quoted from the Clayton Act of October 1914, which was supposed to, but did not, exempt organized labor from the Sherman Anti-Trust Law. Its deeper meaning, as Gompers stressed, was that, contrary to Marx, American workers were free. It was daily refuted by the fact that tens of millions of workers, acting under severe restraints, sold their labor power to their employers. The bosses, enjoying the reality of the wage system, which Gompers endorsed, were willing to allow the latter his demagogic assertion that labor power was not bought and sold in the United States.

In addition to committing the labor movement generally to the war, the biggest service of the Gompers bureaucrats to the imperialists was to stifle the wartime efforts of the workers to organize and strike. Through the War Labor Board and National Defense Council, the A.F. of L. and Railroad Brotherhood leaders gave up the right not only to strike, but even to organize the open-shop basic industries. Lorwin says, "Organized labor relinquished its right to strike," and there was "the understanding at Washington that the status quo in industrial relations should not be disturbed."[1] Thenceforth, the Gompers war policy was to smother strikes and to sabotage organizing campaigns.

The workers, however, harassed by the rapidly rising living costs and having but little feeling of solidarity with the war, were in a very militant mood and much disposed to organize and strike. In 1917, the first war year, there were 4,233 strikes, or more than in any other previous year in American history. Consequently, despite its leaders' ruinous policies, the A.F. of L. grew by 650,000 members during 1917-18. Had it not

[1] Lorwin, *The American Federation of Labor*, pp. 161, 165.

been for the treacherous Gompers no-organizing, no-strike agreement with the bosses and the government, the A.F. of L. could readily have organized at least ten million workers during the war and thus have accomplished the unionization of the basic and trustified industries—a job, however, that had to await the arrival of the C.I.O., almost two decades later.

THE SOCIALISTS AND THE WAR

As the United States entered the war on April 6th, the S.P. held its Emergency Convention in St. Louis to shape its policy to meet the situation. The sentiment in the party had been demonstrated by the adoption, by a vote of 11,041 to 782 in a national referendum, of a resolution proposing to expel any and all Socialists holding public office who should vote money for the war. The party was slowly recovering from the blow of the 1912 split. Workers from the basic industries were again joining it. Membership increased from 79,374 in 1915 to 104,822 in the first three months of 1919.

The St. Louis convention was heavily anti-war. This was basically because of the tragic lessons of the socialist betrayal in Europe, the influences of the developing Russian revolution, and the anti-war attitude of the new proletarian elements which had come into the party. Consequently, the outright pro-war Socialists were swamped, and the Hillquit centrists also had to bend before the anti-war storm.

At the convention three resolutions were presented on the war question. The majority resolution, submitted by Hillquit, branded "the declaration of war by our government as a crime against the peoples of the United States and against the nations of the world," and declared the party's "unalterable opposition to the war." It stated that "the only struggle which would justify the workers in taking up arms is the great struggle of the working class of the world to free itself from economic exploitation and political oppression, and we particularly warn the workers against the snare and delusion of so-called defensive warfare." It proposed that the war be fought by "continuous, active and public opposition to the war, through demonstrations, mass petitions and all other means within our power."[1] The second resolution, presented by Louis Boudin, varied but little from Hillquit's. The third resolution, by John Spargo, was openly pro-war, stating that "having failed to prevent the war, we can only recognize it as a fact and try to force upon the government through pressure of public opinion a constructive policy."

[1] Fine, *Farmer and Labor Parties in the U.S.*, p. 313.

The convention vote was as follows: for the Hillquit resolution, 140 votes; for Boudin's, 31 votes; and for Spargo's, 5 votes. Later on, in a national referendum, the majority resolution was endorsed by a vote of 21,000 to 350.[1]

The Party's resolution was a product of a compromise between the center and the left. Ruthenberg was the outstanding leader of the left at the convention.[2] He had also been a factor in the 1912 convention. Moreover, along with Wagenknecht, he had built a powerful Party organization in Ohio, and he was increasingly active in fighting against the war. As secretary of the subcommittee which drafted the majority resolution, Ruthenberg was responsible for most of its fighting clauses. Hillquit's original draft was merely pacifist. Major weak spots in the resolution were that it did not more clearly distinguish between just and unjust wars, that it did not condemn the social-chauvinists abroad, and that it did not provide a definite program for anti-war struggle.

Following the convention, the pro-war elements—Simons, Benson, Stokes, Walling, Spargo, Hunter, Ghent, Russell, Gaylord, Frank and William Bohn, et al.—quit the Party and joined the openly pro-war forces.[3] Also many Socialist trade union leaders, while formally remaining within the Party, carried out the Gompers war line. Relatively few rank-and-file members were included in these defections.

The centrist Hillquit leadership of the Party, while adopting the anti-war resolution, did little to apply it. This lip service was necessary in order to cover up its betrayal in practice. Centrism was the dominant form of opportunist leadership in the S.P. in 1916-17, because the war was already two years old, revolutionary moods were rising in the ranks of the workers and soldiers in Europe, and this fighting spirit was reflected in the United States. The radicalism of centrism was designed to deceive these militant workers. The left elements, however, pushed the anti-war campaign vigorously, Debs, Ruthenberg, Wagenknecht, and others boldly speaking out against the war. Consequently, in the 1917 local elections the Party polled high votes in New York, Chicago, Cleveland, and other centers, and its membership grew rapidly. Divergent attitudes toward the war created a growing friction between the right and left wings.

[1] For text of all three resolutions, see Trachtenberg, ed., *American Labor Year Book*, 1917-18.
[2] Oakley Johnson, *The Day Is Coming: The Biography of Charles E. Ruthenberg*, unpublished manuscript.
[3] Some of these and other pro-war elements were either expelled or resigned even before the St. Louis convention.

THE I.W.W. AND THE WAR

The I.W.W., from the outset, took a position of opposition to World War I and maintained it courageously. A couple of months after the war began, by convention resolution the organization condemned the war and refused participation in it. It declared that "We, as members of the industrial army, will refuse to fight for any purpose except for the realization of industrial freedom."[1] This abstentionist attitude remained essentially the position of the I.W.W. throughout the war. It was in sharp contradiction to the pro-war position of the French and other syndicalists.

Paying but little attention to the political aspects of the war, the I.W.W. devoted its main efforts to the prosecution of economic struggles and to building its own membership. Its operations concerned mostly agricultural workers, miners, and lumber workers. In carrying out this economic line, which was accompanied by anti-war agitation, the I.W.W. encountered fierce opposition on the part of the government, the employers, the labor misleaders, and self-constituted vigilante gangs.

The Agricultural Workers Organization (I.W.W.) during the war years had an estimated 20,000 members. It conducted strikes of farm workers in many parts of the West—largely successful. One thing to which it paid special attention was halting the prevalent terrorizing and robbing of transient workers by railroad brakemen. It became so that a card in the A.W.O. was good to ride freight trains almost anywhere throughout the West.

In June 1916, the I.W.W. conducted a strike on the Mesabi iron range in northern Minnesota. All the miners in the district came out—some 16,000. Several strikers were killed, the leaders were arrested, and the strike was broken. Later, however, the companies had to improve the conditions of the workers. In Everett, Washington, in November 1916, the I.W.W., engaged in a campaign of organizing lumber workers, came into head-on conflict with local vigilantes. Five I.W.W. members and two vigilantes were killed. The militant I.W.W., however, pressed its work, and during 1917 it led strikes of some 50,000 lumber workers in Washington, Idaho, and Montana. Out of these fights eventually came the eight-hour day for the industry.

In 1917, the I.W.W. also conducted big strikes of copper miners—24,000 in Arizona and 14,000 in Butte, Montana. The companies fought the strikes violently. In Bisbee, Arizona, 2,000 strikers were seized, transported far out into the desert, and left there with no food or water. This outrage provoked a national protest. In the hard-fought strike in

[1] *Solidarity*, Oct. 3, 1914.

Butte, on August 1, 1917, several gunmen kidnapped Frank H. Little from his hotel and hanged him from a railroad bridge on the outskirts of the city. Little, a member of the General Executive Board of the I.W.W., was laid up with a broken leg when the lynch gang seized him. At the end of the war the I.W.W.'s membership was variously estimated at up to 120,000.

THE I.T.U.E.L.

The International Trade Union Educational League was formed in St. Louis, on January 17, 1915, at a conference of a dozen former members of the Syndicalist League from Chicago, Omaha, St. Louis, and Kansas City. Chicago was chosen as headquarters, and William Z. Foster was elected secretary. Its principal papers were the San Diego *International*, the Omaha *Unionist*, and the Chicago *Labor News*. The organization never really got established, however, basically because the left wing at the time, firmly wedded to the policy of dual unionism, had no use for the I.T.U.E.L.'s program of working within the old craft unions.

A syndicalist organization, the I.T.U.E.L. was anti-political, endorsed industrial unionsm, and opposed the war.[1] It held the opinion that the trade unions as such were essentially revolutionary, whether led by conservatives or revolutionaries. This was true, it argued, because they were class organizations, which followed a policy of securing all the concessions they could wring by force from the employers. In view of the ever-growing strength of the trade unions, the I.T.U.E.L falsely assumed that this policy would eventually culminate in the overthrow of the capitalist class by the economic power of the workers; whereupon, the unions would take over the control of society. This syndicalism, of course, expressed a gross overestimation of the power of trade unionism and an equally great underestimation of the power of the capitalist state. It also underestimated the disruptive capacity of reactionary Social-Democracy, and it did not give necessary weight to the need for a class-conscious ideology and a vanguard political party.

By the spring of 1917 the I.T.U.E.L. had disappeared as an organization, about all that was left of it being a loose group of a couple of dozen militants in Chicago and a scattering of active workers in other cities. Most of the Chicago group, however, were leaders in their local unions and also delegates to the Chicago Federation of Labor. There they constituted a very important influence.

The former League members had fought against the war and Amer-

[1] For its program, see William Z. Foster, *Trade Unionism: The Road to Freedom*, Chicago, 1916.

ican participation in it, and had taken the general position that the outbreak of the war should have been countered by a revolutionary general strike. When the United States entered the war in April 1917, they took the position that, inasmuch as the revolution had been betrayed by the reactionary Social-Democrats and syndicalists, the main task during the war was to organize the great unorganized masses into the trade unions. The trade unions, they held, were the all-important basic organizations that would one day emancipate the working class. The war situation, with the great demand for labor and the government's basic need for all possible production, presented an exceptionally favorable opportunity for such union-building work. This should be based on an active strike policy. Every other consideration in the war period was to be sacrificed to the central task of building the unions. Foster led this group.

This, of course, was a highly opportunistic conception. While it did not involve actual support of the war, it nevertheless was an incorrect compromise. It was a sort of economism, an attempt to by-pass the war and to focus the struggle upon immediate trade union questions. The very active unionizing and strike campaigns of the Chicago I.T.U.E.L. group did, however, conflict directly with the no-organizing, no-strike policies of the pro-war Gompers machine.

The Chicago group of militants were in a favorable position to get results in their aggressive unionizing campaigns. For several years they had been winning support in the Chicago Federation of Labor, and they had good working relations with the progressive Fitzpatrick-Nockels leadership. It was largely because of the work of this militant group that the C.F. of L. became the most progressive central labor union in the United States. The left forces, by their influence, made the C.F. of L. the national labor center in the big fight to save Mooney and Billings; it became the leader in the national labor party movement from 1917 on; it hailed the Russian Revolution and demanded the recognition of the Soviet government; it fought the Gompers machine on many fronts; and it became identified with every progressive cause. Significant of the left-wing influence in all this radicalism was the fact that when later on, in 1923, the left-center alliance in Chicago was broken, the C.F. of L. soon degenerated into a routine, conservative Gompers organization.

The first important wartime unionizing work tackled by the Chicago militants was in the railroad industry. Through the Railroad Labor Council, set up by a number of A.F. of L. and Brotherhood local unions which they led, the left forces organized some 25,000 workers locally into the railroad craft unions during 1916-17. This general movement, under the leadership of L. M. Hawver, a League member, finally culminated in the unofficial 1919 national strike of 200,000 railroad shopmen.

The next and still bigger campaign of organization undertaken by the Chicago militants, former members of the I.T.U.E.L., was to organize the national meat-packing industry. For thirteen years this great industry had remained almost completely without unions, and was considered by the A.F. of L. to be impossible to organize. But the Chicago group pushed through the work successfully, on the basis of a federation of the dozen craft unions in the industry and an active organizing and strike policy. John Fitzpatrick was chairman of this national committee and William Z. Foster was its national organizing secretary. Jack Johnstone, organizer for the C.F. of L., eventually became secretary of the Chicago Stockyards Council, with 55,000 members. Joseph Manley and various other left-wingers held key posts. The campaign began on July 11, 1917, and after striking the national industry once and taking another national strike vote, it ended successfully on March 30, 1918, with an arbitration award by Federal Judge Altschuler, granting big wage increases, the eight-hour day, union recognition, and other improvements. At these arbitration hearings the nation was amazed by the dramatic exposure of the horrifying wage and working conditions prevailing in the meat-packing industry.

One of the greatest achievements in this packinghouse campaign was the organization of the Negro workers. They formed at least 20,000 of the 200,000 workers who were organized nationally. Their organization was of major importance and also unique in trade union history. They constituted the largest body of organized Negro workers anywhere in the world. Thus, the "hopeless" national packing industry, the despair of organized labor for many years, became organized. The whole labor movement was thrilled. And the prestige of the Chicago Federation of Labor and its left wing soared.

The next big wartime organizing task which the Chicago I.T.U.E.L. group set itself was the organization of the national steel industry, the toughest of all tasks confronting the labor movement. This campaign was begun on April 7, 1918, only a week after the Altschuler decision in the packing industry. The left-wingers presented the resolution on organization to the Chicago Federation of Labor, which endorsed it. Foster was elected delegate of the C.F. of L. to the A.F. of L. convention at St. Paul, in June 1918, and he had the steel resolution adopted there. The organizing campaign began under a national organizing committee of representatives of 23 unions, with three million members. Gompers was chairman and Foster was organizing secretary. Later on, as the strike approached, Gompers got cold feet, resigned the chairmanship, and put John Fitzpatrick in his place.

The campaign was marked with the characteristic Gompers sabotage, employer violence, and government repression. Nevertheless, the organizers managed to unite 250,000 steel workers in all the major steel centers of the country. The plan of the lefts had been to force a favorable settlement through a strike in wartime,[1] but owing to lack of funds the campaign was slowed and the national strike of 367,000 steel workers did not come about until September 22, 1919, about ten months after the war's end. The strike was crushed, after nearly four months, by a combination of sabotage by the Gompers machine and wholesale strikebreaking and violence by the employers and the government. Although the great strike was lost the employers had to abolish the twelve-hour day and seven-day week and to introduce many improvements in wages and working conditions. The 1919 strike, by proving that the steel industry, the greatest of all trustified, open-shop, company-unionized industries, could be organized, paved the way for the completion of this basic task fifteen years later by the C.I.O.

The Chicago group felt that all these big organizing successes constituted a brilliant justification of its long-advocated policy of working within the old unions, but the S.P. left wing and I.W.W. militants still remained fascinated by the dual union policy, which had been traditional for some twenty-five years past.

GOVERNMENT TERROR AGAINST THE LEFT

The government, under the "liberal" Wilson, fearing the anti-war moods among the masses, immediately after pushing the country into the war, adopted a body of reactionary legislation directed at curbing the anti-war left. The first of these laws was the Espionage Act of June 15, 1917, a sort of grab-all law aimed at curbing a host of labor activities. This infamous law was eventually followed by the Trading with the Enemy Act, Conscription Act, and so on, as well as by dozens of anti-sedition and anti-syndicalism laws in the various cities and states. The sum total of all this legislation was to strip the American people of rights of free speech which at least the whites, if not the Negroes, had practiced ever since the founding of the Republic almost a century and a half before. Under these Draconian laws the government, through Attorney General A. Mitchell Palmer, proceeded ruthlessly against the left wing of the labor movement.[2]

The I.W.W. was the organization to suffer the heaviest blow. On

---
[1] William Z. Foster, *The Great Steel Strike and Its Lessons*, N. Y., 1920.
[2] Trachtenberg, ed., *American Labor Year Book*, 1919-20, pp. 92-113; Robert W. Dunn, ed., *The Palmer Raids*, N. Y., 1948.

September 5, 1917, simultaneous raids, with vigilante participation, were made by Department of Justice agents upon I.W.W. headquarters all over the country. Private homes were broken into and records seized. Bill Haywood, general secretary-treasurer of the I.W.W., estimated that up to February 1918, 2,000 members were under arrest. The mass arrests covered all the members of the I.W.W. General Executive Board, secretaries of industrial unions, editors, and prominent local leaders. In Omaha, the whole convention of the Construction Workers Industrial Union—164 delegates—was arrested. Substitute sets of leaders were also arrested nationally. Everywhere the I.W.W.'s were railroaded to jail for long sentences, charged with general obstruction of the war. The raids culminated in mass trials in Chicago (165), Sacramento (146), Wichita (38), Tacoma (7), Omaha (27), Spokane (28). In the big Chicago trial, in April 1918, under the notorious Judge Kenesaw Mountain Landis, 15 I.W.W. members got 20 years, 35 got 10 years, 33 got 5 years, and 12 got one year, and $2,300,000 in fines were levied against the convicted men. In Sacramento, of the I.W.W.'s on trial, 26 got 10 years each. Similar savage sentences were levied elsewhere.

Many wartime raids and arrests were also directed against the Socialist Party. In September 1917, the national headquarters of the Party was raided. Dozens of Socialist papers, including the *Appeal to Reason, International Socialist Review, The Socialist, New York Call* and *The Masses*, were prosecuted, threatened with denial of second-class mailing privileges. Many of the papers died. Debs was arrested for a speech he made in Canton, Ohio, against war, on June 16, 1918, and was sentenced to 10 years imprisonment. Scores of others—Charles E. Ruthenberg, Alfred Wagenknecht, Kate Richards O'Hare, J. O. Bentall, Scott Nearing, Rose Pastor Stokes, and many more—were jailed and given sentences ranging from one to three years. Molly Steimer, a young girl, got 15 years in jail for distributing leaflets against intervention in Russia.[1] The National Executive Committee of the S.P. was indicted through its officers—Victor Berger, Adolph Germer, J. Louis Engdahl, Irwin St. John Tucker, and William Kruse—but they did not serve time.

Besides the I.W.W. and S.P. cases, there were many other wartime arrests. Among them, Alexander Berkman and Emma Goldman were sentenced to two years for obstructing the draft. There were also various pacifists, concientious objectors, and others jammed into the crowded jails. It has been estimated that 1,500 were sent to prison during the war. Debs went to jail on April 12, 1919, and got out on December 25, 1921. It was not until December 1923 that the last of the I.W.W. war

[1] For wartime arrest cases, see Trachtenberg, ed., *American Labor Year Book*, 1919-20, p. 92 *ff.*

prisoners were set free under the pressure of a strong, united front mass campaign for their release. The wartime terrorism against the left was the first fruit of the imperialist war "to make the world safe for democracy." It was, however, only a foretaste of the still more bitter fruits that were to come, after victory was won and presumably democracy had been assured.

The great war, precipitated by the uneven development of world capitalism, made that unevenness even more pronounced. The United States, the real capitalist victor in the war, enormously expanded its industries during the war. It entered the war a debtor nation and emerged a great creditor nation, with $20 billion in outstanding loans. The dollar had defeated the pound and the mark, and the center of gravity had definitely shifted from Europe to the United States. Imperialist Wall Street was well on its march to world capitalist domination. World War I sowed the seeds for World War II.

10. The Russian Revolution
(1917-1919)

The great Russian Revolution of November 7, 1917, born of the deepening general crisis of world capitalism, was the first Socialist breakthrough of the fortifications of the international capitalist system. The revolutionary masses of workers and peasants, led by the Bolshevik Party, which was headed by the great Lenin, smashed tsarism-capitalism in Russia and thereby dealt a mortal blow to the international capitalist system. World imperialism was broken at its weakest link. The Revolutions of 1905 and of March 1917 had been but preliminary to the very basic Bolshevik Revolution of November 1917. A new era of world history was now ushered in—the era of proletarian and colonial revolutions and the decline of world capitalism.

With revolutionary energy the new Soviet government carried through the great tasks that the Kerensky provisional government could not and would not do. "In order to consolidate the Soviet power, the old, bourgeois state machine had to be shattered and destroyed and a new, Soviet state machine set up in its place. Further, it was necessary to destroy the survivals of the division of society into estates and the regime of national oppression, to abolish the privileges of the church, to suppress the counter-revolutionary press of all kinds, legal and illegal, and to dissolve the bourgeois Constituent Assembly. Following on the nationalization of the land, all large-scale industry had also to be nationalized. And, lastly, the state of war had to be ended, for the war was hampering the consolidation of the Soviet power more than anything else. All these measures were carried out in a few months, from the end of 1917 to the middle of 1918."[1] The Soviets withdrew from the war and called upon the world to make peace.

The Russian Revolution sent a thrill of joy through the hearts of hundreds of millions of the exploited and oppressed all over the world. Its influence was decisive in the profound wave of revolution which swept eastern and central Europe upon the end of the war. Kings and emperors toppled as this revolutionary upsurge went through Germany, Austria-Hungary, and the Balkans. The whole of European capitalism was shaken to its foundations.

[1] *History of the Communist Party of the Soviet Union*, p. 214.

UNITED STATES INTERVENTION

If the peoples of the world were inspired by the Russian Revolution, the capitalists of all countries were profoundly shocked by it. In their fright they trembled at the threatened destruction of their whole system of exploitation and robbery. So they lost no time in taking drastic measures to try to checkmate and defeat the revolution. Immediately at the close of the war the victorious Allied powers began to pour their troops into Soviet Russia and to stimulate and organize the domestic counter-revolutionists to fight the Soviet government. Great Britain, France, Japan, the United States, Germany, Poland, and Czechoslovakia all had a hand in this counter-revolutionary intervention.

The consequence was a tremendous civil war. The revolutionary Soviet people, although harassed by economic breakdown, famine, blockade, and general exhaustion from the world imperialist war, rallied their forces, built up a powerful Red Army, and with unparalleled heroism, beat back all their foreign and domestic enemies. In this desperate struggle they battled through a thousand Valley Forges. At one time by far the greater portion of the country was in the hands of the interventionists and their Russian counter-revolutionary allies. But the Red Army finally defeated them all, smashing Denikin, Kolchak, Yudenich, Wrangel, and the host of other tsarist and foreign generals. Consequently, at the end of 1920 Great Britain, France, and Italy had to lift their blockade, and soon thereafter Japan was forced out of Siberia. The United States troops had to get out, too. The revolution had won a decisive victory in its life-and-death struggle.

The bases for this immense victory were the indomitable revolutionary spirit of the Russian people, their all-out support of the Soviet Red Army, the invincible power of the Communist Party, and the brilliance of its great leader, Lenin. Not the smallest factor in winning the victory was the supporting spirit among the workers in many other countries, which prevented the respective capitalist governments from mobilizing their full strength against the embattled Soviet people.

The United States government, dominated by reactionary monopoly capital, took a leading part in the counter-revolutionary intervention against Soviet Russia during 1918-20. The "liberal" President Wilson, without even asking any authorization whatever from Congress, arbitrarily sent armed American expeditions to Siberia and north Russia. The alleged purpose of the one to Siberia was to guard against the danger from large numbers of German and Austrian prisoners, freed by the Revolution; whereas the stated purpose of the expedition to north Russia was to attack Germany from the rear. But the whole intervention was nothing but a brazen attempt to overthrow the young Soviet government and to restore capitalist reaction to power.

The Siberian expedition of some 7,000 men, under General W. S. Graves, co-operated with the Russian reactionaries and the Japanese to overthrow the local Soviet in Vladivostok. President Wilson supported the tsarist General Kolchak in his efforts to smash the Soviet government and to make himself dictator of Russia. The Siberian adventure came to an inglorious end when Kolchak's forces were wiped out by the Red Army.

The adventure in north Russia, centering around Archangel, was carried out in conjunction with the British, French, and White Guard Russians. About 5,000 American soldiers, under Colonel Stewart, made up this country's armed forces. The aim of the allied expedition was the capture of Petrograd and the overthrow of the Soviet government.

But the northern invaders were defeated and in danger of annihilation. "On March 30, 1919, Company 'I' of the 339 U.S. Infantry refused to obey orders to proceed to Archangel." The men yielded only after one of their number who had been arrested was released. This unrest was blamed upon "Bolshevik propaganda." "Fear of a general mutiny was expressed, and General March, Chief of Staff, pledged the withdrawal of the American forces by June,"[1] which was carried out.

Lenin roundly condemned this reactionary United States intervention, declaring that "the British and Americans are acting as hangmen and gendarmes of Russian freedom, in the same sense in which the role was played under the Russian hangman, Nicholas I."[2]

This was only the first of a generation-long series of United States aggressions against Soviet Russia, including also economic blockade and diplomatic boycott—all of which were defeated by the unconquerable revolutionary Russian people. The United States refused even to recognize the U.S.S.R. diplomatically until 1933, in Roosevelt's day. This bitter anti-Soviet hatred on the part of the ruling monopolists of the United States, implacable and never-ending, has finally culminated in Washington's present attempt to organize an all-out capitalist war against the U.S.S.R.

THE SOCIAL-DEMOCRATS BETRAY THE REVOLUTION

Inspired by the Russian Revolution and horrified by the butcheries of World War I, the world's workers were swept by a great wave of revolutionary spirit, especially in Europe. Given proper leadership, the

---

[1] F. L. Schuman, *American Policy Towards Russia Since 1917*, pp. 136-37, N. Y., 1928.
[2] Cited by P. M. Pospelov in *For a Lasting Peace* . . . , Jan. 26, 1951.

latter were ready to follow the example of the Russian workers. They were ripe for Socialist revolution. But the right-wing leaders of the big European Social-Democratic parties, strongly entrenched in all the organizations of the working class, had quite different ideas. To them the proletarian revolution, both in Russia and in their own countries, was a terrible nightmare—no less so than to the employers. It went violently counter to their whole outlook and program, which was to patch up capitalism here and there with minor reforms. They were committed, in reality, to the continuation of the capitalist system, and the very last thing they wanted was to see this system overthrown and a real Socialist system substituted. Therefore, just as these elements had rushed to the support of their respective capitalist classes during World War I, so now they hurried to the defense of the capitalist system itself, threatened as it was with revolution. Joining forces with the capitalists, these pseudo-Socialists proceeded to attack with fire and sword the entire revolutionary movement among the proletarian masses in all its manifestations, both at home and in Russia.

The dominant and traitorous European right-wing leaders were typified by such figures as Legien, Noske, and Scheideman in Germany, Henderson, Hyndman, and MacDonald in England, Guesde and Thomas in France. Another group of Social-Democratic leaders, the centrists, were typified by Kautsky, Hilferding, Bauer, Longuet, Fenner Brockway, Hillquit, and Ledebour. The latter group was long on revolutionary phrases and short on revolutionary struggle. Lenin characterized Kautsky as "In words everything, in deeds nothing." The substance of the centrists' policy was to give lip service to the revolution while fighting against it in fact. The general effect of this policy was to paralyze the action of the revolutionary workers, while the right forces, in open alliance with the capitalists, virtually cut the revolution to pieces. It was these centrist elements who set up so-called left Socialist parties to block the Communist parties in various countries. In February 1921, in Vienna, they formed the International Working Union of Socialist Parties, nicknamed the "Two-and-a-Half International," as a counterweight to the Communist International. After the depth of the revolutionary crisis in central Europe had passed, the centrists and their phony international went back where they belonged politically, into the Second International.

The apparently divergent policies of the right-wing leaders and the centrists were, in fact, only a division of labor, the basic aim of which was to defeat the revolution in central and western Europe. This they accomplished together, working hand in hand with the capitalist generals and politicians. They shot down the revolution in Germany, Hungary, Austria, and Italy, and only the strong fist of the Red Army prevented them from doing the same thing in Soviet Russia. The right and centrist Social-Democratic leaders saved capitalism in middle Europe, and thereby also in western Europe. Upon the heads of these betrayers of socialism, therefore, rests the responsibility for all the evils that have since followed—the rise of fascism, World War II, and now the threat of another great world conflagration.

IMPACT OF THE REVOLUTION UPON THE AMERICAN LABOR MOVEMENT

In the United States, as in other countries, a wave of fighting spirit was generated among the masses by the advent of the great Russian Revolution, but, unlike eastern Europe, it did not reach the intensity of a tornado. At last the workers had succeeded in smashing their way through the fortifications of the hated capitalist system and had opened up the way to socialism. Even the more conservative categories of workers realized that a great blow had been struck for freedom. Crowded meetings of workers in American cities, hungry for every scrap of information about the First Workers Republic, made the rafters ring with applause at every mention of the Bolsheviks and their great leader, Lenin. Debs, with his genius for revolutionary expression of rank-and-file spirit, declared, "From the crown of my head to the soles of my feet I am a Bolshevik, and I am proud of it. The day of the people has come."[1] The Seattle longshoremen, in the spirit of the period, struck against loading munitions to be used against Soviet Russia. The broad masses of the American proletariat distinctly felt that the great victory in Russia was also their victory. This was especially the case among the huge armies of immigrant workers.

But the opportunist leaders of the American Social-Democracy, like their kind in Europe, took an altogether different attitude toward the Russian Revolution. The A.F. of L. top leaders, for example—an undeveloped brand of Social-Democrats who, because of the ideological undevelopment of the American working class, do not need to make demagogic use of Socialist slogans[2]—condemned the revolution from the

[1] *The Liberator*, May 1919.
[2] Lenin made no basic distinction between the A.F. of L. leaders and the European right-wing Social-Democrats. For example, he said in his letter to the Socialist Propaganda League in 1916: "Such men, however, as Mr. Legien in Germany and Mr. Gompers in the U.S.A. we consider to be bourgeois, and their politics are not socialist but national middle class politics. Mr. Legien, Mr. Gompers and the like represent not the working class but the aristocracy and the bureaucracy of the working class." (*Collected Works*, Vol. 18.)

outset. Their instinct, as labor tools of the capitalists, was as unerring in their hatred of living socialism as that of the big monopolists themselves. The 1919 convention of the A.F. of L. refused its endorsement of the Soviet government of Russia, and subsequent conventions, becoming bolder in their reaction, attacked the Soviets with unlimited violence and slander. From the earliest period right down to the most recent days, the big bureaucrats of the A.F. of L. have been outstanding and relentless instigators of every capitalist assault against the Soviet Union.

The leaders of the Socialist Party, at the outset, were more circumspect. They were mostly centrists of the Hillquit brand—the bulk of the extreme right-wing leaders having quit the Party after their failure to win it for a pro-war policy. The centrist opportunists, who also in their hearts deeply hated the Soviet government and considered it the repudiation of all their political plans and programs, adopted a policy of maneuvering regarding it, against the pressure of the militant rank and file of the Party. Consequently, they weakly hailed the Revolution, and in their 1919 convention, tongue-in-cheek, pledged "our support to the revolutionary workers of Russia in the maintenance of their Soviet government."[1] They also, pushed on by the rank and file, lodged a formal protest against the armed intervention of the United States and other capitalist powers in Soviet Russia. But when, as the sequel showed, the hypocrisy of these pretenses was unmasked, Hillquit and his co-leaders became no less violent in their opposition to the Soviet Union than were their political kin, the reactionary leaders of the A.F. of L. Hillquit later pronounced the Soviet government "the greatest disaster and calamity that has ever occurred to the Socialist movement."[2]

The left wing tirelessly challenged the treacherous attitude of the Hillquit leadership toward the Russian Revolution, bringing to the masses, as best it could, the lessons of this tremendous political forward leap of the world's working class. And the Communist Party, born from the left wing of the Socialist Party, throughout its 32 years of life, has never flagged in its efforts to have the masses of workers understand the constructive meaning of this gigantic political development.

THE TEACHINGS OF MARXISM-LENINISM

The Russian Revolution, and the long revolutionary struggle preceding it, resulted in the formulation of tremendous contributions to the body of Marxist social science. These were expressed in the reality of

[1] Trachtenberg, ed., *American Labor Year Book*, 1919-20, p. 414.
[2] *New Leader*, Feb. 4, 1928.

the great Revolution itself and, inseparably, in the brilliant scientific writings of Lenin. The sum and substance of this whole theoretical development was to raise Marxism to the level of Marxism-Leninism. This, in a scientific sense, is the greatest of all the contributions of the Russian Revolution to world humanity.

"Leninism," says Stalin, "is the Marxism of the era of imperialism and of the proletarian revolution."[1] There are two major aspects to the theoretical work of Lenin. First, Lenin re-established the principles of Marxism, as already stated by Marx and Engels in *The Communist Manifesto* and their other works. These principles the right-wing theoreticians of the Second International had been busily tearing down and burying for the previous half century. Second, Lenin further greatly developed Marxism, adding to it the basic lessons to be learned from the present period of imperialism and proletarian revolution. His work summed up to a complete theory of the Socialist revolution.

In the first aspect of Lenin's work, namely, the freeing of Marxism from opportunist revisionism, Lenin restated Marx's basic proposition that the present state is a repressive instrument of capitalism, the "executive committee of the capitalist class," thereby theoretically destroying the current Social-Democratic revisionist conception that the modern state under capitalism is a sort of people's state, without specific capitalist class domination. Lenin also proved the correctness, under modern conditions, of Marx's fundamental contention that the capitalist state, because of ruling class violent resistance to all democratic advance, would have to be abolished before socialism could be established. He declared that all the right-wing Social-Democratic chatter about capitalism being gradually transformed step by step into socialism was opportunism. At the same time, Lenin showed the growing over of the bourgeois democratic revolution into the socialist revolution.

Lenin, too, demonstrated irrefutably the fundamental correctness of Marx's conception of the dictatorship of the proletariat being the state form of the workers' rule under socialism,[2] and he shattered all revisionist nonsense about socialism—or what the opportunists miscall socialism—being only a continuation, in a more advanced form, of bourgeois democracy. Lenin also brilliantly revalidated the great Marxist principle of the class struggle, as against the mess of class collaborationism, which actually means working class subordination to capitalist class domination, into which the revisionist theoreticians of the Second International had bogged down the Socialist movement. Finally, to mention no more of Lenin's tremendous rebuttressing of Marxism, he restated Marx's funda-

[1] Joseph Stalin, *Foundations of Leninism*, p. 10, N. Y., 1939.
[2] Karl Marx, *Critique of the Gotha Program*, p. 18, N. Y., 1938.

mentals of dialectical materialism,[1] in opposition to the welter of bourgeois idealism and eclecticism which the degenerate Social-Democratic theoreticians of the Second International had absorbed from their bourgeois masters.

In the second major aspect of Lenin's theoretical accomplishments, namely, the development of Marxism to encompass the many problems of modern monopoly capitalism and proletarian revolution, Lenin performed a prodigious amount of pioneering theoretical work. Here we can give only the barest outline of his immense contributions in this respect. Lenin performed the basic task of analyzing capitalist imperialism, dissecting the whole structure of modern monopoly capitalism, and demonstrating that it is moribund capitalism, the final stage of the capitalist system. In doing this work, Lenin laid bare the basic causes of modern war. This general analysis he further strengthened by his profound discovery of the law of the uneven development of capitalism: the law which explains how and why the capitalist nations, instead of all developing at an even pace, grow at widely varying tempos, with the result that they periodically readjust by war their changing political relationships. Lenin also successfully challenged the bigwigs of the Second International, who held that socialism must come first in the most industrialized countries and, to be successful, must also occur in several of them at once. He proved that socialism, on the contrary, could be established in one country alone, specifically in backward, predominantly agricultural Russia. Stalin, later on, was also to make brilliant contributions on this key question. Lenin, while pointing out the ingrained warlike character of imperialism, also stressed both the necessity and the possibility of the peaceful coexistence of capitalist and socialist states in the world.

Lenin, along with Stalin, developed the theory of colonial and national liberation revolution. He likewise demonstrated the basic need for co-operation between the colonial peoples and the revolutionary proletariat of the imperialist countries. Repudiating the entire body of Social-Democratic revisionist theory, Lenin also showed the revolutionary potentialities of the peasantry in alliance with and under the general leadership of the proletariat. Lenin, who was as great a strategist and tactician as he was a theoretician, developed the role of partial demands, of trade unionism, and of parliamentarism, thus solving many difficult problems of methods and weapons in the general fight of the working class for socialism. Lenin, throughout his entire work, thoroughly unmasked the opportunist Social-Democrats, showing them to be wedded to the capitalist

[1] V. I. Lenin, *Materialism and Empirio-Criticism*, in *Selected Works*, Vol. 11; Joseph Stalin, *Dialectical and Historical Materialism*, N. Y., 1940.

system, and exposing the economic and political reasons why this was so.

To cap his immense theoretical achievements, Lenin was also the architect and chief organizer of the great Russian Communist Party, which led the Russian people in their historic victory over capitalism. Lenin called this "a party of a new type." It is incomparably the most highly developed political organization in the history of mankind. The Communist Party is composed of the best, most advanced elements of the working class, peasantry, and intellectuals. It is highly disciplined, yet it practices a profound democracy. It employs a regenerating self-criticism —learning from its own mistakes—which invigorates it in every phase and stage of its work. Its membership is inspired by the highest qualities of courage, devotion to the Soviet people's interests, and loyalty to the great cause of socialism. This great Party, the nightmare of capitalists and their Social-Democratic henchmen all over the world, is an imperishable monument to Lenin's theoretical skill and organizing ability and also to the profound revolutionary spirit of the Soviet people.

Lenin, like Marx, incorporated his theoretical work in many powerful books. And Lenin, again like Marx, also found the greatest justification of his writings, not only in their strong argumentation, but especially in the supreme test of experience in life itself. Lenin not only worked out revolutionary theories, but he also stood at the head of the masses of the Russian people in carrying through, in line with these theories, the greatest revolution in all of human history. His closest co-worker in this tremendous movement was Stalin. Lenin's theories and Marx's are now being profoundly justified by the present whole course of world political development, by the rapid decline of capitalism and rapid rise of socialism.

MARXISM-LENINISM AND THE AMERICAN MARXISTS

Marxism-Leninism is universal in its application. It is as naturally international as are all other branches of science. Its principles and policies apply to all countries, in all stages of capitalist or Socialist development. But, following the dictum of Engels, and as every Communist theoretician has pointed out time and again, Marxism-Leninism is not a dogma, but a guide to action. It is not to be applied as a blueprint in every situation, as a readymade panacea. The value of Marxism-Leninism can be realized in a given country only if its principles and policies are flexibly adapted to the specific situation prevailing in that country. As Lenin put it in 1918, "the revolution proceeds with a different tempo and in different forms in different countries (and it cannot be otherwise)."[1]

[1] Lenin, *A Letter to American Workers*, p. 21.

Marxism-Leninism made its impact upon the American left Socialist movement not only by means of the practical example of the Russian Revolution and Lenin's major writings, but also by direct counsel from Lenin himself. Lenin knew the American situation profoundly and was deeply interested in it. He wrote a basic work on American agriculture,[1] and twice he sent major political letters directly to the American working class—once, in 1916, in answer to a manifesto of the Socialist Propaganda League, and the second time in 1918, in his famous *A Letter to American Workers*. Also, during the early years of the Communist International, Lenin often spoke about the "American question."

The initial influence of Marxism-Leninism on American Marxist thinking was tremendous. Lenin provided the basic answers to many complicated problems of theory and practice which for decades past had confused and crippled the American Socialist movement. This clarification, besides acting with crushing effect upon the right-wing sophistries, also tended to liquidate the traditional sectarian errors of the left wing. Lenin exposed the De Leonite theories, syndicalist and sectarian, which had dominated and plagued the left wing ever since the death of Engels almost a quarter of a century earlier. Lenin provided a solid theoretical basis for the left's fight against Gompersism in the trade unions, and he also refuted the pseudo-Socialist pretenses of all sections of right-wing Social-Democracy—including its Bernsteinian and Kautskyan varieties. This had a clarifying and strengthening effect upon the American Marxist movement.

Highly important from the American standpoint was Lenin's scientific analysis of imperialism. With powerful emphasis, Lenin pointed out the qualitative differences that develop within the whole structure of capitalism with the growth of monopoly. Previously, without clearly differentiating itself from the right wing on this question, the left wing had tended to consider the growth of monopoly as merely a quantitative development of capitalism, and its "expansionism" (imperialism) as simply a secondary policy manifestation, instead of a basic expression of monopoly capitalism. This error led to a profound underestimation of the aggressive character, reactionary aims, and war-making potentialities of imperialism. Lenin cleared up all this confusion.[2]

Lenin also made clear the road of all-out political mass struggle to socialism. In so doing, he annihilated for Americans the prevalent De Leonite, syndicalist ideas that the workers would win their way to power by "locking out the capitalists," or by means simply of a general strike, and other kindred illusions. He also smashed the syndicalist conception,

[1] Lenin, *Capitalism and Agriculture in the the U. S.*
[2] V. I. Lenin, *Imperialism, the Highest Stage of Capitalism*, N. Y., 1939.

previously held almost unanimously by all sections of the American left wing, to the effect that after the workers had secured political power the Party would dissolve itself and the unions would take over the management both of the industries and of society as a whole. Lenin with the reality of the Russian Revolution to back up his words, clearly outlined the Soviet form of the dictatorship of the proletariat, pointed out that it is incomparably more democratic than the bourgeois dictatorship, and stressed the decisively leading role of the Party in every stage of the struggle, both before and during the existence of socialism.[1] Lenin also, in his masterly analysis of the national question, with the able co-operation of Stalin, laid the basis for a fundamental understanding of the Negro question in the United States, a problem that had baffled left-wing thinking up to that time. With his historic doctrine that "Without a revolutionary theory there can be no revolutionary movement," Lenin struck hard, too, at the traditional American tendency to minimize theory.

Among his many other contributions to the American revolutionary movement, Lenin clarified the question of the role of the farmers, which had always been a weak spot in S.L.P. and S.P. policy, especially after the advent of De Leon. Lenin stressed the vital necessity of labor co-operating with the oppressed and exploited strata of these toilers, and he indicated the basic conditions under which such co-operation, with working class leadership, should be carried out. Lenin, also, with his strong anti-sectarian position and his supreme genius for mobilizing all the potential strength of the anti-capitalist forces, laid the basis for a clarification of the question of the labor party. Smashing through the crippling De Leonite policy of non-participation in the broad, elemental mass movements of struggle, Lenin categorically, like Engels long before him, supported participation in such movements. Lenin likewise clarified the knotty question of partial political demands, which had also been a bone of contention in left-wing ranks for many years, especially under De Leon's intellectual tutelage. Indeed, Lenin had made this question quite clear in Russian practice, long before the Bolshevik Revolution. He showed that partial demands are an integral part of the workers' whole struggle. And Stalin, in his *Foundations of Leninism,* points out that reforms are by-products of revolutionary struggle and reforms can and must be used in the fight for socialism.

Lenin also clarified American Marxists on the question of religion. The Socialist Party, from its inception, had a confusion of policy on the matter, ranging from a cultivation of petty-bourgeois "Christian socialism" to the placing of "God-killing" as the main task of the Party. Lenin, reiterating Marx's statement that "Religion is the opium of the people,"

[1] Lenin, *State and Revolution.*

stressed its class role in the exploitation of the workers, and declared: "We demand that religion be regarded as a private matter so far as the state is concerned, but under no circumstances can we regard it as a private matter in our own party." Lenin insisted, on the one hand, upon the complete separation of Church and State, and on the other, on an educational campaign by the Party. However, "the propaganda of atheism by the Social Democracy must be *subordinated* to a more basic task— the development of the class struggle of the exploited masses against the exploiters." The Party should not write atheism into its program. It should, however, freely admit religious-minded workers to membership and then educate them to a scientific outlook on life.[1]

The writings of Lenin, the master Party builder, clarified the American left-wing movement about the structure, practice, and role of the Communist Party. In this respect he also made crystal-clear many problems which had worried and handicapped the left for many years. Lenin's basic teachings on the Party were especially needed in the United States, because of the long prevalence of syndicalist and semi-syndicalist ideas, the heart of which was a belittlement of the Party and an underestimation of political action.

To all these great contributions of Lenin to the American movement must be added at least another. It was Lenin, above all others, who finally knocked on the head that chronic American sectarian disease, the dual union illusion. As we have seen earlier, ever since the days of Debs' American Railway Union in 1894 and De Leon's Socialist Trades and Labor Alliance in 1895, American left-wingers had been obsessed with the idea that the way to revolutionize the labor movement was to withdraw from the conservative trade unions and to organize independent, theoretically perfect industrial unions. The general effect of this policy had been to leave the Gompers machine in virtually unchallenged control of the basic mass economic organizations of the working class and to waste the strength of the dynamic left-wing fighting trade unionists in innumerable utopian industrial union projects.

Lenin had encountered the problem of such abstention from the unions in Russia in 1908, on the part of the Otzovists, a group among the Bolsheviks. These elements, among other wrong tendencies, refused to work in the trade unions and other legally existing societies. Lenin, with his keen ability to go straight to the heart of a problem, and, thus with a penetrating analysis to settle it once and for all, sailed into the Otzovists and destroyed their position completely.[2] Lenin dealt again and crushingly with this particular sectarian abstentionist tendency

[1] V. I. Lenin, *Religion*, pp. 11-20, N. Y., 1933.
[2] *History of the Communist Party of the Soviet Union*, p. 135.

shortly after the beginning of the Russian Revolution, when "ultra lefts" in Germany, Holland, England, and other European countries, in the exuberance of their revolutionary spirit, had no patience for work in the old trade unions, but sought short cuts by setting up new revolutionary labor organizations. Lenin sharply denounced this practice as a serious form of sectarianism. He declared that "To refuse to work within reactionary trade unions means leaving the insufficiently developed or backward working masses under the influence of reactionary leaders, agents of the bourgeoisie, labor aristocrats, or 'bourgeoisified' workers."[1] This criticism applied with triple force to the United States, where the dual union fallacy had reigned almost unchallengeable in left circles for many years, thereby doing incalculable damage to the revolutionary movement.

Lenin, in fighting for a correct political line, fought on two fronts. That is, he combated both the right danger and all forms of pseudo-leftism. This two-front fight was particularly necessary in the United States, with its ingrained historical right weakness of American exceptionalism and its long affliction of "left" sectarianism.

The long-continued sectarianism of the left wing was basically an immature political reaction against the extreme opportunism of the S.P. and A.F. of L. leaders, which was bred of the especially corrupting influences of American political life. The left's dual unionism, anti-labor party, anti-farmer, anti-immediate demands, anti-parliamentary, and other ultra-revolutionary policies and attitudes were short-cut methods aimed to create powerful trade unions, a militant workers' party, and a mass Socialist ideology. A historical influence, too, producing left sectarianism was the pressure of the vast body of foreign-born workers, who were as yet little integrated into American economic, political, and social life.

Important also in this general respect was the fact that the American Marxist movement, in the imperialist epoch, had produced no outstanding Marxist theoretician, capable of immediately and basically solving the many complex problems faced by the working class. During many years, from the 1890's on, the great Lenin was developing Marxism into Marxism-Leninism and building the core of the eventual powerful Bolshevik Party. At this time, the American Socialists, in an extremely difficult objective situation, were being gravely hindered in their development by the powerful but revisionist influence of the ultra-left sectarian and semi-syndicalist theoretician, De Leon.

The sudden impact of Lenin's profound and comprehensive writings, supported as they were by the tremendous reality of the Russian Revolution, revolutionized the thinking of the Marxist forces in the United

[1] Lenin, *"Left-Wing" Communism, an Infantile Disorder*, p. 36.

States. The left moved rapidly toward a position of scientific communism. As Alexander Bittelman put it: "The formative period in the history of our Party appears as a development from Left Socialism to Communism. The essence of this development consisted in this, that the Left wing of the Socialist Party (1918-1919) was gradually freeing itself from vacillation between reformism and ultra-Left radicalism by means of an ever closer approach to the positions of Marxism-Leninism."[1]

Manifestly, Marxism-Leninism applied completely to the United States, but not as a blueprint. For this country is no "exception"; it is flesh and blood of the world capitalist system and is subject to that system's laws of growth and decline. But to adapt this tremendous body of scientific Marxist-Leninist principles to the specific conditions prevailing in the United States—that is, for the strengthening of every phase of the American workers' struggle for a better life—was a task of very large proportions. And as the sequel showed, many mistakes were to be made in this adaptation. Long-continued modes of incorrect thinking and of sectarian policies were not be overcome in a day. To build a mature Communist Party in any capitalist land is a very difficult political task, but most of all, in the United States, the stronghold of world capitalism.

[1] Alexander Bittelman, *Milestones in the History of the Communist Party*, p. 27, N. Y., 1937.

11. The Split in the Socialist Party (1919)

The split in the Socialist Party, which gave birth to the Communist Party, came to a head in the fall of 1919. It had its origin in the long struggle between the right and left which had gone on in the Party, with constantly greater intensity, ever since the foundation of the organization in 1901. Historically, this struggle had turned around many issues, covering practically every phase of the Party's program, its every-day activities, and its composition. It was the struggle of the militant proletarian left of the Party, striving to make the Socialist Party into the fighting Party of the working class, against the opportunist right which wanted to make it into a Party of petty-bourgeois reforms. That these two incompatible groups should eventually find themselves in separate parties was inevitable.

THE LONG INTERNAL STRUGGLE

In the present history we have already briefly reviewed some of the outstanding features of this long and ever-growing struggle within the S.P. Among these were the persistent fights against the control of the Party by petty-bourgeois opportunists; the many years' battle against Berger's "Milwaukee socialism"; the struggle against pro-Gompersism in the Party leadership; the persistent effort of the left to make the Socialists active workers in strikes, labor defense cases, and other working class battles; the struggle against white chauvinism and the oppression of the Negro people; the fight for the organization of the unorganized into trade unions; the endless battle over industrial unionism; the struggle for a strong anti-war policy; and the attempt to give the Party a sound position on the Russian Revolution. It was a continuous battle against an insolent and aggressive Bernsteinism, a corrupt Gompersism, and a tricky Kautskyism, by a militant left wing working to create a fighting Marxist policy and party.

Toward the end of World War I the dominant Party leadership had crystallized into two opportunist groups. One, the extreme right, the outright Bernsteinians, although weakened by the right-wing split on the war, were typified by Berger, Cahan, Germer, Hayes, Van Lear, Stit

Wilson, Harriman, and the like. The other group, the centrists—Kautskyans, who were long on revolutionary phrases and short on revolutionary deeds—was typified by Hillquit, Oneal, and Lee. As the struggle against the left developed, these two groups tended to merge into one general right wing, resolved at all costs to prevent the Party from becoming a fighting Socialist organization.

The constant internal struggle led, through the years, as we have seen, to a number of heavy political-organizational collisions between the right and the left. During the earlier days of the Party there were sharp local struggles in many cities and states—Texas, Nebraska, Oklahoma, and especially Washington in 1909. Then came the big national battle at the 1912 convention in Indianapolis over the moot question of the Party's rejection of the use of sabotage in the class struggle. Next, there followed the struggle at the 1917 St. Louis Emergency Convention and afterward, with the Party's anti-war policy as the main bone of contention. And finally, there came the decisive 1919 Chicago convention, when the whole life and line of the Party were at stake.

During this long struggle the left wing, although not able to control the Party, had been growing in political strength and maturity. While still largely a prey to "left" sectarianism, it had nevertheless clarified itself on many questions. It was also developing organizationally. Its growing consolidation as a definite national force was seen in its strong grouping in pre-war days around the *International Socialist Review*. And, after the *Review* had been destroyed during the war, around the Socialist Propaganda League, which had been launched in Boston in November 1916, with S. J. Rutgers (who later returned to his homeland, Holland) as its leader. Finally, in Chicago, in September 1919, the left wing could and did establish its own independent political organization. This was an historical political necessity. The American Communist movement, fundamentally the product of a long evolution in the intense class struggle of the United States, had at last reached its natural goal by becoming an independent party.

THE IMMEDIATE CAUSES OF THE 1919 SPLIT

Various powerful political forces combined to bring about the split in the Socialist Party at the precise time it occurred. Fundamentally, these were products of World War I and the Russian Revolution. The United States, under its own specific conditions, felt the terrific shock of these basic events which were undermining the whole structure of world capitalism. Among the manifestations of this shock were the break-up of the Socialist Party and the birth of the Communist Party.

A major immediate factor leading to the split within the Party was the acute discontent among the rank and file at the way the opportunist Party leadership had met the issue of the war. This was directed not only at the seceding pro-war leaders of the right, but also at the Hillquit group. There had been great enthusiasm after the St. Louis convention, with its militant anti-war resolution—even the left wing being more or less taken in by Hillquit's anti-war demagogy. But soon thereafter disillusionment set in among the lefts, because many of the Party leaders who had voted for the St. Louis resolution either failed to back it up in practice or came out in open support of the war. This course deeply outraged the proletarian membership, who ardently wanted the Party to conduct a militant struggle against the imperialist war.

Added to this rank-and-file discontent was an even greater resentment of the left-minded membership at the compromising manner in which the right-centrist Hillquit leadership handled the central question of the Russian Revolution. The militant membership of the Party rightly looked upon the Revolution as a supreme Socialist triumph of the Russian working class, and they were determined to give it all the support and protection they could against the armed intervention and other attacks being made upon it by the capitalists of the United States. Consequently, the proletarian members of the Party were not slow to understand that the Hillquit leaders of the Party, with their weasel-worded, opportunistic endorsements of the Soviet government and their feeble protests against American intervention in Soviet Russia, were in reality enemies of the Russian Revolution.

Additional fuel was added to the fire of Party discord by the specific controversy over the question of the international affiliation of the Party. This began to take shape during the war in connection with the wartime conferences in Zimmerwald and Kienthal, with the left wing pressing for active support of Lenin's fight for a sound international working class policy. It became even more acute when in Moscow, under Lenin's direct leadership, on March 2-6, 1919, nineteen left-wing groups and parties established the Third, or Communist, International.[1] This was an indispensable development, growing out of the whole international situation —with the Second International broken down by the war treason of its leaders and the revolutionary workers of Europe on the march, demanding a new international organization.

The left wing of the American Socialist Party insisted that the Party affiliate to the Communist International. But again the slippery Hillquit leadership, while speaking softly about the new organization, took an

---

[1] Boris Reinstein was the unofficial representative at this conference.

active initiative in trying to put the shattered Second International back on its feet. The latter elected delegates to the proposed Stockholm conference of 1917 (which never assembled), and they also supported the Berne conference of September 1918—both of which were designed to disinter the dead Second International. These actions caused deep resentment in the Socialist Party of the United States.

Still another factor intensifying the inner-Party tension was the urgent need to develop a fighting program to support the current big struggles of the workers and to counter the post-war offensive of the employers. This was the time of the Seattle general strike (January 1919), of the Winnipeg general strike (April 1919), and of the great steel strike (September 1919). Many other strikes were looming on the horizon. On all sides, too, the employers were obviously preparing for an aggressive anti-labor drive. The opportunist Hillquit leadership, to the deep discontent of the rank and file, was quite incapable of developing a program of militant action which would place the Party in the vanguard of the tremendous class struggles which were then in the process of taking place.

THE RELATIONSHIP OF THE PARTY FORCES

The left wing of the Party was in a strong position in the growing internal fight. Its supporters had been basically educated in the fight against the war, and they were also profoundly inspired by the great Russian Revolution. Most important in strengthening the ideology of the left wing during this critical situation was the initial publication in the United States during 1918 and 1919 of such fundamental documents of Lenin's as *A Letter to American Workers, The Soviets at Work, State and Revolution,* and *Imperialism, the Highest Stage of Capitalism.*

The left clearly had behind it a majority of the Party membership. It drew its strength from all sections of the Party, but its main strongholds were in New York, Ohio, Michigan, Illinois, and Massachusetts, and especially in the "language federations." Of these organizations, the Russian Socialist Federation, with about 8,000 members, was the largest and most militant. The Party membership had gone up from 80,379 in 1917 to 104,822 in the first months of 1919, and most of these new members, workers who had been recruited by the federations, were definitely left in their thinking.

Regarding the Party press, the right-wing leadership eventually managed to hang onto control of the New York *Call* and most of the other English-speaking organs. The non-English press, however, with the notable exception of the *Jewish Daily Forward,* almost solidly supported the left wing. During the struggle the left wing created several new

English-language papers, the most important of which were *The Class Struggle* (1917) and *The Communist* (1919) in New York; *The Revolutionary Age* (1918) in Boston; *The Proletarian* (1918) and *The Communist* (1919) in Chicago; and *The Socialist News* in Cleveland. *The Revolutionary Age* served as the central organ of the S.P. left-wing movement.

During the previous few years the left wing had also been building up many new leaders. Outstanding among these were Charles E. Ruthenberg of Cleveland and John Reed of New York. These new leaders could be depended upon to fight for a sound program. While the old left-wing leader, Debs, spoke militantly against the war and for the Russian Revolution and also supported other policies of the left, he nevertheless refused to carry on the indispensable struggle against the right-wing opportunists who held the leading posts in the Party. Haywood, outside of the Party, belonged to the I.W.W.

The right wing in the Party, in contrast to the left, was in a very difficult situation. It was definitely in the minority, and besides, it had lost many of its ablest writers and speakers through the wartime defection of these pro-war elements. But what the rights lacked in numbers and ability they hoped to make up in a ruthless use of their key posts in the Party. As reactionaries always do in such situations, they decided to defeat the democratic will of the membership by violence, and to hold on to the party leadership at all costs.

To achieve their own program, the left wing sought, as the fight grew, to function through the democratic workings of the Party. But the Hillquit-Berger leadership, with their desperate policies, would have none of Party democracy under these conditions. *The Revolutionary Age* expressed the situation thus: "The slogan of the moderates is: Split the Party for moderate Socialism! The slogan of the Left-Wing is: Conquer the Party for revolutionary Socialism—for the Communist International."[1] Along these lines the fight was conducted. In view of the right wing's complete suppression of Party democracy the split was inevitable.

THE DEVELOPING STRUGGLE

With the beginning of the fateful year, 1919, the internal Party struggle became more and more intense. By then the central issues between the two major Party groupings had become clearly crystallized—class struggle against class collaboration, proletarian internationalism against national chauvinism, proletarian dictatorship against bourgeois democracy, the Third International against the Second International.

In New York the left wing was making rapid headway in winning

[1] *The Revolutionary Age*, May 24, 1919.

locals, only to have them immediately reorganized and screened under right-wing leadership by the Party bosses. Nevertheless, the Party branches in Brooklyn, the Bronx, and Queens quickly came under left-wing leadership. On February 15, 1919, when the Central Committee of the Greater New York locals of the Socialist Party, dominated by Julius Gerber, refused to censure the local Socialist aldermen for supporting the war, the representatives of twenty left-wing locals from various parts of the city came together in a conference to take action. After listening to talks by John Reed, Jim Larkin, Rose Pastor Stokes, and by representatives of various federations, the conference organized itself as the Left-Wing Section of the Socialist Party and elected officers. The conference also decided to publish a Manifesto,[1] and to issue a paper, which appeared on April 19, 1919, as the *New York Communist*, with John Reed as editor. The left wing can be said to have come into being as an organized force at this date. Chicago, Boston, Cleveland, and other centers, taking the New York Manifesto as their basis of policy, soon followed New York's example.

Meanwhile, important events quickly followed one another in the national sphere. For one thing, in answer to the call for a conference in March in Moscow to organize the Communist International, the left wing had submitted to the S.P. in good time a referendum proposal to the effect "That the Socialist Party should participate in an international congress or conference called by or in which participate the Communist Party of Russia, and the Communist Party (Spartacus) of Germany." The referendum carried by a huge majority, but the wily Hillquit held up the returns until May, two months after the founding conference of the Comintern had been held.

Then came the national elections within the Party, which were also, as usual, conducted by referendum vote. Held early in the spring of 1919, the elections resulted in a sweeping victory for the left wing. Even such outstanding right-wing leaders as Hillquit and Berger went down to ignominious defeat. But Hillquit, with his rule-or-ruin policy, refused to make public the unfavorable returns. The election figures, as finally authenticated by the left wing, showed that for the post of international secretary Hillquit had received only 4,775 votes, as against 13,262 for Kate Richards O'Hare; and for the Second International representative, Berger had been swamped by John Reed to the tune of 17,235 votes to 4,871. The left wing also elected 12 of the 15 members of the National Executive Committee. Ruthenberg and Wagenknecht were elected to the National Executive Committee with over 10,000 votes each, or from three to five times as many as the corresponding right-wing candidates.

[1] James Oneal, *American Communism*, p. 375, N. Y., 1947.

HILLQUIT'S "PINK TERROR"

The significance of these events was not lost upon the Party's official leaders. They saw clearly that if inner democracy were to be continued, the left wing would surely win national control of the Party. Therefore, resolved to hold on come what might, they embarked upon a policy of expulsions which had never been equaled, even by the ultra-reactionary A.F. of L. leadership. The expelled members and organizations were given no semblance of trials, nor were formal charges even preferred against them.

The National Executive Committee, in its May 24-30, 1919, meeting, arbitrarily expelled the Michigan state organization with 6,000 members, and it suspended (expelled) the Russian, Lithuanian, Polish, Lettish, Hungarian, Ukrainian, and South Slav federations, with a total of over 40,000 members.[1] The right-wing leadership especially wanted to get rid of the rapidly growing federations, whose militant spirit, based on abominable conditions in American industry, also largely reflected the revolutionary situations in their respective native countries.

In the succeeding weeks the state organizations of Massachusetts and Ohio were also expelled,[2] and along with them the Party organization in Chicago and whole groups of locals in New York and in various other centers. In all these sections of the Party the left held large majorities. Finally, a total of at least 55,000 members had been dictatorially driven out of the Party. At the same notorious May meeting the National Executive Committee set aside the results of the national election referendum and transferred the entire property of the Party to a corporation of seven members.

The men who committed this crime against Party unity and democracy were A. Shiplacoff, James Oneal, G. H. Goebel, Fred Krafft, Seymour Stedman,[3] Dan Hogan, John M. Work, and M. Holt. The two left-wing members present at this infamous meeting—Alfred Wagenknecht and L. E. Katterfeld—were powerless to halt the outrageous proceedings. Five National Executive Committee members were absent.[4] Hillquit, then sick in the hospital, engineered the whole shameful business.

Meanwhile, on May 5th, a call had gone forth summoning a national conference of the left wing to take action in the Party crisis. It was signed by Local Boston, Local Cleveland, and the Left Wing Section of the S.P. of New York. The call aroused tremendous enthusiasm within

---

1 *The Revolutionary Age*, June 7, 1919.
2 Fine, *Labor and Farmer Parties in the U.S.*, p. 344.
3 Stedman joined the C.P. several years later.
4 *The Revolutionary Age*, June 7, 1919.

the Socialist ranks, and the membership rallied to support it. The wholesale expulsions perpetrated by the National Executive Committee majority served to intensify the conflict.

THE NATIONAL LEFT-WING CONFERENCE

The National Conference of the Left Wing met in New York, at Manhattan Lyceum, on June 21, 1919. Present were 94 delegates from 20 cities, including New York, Boston, Buffalo, Cleveland, Rochester, Philadelphia, Pittsburgh, Hartford, Minneapolis, Duluth, St. Paul, Detroit, Kansas City, Denver, and Oakland. The delegates represented the bulk of the membership of the Socialist Party.

The main purposes of the gathering, as stated in the call under which the conference had assembled, were "to formulate a national declaration of Left Wing principles, form a national unified expression of the Left Wing (a sort of general council—not a separate organization) and concentrate our forces to conquer the Party for revolutionary Socialism."[1] Hardly had the conference gotten under way, however, when a serious division took place within it. This was caused by a statement by Dennis E. Batt of Detroit (later a renegade) to the effect that immediate steps were being taken by his group to form a Communist Party on September first in Chicago, and proposing that this be the line of the conference. Behind Batt's proposition stood the Michigan District and the seven ousted federations. This was the beginning of a deep split in American Communist ranks which took two and a half years to heal.

Those who advocated forming a Communist Party at once took the position that there was little or no prospect of capturing the S.P. special convention, scheduled for Chicago on August 30th; that the right-wing officials would hang onto control despite all attempts to oust them; that it was useless to capture a completely discredited Party; and that the historic moment had now struck to form the Communist Party. The opposing group, which included such as John Reed, Charles E. Ruthenberg, Alfred Wagenknecht, Alexander Bittelman, W. W. Weinstone, and Charles Krumbein, maintained, on the contrary, that the present tactic of fighting to secure control of the S.P., in the name of the Party majority, was winning the support of the mass of the rank and file; that it was exposing the Hillquit leaders, with their ruthless expulsions, as the real splitters; and that, in order to win over the still wavering groups in the Party, this policy should be continued up to the August 30th convention. The latter, undoubtedly the more flexible and more correct

[1] *The Revolutionary Age,* June 26, 1919.

position, was calculated to win the greatest body of supporters for the new party.

The dispute over tactics occupied the main attention of the left-wing national conference. After three days of deliberation, Batt's proposal to quit the struggle inside the S.P. and to proceed directly to launch the C.P. was voted down, 55 to 38. The majority decided that "This conference shall organize as the Left Wing Section of the Socialist Party and shall have as its object the capturing of the Socialist Party for revolutionary Socialism." This was carried by a vote of 43 to 14, with 14 abstaining. The Conference, as part of its general tactical line, also decided that it would elect Left Wing delegates, including the expelled organizations, to the S.P. convention; that it would seek to have the S.P. convention adopt the Left Wing Manifesto as the basis of its program; that it would fight for affiliation of the S.P. to the Communist International; that the results of the national election referendum should be accepted; and that, if through the courts and the police, the right-wing leaders should maintain control of the convention, then the Communist Party should be formed at once.

The Michigan-federation group refused to abide by these decisions. They let it be known to the conference that, regardless of that body's decisions, they were going to abandon work within the S.P. and in any event would orient themselves toward launching the Communist Party in Chicago on September first. The Communist ranks were deeply split.

The National Left Wing Conference provided for the publication of a manifesto and program. It also established headquarters in New York and made *The Revolutionary Age* its official organ. The conference selected a National Council of Nine. Among these were Charles E. Ruthenberg, John Ballam, I. E. Ferguson, James Larkin, and Eadmonn MacAlpine. Ferguson was chosen national secretary. The conference also issued a call for a convention in Chicago, on September first, of all revolutionary elements that would unite with a revolutionary Socialist Party or with a new Communist Party.

The S.P. leaders, as the date of their Chicago convention approached, intensified the expulsion campaign, and the left wing also busily mobilized its forces. Meanwhile, on July 26-27, the left-wing National Executive Committee members who had been elected in the national referendum, but not recognized by the S.P. controlling clique, held a meeting in Chicago. This meeting claimed to be the legitimate National Executive Committee of the S.P., and it elected L. E. Katterfeld Party chairman, and Alfred Wagenknecht, national secretary. Adolph Germer, S.P. executive secretary, was removed and instructed to turn over the effects of the Party to Wagenknecht. But this line of policy was not aggressively pushed, and the new left-wing National Executive Committee of the S.P. played little part in the big struggle now rushing fast to a climax.[1]

In an effort to heal the breach in the Communist ranks, a conference of both Communist factions was held in August. This meeting, by a vote of seven to two, decided to support the proposition of launching the C.P. on September first, Ruthenberg and other Council leaders, in the meantime, having gone over to the Michigan-federations policy. Therefore, a joint call for a Communist Party convention on September first was issued, signed by the National Left Wing Council and the National Organizing Committee (Michigan-federations group).[2] But the National Council minority, headed by John Reed and Alfred Wagenknecht, refused to accept this decision and continued with the original policy of the Council, to try to win control of the S.P. Unity had not been achieved, and the two Communist factions continued to work at cross purposes.

THE LEFT WING MANIFESTO

At this point it may be well for us to make a brief analysis of the National Council's Left Wing Manifesto, upon the basis of which the American Communist movement was being organized. This Manifesto, differing little from the original New York Left Wing Manifesto, eventually served also, with only minor changes, as the basis for the programs of the two Communist Parties soon to be born.[3]

The Manifesto correctly condemned the whole political line, root and branch, of the right-wing S.P. leadership. It accused Hillquit and company of basing the Party program upon the petty bourgeoisie and the skilled aristocracy of labor; of failing to support industrial unionism and the workers' economic struggles; of surrendering to Gompersism; of carrying on an opportunist parliamentary policy; of sabotaging the struggle against the war; of opposing the Russian Revolution; of accepting a Wilsonian peace; of supporting the decayed Second International; and of generally carrying on a policy of reform which led, not to socialism, but to the perpetuation of capitalism.

As against this policy of reformism and class collaboration, the Left Wing Manifesto outlined a policy of militant struggle in both the industrial and political fields. It proposed basing the Party and its program

[1] *The Revolutionary Age*, Aug. 2, 1919.
[2] *The Revolutionary Age*, Aug. 23, 1919.
[3] For the text of these two manifestoes, see *Revolutionary Radicalism* (Report of Lusk Committee), Part 1, pp. 706-38, Albany, 1920.

upon the proletariat; full support of industrial unionism; relentless war against Gompersism; revolutionary parliamentarism; support of the Russian Revolution; affiliation to the Communist International; and a program aimed at the abolition of the capitalist system and the establishment of the dictatorship of the proletariat.

The Manifesto registered a long stride by the Left Wing toward a Marxist-Leninist policy. It was an enormous qualitative advance over pre-war programs of the left, such as the "Industrial Socialism," Haywood-Bohn platform of 1911. The previous left line had been saturated with sectarianism and syndicalism, whereas the 1919 program was predominantly Marxist-Leninist. Among its good points, the Manifesto presented an essentially sound analysis of American imperialism, a lack of which in years past had been a grave weakness of the left. The Manifesto also made a clear analysis of the recent imperialist war, which was also a vast improvement over the pacifist conceptions that had hitherto prevailed in the Party, even in its left wing. Another big step forward in the Manifesto was its Marxist analysis of the state, both in its capitalist and socialist forms. In particular, its presentation of the dictatorship of the proletariat, while exhibiting some hangovers of De Leonism, was a marked advance over the previously prevailing syndicalist ideas of a labor union state. The program of organized mass action, as the way to socialism, showed the left wing was beginning to free itself of De Leonite illusions about "locking out the capitalists," folded arms general strikes, and other fantasies. The Manifesto also laid great stress upon the leading role of the Party, as against a gross underestimation of the Party in the past.

That is to say, the Manifesto (aside from such theoretical weaknesses as its failure to analyze Social-Democracy correctly) marked real progress toward grasping the general theoretical principles of Marxism-Leninism, in the broad sense indicated above. On the negative side, however, the Manifesto showed little skill in applying these correct fundamentals to the specific situation in the United States. The American Communists had gotten a first grasp upon the powerful weapon of Marxist-Leninist analysis, but they had not yet learned how to use it correctly. They were still far from having mastered Lenin's great lesson that Marxism is not a dogma, but a guide to action—a weakness that was to plague the Party for many years. Particularly with regard to the basic question of the road to the abolition of capitalism and the establishment of socialism, there was a tendency to overlook specific American conditions and to think mechanically in terms of the experience of the Russian Revolution. This weakness made for political rigidity, and it tended to stimulate long-existing sectarian tendencies.

The Manifesto, in its theoretical approach, dealt decisive blows against the opportunist right wing and also against sectarian errors of the left in the past; but on its practical side it did not even partially liquidate the "leftist" sectarianism which had always been a heavy handicap to the American Marxist movement, especially since the theoretical predominance of De Leon after 1890, by blocking broad united coalition action on immediate political, economic, and legislative issues.

The Left Wing Manifesto, in fact, fairly reeked with this traditional sectarianism in practice. It continued the incorrect line of attempting to desert the old trade unions and to replace them with ideally conceived, dual industrial unions. It also took a narrow position toward the labor party, repudiating it as a danger to the working class. It likewise failed completely to develop a program of united front action with labor's natural allies, especially the Negro people and the farmers, considering the anti-capitalist struggle to be one for the working class alone. It ignored generally the basic Negro question. It also left the matter of partial demands completely out of the picture, and it reduced its parliamentary activity simply to one of agitation. The conception of an immediate, as well as an ultimate, program did not enter into the document. As Alexander Bittelman says, "The Left Wing did not seem to realize that revolutionary mass action grows out only of the real living issues of the class struggle, as it develops day by day."[1]

Thus, it will be seen from the Manifesto that the Communist Party (in its two sections) was born while in the midst of absorbing the great meaning of the Russian Revolution and of learning the basic essentials of Marxism-Leninism.[2] This indefinite position was a handicap to it and was basically responsible for the Party's later struggles to heal the split and to achieve a more correct, broad mass program. Ruthenberg noted this fact,[3] remarking that most of the European Communist parties were organized at later periods than ours—to their advantage. Whereas the American Communist Party was born in September 1919, the dates of other Communist parties were: England, August 1920; Germany, early in 1921; France, January 1921; Italy, 1921. By their later dates of birth these parties were far better prepared ideologically to take up the tasks of independent parties than was the case in the United States. But the general situation in the United States, as we have seen, con-

---

[1] Bittelman, *Milestones in the History of the Communist Party*, p. 42.
[2] The first installment of Lenin's *State and Revolution* was not published until two months before the Left Wing National Conference (*The Communist*, February 1919) and Lenin's famous *"Left-Wing" Communism, an Infantile Disorder*, with its devastating attack upon all forms of sectarianism, was not published until 1920, almost a year after the 1919 Party convention.
[3] Charles E. Ruthenberg in *The Communist*, July 1921.

ditioned irresistibly the birth of the Communist Party at the time it actually took place; it could not have been delayed.

THE DECLINE OF THE SOCIALIST PARTY

The split, now so rapidly coming to a crisis, was to prove disastrous to the Socialist Party. After the break the membership dropped swiftly from 104,822 in 1919 to but 26,766 in 1920. The decline continued, until it had sunk to 7,425 in 1927. At the present time, in 1952, the S.P. has probably not over 4,000 members. The Party's mass influence also tobogganed; it became a prey to internal dissensions, and finally splitting in 1936, it gave birth to the bourgeois Social-Democratic Federation. Moreover, the S.P. has degenerated politically to the extent that, as we shall see, it has become an unblushing supporter of warlike American imperialism.

The Socialist Party came into existence as a sound reaction against the sectarian dogmatism of the Socialist Labor Party. After twenty-five years of existence the latter had remained a skeleton organization, made up mainly of foreign-born workers, propagating socialism abstractly, and carrying on few activities related to the everyday problems of the American working class. The S.L.P.'s chronic failure to measure up to the needs of the period became especially glaring as the United States entered the stage of imperialism and the working class embarked upon broad mass struggles. Manifestly, the S.L.P. could not be the vanguard party of the working class in this situation; hence the flag of Socialist leadership passed to the Socialist Party.

In its earlier stages the Socialist Party displayed great activity in the class struggle. In the innumerable strikes of the period the Socialist workers were most active. Large numbers of trade unions were organized by Socialists, and Party members were always prominent in unionizing campaigns, labor defense cases, farmers' struggles, and the like. For many years the Party, which was composed overwhelmingly of workers, fought the corrupt and reactionary Gompers machine. The Party also carried on much valuable anti-capitalist propaganda among the workers. This is why it grew so rapidly and became an important political factor in the country. The healthy aspects of these accomplishments were the work primarily of the Party's proletarian left wing.

But, as we have seen, the Socialist Party, despite its considerable early achievements, also failed to live up to the tasks placed upon it by history, specifically by the era of imperialism into which it was born. It was not the needed "party of a new type," but was patterned after the opportunist-dominated Social-Democratic Party of Germany. From the outset it was crippled by a petty-bourgeois leadership and afflicted with a bourgeois ideology rather than that of Marxist socialism. The reformist Party leaders proved incapable of giving the necessary economic and political leadership to the working class. The Party also suffered from strong sectarian and syndicalist tendencies in its left wing, which greatly hindered its development.

The failure of the Party, under opportunist leadership, to act as the vanguard of the working class inevitably produced within it the development of a strong left wing, fighting for a real class struggle policy. The growth of this left wing was the gestation of the Communist Party. The new Party finally and inevitably came to birth in the fire of World War I and the Russian Revolution. The S.P. opportunist petty-bourgeois leadership had especially failed to understand the political lessons of these great events; but, in meeting them it definitely exposed itself instead as an enemy of the Socialist system that had just been established. The leadership of the Socialist movement in the United States, therefore, had to and did pass from the Socialist Party to a new organization, one truly Socialist in character, the Communist Party.

12. The Formation of the Communist Party (1919-1921)

The Socialist Party convention opened on August 30, 1919, in Machinists' Hall, 113 South Ashland Boulevard, Chicago. The Hillquit clique had complete control of the Party apparatus, and from the outset they used this control drastically. Their Contest Committee, passing on challenged credentials, refused seats to delegates of the left wing from a dozen states. When John Reed and other left-wingers nevertheless tried to take their seats, Executive Secretary Germer called in the police to expel them. At this outrage the left-wing delegates walked out. The long-brewing division between the right and left wings had now reached the final stage of an open, organizational split.[1]

THE TWO COMMUNIST CONVENTIONS

Meanwhile, the two Communist groups went ahead with organizing their separate conventions. Sharp criticisms were flying back and forth between the factions. The Reed-Wagenknecht group, after their expulsion from the S.P. convention, at first claimed to be the legitimate S.P., but on the day following, August 31st, they went to the I.W.W. hall, 129 Throop Street, and formed themselves into the Communist Labor Party of America. A day later, on September 1st, at 1221 Blue Island Avenue, the Michigan-federations group organized the Communist Party of America.[2]

The C.P., containing the federations, was much the larger of the two new parties. It had 128 regular and fraternal delegates and claimed a membership of 58,000. The C.L.P. had 92 delegates at its convention. It issued no figures as to membership, which was mainly American-born, but it was obviously very much smaller than the C.P. The C.P. asserted that the C.L.P. had about 10,000 members. Efforts were made to unite the two conventions, especially by Ruthenberg, but without success. The C.P. criticized the C.L.P. as centrist, and declared that if the latter wanted unity the C.L.P. delegates could come over to the C.P. conven-

[1] *The Communist*, Sept. 27, 1919.
[2] In Canada, the Communist Party was also born in two sections at the same general time and for the same general reasons.

tion and participate there as fraternal delegates. This proposition, of course, the C.L.P. scorned.

Meanwhile, the Michigan group at the C.P. convention, led by Batt and Keracher, took exception to the strong control exercised by the federation leaders and refused to vote for the C.P. program. This group was expelled on December 2nd, after which in June 1920, they organized themselves as the Proletarian Party, a wisp of a party which still exists. Ruthenberg was elected executive secretary of the C.P. and Wagenknecht was chosen for the same position in the C.L.P. *The Communist* became the organ of the C.P., and *The Toiler* (formerly the *Socialist News*) the journal of the C.L.P. The C.P. set up its headquarters in Chicago and the C.L.P. moved to Cleveland. The C.P. had 12 publications in its "language" federations.

Both U.S. Communist Parties extended their organization into Canada. In June 1921, however, the two groups were fused into one Communist Party, which was born "underground."[1] The Workers Party of Canada was founded in February 1922. In June 1943 the C.P. of Canada was reorganized into the present Labor-Progressive Party.

THE COMMUNIST PROGRAMS

The programs of the two parties were essentially the same.[2] Their strengths and weaknesses were those of the Left Wing Manifesto, upon which they were based and which we analyzed in the preceding chapter. That is, they developed a basically correct Marxist-Leninist position on such general questions as the state, imperialism, the war, and proletarian dictatorship; but they failed in applying Marxist-Leninist principles to the concrete American situation. In the latter respect, they largely remained clamped in the traditional sectarianism and "leftism."

Thus, on the trade union question, dualism expressed itself in both parties. The C.P., for example, proposed the formation of a "general industrial union organization embracing the I.W.W., W.I.I.U.,[3] independent and secession unions, militant unions of the A.F. of L., and the unorganized workers, on the basis of the revolutionary class struggle. The C.L.P. also took a dual union line.

The C.L.P. did not mention the Negro question at all, and the C.P. outlined the incorrect, but generally-held opinion in the word-for-

[1] Tim Buck, *30 Years, the Story of the Communist Movement in Canada*, pp. 21-23, Toronto, 1952.
[2] For both programs, see Trachtenberg, ed., *American Labor Year Book*, 1919-1920, pp. 414-19.
[3] Socialist Labor Party, *The Workers International Industrial Union*.

word De Leonite formula that "The racial expression of the Negro is simply the expression of his economic bondage and oppression, each intensifying the other. This complicates the Negro problem, but does not alter its proletarian character."[1]

Both parties proposed to have nothing to do with partial, immediate political demands. The C.P. said that its parliamentary representatives "shall not introduce or support reform measures," and the C.L.P. declared that its platform "can contain only one demand: the establishment of the Dictatorship of the Proletariat." Parliamentary action was thus reduced to a question of agitation of revolutionary formulas.

The parties' platforms were also incorrect in their approach to the question of the workers' potential united front allies in the class struggle. For example, said the C.P.: "The Communist Party, accordingly, in campaigns and elections, and in all its other activities, shall not cooperate with groups or parties not committed to the revolutionary class struggle, such as the Socialist Party, Labor Party, Non-partisan League, People's Council, Municipal Leaguers, etc." The C.L.P. was no less "leftist."

Both parties declared for affiliation to the Communist International. Both also stressed the leading role of the Party, but this they did in an abstract manner, failing to realize that the Party had to be the leader not only in periods of revolutionary struggle but also in every day-to-day issue of the working class, no matter how small.

The political basis of the "leftism" that prevailed in both parties was a wrong estimate of the general political situation in the United States. The tacit assumption of both parties was that the country was approaching a revolutionary crisis. Thus, the C.L.P. program "realizes that the time for parleying and compromise has passed; and that now it is only the question whether all power remains in the hands of the capitalists or is taken by the working class." The C.P. program expressed a similar spirit of revolutionary urgency. Little analysis was developed at the time of this key proposition, however.

Much of Europe then was in a revolutionary situation. Moreover, the revolution in Germany, had it not been betrayed by the Social-Democrats, could have spread widely, thereby directly affecting the United States. It was therefore quite correct for the American Communist Parties to have a general Socialist perspective. Their mistake was in conceiving this in an altogether too immediate sense and in a mechanical fashion. They failed to make a clear distinction between a Europe devastated by the war and the scene of active revolutionary struggle, and a capitalist America enriched by the war and by no means ready

[1] Alexander Trachtenberg, ed., *American Labor Year Book*, 1919-1920, p. 419.

for socialism. This faulty analysis contributed directly to the young Communist parties' underestimation and neglect of the daily struggles of the workers for partial demands. Raising the slogan of Soviets for the United States was a serious political error, indicating the political immaturity of the Party.

The two conventions, between them, laid the organizational and political foundations for the eventual Communist Party of the United States. But many urgent tasks confronted this young and split movement. The first and most important of these was to bring about unity between the two Communist parties. There were also very many left-wing elements still to be assembled, including sections remaining in the S.P., the more advanced I.W.W. members, the militants in the A.F. of L., and other groupings moving toward Marxist socialism. Above all, there was the necessity of securing a better grasp upon the great theoretical principles of Marxism-Leninism so newly come to the knowledge of the American left wing. But before these urgent tasks could be done the movement was to undergo its first test by fire.

THE PALMER RAIDS

The Communist Party of the United States was born in the midst of sharp economic and political struggles, both abroad and at home. The Russian Revolution was surging ahead, smashing the armies of the counter-revolutionary interventionists, and Germany and all of central and eastern Europe were stirring with revolutionary spirit. In the United States the workers, reflecting something of the revolutionary mood of the working class in many countries, were fighting on the offensive. The historic Seattle and Winnipeg general strikes were still fresh in memory, and the great steel strike, a thrust by over a third of a million workers at the very heart of the open-shop industries, was just beginning. In this situation came the formation of the Party, the most advanced expression of the workers' militancy and fighting spirit.

The capitalists, frightened at all these threatening developments, were beginning their intense post-war offensive to give the workers another bitter taste of the "democracy" they had saved by winning the war. They arbitrarily used the state power for the illegal suppression of the people's rights. This growing employers' offensive hit the Communist parties with full force in the infamous Palmer raids at the end of 1919.

On October 16th of that year the police pushed into the C.L.P. headquarters in Cleveland and arrested the Party leadership, and on November 8th, in New York, 700 police invaded mass meetings celebrating the anniversary of the Russian Revolution, seizing several hundred workers. But

FORMATION OF THE COMMUNIST PARTY

these raids were only dress rehearsals for the big outrages yet to come. Suddenly, during the night of January 2, 1920, the Department of Justice struck nationally in 70 cities, dragging workers from their homes, slugging them, and throwing them into crowded jails, often without proper food and toilet facilities. These monstrous raids, authorized by the "liberal" President Wilson, were carried out by Attorney General A. Mitchell Palmer and his hatchet man, J. Edgar Hoover. Allegedly, the country was on the brink of a revolution and this was the way to save it, regardless of law and constitutional rights.

An estimated 10,000 were arrested.[1] Most of the two Communist parties' leaders were in jail, 39 of the officials of the C.L.P. being indicted. Eventually, Ruthenberg, Larkin, Winitsky, Whitney, and others, arrested during the period of the raids, were sentenced to long terms in the penitentiary. The government struck hardest at the foreign-born workers, whom it considered the most dangerously revolutionary. Under the Wartime Deportation Act over 500 aliens were summarily deported. On the steamer *Buford*, sailing from New York, there were 249 deportees, including Alexander Berkman and Emma Goldman. In the prevailing hysteria Victor Berger, although regularly elected, was refused a seat in the House of Representatives, and five Socialist Assemblymen were denied their places in the New York State Legislature.[2]

This terrorist attack, accompanied by rulings of the Department of Labor that foreign-born members of the Communist movement were deportable as such, deprived the two Communist Parties of their basic rights of free speech and free assembly. It forced them to close their national headquarters and to take other elementary steps to protect their members, branches, press, and leading committees from arbitrary raids and terrorist victimization. That is, faced by illegal attacks designed to outlaw the Communist movement and to drive it underground, the two Parties reacted as various other labor and progressive movements before them had done in American history when facing similar persecution. They adopted protective measures and pursued their legitimate activities as best they could under the circumstances. No constructive political movement will allow itself to be destroyed by police persecution.

The term "underground," in relation to the Parties' position during these years of persecution, was greatly exaggerated and distorted in the press. The fact was, however, that A. Mitchell Palmer, J. Edgar Hoover, and the others carrying out the offensive against the Communists did not succeed in stopping completely the open and public activities of the Communist movement, which persisted in spite of the government's ef-

1 Senator T. J. Walsh in *Congressional Record*, 67th Congress, Fourth Session, p. 3005.
2 Robert W. Dunn, ed., *The Palmer Raids*, N. Y. 1948.

forts to drive it underground. Despite violence, threats of violence, vigilante action, and similar illegal policies, either practiced directly or condoned by the authorities, the Parties openly published various journals, such as *The Toiler* of the U.C.P. and *Der Kampf*, the first Jewish Communist paper in the United States. Books and pamphlets were also sold openly, and the "language federations," for the most part, managed to operate their "homes" and keep their papers going. The Workers Council also functioned openly and published its paper.

The term "illegal," as applied to the status of the two Parties during this period, was a misnomer. In reality, the advocacy of the Parties' programs and the practice of their general activities were legal, in that they were entirely within the Constitution, but because of the prevailing violent and illegal suppression the Party was unable to exercise these democratic rights openly. Proof of the correctness of this analysis was to be seen in the fact that once the Palmer terror was over and the Communist Parties had succeeded in practice in establishing their democratic rights, the legal status of the Communist Party was not challenged by the national government for 25 years; that is, until a new governmental terrorism was launched as an integral part of Wall Street's present drive to master the world.

During the following months the Communist Parties, both of which had moved to New York, were busily occupied reorganizing themselves—their branches, papers, and leading committees—in accordance with the new situation. When, later on, in their 1920 conventions the parties took stock of their membership, they found that they had held together only about 10,000 out of the approximately 60,000, who had earlier flocked to the standard of the left wing. The Palmer raids had seriously weakened the parties' numerical strength, but had by no means broken their backs. They were now reduced to the hard core of resolute Communist fighters. Their reduction in size after the government's ruthless onslaught was not surprising. During the terror following the 1905 Revolution in Russia, for example, the Bolshevik Party was greatly reduced in numbers. Similar shrinking in size, but not in revolutionary spirit, was later to be observed of the Communist Party of China under Chiang Kai-shek's terror, and also of the parties in many European countries under the ruthless fascist regimes. The 50,000 or so of erstwhile members who dropped out of the Communist parties in the United States under the Palmer terror generally became non-member supporters and sympathizers of the Party.

FORMATION OF THE UNITED COMMUNIST PARTY

Obviously, Party unity in the United States was a burning necessity. The leaders of the Communist Labor Party, from the time of the conventions, pressed for a consolidation of the two parties; but the federation leaders in the Communist Party were reluctant. Their unity proposition to the C.L.P. was, in substance, that the latter should join up with the C.P. as individuals and locals. "Unity with the C.L.P. as a party of centrists," said they, "was impossible."[1] The federation leaders raised two definite issues, which stood in the way of unity. First, they charged that the C.L.P. leaders were opportunists, holding that their own members, mostly foreign-born, were imbued with a more revolutionary spirit than the predominantly American-born C.L.P. membership. Second, they feared that the C.L.P. leaders, underestimating the role of the foreign-born generally in the class struggle, would destroy the "language federations," not realizing what a powerful means these were for organizing the foreign-born workers of the respective national groups, most of whom at that time did not speak English. A further general bar to unity was the fact that, since they were in the process of grasping the great body of Marxist-Leninist thought, there was a tendency in both parties to magnify the importance of every detail of difference, to dispute over minor points with rigidity, and to apply Marxism-Leninism to the United States in a blueprint fashion, rather than upon the basis of actual American conditions. This sectarian attitude led to secondary splits in the parties during this formative period.

Notwithstanding these differences the two parties, early in 1920, began unity negotiations.[2] Ruthenberg, executive secretary of the C.P., was an ardent advocate of Party unity in that body. Despite these efforts, the unity proceedings dragged on without any results, with each side voting down the proposals of the other. Finally, the C.P. itself split over the unity question, with a large section of that organization, led by Ruthenberg, joining up with the C.L.P. Segments broke off from several of the federations, and the bulk of the Jewish Federation, led by Alexander Bittelman, disaffiliated from the C.P. and joined the C.L.P. A unity convention was held at Bridgman, Michigan, in May 1920. As a result, the United Communist Party of America was born. Ruthenberg was elected executive secretary, and the new Central Executive Committee was made up of five members from the C.P. and five from the C.L.P.

The U.C.P. made no important changes in political policy from that

1 *The Communist*, Aug. 1, 1920.
2 *Communist Labor* (official organ of the C.L.P.), May 15, 1920.

of the C.L.P. and C.P. The big question at issue in the convention was the role of the federations. The C.P. was practically a "federation of federations"; these bodies had a high degree of autonomy, holding their own conventions, electing their officials, and having the power (used upon occasion), if they saw fit, to withdraw from the Party. The U.C.P., on the other hand, was opposed to this loose system. While authorizing federations, the U.C.P. declared that these would hold national conferences, not conventions, and that their decisions, activities, officials, and journals were all to be under the direct control of the Central Executive Committee. The basic Party unit was set by the convention at not more than ten or less than five members.

The C.P., in turn, held its convention of 34 delegates (also "underground") in July 1920, in New York City. There was much bitterness over the recent "unity" proceedings, which had split the C.P., and the new U.C.P. was dubbed the "United Centrist Party." No important programmatic changes were made by the C.P. Incorrectly, however, the U.C.P. was accused of giving undue prominence to the Negro question in its convention by considering it as a separate item. Reports to the C.P. convention showed that whereas the total dues payments of the C.P. for the last three months of 1919 averaged 23,744 per month, the number was down to 5,584 for the first four months of 1920. The estimated membership at convention time was 8,500. It was reported that 18 percent of the membership had been lost to the U.C.P. in the "unity" proceedings. Charles Dirba was elected executive secretary of the C.P.

THE ROLE OF THE COMMUNIST INTERNATIONAL

Founded in March 1919, the Comintern, by the time of its second congress in July 1920,[1] was actively functioning. Henceforth, during the next twenty years, the American Communist movement was to have the invaluable advantage of the advice and experience of the Marxist-Leninists of the world in the development of Communist policy in the United States. This was of great importance because the American left had been practically isolated from the left wing in other countries since the death of Engels in 1895.

The Communist International, made up in its congresses and leading committees of worker delegates from all over the world, was a highly democratic organization—far more so, in fact, than the Second International had ever been. No decisions were arrived at without the most thorough discussions with the delegations directly concerned. Charges by Social-Democrats and other capitalist agents that the Comintern issued

[1] John Reed, a delegate, died shortly after this congress, on October 11th, in Moscow.

FORMATION OF THE COMMUNIST PARTY 179

arbitrary orders and directives to its affiliates were only so many examples of the current anti-Communist slander campaign. Stalin, years ago, answered this calumny: "The assumption that the American Communists work under orders from Moscow is absolutely untrue. There are no Communists in the world who would agree to work 'under orders' from outside against their own convictions and will and contrary to the requirements of the situation. Even if there were such Communists they would not be worth a cent."[1] The Comintern was a disciplined organization, and international capitalism dreaded its decisive action; but its Leninist discipline was based upon a profound democracy throughout its entire structure.

Enemies of communism also made many fantastic charges about the Comintern sending its "agents" to various countries, including the United States. These delegates were painted in an especially sinister fashion. In reality, however, with respect to its representatives traveling to various countries, the Comintern functioned much like any other international labor body. Such representatives, members of brother Communist parties, simply undertook to give the parties concerned the benefit of their own particular experience in the light of the general policies and decisions of the Comintern.

Stupid and baseless also was the charge that the existence of the Communist International (and now of the respective Communist parties, since the Comintern was liquidated) constituted interference by the Soviet Union in the internal affairs of other countries. The Comintern was a movement, based on the Communist parties of all the major countries in the world and growing out of the Socialist movement, which had been developing for at least 75 years before the U.S.S.R. was born.

Among its many general decisions, the second congress of the Comintern, in July 1920, formulated three of special importance. These were the well-known "21 points," the colonial resolution, and the development of the policies laid down in Lenin's famous pamphlet, *"Left-Wing" Communism, an Infantile Disorder.*

The "21 points" laid down the working principles of the Communist movement, both on a national and international scale, in the intense revolutionary situation then existing. The points provided for a revolutionary Party--in regard to its membership, leadership, policy, press, and discipline. Their primary purpose was to establish what a Communist Party should be in order to lead the masses in the revolutionary struggle then rapidly developing in Europe. The "points" were guides, not inflexible rules. In the practice of the various Communist parties

[1] Joseph Stalin, *Interview with the First American Trade Union Delegation to Russia*, N. Y., 1927.

they were widely varied. At this time the two American Communist Parties were only in fraternal affiliation with the Comintern, and the Communist movement of the United States, after its eventual unity, never officially endorsed the 21 points.

If the "21 points" were a devastating blow against the right, Lenin's *"Left-Wing" Communism, an Infantile Disorder* was no less sharp an attack against the "ultra-left." It was a slashing assault upon sectarianism among Communists, in all its forms. In this great booklet Lenin especially demolished the illusion of dual Socialist unionism, using among other illustrations the experience in this matter in the United States. Lenin also cracked down on such virulent forms of "leftism" as non-participation in bourgeois parliaments, refusal to fight for partial demands, failure to develop fighting alliances with labor's small farmer and other allies, tendencies to try to apply the Russian experience mechanically in other countries, and the like.

The colonial resolution, written by Lenin, was of major importance. It explained the relations between the struggle of the working class in the imperialist countries and those of the colonial peoples fighting for national independence. It clearly forecast the immense revolutionary struggles now shaking the whole colonial world.

PARTY UNITY ACHIEVED

Despite the failure of the U.C.P. convention of May 1920 to establish Party unity, strong rank-and-file pressure continued in that direction. The U.C.P. leadership also redoubled its unity agitation. A Communist Unity Committee, headed by Alexander Bittelman, member of the U.C.P., criticized the leadership of both parties and insisted upon immediate Party unification. Moreover, the Comintern lent its influence. The C.P. federation leaders yielded under the strong unity urge in the Party.

Consequently, unity negotiations were begun shortly after the first U.C.P. convention, but they dragged along slowly, deadlocks occurring over the matter of representation at the proposed unity convention. The C.P. also insisted upon autonomy for the federations, asserting besides that the U.C.P. was "not sufficiently revolutionary." The separate conventions of the U.C.P. in January, and of the C.P. in February 1921 (both held without any open publicity) gave new strength to the movement for unity. Finally, after much negotiation, the general convention to unify the C.P. and U.C.P. took place in May, at Woodstock, New York.[1]

[1] For convention proceedings, see the July 1921 issue of *The Communist*.

FORMATION OF THE COMMUNIST PARTY

Each Party was represented by 30 delegates. The convention lasted for two weeks. The U.C.P. reported 5,700 members, organized into 667 groups, and 35 publications. The C.P. reported a dues-paying membership of 6,328 and 19 newspapers. Each Party stated that it had issued some two million copies of leaflets during the past few months.

The debates at the convention, although heated, brought forth no important political differences between the two groups. The main discussions turned around questions of tactics, especially on how to break the parties' isolation and how to apply the principles of Marxism-Leninism in the sharp class struggles then going on. On this question the influence of Lenin's writings, particularly his *"Left-Wing" Communism, an Infantile Disorder,* was in evidence. The most important change in policy adopted by the convention was the abandonment of the historic left-wing policy of dual unionism. In this respect, the convention declared that "The policy of the I.W.W. and similar organizations of artificially creating new industrial unions has been shown by experience to be mistaken." And "The Communist Party condemns the policy of the revolutionary elements leaving the existing unions."

This stand against dual unionism constituted a heavy blow against sectarianism. But the Party was not yet prepared to draw the full implications from its new tactical line, particularly as expressed in Lenin's pamphlet against leftism. While endorsing the principle of partial demands, it developed no program of such demands. The Party also, in its Unity Convention, while speaking for co-operation with the exploited rural masses, worked out no practical united front policies for so doing. Nor was it, as yet, prepared to endorse the labor party movement. And as for the Negro question, little or no progress was made on this. The matter was not included in the Party's program, but was referred to the manifesto. Despite these many shortcomings, however, the convention's proceedings, above all in the abandonment of dual unionism, went far toward the elaboration of a sound Marxist-Leninist mass policy for the United States.

A serious dispute at the U.C.P.-C.P. Unity Convention took place over Party structure. The role of the federations was the principal bone of contention. Finally, a compromise was arrived at which held the federations under general Party control, while allowing them considerable autonomy. Henceforth, the federations would hold conferences, not conventions; they would be subject to general supervision of the Central Executive Committee; and their members would have to pay their dues directly to the Party. The fused organization was called the Communist Party of America, and its headquarters was established in New York. Ruthenberg was elected executive secretary. The Central Executive Committee, instead of the proposed nine members, had to be enlarged to ten—five from each constituent party.

It was a joyous delegation that completed the arduous work of this long and decisive convention. Amid the general enthusiasm of the convention, "Party lines melted away. Comrades, who had been separated for years, embraced each other; hands clasped hands; the delegates sang the International with as much energy as could be mustered after the trying 48-hour continuous sessions."[1]

CONCENTRATING THE COMMUNIST FORCES

Meanwhile, as the former left wing of the Socialist Party, now crystallized into the Communist Party, went ahead unifying itself and developing an American Marxist-Leninist program, it was also absorbing strength from other militant currents. First, there was the I.W.W. From the outset, the Communists exerted great effort to win over members of this fighting organization. In January 1920, the Comintern addressed a special letter to the I.W.W., polemizing against its syndicalist illusions and offering it "the hand of brotherhood." Many of its outstanding leaders turned to the Party, including William D. Haywood, George Hardy, Art Shields, and Roy Brown. Elizabeth Gurley Flynn, who joined the Party some years later, also came from the I.W.W. Haywood declared, "As soon as the consolidation of the Communist Party in the United States was effected, I became a member."[2] He died in Moscow in 1928, where, a sick man, he had gone to avoid a 20-year prison sentence for his anti-war stand.

In 1920 the I.W.W. General Executive Board formally endorsed the Communist International. However, because most of the I.W.W. leaders were nevertheless opposed to communism, they finally succeeded in driving a wedge between the I.W.W. and the Communist Party. In the spring of 1921 the I.W.W. sent a delegate to the first congress of the Red International of Labor Unions in Moscow. But upon receiving an unfavorable (highly biased) report from its delegate, George Williams, on what had happened there, the I.W.W. decided not to affiliate to the new labor international. Like a number of other syndicalist organizations in Europe and Latin America, the I.W.W. oriented toward the so-called Berlin syndicalist international, which was being organized at the time. Despite the I.W.W.'s strong syndicalist trend, however, considerable numbers of its members became Communists. Gambs says, "Possibly

1 *The Communist*, July 1921.
2 J. G. Gambs, *The Decline of the I.W.W.*, p. 75, Denver, Colo., 1932.

the I.W.W. have lost as many as 2,000 members to the Communist Party."[1]

The Socialist Labor Party furnished but few members to the Communist Party—Boris Reinstein, Caleb Harrison, and some others. The S.L.P., immersed in the sectarian dogmas of De Leon, was totally unable to understand the Russian Revolution and its profound implications for the world labor movement. It condemned the Revolution as "premature" and ridiculed the C.I. as "only a circus stunt."[2] The S.L.P. soon degenerated into a frenzied redbaiting and Soviet-hating sect.

An important development of this period, signalizing the beginning of one of the—eventually—most important of all the membership sources of the Communist Party, was the growth of the Communist movement among the Negroes, in New York. This took place chiefly around the journal, *The Messenger*. This paper, of which we shall have more to say in a later chapter, was established in 1917 by a group of Negro intellectuals and trade unionists, including A. Philip Randolph, Chandler Owen, Richard B. Moore, and Cyril Briggs.

The Messenger, which had the backing of many Socialist-led trade unions, followed an essentially left line. It opposed the war, supported the Russian Revolution, and was in favor of an active fighting policy for labor and the Negro people. During the period of the S.P. 1919 split, the editorial board of *The Messenger* was divided, the lefts, Briggs and Moore, resigning. Randolph, hanging onto the paper, transformed it into a typical right-wing Socialist journal. Eventually, in 1925, it became the official organ of the newly-organized Brotherhood of Sleeping Car Porters. Out of *The Messenger* group came several pioneer Communists.

The youth were also a source of strength for the gathering Communist forces. The profound events which had resulted in the split in the Socialist Party and the organization of the Communist Party naturally had its repercussions among the Socialist young people. The S.P., in April 1913, after several years of preliminary work of the Intercollegiate Socialist Society, had constituted the Young People's Socialist League. The Y.P.S.L. in 1916 consisted of 150 clubs and 4,000 members. It published *The Young Socialist* and carried on educational and social work.[3] During the war the organization, leftward-inclined, held many anti-war meetings and made much agitation against conscription.

The treacherous attitude of the Social-Democratic leaders of the Second International, toward the Russian Revolution and the war, pro-

[1] Gambs, *The Decline of the I.W.W.*, p. 89.
[2] *The S.L.P. and the Third International*, N. Y., 1926.
[3] Trachtenberg, ed., *American Labor Year Book*, 1916.

duced profound repercussions in the Y.P.S.L., as in other sections of the American Socialist movement. At the Y.P.S.L.'s first national convention, held in May 1919, this left spirit in the organization found expression. The convention passed resolutions condemning the Second International and supporting the Third International. In December 1919, after the Socialist Party had split in September, the Y.P.S.L. held a special convention, in response to left-wing demands. It thus set itself up as an independent organization, declaring for the Young Socialist International, which was then in the process of transforming itself into the Young Communist International. When the Palmer raids against the labor and Communist movement took place, the independent Y.P.S.L. disintegrated as a national organization, although some of its sections remained in existence. Wm. F. Kruse, the head of the Y.P.S.L., joined the Workers Party at its formation in December 1921, and many former Y.P.S.L. members also took part in forming the Young Communist League. The Y.C.L. came into existence, at a convention in April 1922, in "underground" conditions. The Young Workers League was organized in May 1922,[1] out of the numerous youth groups then existing. Among its leaders were Harry Gannes and John Williamson.

In the breakdown of the Socialist Party and the formation of the Communist Party in 1919, women Socialist fighters also played an important role. Most of them went over to the new party, or became active sympathizers. At the founding convention of the C.P. and C.L.P., there were several women delegates. Among the most outstanding of the pioneer women Communists may be mentioned Ella Reeve Bloor, Anita Whitney, Margaret Prevey, Kate Sadler Greenhalgh, Rose Pastor Stokes, Hortense Allison, Sadie Van Veen, Jeannette Pearl, Rose Wortis, Margaret Krumbein, Rose Baron, Becky Buhay, Dora Lifshitz, Clara Bodian.

Another important source of recruits for the Communist Party was the Trade Union Educational League. The T.U.E.L., the successor to the old Syndicalist League and International Trade Union Educational League, was founded in Chicago, in November 1920. After the loss of the big national steel strike, the group of Chicago militants who were behind that movement more than ever felt the need to organize the "militant minority" in the trade unions. The organization also included trade unionists in Canada.

The T.U.E.L. was not so definitely syndicalist as its predecessors, the S.L.N.A. and I.T.U.E.L., had been. Its members and leaders were decisively influenced by the lessons of the great Russian Revolution and by the writings of Lenin. The Chicago syndicalist group was a revolt

[1] Helen Allison and Carl Winter, unpublished manuscript.

not only against Gompersism in trade unionism, but also against the right opportunism of the Socialist Party; hence the works of Lenin had a tremendous impact upon it, even as upon all other sections of militant workers. The group's anti-politicalism was breaking down, and it had played an important part in the labor party movement which centered nationally in Chicago. It was rapidly moving toward Marxism-Leninism. In 1920 the chief remaining barrier between the T.U.E.L. militants and the Communist Party was their difference over the trade union question, the T.U.E.L. being unshakably opposed to dual unionism, which the Communists still supported. This obstacle, however, was removed when Lenin's pamphlet, *"Left-Wing" Communism, an Infantile Disorder*, appeared in the United States in January 1921. From then on dual unionism was finished as Communist policy. William Z. Foster, the head of the T.U.E.L., whose thinking had been revolutionized by Lenin, was invited to come to Moscow for the first congress of the Red International of Labor Unions, held on July 3, 1921. There the R.I.L.U. definitely repudiated dual unionism. In the summer of 1921 Foster and other T.U.E.L. militants joined the Party. This brought in a considerable group of active and experienced trade unionists, among them Jack Johnstone, Jay Fox, Joseph Manley, David Coutts, Sam Hammersmark, and many others. The T.U.E.L., however, remained an independent, broad united front organization, made up of left-wingers and progressives generally.

13. The Workers Party (1921)

The years immediately following World War I were years of virulent capitalist reaction. We shall deal with this offensive of capital more fully in the next chapter. During this period the United States went through many hard-fought strikes, numerous "race riots," and labor frame-up cases. The labor movement was fighting for its very existence. The severe economic crisis of 1920-21 sharpened the class struggle. This was the time when the Ku Klux Klan, flourishing as never before, claimed to have five million members. In order to play an important part in the current big class struggles, it was necessary that the Communist Party should carry on public activities in all kinds of tasks so far as possible under the existing circumstances. The fusing together of the two "underground" Communist Parties at the May 1921 convention was a long stride in this general direction.

But to get the Party fully into the open was no small problem. In fact, it was a unique task, which was to take nearly two years to accomplish. The basic difficulty, of course, was to develop the mass work of the Party in the face of the reactionary capitalist offensive then going on. There was little known Communist experience to serve as a guide in this specific situation. Of course, there were cases of Communist parties which, forced underground by capitalist terrorism, had emerged into legality during periods of revolutionary upheaval. Striking examples of this were given by the Bolsheviks during the 1905 and March 1917 revolutions in Russia, and also by the parties in the Balkans after World War I. There were similar experiences later in many European countries upon the defeat of Hitler and the revolutionary upsurge of the working class in the aftermath of World War II. But few, if any, examples were to be found then of Communist parties that had legalized themselves during periods of sharp reaction, such as existed in the United States.

Besides these objective difficulties to the Party's assuming a fully open status in the face of the current capitalist reaction, there were also subjective reasons making this task even more difficult. That is, the sectarianism still prevailing in the Party—the tendency to stand apart from the daily struggles of the masses and to deal only with Socialist agitation, under the pressure of the force and violence of the authorities—led to the tacit acceptance of "underground" conditions, to the idea that of necessity a Communist Party had to be illegal in a capitalist country. Such false conceptions were strengthened by the fact that the left-wing non-citizen immigrant workers were victimized by arbitrary deportation and needed all possible protection from ruthless reaction.

THE AMERICAN LABOR ALLIANCE

The Communist Party, as the basic champion of democracy, always strives to carry on its activities in the greatest possible publicity, in order most effectively to reach the masses with its message. This was the fundamental orientation of the C.P.U.S.A. during this difficult formative period. The Party, as best it could, moved toward winning for itself the prevailing popular democratic rights of free speech and free assembly, in spite of all the barbarous persecution to which it was subjected. And it eventually succeeded in this endeavor.

Nevertheless the opportunities for mass Communist work were being neglected because of sectarian moods in the Party. The May 1921 C.P. convention correctly declared, "Far greater and much more effective use of legal channels can and must be made. Our legal activities, always under the control of the Central Executive Committee of the C.P., should be amplified and intensified."[1] In line with this decision, the Workers League was set up in New York City, and it ran candidates in the Fall elections of 1921. Attempts by the local election board to disqualify these candidates on the grounds that they were either in jail or indicted were defeated. The Party also began to take an active part openly in various current local political struggles.

The Party's first organizational step toward a fully open status, however, was taken with the establishment of the American Labor Alliance. This body was set up, rather tentatively to begin with, at an open convention in New York City, in July 1921. There were 15 organizations present, including the Irish American Labor League, National Defense Committee, Finnish Socialist Federation, Associated Toiler Clubs, American Freedom Foundation, Ukrainian Workers Clubs, Independent Socialist League, Marxian Educational League, Hungarian Workers Federation. The A.L.A. convention elected Elmer L. Allison as secretary and established headquarters at 201 West 13th Street.

The Alliance declared that its aim was to "unify, through a central body the great mass of discontented 'left' political and economic forces

[1] Proceedings of the Convention of the Communist Party in *The Communist,* July 1921.

of the country and rally them about a common aim."¹ Later, and more specifically, the A.L.A. stated that it "is of the opinion that the time is ripe for the organization of the class conscious workers of America into a new revolutionary Party and it announces that in the near future it will call a national conference to form such a Party."² To this general end, one of the essential moves of the A.L.A. was to come to an agreement with the Workers Council.

THE WORKERS COUNCIL

After the big split in the Socialist Party in 1919, which led to the formation of the two Communist parties, there remained a number of opposition elements within the S.P. who were still nursing the hope of using that organization as the working class Party. This tendency was led by J. Louis Engdahl, Alexander Trachtenberg, William Kruse, Margaret B. Prevey, and M. Olgin. Numerous centrists also went along, including Salutsky, and others. The lefts in this group made the serious error of not leaving the S.P. with their following immediately upon the formation of the Communist Party in 1919.

At the Chicago S.P. convention, in September 1919, this group was responsible for the passage of a resolution making a qualified (originally unqualified) application for affiliation to the Comintern. The latter sharply rejected this, stating that "The Socialist Party of the United States is not a working class Party, but an auxiliary of the American bourgeoisie, of American imperialism."³ At the New York convention of the S.P., in May 1920, the Engdahl-Trachtenberg group was again defeated, although Trachtenberg, candidate for international secretary against Hillquit, received one-third of all votes cast. This group supported the nomination of Debs, then in jail, by the convention—Victor Berger, who favored Hoan, declaring that no American would vote for a man in jail. At that convention, the group functioned as the "Committee for the Third International," which it had previously organized to carry on propaganda within the S.P. They also formed, in May 1921, the Workers Council, which was a functioning political organization, claiming the support of the Jewish, Finnish, and Czech federations, the German Workers Educational Society, and a part of the Italian Federation. It also received the support of groups of English-speaking members throughout the country who still belonged to the Socialist Party and who were in favor of affiliation with the C.I. In June 1921, the S.P. held its convention in

1 *The Toiler*, N. Y., Aug. 6, 1921.
2 *The Voice of Labor*, Chicago, Sept. 30, 1921.
3 *The Communist* (U.C.P.), No. 10, 1920.

Detroit. The convention declared against the Communist International, against the dictatorship of the proletariat, and against mass action.

Whereupon, the Workers Council group belatedly quit the Socialist Party. In an article in their official journal, entitled "Farewell to the Socialist Party," they declared, "The Committee for the Third International sees no further reason for staying in the Socialist Party. It believes that the Socialist Party has completely and beyond recovery outlived its usefulness as an agency for propaganda and as an instrument for the realization of socialism."[1]

During this period the S.P. suffered a series of losses, in addition to the withdrawal of the Workers Council. Most important, the Finnish Federation, with several thousand members, seceded on December 20, 1920; the Jewish Federation followed suit in September 1921; and one week prior to this the Bohemian Federation had voted by ten to one to withdraw from the Socialist Party.[2] From 1920 to 1922, the S.P. declined from 27,000 to 11,000 members.

The wholesale splittings from the Socialist Party in 1919-21 left Debs almost the sole prominent "left" still within the Party. He cut a tragic figure, this one-time battler for the left who had been such a brilliant propagandist for socialism but who was now unable to follow the path toward socialism. When the big Communist split was developing early in 1919, Debs kept silent, making no statements as to his position in the basic conflict within the Party. Evidently, however, while supporting the Russian Revolution, he did not understand the dictatorship of the proletariat because of his bourgeois-democratic prejudices, nor could he realize that his old co-workers in the leadership of the S.P. were in actuality enemies of socialism. He was in jail when the 1919 split took place. D. Karsner, who visited Debs at his home and at the Atlanta penitentiary, states that the latter said to him, "I do not see any difference between the Workers Party and the Socialist Party," and he proposed a fusion of the two parties. Debs is also reputed to have told Karsner, "I have arrived at the definite conclusion that my place in the future as in the past is in the Socialist Party."[3] Whatever he may have said to Karsner, the fact is that Debs remained in the bankrupt Socialist Party until he died on October 20, 1926.

FORMATION OF THE WORKERS PARTY

The American Labor Alliance, with the active support of the Com-

---

1 *The Workers Council*, Sept. 25, 1921.
2 *American Labor Year Book*, 1922-23, p. 406.
3 David Karsner, *Talks with Debs in Terre Haute*, pp. 28-33, N. Y., 1922.

munist Party, began, in August 1921, to charter locals for a new organization. At the same time the Workers Council, which supported the plan for such a party, also began organizational work to the same end. On October 15th, the Workers Council issued a call for a conference to consider the possibilities of forming the new Party. In consequence, the American Labor Alliance and the Workers Council, after considerable negotiation, got together and issued a joint call to establish a new Party.[1]

The call was endorsed by the following organizations: American Labor Alliance, and its affiliated bodies, the Finnish Socialist Federation, Hungarian Workers Federation, Italian Workers Federation, and the Jewish Workers Federation, the Workers Council of America, Jewish Socialist Federation, and Workers Educational Association (German). The call was signed by Elmer L. Allison, for the Workers Party Convention Committee.

Accompanying the convention call was a statement of principles, which the participating organizations were required to approve. It read:

"1. *The Workers' Republic*: To lead the working masses in the struggle for the abolition of capitalism through the establishment of a government by the working class—a Workers' Republic in America.

"2. *Political Action*: To participate in all political activities, including electoral campaigns, in order to utilize them for the purpose of carrying our message to the masses. The elected representatives of the Workers Party will unmask the fraudulent capitalist democracy and help mobilize the workers for the final struggle against their common enemy.

"3. *The Labor Unions*: To develop labor organizations into organs of militant struggle against capitalism, expose the reactionary labor bureaucrats, and educate the workers to militant unionism.

"4. *A Fighting Party*: It shall be a party of militant, class conscious workers, bound by discipline and organized on the basis of democratic centralism, with full power in the hands of the Central Executive Committee between conventions. The Central Executive Committee of the Party shall have control over all activities of public officials. It shall also co-ordinate and direct the work of the Party members in the trade unions.

"5. *Party Press*: The Party's press shall be owned by the Party, and all its activities shall be under the control of the Central Executive Committee."

The convention for the new Party was convened at the Labor Temple on East 84th Street, New York, December 23-26, 1921. There were 150 delegates from all over the country. Among the most important organizations represented, with power to affiliate, were, in addition to the Ameri-

[1] *The Workers Council*, Dec. 15, 1921.

can Labor Alliance and the Workers Council proper, the Russian, Finnish, South Slavic, Ukrainian, Irish, German, Greek, Jewish, Italian, Esthonian, Spanish, Armenian, Lettish, Scandinavian, and Hungarian federations and sections. There were also fraternal delegates from such organizations, among others, as the Proletarian Party, Left Poalei Tsion, Young Workers League, and the African Blood Brotherhood. The convention acted for a combined membership of some 20,000 in the fully accredited organizations, which issued nine daily and 21 weekly publications.

The convention was opened by J. Louis Engdahl, who in a short address greeted the delegates and dealt with the historic significance of the gathering as "opening a new epoch in the struggle of the American working class." He welcomed the delegates from the various groupings, "who for many years had been traveling different roads and had finally come together and found common ground in the joint effort to build a real revolutionary Party in America."

The three days of discussion that followed revealed substantial agreement on all major questions of principles and tactics. The only important differences were those raised by the three fraternal delegates from the Proletarian Party. They criticized the whole project of the convention from a narrow "leftist" sectarian viewpoint, claiming that their own tiny organization would suffice as the party of the working class. The Proletarian Party later refused to affiliate with the new Party.

The new organization was named the Workers Party of America. Plans were made for the early publication of an official organ, *The Worker*. A Central Executive Committee of 17 members was elected; Ruthenberg was chosen secretary, but since he was in jail, Caleb Harrison, appointed assistant secretary, was named to serve as acting secretary. New York City was designated as the seat of the national headquarters.[1]

THE WORKERS PARTY PROGRAM

The Workers Party convention of 1921 constituted a very important stage in the history of the developing Communist Party of the United States. It established the long-sought unity of practically all the Communist forces in the country, and it also marked the conclusion of the founding phase of the Communist Party. It ended the period of almost exclusively Socialist propaganda and initiated the new Party into the beginnings of mass work. It dealt a number of blows at the traditional sectarianism of the left wing by working out an elementary program of

[1] For convention proceedings, see *The Toiler*, Jan. 14, 1921, and *American Labor Year Book*, 1923-24, p. 159.

immediate demands. It marked, especially, an important step in the open work of the Party. In short, the convention registered real progress in the adaptation of Marxism-Leninism to the specific conditions of the class struggle in the United States. Enemies of the Party, such as James Oneal, have tried to interpret the founding of the Workers Party and the adoption of its specific program as an abandonment of the Leninist line of the Communists. But this was nonsense. The whole development represented the normal growth of the Party in its historic task of combining Socialist propaganda with a militant struggle for the everyday needs of the workers and the masses of the people.

The W.P. program, for the first time in a generation of left-wing history, contained what might properly be termed both a maximum and a minimum program. It did not confine itself simply to outlining the basic program of communism. The main principles of the organization were stated in the document that accompanied the call for the convention. These (see page 190) expressed in simple terms the general Socialist aims of the Party without, however, defining in detail the general perspectives and strategy of the Party, which had so much occupied the attention of previous Communist conventions.

In this respect, the program declared, "The Workers Party will courageously defend the workers and wage an aggressive struggle for the abolition of capitalism." The convention also gave a ringing endorsement to the Russian Revolution, which had ushered in a new period, "the era of Workers Republics," and it demanded recognition of the Soviet government by the United States. After making a concrete analysis of the world setting in which the United States found itself and of the general position of American imperialism, the program proceeded to outline a course of practical mass struggle.

The trade union question occupied nearly half the space in the program. After dealing with the shameful desertion of the workers by their Social-Democratic leaders in the current bosses' offensive, the program called upon all workers to join the union of their trade, to form minority groups of left-wing workers within the unions, to work for fighting programs in the organizations, and to depose the reactionary union leadership. The program condemned dual unionism and all ideas of destroying the old craft unions. It supported the amalgamation of the trade unions into industrial organizations.

On the Negro question much progress was registered over the past neglect of this vital matter. Under the head of "The Race Problem," the program, beginning with an analysis of the history of Negro oppression in the South, went on to say that "The Workers Party will support the

Negroes in their struggle for liberation, and will help them in their fight for economic, political, and social equality. It will point out to them that the interests of the Negro workers are identical with those of the white. It will seek to end the policy of discrimination followed by organized labor. Its task will be to destroy altogether the barrier of race discrimination that has been used to keep apart the black and white workers, and weld them into a solid union of revolutionary forces for the overthrow of their common enemy." While falling short of an understanding of the Negro question as a national question, this was the most advanced resolution on the matter ever adopted by any Marxist party in the United States up to that time.

The resolution on the youth provided that "The C.E.C. [Central Executive Committee] of the W.P. appoint a provisional national organization committee to amalgamate all existing militant young workers' organizations, to create new ones wherever possible, and to carry on all work preparatory to the calling of a national convention which will unite these forces and officially launch the Young Workers League of America." Pursuant to this resolution, a conference was held a couple of months later and the proposed league was established.

A further resolution declared that "The Workers Party recognizes the necessity for an intensified struggle to improve women's conditions and to unify them in the common struggle with the rest of the working class against capitalism." It was to take the initiative in organizing and leading them in struggle. The convention pledged its support to the workers in agriculture. It also denounced the frame-ups against Mooney and Billings, and Sacco and Vanzetti, and it called upon the workers to fight for their freedom. Debs had been freed by President Harding, under strong mass pressure, and to him the convention said: "We greet with joy your homecoming [from prison] and fervently hope that you will soon again be fighting in the ranks of the American working class in their struggle for emancipation."

On the question of parliamentary action the program, while pledging participation in elections and in the general political life of the country, still displayed heavy indications of the traditional "left" sectarianism by considering parliamentary action exclusively as a means of exposing capitalism and of conducting Socialist agitation. The partial demands worked out for the elections and for other phases of the workers' struggles were altogether inadequate and in no sense presented a rounded-out program for the day-to-day struggle. The Party, as yet, also took no steps toward participation in that broad mass political activity of the American working class, the labor party.

THE PARTY ASSERTS ITS DEMOCRATIC RIGHTS

The establishment of the Workers Party was an important step in winning the democratic rights of the Communist movement after it had been stripped, in its two original sections, of free speech and assembly by the ferocious Palmer raids of January 1920. But this progress was not achieved without a serious split in the Communist Party. Three members of the Central Executive Committee, believers in the theory that, of necessity, the Communist movement had to be "underground" in a country such as the United States, took the position that the very existence of the Workers Party would tend to liquidate the Communist Party both programmatically and organizationally. So they took a flat stand against this policy and developed a factional struggle to support their point of view. All attempts at resolving the differences having failed, the rebellious dissident group was suspended on November 2, 1921.

On February 3, 1922, the ousted group, under the name of the Workers Defense League of New England, issued a call for a national conference, to be held in New York City on February 18th. Here was formed the United Toilers of America, which, with a "leftist" line, was sharply opposed to the newly organized Workers Party. The new Party set up headquarters in New York and issued *The Workers Challenge* as its official organ. The United Toilers had a small following, mostly in the New York area, but it claimed a membership of 5,000. The movement was liquidated at the Bridgman C.P. convention of August 1922, nearly all of its members returning to the Party.

After the formation of the Workers Party in December 1921, the fight to establish in practice the democratic rights of the Communist Party proceeded apace. This question was the central issue at the Party convention in Bridgman, Michigan, in mid-August of 1922. Given the continuing post-war offensive of the employers against the whole labor movement, however, the convention, by a close vote, decided against liquidating the "underground" aspects of the Party. In the existing factional line-up, the majority group, led by Katterfeld and others, were known as the "Goose caucus," and they called the minority group, led by Ruthenberg, the "Liquidators."[1]

As an indication that the government's attempt to outlaw the Party was not yet over—the Party convention was raided on August 22nd by agents of the F.B.I. and the State of Michigan, just as it had concluded its deliberations and was dispersing. Seventeen delegates were arrested with 40 more jailed later on. They were all charged with violating

[1] For programs of the "Goose" and "Liquidator" caucuses, see *The Communist*, July 1922.

the Michigan anti-syndicalist law—concretely, with "unlawful assembly." This was the beginning of a long legal fight (see next chapter) to win for the Party the elementary democratic right of freely presenting its program to the American people.

However, the conditions, marked by the illegal force and violence of the authorities, which had deprived the Party of its democratic rights, were changing. A new turn was developing in the general political situation (as we shall see in ensuing chapters), with the employers' offensive against the working class assuming less violent forms. The opportunity was, therefore, at hand for the Party to reach its desired goal of a completely public existence. Consequently, on April 7, 1923, the Communist Party declared its full consolidation with the Workers Party. Thus, the "underground" period of the Communist Party, forced upon it by the barbarities of the Palmer raids, came to an end after 29 months. At its 1925 convention the Workers Party changed its name to the Workers (Communist) Party and, finally, at its 1930 convention, to the Communist Party of the United States. The winning of its elementary legal rights of free speech and assembly by the Communist Party was an important victory for democracy in the United States.

14. The Communists and the Capitalist Offensive
(1919-1923)

Immediately after their foundation, the young Communist parties had to face a most vicious employers' offensive. American imperialism, as we have remarked, emerged from World War I as the leading world power in a capitalist system which, as the sequel has showed, had received a blow during the war from which it would never recover. It was stricken with an incurable, deepening general world crisis. The United States, now more firmly controlled by monopoly capital, and greatly enriched and centralized as a result of the war, was powerful, arrogant, and reactionary. It took a decisive hand in writing the Versailles imperialist treaty, and then stayed out of the League of Nations in order to preserve its own complete freedom of action. With its successive Dawes and Young plans,[1] the United States largely dominated the economic life of the conquered countries of Europe. It asserted its growing power in the Pacific in the Nine-Power Pact. Under the "Open Door" policy it maneuvered to seize hold of war-torn China. With an active trade and political offensive in Latin America, it strengthened its grip in that great area at the expense of the Latin American peoples and of its weakened imperialist rivals, Great Britain and Germany.

Animated by the reactionary spirit which was soon to produce fascism in Europe, sensing its new position as the leading world capitalist power, and panic-stricken at the revolutionary spirit of the workers in Russia and elsewhere in Europe, Wall Street undertook to cripple the organization of the militant American workers. Consequently, during the first four post-war years there developed the most violent anti-labor drive in American history.

This offensive, aimed at every phase of the labor movement, had as its main objectives to cut the heart out of the trade unions and to destroy the newly-born Communist movement. During the war the workers, despite the treacherous attitude of the top leadership of the A.F. of L. and Railroad Brotherhoods, had won the eight-hour day in many areas of industry and had managed to extend trade unionism into various

[1] Wall Street financial plans ostensibly to save European capitalism.

THE CAPITALIST OFFENSIVE 197

sections of the forbidden open-shop territory, the trustified industries. The most important of these advances were in steel, railroad, mining, marine transport, meat-packing, lumber, and textiles. Therefore, monopoly capital set out to drive the unions from these advanced posts and, if possible, still further back than they had been before the war. The capitalists would demonstrate in practice just how cynical had been their wartime slogan, "Make the world safe for democracy." They would give the workers a real taste of democracy, Wall Street brand.

Big capital in the United States deliberately sought to destroy the trade union movement and to replace it by its own system of the "open," anti-union shop and company unionism. Company unions, first suggested by one J. C. Bayles in 1886, began to grow after 1900.[1] By the end of World War I there were 250 company unions, in the metal trades, on the railroads, and in the trustified industries. Generally, the employers built these company unions as barriers to the spread of the trade unions proper. The post-war plan was to extend this poisonous system as far as possible, thereby rendering the trade union movement virtually powerless. In developing this system of employer-controlled unions, American big business gave the lead to Mussolini and Hitler with their later, fully developed, fascist unions.[2]

Hardly had the war ended when the employers began their drive against the trade unions, but it only got really under way during the great steel strike of September 1919. This offensive was in evidence at the National Industrial Conference of October 1919, called by President Wilson presumably to adjust the stormy industrial situation. At this conference the big industrial dictators not only refused to settle the current steel strike, but they virtually declared war upon all organized labor. "Labor unions are no longer necessary," had said the arrogant Judge Gary, head of U.S. Steel, and the conference acted in this sense. The open shop movement, with its slogan of "the American plan," was soon raging throughout the country. All the big employers' associations —National Association of Manufacturers, United States Chamber of Commerce, and many powerful bodies in the individual industries— were in it, backing the National Open Shop Association. "By the autumn of 1920," say Perlman and Taft, "the country was covered with a network of open shop organizations. In New York State alone at least 50 open shop associations were active."[3] In the Middle West and West the drive was no less malignant than in the industrial East.

[1] *The Workers Monthly*, Sept. 1925.
[2] Robert W. Dunn, *The Americanization of Labor*, p. 127 ff., N. Y., 1927.
[3] Perlman and Taft, *History of Labor in the U.S.*, Vol. 4, p. 491.

THE FIRST BLOW FALLS UPON THE LEFT

The first to feel the blow of the capitalist offensive were the more advanced and militant workers. The employers understood very well then, as they do now, the fighting role of the most class-conscious among the workers, and they always give them the heaviest and earliest blows. The capitalists particularly feared and hated the new Communist movement, which they sensed was the vanguard of the working class. We have already seen how the two young Communist parties were assailed and violently persecuted by the ferocious Palmer raids of 1919 and 1920. And over two years later, in August 1922, the government showed that it was still striving to wipe out the Communists by raiding the national convention of the Communist Party, held in Bridgman, Michigan.

The wartime attack upon the I.W.W. was also continued into the post-war period, with added fury. In Centralia, Washington, on Armistice Day, November 11, 1919, during a parade of the American Legion, a gang of hoodlums attacked the I.W.W. hall and in the ensuing armed battle three Legionnaires were killed. One I.W.W. member was lynched and eight others were sentenced to from 25 to 40 years in jail. This was the signal for violent attacks upon the I.W.W. all over the West. As it turned out, the Communists, with the benefit of world experience at their hand, were able to save their organization during the post-war drive by protective measures, but the I.W.W. was largely cut to pieces. Partly from these attacks and partly from its failure to learn the general political lessons of the Russian Revolution, the I.W.W. from this period on ceased to be a real factor in the labor movement.

THE DRIVE AGAINST THE TRADE UNIONS

During the decade of the war and post-war period the working class had greatly changed. The number of workers engaged in industry was up by 31.6 percent. The sharp dividing line between skilled and unskilled was greatly blurred by the growth of mass production. A considerable Negro proletariat had grown up in the northern industries. And with immigration shut off, the speed of Americanization of the foreign-born workers had been hastened. All this made for a greater homogeneity and solidarity among the workers.

The workers, coming out of the war and harassed by the rapidly rising cost of living, were in a militant mood. Besides having their own immediate grievances, they also reflected to a considerable extent the revolutionary spirit of the workers in Eastern Europe. During 1919, 4,160,348 workers engaged in strikes (the largest number in any one year

THE CAPITALIST OFFENSIVE 199

in previous American history). This worker militancy produced, among many other struggles, the notable general strikes in Seattle (February) and in Winnipeg, Manitoba (August), the Boston police strike (September), the unofficial strike of 200,000 railroad shopmen, and the great coal and steel strikes (September).[1]

These strikes, while bringing certain economic concessions to the workers in each case, were all beaten to a greater or less extent by the aggressive employers, with the help of the government, the police, and the courts. The coal strike was peremptorily outlawed by an injunction issued by Federal Judge Anderson, who forbade the national officers of the U.M.W.A. to do anything that would further the strike. John L. Lewis then called off the strike, making his well-known statement, "I cannot fight the government." The miners continued to fight on, however, and eventually won livable agreements. The big steel strike of 367,000 workers was fought out under terroristic conditions. The whole of the steel areas was overrun with strikebreakers, armed guards, police, deputy sheriffs, and troops. Pickets were arrested on sight, and in the great Monongahela River district outside of Pittsburgh, where 200,000 steel workers were employed, not a single mass meeting of strikers was permitted during the nearly four months of the strike. Finally, the strike was broken and the unions completely smashed. Among the 22 killed in this strike was Mrs. Fannie Sellins, U.M.W.A. organizer in the steel campaign, who was brutally murdered by steel trust gunmen at New Kensington, Pennsylvania.[2]

The strikes of 1920-21 were sharpened by the outbreak of a severe economic crisis. This was caused primarily by difficulties in the changeover from war to peace production and by a heavy falling off of American exports—from $6,516,000,000 in 1920 to $3,771,000,000 in 1921. Industrial production dropped 25 percent, and by October 1921, there were 5,750,000 unemployed. Although profits remained at levels 100 percent higher than in 1913, the employers took advantage of the situation by slashing wages from 25 to 50 percent and by intensifying their assaults upon the trade unions.

The workers did not take these wage cuts unresistingly, and the years 1920-21 were marked by many hard-fought strikes. Notable among them was the "outlaw" switchmen's strike of April 1920, beginning in Chicago, fanning out all over the country, and paralyzing many of the biggest railroads. This spontaneous rank-and-file revolt was led by John Grunau. In West Virginia, during 1920-21, virtual civil war existed in the mining

[1] For a general account of the strikes of this period see Perlman and Taft, *History of Labor in the United States*, Vol. 4, pp. 434-54.
[2] William Z. Foster, *The Great Steel Strike and Its Lessons*, N. Y., 1920.

regions. In May 1921, the Atlantic Coast seamen went out, in the biggest strike in the history of that industry, a strike which was broken by employer violence. During 1921-22, the Typographical Union led a whole series of hard-fought strikes in many localities, and the building trades, notably in Chicago and New York, fought hard struggles against the open shop during 1921. The year ended with the defeat, in December, of 45,000 packinghouse workers in 13 cities, resulting in the nation-wide break-up of the unions in that industry.

The big post-war open-shop drive came to a climax in 1922. This year saw many big strikes, chief of which were those of the New England textile workers, the coal miners, and the railroad shopmen. The textile strike began in January, and it lasted six months, in the face of wholesale use of strikebreakers, court injunctions, and troops by the employers and the government. The workers were largely defeated.

The coal strike, starting on April 1, 1922, involved 600,000 hard and soft coal miners. This strike, as usual with miners' strikes, was marked with extreme violence on the part of the employers' thugs. But in Herrin, Illinois, these gunmen bit off more than they could chew. In June they murdered a couple of strikers there in cold blood, whereupon the miners mobilized, killed 19 gunmen, and drove the rest out of the community. Result, 214 miners were indicted for murder, treason, and conspiracy, but in the strongly union coal country it proved impossible to convict them. The national strike resulted in an agreement which, however, left out the 100,000 unorganized miners who had struck in Western Pennsylvania, a disastrous betrayal by Lewis, as it turned out later.

The strike of the 400,000 railroad shopmen began on July 1, 1922, against repeated wage slashes put through by the Railroad Labor Board. The Harding Administration, which was bringing the country "back to normalcy," announced that it would break the strike by every means necessary. It was helped by the train service unions, which remained at work while the shopmen were striking, and by the Maintenance of Way Union, 350,000 strong, which pulled out of the strike movement on the eve of the strike date. On September first, Attorney General Daugherty secured a federal injunction virtually outlawing the strike. These blows were too much, and on September 13, with the strike practically broken, some 225,000 of the men were signed up in a surrender agreement known as the B. & O. plan—of which more later. About 175,000 went back without any agreements or unions.

All told, some ten million workers were on strike during the four years of intense struggle from 1919 to 1922 inclusive. Organized labor lost much hard-won ground. The unions in the steel, meat-packing, lumber, and maritime industries were almost completely wiped out. Working conditions suffered accordingly. Even such well-established organizations as those in the coal, railroad, printing, building, textile, and clothing industries were deeply injured. As a result, the membership of the A.F. of L. dropped from 4,160,348 in 1920 to 2,926,462 in 1923. It was the most serious defeat ever suffered by the American labor movement.

MISLEADERS OF LABOR

The top leaders of the A.F. of L. and Railroad Brotherhoods—lazy, incompetent, corrupt, and reactionary—were shocked and demoralized by the big offensive from their capitalist friends of wartime. Their policy to meet the offensive was a combination of crass betrayal and cowardly flight. In the midst of the drive, on February 23, 1921, the A.F. of L. Executive Council called a meeting of high officials to consider the critical situation, "to combat the problems arising from unemployment, reaction, and Bolshevism." The conference proposed nothing but a publicity campaign to win popular support. As Lorwin says, it "could offer little tangible aid to the unions. Each international union had to face its own problems."[1]

This was bankruptcy in the face of the aggressive enemy. The leaders of each union tried to save themselves at the expense of the other unions. An orgy of labor betrayal and "union scabbing" took place. In the steel strike the workers were shamelessly abandoned to their fate by the A.F. of L. leaders. In meat-packing the A.F. of L. leaders split the federation that had organized the industry, expelled the Stockyards Labor Council, and alienated the Negro workers. In printing, the Typographical Union fought for its life,[2] all the other unions in the industry continuing at work, trying to profit at the striking union's expense. When the Pressmen struck, on rank-and-file initiative, the ultra-reactionary leader, Berry, cynically replaced them with union scabs. The betrayal of the 100,000 unorganized striking miners in Western Pennsylvania in the settlement of 1922 ultimately became a disaster to the U.M.W.A. During the railroad shopmen's strike, the union scabbing reached its lowest depths. While the shopmen fought desperately against the companies and the government, not only did the Maintenance of Way Union pull out of the movement and make its own terms, but the four strategically situated Operating Brotherhoods remained at work, and worse yet, actually made new agreements at the expense of the striking shopmen. Small wonder, then, that organized labor in general suffered such a big defeat.

[1] Lorwin, *The American Federation of Labor*, p. 204.
[2] *The Labor Herald*, March 1922.

The initiative in the struggle during this crucial period came from the rank and file and the lower officialdom. During the war, with the top leaders tied up with pro-war, no-strike, no-organizing agreements with the government and the employers, the organizing campaigns and strikes had been led by the workers. For example, the big meat-packing and steel campaigns were the work of the workers themselves, against the will of the upper union leadership. After the war, in the face of the employers' offensive, this rank-and-file initiative continued. While the reactionary top leadership ran for cover from the storm, it was the workers themselves who developed the struggle. Their fighting spirit and initiative were especially manifested by the "outlaw" shopmen's strike, "outlaw" switchmen's strike, "outlaw" pressmen's strike, the spontaneous strikes of the unorganized coal miners of Western Pennsylvania, of New England textile workers, and by strikes of various other groups of workers.

THE COMMUNIST PARTY BREAKS ITS ISOLATION

Unfortunately, throughout most of this great struggle there was no organized left wing in the unions to give leadership to the militant workers, betrayed by their high-paid, capitalist-minded officials. The T.U.E.L. was not formed until the end of 1920, and it took a year really to get under way; and the Communist Party was as yet too young and unready to register its latent strength in the struggle. The Party, itself the object of heavy blows from reaction, was fighting to unify itself and to secure its democratic rights to a legal existence.

But the greatest difficulty of all for the young Communist movement in this critical period was that it had not yet hammered out its Marxist-Leninist program. It was still primarily a party of Socialist agitation, with little or no program of partial demands and immediate struggle. The Party was also especially hampered by its long-time policy of dual unionism. Ruthenberg remarked later, "The Communist Party of 1919 stood outside of the labor movement, endeavoring to draw the workers into its ranks through agitation and propaganda which pointed to the necessity of a revolutionary party fighting for the overthrow of capitalism"; and, "The Party in 1919, and during 1920, was isolated from the trade union movement."[1]

During this period the Party (in its two split sections) participated in a number of strike situations—in the 1919 steel strike, in the 1920 coal strike, and others. But in doing so it dealt almost exclusively with revolutionary objectives. In steel, for example, with the city of Gary

[1] *Workers Monthly*, Sept. 1926.

under martial law, the Party declared, "The workers must capture the power of the State. . . . The answer to the Dictatorship of the capitalists is the Dictatorship of the Workers."[1] This was theoretically correct long-range advice, under radically different objective conditions, but with the workers fighting desperately to establish their unions and to abolish the twelve-hour day and the seven-day week within the framework of capitalism, it fell upon deaf ears.

It was not until late in 1921, with the achievement of Party unity and especially with the abandonment of the crippling policy of dual unionism, that the vigorous young Communist movement, now called the Workers Party, began to play a real part in the struggles of the hard-pressed working class. As Ruthenberg said in his above-quoted article, "In 1921 the Party revised its trade union policy and adopted the correct Communist policy of working within the existing trade unions." This shift in policy mainly took the practical form of all-out support to the Trade Union Educational League.

In this general respect the practical experience and union prestige of the group of T.U.E.L. militants, now become Communists, who had led the big meat-packing and steel organizing campaigns as well as many other progressive causes in Chicago, was of great advantage to the Party. Their effectiveness was further enhanced by the important fact that this group had a close, working united front with the Fitzpatrick-Nockels leadership of the Chicago Federation of Labor, a body of 325,000 members and the leading progressive labor center in the American trade union movement.

EARLY ACTIVITIES OF THE T.U.E.L.

The T.U.E.L., although organized in November 1920, did not become a real factor among the trade unions until early in 1922. Its official organ, *The Labor Herald,* appeared in March of that year. Its program, printed in the first issue, assailed the reactionary bureaucracy and proposed a fighting policy instead of class collaboration, amalgamation of the craft unions into industrial unions, organization of the unorganized, independent political action, affiliation to the Red International of Labor Unions, recognition of Soviet Russia, and the abolition of capitalism and the establishment of a workers' republic. As its organizational forms, the T.U.E.L. set up groups of progressives and left-wingers in the unions of the various crafts, industries, localities, and regions on a non-dues-paying basis to promote its general program. The entire trade

[1] *The Communist,* Oct. 11, 1919.

union strength of the Workers Party was mobilized in the T.U.E.L., and most of the latter's leaders were Communists.

The T.U.E.L. was well received and soon developed a broad left-progressive coalition. Militant workers all over the country, disgusted with Gompersism, quickly became interested in its program. Among others, Alex Howat, Kansas mine leader, became a League member, and so did J. G. Brown, national head of the Labor Party, while John Fitzpatrick and Ed Nockels looked upon the organization with a friendly eye. Debs endorsed the League and wrote, "The Trade Union Educational League is in my opinion the one rightly-directed movement for the industrial unification of the American workers."[1]

The T.U.E.L. quickly established flourishing local and national groups in various industries: mining, textile, building, clothing, food, leather, etc. At its national railroad conference in Chicago, in December 1922, there were 425 delegates from all over the country. Otto Wangerin led this strong movement. T.U.E.L. groups were also established in Canada under the general leadership of Tim Buck.[2]

Almost at once the League began to exert a strong influence in many situations. In Chicago T.U.E.L. militants, Charles Krumbein, Nels Kjar, and others, were largely responsible for a union demonstration of 125,000 workers against the infamous Landis building trades award. At the Detroit convention of the Maintenance of Way Union in 1922 the aroused delegation, led by a few T.U.E.L. members, fired Grable, the union president, and his entire administration, for their crass betrayal of the railroad shopmen's strike. In the current Machinists' Union national election the left-wing nominee for general president, the T.U.E.L. candidate, polled 14,598 votes against 41,837 votes for the incumbent, William H. Johnston. Andrew Overgaard led this movement. In the needle trades the left wing at once became an important factor.

In the national coal strike of 1922, League militants, by calling huge protest meetings of miners, prevented Frank Farrington, the Illinois district U.M.W.A. leader, from making a separate settlement that would have broken the strike. At the U.M.W.A. convention of that year the League members, working jointly with Alex Howat on the question of the latter's expulsion because of his all-out fight against the infamous Kansas Industrial Court law, polled a majority of convention votes

---

1 *The Labor Herald*, Apr. 1923.
2 A dual unionist deviation from Communist trade union policy at this time was the formation of the United Labor Council of America, in New York in November 1921, by a group of Communists. This organization assembled a number of the many small independent industrial unions of the period, but it soon passed out of existence. See *The Toiler*, Nov. 11, 1921.

against John L. Lewis. Early in 1923 Joseph Manley and Margaret Cowl were instrumental in preventing a split of some 50,000 foreign-born workers from the U.M.W.A. throughout the Pennsylvania anthracite regions. This secession movement was provoked when the conservative district leadership suddenly decided to change the union organization from a language to a mine basis, the purpose of which was to throw the union's control into the hands of conservative English-speaking elements. Pat Toohey and Tom Myerscough were the League's outstanding leaders among the miners.

The League members were especially active in the 1922 national railroad shopmen's strike. While on a national tour to strengthen the strike, Foster, the secretary-treasurer of the T.U.E.L., was kidnaped from a hotel in Denver by the Colorado Rangers (state police), held several days, spirited all the way across Colorado and Wyoming, and dumped out at the Nebraska state line. Debs wired Foster his support. This case was the central issue in that fall's elections in Colorado, with the result that the incumbent governor was defeated and the State Rangers were abolished during the new governor's term.

MASS CAMPAIGNS OF THE T.U.E.L.

The Workers Party, in line with its growing role as the vanguard party of the working class, projected as the three most basic issues confronting the workers, the amalgamation of the trade unions into industrial unions, the formation of a labor party, and the recognition of Soviet Russia. These corresponded to the most pressing needs of the labor movement. In the trade unions directly, the Communists advocated these issues through the united front T.U.E.L.

The League concentrated its fight nationally around these three major issues. The great rank and file of organized labor, disgusted and indignant at the shameful bankruptcy of their leaders in the face of the employers' offensive, gave the three issues powerful support. "Amalgamation or Annihilation," "Amalgamation and a Labor Party," "Recognize Soviet Russia," were slogans that ran like wildfire throughout the labor movement during 1922-23. The Workers Party, through its extensive organization and press, rallied its forces actively for all these struggles.

The big campaign for amalgamation began with the adoption by a vote of 114 to 37 of a resolution by Johnstone and Foster at a meeting of the Chicago Federation of Labor, on March 19, 1922. At the following meeting the reactionaries, who hoped to rescind the resolution, were again defeated, this time by 102 to 14. Alarmed at these developments, on April 11th, Gompers came to Chicago and, fearing to attend the C.F. of L. session, called a meeting at the Morrison Hotel of several hundred hand-picked union officials. Putting out the slogan, "Capture the C.F. of L. from the Reds," he advocated what meant a violent attack on the local federation. But nothing came of this desperate proposal. The C.F. of L.'s endorsement of amalgamation stood fast.

The progressive prestige of the Chicago Federation of Labor was high, because of its sponsorship of the big meat-packing and steel campaigns, its leading role in the labor party movement, its active support of Mooney and Billings, and its general reputation as an anti-Gompers organization—so that when it endorsed amalgamation, this had a tremendous influence nationally. Trade union organizations all over the country, wherever the Party and the T.U.E.L. had contacts, began to adopt resolutions for amalgamation. The movement ran like a prairie fire, with the confused and alarmed Gompers machine unable to halt it. The rank and file saw in the amalgamation movement the labor solidarity and fighting policy so shamefully lacking in the bitter strikes of the period. The top union leadership saw in it a deadly menace to their whole corrupt position.

Sixteen international unions during the next 18 months endorsed amalgamation, including such organizations as the Railway Clerks, Maintenance of Way Workers, Typographical, Molders, Amalgamated Clothing Workers, Furriers, Bakery, Lithographers, Brewery, Butcher Workmen, and others. Seventeen state federations, including Pennsylvania, Ohio, Indiana, Michigan, Minnesota, Washington, and others took similar action. Scores of large city central bodies and trade councils also went for amalgamation, as did thousands of local unions—3,377 in the railroad industry alone. Tim Buck also reported, "Amalgamation resolutions have been endorsed during the past year by almost every kind of union in every part of Canada." The League was well within the truth when it claimed that two million organized workers had endorsed amalgamation, or more than half of the whole labor movement.[1]

The Workers Party campaign for the labor party, which was also being advocated militantly all over the country by the T.U.E.L., was almost as successful as that for amalgamation. The workers drew correct lessons from the outrageous policies of the government in the political situation. A whole string of international unions and state and local labor bodies, in response to the Party's and the League's campaign, went on record for the labor party. In March 1923, the T.U.E.L. put out a national labor party referendum directly to 35,000 local unions of

[1] Jay Fox, *Amalgamation*, Chicago, 1923.

the A.F. of L. and Railroad Brotherhoods.[1] Although this met with active opposition from the reactionaries, 7,000 locals replied favorably to the League, and doubtless many thousands more took affirmative action without notifying the T.U.E.L. In the following chapter we shall deal further with the labor party movement and the key role played in it by the Workers Party.

From its inception the Workers Party had made a continuous and resolute fight for the recognition of Soviet Russia. This, too, the T.U.E.L. took up as a central issue. The fight was widely successful among the masses. Many international unions, including the Miners, Stationary Firemen, Locomotive Engineers, Machinists, Painters, Amalgamated Clothing Workers, and so on, as well as innumerable central bodies, supported this demand. In 1919, in New York, the American Labor Alliance for Trade Relations with Russia was formed—its president was Timothy Healey, head of the Stationary Firemen's Union—and many trade unions were affiliated to it.[2] In addition to the Workers Party and the T.U.E.L., big factors in the recognition campaign were the Trade Union National Committee for Russian Famine Relief, headed by Joseph Manley, and the Friends of Soviet Russia, led by Alfred Wagenknecht. The latter organization, in its several years of very effective work, raised two million dollars for famine relief and technical aid for Soviet Russia, then fighting to live and develop in the face of a world of capitalist enemies.

Under the stimulus of its three big integrated campaigns for amalgamation, the labor party, and recognition of Soviet Russia, the influence of the Workers Party soared and the T.U.E.L. grew rapidly. For the Communists, this situation was indeed a far cry from that of but a short while ago, in the days of the Party's "underground" status, of its purely Socialist agitation, and its isolation from the labor movement.

THE A.F. OF L. CONVENTION OF 1923

The big rank-and-file movement that the Workers Party and the T.U.E.L. had created came to a head-on collision with the bureaucratic machine at the A.F. of L. convention in Portland, Oregon, in the fall of 1923. By this time the A.F. of L. leaders, recovering from their initial fright and confusion at the sudden appearance of the strong Communist-progressive opposition, were again organized and in full control of their situation. In the convention, made up almost completely of top officials of the international unions, there was no trace of democ-

[1] *Labor Herald*, March 1923.
[2] Alexander Trachtenberg in *The Communist*, Sept. 1939.

racy. That over half the rank and file of organized labor had voted for basically new policies, meant nothing to these misleaders. With old man Gompers in the driver's seat, they proceeded cynically to violate the mandate of their members and to disregard the entire rank-and-file movement. In this policy the Social-Democratic union leaders at the convention fused completely with the Gompersites. The whole outrage was staged amid an orgy of redbaiting, designed to terrorize the delegates into compliance with the will of the Gompers machine.

Amalgamation was condemned as "communistic," with no discussion or roll-call vote permitted. The labor party resolutions were steamrollered to defeat, as "un-American," the vote on them being 1,895 for and 25,066 against. The resolution for recognition of Soviet Russia got the most support, Hayes of the Typographical Union, Healey of the Firemen, Smart of the Switchmen, Johnston of the Machinists, and others all speaking for it; but it too was swamped by the machine vote. Thus, the A.F. of L. leaders, faithful to the interests of their capitalist masters, cold-bloodedly condemned a program that would have brought real life to the labor movement, which they had nearly ruined by their reactionary policies. To cap the climax, a Communist delegate at the convention was illegally and dramatically expelled from the convention upon the motion of Philip Murray, then of the Miners Union.

A number of forces combined to make it possible for the A.F. of L. leaders to succeed with this monstrous flouting of rank-and-file wishes. First, the economic situation had ameliorated somewhat and the violent union-wrecking campaign of the bosses had also materially slowed down. Second, the A.F. of L. leaders at this convention came forth with a whole new program of class collaboration, of "union-management co-operation" (of this more later), which they elaborately paraded as a constructive and progressive policy. Third, the Workers Party and the T.U.E.L. had much too loose a following to back up their wide agitational support by vigorous organized action. Fourth, and highly important, was the fact that three months before, the Workers Party had a serious split with its progressive allies of the Fitzpatrick group over the labor party, and the Gompersites were able to take advantage of this split situation and to carry out the attack against the left wing. The Portland convention was the signal for a violent assault upon the Workers Party, the T.U.E.L., and all their friends and supporters throughout the labor movement.

DEFENSE OF CLASS WAR PRISONERS

Labor defense was a very important activity of the Workers Party during the period of intense capitalist offensive after World War I.

There were the numerous I.W.W. cases of the war and early post-war periods: the cases of Debs, Ruthenberg, and many others arrested in connection with the war; the historic Mooney-Billings case; the famous McNamara-Schmidt case; and various others. Then there were scores of cases of foreign-born workers arbitrarily jailed or deported by the reactionary Wilson and Harding governments. At first the Party either organized or co-operated with special defense committees around these various cases, but on June 23, 1925, in Chicago, it took the initiative, with other forces, in establishing the International Labor Defense, a united front organization on a mass basis. Prominent in this work were Elizabeth Gurley Flynn, Anna Damon, and Rose Baron. In the same period the Council for the Protection of the Foreign Born was established.

On May 5, 1920, another celebrated case was added to the many frame-ups that were already disgracing American democracy. This was the arrest in Massachusetts of Nicola Sacco and Bartolomeo Vanzetti. They were anarchists and both foreign-born, the first a shoemaker and the other a fish peddler. They were falsely charged with committing a $15,000 payroll robbery in South Braintree, Massachusetts, during which a guard was killed. After a farcical trial, marked by the most cynical redbaiting and national chauvinism, the two defendants were convicted and sentenced to the electric chair. The Workers Party became the heart of the fight to save them.

The outrageous frame-up aroused indignation in labor and liberal circles all over the world. For the next seven years demonstrations, strikes, and protests against the legal lynching took place in many cities, with Communists everywhere playing a leading role. But the ruthless capitalists refused to let their prey escape, the conviction of Sacco and Vanzetti being sustained all through the courts despite its obvious injustice. The two victims of class hatred were finally executed on August 23, 1927, in the midst of a great international protest. There were demonstrations in many cities in the United States, and also in Panama, Manila, Brussels, Havana, Mexico, Buenos Aires, Montreal, Warsaw, Belgrade, Melbourne, Cairo, and the Soviet Union. In Geneva, Switzerland, 50,000 demonstrated. Armed guards were posted at United States embassies all over the world. After the executions, 150,000 marched on the United States embassy in Paris and fought the police from barricades. In Boston, 250,000 turned out for the funeral in a downpour of rain.[1] The Sacco-Vanzetti lynching was one of the bitter outrages for which the workers will one day exact retribution.

Then there was the defense of the 57 Communist leaders arrested and indicted in connection with the Communist convention in Bridg-

[1] *National Guardian*, March 28, 1951.

man, Michigan, in August 1922. The Labor Defense Council was set up to lead in the defense. This was a broad united front movement, including in its executive committee such figures as Eugene V. Debs, Max S. Hayes, Robert M. Buck, Rev. John A. Ryan, J. G. Brown, Roger N. Baldwin, R. D. Cramer, F. Fisher Kane, and George P. West. The chief counsel was the well-known attorney, Frank P. Walsh. The defense had the active support of the Chicago Federation of Labor and of trade union bodies in many other cities.

The trials took place in St. Joseph, Michigan, beginning in February 1923. Each of the three score defendants demanded and secured a separate trial under the state law. Foster was the first tried. After a three weeks' trial the jury was hung, six and six. Ruthenberg was tried next and, more drastic frame-up methods having been found necessary, he was quickly convicted. He was sentenced to three to 10 years for "illegal assembly." His conviction was sustained all through the courts, including the Supreme Court, but his death took place before he could actually begin serving his sentence. Meanwhile, the authorities in Michigan, facing the prospect of endless individual trials, abandoned the whole unprofitable business. Finally, in 1934, a dozen years later, the indictments were dropped by a New Deal attorney general in Michigan.

15. The Communists and the LaFollette Movement
(1922-1924)

The general resistance of the workers to the capitalist offensive in the years immediately following World War I crystallized in a big farmer-labor movement, and culminated in the independent candidacy in 1924 of Senator Robert M. LaFollette for the presidency of the United States. This was the biggest effort ever made, before or since, by the rank-and-file American workers and their class allies to set up an independent political organization in the face of official betrayal. The Workers Party, the Communist Party of the period, played a most important role in this significant development.

For the past century and a half one of the American capitalists' most powerful means of dominating the workers has been to keep them affiliated to, or under the domination of, the capitalist political parties. Since Civil War times this device of the capitalist rulers has manifested itself in the so-called two-party system. Throughout all these years the advanced workers repeatedly rebelled against this infamous political control by organizing labor parties, but these attempts did not succeed. Various reasons combined to bring about their failure. Basic among these were the following: the political immaturity ideologically and organizationally of the working class; its lack of homogeneity, made up as it was largely of great masses of workers with different languages, religions, and cultural backgrounds; the persistence of petty-bourgeois illusions among the workers; the stubborn opposition of the trade union bureaucracy since the rise of the A.F. of L.; and last, but not least, the lack of a clear lead from the Marxists, chiefly because of sectarian reasons.

In the decades immediately following the Civil War, the early American Marxists, with the personal advice of Marx and Engels, did in general follow the sensible policy of participating in these elementary working class parties and of co-operating with the closely affiliated farmer political organizations, although not without making many sectarian and opportunist mistakes. Lenin wrote: "Marx and Engels taught the socialists to break *at all costs* with narrow sectarianism and *affiliate* with the labor movement, so as to *rouse politically* the proletariat, since the proletariat displayed *almost* no political independence either in England or America in the last third of the 19th century."[1] From 1890 on, however, the sectarian De Leon put an end to this essentially correct mass policy, holding that the labor and farmer parties were basically reactionary and that the Socialist Labor Party alone sufficed as the party of the working class. The Socialist Party continued this narrow line, and it was not until as late as 1921 that it began to look upon the spontaneous labor party movement as anything but a rival. The Workers Party inherited from the Socialist Party the long-standing hostile attitude toward the labor party.

In 1922, however, the Workers Party broke sharply with the thirty-year-old anti-labor-party policy of the S.L.P. and the S.P. and took its place in the forefront of the growing struggle for a labor party. The Workers Party, through discussions at home and with European Marxists in Comintern sessions, understood that the political development of the working class in the United States was not following an identical pattern with that in Continental Europe. In Europe, where the trade unions were organized either after, or simultaneously with, the Socialist Party, this Party developed independently with an individual membership, a Social-Democratic program, and a recognized political leadership of the working class. On the other hand, in certain countries, owing to factors specifically retarding the political development of the workers, the trade unions came before the political party in the development of working class organization. There the workers, seeking to wage a political as well as an industrial struggle, eventually came to set up a labor party based primarily upon the trade unions. This latter course has been true of Great Britain and its several dominions—Australia, Canada, New Zealand, South Africa—and also of the United States. Here the general line of development is also toward a broad party based on the trade unions, but the tempo of its growth is far slower because the retarding political factors have been much greater. Further elaboration upon this point is to be found in Chapter 37. Over many years the American Marxists failed to understand the foregoing facts, finally pointed out by Stalin, about the general line of working class political development, and the role of the labor party in it.

By 1922 the Workers Party had come to understand the vital importance of supporting the labor party as a break on the part of the workers with the two-party system and bourgeois political domination. This was a big stride away from sectarianism and into broad mass work. At its second convention, held in New York City in December 1922, the delegates, therefore, confirmed the earlier decision by the Central Executive Committee in May 1922, and declared:[2] "The Workers Party favors the forma-

[1] V. I. Lenin, *Marx, Engels, Marxism*, p. 108, N. Y., 1933.
[2] Charles E. Ruthenberg in *The Liberator*, Feb., 1923.

COMMUNISTS AND LAFOLLETTE MOVEMENT 213

tion of a labor party—a working class political party, independent of, and opposed to, all capitalist political parties. It will make every effort to hasten the formation of such a party and to effect admittance to it as an autonomous section." It added: "A real labor party cannot be formed without the labor unions, and organizations of exploited farmers, tenant farmers, and farm laborers must be included."[1]

The political situation at this time was propitious for the formation of a labor party. The workers in the United States, passing through the bitterest offensive of big capital, had carried out a whole series of fierce strikes. They had been largely disillusioned by Wilson's "liberalism" and, of course, they had no use for Harding's brand of reaction. Besides, the Gompers leaders had been deeply discredited in the whole post-war struggle, and they were little able to stem the strong tide for independent working class political action. Also, for the first time in over 35 years the Marxists, in the Workers Party and the T.U.E.L., were making a real fight for a labor party. Consequently, the workers turned sharply toward independent political action.

THE DEVELOPING LaFOLLETTE MOVEMENT

Four main streams of mass political organization finally culminated in the movement behind the LaFollette presidential candidacy of 1924. These were: (a) The group of local labor parties that grew up during 1918-19 in Chicago, New York, Bridgeport, and other cities, with state parties in Illinois, Connecticut, Michigan, Utah, Indiana, and Pennsylvania. The Chicago Federation of Labor was the recognized leader of this movement. (b) The Nonpartisan League, founded in 1915 as a left wing in the Republican Party and headed by A. P. Townley, formerly an S.P. organizer. The N.P.L. claimed 188,365 members in 1918. It was centered in the Dakotas, and loosely grouped around it were a number of state farmer parties in the Middle West and Northwest. (c) The Committee of Forty-Eight, founded in 1918 and headed by J. A. H. Hopkins. This was an extensive petty-bourgeois liberal organization. (d) The Plumb Plan movement, which was organized in 1919. Its leaders were Warren S. Stone and William H. Johnston, the heads of the Locomotive Engineers and Machinists Unions respectively. It was based on the sixteen railroad unions and had a program calling for "government ownership and democratic operation of the railroads." The N.A.A.C.P. eventually also endorsed LaFollette.

In November 1919, the various state and local labor parties met in Chicago and combined into the National Labor Party. The pre-T.U.E.L.

[1] Bimba, *History of the American Working Class*, p. 318.

group in Chicago was active in this movement, and the national secretary of the National Labor Party, J. G. Brown, later became a member of the T.U.E.L. In 1920, again in Chicago, the National Labor Party took part in a merger of the Committee of Forty-Eight and a number of state farmer parties, emerging as the Farmer-Labor Party, again with Brown as secretary. The Chicago left-wingers were also very active in this convention—in fact, actually bringing about the amalgamation of the two main groups by rank-and-file action when their leaders vacillated. The F.L.P. sought LaFollette for its candidate in the 1920 elections; but its program was "too radical" for him and the "lefts" objected to LaFollette's white chauvinism. Parley Parker Christensen, who was comparatively unknown, was nominated and polled some 300,000 votes.

The next big step in the developing LaFollette movement was taken when the Plumb Plan movement, in February 1922, transformed itself into the Conference for Progressive Political Action (C.P.P.A.). Attending its founding meeting in Chicago, besides the representatives of the sixteen railroad unions, were representatives of the miners, needle trades, nine state federations of labor, and other union bodies, and also the National Farmer-Labor Party, Socialist Party, Nonpartisan League, various state labor parties, the National Catholic Welfare Council, Methodist Federation for Social Service, and so on. All told, about 2,500,000 were represented. Dodging the labor party issue, however, the conference decided that each state should use such plan of organized political action as it saw fit, working either as a minority within the old parties or as an independent political party. J. G. Brown and Morris Hillquit were members of the national organizing committee.

In December 1922, the C.P.P.A. held another conference in Cleveland. Here, however, the question of forming an independent labor party thrust itself forward and occupied the center of attention. The labor party resolution was finally voted down, 64 to 52; whereupon the Farmer Labor Party, led by Fitzpatrick, decided to withdraw from the C.P.P.A. The Communists advised against this action,[1] the Workers Party having sent two delegates to this Cleveland conference—Ruthenberg[2] and Foster. The Socialist Party, joining with the reactionaries, issued a statement demanding that the Workers Party be barred.[3] The whole Chicago Farmer-Labor group insisted that Ruthenberg and Foster be accepted as full participants. But the conference, controlled by conservative union leaders, voted not to admit the representatives of the Workers Party.

1 *Proceedings of the Third National Convention, Workers Party, December, 1923*, p. 15, Chicago.
2 Ruthenberg, who had been in prison since early in 1921, was released in July 1922.
3 Fine, *Labor and Farmer Parties in the U.S.*, p. 405.

THE WORKERS PARTY AND THE FARMER-LABOR PARTY

The Workers Party and the T.U.E.L. meanwhile were actively pushing among the masses their agitation for a labor party. The T.U.E.L.'s national referendum on the labor party was a big success. All over the country unions voted favorably upon the T.U.E.L.'s proposition to establish a labor party forthwith. *The Labor Herald* reported that "the unions now on record in the League vote extend over 40 states and 47 international unions. In the thousands of locals in which the issue has been raised we have been informed of less than a dozen which failed to approve of a labor party."[1] The leaders of the Chicago Federation of Labor endorsed this referendum.

It was during this time, in April 1923, that the Communist Party, at a special convention, liquidated its "underground" phase. The Workers Party now became in fact, if not in name, the Communist Party. The Workers Party moved its headquarters from New York to Chicago in July. At its third convention, in December 1923, the Party reported a membership of 25,000.

Meanwhile, definite working relations were developing nationally between the Workers Party and the Fitzpatrick-Nockels-Brown group. The ten years of co-operation between the Federation leaders and the Chicago T.U.E.L. militants, which had resulted in so many constructive national campaigns, was now developing finally into a united front between the Workers Party and the Farmer-Labor Party.

By mutual agreement of the two parties, a call was issued by the Farmer-Labor Party for a general convention to take place in Chicago, on July 3, 1923, of "all economic and political organizations favoring the organization of a Farmer-Labor Party." The W.P. and F.L.P. leading committees agreed upon the basis of representation, the construction and the number of the future party's leading committee, and also upon certain resolutions to be proposed, including the recognition of Soviet Russia. They also agreed that if there were half a million workers represented at the convention the new party should be formed. The W.P. and the F.L.P. shared the costs of the sending out of the convention call. On the agreed upon basis invitations were extended nationally to all trade unions, local and state labor and farmer parties, and the Socialist, Socialist Labor, and Proletarian parties, in addition to the two sponsoring parties.[2] The S.P. declined the invitation, but the general response was excellent. The movement grew in many directions.

1 *Labor Herald*, June 1923.
2 *Proceedings of the Third National Convention, Workers Party*, pp. 15-17.

As the July 3rd convention approached, however, the Fitzpatrick group began to waver and to grow visibly cool toward it. The A.F. of L. had cut off its subsidy to the Chicago Federation of Labor, and many LaFollette-inclined forces were trying to induce Fitzpatrick and his group to cut loose from the coming convention. The latter weakened under these pressures. Nevertheless, they went into the convention without openly repudiating their agreement with the Workers Party.

THE FEDERATED FARMER LABOR PARTY CONVENTION

The convention of July 3, 1923, brought together an estimated 600,000 workers and farmers, represented by 650 delegates. Of these, the Communists made up but a very small minority. The enthusiasm for the proposed federated party swept the gathering, which was composed mostly of rank-and-filers. From the outset the Fitzpatrick group maneuvered against the convention's establishing a party. First, they tried to reject the credentials of the Workers Party, but this move was defeated almost unanimously by the convention. Then they sought, through an out-of-town delegate, to transform the convention into simply a consultative conference. This move was countered by an amendment to form the new party, made by Joseph Manley, a Workers Party member representing Local 40 of the Structural Iron Workers Union, and supported by Ruthenberg.

Only on the night of the third and last day of the convention did the confused Fitzpatrick group bring in a definite proposition as to what they wanted done. They then proposed that all the organizations present should affiliate to the Farmer Labor Party as autonomous units, except that the revolutionary elements, meaning the Workers Party, should be excluded. The F.L.P. proposal said "it would be suicide ... to bring into such affiliation any organization which advocates other than lawful means to bring about political changes"—strange charges indeed coming from the radical Fitzpatrick group, which had invited the W.P. to this convention and which only a few months before had voted to seat Ruthenberg and Foster at the C.P.P.A. gathering in Cleveland. The convention rejected the Fitzpatrick proposition with a roar and decided by a vote of about 500 to 40 to organize the Federated Farmer Labor Party, which was done.[1] As Fine says, the Fitzpatrick group wanted to bolt, "but they did not have enough of a following for that."[2] A representative group of workers and farmers were then elected as the

[1] *Proceedings of the Second Convention, Workers Party, 1923*, p. 19; *The Labor Herald*, Aug. 1923.
[2] Fine, *Labor and Farmer Parties in the U.S.*, p. 431.

Executive Committee. Joseph Manley was chosen secretary-treasurer, and the F.F.L.P. established its headquarters in Chicago.

The program of the F.F.L.P. proposed to "free the farm and industrial worker from the greedy exploitation of those who now rule this country and to win for them the right to life, liberty, and the pursuit of happiness which their exploiters deny them." The new party demanded "the nationalization of all public utilities and all social means of communication and transportation" and that these industries be operated democratically, eventually by the economic organizations of the workers and farmers. For labor the demands were the eight-hour day, the abolition of child labor, and a federal minimum wage. For veterans, the bonus. For all city and rural workers, the establishment of a general federal system of social insurance, covering sickness and other disabling causes. For the farmers, the demand that the land be assured to the users, as well as the issue and control of all money by the government, the payment of war debts by an excess profits tax, and a moratorium on all farm debts. The program made no specific demands for the Negro people.[1]

The organizations which voted to form the Federated Farmer Labor Party on July 3rd, represented approximately 600,000 members—some 50,000 miners, 10,000 machinists, 100,000 needle workers, 7,000 carpenters, 10,000 metal workers, the West Virginia Federation of Labor with 87,000 members, the A.F. of L. central bodies of Detroit, Buffalo, Minneapolis, and Butte, with 140,000, 40,000, 20,000, and 10,000 affiliated members. The farmer-labor parties of Washington, Ohio, California, Illinois, Wisconsin, and elsewhere added many additional thousands. But when it came later on to actually affiliating with the F.F.L.P., only some 155,000 did so, and these were mostly the more advanced organizations.[2] In short, the F.F.L.P. had failed to win the masses. The attraction of the C.P.P.A., plus the Fitzpatrick split—both with the help of the redbaiting capitalist press all over the country—succeeded in keeping the more conservative trade unions at the convention from joining up with the F.F.L.P. The latter organization gradually dwindled in strength.

THE FARMER-LABOR PARTY

Labor party sentiment continued strong, however, and a fresh attempt was made by the Workers Party to get such a party established on a broad basis. This new effort was organized in conjunction with the well-established Minnesota Farmer-Labor Party, with which the Workers Party had built up friendly relations. A general convention was held in St. Paul,

[1] *American Labor Year Book*, 1923-24, p. 158.
[2] *Proceedings of the Third National Convention, Workers Party*, p. 21.

Minnesota, on July 17, 1924, for the purpose of setting up a national farmer-labor party. This convention assembled 542 delegates from 29 states, representing largely farmers. After adopting a program similar to that of the F.F.L.P., it elected as its executive secretary C. A. Hathaway, an influential Minnesota Communist machinist. The convention chose as its candidates in the approaching national elections, for president, Duncan McDonald, former U.M.W.A. head in Illinois, and for vice-president, William Bouck, chief of the Western Progressive Farmers League of Washington.

At the St. Paul convention, despite the overwhelming decision to form the new Farmer-Labor Party, there was much sentiment for LaFollette, and proposals were carried for negotiations with the Conference for Progressive Political Action on the question of joint support for a LaFollette ticket. The Workers Party, looking askance at LaFollette as a petty-bourgeois reformist, declared to the St. Paul convention that "the only basis upon which the Workers Party will accept LaFollette as the candidate is that he agree to run as a Farmer-Labor candidate, to accept the party's platform and its central control over the electoral campaign and campaign funds."[1] LaFollette rejected these terms.

A couple of weeks after the St. Paul convention, on July 3rd, at Cleveland, the C.P.P.A. nominated Robert M. LaFollette and Burton K. Wheeler to run for president and vice-president. The convention represented at least four million organized workers, farmers, and middle class groupings. The A.F. of L., for the first time endorsing independent presidential candidates, gave the movement its official blessing. With the ultra-reactionaries Calvin Coolidge and John W. Davis, running as the Republican and Democratic candidates, the A.F. of L. could not withstand LaFollette pressure among its rank and file. Moreover, the Gompersites had a healthy respect for the railroad unions behind the C.P.P.A., as the latter had given them the worst licking in their career at the 1920 A.F. of L. convention in Montreal upon the issue of the Plumb Plan. But the Executive Council, in endorsing LaFollette, made it clear that this action was in no sense "a pledge of identification with an independent party movement or a third party."[2]

The strong mass sentiment for LaFollette had disastrous effects upon the Farmer-Labor Party just organized at St. Paul. Most of the participants at that convention later mounted the C.P.P.A. bandwagon. Consequently, the Executive Committee of the Farmer-Labor Party deemed it the part of wisdom to withdraw its candidates, McDonald and Bouck, thereby dissolving the F.L.P. as a party. The Workers Party thereupon

[1] *The Liberator*, July 1924.
[2] Lorwin, *The American Federation of Labor*, p. 225.

put up William Z. Foster, the leader of the 1919 steel strike, as its candidate for president. This was the first national Communist ticket, an event of prime historical importance in the life of the working class. The Party got on the ballot in 13 states, made a strong campaign, and polled for the national ticket, according to the unreliable official figures, some 33,316 votes.

In the presidential elections the LaFollette Progressive Independents polled 4,826,382 votes, or about 16.5 percent of the total vote cast. Undoubtedly, large numbers of votes were stolen from the LaFollette column. LaFollette's good election showing and the huge mass organizations behind the C.P.P.A. obviously provided a sufficient basis for a strong national party of workers and farmers; but this was the last thing wanted by the A.F. of L. and railroad union leaders, tied as they were to the two capitalist parties. Consequently, on February 21, 1925, they met in Chicago, and after rejecting proposals to form a labor party, informally dissolved the C.P.P.A. and went back to the old Gompers policy of "reward your friends and punish your enemies." Gompers died on December 13, 1924, shortly after the LaFollette campaign, but his anti-working class policies lived right on after him.

Despite the favorable political situation, the working class was not able, during the crucial period of 1922-24, to make a breakaway from the two capitalist parties and to establish an independent mass political party. This was because of the workers' prevalent ideological and organizational weaknesses mentioned above, the crass betrayal by the trade union leaders and the Hillquit S.P. leadership, and the fact that in 1923 the economic situation began to pick up substantially. The ensuing "prosperity" tended to re-create petty-bourgeois illusions among the masses, and it also strengthened the control over the unions by the reactionary leaders, sworn enemies of the labor party. Errors made by the left wing were also a factor in the failure to organize a labor party.

TACTICAL MISTAKES OF THE WORKERS PARTY

It is clear that in this complicated fight for a labor party the young Workers Party, in its eagerness to help the working class to break out of the deadly two-party trap and to establish a labor party, made some serious errors. The most basic of these was to permit itself to become separated from the broad movement of workers and farmers gathered behind LaFollette. Although the Party was barred from affiliating officially, nevertheless, through the mass organizations, it could have functioned as the left wing of the LaFollette movement, even at the cost of a qualified endorsement of its candidates. The basic reason given by the Workers

Party for not participating in the LaFollette movement—the fear that the small Party would be engulfed by this broad petty-bourgeois-led movement—was not a sound conclusion. The fact that the Party, at the time of this broad movement of workers and farmers, was compelled to put up its own candidates, was proof that a sectarian mistake had been made.

That there was, of course, some danger that the Party might be swamped ideologically by LaFollettism was to be seen right in the Workers Party itself. John Pepper, a Central Executive Committee member, put forward a highly opportunistic evaluation of the LaFollette movement. He called that movement "the third American revolution." Said he, "The revolution is here. World history stands before one of its great turning points—America faces her third revolution . . . the coming third revolution will not be a proletarian revolution. It will be a revolution of well-to-do and exploited farmers, small business men, and workers. . . . It will contain elements of the great French revolution, and the Russian Kerensky revolution. In its ideology it will have elements of Jeffersonianism, Danish co-operatives, Ku Klux Klan, and Bolshevism."[1] The danger of such trends was emphasized by the current petty-bourgeois illusions among the masses.

Of course, in any broad mass movement there will be different ideologies, some even reactionary, but to say, as Pepper did, that the labor-LaFollette movement represented a "third revolution," was not only to overestimate its social character and its strength, but also to give a wrong perspective on the nature of the social change which America faces in the future. The LaFollette movement represented a united front of workers, petty bourgeoisie, and farmers in the struggle against monopoly capital, with the petty bourgeoisie and labor leaders in control. Time, experience, and the work of the Communists were necessary to change that domination. But to withdraw from the movement, as the Communists did, was a political error. The Party should have gone along in critical support of the LaFollette movement. Thus, it could not only have carried on effective work among the masses in motion, but could also have avoided much of the Party's later relative isolation.

Another error, of the same general character, was the split with the Fitzpatrick group over the formation of the Federated Farmer-Labor Party on July 3, 1923. In view of the strong tendency among the masses to turn toward the C.P.P.A. and a LaFollette ticket, which was already then in prospect, and also in view of the vacillating attitude of the Fitzpatrick forces, it was unwise for the Communists to insist upon setting up the F.F.L.P. at that time, even though this was formally in accordance with the pre-convention agreement between the W.P. and the Fitzpatrick-

[1] *The Liberator*, Sept. 1923.

Farmer-Labor Party group. The Workers Party should have been able to realize that under these circumstances there was as yet no solid basis for the new labor party. The result of this mistake was the still-born Federated Farmer-Labor Party. The later formation of the Farmer-Labor Party at the June 17, 1924, convention in St. Paul, merely compounded the original error with another premature party, which had to be abandoned almost at once.

The W.P.-Fitzpatrick split on July 3, 1923, was particularly harmful in that it spread throughout the trade union movement. Eventually it largely divorced the Communists from their center group allies, breaking up the political combination which had carried through the amalgamation and labor party campaigns, not to mention, in its earlier days, the Mooney campaign, the meat-packing and steel organizing drives, and various other progressive movements. The left-center split on July 3rd was one of the basic reasons why the Gompers bureaucrats could ride roughshod over the left wing at the A.F. of L. convention a few months later.

From a policy standpoint what had happened was this: The Workers Party started out with the correct theory that the labor party had to be based on the broad trade union movement. But when its affiliation to the C.P.P.A. was denied, it mistakenly concluded that the left-center combination of the W.P. and the Fitzpatrick group would suffice to build the labor party. And finally, when the ill-advised split came with Fitzpatrick, the W.P. departed still further from its broad and correct labor party policy and undertook to organize the labor party itself, with only its closest allies. This narrowing line was quite futile, as both the July 3, 1923 and June 17, 1924, conventions demonstrated, and as was shown by the relative isolation of the Workers Party.

FACTIONALISM IN THE WORKERS PARTY

The labor party campaign of 1922-24 gave birth to a sharp factional struggle within the Workers Party, which was to continue, with greater or less intensity, until 1929. Grave inner-Party differences developed over the strategy and tactics to be pursued in the fight for the labor party. The Party was split into two major groups which, in the heat of the internal fight, came to act almost like two separate parties, with their specific caucuses and group disciplines. The Bittelman-Foster group, which controlled the majority at the Workers Party convention in 1924, having the support of the great bulk of the trade unionists in the Party, had a background of experience and training in the Socialist Party, the I.W.W., and the A.F. of L. The Ruthenberg-Pepper minority group, on the other hand, came almost exclusively from the left wing of the Socialist Party and had Party and political experience but had done little or no practical trade union work. A number of its leaders were intellectuals, and there also were some intellectuals in the Bittelman-Foster group. The factional struggle was not entirely negative, however. What took place basically during the long internal fight from 1923 to 1929 was a slow process of gradually welding together these divergent Party groups into a united Marxist-Leninist leadership.

The Bittelman-Foster group, themselves not without blame for the July 3rd split, soon thereafter concluded that a serious error had been made in organizing the Federated Farmer-Labor Party, and they wanted to do away with the narrow labor party policy that had brought it about. They argued that this split with the progressive elements was isolating the Party in the trade unions, a situation which they, as active trade unionists, felt keenly. They also maintained that by keeping "left" labor parties in the field, which cost the Workers Party heavily in finances, personnel, and prestige, the Party was in fact tending to liquidate itself. They insisted that a labor party should be established only when this could be done on a broad trade union basis. But in maintaining that there was then no such broad basis for the labor party, the Bittelman-Foster group made the serious error of proposing that the labor party slogan be dropped, "at least for the time being." This would have had the effect of further isolating the Party from the labor party movement. The statement eventually cost the group the Party leadership.

The Ruthenberg-Pepper group, on the contrary, stoutly refused to admit that the July 3rd split and formation of the F.F.L.P. was a mistake. Instead, they defended the whole political line that had brought this about. Pepper, particularly, devised a set of opportunist theories to this effect. He argued that of necessity the labor party in its initial stages had to be a "left," or "class" party; that this "left" labor party would transform itself gradually into a mass Communist Party; that the trend was for the various labor groupings each to organize its own labor party —the progressive labor unionists, the Socialists, and the Communists each having a separate labor party or striving to build one; that the united front with the Fitzpatrick group was opportunistic anyhow and had to collapse eventually.[1]

The fight over labor party policy spread into all branches of Party work, involving also the national groups and the Young Workers League. A bitter struggle developed between the two factional groups for control

---

[1] For the points of view of the two main factions in the labor party controversy, see *The Workers Monthly*, 1924-25, and Proceedings of the 1925 Convention of the Workers Party.

of the Party. The issue was taken up in the Comintern. After a long discussion, a resolution was worked out, early in 1925,[1] to the effect, that the Bittelman-Foster group was wrong in proposing to drop the labor party slogan and that the Ruthenberg-Pepper group had placed the labor party question "somewhat too narrowly." It was characteristic of the existing factional situation that both groups claimed that their position had been sustained, and the struggle went right on.

The Bittelman-Foster group won a majority of the delegates at the fourth convention of the Workers Party, on August 21, 1925, in Chicago. The factional fight in this convention was intense. Jay Lovestone, who later became a bitter enemy of communism, at one point tried to split the Party. The Ruthenberg-Pepper group was holding a general meeting, while the waiting convention held up its sessions. Lovestone introduced a motion in the caucus, proposing that the minority should not return to the convention—a move which, if carried out, would have split the Party. But this splitting motion was defeated by one vote.

At this convention the Bittelman-Foster group gave up its majority on the Central Executive Committee (a mistake) because of criticism from Zinoviev, head of the Comintern. For making this criticism, which was flatly against the thoroughly democratic procedure of the Comintern, Zinoviev was later severely condemned. A "parity" Central Executive Committee was elected by the convention, which soon became a Ruthenberg-Pepper majority. And the factional fight continued. An important constructive measure of the 1925 convention was the expulsion of the small Lore group of right opportunists. The Party also added the word "Communist" to its name, becoming the Workers (Communist) Party.

THE DEATH OF LENIN

On January 21, 1924, the peoples of the Soviet Union and the world suffered a tremendous loss by the death of the great Lenin, at the age of 54. Lenin, who stands in history as a peer of the brilliant Karl Marx, was extraordinarily gifted as a theoretician, organizer, and practical leader. Lenin developed the Marxist analysis to explain monopoly capitalism, imperialism, the final stage of the moribund capitalist system, and he expanded and applied in the actual building of socialism Marx's great conception of the hegemony of the working class in political struggles and of the dictatorship of the proletariat. He fought against all the bourgeois idealist schools of thought. It was he, too, who worked out the basic principles for the organization of the resolute, disciplined, flexible Communist Party, the party of a new kind, dreaded the world over by the

[1] *Daily Worker*, May 29, 1925.

capitalists and their labor leader lackeys. It was Lenin, also, who taught the workers the indispensability of the peasants and the colonial peoples as revolutionary allies. To climax his innumerable achievements, theoretical and organizational, Lenin demonstrated the correctness of all his work by leading in person the great Russian Revolution to a shattering socialist victory over world capitalism. Lenin was the capable continuer and developer of the historic work of Marx and Engels. Stalin, the present brilliant head of the Soviet people, who has further enriched and expanded Marxism-Leninism, was the ablest pupil of Lenin. Lenin, a devoted son of the people, and a bold and indomitable leader, was the towering political genius of the twentieth century.

16. Toward Negro-White Labor Solidarity (1919-1924)

One of the most important developments of the World War I and post-war period was the beginning of an active co-operation between the Negro people and the labor movement. A number of factors combined to produce this most significant movement. Not the least of these factors was the educational work of the Workers Party, and a more correct attitude toward the Negro question on the part of the broad left wing of the labor movement. An important element, too, was the growth of a substantial body of Negro workers in the North.

During the period from 1910 to 1920 there was a migration of well onto a million Negroes from the South to the North. Conditions were so terrible for the Negro people in the southern states that they sought in great masses to escape from them by fleeing north where, however, things were not radically better. The Negro population during these years increased in New York by 66 percent, in Chicago by 148 percent, in Detroit by 611 percent, and in other cities similarly. The Negro migrants flocked into the industries—such as were open to them. The existing body of Negro wage workers was greatly increased. According to the federal census figures, the number of Negro workers in manufacturing industries rose from 631,280 in 1910 to 886,870 in 1920, a 40 percent increase. The principal industrial strongholds of the Negro workers in 1920 were in steel—17 percent, meat-packing—15 percent, railroads—8 percent, and coal mining—7 percent. The growth of the Negro proletariat was one of the most significant political features of this general period.

The Negro people suffered most in the wave of reaction unleashed by the capitalists during and after the war. The lynchers were abroad with gun and torch and rope. Not a week passed but sadistic lynch horrors were splashed in the newspapers. In 1917 at least 38 Negroes were lynched; in 1918 the number went up to 58, and in 1919 to 70. In the 45 years from 1885 to 1930 there were 3,256 lynchings, or an average of 73 per year. "Race riots" were precipitated by the employers and their lackeys in scores of towns and cities, including Chicago, Detroit, East St. Louis, and Washington. The Ku Klux Klan, huge in size and bold and ruthless, attacked the Negro people, the foreign-born, and the Communists as its main targets. The Klan invaded many northern states and insolently announced that it would eventually seize control of the national government.

But the lynchers and white supremacists unexpectedly encountered a very militant Negro people, who frequently fought arms-in-hand against their persecutors. In the great East St. Louis riot of July 1917, which cost 40 lives, many of those who perished were whites. The same was true of the 13-day riot in Chicago in July 1919, where, with 13 officially listed as dead, the Negroes successfully defended themselves from the lynch mobs. In Elaine County, Arkansas, an estimated 100 Negro sharecroppers were butchered by armed thugs in a bitter battle. Illustrating the Negro people's militant spirit, in August 1917, a Negro regiment in Houston, Texas, goaded beyond endurance by attacks of the Jim Crowers, defended itself, killing 17 attackers. The fact that 19 Negroes were hanged for this affair and 41 imprisoned for life did not quell the fighting spirit of the Negro people.

The sharp spirit of resistance of the Negro masses was akin to the militant mood generally of the workers during this period. And much of it was to be attributed to the fighting line of the Workers Party, although it also had other sources. The Negro people were outraged and aroused by the brutal regime of Jim Crow and persecution under which they lived. In France, too, the Negro troops, themselves segregated into Jim Crow regiments, had been received by the masses of the people with far more of a spirit of fraternity than they had ever known in the United States. Hence, when the soldiers returned home they were resolved not to submit to the monstrous Jim Crow spirit prevailing in both North and South. Also, very important in producing militancy among the Negro masses was the stimulating example of the great Russian Revolution. In the U.S.S.R., the American Negro people, as well as the oppressed nations all over the world, saw before their eyes the tremendous example of the many peoples who make up the Soviet Union living together in harmony and equality. Soviet influence upon American Negroes in this respect has been far greater than is generally recognized.

THE GARVEY MOVEMENT

The first important step taken by the harassed Negro people in an organized manner to defend themselves during the war and post-war years was the Universal Negro Improvement Association, the so-called Garvey movement. Its founder, Marcus Garvey, a brilliant Negro leader, born in Jamaica in 1887, was originally a printer and editor. He launched his movement in the British West Indies in 1914, and it was designed to appeal to the Negro peoples of the world. Garvey came to the United

States in 1917, establishing the first section of the U.N.I.A. in New York during that year. The movement showed vitality, grew rapidly, and it held its first organized national convention in 1920.

During the initial stages of his movement, Garvey, in line with the militant spirit of the American Negro people, developed a bitter bill of grievances. Among these, as he outlined them in 1920, were inequality in wages of Negro and white workers, exclusion from trade unions, deprivation of land, taxation without representation, unjust military service, Jim Crow laws, and lynching. The U.N.I.A. demanded "complete control of our social institutions without interference by any alien race or races." It originally favored the U.S.S.R., supported self-determination of peoples, and repudiated the League of Nations because "it seeks to deprive Negroes of their liberty." It declared also that "the Negro should adopt every means to protect himself against barbarous practices inflicted upon him because of color."

Garvey had no faith in the possibilities of Negroes securing just treatment in any country, including the United States, where they constitute a minority. Although his program stimulated the American Negro people to fight gross injustices, Garvey's real objective was eventually to get the Negro masses to return to their original homeland. "Back to Africa" was his central slogan.

The Negroes of the United States joined the Garvey movement in substantial numbers. During the early 1920's, the U.N.I.A. claimed half a million members, and it was by far the largest Negro political organization in the country. Negro militants were attracted to the movement chiefly, however, because of its fighting spirit, but without attaching basic importance to its "Back to Africa," "Negro-Zionist" aspect. The Negro masses, Americans of many generations standing, were obviously determined to fight for their rights in the land of their birth. The "Back to Africa" slogan was purely utopian.

Soon the U.N.I.A., opportunistically led by Garvey and his group, began to yield to reactionary capitalist pressures and to shed its early radicalism. As Robert Minor describes it, "By a process of elimination, all demands which were offensive to the ruling class were dropped one by one, and the organization settled down to a policy of disclaiming every idea whatever of demanding any rights for the Negro people in the United States—the policy of declaring that the Universal Negro Improvement Association was . . . trying only to construct an organization of a 'home for the Negro people in Africa.'"[1] Eventually its policy degenerated to the point where the organization quit real fighting for equality for the Negro in this country. This reactionary line eventually killed the

[1] Robert Minor, in *The Workers Monthly*, Apr. 1926.

Universal Negro Improvement Association among the Negro people.

From 1921 on the main activities of the U.N.I.A. leaders were centered around selling stock in the Black Star Line of steamships, which was to render a triangular service between the West Indies, Africa, and New York. About $500,000 was collected for this purpose. The steamship line not materializing, however, Garvey was arrested by the federal government, convicted, and sent to Atlanta federal penitentiary in 1925 for two years. The big movement which he had built, torn with factionalism during his imprisonment, gradually fell to pieces. As Harry Haywood points out in his book, however, the disintegrated Garvey movement left many small organizations behind it.[1]

The central political significance of the Garvey movement was its national content. Garvey cultivated a national spirit, although it was a bourgeois nationalism, among the Negro people of the United States. His movement, being basically utopian, could not serve the aspirations of the Negro people, but it did help to raise them to a new level of unity and consciousness. The Negro national spirit vaguely voiced by Garvey reached its full development in present-day Communist policy, which is based upon the reality that the Negro people in this country constitute an oppressed nation.

The Workers Party generally adopted a friendly, although critical, attitude toward the Garvey movement. In 1924 the Central Committee sent a letter to the U.N.I.A., offering the support of the Workers Party and urging co-operation between Negroes and whites. In this letter, however, the Party still handled the question, not from a national but from a class and race standpoint.[2]

ATTEMPTS TO DIVIDE NEGRO AND WHITE WORKERS

Employers have long used the policy toward their workers of divide and rule. They have systematically played off one group against another, to the detriment of all: native-born against immigrants, men against women, skilled against unskilled, members of one nation or religion against those of another. Negro workers have been especially the victims of this disruptive policy. For many years the employers made it impossible for Negroes to work in various industries—steel, auto, rubber, textile, lumber, electrical, etc., or to secure jobs at skilled trades, unless they would agree in practice to take the jobs of striking white workers. The heart of the Communists' policies has always been to combat and defeat these divisive tactics of the employers.

[1] Haywood, *Negro Liberation*, p. 203.
[2] *Daily Worker*, Aug. 5, 1924.

The conservative trade union leaders, however, as lieutenants of capital in the ranks of the workers—and particularly the Gompers clique of bureaucrats—went right along with the infamous anti-Negro policy of the employers. Themselves experts at discriminating against various sections of the working class—against women, young workers, the unskilled, and the unemployed—these labor officials practiced the worst exclusionism against Negro workers. They did their utmost to prevent Negroes from getting a foothold anywhere in the industries, especially in the skilled trades. Dozens of trade unions cynically barred Negro workers from membership by constitutional provisions, while many more excluded them in practice. These treacherous policies were made all the more disgraceful by the hypocritical official pretenses of the A.F. of L. to organize all workers, "regardless of race, creed, or color," while its leaders refused to stir in order to compel its affiliated unions to admit Negroes into the industries and the unions. The anti-Negro policies of the Gompers clique constitute the most shameful of all the disgraceful pages in the history of these misleaders of labor. The essence of the latter's position, like that of the employers, was that if the Negro workers were to get into the industries, and particularly the skilled trades, it could only be by taking strikers' jobs. And the tragedy was that such reactionary policies of the union leaders had a certain amount of support from the more backward and chauvinistic sections of the white workers.

To make the position of the Negro workers still more difficult, some of their own people to whom they then looked for leadership—conservative petty-bourgeois elements, who were outraged by the shocking conditions of discrimination practiced against Negroes in the industries and the unions—also took a position that the only way the Negro worker could get into industry and skilled work was by disregarding the unions. Spero and Harris give many examples of this attitude, which was sharply marked during the World War I period.[1] Booker T. Washington saw no hope in trade unionism for the Negro worker. Nor did Garvey. The latter's attitude, say the above-mentioned writers, was that the Negro should "beware of the labor movement in all its forms." Kelly Miller, a Negro professor at Howard, dealing with the Negro and trade unionism, said, "Whatever good or evil the future may hold for him, today's wisdom heedless of logical consistency demands that he stand shoulder to shoulder with the captains of industry." There was also anti-trade union sentiment in such organizations as the Urban League and the N.A.A.C.P. a quarter of a century ago. And every practical trade union organizer of those days knew that a number of the Negro petty-bourgeois leaders, sickened by the Jim Crow policies of many trade unions, were

[1] S. D. Spero and A. L. Harris, *The Black Worker*, pp. 138-46, N. Y., 1931.

sure to take a stand advising the Negro workers to have nothing to do with the labor movement. Cayton and Mitchell say, "Toward the labor movement the Negro upper class has generally been antagonistic."[1] Many of these intellectuals, too, precisely because of their weak class position in relation to the white bourgeoisie, tended to sell out the interests of the workers to the latter.

GROWING UNITY BETWEEN NEGRO AND WHITE WORKERS

It is to the great honor of the Negro workers that they have been able largely to win their way into the unions and industries and to create, during our years, a body of almost one million solid trade unionists from their ranks. And they have accomplished this in spite of the Jim Crow policies of the employers and their lackey trade union leaders, as well as the unwise advice of many petty-bourgeois Negro leaders. Of course, some Negro workers were misused as strikebreakers in the post-World War I years, but this development has geen grossly exaggerated by enemies of the Negro people. Strikebreaking was far more prevalent among the whites. For every Negro strikebreaker there were scores of white ones.

The solidarity between Negro and white workers was greatly increased during the World War I period. This was the work of the most advanced elements among the Negroes and the left-wing whites, and it was accomplished in the face of strong opposition from the forces described above. The Communist Party is particularly proud of the fact that it was a dynamic factor in this whole crucial development.

The first major concrete step in developing Negro-white trade union co-operation during this period was in the big meat-packing organizing campaign and strike movement of 1917-18, which we have outlined in Chapter 9. This key movement was led by William Z. Foster and J. W. Johnstone, who eventually became Communists. The unionizing drive succeeded in bringing into the labor organizations some 20,000 Negro workers, out of a total of about 200,000 workers organized all over the country. This achievement surpassed anything that had previously been accomplished by labor unions friendly to Negroes, such as the I.W.W., Miners, Longshoremen, and others. It is today a cherished tradition of the Communist Party.

The packinghouse success was all the more significant because it was achieved in the face of powerful opposition not only from the packers'

[1] H. R. Cayton and G. S. Mitchell, *Black Workers and the New Unions*, p. 378, Chapel Hill, N. C., 1932.

trust and the Jim Crow leaders of the A.F. of L., but also because it had to counter a strong resistance on the part of many Negro petty-bourgeois intellectuals. The latter, judging from past experiences, feared that the packinghouse union campaign would be only another trap for the Negro workers. Many also feared to lose their own leadership among the Negro masses to the unions. But the strong proletarian sentiments of the workers overcame all this opposition and led them to grasp in friendly solidarity the hands of the white workers outstretched to them.

The newly-developed solidarity of Negro and white workers in the packing industry had a real test of fire during the severe Chicago "race riots" of July 1919. This anti-Negro pogrom was organized by agents of the packers, who above all wanted to force the Negroes out of the unions and to drive a wedge between the Negro and white workers in their plants. The Chicago Stockyards Labor Council, then headed by J. W. Johnstone (Foster having left the packing industry to work in steel), saw the storm coming and mobilized the union membership to head it off. On July 6th a big parade of white and Negro packinghouse workers marched through the Negro districts of the South Side of Chicago, in an effort to allay the grave tension. Nevertheless, on July 27th, as a result of direct provocation by packer-organized hoodlums, the storm burst. Virtual civil war raged for two weeks in the whole area, with 6,000 police and soldiers mobilized to intimidate the Negro people. Meanwhile, 30,000 white stockyards union workers met, protested, pledged solidarity with their Negro brother workers, and demanded the withdrawal of the armed forces, which had done most of the killing. The splendid stand of the Stockyards Labor Council during this crisis, and especially of Jack Johnstone, stands forth as one of the very finest events in the history of the American labor movement. It did much to cement Negro-white labor solidarity over the country.[1]

A second basic development in this general period, making for Negro-white labor solidarity, was the wartime growth of *The Messenger* group of New York Negro workers and intellectuals. In Chapter 12 we have sketched an outline of this important movement. Its main significance, particularly with regard to Negro-white labor co-operation, rested in the fact that it challenged current Negro petty-bourgeois opinion that trade unionism was injurious to the Negro workers and it boldly urged Negroes to get into the unions. The group tirelessly exposed the indignities and injuries inflicted by the A.F. of L. Jim Crow system and demanded the admission of Negro workers into all unions on the basis of full equality. Besides, it displayed initiative in organizing Negro workers in those callings where they predominated in the working force.

[1] *The Communist*, Jan. 1930.

The *Messenger* group, in whose early and best stages pioneer Negro Communists played a decisive part, gave birth to a whole series of constructive activities and organizations, which we can only list here. It created several papers besides *The Messenger* itself, including *The Crusader*, *The Challenge* and *The Emancipator*. Among the labor organizations growing out of this group's activities were the United Brotherhood of Elevator and Switchboard Operators, National Brotherhood Workers of America, National Association for the Promotion of Labor Unionism among Negroes, the proposed United Negro Trades, the Brotherhood of Dining Car Employees, and the Brotherhood of Sleeping Car Porters. The broad *Messenger* group was also the source of several general Negro organizations of political protest and activity, among them the Friends of Negro Freedom and the African Blood Brotherhood.[1]

The *Messenger* group, particularly in its earlier phases, was essentially a radical, left-wing body. It sounded a high note of fighting militancy for the Negro people, in a period of hysteria when they were being fiercely attacked by capitalist reaction. The "New Negro" of the *Messenger* conception was one who was quite willing to die if need be in defense of himself, his family, and his political rights. He demanded "the full product of his toil." His immediate aim was "more wages, shorter hours and better housing conditions." He stood for "absolute social equality, education, physical action in self defense, freedom of speech, press and assembly, and the right of Russia to self-determination."[2] *The Messenger* was one of the very few Negro papers that opposed World War I. The F.B.I., distorting the paper's militancy, stated that "This magazine threw all discretion to the winds and became the exponent of open defiance and sedition."[3] Such militancy was eventually ironed out, however, by Randolph and his associates in pushing *The Messenger* into the typical right-wing Socialist position. Pressure from *The Messenger* group and from the Communist Party was largely responsible, during the early 1920's, for the more favorable position on trade unionism for Negro workers taken by the N.A.A.C.P. and the Urban League.

THE COMMUNISTS AND NEGRO-WHITE CO-OPERATION

The appearance of the Communist Party upon the political scene, after 1919, raised the whole struggle of the Negro people to a higher level in their fight for fundamental human rights. The Communists in particular strengthened the basic tendency of the Negro masses, the white work-

[1] Harry Haywood, unpublished manuscript.
[2] *The Messenger*, Aug. 1920.
[3] Max Lowenthal, *The Federal Bureau of Investigation*, p. 121, N. Y., 1950.

ers, and progressives generally to work together for the promotion of their common interests. With their customary thoroughness and militancy, the Communists quickly overcame the crass neglect and misunderstanding of the Negro question which had been such a marked weakness in the policies of the Socialist Labor and Socialist parties for the previous forty years, and they made the fight for Negro rights a burning issue throughout the labor movement.

Already during the period of 1920-1921 the Party had increasingly recognized the significance of the Negro question. When the Workers Party was organized at the end of 1921 and brought the Communist movement into legality, it took a better position regarding the Negro people. As remarked earlier, the convention resolution then adopted was the most advanced ever written on the Negro question by any working class party in the United States. At its 1922 convention, the Workers Party restressed the Negro question, adopting a program of full support to the fight of the Negro people for economic, political, and social equality, and waging a fight against white chauvinism and for unity in the struggle against capitalism. The T.U.E.L. in its mass campaigns during the early 1920's also gave encouragement and support to the general movement of the Negro people. In the national elections of 1924, William Z. Foster, presidential candidate of the Workers Party, presented the Communist program on the Negro question in many cities of the Deep South. And from those years right down to the present time there has been no convention or mass campaign of the Communist Party in which the Negro question has not been in the front line of consideration.

Five specific features may be singled out as characterizing the Communist fight on the Negro question, initiated during these early years. First, the Communists understood the key significance to the Negro people of a place in industry and in the unions, and they fought relentlessly to break down every barrier in this respect. Second, there was the special stress that the Communists laid upon the vital issue of social equality. Other movements which had given some co-operation to the Negro masses in their fight for justice almost always dodged and hedged on the matter of social equality. But not the Communists. In their programs and in the life of the Party, they saw in the fight for social equality a basic aspect of the whole struggle of the Negro people. Third, from the outset the Communists also realized the basic need to fight against white chauvinism (white supremacist ideology), not only in the ranks of the established enemy, but also among the white workers, even among those politically well developed. The importance of this position may be realized when one looks back at the outrageously chauvinistic material that formerly appeared unchallenged in the press of the Socialist Party. The fight against this insidious white chauvinism, in the midst of the Communists themselves, has gone on with increasing clarity and vigor ever since. Fourth, the Communists made clear the enormous political significance to white workers of the fight for Negro rights. They knocked on the head the current idea that support of the Negro people was only a sort of generous gesture of solidarity, and made it clear that the white workers could not win their fight without the co-operation of the Negroes. They demonstrated the fact that the Negro people constituted a powerful constructive force which imperatively had to be linked up with that of the whites. And fifth, whereas in the past most forces in the labor movement who were sympathetic to the Negroes' cause at best gave it only a sort of lip service, the Communists, realizing the tremendous importance of the Negro question, have always placed it high on their program and given it all possible support and emphasis. The Party in these years, however, had not yet come to understand the Negro question as a national question.

A NEW STAGE IN THE NEGRO PEOPLE'S MOVEMENT

The foregoing policies the Communists practiced over the years in all their activities on the Negro question, in such bodies as the American Negro Labor Congress, the trade unions, and many other organizations and movements. These Communist activities were a major factor in raising the Negro people's struggle to a higher political level.

The general developments listed above produced marked constructive effects upon the liberation movement of the Negro people. The first of these effects was the beginning of a break-down in the previous isolation of the Negro movement. The isolation of the Negro people had been most sharply cultivated by the Garvey movement, which not only discounted all hope of co-operation with whites, but even proposed that the Negroes should leave this country altogether. However, finding new allies among the white left-wing forces and the broad labor movement, the Negro people, in line with their stand in previous decades of struggle, gradually abandoned the Garveyite idea that they had to make their fight alone. More and more they took their proper place in the front ranks of the broad progressive, democratic forces of the United States.

The second important development in the Negro national movement during the period, arising from the causes with which we have been dealing, was the strengthening of the role of the Negro proletariat in the liberation movement. Not only did the workers become more important because of their growth numerically, but they also played more of the part of leaders of the Negro people. This was a consideration of major importance; for among the Negro people as well as among the American people in general, only the proletariat can successfully lead the toiling masses to freedom.

The third important development in the Negro movement in this period was the acceleration of the growth of Communist influence among the Negro masses. The Communists, who all over the world stand at the head of the fighting working class and the oppressed colonial peoples, were particularly fitted to convey a new strength and leadership to the Negro movement in the United States. In the ensuing years they were to demonstrate this fact very clearly.

17. A.F. of L. Class Collaboration During the Coolidge "Prosperity" (1923-1929)

The period from early 1923 through most of 1929 was one of industrial expansion and capitalist prosperity for the United States. With ups and downs, the "prosperity" lasted practically all through the presidency of the Yankee skinflint and police strikebreaker, Calvin Coolidge, as well as during some six months of the term of the "great engineer," Herbert Hoover, imperialist exploiter of colonial peoples. It was a time of speculation and capitalist arrogance, until finally, in October 1929, the whole dizzy economic edifice went crumbling like a house of cards in the greatest economic crisis in the history of world capitalism.

American industry, fed by the red blood of war, increased its production from 1913 to 1929 by 70 percent.[1] "By 1928 the total volume of (U.S.) production exceeded the production of the whole of Europe."[2] The production of passenger automobiles, the bonanza industry, went up from 895,930 in 1915 to 4,587,400 in 1929, and trucks from 74,000 to 771,000. The production of gasoline increased by 300 percent. During this whole period monopoly flourished, the trustification of industry developed at a rapid speed, and the number of blood-nourished millionaires multiplied. Never before had the world seen the like of this saturnalia of capitalist profit-making. But the living standards of the workers lagged.

Various factors combined to create the Coolidge post-war boom. Among these were the American capital export of $20 billion in war and post-war loans to finance Europe's war and to rebuild its shattered industries; the capture of world markets by the United States from the crippled European powers; the introduction of an intense speed-up, or "rationalization" of industry in the home country; the growth of a huge installment-buying system; the industrialization of the South; the expansion of the automobile industry; and the wide extension of luxury industries. The whole fevered development was based upon the destruction

[1] James S. Allen, *World Monopoly and Peace*, p. 120, N. Y., 1946.
[2] F. Sternberg, *The Coming Crisis*, p. 119, N. Y., 1947.

wrought by World War I. This great war not only tremendously enriched the United States and made it far and away the wealthiest capitalist country, but it also demonstrated that the world capitalist system, including the United States, was sinking into an incurable general crisis, and that in order to keep going even temporarily, it required the fatal stimulant of war.

During the Coolidge "prosperity" period American imperialism was aggressively expansionist and reactionary. Its general predatory spirit was exemplified by the huge growth of military and naval armaments, repeated armed invasions of Caribbean and Central American countries, systematic penetration of Germany through the Dawes and Young plans, violent hostility toward the Soviet Union, and inroads upon China through the device of the "Open Door" policy. It was characterized by such developments on the home front as the passage of reactionary legislation to curb union labor, the systematic encouragement of company unionism, the execution of Sacco and Vanzetti, the continued imprisonment of Mooney and Billings, the unchecked outrage of lynching in the South, the Teapot Dome scandal, the Scopes anti-evolution trial, and the like.

THE SPEED-UP, OR "RATIONALIZATION," DRIVE

The central economic aim of the big capitalists in the United States during this period was to speed up the workers in production, to exploit them to the limit of their endurance. To exploit the workers more intensively is, of course, always the objective of the capitalists; but this was especially the case during the Coolidge years. Their aim was to satisfy the commodity-hungry post-war world markets, with a minimum of new capital investment—the demand for capital export to Europe being very heavy. Hence the speed up or "rationalization of industry," as they called it, became a fetish with the American capitalists during these years.

The heart of the rationalization of industry was the system of mass production. With the assembly line as its characteristic feature, and the reduction of innumerable skilled jobs to the common denominator of the line, this changed the whole lay-out of the plant. This system, stimulated by World War I, was the basis for the eventual great increase in the productivity of American industry. During the 1920's the capitalists strove to drive the workers even faster and to make them helpless in the mass production system.

But to enforce their speed-up of the workers, it was necessary for the employers to break the latter's resistance to being thus ruthlessly driven. Here the conservative trade union leadership came into the picture, as willing servants of the employers. The top A.F. of L. and Railroad Brotherhood leaders had rallied their membership for the employers' imperialist World War I and shamelessly sabotaged the workers' resistance during the big union-smashing drive of the bosses after the war had been won. Now they could be depended upon to perform this new speed-up task for their masters, the employers—and they did just that.

The conservative union leaders were not only willing but eager to carry out the bosses' plans for the "rationalization" of industry. What happened to the workers' living standards in the meantime was not of primary concern to them. These labor bureaucrats were frightened by the serious defeats the unions had suffered during the post-war offensive of the capitalists and by the growth of radical sentiment among the rank-and-file workers. And so the only condition they laid down to the arrogant employers was that they be allowed to maintain some sort of dues-paying mass unions, however enfeebled, that would suffice to pay their over-swollen salaries, not to mention their other financial perquisites.

To this end, the conservative union leaders were ready to go far in the direction of company unionism, and they did. William Green, who succeeded Gompers as the head of the A.F. of L. in 1924, made this willingness very clear in a number of the most servile speeches ever delivered by a labor leader in the United States. He placed the unions of the workers at the disposal of the bosses in the latter's speed-up plans. The Executive Council's report to the A.F. of L. convention of 1927 showed how far the labor bureaucrats were going toward company-unionizing the trade unions. It declared that "there is nothing that the company union can do within the single company that the trade union cannot develop the machinery for doing and accomplish more effectively. Union-management co-operation ... is much more fundamental and effective than employee representation plans for co-operation with management."

Some sections of big, open-shop capital became interested in these offers of the A.F. of L. leaders to have the craft unions "do better" the functions of the company unions than the company unions themselves. William Green reported to the Executive Council, in January 1927, that "the General Motors Company was prepared to agree to the organization of some of its big plants as an experiment in union-management co-operation, provided that there would be no jurisdictional fights."[1] But the 19 unions claiming jurisdiction over the automobile workers could not agree among themselves as to which should get the workers. With the characteristic stupidity of craft unionism, they preferred see the basic industries remain unorganized than to surrender their rival paper

[1] Lorwin, *The American Federation of Labor*, p. 246.

claims over the workers. Therefore the whole scheme fell through. Lorwin says that other big concerns besides General Motors were also interested in Green's plans to company-unionize the American labor movement.

THE UNIONS AS SPEED-UP AGENCIES OF THE BOSSES

The new orientation of the labor bureaucracy toward intensified class collaboration for the speed-up began to manifest itself in the form of the so-called Baltimore and Ohio plan, a scheme for more intensive production, devised by the efficiency experts of that railroad. It was forced upon the defeated shopmen on several roads at the end of their ill-fated strike of 1922. The essence of the B. & O. plan was that if the workers would agree with the bosses to turn out more work they would thereby automatically reap real advantages in the shape of increased wages and more continuous employment.

With the top labor officials bankrupt after the big post-war drive of the employers against the unions, the A.F. of L. convention of 1923 grasped at the B. & O. plan, or union-management co-operation scheme, as manna miraculously fallen from heaven. It offered a way to preserve some semblance of mass organization and it gave them a sort of program to take to the workers, so they made the most of it. The convention, composed almost exclusively of high union officials, hailed the plan as a turning point for the labor movement and the United States. Two years later the 1925 convention of the A.F. of L. developed the plan in great detail as the "new wage policy."

Not content with offering to co-operate with the capitalists for more production, the trade union leaders went into the speed-up business themselves. They put efficiency engineers on the union payrolls and had them devise plans for increasing production. These schemes they then proceeded to force upon the workers and also offered them, free of charge, to the employers. Many labor organizations followed such practices. Indeed, unions that did not do so were looked upon by the bureaucrats as backward and unprogressive. So low had the trade union leadership fallen that it had actually transformed the unions from fighting organizations, designed to protect the workers' interests, into parts of the employers' producing mechanism. Union-management co-operation thus went far beyond even the rosiest dreams of the classical industrial efficiency expert, Frederick Taylor. Before World War I, Taylor's speed-up devices had been condemned with bell, book, and candle by the labor officialdom as the death of all trade unionism; but now these same leaders accepted Taylor's ideas as the gospel of organized labor.

The erstwhile "progressive" or center group in the labor movement vied with the right-wing labor leadership in its enthusiasm for union-management co-operation. The Socialists, too, grabbed it hook, line, and sinker. In fact, in no unions in this country was the speed-up system so highly developed as in the supposedly socialistic needle trades unions. They had complete sets of efficiency engineers, standards of production, and all the rest of the speed-up plans. Leo Wolman, research director of the Amalgamated Clothing Workers, thus explained the role of labor unions in this period: "The primary aim of the labor union is to co-operate with the manufacturer to produce more efficient conditions of production that will be of mutual advantage. In some cases labor unions will even lend money to worthy manufacturers to tide them over periods of distress."

FORD VERSUS MARX

In order to drive ahead with the speed-up, "rationalization" plans and to demoralize the labor movement still further, blatant American imperialism put forth during the Coolidge period a whole series of "prosperity illusions" designed to befuddle and confuse the workers. Never in the whole history of American capitalism did the bosses give birth to so many glowingly utopian ideas of social progress as in the hectic boom times of the 1920's.

For example, Thomas N. Carver, Harvard professor of political economy, came out with a glittering theory to the effect that the workers, because of mass production and the speed-up, not only could become but were becoming capitalists by buying up industrial stocks.[1] "The only revolution now under way," said he, "is in the United States. It is a revolution that is to wipe out the distinction between laborers and capitalists by making laborers their own capitalists and by compelling most capitalists to become laborers of one kind or another." He stated that the savings of the workers were so great that "Any day the laborers decide to do so, they can divert a few billions of savings to the purchase of common stock of industrial corporations, railroads, and public service companies, and actually control considerable numbers of them." Thus, said he, "If the railroad employees would merely save the increase which they had recently received in wages, it would give them $625,000,000 a year for investment. On this basis, if they bought railroad stocks at par, they could, by investing all their savings and dividends in railroad stocks,

1. T. N. Carver, *The Present Economic Revolution in the United States*, pp. 9, 94, 124, Boston, 1925.

buy $3,490,000,000 in five years. This would give them a substantial majority of all the outstanding stocks." But how the workers were to eat in the meantime, Carver did not say.

Professor Tugwell of Columbia, in his book, *Industry's Coming of Age*, developed the perspective that capitalism—monopolized industries and all—was gradually becoming "socialized," with the private ownership feature tending to atrophy and die out. Gillette, the safety razor magnate, in his book, *The People's Corporation*, painted a capitalist-"Socialist" utopia, which the people were gradually creating by buying industrial stocks, a plan akin to Carver's. Foster and Catchings, forerunners of John Maynard Keynes, elaborated plans for "financing the buyer" which supposedly would eliminate economic crises and bring prosperity for all. Stuart Chase, an erstwhile Socialist, pictured a new and glowing mass prosperity inherent in the simple plan of abolishing waste in industry by applying more scientific production methods. Whiting Williams, MacKenzie King, Glen Plumb, Thorstein Veblen, and many others added their voices to the chorus of capitalist economists and industrialists who were about to create a world of plenty for all. It was in this spirit that Herbert Hoover, who was Secretary of Commerce under Coolidge and one of this school of economists, assured the people after his election, in November 1928, that the United States was then on the verge of abolishing poverty. All this demagogy, of course, was but the delirium of optimism (in an extreme degree) always felt by the capitalists when their economic system is in the boom phase of its cycle.

The substance of what all these exuberant boosters of American capitalism were saying was that capitalism in this country, by the natural processes of its evolution, was turning into socialism, if not something far superior. Capitalism in the United States, distinct from that in Europe, had overcome its internal contradictions, had "come of age," was being democratized, and had entered upon an endless upward spiral of development and mass prosperity. It was a sort of "capitalist efficiency socialism." The "New Capitalism," they called it. As these soothsayers would have it, Henry Ford had superseded Karl Marx.

During these hectic years the capitalists of Europe and elsewhere looked with envy and admiration upon the United States, where the capitalists by the magic of mass production and the speed-up had apparently tamed the labor movement and solved all economic problems. In the forefront of these foreign admirers of American monopoly capitalism and imperialism were the Social-Democrats of Europe. Rudolph Hilferding, leading theoretician of German Social-Democracy, said at the Kiel 1927 convention of that party, "We are in a period of capitalism which in the main has overcome the era of free competition and the sway of the blind forces of the market and we are coming to a capitalist organized economy." Karl Kautsky also supported this line. The Social-Democrats outdid each other in praise of the new American mass production and intensified class collaboration, and they sought eagerly to introduce these things into their own countries. In the United States, so they believed, all their Bernsteinian dreams of capitalism turning into "socialism" were coming true.

"THE HIGHER STRATEGY OF LABOR"

The upper officials of the A.F. of L. and the Railroad Brotherhoods fell right in with this campaign of ideologically poisoning the working class, even as they had fully accepted the speed-up program which was the basis for the great flood of capitalist demagogy about everlasting "prosperity." William Green, an apt pupil of Gompers, arch-reactionary and labor sponsor of capitalism, took the lead in pledging loyalty to the capitalist system and in excoriating everything radical or revolutionary. H. V. Boswell, head of the Locomotive Engineers Bank of New York, also expressed the current bureaucratic opinion when he said: "Who wants to be a bolshevik when he can be a capitalist instead? We have shown how to mix oil and water; how to reconcile capital and labor. Instead of standing on a street corner soapbox, screaming with rage because the capitalists own real estate, bank accounts, and automobiles, the engineer has turned in and become a capitalist himself."[1]

To carry out their new speed-up, get-rich-quick orientation, the labor bureaucrats, upon Carver's suggestion, worked out what they grandiloquently called "the higher strategy of labor." Matthew Woll, in *Iron Age,* thus expressed his idea of this newfangled term: "In its early struggles labor sought to retard, to limit, to embarrass production to obtain that which it desired. Now it seeks the confidence that it is a preserver and developer of an economic, industrial, and social order in which workers, employers, and the public may all benefit." And Warren S. Stone, "progressive" president of the Locomotive Engineers, explained it thus: "Organized labor in the United States has gone through three cycles. . . . The first was the period during which class consciousness was being aroused. . . . The second was the defensive struggle for the principle of collective bargaining. . . . The third cycle or phase lies in constructive development toward a system of co-operation rather than war."[2]

The plain English of all this blather was that the "new wage policy" and "the higher strategy of labor" amounted to a speed-up, no-strike

---

[1] Cited in Bimba, *History of the American Working Class,* p. 347.
[2] Cited in *World's Work,* Nov. 1924.

policy. That is, the workers were to produce to the limit and then trust to the "intelligent" capitalists to reward them adequately in friendly conferences with the union leaders. Consequently, the number of strikes and strikers toboganned. In 1922 the total number of strikers was 1,612,562, but by 1929 this had fallen to only 230,463.[1] The workers' living and working standards suffered accordingly.

Along with Wall Street's no-strike policy, dolled up as "the higher strategy of labor," the top labor leadership also accepted the current bourgeois propaganda about the tremendous savings of the workers, and they plunged into business in a big way. During the early twenties they set up a whole maze of labor banks, insurance companies, investment concerns, and the like, more than one of which operated upon a non-union basis. This was "trade union capitalism," as Communists called it. The unions went in especially for labor banking. The international union or important central labor body that did not support labor banking was considered very much behind the times. All told, at the height of this craze, in 1925, there were 36 labor banks, with total resources of $126,356,944. Outstanding leaders in this banking movement were the Locomotive Engineers and the Amalgamated Clothing Workers.

DEGENERATION OF THE LABOR BUREAUCRACY

The top leadership of the American Federation of Labor and the Railroad Brotherhoods, ever since the 1890's, had been noted for its corruption by capitalist influences, its almost total lack of working class integrity. The characteristic A.F. of L. leader of the period (with many honorable exceptions, of course) was one who was devoted to the perpetuation of capitalism, was an inveterate enemy of all radicalism, and looked upon trade union leadership as an easy way of making a good living. Top jobs in the unions were rich sinecures, to be grabbed and held by any means possible. Such posts, among their numerous financial advantages for their holders, provided many opportunities for union leaders to milk employers who wanted guarantees against strikes, and also opportunities for these leaders to develop remunerative alliances with the Republican and Democratic parties. The welfare of the workers who made up the unions was a matter of but secondary consideration. The marvel was how the labor movement could exist at all, much less make real progress, with such a corrupt top leadership.

During World War I, the post-war offensive, and the Coolidge "prosperity" period, the corrupting capitalist influences upon the labor

[1] *American Labor Year Book*, 1929, p. 135.

bureaucracy were particularly strong, and the leaders' morale sank visibly under the pressure. Many of the officials became rich from the plentiful sources of graft open to them. John Mitchell, former president of the United Mine Workers and first Vice-President of the A.F. of L., was a characteristic figure, a real capitalist. When he died in 1919 his wealth totaled $244,295, including investments in many capitalist concerns—coal mines, Armour & Co., the B. & O., the New York Central, the Rock Island—all companies that were noted for their labor-crushing activities. George L. Berry, head of the Printing Pressmen and long an honored figure in the A.F. of L. hierarchy, acquired a million dollars or more by his various brands of skulduggery. There were many like him in the various unions. Dozens of labor leaders were taken over by the capitalists and used as "personnel directors"—as strike-preventers—in their industries.

Corruption was most rampant in the building trades, which formed the backbone of the A.F. of L. during these times. There real gangsterism prevailed. Many building trades leaders sold "strike insurance" freely to the employers and robbed their membership by every known device. Numbers of them also were directly tied up with the underworld during the period of prohibition. They ruled the unions by force and, fighting for control, they periodically carried on murderous gun battles with each other. A star product of this Gompers unionism was Robert P. Brindell of New York, who was credited with amassing a million dollars in the two years before he was exposed by the Lockwood Committee in 1920. Another was Simon O'Donnell, wartime head of the Building Trades Council of Chicago, who was given a spectacular funeral, gangster fashion, with a $10,000 coffin, when he died in 1927. Still another was the notorious "Big Tim" Murphy, also of the Chicago Building Trades. Murphy, who was finally killed in a gangster war, expressed the characteristic A.F. of L. philosophy of labor leadership as follows: "I'm still pretty much of a kid, but I made a millon and spent a million, and I figure I'll make another million before they plant me."[1]

The bosses cultivated this corrupt type of leadership, even though occasionally, to discredit the unions, they would send one or two crooked union officials to jail after a spectacular trial. As for the A.F. of L. Executive Council, it did precisely nothing to eliminate the gangsterism and corruption. On the contrary, the Mitchells, Berrys, Brindells, O'Donnells, and many more of the like were for decades dominant figures in the A.F. of L. Some of them enjoyed honored seats in the Executive Council itself, and generally they crowded the A.F. of L. conventions,

[1] William Z. Foster, *Misleaders of Labor*, Chicago, 1927.

voting down all "red" proposals. This was the kind of labor leadership that so ruthlessly rejected amalgamation, a labor party, and Soviet recognition at the 1923 convention of the A.F. of L., even though the bulk of the organized workers had demanded these policies. It was such labor leaders, too, who were ardent supporters of the Gompers clique in office, and defenders of the "new wage policy," "the higher strategy of labor," "trade union capitalism," and militant struggle against the left wing, during the Coolidge boom period of 1923-1929.

THE BILL OF RECKONING

The intensified class collaboration carried on by the conservative upper leadership of the trade unions during the Coolidge period had a number of very harmful effects upon the workers and their unions. For one thing, the acceptance and propagation by the union leaders of prosperity illusions, put out by the employers, were demoralizing ideologically to the workers. Especially confusing was the boundless flood of propaganda to the effect that economic crises were now a thing of the past in the United States. It left the workers quite unprepared for the economic holocaust that struck in October 1929. The top trade union leaders, deceived by their own propaganda, were even less ready for the great economic breakdown than the workers themselves when it finally came.

The bosses' speed-up program, popularized among the workers by the trade union leaders under the name of the "new wage policy" and "the higher strategy of labor," also operated to the detriment of the working and living standards of the workers. This no-strike policy took all the fight out of the unions. Never in the life of the modern American labor movement was its morale so low as during the Coolidge period of intensified class collaboration. Taking advantage of the cultivated inertia of the unions, the employers naturally grabbed unto themselves all the advantages of the increased production which they were able to wring from the workers under the very convenient plan of union-management co-operation.

There was also a general worsening of conditions in the shops during this period. With the class vigilance of the unions weakened by the pest of class collaboration, the bosses were able, under the sacred sign of industrial efficiency, to strip the workers of many hard-won labor conditions. In a period of industrial activity, when the workers possessed a maximum of latent power with which to improve their wage rates, the employers kept wages down. From 1923 to 1929, although output in industry increased no less than 29 percent per worker and profits doubled and tripled, the workers' wages advanced little, if at all. Wage increases, coming mostly from overtime work, went mainly to the skilled workers, with the wage conditions of the masses of semi-skilled and unskilled either stagnant or declining. The top union officials, now blossoming forth as bankers and industrialists, had little time to waste upon such minor matters as protecting the workers' standards.

The class collaboration policies of the union leaders also had deleterious effects upon the growth of the unions. The Coolidge boom years, although accompanied by considerable unemployment, constituted a period of high industrial activity that should have provided a big increase in union membership. But the unions actually declined numerically during these years. Thus in 1922 the A.F. of L. had 3,195,635 members, whereas in 1929, after several years' dose of "union-management co-operation," the number had fallen to 2,933,545, a loss of 262,090 members. Actually the loss was much greater, as many unions, despite membership decreases, continued for internal political reasons to pay their earlier, top-figure per capita tax to the A.F. of L. For example, in 1928 the U.M.W.A. paid on 400,000 members, as in 1920, but in the meantime it had lost about 200,000 dues-paying members. The 1923-29 period was the first time in labor history that the trade unions failed to grow substantially during a long period of "prosperity."

To make the "new capitalism" policies still more bankrupt, the union leaders made ducks and drakes of the millions of dollars that the workers had so trustingly placed in their hands through the many labor banks and other financial and industrial concerns organized during the epidemic of "trade union capitalism." The whole shaky structure soon collapsed, with losses to the workers of huge sums of money. This financial debacle was brought about by wild speculations in Florida, and by general recklessness and incompetence. Speaking of the breakdown of the Locomotive Engineers' big string of banks, Perlman and Taft say, "On the larger issue of redirecting capitalism the movement for labor banks, as shown by the engineers' fiasco, was little more rational than the children's crusade against the Saracens."[1] The number of labor banks fell off rapidly, in the midst of the growing scandal. By 1932 their number was reduced to seven, and now there are only four of them left. This was the unhappy ending of Professor Carver's scheme for the workers to buy out capitalism—as executed by the capitalist-minded reactionaries heading the A.F. of L. and Railroad Brotherhoods.

[1] Perlman and Taft, *History of Labor in the U.S.*, Vol. 4, p. 578.

18. Communist Class Struggle Policies (1923-1929)

Throughout the Coolidge "prosperity" period the Workers Party, renamed the Workers (Communist) Party in 1925, fought strongly against the whole class collaboration program of the trade union leadership and came forward with a policy of class struggle. This in spite of serious right opportunism—Lovestoneism—in its own ranks. The Party exposed the fallacies, in theory and practice, of the "B. & O. plan," "union-management co-operation," the "new wage policy," "labor banking," "the higher strategy of labor," and all the rest of the current ideological sugar-coating of the employers' speed-up program. It also blasted the crude "American exceptionalism" underlying the entire campaign of confusing and thereby more intensively exploiting, the workers—the notion that somehow capitalism in the United States was different from and superior to capitalism in the rest of the world. The Party showed that the so-called "new capitalism" was just the same old capitalism in the boom phase of its economic cycle, and that, far from having ended all economic crises, this system was at the time definitely heading toward a severe industrial break-down. The Party demonstrated that the entire policy of the official bureaucracy was bringing about lowered living standards and weakened trade unions for the workers.

The Communists and their allies, in spite of severe persecution, fought everywhere against the application of the deadly class collaboration program of the A.F. of L. leadership—on the floors of union halls, in the trade union elections, and on strike picket lines. They cultivated a militant struggle of the workers, Negro people, and farming masses for their elementary demands. Most of the important organizational campaigns and strikes of the period were either directly led or heavily influenced by the Communists and their co-workers. This was because the official heads of the labor movement refused to give leadership to the workers, even on the most elementary questions. This resolute fight against the A.F. of L. class collaboration policies during the Coolidge regime constitutes one of the most effective pages in the history of the Communist Party of the United States.

THE EXPULSION POLICY

A basic necessity for the employers and labor leaders, in order to force the current speed-up program upon the unwilling workers, was to break down all opposition to such a program in the unions. This was what the efficiency expert Taylor had euphoniously called "getting the workers' consent." It implied war to the knife against the Communists and all other opponents of intensified class collaboration. As a general consequence democracy was just about extinguished in the trade unions. A "goon" rule, patterned after the current gangsterism of the prohibition era, and in many cases actually carried out by professional gangsters, was instituted in unions where the left wing had a strong following. Moreover, the employers and the police could also be relied upon to help the reactionary union leaders, should the situation threaten to get out of hand.

The worst feature of this terroristic regime was the leaders' policy of expelling militants from the unions. The Workers (Communist) Party was blasted, the T.U.E.L. was condemned as a Communist organization and a dual union, and membership in either brought expulsion. The Communists, who could not be defeated in honest debate, were ousted from the unions altogether, often to the accompaniment of physical violence. This meant that they were also forced out of the industries where they earned their livelihood. Such terrorism was something new in the American labor movement, for all of its previous record of reaction. Never before had workers been systematically expelled from their jobs and from their unions because of their political opinions. Dozens of union ruling cliques, anticipating by a generation the Smith and McCarran Acts, wrote clauses in their union constitutions specifically barring Communists (often along with Negroes, women, youths, and other "undesirables"). The expulsion campaign, beginning with a few militants here and there, finally reached the stage of ousting thousands at a time.

The Socialists went along with the outright Gompersites in this terror campaign, even as they had swallowed whole the latter's B. & O. plan, new wage policy, speed-up program. Indeed, in their activities the Socialists even outstripped the open reactionaries. For the first of the expulsions took place in the Socialist-led International Ladies Garment Workers Union, and it was also in that organization that the expulsion campaign later reached its highest point, with the ouster of 35,000 New York cloakmakers. No unions in the country were more gang-ridden than the needle trades organizations.

In the shameful class collaboration of the Coolidge period the Socialist leaders finally cemented the open alliance with the Gompers—now Green—bureaucracy that they had been courting for so many years. Schneider and Saposs describe this development in which the Socialists gave up their policy of militant boring-from-within and sought to win the confidence of the A.F. of L. administration.[1] And, says Saposs, "After the world war the Socialist boring-from-within policies and tactics were completely reversed. . . . Instead, they aim to sue for the confidence and good will of the entrenched labor leaders. . . . This new political alignment of the Socialists with the Administration forces marks the end of their leadership of the opposition in the labor movement."[2] Ever since then, the Socialists have been part and parcel of the reactionary clique dominating the American labor movement.

About the close of the "prosperity" period, in May 1929, a group of "left" Social-Democrats and renegade Communists, alarmed at the too flagrant corruption of the Socialist Party leadership, formed the Conference for Progressive Labor Action. It aimed at eventually becoming a rival of the Communist Party. Its chief figures were A. J. Muste, head of the Brookwood Labor School, J. H. Crosswaith, and others. Its program called for an active wage policy, social insurance, trade union democracy, a labor party, workers' education, and recognition of Soviet Russia. The C.P.L.A. was built on the Two-and-a-Half International plan—that is, lots of radical talk but little constructive action. It made a pale effort to pattern its main work after the T.U.E.L. This "Muste movement" existed for several years. It took part in a few textile and mine strikes, but it played no very important role in the labor movement. In October 1934, it merged with the Trotskyites—a short-lived union which hastened its disintegration. The C.P.L.A. served mostly as a fig leaf to cover up the nakedness of the leadership of the Socialist Party and the A.F. of L. The Musteites were the "little brothers of the big labor fakers."

The resentment of the masses of workers at the treacherous class collaboration policies being followed by their unions' leadership was evidenced by the strong support given the Workers (Communist) Party and T.U.E.L. program in many industries, despite the expulsion policy of the top union leaders. Thus, in the Machinists Union elections of 1925 the Anderson progressive-left slate got 17,076 votes, against 18,021 for the administration candidate, William H. Johnston. Undoubtedly, the left actually won the election. And in the Carpenters Union elections of the same year the T.U.E.L. candidate, M. Rosen, was credited with 9,014 votes against 77,985 for the reigning autocrat, Hutcheson.

[1] D. M. Schneider, *The Workers (Communist) Party and the American Trade Unions.* Baltimore, 1928.
[2] D. J. Saposs, *Left Wing Unionism,* pp. 37, 39, N. Y., 1926.

HARD-FOUGHT TEXTILE STRIKES

Among the many industries where the Communist Party and T.U.E.L. forces led strikes during the Coolidge period were the textile, needle trades, and mining industries. These were the so-called sick industries of the period, suffering heavily from unemployment, speed-up, low wages, and—to make matters worse for the workers—reactionary trade union leadership. All these strikes were conducted upon a broad united front basis of Communists, left Socialists, and progressives, through the T.U.E.L. and its specific organizational forms in the various industries.

The first big struggle of textile workers to be initiated by the Party and conducted directly by the T.U.E.L. was the famous Passaic, New Jersey, strike of 1926. At the outset the workers, employed mostly on woolens and worsteds, were almost completely unorganized—of the one million textile workers nationally, not over five percent were unionized at that time. The Party forces energetically set about organizing among them. Characteristic conditions of deep poverty, gross exploitation, and boss tyranny prevailed. The spark that touched off the bitter struggle in Passaic was a 10 percent wage cut in October 1925. The A.F. of L. union in the industry, one of the most incompetent in the labor movement, the United Textile Workers, refused to stir in the matter, so the T.U.E.L. forces, in the form of the United Front Committee, began with success to organize in Passaic.

The strike was precipitated on January 21, 1926, when a committee of 45, presenting the demands of the workers to the Botany Mills, were discharged forthwith. The response of the mass of workers to this brutal treatment of their leaders was immediate and powerful. In two days the 5,000 unionized workers of the autocratic company were on strike, and within a few days the whole Passaic area, with some 16,000 textile workers, was tied up. The bosses, with the characteristic violence that accompanied the "open shop" movement, undertook to break the strike by instituting thug rule in the community. Every known strikebreaking technique was used; but they all failed, the solidarity of the workers was invincible. The official head of the strike was Albert Weisbord, a weakling; but the main strength came from the Party backing, with such militant fighters as W. W. Weinstone, Charles Krumbein, Elizabeth Gurley Flynn, John Ballam, Alfred Wagenknecht, and others.

The strike was very well organized and was fought on both sides with great stubbornness. It attracted national attention. This hard-fought strike sounded a new and militant note in the labor movement, then being choked by the union-management co-operation poison. The struggle lasted thirteen months; it was finally settled by a compromise which restored the wage cut, admitted the right of the workers to organize in the A.F. of L., and gave some recognition to the union grievance committees.

The next big textile strike in which the Party and the T.U.E.L. played a decisive role was the walkout of 26,000 cotton mill workers in New Bedford, in April 1928. This strike was also against a wage cut and the speed-up, and for union recognition. The strike gave birth to a series of further strikes in Fall River, Woonsocket, and surrounding textile centers. After six months of struggle the wage cut was defeated in New Bedford, but the workers were deprived of a real victory by a typical A.F. of L. sell-out. The strike resulted in the formation of a new textile union, the National Textile Workers, affiliated to the T.U.E.L.

The most desperately-fought textile strike of the period, however, was that in Gastonia, North Carolina, in 1929. The National Textile Workers Union sent organizers into the South in February of that year. Their activities started a general movement among the textile workers, who were suffering under extremely low wages, the stretch-out (speed-up), and anti-union shop conditions. The workers involved were almost entirely American-born, for several generations back. The N.T.W. forces concentrated on the Gastonia area, where a strike of 2,500 workers of the Loray mills took place on April 2nd. Later these workers were joined by 1,700 others. The whole membership of 25,000 local textile workers was deeply stirred by the dramatic strike. The Workers (Communist) Party had many of its organizers in the field.

The millowners and the state government officials set out immediately to break the menacing strike by violence. The governor, a textile millowner, ordered several companies of militia to the scene. The American Legion organized vigilantes, and on April 18th, a masked gang of 50 to 75 attacked the union headquarters, wrecked it, and beat up strikers there. On June 7th, another gang of thugs, led by Chief of Police Aderholt, raided the union center; but this time the workers were prepared and defended themselves with gunfire. The police chief was killed and three of his deputies were wounded. This led to the arrest of 100 workers. Eventually seven strike leaders were found guilty of second degree murder and given prison sentences of up to 20 years. During the trial, a vigilante mob ran riot, smashing the union headquarters and assaulting organizers. Ella May Wiggin, a mother and militant strike leader, was murdered. The strike was finally crushed, but the millowners were compelled to make concessions to the workers.

The A.F. of L. was greatly alarmed by the uprisings of the southern textile workers and the growing Communist influence, which affected Tennessee, Georgia, the Carolinas, and other centers, and it sent a flock of organizers into these areas in an effort to head off the movement. William Green toured the South hobnobbing with the millowners and bankers and offering them co-operation of the approved B. & O. plan type. But the textile bosses, mostly representing Wall Street big capital, preferred their own methods of suppressing strikes and union activities by open terrorism. The southern textile workers, however, remained unorganized. At the time the Workers (Communist) Party made a major mistake of concentrating too much of its attention upon Gastonia and not spreading out and challenging the employers and the A.F. of L. misleaders in other key southern textile centers.

The Passaic, New Bedford, and Gastonia strikes represented new high levels of strike organization for the United States. Not only was the strike organization itself highly perfected in each case, but the auxiliary departments were also well developed. There were strong youth sections to mobilize the youth and children. Special attention was paid, too, to the enlistment of women in the strikes, and many women leaders played most active parts. The Workers International Relief (W.I.R.) thoroughly organized national strike relief campaigns, and the International Labor Defense (I.L.D.) conducted vigorous fights for legal defense of the many arrested strikers and union leaders. The Workers (Communist) Party gave vitality and strength to all this work. The strikes, too, were conducted with a keen eye to strike strategy, a subject to which the T.U.E.L., in international affiliation to the R.I.L.U., paid very much attention during these years. The great significance of the strikes was their high fighting spirit at a time when the A.F. of L. was carrying out its no-strike policies. They emphasized the role of a new factor, the Communist Party, in the labor movement.

THE NEEDLE TRADES STRIKES

The needle trades "Socialist" union leaders, as already remarked, were neck deep in the paralyzing A.F. of L. class collaboration and speedup policies of the period of 1923-29. This fact brought them into head-on collision with the Communist and progressive forces, who were strongly organized in the Party and the T.U.E.L. in the industry. The left wing fought for improved wage conditions, the 40-hour week, the shop delegate system, organization of the unorganized, a needle trades industrial union, a labor party, affiliation with the R.I.L.U., defense of the Soviet Union, and against the whole prevailing speed-up, gangster-control regime of the right-wing leaders.

The first decisive collision developed in the Fur Workers Union. After various oscillations in power, the left-center united front made a bitter fight and won solid control of the New York Joint Board, which constituted about 80 percent of the whole union. Ben Gold, who was stabbed by gangsters during the struggle, became head of this Board. In February 1926, some 12,000 New York furriers went out on strike with the 40-hour week as their central demand. The ensuing 17-week strike was one of the hardest fought in the history of New York City.

The Kaufman leadership of the national union sabotaged the strike from the outset. Finally they brought in William Green, A.F. of L. president, who went over the head of the New York Joint Board and arranged a sell-out with the bosses on the basis of the 42-hour week. The left rallied the fur workers so solidly, however, that they refused to allow the betrayal agreement to be put through. Several weeks later, the workers finally won the 40-hour week, the first instance of its establishment in American industry. It was a resounding victory for the workers and the left, and a direct smash in the face of the strikebreaking top leadership of the A.F. of L.

The latter was not so easily disposed of, however. Deeply embarrassed and embittered by their defeat, Green and Co. set up an ultra-reactionary committee, consisting of Matthew Woll, E. McGrady, J. Ryan, J. Sullivan, and H. Frayne, to "investigate" the conduct of the strike. As a result the Furriers' New York Joint Board and its affiliated local unions were "reorganized" in January 1927. The effect of this unheard-of action was to expel 12,000 furriers from their union and to leave the International bankrupt.[1]

The struggle in the International Ladies Garment Workers was no less intense. By 1925, in spite of the top leaders' gangster and expulsion policy, the left-center united front had won control of locals 2, 9, and 22, comprising about 70 percent of the New York Joint Board, backbone of the International. Whereupon, President Sigman cynically expelled the 77 Communists and T.U.E.L. supporters on these locals' executive boards, an action which amounted to ousting 35,000 members from the union. The expelled locals set up the Joint Action Committee, conducted a sharp struggle, and after 16 weeks compelled Sigman to give in and reinstate the three locals. This was a nationwide victory for the left wing of the union. Consequently, when the national convention of the I.L.G.W.U. assembled in Philadelphia in November 1925, the left wing, with 114 delegates, represented 34,762 members, or two-thirds of the convention's real representation. But the Sigman administration had so gerrymandered the union elections that although there were only 15,852 members behind them, they nevertheless had 146 delegates, or the con-

[1] Philip S. Foner, *The Fur and Leather Workers Union*, N. Y., 1950.

vention majority. They used this control to maintain themselves in power.

On July 1, 1926, the left-led I.L.G.W.U. New York Joint Board called a strike of 40,000 cloakmakers against intolerable conditions in the industry. The Workers (Communist) Party gave all-out support to the strike. President Sigman, while officially endorsing the strike, sabotaged it. Finally, in December, after a bitter 20 weeks' strike, Sigman made an agreement with the bosses behind the back of the Joint Board, patterning this maneuver on Green's in the fur situation. This second time, however, the treachery succeeded. There were many fine leaders among the cloakmakers, such as Joseph Boruchovitch, but the key figures of the cloak and dressmakers Joint Boards—Louis Hyman and Charles Zimmerman (who were later rewarded by the International)—did not boldly rally the strikers to defeat the sell-out, as the Gold leadership had done in fur, but tamely yielded. The strike was lost, and 35,000 workers found themselves outside of the union.

The mass expulsions of Communists and other progressives from the Fur Workers and I.L.G.W.U. resulted, on December 28, 1928, in the formation of the Needle Trades Workers Industrial Union (T.U.E.L.). Louis Hyman was elected president and Ben Gold secretary-treasurer. Then followed a bitter seven-years' fight between rival unions for control of the industry. But of this general development more later.

In the long and difficult needle trades struggle women militants played decisive parts. There were no braver pickets or bolder fighters for trade union democracy. When the Needle Trades Workers Industrial Union was formed it had more women than men members.

In the Amalgamated Clothing Workers (and the Cap and Millinery Workers) the struggle between left and right was not so sharp, although in both cases the top leadership (especially Hillman) was tied up with the B. & O. plan, the "new wage policy," labor banking, standards of production, speed-up, and the general class collaboration program of the A.F. of L. The A.C.W. also expelled a number of militants for T.U.E.L. membership. However, Sidney Hillman, head of the organization, was inclined to follow some elements of a progressive political policy, A.C.W. conventions commonly adopting left resolutions on non-economic questions. The union also displayed friendship for embattled Soviet Russia; in 1921 it organized the Russian American Industrial Corporation, with Robert W. Dunn in charge, to aid in establishing the clothing industry in that country. The A.C.W., then an independent union, also maintained a fraternal affiliation with the R.I.L.U. On many political questions the left had a united front with Hillman, but, as in many such cases, the left was not skillful enough to build up its own forces while working in the united front. Today, under the Potofsky leadership, the A.C.W. is just another dry-as-dust A.F. of L. union, but a generation ago, as an independent union born in struggle in 1914 against A.F. of L. crooks, it enjoyed great prestige with the left wing. Indeed, most of the independent industrial unions of the period—in metal, textile, food, shoe, tobacco, etc.—included in their titles the word "amalgamated." The direct strength of the Communist and T.U.E.L. forces in the A.C.W. was indicated at its 1924 convention when Phil Aronberg, Communist candidate for the general executive board, received 8,897 votes against 17,362 for his opponent.

THE STRUGGLE IN THE MINING INDUSTRY

The United Mine Workers sank almost into a death crisis during the Coolidge "prosperity" period. The coal industry, a "sick" one, partly owing to swift mechanization, suffered from heavy unemployment which sapped the economic power of the union. The mine operators, realizing their advantage in this situation, proceeded to stick the harpoon into the weakened union. John L. Lewis, U.M.W.A. president, made the situation worse by a lot of leadership sins of commission and omission. Instead of fighting resolutely against unemployment, he raised the reactionary slogan, "200,000 miners must go." In 1922, also, Lewis abandoned the key miners of the unorganized districts in the strike settlement of that year, and he also refused to make a serious effort to organize the strategic mines in the southern states. To make a bad situation worse, Lewis expelled Freeman Thompson, Pat Toohey, Frank Borich, Dan Slinger, Tony Minerich, and hundreds of other Communist union fighters, who had dared speak out against his ruinous policies.

The T.U.E.L., with the active support of the Party, began activities early in the mining industry (see Chapter 13). In Pittsburgh, on June 2-3, 1923, it organized the Progressive International Committee of the U.M.W.A. This broad left-progressive committee put forward demands, major among which were the six-hour day, five-day week, enforcement of the union scales, unemployment relief and insurance, organization of the unorganized miners, opposition to arbitration and speed-up agreements, a national contract for all coal miners, restoration of union district autonomy, nationalization of the mines, and a labor party. In furthering this program the left-progressives nominated an election slate, headed by George Voyzey, a Communist rank-and-file Illinois miner, against the Lewis ticket. In the final election tabulation Lewis credited Voyzey with polling 66,000 votes, as against 136,000 for himself. The opposition claimed that Voyzey had actually been elected.

Meanwhile the union's position in the industry deteriorated rapidly.

The Jacksonville agreement of February 1924 was supposed to run until April 1927, but in 1925 the big operators of West Virginia and Western Pennsylvania, including the Pittsburgh Coal Company, the largest of them all, began freely to violate the union agreement and to operate open shops. The union rapidly disintegrated in Pennsylvania, Ohio, West Virginia, Kentucky, Alabama, and other bituminous districts. When the crucial strike of April 1, 1927, began, the U.M.W.A. controlled only 40 percent of soft coal production, as against 60 percent in 1924.

In 1925, the T.U.E.L. forces in the industry, to counteract the catastrophic decline of the union, put out the slogan, "Save the Union," and organized a broad united front committee by that name. Pat Toohey was secretary, and Frank Keany, former head of the U.M.W.A. in West Virginia, was editor of *The Coal Digger*. The T.U.E.L. carried out a three-phase campaign in the mining areas. The first stage of this was to push for the organization of the vital West Virginia, Kentucky, and southern mine fields in preparation for the coming strike. Nothing came of this, however, as Lewis, despite the demands of many scores of local unions, refused to budge toward doing the job.

The second stage of the Save-the-Union campaign was to put up a national ticket of progressives against the Lewis slate in the 1926 U.M.W.A. elections. The chief Save-the-Union candidates were, for president, John Brophy, president of District 2; and for secretary-treasurer, William J. Brennan, former president of District 1 in the anthracite region. This was a very broad united front movement. The left-progressive opposition made a vigorous campaign, for which Lewis allowed 60,661 votes for Brophy and counted 173,323 for himself. Brophy protested that gross frauds had been practiced and claimed he had been elected.[1]

The third stage of the Save-the-Union program was all-out support of the strategic 1927 bituminous strike. The progressive opposition mobilized its strong forces everywhere to man the picket lines and to hearten the strikers. The Penn-Ohio Strike Relief, headed by Alfred Wagenknecht, was set up and conducted a vigorous national campaign. After the strike had been going on for a full year, on April 1, 1928, the Save-the-Union Committee held a mass conference in Pittsburgh, for the purpose of strengthening and extending the strike. Present were 1,125 delegates representing 101,000 miners, or about half the total of the U.M.W.A. membership. The conference issued a call to the miners in the non-striking fields to come out, and there was a considerable response.

But the strike was beyond saving. Shortly afterward Lewis signed a

[1] *Labor Unity*, June 15, 1927.

separate agreement for the Illinois district, after which the other districts straggled back to work as best they could. Wages and working conditions won in 30 years of struggle were lost almost overnight. Then, indeed, the union crumbled. Splits and dual unions developed in Pennsylvania, West Virginia, Colorado, and elsewhere. During this period of collapse of the U.M.W.A. the Save-the-Union forces, except for the Brophy group, drew their supporters together and, in September 1928, founded the National Miners Union in Pittsburgh. John Watt was elected president, William Boyce, vice-president, and Pat Toohey, secretary-treasurer, of the new miners' organization.[1]

FORMATION OF THE T.U.U.L.

The Trade Union Unity League was founded in Cleveland, Ohio, August 31-September 1, 1929. It developed as a reorganization of the T.U.E.L. at the latter's fourth national convention. In attendance were 690 delegates from 18 states. Some 322 delegates came from the three newly-organized national industrial unions in the textile, needle trades, and mining industries, which together had a membership of about 57,000; 159 delegates were from left-wing groups in craft unions; 107 from small groups in unorganized industries; and 18 came directly from A.F. of L. local unions. Of the delegates, 64 were Negroes, 72 women, and 159 young workers. The average age was 32 years. A National Executive Board of 10 and a National Committee of 53 were elected. *Labor Unity* was the official organ and New York was chosen as national headquarters. William Z. Foster was elected general secretary.[2]

The program of the T.U.U.L. followed the general lines of the old T.U.E.L. It was a broad, independent, united front movement of Communists and progressives. It made a head-on collision with the class collaborationism of the A.F. of L. leadership, basing itself on the class struggle. Its central slogan was "Class against Class." Concretely, the program called for the seven-hour day, the five-day week, the organization of the unorganized, industrial unionism, social insurance, full economic, political, social equality for the Negro people, affiliation to the R.I.L.U., world trade union unity, struggle against fascism and imperialist war, defense of the Soviet Union, and socialism.

The major difference between the T.U.U.L. and T.U.E.L. was that whereas the old T.U.E.L. placed the main stress upon the work within the conservative trade unions, the new Trade Union Unity League put its main emphasis upon the organization of the unorganized into indus-

[1] Perlman and Taft, *History of Labor in the U.S.*, Vol. 4, pp. 564-68.
[2] *Labor Unity*, Sept. 14, 1929.

trial unions. As we have seen, this new orientation had been developing through 1927-28 in the work of the T.U.E.L.; in fact, the scenes of its sharpest struggles—textile, needle, and mining—had produced three new independent industrial organizations, based on the principle of "one factory, one industry, one union."

Three basic considerations made necessary this radical change in trade union policy represented by the difference in line between the T.U.U.L. and the T.U.E.L. First, the class collaboration, speed-up policy of the A.F. of L. and railroad union leadership was violently contrary to the interests of the workers, and it destroyed the fighting qualities of the unions. As the program of the T.U.U.L. declared, "the trade union movement of pre-war days, despite its corruption, backwardness and general weakness, was a fighting organization in comparison with the degenerate A.F. of L. of today." Second, the A.F. of L. unions, misled and betrayed into the hands of the employers, were in serious decline. They had lost out in many important sections of industry, particularly its trustified areas—steel, auto, meat-packing, textile, lumber, railroads, coal mining, etc. Now more than ever, they were becoming restricted to skilled workers and did not represent the great masses of unskilled and semi-skilled workers or protect their interests. Third, the expulsion of large numbers of Communists and militant rank-and-file workers from the old unions posed the question of independent unionism in an acute form. It was these general reasons which led the Communists and their progressive allies at this time, through the T.U.U.L., to put the main stress upon organizing new unions in the unorganized or semi-organized industries.

This sharp departure in labor policy was not supported by the Workers (Communist) Party without very considerable discussion.[1] Jay Lovestone and his followers generally opposed the new trade union line. The R.I.L.U. also spoke on the question, as the world-wide expulsion and splitting policies of the Social-Democrats were everywhere making the question of independent unionism an urgent matter.

This changed labor policy did not signify that the Communists were reversing themselves and going back to dual unionism, as Muste and other enemies maintained. Undoubtedly, under the circumstances there was a wide base for independent unionism. During the next few years, however, there were considerable sectarian tendencies to build independent unions in situations where there were no grounds for them, and also to consider the T.U.U.L. as a national labor center that would eventually supersede the A.F. of L. Nevertheless, the T.U.U.L. unions led many

---

[1] *The Communist*, July 1928.

important strikes, organizing campaigns, and unemployment fights. In particular, they did invaluable pioneering work in preparation for the tremendous organizing drives of the middle 1930's.

INTERNATIONAL LABOR UNITY

Communists, as conscious internationalists, are always ardent supporters of world trade union unity. This issue, in various forms, was important during the Coolidge period. One manifestation was the campaign during those years for trade union affiliation to the R.I.L.U. The most important action in this respect was the vote for affiliation of the Nova Scotia miners in 1923, for which, among other things, they were expelled from the U.M.W.A. Another important international activity was the going of labor delegates to Soviet Russia to study the new socialist republic at first hand. The most important of these delegations was that in 1927, consisting of James H. Maurer, John Brophy, F. L. Palmer, J. W. Fitzpatrick, and A. F. Coyle, all well-known trade union figures—together with economists—Robert W. Dunn, Stuart Chase, Paul Douglas, and others. The delegation submitted a favorable report, which was well received by the rank and file of organized labor.

During these years, the Russians made a big fight to establish world trade union unity. The policy of the Social-Democratic International Federation of Trade Unions was to keep the Russian unions isolated from the labor movement of the West. Therefore, after several ineffectual tries for general unity, the Russian trade unionists got together with the British union leaders and formed the Anglo-Russian Committee. The British leaders were the more willing to do this, as Great Britain was anxious to gain access to the great Russian markets. The A.F. of L., violently anti-Soviet, was radically opposed to the new committee, which opened up promising perspectives for a united trade union international. Hence, when A. A. Purcell, head of the British Trades Union Congress, came to the A.F. of L. convention of 1925 as a fraternal delegate and spoke for world labor unity, he was denounced as a "red" by the Green bureaucrats and virtually treated as a pariah. The Workers (Communist) Party vigorously supported and popularized the Anglo-Russian Committee. The Committee was dissolved, in September 1927, by the British union leaders, on the pretext of the Soviet trade union leaders' criticism of their treacherous betrayal of the workers in the great English general strike of 1926.[1]

[1] Lewis L. Lorwin, *Labor and Internationalism*, pp. 313-15, N. Y., 1929.

19. Building the Party of the New Type (1919-1929)

To cope with the tasks of the American class struggle the working class needs what Lenin called a party of a new type. This party, as Stalin explains it, must be a party able to "see farther than the working class; it must lead the proletariat and not follow in the tail of the spontaneous movement. . . . The Party is the political leader of the working class." It must be "a militant party, a revolutionary party, one bold enough to lead the proletarians to the struggle for power, sufficiently experienced to find its bearing amidst the complex conditions of a revolutionary situation, and sufficiently flexible to steer clear of all submerged rocks on the way to its goal."[1] The party, self-critical, democratic, and disciplined, must fight in the vanguard of the struggle, yet be most intimately interwoven with every fiber of the proletariat. It is a party which does not substitute wishful thinking and empty slogans for the real situation, objectively or subjectively. The party of the new type stays with the working class and the people at every stage in their struggle, providing the best solutions for all the problems of a given period, leading to the final stage where the toiling masses find it necessary to change the basic social relations.

During the decade from 1919 to 1929 the Communists laid the first foundations of such a Leninist party in the United States, the stronghold of world capitalism; that is, they largely absorbed the general principles of Marxism-Leninism, united the Communist forces, withstood the first great attack of the government, fought their way to legality, began to learn to practice self-criticism and discipline, and cleansed their ranks of various opportunist elements. They also participated in many broad, united front mass struggles, displaying, as we have seen, no little Leninist initiative in so doing. The Communists were establishing political contacts with the working class, and specifically with the trade unionists, Negro workers, women, youth, and foreign-born. They had begun to master the Leninist task of combining the fight for socialism with the everyday struggles of the masses. The Party also displayed a real international spirit, with its fight for the defense of the Soviet Union, its energetic "Hands Off China" campaign, its vigorous fight with the Com-

[1] Stalin, *Foundations of Leninism*, pp. 108-09.

munists in Latin America against American imperialism, its constant co-operation with the Canadian Communists, and its active support of the work of the Red International of Labor Unions and the Communist International. All these tasks in the building of a party of the new type were comprised in the general slogan, "Bolshevization of the Party." Nevertheless, at the end of the decade, the Party was still too largely agitational in character and it retained many sectarian weaknesses.

In 1925, at the fourth convention of the Party, then called the Workers (Communist) Party, an important organizational step was taken in the Bolshevization of the Party by the reorganization of the Party from its old "language federation" basis to one of shop and street branches with fractions of the national groups to work among their specific organizations. In this convention the Party contained 18 "language federations" (national minority group organizations), the largest of which were the Finns, 6,410; Jewish, 1,447; South Slavs, 1,109; Russians, 870; Lithuanians, 850; and Ukrainians, 622.

Twenty-seven papers were reported as left-wing papers. They operated upon an independent basis, being usually owned by broad united front groups. (See table on page 262.)

During these years, especially after the organizational changes of 1925, the Party's membership fluctuated considerably. The statistics show: 1923, 15,395; 1925, 16,325; 1929, 9,642. The Y.C.L. ranged from 1,000 members in 1922 to 2,500 in 1929. In 1929 the Party had 25 shop papers. On Friday, June 21, 1929, the *Daily Worker* suspended publication for one day, the only time in its 28 years of stormy life. The Workers School, established in October 1923, had at this time about 1,500 students. On January 24, 1927, the Party moved its headquarters from Chicago to New York, and at its 1930 convention it changed its name to the Communist Party of the United States.

The fourth and fifth conventions of the Party (in 1925 and 1927) laid great stress on more completely involving the Party membership in trade union work. The main bulk of the Party workers, foreign-born, worked in unorganized industries, and traditionally had devoted themselves chiefly to political agitational work. This situation was largely changed by decisions to form shop groups and have trade union secretaries in Party branches, by the establishment of mixed nationality branches, and by stress upon the need to give leadership in the workers' economic struggles.

These and ensuing conventions put growing emphasis upon concentration work; that is, the strengthening of the Party's work among the miners, steel workers, railroaders, maritime workers, chemical workers, and others employed in the basic and trustified industries. These are the

THE LEFT-WING PRESS

Language	Name of Paper	Frequency	Circulation
Armenian	The Proletarian	Weekly	1,200
Bulgarian	Saznarie	Tri-monthly	1,900
Czechoslovak	Obrana	Weekly	1,500
Czechoslovak	Delnik	Weekly	1,150
English	Daily Worker	Daily	17,000
English	Workers Monthly	Monthly	16,000
Esthonian	Uus Ilm	Weekly	600
Finnish	Tyomies	Daily	8,000
Finnish	Eteenpain	Daily	8,000
Finnish	Toveri	Daily	4,500
Finnish	Uusi Kotimaa	Semi-weekly	6,000
Finnish	Toveritar	Weekly (women)	11,000
Finnish	Punikki	Semi-monthly	10,000
German	Volkszeitung	Daily	10,000
Greek	Empros	Weekly	4,700
Hungarian	Uj Elore	Daily	9,000
Italian	Il Lavoratore	Weekly	13,500
Jewish	Freiheit	Daily	22,000
Lithuanian	Laisve	Daily	8,000
Lithuanian	Vilnis	Semi-weekly	5,000
Polish	Tribuna Robotnicza	Weekly	1,500
Romanian	Desteptarea	Weekly	1,200
Russian	Novy Mir	Daily	10,000
Scandinavian	Ny Tid	Weekly (agrarian)	2,500
South Slavic	Radnik	Tri-weekly	8,500
Slovenian	Delavska Slovenija	Weekly	4,000
Ukrainian	Daily News	Daily	6,000

heart of the working class, and without their support no trade union movement or workers' political party can succeed in either its immediate or ultimate goals. It was upon the basis of this concentration principle that generally European Marxist parties and the trade unions, historically, have always devoted special efforts to winning the affiliation of the workers in the basic industries. By the same principle, in reverse, the basic weakness of the American trade union movement was expressed in the fact that it long refused to concentrate and to base itself upon the workers in the trustified industries. When the C.I.O. finally did successfully achieve this concentration, the effect was too raise the whole American labor movement onto a higher plane. The Communist Party, in its concentration work, is simply applying with characteristic Communist clarity and vigor the long-established labor principle of centering upon the workers in the key and basic industries, who are the main foundations of the working class.

In the 1928 presidential elections the Workers (Communist) Party put up national candidates, with William Z. Foster heading the ticket. The Party was on the ballot in 32 states; it put on a very active campaign, and polled 48,228 votes, an increase of 15,000 over 1924. In this campaign, the Party fought against the war danger and aggressive American imperialism; it demanded farm relief and social insurance for the workers; it advocated a labor party; and it called for the repeal of the Volstead Act and the Eighteenth Amendment (prohibition).

The gravest weakness of the Party during this whole period was the prolonged internal factional fight. As we have seen, this fight began in 1923 over the question of the labor party. Although this specific question, after the LaFollette campaign of 1924, ceased to be a matter of sharp dispute within the Party, the factional struggle nevertheless continued around many other questions, hampering the Party in all its activities. Time and again efforts were made by the main Ruthenberg-Pepper and Bittelman-Foster groups to compose their differences and to establish Party unity, but to no avail. Further events were to show that Party unity could be achieved only by the elimination of the disruptive non-Communist elements from the Party—the Cannonites and Lovestoneites.

PARTY WORK AMONG WOMEN AND THE YOUTH

As an essential phase of building itself into a true Leninist organization, the Party during its first decade paid increasing attention to work among the masses of women. In 1921 the Party set up a National Women's Commission. The Party based its main orientation upon women in industry, but it also conducted considerable activities among housewives. United front Women's Councils were a factor in these years. All the national group federations, in their respective spheres, interested themselves in women's work. During the 1920's the number of women in the Party did not exceed 20 percent, although in the 1930's it reached almost double that number.

Communist women workers, besides being generally active politically, were a very important force in many strikes during this period, particularly in the needle trades and the textile industry. Women displayed great activity in labor defense work. In such notable struggles as those for Mooney and Billings, Sacco and Vanzetti, and MacNamara and Schmidt, they led the fight all over the country. Women were also outstanding fighters against the high cost of living and all forms of militarism.

During the early 1920's the Party took a sectarian position regarding special protective legislation for women, and it was neglectful of the particular demands of Negro women in industry. The Party organ, *The Working Woman,* for March 1929, had as slogans, for International Woman's Day, equal pay for women; higher wages and shorter hours; better working conditions; an end to child labor; maternity leave and benefits for working mothers; social insurance for unemployment, sickness, accident, old age, and maternity; opposition to the high cost of living, the open shop, the war danger, and "imperialism that breeds war."

The Young Communist League, the name of which varied with the changing titles of the Party, shared most of the weaknesses and strengths of the Party. About 1923, breaking somewhat with its early sectarianism, it started to develop specific youth demands and to lay the basis for children's organizations and sports activities. Its 1927 convention showed a marked orientation toward trade union work, with active youth participation in a number of strikes. The League had the disadvantage of having a weak industrial base, most of its members being students. The factional strife in the Party reflected itself in the League and hindered its development. A special brand of youth sectarianism, "vanguardism," was stimulated by the factionalism in the Party. This deviation, based on the notion that the youth, just because they are young, are more class-conscious than adult workers, tended to narrow down the League from the broad organization that it should have been into a sort of "junior Communist Party."

THE DEATH OF RUTHENBERG

On March 2, 1927, the Party suffered a grievous loss in the death of its general secretary, Charles E. Ruthenberg. He died of appendicitis, which in his overwork he had neglected. Ruthenberg, 45 years old at the time of his death, was the outstanding founder and leader of the Communist Party. He was a sincere, determined, and intelligent fighter. Joining the Socialist Party in 1909, Ruthenberg was especially influential in Ohio. He came to national attention during the well-known "Article 2, Section 6" fight at the S.P. convention of 1912, and he also played a decisive role in the emergency, anti-war convention of the S.P. in St. Louis, in April 1917, as well as generally in the fight against the war. He was particularly effective in the struggles to form the Communist Party, to unify it, and to win it a legal status. He was active also in the

Party's early mass struggles, notably around the question of the labor party. His bold testimony on the stand in the 1917-20 and 1922 Communist trials was an inspiration to the Party. During the factional fight Ruthenberg enjoyed the confidence of both warring groups, so that even during its bitterest phases he remained general secretary.

Ruthenberg was deeply hated and attacked by capitalist reaction, and he spent several years in prison. He was an outstanding student of Marx and Lenin, and he was a powerful influence in giving the young Communist Party a fundamental theoretical grounding. He was widely known and respected among the Communists of the world.

THE SIXTH WORLD CONGRESS OF THE COMINTERN

One of the main international events of this general period was the sixth congress of the C.I., held in Moscow, July-August, 1928. Bringing together leading Marxists from all over the world, it sounded a note of militant struggle. The C.I. Executive Committee, at its meeting of March 1925, had declared that Europe, with American financial help (Dawes plan, Young plan, etc.), had succeeded in "relatively," "partially," and "temporarily" stabilizing itself, after the revolutionary storm of the previous few years. But the sixth congress, three years later, pointed out that even this "relative, partial, and temporary" capitalist stabilization had already come to an end and that the world perspective was one of a deepening of the general crisis of capitalism and a sharpening of the class struggle internationally.

The sixth Comintern congress, at which the first complete program of the C.I. was formulated, analyzed the post-World War I international situation in three periods. The first of these periods, lasting approximately from March 1917 to the end of 1923, was marked by a series of revolutions and revolutionary struggles in Russia, Germany, Hungary, Turkey, Bulgaria, China, India, Korea, and elsewhere. The second period, from early in 1924 to the end of 1927, the time of "relative, partial, and temporary stabilization," was signalized by a growing offensive on the part of the employers and by a comparatively defensive struggle by the proletariat and its allies. The third period, beginning in 1928, when the precarious capitalist stabilization came to an end, opened up a new wave of struggles—between workers and employers, between capitalist countries and colonies, among the imperialist powers, and between the capitalist and socialist sectors of the world.

The concept of the "third period" was hotly debated in the labor movement all over the world, including the United States. It was at the sixth world congress that the fight against the Bukharin group in the

U.S.S.R. began to take definite shape in the C.I. over questions of the stabilization of capitalism, the fight against the right wing, etc.—but of this more later. The soundness of the Congress line of intensified struggle was ultimately and dramatically demonstrated by the facts that within the next decade there developed the great world economic crisis, fascism spread over most of Europe, and World War II broke out.

The Comintern congress of 1928 called for a sharpening of working class struggle on every front. It urged a militant fight against the right-wing elements in the Communist parties, and it intensified the attack against the opportunist Social-Democrats, who were stigmatized as "social fascists" because, in the name of socialism, they were breaking down the workers' resistance before advancing fascism. The central slogan of the congress was "Class Against Class." The right was the main danger, because these opportunist elements in the parties and throughout the labor movement had assumed that the previous partial stabilization of capitalism indicated a permanent healing of the diseases of that social system and therewith a softening of the class struggle.

THE NEGRO QUESTION AS A NATIONAL QUESTION

A development of prime importance at the sixth congress was the profound discussion of the colonial question. The American delegates, as well as those of many other countries, participated deeply. Out of this discussion came the analysis of the Negro question in the United States as a national question. Whereas, the Marxists in the United States had traditionally considered the Negro question as that of a persecuted racial minority of workers and as basically a simple trade union matter, the Party now characterized the Negro people as an oppressed nation entitled to the right of self-determination. This position was developed in full in a further resolution in 1930. This new understanding of the Negro question raised the Party's work among the Negro people to a far higher Leninist level.

This view of the Negro question was founded upon the actualities of the situation of the Negro people and the principles previously evolved by Lenin and Stalin, the world's two leading authorities on the national question. Lenin, in the colonial theses of the second congress of the Comintern, which he wrote in June 1920, already recognized the position of the American Negroes as that of an oppressed nation. The theses called upon the workers of the world "to render direct aid to the revolutionary movements in the dependent and subject nations (for example, in Ireland, *Negroes in America,* etc.), and in the colonies." (Italics mine—W.Z.F.).[1]

[1] Lenin, *Selected Works,* Vol. 10, p. 235.

THE PARTY OF THE NEW TYPE

Stalin, who is the world's greatest living expert on the subject, has defined a nation as an "historically evolved, stable community of language, territory, economic life, and psychological make-up manifested in a community of culture."[1] These are scientific bases of nationhood. According to these criteria the Negro people in the so-called Black Belt in the American South, where they form the majority of the people, constitute an oppressed nation. Commenting upon the Negro people's development of nationhood, Allen says: "Slavery contributed a common language, a common territory, a common historical background and the beginnings of a common ideology, characterized chiefly by aspirations for freedom. In the period of capitalist development, unhindered by chattel slavery, the conditions arose which made it possible for the Negro people to develop more fully along the lines of nationhood. The Negroes were drawn more directly within the process of capitalism, thus evolving the class relationships characteristic of all modern nations."[2] The Negroes in the North, under this general definition, are an oppressed national minority.

Haywood elaborates further: "Within the borders of the United States, and under the jurisdiction of a single central government, there exist, not one, but two nations: a dominant white nation, with its Anglo-Saxon hierarchy, and a subject black one. . . . The Negro is American. He is the product of every social and economic struggle that has made America. But the Negro is a special kind of American, to the extent that his oppression has set him apart from the dominant white nation. Under the pressure of these circumstances, he has generated all the objective attributes of nationhood."[3]

The practical consequences, in policy, of the Communist Party's new position on the Negro question were that, in addition to pressing as before for full economic, political and social equality in all their ramifications for the Negro people, the Party also raised the slogan that the Negro people should have the right of self-determination in the "Black Belt" of the South on the basis of the break-up of the plantation system and the redistribution of the land to the Negro farmers. The demand for self-determination did not mean, however, that the Party advocated the setting up of a "Negro republic" in the South, as its enemies asserted. But it did mean that the Party, henceforth, would insist that the Negro nation should have the right of self-determination, to be exercised by it whenever and however it saw fit to use this right.

---

[1] Joseph Stalin, *Marxism and the National Question*, p. 12, N. Y., 1942.
[2] James S. Allen, *Negro Liberation* (pamphlet), p. 21, N. Y., 1938.
[3] Haywood, *Negro Liberation*, pp. 140-41.

THE AMERICAN NEGRO LABOR CONGRESS

As we have seen in earlier chapters, the Communist Party from its foundation has increasingly interested itself in the fight for justice for the bitterly exploited and harassed Negro people. Among the earliest organized expressions of this Communist policy was the formation of the African Blood Brotherhood, with its paper, *The Crusader*. This body, an offshoot of *The Messenger* group in New York during the early 1920's, together with split-offs from the left wing of the Garvey movement, made a militant fight for Negro rights. It participated in the Negro Sanhedrin, held in Chicago in February 1924. The organization, however, did not achieve a mass basis; and in Chicago, in October 1925, the American Negro Labor Congress was launched.[1] Its outstanding leader at this time was Lovett Fort-Whiteman, and its journal, *The Negro Champion*.

The central significance of the American Negro Labor Congress was its indication of the growing importance of the proletariat in the developing struggle of the Negro people. The A.N.L.C., in advocating aggressively its demands for full economic, political, and social equality for Negroes, laid special stress on the trade union question. It especially fought for the admission of Negro workers into the unions. Its general organizational form was that of local councils composed of Negro labor unions, trade unions that did not discriminate against Negroes, and groups of unorganized Negro workers.[2]

The A.N.L.C. did valuable agitational work for several years but it, too, remained small and was largely limited to Communists in its membership. In this organization's work, new leaders of the Negro people came to the front, including James Ford, Harry Haywood, Maude White, and many others. Cyril Briggs, in describing Communist work in this period, says, "The Party led the Negro fig and date workers' strike in Chicago, the laundry strike in Carteret, N. J., the Colored Moving Picture Operators strike in New York. In addition, we organized the Negro Miners Relief Committee, captured the Tenants League from the Socialists, held classes and forums in New York City, Chicago, Philadelphia, etc."[3]

The A.N.L.C. was superseded in 1930 by the League of Struggle for Negro Rights. The latter's national secretary was Harry Haywood, and its journal was *The Negro Liberator*. The League, in making its fight for Negro rights, based itself upon a general struggle for Negro national liberation. This organization did much pioneering work in the South during the ensuing years.

---

[1] Robert Minor in *The Workers Monthly*, Dec. 1925.
[2] *Program of the American Negro Labor Congress*, N. Y., 1925.
[3] Cyril Briggs in *The Communist*, Sept. 1929.

The tireless and resolute fight of the Communist Party during the Coolidge period won much attention and support from the masses of the Negro people. Gradually a substantial body of Negro Communists was built up. The growth of Communist influence among the Negro people was particularly marked after the Party's recognition of the national character of the Negro question and its application. At the Communist Party's sixth convention, in March 1929, Jack Stachel reported that there were about 200 Negro members, but a year later, in the membership drive beginning March 6, 1930, which brought in a total of 6,167 recruits, no less than 1,300 of these were Negroes—so rapidly was Communist sentiment growing among the Negro masses.

THE EXPULSION OF THE TROTSKYITES

Among the major steps taken during this decade of 1919-29 toward the building of the Party of a new type was the expulsion of the Trotskyites on October 27, 1928. This group was led by James Cannon, who had long played an active part in the Party leadership (Bittelman-Foster group) as an inveterate factionalist. This Trotskyite development also had a direct relationship to the sixth congress of the Communist International.

For several years prior to the sixth Comintern congress Trotskyism, which Lenin had long fought, had become a malignant pest in the Soviet Union. Leon Trotsky, always an opportunist and adventurer, made a reckless grab for the leadership of the Communist Party after the death of Lenin in 1924. The substance of his "ultra-revolutionary" program was the provocation of a civil war against the Soviet peasantry as a whole and the unfolding of an aggressive foreign policy that could only have resulted in bringing about a war between the capitalist powers and the Soviet Union. Trotsky's central argument was that socialism could not be built in one country and that, consequently, an immediate European revolution was indispensable. His policies to force such an artificial revolution would have been fatal to the Russian Revolution and would have brought about the restoration of capitalism in Russia.[1]

The Soviet people wanted none of Trotsky's destructive program. The brilliant Stalin proved in theory (and the experience of the ensuing quarter of a century has completely demonstrated his correctness in practice) that it was possible to build socialism in one country, the Soviet Union, and that the Communist Party's policies were leading to precisely

[1] Trotsky also condemned Comintern policy in China, but Mao Tse-tung and other Chinese leaders have repeatedly affirmed that the Chinese Revolution was fought to a victorious conclusion primarily along the lines suggested by Stalin many years ago.

that goal. As a result the Communist Party, the Soviets, the youth, the trade unions, and the various other mass organizations overwhelmingly defeated the Trotsky program, which had been given strong support by the opportunist Zinoviev-Kamenev group.[1] Inasmuch as all these elements, in their struggle against the Party, had proceeded to criminal means of sabotage and other violence, this whole group of leaders were expelled as counter-revolutionaries by the fifteenth congress of the Communist Party of the Soviet Union in December 1927.

At the time of the sixth congress of the Comintern in 1928 Trotsky was in exile, as a criminal against the Revolution. He made an appeal to the congress to try to get it to repudiate the decision of the Communist Party and the government of the Soviet Union. The congress, however, overwhelmingly rejected this insolent proposal. Nevertheless the scheme found a secret supporter in James Cannon, one of the Communist Party delegates from the United States. Upon Cannon's return to this country he began at once to spread clandestine Trotskyite propaganda with his friends. They advocated withdrawal from the existing unions, abandonment of the united front, and carried on a bitter factional struggle. The Bittelman-Foster leaders, learning of what was going on, preferred charges against Cannon, Max Schachtman, and M. Abern, and all three were promptly expelled by the Party as splitters, disrupters, and political degenerates. About 100 of Cannon's followers were also finally ousted from the party.

Upon their expulsion the Trotskyites formed themselves into an opposition league, which, after several internal splits and two slippery amalgamations—the first with the Musteites in 1934, and the second with the Socialist Party in 1936—finally emerged, in January 1938, as the Socialist Workers Party, an organization which has since averaged only a thousand or two members. The reason-for-being of this party, which is the American section of the so-called Fourth International, with its pathological antagonism toward the Communist Party and the Soviet Union, is to serve as a tool of reaction. It carries on its counter-revolutionary work against the Party and the U.S.S.R. under cover of a cloud of super-revolutionary phrases.

LOVESTONE AND EXCEPTIONALISM

The sixth world congress of the Comintern was followed by the expulsion, in June 1929, of the Lovestone group of right opportunists, numbering some 200 members, including Lovestone himself, B. Gitlow, B. Wolfe, and H. Zam, the latter being head of the Y.C.L. Jay Lovestone, a

[1] Joseph Stalin, *Problems of Leninism*, N. Y., 1934.

petty-bourgeois intellectual, came into the Party from the Socialist Party at the beginning. Like Cannon, Lovestone was a professional factionalist and intriguer. Upon the death of Ruthenberg in 1927, he, as a leading member in the Ruthenberg-Pepper group, managed by factional methods to become executive secretary of the Party, a position which he held for two years.

Lovestone's opportunism was brought to a head by the penetrating analysis and fighting perspective developed by the sixth congress of the Comintern. The substance of Lovestone's political position was that while the "third period" of growing capitalist crisis and intensifying class struggle, as outlined by the congress, was valid for the rest of the world, it did not apply to the United States. To justify this contention, Lovestone restated in Marxist phraseology, the traditional bourgeois theory of "American exceptionalism." That is, that in its essence capitalism in the United States is different from and superior to capitalism in other countries and is, therefore, exempt from that system's laws of growth and decay. What Lovestone did was to found his analysis upon the specific features of American capitalism, upon its minor differences from capitalism in other countries, instead of upon its basic sameness with capitalism the world over. Lovestone sought to buttress his opportunist conclusions by arguing that his theory of American exceptionalism fitted in with and was based upon Lenin's law of the uneven development of capitalism. The main practical conclusions from Lovestone's position were that while capitalism in the rest of the world was in deepening crisis and could anticipate revolutionary struggles from the workers, capitalism in the United States was definitely on the upgrade and no sharpening of the class struggle could be expected. Lovestone was supported in his opportunistic theories with especial vigor by Pepper and Wolfe.

These opportunists had already been developing their exceptionalist theories before the sixth congress, and they intensified them after that gathering. At first they wrote in terms of cunning implications, but gradually they grew bolder in their expressions. The May 28, 1928, plenum of the Central Executive Committee, where they had the majority, officially accepted the Pepper idea that "An analysis shows that there is a basic difference between European and American conditions at present." Wolfe outlined a glowing "Program for Prosperity," grossly exaggerating the economic perspectives of American capitalism. Lovestone developed a whole body of revisionist theory—that the industrialization of the South would automatically wipe out the Negro question as such by making proletarians of the Negro masses; that the "Hooverian Age" of American capitalism corresponded to the "Victorian Age" of British capitalism;

that American imperialism was a "cat's-paw" of British imperialism; that in analyzing world capitalism primacy had to be given to the external contradictions—the latter an expression of Lovestone's position that American capitalism, unlike capitalism elsewhere, was sound at heart; that there was no prospect of an economic crisis in the United States, and so on.[1]

Meanwhile Lovestone had been intriguing with the right-wing forces throughout the Comintern who were fighting against the political line of the sixth world congress. At the same time he absorbed the Trotskyite position that the leadership of the Comintern and Soviet Communist Party were in decay and that the Russian Revolution was being destroyed by a Thermidorean reaction. Lovestone sewed up an alliance with Bukharin, the leader of the international right wing, who was then developing his opportunist fight against the leadership of the Communist Party of the Soviet Union.

The Soviet Communist Party, at the outset of the first five-year plan, was aggressively pushing the work of industrialization, farm collectivization, and struggle against the kulaks (big farmers) and village usurers. Bukharin and his group, on the way to counter-revolutionary activities, held to the theory that world capitalism had definitely stabilized itself and was becoming "organized." They directly opposed the Party line, proposing instead to slacken industrialization, to halt farm collectivization, to abandon the struggle against the kulaks, and to liquidate the state foreign-trade monopoly. Stalin demonstrated to the Party the fatal consequences of Bukharin's policy, and the defeated Bukharin early in 1929 formed his unprincipled, and eventually fatal, bloc with the expelled Trotsky-Zinoviev counter-revolutionary cliques. These elements reflected the interests of the remnants of the former ruling classes in Russia. It was with these reactionary forces that Lovestone and Pepper aligned themselves.[2] This pair reflected these renegade currents in the American Communist Party.

In the field of practical Party work Lovestone's revisionism manifested itself in tendencies to concentrate upon struggles over inner-Party control rather than mass work, to neglect the fight for Negro rights, to underestimate the role of the new T.U.U.L. industrial unions, to fail to give full support to left-led strikes and organizing campaigns, to underestimate the importance of the fight against Social-Democracy, and to soften the Party's ideological attack upon the current intensive class collaboration policies and prosperity illusions of the top trade union bu-

---

[1] For material on the Lovestone controversy, see *The Communist* for 1927-29.
[2] *History of the Communist Party of the Soviet Union*, pp. 291-95.

reaucracy. Lovestoneism definitely slowed down the mass struggles of the Party in the crucial 1927-29 period.

The development of Lovestone-Pepper revisionism greatly sharpened the factional fight within the American Communist Party. The Bittelman-Foster group actively challenged the whole Lovestone-Pepper line, arguing that it gave a wrong estimation of the international situation, of domestic economic perspectives, of the position of Social-Democracy, and of the radicalization of the workers; in other words, that it contradicted flatly the realities of the political situation and the validity of the sixth congress political analysis in the United States. The internal controversy came to a crisis at the sixth convention of the Party, held in New York, beginning on March 10, 1929, at which the Lovestone-Pepper group had behind them a majority of the delegates. After futile discussion, the convention unanimously decided to seek the advice of the Comintern in the solution of this problem.

During the next weeks the C.I. held elaborate discussions on the questions submitted to it by the American Party. The Party's persistent internal struggle attracted wide attention among all delegations. Leading Marxists from many countries participated in the discussion—from France, Germany, Britain, China, Czechoslovakia, Canada, U.S.S.R. Stalin, who was a delegate, spoke on the question.[1] He criticized both groups for their narrow factional attitudes and for their overestimation of the strength of American imperialism. He said, "Both groups are guilty of the fundamental error of exaggerating the specific features of American imperialism. . . . This exaggeration," he stated, "lies at the root of every opportunistic error committed by both the *majority* and *minority* groups." He also remarked that "this is the basis for the unsteadiness of both sections of the American Communist Party in matters of principle."

Further, on the key question of American exceptionalism, Stalin said: "It would be wrong to ignore the specific peculiarities of American capitalism. The Communist Party in its work must take them into account. But it would be still more wrong to base the activities of the Communist Party on these specific features, since the foundation of the activities of every Communist Party, including the American Communist Party, on which it must base itself, must be the general features of capitalism, which are the same for all countries, and not its specific features in any given country." Stalin also gave a brilliant Marxist forecast of the coming American economic crisis. Said he: "The three million now unemployed in America are the first swallows indicating the ripening of the economic crisis in America." This he said on May 6, 1929, at a time when the bourgeois and Social-Democratic theoreticians, glowing with

[1] Joseph Stalin, *Speeches on the American Communist Party*, N. Y., 1929.

enthusiasm for the "new American capitalism," were shouting all over the world that economic crises were now a thing of the past for the United States.

Stalin heavily stressed the menace of factionalism in the American Party. He said that "factionalism is the *fundamental evil* of the American Communist Party." The long struggle, become a fight for power between the two groups, he characterized as "unprincipled." He declared further that such "factionalism is dangerous and harmful, because it weakens communism, weakens the offensive against reformism, undermines the struggle of communism against Social-Democracy in the labor movement." Democratic centralism requires free discussion in the Party, combined with sound discipline; but the type of struggle that went on in the American Communist Party had become destructive.

The commission, made up of delegates from Communist Parties from many countries, finally outlined its position in an "Address to the C.P.U.S.A."[1] This statement developed the explanation of the validity of the sixth congress analysis for the United States, indicating the approach of an economic crisis, with an intensified class struggle. On "American exceptionalism" it said: "The ideological lever of the right errors in the American Communist Party was the so-called theory of 'exceptionalism,' which found its clearest expression in the persons of comrades Pepper and Lovestone, whose conception was as follows: a crisis of capitalism, but not of American capitalism; a swing of the masses to the left, but not in America; a necessity of struggling against the right danger, but not in the American Communist Party."

THE UNIFICATION OF THE PARTY

Lovestone and Gitlow rejected this outcome, and upon their return to the United States, they made a determined attempt to split the Party. But in this they failed completely, almost their entire group repudiating them and rallying to the support of the Party. Finally, as we have already noted, a couple of hundred of them were expelled by the Party for factionalism and disruption. The Central Executive Committee issued an extended statement explaining the basis for their expulsion.

During this period the Central Executive Committee set up a leading secretariat of four: Robert Minor, Max Bedacht, W. W. Weinstone, and William Z. Foster—that is, of representatives of the former inner groupings in the Party. This secretariat then proceeded to do away with the remnants of factionalism and to unite the cleansed Party. It was the

[1] *Daily Worker*, May 20, 1929.

beginning of a Party unity which, not without many flaws, was to last for almost fifteen years. The elimination of the unhealthy, non-Communist Trotskyite and Lovestone elements, who were basically responsible for the unprincipled aspects of the factional fight, had finally made it possible to unify the Party. Thus, the six long years of sharp factionalism from 1923 to 1929 came to an end. The achievement of Party unity was another long stride toward the building of a Leninist Party of a new type in the United States.

The future course of events quickly and fully justified both the political and organizational line taken by the Party during this situation. The outbreak of the great economic crisis in October 1929, only a few months after Lovestone's expulsion, dealt a smashing blow to the bourgeois theory of "American exceptionalism," and it was also a conclusive demonstration of the fundamental correctness of the analysis of the sixth congress. As for the Lovestoneite leaders, they soon fell into the political degeneration which is the common fate of renegades from communism. For a few years, making pretenses of being Marxist-Leninists, the Lovestoneites maintained an organization conducting anti-Party propaganda, but eventually the group fell apart in complete political demoralization. Lovestone became an open enemy of communism and the Soviet Union. He is now an anti-Communist expert and specialized booster of American imperialism in the service of the reactionaries, David Dubinsky and Matthew Woll. Wolfe, become a professional defender of capitalist "democracy," busies himself publicly with devising plans on how American imperialism might overthrow the Soviet Union and the Chinese People's Republic. And as for Gitlow, he has degenerated into just another bought-and-paid-for government, anti-Communist stoolpigeon.

20. The Communist Party and the Great Economic Crisis (1929-1933)

The golden era of "permanent prosperity" in the United States was brought to a sudden end by the terrific stock-market crash of October 1929. This was accompanied by a headlong fall in all spheres of the national economy, a decline which continued without let-up for the next four years. Over $160 billion in stock-market values were wiped out, basic industry production sank by 50 percent, 5,761 banks failed, and the value of farm products fell from $8.5 billion to $4 billion. Wage cuts for all industries ran to at least 45 percent. By 1933 some 17 million workers were walking the streets unemployed, and many millions more were on part time.[1]

This great cyclical crisis, beginning in the United States, spread rapidly throughout the capitalist world. The other countries of the Americas, Europe, Asia, and the colonies were all engulfed by it. Capitalist world production dropped 42 percent and foreign trade 65 percent. The number of unemployed throughout the world reached the staggering total of 50 million.

The crisis was one of overproduction—an explosion of the basic capitalist internal antagonism between the private ownership of industry and the social character of production. That is, rapidly expanding production had far outrun the limited power of the capitalist markets to absorb this output, owing to the systematic exploitation of the toiling masses by the robber capitalists. This condition was accentuated by the anarchy of capitalist production. Hence the general economic glut and violent crisis catastrophe resulted.

The cyclical crisis was far and away the most severe in the history of world capitalism, in its depth, duration, and universality. This exceptional severity was due to the fact that the breakdown took place within the framework of the deepening general crisis of the world capitalist system. That is to say, the crisis occurred in the midst of a prolonged international agricultural crisis, of great political upheavals in the colonial world, and of the tremendous growth of socialism in the Soviet Union. The cyclical economic crisis, in turn, greatly deepened the general crisis of

[1] See Labor Research Association, *Labor Fact Book 2*, N. Y., 1934.

world capitalism and had the effect of intensifying the decay of that economic and political system.

The capitalists of the world and their Social-Democratic lackeys were profoundly shocked and demoralized by the great crisis, particularly those in the United States. All their dreams of the "new capitalism," which was to establish permanent capitalist "prosperity" and to put an end forever to the menace of socialism, were destroyed overnight by the terrific economic hurricane. The capitalist leaders were confused, frightened, and planless, and so they remained throughout the crisis.

Many capitalist spokesmen became panicky. Whereas only a short while before they had seen a capitalist heaven at hand, now they heard the Socialist revolution knocking at their doors. The leading Wall Street economist, Dr. Irving Fisher of Yale, warned that the United States was in danger of being "devoured by some form of socialism." Judge Brandeis declared that "The people of the United States are now confronted with an emergency more serious than war." Representative Rainey, in the House, stated that the United States is "right up against Communism"; and the capitalist press generally was filled with the most lugubrious forebodings.

To make the capitalist-Social-Democratic discomfiture worse, not only was their supposedly crisis-proof capitalist system broken down, but the Soviet economic system, which the bourgeois economists had long since condemned as unworkable, went right on throughout the crisis, growing and flourishing like a bay tree. Between 1929 and 1933, when world capitalist production was cut almost in half, that of the Soviet Union increased by 67 percent; the number of wage earners jumped from 11,500,000 to 22,800,000; wages were doubled; and unemployment became non-existent. The first five-year plan, which all the economists and labor leader flunkeys of capitalism had sneered at, was finished in four years. Triumphing over tremendous difficulties—fifteen years of imperialist and civil wars, intervention, and blockade—the Soviet Union leaped forward from a predominantly agricultural country, almost medieval in its backwardness, to first place among the industrial nations in Europe. And it did all this while world capitalism, caught in the tangle of its own contradictions, lay economically prostrate. Altogether it was a world-shaking demonstration of the superiority of socialism over capitalism.

MARXISTS ANTICIPATE THE CRISIS AND GIRD FOR THE STORM

The outbreak of the economic crisis did not take the Marxists of the world by surprise. They had understood from the outset of the Coolidge boom period that the capitalist "prosperity" was built upon sand. Repeatedly during these years the Marxists, notably in the speeches of Stalin, had pointed out the coming of an economic crisis in the United States. The American Communist Party had analyzed indications of the approaching crisis, namely, the prolonged agricultural depression, the big unemployment in coal mining, textiles, and other industries, and the deadly overproduction effects of the speed-up and low-wage policies of the bosses and their agents, the top trade union leaders. At its meeting in February 1928, the Central Committee of the Communist Party warned that serious cracks were appearing in the American economy and that these would grow and have far-reaching effects. In the presidential election campaign of that year the Party made a central issue of the question of unemployment. Also, during the fight against Lovestone in 1927-29, a key matter of dispute was precisely the economic prospects of the United States. Lovestone contended that whereas other parts of the world might become involved in economic crisis, the United States, in an exceptional position, would continue indefinitely upon an upward spiral of development; whereas the Marxists in the Party maintained that a great American economic crisis was in the making.

The Party repudiated Lovestone and his bourgeois prosperity theories in good time. At the October 1929 meeting of the Central Committee the Party leadership examined the existing situation and declared that it showed "the clear features of an oncoming economic crisis which would shake the very foundations of the power of American imperialism." The Central Committee called upon the Party membership to get ready for the storm, to root out all passivity and indifference, and to adopt the methods and forms of struggle demanded by the new period. Hardly had the plenum adjourned when its analysis was confirmed by the roar of the great stock-market crash that was heard around the world.

The Wall Street magnates, and their little brothers, William Green, Norman Thomas, Jay Lovestone, *et al.*, still refused to take this foreboding event seriously and predicted that capitalism, basically sound, would soon resume its upward growth. But the Party rejected such rosy prophecies. At its January 1930 meeting the Central Committee pointed out that the stock-market crash was but the opening phase of a serious economic breakdown. It said, "We are dealing with the most far-reaching economic crisis in the history of capitalism, involving the whole world." This correct analysis was an indication of the growing Marxist-Leninist development of the Party leadership.

HOOVER'S STARVATION POLICIES

With the outbreak of the economic crisis the bourgeoisie immediately embarked upon the same course that it had followed during all previous crises; namely, to unload the burden of the economic breakdown upon the shoulders of the workers and poorer farmers. Without the slightest concern for the welfare of their wage slaves, out of whose labor they had amassed their fortunes, the capitalists proceeded to throw millions of workers out on the streets without any relief, much less unemployment insurance, such as prevailed in most European countries.

President Hoover, who took office seven months before the crash, while spouting demagogic phrases that poverty was about to be abolished and that he would put a chicken in every pot and a car in every garage for the workers, did nothing to relieve the ghastly situation of mass starvation. Hoover's idea was to let the economic hurricane blow itself out, as such storms had always done in the past. So he threw the power of the government behind the employers' wage-cut program, used the armed forces to intimidate the unemployed, relegated the stingy relief program entirely to the individual states, and filled the country with Pollyanna propaganda to the effect that the return of prosperity was "just around the corner." He used every means to protect the interests of the employers. A major device in this respect was the organization of the Reconstruction Finance Corporation, which handed out two billion dollars to the railways, banks, and industries, to the tune of his assertions that the benefits of these subsidies would "trickle down" to the workers.

Meanwhile, the economic situation steadily worsened all through 1930-32, and myriads of workers and poor farmers fell into actual starvation. The United States had a dramatic example of the workings of the Marxist principle of the absolute impoverishment of the workers through the operation of the capitalist system. Bread lines and soup kitchens multiplied all over the country. "Hoovervilles"—horrible shanty towns built by the unemployed—sprang up on city dumps and vacant lots everywhere. Vast masses of workers were evicted from their homes—typically, 100,000 in Ohio alone during the first two years of the crisis. Millions of homeless workers drifted aimlessly on the railroads in a fruitless search for work. Although wages dropped almost 50 percent, retail food prices went down only 12 percent. The United States, erstwhile land of boasted capitalist prosperity, became a nightmare of hunger, sickness, destitution, and pauperization. Under these heavy pressures petty-bourgeois illusions among the workers were weakened and a fighting spirit grew.

Worst of all stricken were the Negroes. In the industrial centers unemployment among them ran about twice as high as among the whites. Negro workers were laid off and whites given their jobs at lower wages. Wages for Negro workers averaged 30 percent less than for whites. Also in the matter of relief the Negroes got much the worst of it, being either denied assistance altogether, given less of such aid, or discriminated against otherwise in the distribution process. Always the poorest paid in industry, the Negroes had few or no reserves with which to meet the crisis, and conditions among them beggared description. During the four crisis years 150 Negroes were lynched.

Meanwhile, the capitalists occupied themselves with destroying the huge surpluses that were glutting their production system. Among many such examples, great masses of oranges in California were soaked with kerosene to prevent their being eaten; in the Middle West vast amounts of corn were used to fire furnaces, and cattle and hogs were destroyed, and in the South big amounts of cotton were plowed under. And all the while the people starved. Capitalism in the United States had become idiotic in its chaos.

A.F. OF L. AND S.P. POLITICAL BANKRUPTCY

The A.F. of L. leaders were no less shocked and demoralized by the crisis than were the capitalists themselves, and for the same basic reasons. Their stupid capitalist dreams had exploded in their faces. They developed no program whatever to protect the workers' interests in this unprecedented economic holocaust. Their whole impulse was to tail along after the capitalists, as the latter floundered about, trying to find some way out of the crisis.

The Green bureaucracy followed Hoover's general line. They weakened the workers' militancy by re-echoing Hoover's demagogy to the effect that economic recovery was right at hand. They adopted the Hoover "stagger plan" of employment, which meant pauperizing the whole working class. They surrendered to Hoover's wage-cutting program. Consequently, never in the history of the American labor movement did the trade unions submit so unresistingly to slashing wage cuts in an economic crisis as they did during 1929-32 under the misleadership of the A.F. of L. officialdom.

The A.F. of L. leaders especially supported the capitalists in combating the mass demand for unemployment insurance. With incredible brass and stupidity, they denounced this vitally needed measure as "the dole," as "subsidizing idleness," as "degrading the dignity of the working man," and as "a hindrance to real progress." President Hoover and the many generals, bishops, and capitalists who crowded the platform of the 1930 A.F. of L. convention, had good reason to congratulate—as they did—Green, Woll, and company for so energetically combating the demand for unemployment insurance then being raised insistently all over the country by the Communists and the hungry working people. It was not until July 1932, after nearly three years of bitter crisis, that the well-paid A.F. of L. leaders finally yielded to the great mass pressure and reluctantly endorsed unemployment insurance.[1]

The Socialist Party leaders, firmly wedded to the Green bureaucracy and its bourgeois ideology, followed a similar line during the crisis years. It was four years before they showed any life on the unemployment question. They supported the Hoover "stagger plan"; they made no fight for unemployment insurance, although the S.P. had endorsed it long before; they gave no support to strike resistance against the universal wage cuts; they counseled patience and predicted an early return of "good times." In "Socialist" Milwaukee, workers were evicted and starved, as elsewhere. The surrender policies of the Socialists were well illustrated by Norman Thomas who spoke with J. P. Morgan on the radio in support of Hoover's "block-aid" policy, a system of neighborly mutual aid, whereby presumably Morgan would help his needy neighbors on Park Avenue, while the starving unemployed did the same in the slums and "Hoovervilles" of Harlem and the East Side. The S.P., like the A.F. of L., had abandoned the unemployed.

THE COMMUNISTS LEAD THE MASS STRUGGLE: MARCH 6TH

There was only one party in the United States from which leadership could and did come for the unemployed—the Communist Party. With relatively few members,[2] but with a clear head and a stout heart, the Party boldly organized the famished unemployed. The first major result was seen upon the death of Steve Katovis, a striking bakery worker who had been brutally killed by the New York police in January 1930. His funeral procession, essentially a protest of the unemployed, massed 50,000 indignant workers.

Then on March 6, 1930, came the historic national unemployment demonstration, led by the Communists. The Communist Party, the Young Communist League, and the Trade Union Unity League threw their united forces into the preparations. A million leaflets were circulated and innumerable preliminary meetings were organized. The national demonstration was held under the auspices of the T.U.U.L. The central demand was for unemployment relief and insurance, with stress upon demands for the Negro people, against wage cuts, and against fascism and war.

[1] Lorwin, *The American Federation of Labor*, p. 294.
[2] The C.P. convention of 1929 reported a membership of 9,642.

Among the mobilizing slogans were "Work or Wages!" and "Don't Starve —Fight!" The city authorities everywhere massed their armed forces against the demonstration, as though to put down a revolutionary uprising—in New York 25,000 police and firemen were concentrated against the Union Square demonstration. Obedient to their capitalist masters, the A.F. of L. leaders cried out that it was all a Moscow plot—Matthew Woll shrieking that the T.U.U.L. had just received two million dollars from Russia to finance the great conspiracy against the United States.

The March 6th turnout of the workers was immense—110,000 in New York; 100,000 in Detroit; 50,000 in Chicago; 50,000 in Pittsburgh; 40,000 in Milwaukee; 30,000 in Philadelphia; 25,000 in Cleveland; 20,000 in Youngstown, with similar huge meetings in Los Angeles, Boston, San Francisco, Seattle, Denver, and other cities all over the country. All told, 1,250,000 workers demonstrated against the outrageous conditions of hunger and joblessness. In the demonstrations Negro workers were a pronounced factor. Everywhere the unemployed had to face police brutality; in New York, for example, the police, refusing to permit the demonstrators to present their demands to the playboy "tin box" mayor, James J. Walker, violently dispersed the monster meeting. William Z. Foster, Robert Minor, Israel Amter, and H. Raymond, leaders of the demonstration, were arrested and railroaded to the penitentiary for indeterminate three-year terms.

The gigantic March 6th demonstration startled the entire country. Under the leadership of the Communists, the unemployed had stepped forth as a major political force. The great demonstration at once made the question of unemployed relief and insurance a living political issue in the United States. It showed that the masses were not going to starve tamely, as the bosses and reactionary union leaders had thought they would. The bourgeois and imperialist press grudgingly admitted that the Communists were leading the unemployed masses. The vast turnout gave a new sense of political strength to the Party. Altogether it was a magnificent demonstration of the Leninist leading role of the Communist Party.

UNEMPLOYED COUNCILS AND HUNGER MARCHES

The National Unemployed Council, made up of workers of all political affiliations, was organized in Chicago, on July 4, 1930, at a convention of 1,320 delegates. It was fully backed by the C.P., T.U.U.L., and Y.C.L. Local unemployed councils were set up in scores of cities all over the country. Besides the unemployed, the movement also included trade unions, fraternal societies, Negro organizations, and other sympathetic groupings. The councils fought for unemployment insurance, immediate cash and work relief, public work at union wages, food for school children, against eviction, against Negro discrimination, and so on. They used mass meetings, parades, petitions, picketing, hunger marches, and many other forms of agitation and struggle; they formed block committees to organize the workers in their homes. The main instrument for work inside the A.F. of L. was the A.F. of L. Committee for Unemployment Insurance and Relief, headed by Louis Weinstock of the Painters Union, which won the direct support of 3,000 local unions, 35 city central labor councils, 6 state federations, and 5 international unions. This movement concentrated its general political demand on the Workers Unemployment Insurance Bill (H.R. 2827).

The Unemployed Councils, in the face of widespread police brutality, conducted a mass of activities to bring pressure upon employers, local relief boards, and the city, state, and national governments. They led hundreds of demonstrations on a local and national scale. Some of the most important national mass movements were those on May 1, 1930, with 350,000 participating; on National Unemployment Insurance Day, February 25, 1931, with 400,000 demonstrators, and the turnout, on February 4, 1932, with 500,000 in the nationwide mass meetings. Three times mass petitions with a million signatures or more were presented to Congress. There were also hunger marches from the industrial centers to the capitals in many states. And then there were the two national hunger marches to Washington on December 7, 1931 (1,800 marchers) and December 6, 1932 (3,000 marchers).

These national hunger marches attracted tremendous attention. They were highly organized. The marchers traveled in old automobiles, which had been collected; the participants were registered, and each car, detachment, and column had a leader. The strictest discipline prevailed. Columns started from St. Louis, Chicago, Buffalo, Boston, and elsewhere, with regularly scheduled and organized stop-over places. All the columns converged upon Washington with clockwork precision. The return journey was made in an equally disciplined and organized manner. Attempts of American Legion elements and assorted hoodlums to break up the marches en route failed.

In Washington the marchers were a sensation. Their band played *The International* on the great plaza before the Capitol. Thousands of police and detectives had been mobilized from all over the country. Troops at nearby forts were held in readiness. One would have thought the marchers were going to try to overthrow the government. As the first hunger march went along Pennsylvania Avenue from the Capitol to the White House (and later to the A.F. of L. building) to lay its demands before Hoover (and Green), the parade was flanked on both sides by rows of marching policemen who outnumbered the hunger marchers by at least two to one. The Party concentrated its entire forces upon making these national marches successful.

The manifold activities of the Unemployed Councils, besides making a burning national issue of unemployment insurance, also resulted in securing many immediate relief concessions to the unemployed all over the country. The frightened capitalist class saw that the old game of letting the workers starve it out during economic crises would no longer work. They were dealing with an awakening working class, one which in the next few years would write some epic labor history.

THE FIGHT AGAINST WAGE CUTS

While the unemployed, under the leadership of the Communists, were thus militantly fighting against starvation, the masses of organized workers, locked in the grip of the Green misleaders, were yielding, almost without any resistance, to the repeated, deep-cutting wage slashes of the crisis years. Like Hoover, the top union leaders (though they made wordy complaints to the contrary) believed that the wage cuts were economically necessary; hence they helped the bosses put them through. This was quite in line with their no-strike, class collaboration policies of the previous Coolidge "prosperity" period. The union leaders' spinelessness and corruption in this respect were illustrated by the fact that when the railroad unions accepted a national 10 percent wage cut without a strike, Matthew Woll hailed it as one of the greatest industrial achievements in the history of the country. Consequently, during the crisis years the number of strikes fell to a record low, in contrast to the flaming resistance of the workers during the crises of 1877, 1893, and 1921. Hoover, at the A.F. of L. convention in 1930, might well gloat that "For the first time in more than a century of these recurring depressions, we have been practically free of bitter industrial conflicts." Small wonder that during the crisis the Federation lost about a fifth of its membership.

With the Communist Party so heavily engaged in leading the unemployed all over the country, the lefts and progressives were unable also to secure the leadership of the employed, to smash the no-strike policy of the Green bureaucracy, and to develop a solid resistance against the sweeping wage cuts of the period. Nevertheless, during this period the T.U.U.L. unions, most of whose leaders were Communists, did lead a number of important strikes. These included several textile strikes against wage cuts in New England, involving some 75,000 workers. A very important and successful strike was that of 1,500 steel workers led by the T.U.U.L. in October 1932, at the Republic Steel plant at Warren, Ohio. Then there were numerous small strikes among the needle trades workers in various cities, together with T.U.U.L. strikes in food and other industries. Important, too, were big T.U.U.L.-led strikes of 7,000 agricultural workers in Imperial Valley, California, in 1930, and 18,000 Colorado beet workers in 1932.

But the most important T.U.U.L. strike of the crisis period was that of 42,000 coal miners, 6,000 of whom were Negroes, in the Pittsburgh area, beginning in May 1931. This was the largest strike ever led by a left-wing union in the United States. The fierce struggle, with its slogan of "Strike against Starvation," was conducted by the National Miners Union—T.U.U.L. The miners, whose U.M.W.A. union had been destroyed locally in the great strike of 1927-28, were at the last extreme of hunger and desperation. The strikers fought in the face of violence from the mine operators, the government, and the U.M.W.A. leaders. After a desperate struggle of four months the strike was broken. An aftermath of this bitter fight was a strike of 8,000 Kentucky miners, on January 1, 1932, also under the leadership of the N.M.U. Guerrilla war conditions prevailed, with the whole union leadership arrested in Pineville. This strike, too, was beaten. Harry Simms, Y.C.L. organizer, was killed in this Kentucky strike.

The Labor Research Association listed 23 workers brutally murdered by the police, company gunmen, and vigilante thugs in the many struggles of the Communist Party, Unemployed Councils, and Trade Union Unity League during 1929-32. Eight of these were killed in strikes and 15 in unemployed demonstrations. Hundreds more were slugged and jailed. Five workers were killed by police in the famous hunger march to the Detroit Ford plant on March 7, 1932, including Joe York, Y.C.L. organizer and Joseph Bussell, 16-year-old Y.C.L. member. Three Negroes were shot down in an anti-eviction fight in Chicago on August 4, 1931. Unemployed Council and T.U.U.L. headquarters were raided repeatedly. Two national secretaries of the National Textile Workers Union, William Murdock and Pat Devine, were deported to England as Communists. The Food Workers Industrial Union had 110 injunctions issued against it in New York strikes, and 100 T.U.U.L. agricultural strikers were arrested, with eight of their leaders being sent to the penitentiary for terms of from 3 to 42 years. It was during this period, in May 1930, that the House of Representatives established the Fish Committee, forerunner of the notorious Dies, Thomas, Wood, Rankin, and McCarran thought-control committees of later years.

THE PENETRATION OF THE SOUTH

One of the greatest achievements of the Communist Party during the big economic crisis was its penetration of the South. During the

Coolidge years the Party had carried on considerable work in the South —the building of scattered branches, the Foster election tours of 1924 and 1928, and so on. But its real work there began when, on August 30, 1930, it established the *Southern Worker* at Chattanooga, Tennessee with James S. Allen as editor. Conditions in the South at the time were shocking—huge unemployment, sharecropper farmers at the point of starvation, and the country overrun with a plague of terroristic organizations—K.K.K., Blue Shirts, Silver Shirts, Black Shirts, Crusaders, White Legion, and others.

The Party worked bravely in this extremely difficult situation. It carried on unemployed demonstrations among the textile workers in the area from Virginia to Georgia, and also in various other centers. It actively led the heroic strike of the Negro and white miners of Kentucky and Tennessee early in 1932, under the auspices of the National Miners Union. In this bosses' civil war many were killed. The Harlan County mine operators association posted a reward of $1,000 for the arrest of Frank Borich, Communist president of the N.M.U., dead or alive.[1] For a worker to carry a card in the N.M.U. or the Communist Party subjected him to a charge of criminal syndicalism. The Party was also very active among the Negro and white steel workers and miners of the Birmingham, Alabama, area.[2]

The greatest struggle that developed out of the Party's southern penetration was the international fight to save the nine Scottsboro youths. On March 25, 1931, nine Negroes—mere boys—were jailed in Scottsboro, Alabama, charged with having raped two white girls on a freight train. Actually the rape never occurred, as Ruby Bates, one of the girls concerned, later publicly testified.[3] Nevertheless, as part of the general terrorism directed against the Negro people, the nine boys—C. Norris, C. Weems, H. Patterson, O. Powell, O. Montgomery, E. Williams, A. Wright, W. Roberson, and Roy Wright, were quickly convicted in a lynch atmosphere, and all except Wright (who was 13 years old) were sentenced to die in the electric chair.

On April 9th, the International Labor Defense wired Governor Miller, demanding a stay of execution, and sent its lawyer, the veteran Communist Joseph Brodsky, to Alabama to defend the Negro youths about to be legally lynched. Meanwhile, the Communists moved promptly to make the case known all over the country, which action saved the boys from death. However, the A.F. of L., S.P., A.C.L.U., and even the N.A.A.C.P. displayed no interest in the case.

1 *The Southern Worker*, Feb. 27, 1932.
2 Mary Southard, unpublished manuscript.
3 *Daily Worker*, Apr. 6, 1935.

COMMUNIST PARTY AND THE CRISIS 287

Then began a great legal mass struggle lasting for many years and paralleling the famous Mooney fight. The case was fought back and forth in the courts. Mass meetings were held all over the country. The C.P. led all this work. Liberal and labor organizations finally interested themselves. In 1934, the American Scottsboro Committee, led by S. Leibowitz, was set up, and in 1935 the united front Scottsboro Defense Committee was organized; it was made up of the I.L.D., N.A.A.C.P., A.C.L.U., L.I.D., Methodist Federation for Social Service, and other organizations. This defense committee waged the legal battle, while the I.L.D. conducted the mass campaign. J. Louis Engdahl, general secretary of the I.L.D., died of pneumonia while touring Europe, speaking on the case. After the lynchers were frustrated in their attempts legally to murder the Negro youths, then came the fight to save the latter from the ferocious prison sentences —up to 99 years—that were inflicted on them. Actually, it was not until 1950 that this scandalous frame-up came to an end, with the release of the last of the innocent Scottsboro prisoners.[1] William L. Patterson was I.L.D. national secretary during most of this big struggle.

The great Scottsboro fight made the Communist Party known and respected by the Negro people everywhere. An aftermath of Scottsboro was the bitter fight of the sharecroppers at Camp Hill, Alabama, on July 16, 1931. With cotton selling at nine cents per pound and costing 17 cents to produce, the economic conditions of the sharecroppers were terrible. The landlords were raising rents, seizing more and more of the tenants' crops, and even robbing the small farmers of their livestock. The Party in the South, undertaking to organize the Negro and white sharecroppers, proposed as an emergency program 50 percent reduction in rents and taxes, a five-year stay on all debts and mortgages, and a cash advance from the government to the small farmers.[2]

An important struggle began in January 1931, by a march to England, Arkansas, of 500 Negro and white sharecroppers, who forced the local planters and merchants to give them food. Meanwhile, Communist Party members initiated the formation of the Share-Croppers Union in Tallapoosa County, Alabama. A heavy clash came at Camp Hill in July when a meeting of the union, called to protest the Scottsboro outrage, was broken up by a white mob and the meeting place, a church, was burned to the ground. Captured after a gun battle in which the sharecroppers had defended themselves against mob violence, the Negro leader, Ralph Gray, was cold-bloodedly murdered by the mob. Scores of Negroes were slugged and arrested. But the Share-Croppers Union grew. By the end of 1932 it numbered 1,500 members, and it was

[1] Haywood Patterson and Earl Conrad, *Scottsboro Boy*, N. Y., 1950.
[2] *The Southern Worker*, March 21, 1931.

to play an important part in the tenant farmers' struggles during the New Deal years.

Another big battle growing out of these early years of the Party's work in the South was the Angelo Herndon case. Herndon, a member of the Y.C.L., was arrested in Atlanta, on July 11, 1932, because of his activities in behalf of the Scottsboro boys and the unemployed. He was charged with incitement to insurrection (under a law of 1861) and after a kangaroo trial was sentenced to 18 to 20 years in prison. The I.L.D. led the broad united front fight, and the leading lawyer was Benjamin J. Davis, Jr., now in prison as a member of the National Committee of the Communist Party. It was a long legal battle, backed by innumerable mass meetings and a huge petition campaign. The Supreme Court at first sustained the conviction but eventually reversed itself by a five-to-four decision. Herndon, out on $18,000 bail, was finally freed in 1937 from the clutches of the white supremacist lynchers.

During this period one of the most dramatic episodes in the Communist Party's fight against white chauvinism, both within and without the ranks of the Party, was the public trial of a Party member, A. Yokinen, in March 1931, in New York City. Yokinen, charged with practicing social discrimination against Negroes, was given an open hearing, at which were present 211 delegates from 133 mass organizations, as well as 1,500 spectators. Found guilty by the workers' jury, he was expelled, but promised to change his course thereafter.[1]

While the Communist Party was thus battling bravely and energetically for rights of the Negro people, the reactionary spirit of the Socialist Party was shown by the following scandalous item in its official organ: "Almost all the Southerners believe in segregating the Negro and depriving him of the social and political rights that whites enjoy. The Southern Socialists must adjust themselves to this state of affairs. It is certain that there never will be a thriving movement in the South unless it is conducted in southern style."[2] Top A.F. of L. policy also remained at a similar reactionary Jim Crow level.

THE FARMERS' REVOLT

The farmers of the West and Middle West fought back against the economic crisis hardly less militantly than the unemployed workers and the Negro people. They faced impossible conditions. Not only had the farmers' income been cut to less than one-half, but the banks and insurance companies were actively foreclosing on mortgages. From 1929

[1] *Race Hatred on Trial*, N. Y., 1931.
[2] *New Leader*, June 21, 1930.

to 1933, some 1,019,300 farmers accordingly lost their property.[1]

The farmers developed an aggressive fight against these barbarous conditions. They organized milk strikes, carried on demonstrations, demanded relief. One of their most effective weapons was the so-called "penny sale." That is, when a foreclosed farm was put up for auction a friendly neighbor would bid a penny for it and the farmers assembled would prevent anyone else from going above this bid. The revolt against foreclosures reached the point of open resistance in many places.

The Communist Party was very active in many rural areas and actively supported this strong farmers' movement. Mainly upon its initiative, the Farmers' National Relief Conference was organized in Washington on December 7, 1932, side by side with the Second National Hunger March. Present were 248 delegates from 26 states, representing 33 organizations and unorganized farmers. The Conference set up a Farmers' National Committee of Action. In November 1933, this Committee of Action met in Chicago; the conference had 702 farmer delegates from 36 states, representing the Farm Bureau, Farmers Union, Farmers Holiday Association, and others. Communist and other left influences was responsible for its program, which called for cancellation of the debts of small and middle farmers, no forced sales or evictions, cash relief for destitute farmers, reduction in rents and taxes, reductions in prices of things the farmers must buy, and abolition of the system of oppression of the Negro people. This militant movement had much to do with developing the important role played by the farmers during the oncoming New Deal years.

THE NATIONAL "BONUS MARCH"

One of the most significant and dramatic events of the crisis years of 1929-33, was the national bonus march of the war veterans to Washington in July 1932. The ex-servicemen, suffering the full blows of the deep economic crisis, betrayed by the American Legion officials, and kicked around politically by the Hoover Administration, took a leaf from the book of the unemployed and en masse presented their grievances to the heads of the federal government. The call for the national march to Washington was made at a hearing of the House Ways and Means Committee in April 1932 by representatives of the Workers Ex-Servicemen's League (W.E.S.L.). This organization was led nationally by the well-known Communists Emanuel Levin, Peter Cacchione, James W. Ford, and others.

There was a tremendous response by the veterans to the call for the

[1] Labor Research Association, *Labor Fact Book 2*, p. 148.

march. Unorganized groups of veterans poured into Washington from all over the country, occupying empty buildings and setting up a great shack camp on the Anacostia flats. Attempts by the Administration, reactionary American Legion officials, and the A.F. of L. leaders to head off the demonstration only increased it. Many Negro workers were in the march, and there was no Jim Crow at Anacostia. The press shrieked "reds" and "revolution."[1]

The marchers in Washington eventually reached a total of 25,000. They shouted, "We Fought for Democracy—What Did We Get?"; "Heroes in 1917—Bums in 1932." Their central demand was the payment of their adjusted service pay—miscalled a bonus.[2] This demand the Communist Party actively supported in the face of strong opposition from the Socialist Party and A.F. of L. leadership. Eventually the "bonus" was realized under the Roosevelt New Deal.

The Hoover Administration, highly embarrassed by the ex-soldier marchers and unable to induce them to leave Washington with their demands unmet, finally ordered out the armed forces against them. General Douglas MacArthur, nowadays posing as an ultra-patriot, military genius, and peerless statesman, thereupon, had his troops, armed with bayonets and tear gas, violently drive the ex-soldiers from their camp and burn it down. General Dwight D. Eisenhower, then an aide of MacArthur and now an eager aspirant for the U.S. presidency, also participated in this dastardly affair. Two veterans were killed and scores wounded. This was the infamous "Battle of Washington." It proved to be a nail in the political coffin of President Hoover. It now rises to menace the hopes of General MacArthur to be the first fascist ruler of America.

The Communists played a very important part in this great movement of the veterans. The W.E.S.L., however, with its very small forces, was not able to maintain the leadership of the swiftly developing struggle. Another factor in this inadequacy was some initial hesitation in the Party leadership as to the potentialities of the movement.

THE PRESIDENTIAL ELECTIONS OF 1932

At election time in 1932 the country, after 37 months of economic crisis, remained industrially paralyzed. The Republican Party, with Hoover as its candidate, proposed nothing but a continuation of the latter's fruitless policies. The Democrats, with Franklin D. Roosevelt, outlined a platform differing little from that of the Republicans; Roose-

[1] Statement of the Communist Party in *The Communist*, Sept. 1932.
[1] Jack Douglas, *Veterans on the March*, pp. 16-18, N. Y., 1934.

velt proposing government economy, a balanced budget, sound currency, and making general promises of unemployment relief. Roosevelt gave no indication of his later extensive reform program, but he did refer in his speeches to "the forgotten man," and he proposed vaguely a "new deal." The A.F. of L. leaders leaned toward Roosevelt, but still clung officially to their antiquated Gompersite nonpartisan policy. The election, a foregone conclusion, went overwhelmingly to Roosevelt by the record plurality of seven million. He carried all the states but six.

The Communist Party put up as its candidate for president William Z. Foster, and for vice-president James W. Ford, a Negro and former Alabama steel worker, whose grandfather had been lynched by klansmen. The Party's election platform included demands for unemployment and social insurance at the expense of the state and employers; opposition to Hoover's wage-cutting policy; emergency relief for the hard-pressed farmers without restrictions by the government and banks; exemption of impoverished farmers from taxes, and no forced collection of rents or debts; equal rights for Negroes and self-determination for the Black Belt; opposition to capitalist terror; opposition to all forms of suppression of the political rights of the workers; opposition to imperialist war; defense of the Chinese people and the Soviet Union. The Party, on the ballot in 40 states, campaigned aggressively, holding hundreds of meetings, distributing seven million leaflets, and selling a million pamphlets. In the midst of the campaign Foster suffered a heart attack, which was to lay him up, more or less, for several years. The Party's national vote was 102,991.

THE STATUS OF THE PARTY AND THE Y.C.L.

Obviously the Communist vote in the election, although more than double that polled by the Party in 1928, was in no sense proportionate to the big struggles led, and militant leadership showed, by the Party and other left-progressive organizations during the crisis years. The basic explanation for this disproportion was that although the workers in masses willingly followed Communist leadership in the bitter fights for their daily demands—relief, wages, etc.—they were not yet ready to make the break with capitalism as such, which they felt that a vote for the Communist candidates would imply. Also, caught in the trap of the two-party system, they did not want to "throw away their votes" on minority candidates.

The Party itself tended to restrict its vote and general mass influence by failing to develop a broad united front election campaign around the burning issues of the period, summarized in its platform. It should have kept these immediate questions far more to the front in its election work. Instead, it laid altogether too much stress upon such advanced slogans as "The revolutionary way out of the crisis," and "A Workers and Farmers Government." This was a leftist sectarian error, into which the Party was led by its failure more skillfully to develop a Leninist line to meet the devastating economic crisis situation.

At the seventh Party convention in June 1930, the secretariat was reorganized to consist of W. W. Weinstone, organization secretary; William Z. Foster, trade union secretary; and Earl Browder, administrative secretary. Browder was formerly editor of the *Labor Herald* and *Labor Unity* and had long been a member of the Central Executive Committee.

During the crisis years of 1929-33, the membership of the Communist Party went up from somewhat less than 10,000 members to 18,000, and that of the Y.C.L. reached about 3,000. These figures, however, also bore but little relationship to the extensive influence of the Communists in the broad mass struggles of the period. The workers, still believing in capitalism, while following the Communists in daily fights, were not yet disposed to join up with militant Communist organizations in large numbers, even as they were not ready to vote the Party election ticket.

Nevertheless, far greater membership gains could have been registered had it not been for inadequate organizational work, especially due to the effects of a stubborn tendency to believe that Party recruiting could not be carried on during mass struggles. The Party, in fact, was beginning to fall into the bad habit of doing nearly all of its recruiting during special membership drives, usually held during less tense political periods. Other negative factors of major significance in keeping down the Party's numbers were a lingering underestimation of the importance of specific youth organization and also, even among Communists, a failure to grasp fully the all-decisive importance of building a powerful mass Communist Party. The latter weaknesses have been particularly strong in the United States, where the trade unions have been the chief leading organizations of the working class and where the workers' parties historically have played much less of a role.

21. Early Struggles Under the New Deal (1933-1936)

When Franklin D. Roosevelt became president on March 4, 1933, American capitalism, lately hailed enthusiastically all over the world by capitalist and Social-Democratic economists as crisis-proof, was still prostrate after more than three and a half years of the great economic crisis. Industrial production was reduced by half, and so was foreign trade. Roosevelt had to close every bank in the country; seventeen million workers walked the streets jobless; millions of skilled workers, farmers, and middle class people had lost their savings, homes, and farms through bank crashes and mortgage foreclosures. And the masses were bitterly disillusioned and resentful at the starvation conditions so brutally thrust upon them by the employers. The country was alive with unemployment demonstrations, strikes, and bonus marches, and the horizon loomed with the sharpening class struggle. Never in all their history had the American capitalists been so confused and frightened as they were now at the appalling economic and political situation. Not prosperity for them, but "revolution," seemed to be "just around the corner."

To meet this chaotic condition Roosevelt proceeded with fantastic speed to introduce his "New Deal," about which he had said almost nothing during the election campaign. Bills were shot through Congress so fast by the panicky capitalist politicians that many of the legislators had only the vaguest ideas of what they were voting on, even if they actually read the many projects. This flood of legislation was chiefly the product of Roosevelt's "Brain Trust"—Moley, Tugwell, Berle, *et al.*

The New Deal, as expressed in the score of alphabetical laws and bureaus of its first couple of years, constituted a greatly increased centralization of the federal government and its intensified intervention in the economic life of the country for the following specific purposes: " (a) to reconstruct the shattered financial banking system; (b) to rescue tottering business with big loans and subsidies; (c) to stimulate private capital investment; (d) to raise depressed prices by setting inflationary tendencies into operation; (e) to overcome the agricultural overproduction through acreage reduction and crop destruction; (f) to protect farm and home-owners against mortgage foreclosure; (g) to create employment and stimulate mass buying power through establishing public works; (h) to provide a minimum of relief for the starving unemployed."[1]

The general purpose of this mass of often contradictory reform legislation was to give a shot in the arm to the sick economic system. It also had a major political objective, namely, to keep the militant-minded masses from taking much more drastic action. Varga points out that, "The aim of the New Deal consisted first and foremost in holding the farmers and workers off from revolutionary mass action."[2] Indeed, had it not been for Roosevelt's program, the workers during this period would have gone much further than they did and almost certainly would have broken away from the two-party system and launched a political party of their own.

The Communist Party, while demanding many of Roosevelt's reforms, clearly pointed out that the New Deal was not a program of steps toward socialism, as Social-Democrats all over the world declared. There was nothing whatever socialistic about it. The capitalists were left in complete control of the banks, factories, and transportation systems, to exploit the workers as before. Nor was the New Deal a program of "progressive capitalism," as the labor leaders, liberals, and eventually Earl Browder called it. Economically, it was simply a plan to shore up broken-down capitalism in this country, to recondition American imperealism so as to help it to survive in a world capitalist system enmeshed in its deepening general crisis. For the most part the New Deal was based upon the ideas of the noted British economist, John Maynard Keynes, whose theory it was that capitalism in its monopoly phase, having ceased to be a self-regulating economic system, must either adopt a policy of direct government intervention and subsidies to industry, or else fall into hopeless ruin.[3]

President Roosevelt, himself a wealthy man, was a frank supporter of the capitalist system, and the avowed purpose of his New Deal was to preserve and strengthen that social order, with certain liberal trimmings. In working out his program, Roosevelt carefully avoided all measures which could in any way tend to undermine the capitalist system. His whole regime worked out to the advantage of monopoly capital, of American imperialism. Profits were never better for the capitalists, trustification went on at an accelerated pace, there was a rapid integra-

[1] William Z. Foster, *Outline Political History of the Americas*. p. 422, N. Y., 1951.
[2] Eugene Varga, *Two Systems*, p. 135, N. Y., 1939.
[3] John Maynard Keynes, *The General Theory of Employment, Interest, and Money*, N. Y., 1935.

tion of the monopolies with the government—into a state monopoly capitalism. Under Roosevelt's presidency Wall Street monopoly capital made many strides ahead, at home and abroad, and these finally placed it in a position to make its present desperate bid for the mastery of the world.

WHY NOT FASCISM IN THE UNITED STATES?

Five weeks before Roosevelt took office in the United States Adolph Hitler, on January 30, 1933, grabbed power in Germany. Hitler, the agent of German monopoly capital, came to government domination directly as a result of the workings of the so-called "lesser evil" policy of the Social-Democrats. That is, refusing to unite with the Communists on an anti-Hitler ticket and struggle, the Social-Democrats voted for and helped to elect as president the reactionary General von Hindenburg, who was supposed to be a lesser evil than Hitler. Whereupon, von Hindenburg, once in office, promptly made Hitler his chancellor. Thus the Nazis came to power. The Social-Democrats, to make their treason to the working class even more flagrant, stated that Hitler had gotten power legally and they voted to support him on that basis. Then the fascist lightning hit, wrecking Social-Democracy, as well as the Communist Party, trade unions, co-operatives, and all other democratic organizations and institutions.

When Hitler took office in Germany, the country was in a mess from the great economic crisis. There was a complete economic breakdown, with about eight million famished unemployed and an impoverished middle class. The big monopolists, now in full control with Hitler, at once established a fascist dictatorship by smashing the labor movement and destroying bourgeois parliamentary government. To put the halted industries into operation, they plunged into a big campaign of rearmament. Then they set out to master the world—a wild fascist dream which finally landed them in the shattering debacle of World War II.

The fascist course taken by the German bourgeoisie was not something peculiar to Germany alone. It was more or less the general orientation of monopoly capital internationally. It was the way the big bankers, manufacturers, and landlords figured to overcome the general crisis of capitalism and to liquidate once and for all the menacing threat of socialism, on both a national and international scale. Undoubtedly the big capitalists, the most reactionary elements among them, dreamed of establishing a fascist world. All over Europe these ruling strata were saturated with fascist conceptions. This was particularly true in Italy, Spain, Poland, Hungary, and the Baltic and Balkan countries. In France, and to a lesser extent in Great Britain as well, there were powerful pro-fascist currents in the ruling class. In the United States, as we shall see later, finance capital was also permeated with a fascist spirit.

Why, then, was there no fascist regime organized here? If the United States, ruled by big business, did not reach the stage of actually trying the desperate fascist solution to its devastating economic crisis, this was because of a number of factors which lessened the capitalist drive toward fascism: (a) U.S. capitalism was not as deeply affected by the general crisis of the system as was German capitalism; (b) U.S. capitalism did not face an imminent proletarian revolution as did German capitalism; (c) U.S. capitalism belonged during that period to the group of imperialist powers that temporarily favored the maintenance of the status quo in the world relation of forces in the imperialist camp, and it was not actively preparing for a world war to redivide the world as was German capitalism; (d) U. S. capitalism, unlike that of Germany, still possessed the financial means to carry out a reform program such as the New Deal, instead of turning to the fateful weapon of fascism.

Undoubtedly the foregoing factors greatly reduced the urge and push of American finance capital toward fascism; but it is indisputable that it nevertheless displayed strong tendencies in this direction. In checking this fascist danger, the mass resistance of the people—workers, Negroes, poor farmers, and lower petty bourgeoisie—played a decisive role. While not revolutionary, they acted in the best traditions of the American people and conducted a whole series of economic and political struggles which largely escaped the controls of the confused employers and their trade union bureaucratic lackeys. The Communist Party considered its main task to stimulate this resistance and to squeeze all possible concessions from the employers and the government. The mass struggles of these years definitely balked the growing fascist tendencies among the ruling class and forced them to make serious concessions to the impoverished and resolute toilers. In short, although in less acute conditions of political struggle, the American workers, like those of France and other European countries, halted the advance of fascism in this country.

THE NATIONAL INDUSTRIAL RECOVERY ACT

The keystone of the early Roosevelt program was the National Industrial Recovery Act, passed by Congress on June 13, 1933. This law (N.I.R.A.) provided for the setting up of industrial price and labor codes in the various industries. Its professed aim was to establish "fair competition" in business and agriculture. The workers were theoretically granted ambiguous rights to organize under Section 7 (a), which stated that the workers had "the right to organize and bargain collectively through representatives of their own choosing." The whole code-making machinery was handled by the National Recovery Administration (N.R.A.), in which the workers were conceded consultative rights in the Labor Advisory Board. But actually, of 775 code-making bodies set up labor was represented on only 26. Big business controlled the whole thing.

This elaborate scheme expressed the strong fascist sentiment current at this time in American big business. N.I.R.A. originated with the United States Chamber of Commerce and it was patterned after Mussolini's "corporative state." The plan proposed generally a state-controlled industrial system and labor movement. The man put in charge of it, General Hugh Johnson, was a reactionary and a frank admirer of the fascist dictator of Italy, Mussolini. Roosevelt gave this dangerous fascist-like plan his hearty endorsement.

The N.I.R.A. was launched in 1933 amid a great ballyhoo, with the backing of an all-class national front. The monopolists, seeing an opportunity to strengthen their industrial control, to extend company unionism, and to reduce organized labor to impotence, were for it. The farm and middle class leaders were allured by its vivid promises of industrial recovery. The A.F. of L. leaders, including the "Socialists," hoping to build up a big dues-paying membership, even on a company union basis, hailed it joyously. Huey Long, Father Coughlin, and other fascist demagogues also ardently supported the N.I.R.A. The Blue Eagle, symbol of N.I.R.A., became at the time the very mark of patriotism and good citizenship. An intense campaign was carried on to put N.I.R.A. across. "Chiselers" on the industry codes were denounced virtually as traitors to the country. Only the Communists opposed N.I.R.A. consistently.

BEGINNING OF THE MASS STRUGGLE

According to the theory behind N.I.R.A. the workers were supposed to sit quietly while their leaders, in brotherly conference with the capitalists in the N.R.A. code-fixing and labor boards, would hand them down an assortment of improved wages and working conditions. Roosevelt and Johnson declared that there must be no strikes, as they would hamper "recovery." The trade unions and Socialist leaders, also with this idea in mind, established what was virtually a no-strike policy. Strikes, in fact, were denounced as a sort of treachery to the existing "national front" behind N.I.R.A. But the masses of the workers had quite other ideas. They observed that although prices under the new codes were rapidly rising, their wages lagged far behind. Hence, in the general spirit of rebellion generated by the great economic crisis, after a short strike lull during the first months of the Roosevelt Administration, they proceeded, despite their "leaders," to develop a rising strike movement. The biggest mass movement of the workers in American history began to get under way.

The Communist Party gave every possible encouragement and leadership to the growing strike movement. From the outset the Party had condemned the N.I.R.A. and all its practices. It warned of the grave dangers of fascism in this early program of the Roosevelt Administration—especially in the light of the tragic course of events in Germany under Hitler. In July 1933, the Party called an Extraordinary Conference of 350 delegates in New York.[1] This conference addressed an Open Letter to the Party, outlining a program of militant struggle, stressing the need to concentrate upon building Party units and trade unions in the basic industries and to give all support to the growing mass strike movement. The conference urged the workers to "Write your own codes on the picket line." It played a vital role in preparing the Party for the big mass struggles ahead.

In 1933 the total number of strikers ran to 900,000, or more than three times as many as in 1932. The T.U.U.L., headed by Jack Stachel (with Foster sick), led 200,000 workers in strikes, as compared with 250,000 independent union strikers, and 450,000 in the A.F. of L. The most important of the many T.U.U.L. strikes of that year were those of 16,000 auto workers in Detroit, 5,000 steel workers in Ambridge, 3,000 miners in Western Pennsylvania, 12,000 shoe workers in New York, 15,000 needle workers in New York, 18,000 cotton pickers and 6,000 grape pickers in California and Arizona, and 2,700 packinghouse workers in Pittsburgh.[2] During these years, all the unions began to grow, the A.F. of L. by 500,000, independents by 150,000, and the T.U.U.L. by 100,000, giving the latter a membership of some 125,000.[3]

THE BIG STRIKE MOVEMENT OF 1934-36

The mass strike movement that got under way in 1933 varied widely from the traditional craft patterns of the A.F. of L. It reflected clearly the principles, strategy, and tactics that had been so vigorously propa-

[1] William W. Weinstone in *Political Affairs*, Sept. 1949.
[2] *Report to the Eighth Convention, C.P.U.S.A.*, Apr. 2, 1934.
[3] The principal T.U.U.L. unions were needle, 25,000 members; metal, 21,000; agricultural, 20,000; coal, 10,000; food, 10,000; shoe, 9,000; furniture 8,000; marine, 7,000; textile, 7,000; auto, 5,000; lumber, 3,500; fishermen, 2,000; tobacco, 1,400.

gated by the Communist Party and the T.U.U.L. The strikes penetrated the hitherto closed trustified industries—steel, auto, aluminum, marine transport, etc.; they ignored the A.F. of L. dictum that union contracts justify union scabbery; they were industrial in character; they embraced Negroes, unskilled, foreign-born, women, youth, and white collar workers; they struck a high note of solidarity between employed and unemployed; they used mass picketing, shop delegates, broad strike committees, sit-down strikes, slow-down strikes, and other left-wing methods; they took on an increasingly political character; and they developed over the opposition of reactionary labor officials who wanted to stifle them.

The years 1934-36 intensified this radical mass strike trend. The number of strikers was high and so was their militancy—1,466,695 strikers in 1934; 1,141,363 in 1935, and 788,648 in 1936. It was a time of both national industrial strikes and local general strikes. The workers fought mainly for wage increases and trade union recognition. Mostly their strikes were successful. During this period the strikes had been largely aimed by the workers "to enforce the codes," but in reality the workers pushed their demands beyond anything contemplated by N.I.R.A. As the Communist Party militantly urged, the workers were indeed writing their own codes on the picket lines.

The employers countered the rising strike movement, as usual, with a policy of violence. They mobilized their armed company gunmen against the strikers, they used the local police forces to beat and jail workers, they had the troops out in dozens of strike situations. In the big national textile strike, 16 workers were killed; many more were killed in the coal strike, the San Francisco strike, and in other bitter economic fights. All told, in 1934-36, 88 workers were killed in mass struggles. But the workers fought back and the strike wave continued to mount.

Of much importance in the strike movement during these early New Deal years were the activities of the National Unemployed Council. This organization kept up its steady agitation for unemployment relief and insurance, and insistently promoted solidarity between the unemployed and employed. It was active in every important strike, strengthening the fighting lines. The Socialists had organized the Workers Alliance, and this also was a factor among the unemployed. In April 1936, in Washington, the Unemployed Councils, Workers Alliance, and National Unemployed League, upon the proposal of the Communists, united in one organization, with an estimated membership of 500,000.[1] In 1938 its membership reached 800,000. The Communists became the most influential element in the new organization and its leadership. The result of the active work among the unemployed was that for the first time in

[1] Labor Research Association, *Labor Fact Book 3*, p. 154, N. Y., 1936.

American labor history scabs could be recruited only with difficulty during an economic crisis. Although the number of unemployed never dropped below thirteen million during 1933-36, they refused to take the jobs of strikers. Owing largely to the militant leadership of the unemployed by the Communist Party, this marked a new high level of working class solidarity in the United States.

The biggest and most significant national industrial strikes during 1934-36 were those of the textile workers and the bituminous coal miners, both A.F. of L. strikes. The national textile strike, led by the United Textile Workers in September 1934, embraced 475,000 workers in 11 states, including large numbers of workers in the South. The strike faced great violence from the employers and the government. It was largely lost when the demands of the strikers were referred to an arbitration board and the strike was called off. The national bituminous coal strike of September 1935 brought out 400,000 miners, tying up nearly every important soft coal field. Within a few days the strike resulted in a victory. It put the U.M.W.A. back on its feet as a powerful organization, after it had been almost demolished in the fateful strike of 1927-28. There was also the left-led National Lumber Workers strike of 41,000 lumbermen in the Pacific Northwest. Another highly important strike early in 1936, significant of the great wave of strikes soon to come in the trustified industries, was the successful strike of the rubber workers in Akron.

Important local general strikes and near-general strikes, which cut right across A.F. of L. "sacred" contracts, were a pronounced feature of these years. In Milwaukee (February 1934) and Minneapolis (May 1934) small bodies of strikers quickly attracted the support of the local labor movements when attacked by employer violence, and general walk-outs were averted only by timely settlements. In Pekin, Illinois, during the same year, there was another such general strike movement. In Toledo (May 1934) when the bosses tried to smash a strike of 1,500 metal workers, the local labor movement came to their active support, 83 of 91 A.F. of L. local unions, to the outrage of their conservative leaders, voting to strike. In Terre Haute (July 1935) a two-day strike of 48 A.F. of L. locals with 26,000 workers took place in support of 600 hard-pressed metal workers. In all these situations the Communists were highly active.

THE SAN FRANCISCO GENERAL STRIKE

The great general strike in the San Francisco Bay area, embracing 127,000 workers, took place during July 16-19, 1934. It grew out of a coastwise strike of 35,000 maritime workers. The Communist Party, which had a strong organization in California, gave the strike its full support and its influence was of major importance in the struggle. The historic strike gave an enormous impetus to the whole American labor movement.[1]

The movement began in a drive from 1932 on, led by Communists and progressives, to organize the marine workers of the Pacific Coast. This drive culminated in a strong A.F. of L. longshoremen's union with Harry Bridges at its head, a demand for better conditions, and a coastwise strike of 12,000 of these workers on May 7, 1934. The Marine Workers Industrial Union (T.U.U.L.), headed by Harry Jackson, which won the leadership of decisive sections of the seamen, also called them on strike, and by May 23rd, the eight A.F. of L. maritime unions were out all along the coast. For the first time West Coast shipping was at a complete standstill. The conservative A.F. of L. leadership tried desperately to check the powerful movement, but in vain. Joseph Ryan, dictator of the Longshoremen's Union, was forced to abandon the strike and left the city. Bridges, head of the rank-and-file committee of 75, in tune with the militant workers, brilliantly outgeneraled the labor misleaders at every turn.

Enraged at the employers' violent efforts to break the maritime strike and also at their obvious determination to make the city open shop, the workers of San Francisco developed a strong fighting spirit. The Communist Party, which had many members and supporters in key A.F. of L. local unions, urged a general strike in all the cities along the Pacific Coast. To no avail, the top union leadership opposed the rising general strike spirit among the workers. In mid-June, Painters' Local 1158 sent out a letter for a general strike. By early July the influential Machinists Local 68, along with many other local unions, had endorsed the proposed strike. The police killing of two waterfront workers on July 8th—one of them Nick Bordois, a Communist—added fuel to the flames, with 35,000 angry workers turning out to the funeral. On July 10th the Alameda Labor Council called for a general strike; on July 12th the San Francisco and Oakland teamsters went out; and on July 16th 160 A.F. of L. unions, 127,000 strong, tied up the whole San Francisco Bay region.

The strike was highly effective. Practically the entire industrial life of the great bay community came to a halt. The workers were powerfully demonstrating their resentment at the great economic crisis and their determination to have a better day under the promised "New Deal."

[1] For details and interpretations of the strike, see Labor Research Association, *Labor Fact Book 3*; Mike Quin, *The Big Strike*; and George Morris, *Where Is the C.I.O. Going?*

Not a store could open, not a truck could move, not a factory wheel could turn, without the permission of the General Strike Committee. Never was any American city so completely strike-bound as was the whole San Francisco Bay community during this great strike.

The government—local, state, and national—turned all its guns upon this—to the capitalists—highly dangerous strike. Mayor Rossi swore in 5,000 deputies and police; Governor Merriam ordered out 4,500 militia to dominate the area; President Roosevelt denounced the strike, and his agents, Hugh Johnson of N.R.A. and Secretary of Labor Frances Perkins, were on the spot to try to disintegrate it. The press whipped up the whole region with frantic redbaiting and yells that the Communist revolution was at hand. Vigilante gangs raided and wrecked the headquarters of the Communist Party, the *Western Worker,* and various labor and left-wing mass organizations. Over "400 men and several women were arrested and thrown into a jail so crowded that most of them had to sleep on the floor," reported the *New York Times,* on July 29, 1934. For several weeks the Communist Party was virtually outlawed in California.

While the government attacked the strike from without, the A.F. of L. leaders assailed it with more deadly effect from within. William Green blasted the strike as "unauthorized" and as the work of the Communists; Joseph Ryan and other national labor fakers tried to force their members back to work; and Howard of the Typographical Union managed to keep his men on the job on the basis of a last-minute 10 percent wage increase. As for the local top union leaders in San Francisco—Vandeleur, Kidwell, Deal, and others—when they saw that they could not forestall the general strike, they joined it in order to strangle it. With control of the General Strike Committee in their hands, they refused to halt publication of the capitalist newspapers and the operation of telephone and telegraphic services; they issued large numbers of permits to restaurants to open, and to trucking outfits to operate; they made no attempt to police the city with the strikers; they gave their endorsement to the bosses' strikebreaking and redbaiting campaign. And when they felt that they had things well enough in hand, they suddenly moved to call off the strike. But with all their maneuvering they could carry the anti-strike motion only by a standing vote of 191 to 174, not daring to risk a roll call vote. The historic strike was over.

The maritime workers were left to fight alone. On July 30th these 35,000 strikers went back to the job, after a three-month walkout. Their demands were referred to arbitration, out of which they secured a partial victory. In this epoch-making strike the West Coast longshoremen and their leader, Harry Bridges, laid the basis for one of the finest labor unions in the capitalist world, the International Longshoremen's and Warehousemen's Union.

The key to winning the great San Francisco strike was to spread it all over the coast, and still farther. This extension was indispensable in order to checkmate the co-ordinated attempts of the government, the employers, and the A.F. of L. leadership to localize, isolate, and strangle the strike. The Communists and the other left and progressive elements, despite numerous minor mistakes, were quite aware of this imperative need to spread the strike, and they tried to do just that. But their forces were too small to accomplish it in the face of the formidable opposition. The "lost" San Francisco strike, in spite of all lugubrious predictions, had a stimulating effect upon the labor movement in California and all over the United States. The strike created one of the most glorious traditions in the entire history of the American labor movement.

THE T.U.U.L. MERGES WITH THE A.F. OF L.

During the first two stormy years of the New Deal about one million workers, largely unskilled and foreign-born from the basic industries, poured into the A.F. of L. unions. Naturally these workers preferred to join the recognized and established labor unions if there was a possibility of getting results from them. This influx radically changed the situation in those organizations. It broke down the officials' no-strike policy, brought in a breath of democracy, weakened the bureaucrats' control, and made it more difficult to enforce the anti-Communist clauses against the left. Besides, sections of the top leadership began to interest themselves in organizational work.

Recognizing that the conditions that had originally caused the formation of the T.U.U.L. were now breaking down, the Communists and other lefts, always ardent champions of labor unity, began at once to shift their orientation toward a return to the A.F. of L. Already, early in 1933, they joined forces with the miners in their drive to re-establish the U.M.W.A., and in September 1934, the T.U.U.L. proposed trade union unity to the A.F. of L. In various industries T.U.U.L. bodies began to join up with corresponding A.F. of L. unions. This unity trend, however, did not sit well with the A.F. of L. top leaders, and William Green sent out a letter warning against the unity moves of the T.U.U.L.

In the spring of 1934[1] the Communist Party advanced the slogan, "For an Independent Federation of Labor," to be composed of the 400,000 members of the T.U.U.L. and other independents, but this policy was

[1] *Labor Unity*, June 1934.

soon perceived to be incorrect and it was dropped. Instead, the trend toward general labor unity was pushed vigorously by the Party everywhere. Early in 1935 the T.U.U.L. steel, auto, and needle trades unions voted to affiliate with the A.F. of L., the workers joining as individuals where they could not affiliate in a body. On March 16-17, 1935, at a special convention, the T.U.U.L. resolved itself into a Committee for the Unification of the Trade Unions, with the objective of affiliating the remaining T.U.U.L. organizations to the A.F. of L..[1] Four months later the T.U.U.L. disbanded altogether.

Although it displayed some sectarian and dualist tendencies, the T.U.U.L. nevertheless played an important and constructive role in the labor movement. All through the great economic crisis, when A.F. of L. militancy was at its lowest point, the T.U.U.L. did heroic and effective work, as we have seen, in leading the employed and unemployed workers in struggle. Its militant advocacy of industrial unionism over several years was highly educational to the workers. The contacts it had established in the basic industries, together with the shop units of the Communist Party, were fundamental factors in developing the great C.I.O. organizing campaign of the next few years. The Party was basically correct in supporting the T.U.U.L. as it did.

THE FORMATION OF THE C.I.O.

The big labor struggles of the early New Deal years came to a sharp climax with the formation of the Committee for Industrial Organization (C.I.O.) in November 1935. This body was originally composed of representatives of the coal miners', textile, ladies' garment, men's clothing, printing, oil-field, cap and millinery, and metal miners' unions, with a combined membership of about one million. The Committee's purpose was the unionization of the almost totally unorganized millions of workers in the basic trustified industries. It was truly a momentous development, and the Communist Party gave its most active support from the start.

The dominant leaders among the Green A.F. of L. bureaucracy had looked with grave misgivings and alarm upon the tremendous mass movement toward unionism that developed during the last months of the economic crisis and the early period of the New Deal. They feared it hardly less acutely than did the employers themselves. They were afraid that the huge numbers of new unskilled and foreign-born union members, with their radical conceptions of what labor unions should be and do, would spoil the long-time picnic of the bureaucrats by eliminating the

[1] *Daily Worker*, March 11, 16, 17, 1935.

skilled workers as the dominant trade union element, by breaking down craft lines and transforming the craft unions into industrial unions, by forcing the labor movement from its class collaboration basis onto one of class struggle, and by selecting for themselves new and presumably radical leaders. To avoid all these threatening disasters and yet to profit from the mass upheaval, the policy of the Green bureaucrats was to grab off the skilled workers and let the rest go—in the time-honored A.F. of L. fashion.

Significantly, the eight A.F. of L. unions that launched the C.I.O. were all either industrial or semi-industrial in form. Their leaders— John L. Lewis, Philip Murray, Sidney Hillman, *et al.*—while basing themselves, like the Green bureaucrats, primarily upon the skilled workers, had learned that this policy did not necessarily involve excluding the unskilled from the unions. Because of the bitter experience of the post-World War I and economic crisis years, and also because of the great pressure of the rank-and-file workers for organization, they had become convinced that the unionization of the basic industries was an absolute necessity if the labor movement was to survive and progress. Later on, under the weight of the newly organized masses, this position led these leaders to adopt many progressive measures. Only in this narrow sense could they themselves be called progressives. The sequel was to show that they did not depart from their basic role as defenders of the capitalist system against the elementary interests of the workers (see Chapter 34).

The split in the ranks of the labor bureaucracy greatly accelerated the tempo of trade union progress. The Communists, who were a considerable factor in the A.F. of L., gave the opposition leaders all possible co-operation and support in their new progressive role. In 1933, when the organization spurt began, the A.F. of L. leaders had tried to sort out the new union recruits according to crafts and distribute them among the respective unions, but this proving impossible, they assembled the workers into miscellaneous federal local unions. At the 1934 A.F. of L. convention, with 2,000 such locals existing, however, the issue had to be settled. There was a powerful sentiment for industrial unionism, with 14 resolutions demanding this measure. The Communist Party vigorously stimulated this movement among the rank and file. Even the hard-boiled officials that make up A.F. of L. conventions knew that a maneuver had to be made. So the leadership put through a unanimous resolution which, while endorsing craft unionism, "wherever the lines of demarcation between crafts are distinguishable," vaguely recognized the need for industrial unionism and instructed the Executive Council to issue charters in various industries. The progressives assumed that these charters would be of an industrial character. This A.F. of L. convention was held in San Francisco only a short while after the great San Francisco General Strike, in which the lefts, all industrial unionists, had such an important part.

During 1935 the Executive Council gave limited industrial charters to the United Auto Workers and the United Rubber Workers, but they refused national charters to the many new local unions in radio, cement, aluminum, and other basic industries. They also did nothing to advance the projected campaign to organize the steel industry, although large numbers of steel workers had literally forced their way into the unions. In short, the Council brazenly sabotaged the 1934 convention resolution. All of which greatly enraged the advocates of industrial unionism.

At the 1935 convention in Atlantic City, beginning October 7th, therefore, John L. Lewis and five other leaders introduced a resolution calling for the organization of the basic industries into industrial unions. The resolution sharply condemned A.F. of L. craft unionism as futile in trustified industries and declared that "in those industries where the work performed by a majority of the workers is of such nature that it might fall within the jurisdictional claim of more than one craft union, it is declared that industrial organization is the only form that will be acceptable to the workers or adequately meet their needs." After a long and bitter debate the Lewis resolution was defeated by a vote of 18,025 to 10,924. The A.F. of L. leaders were willing to keep the industries unorganized, just so their own jurisdictional claims remained intact.

Undeterred by their convention defeat, the Lewis group a month later organized the C.I.O. and began the work of unionization. They launched active national campaigns in steel, auto, rubber, textile, and coke-processing. Huge sums of money were pledged by the eight co-operating unions. National organizing committees were set up, and new industrial unions were to be formed. The basic industries would be organized in spite of the A.F. of L. leadership.

The Green bureaucrats promptly condemned the C.I.O. for this action, and after considerable maneuvering, suspended its eight unions on August 5, 1936, for "dual unionism and insurrection" against the A.F. of L. This suspension, which amounted to the expulsion of over one million members (about 40 percent of the A.F. of L.), was endorsed by the A.F. of L. convention, despite strong opposition, at Tampa, Florida, in October 1936. Wide protests from local unions, city central bodies, and state federations all over the country were unavailing to halt the Green-Woll-Hutcheson splitters. They were ready to wreck the labor movement rather than depart from their decrepit craft unionism.

Lewis, apparently taking it for granted that the organizational work had to be done outside of direct contact with the Green reactionaries, made no determined fight to maintain affiliation with the A.F. of L. On this tactical question the Communists disagreed with him. The Communists believed that inasmuch as Lewis had 40 percent of the A.F. of L. unions behind him and a vast following among the rest of the labor movement, it would have been possible for him to beat the Green machine by a resolute fight. As it was, Lewis did not even have his C.I.O. delegates at Tampa. If the split could not be avoided, the Communists said, at least it could be made to take place under far more favorable conditions for the C.I.O. The Party opposed the split and its slogan was "For a United, Powerful A.F. of L."[1] It gave everything it had, however, to the building of the C.I.O. at all stages, and in the organization of the basic industries for which it had fought so long and militantly.

THE GROWING COMMUNIST PARTY

During the years 1933-36 the Communist Party, deeply involved in all the mass struggles of the period, made considerable growth, not only in mass influence but also in numerical strength. It concentrated its efforts more and more upon the basic industries. At the eighth convention of the Party, in Cleveland, April 2-8, 1934, the membership was 24,500, as against 14,000 in 1932. Of the 233 regular delegates, 119 came from basic industries. There were 39 Negro delegates, and 2,500 Negro Party members. The increasing percentage of native-born was also indicated by the fact that 145 of the convention delegates were born in the United States. At this time the Y.C.L. had grown to 5,000 members, also a substantial increase over 1932. By the time of the ninth Party convention, held in New York, June 24-28, 1936, the Party membership had gone up further to 41,000, and there were 11,000 in the Y.C.L.

The Socialist Party, Musteites, Lovestoneites, Trotskyites, S.L.P., and Proletarian Party—all remained small and mostly stagnant sects. For a while in the middle of the 1930's, the Socialist Party began to show some life and growth. But the new "left" trend, led by the opportunist Norman Thomas of all people, soon petered out, and the S.P., wracked by Trotskyites and right opportunist Social-Democrats, Musteites, and Lovestoneites, went on to a confused split in 1936, which reduced it to still greater helplessness. The leadership of the Communist Party as the vanguard party of the militant forces in the labor movement had become clear and indisputable.

[1] Statement of the Central Committee of the Communist Party in *The Communist*, March 1936.

22. The Broad Democratic Struggle (1933-1936)

The early New Deal years saw, along with the great trade union upsurge, the development of various other mass democratic struggles. The Communist Party, with its broad united front policy and in its growing role as the vanguard of the working class, played a major part in initiating and stimulating many of these movements. The Roosevelt Administration, increasingly needing popular support in its fight against extreme reaction, also tolerated and, in some cases, supported them. All these forces went to provide the democratic basis of the great political coalition that carried Roosevelt four times to the presidency.

THE NATIONAL NEGRO CONGRESS

These years marked a great political advance by the Negro people. The Negro masses battled militantly against job discrimination, Jim Crow, and lynching; they forged ahead and won national distinction in the fields of science, literature, the theater, and sports;[1] they broke down the segregation walls of the labor movement and laid the basis for the present splendid army of a million Negro trade unionists; they stood in the front ranks of the democratic masses generally in every sphere of the class struggle.

The rising spirit of struggle among the Negro people during these years reflected itself in the National Negro Congress, organized in Chicago, February 14-16, 1936. The N.N.C. grew out of a conference held previously under the auspices of Howard University and the Joint Committee on National Recovery.[2] The Congress, which included also whites, was a broad united front of Negroes from all democratic strata. There were Republicans, Democrats, Socialists, and Communists at the Congress; there were churchmen, workers, professionals, businessmen. All told, 817 delegates attended, coming from 28 states and representing 585 organizations with a "combined and unduplicated" membership of

---

[1] It was during this time that the Communist Party began its long, tireless, and finally (in 1947) successful campaign to break down Jim Crow in major league baseball. The Negro press was very active in this fight.

[2] James W. Ford in *The Communist*, April, May, June 1936.

1,200,000. Among those present were such notables as Ralph Bunche, W. E. B. DuBois, A. Philip Randolph, R. A. Carter, John P. Davis, James W. Ford, and others. A majority of the delegates came from the civic (226), educational (14), and religious groups (81). Eighty-three unions were represented and 71 fraternal organizations. The national president was A. Philip Randolph and the secretary John P. Davis.

The Communists played an important part in the organization of this significant Congress. The idea for the Congress was suggested two years before by James W. Ford, well-known Communist, in a debate with Oscar De Priest and Frank Crosswaith. Party forces also spent much effort in popularizing the Congress and in doing the extensive organizational work to bring the convention together. At the convention itself Ford and other Communists and sympathizers were very influential. In the National Council of 75 elected by the Congress, there were several Communists.

The Congress adopted a progressive program meeting the most pressing needs of the Negro people. It urged the participation of Negroes in trade unions, endorsed trade union unity, condemned the Jim Crow system and all types of reaction, and demanded full rights for Negroes. It supported the developing fight against fascism and war, and it repudiated the "neutral" attitude of the United States toward the invasion of Ethiopia. It proposed a plan for consumers' and producers' co-operatives and also the extension of the Workers Alliance. The Congress favored a world congress of the Negro people, and the church panel recommended that churches should devote every fifth Sunday to advancing the work of the Congress. On political action, the Congress voted for the ultimate formation of a farmer-labor party; however, in the meantime it declared, "We do not support any candidates, but we give you their records." The Congress did not take any stand as to its ultimate political goal, nor did it raise the question of the Negro people as a nation.

The National Negro Congress, a broad movement uniting Negro workers and middle class elements, had local councils in many cities. It became a vehicle for the expression of the leading role of the Negro working masses in the general movement of the Negro people. During the next years it was to prove an especially important agency for building the C.I.O. and for promoting trade union organization generally among Negro workers.

THE AMERICAN YOUTH CONGRESS

One of the most vital of all the mass movements that developed during the early New Deal years was the American Youth Congress. The United States had never before seen anything like it. Organized in 1934, the movement encompassed about 4,600,000 young people by the outbreak of World War II. Animating it was a militant protest of American youth against the bitter hardships of the young people during the great economic crisis, against the general neglect of their interests by the government, and against the looming prospect of fascism and another world war.[1]

The Roosevelt Administration early undertook to control this new and dynamic national force of the organized youth. Consequently, it selected as its agent a young woman, Viola Ilma, who with the backing of Mrs. Roosevelt, half a dozen governors, Mayor La Guardia, and other Administration forces, called a general youth convention in New York, in August 1934. The response was heavy, at least 1,500,000 organized young people being represented, including the Y.M.C.A., Y.W.C.A., Y.M.H.A., and many other religious and fraternal youth organizations. The Catholics were there as observers. Both the Y.P.S.L. and Y.C.L. were present.

Miss Ilma, who had just returned from fascist Germany, obviously had acquired her ideas for the type of new youth organization from the Hitler youth. She seemed to think that the young people had come to the convention in order to be told what to do—as they were in school, in the factories, and in the army. But she entirely underestimated the new democratic spirit of the youth. Hence, when the convention tried to elect its own chairman and she refused even to entertain the motion, the convention overrode her arbitrariness and voted her down. She then quit cold, crying out in the newspapers that the Communists had captured the youth movement. Mrs. Roosevelt was stunned at the unexpected course of events, but the stakes were very high and she went along with the American Youth Congress then being formed. Gilbert Green, head of the Young Communist League, was a member of the National Board that was set up.

The next few years were full of activity for the Youth Congress. The A.Y.C. took an active part in the trade union organization of young people, fought for improved conditions in the government Civilian Conservation Corps youth relief camps, demanded a more enlightened program from the National Youth Administration (which was established in June 1935), condemned in unmeasured terms all discrimination against the Negro people, and fought against the rising dangers of fascism and war. The A.Y.C. formulated its immediate program of political youth demands in the American Youth Act, introduced in Congress on January

[1] Dave Doran, *Highway of Hunger*, N. Y., 1933.

13, 1936.[1] This bill elaborated an extensive plan of vocational training and student aid, financed by the government and managed by the students. Although the bill never became law, it was widely popularized and served as the basis for much state and federal youth legislation.

Almost overnight the organized youth became a power in the land. Youth leaders—Waldo McNutt, William Hinckley, Joseph Cadden, Gilbert Green—were figures to be reckoned with. Even the A.F. of L. had to recognize the new youth movement at its 1935 convention, where for the first time in its history it gave favorable consideration to a series of youth proposals. The C.I.O. also sent delegates to the A.Y.C. congresses, cultivated youth strike demands, and otherwise actively supported the movement. Many trade unions and state farmer-labor parties developed youth sections, activities, and demands. Both the Republican and Democratic parties paid much attention to youth work of their kind.

An important development in the youth movement of this period was the formation in Columbus, Ohio, in December 1935, of the American Student Union, through the amalgamation of the National Student League (Communist-led, founded in 1932) and the much weaker Student League for Industrial Democracy (Socialist-led, founded in 1905). Characteristic of the A.S.U.'s many and various activities, it led a national anti-war strike of 184,000 students on April 12, 1937. Such strikes were continued until April 1941, those in 1938-39 totaling several hundred thousand students. Another, and very important, youth development of the period was the formation of the promising united front Southern Negro Youth Congress in Richmond, Virginia, in February 1937. Edward Strong was chairman. James W. Ford, James Jackson, and Henry Winston were also leaders in this vital movement, which for the next few years, throughout the South, carried on widespread educational work, supported strikes, popularized the National Youth Act, and generally struggled against Jim Crow. By 1939 this organization and the Southern Conference for Human Welfare represented at least 500,000 Negro youth in the South. Communists were very active in the work of these organizations.

Communist influence was powerful in the American Youth Congress, which followed an advanced policy. In particular, the young leaders of the broad organizations of young men and women were greatly attracted by the militancy of the Communists, by their understanding of the general youth question and specific youth demands, by their skill in developing the broad united front movement of elements which were widely divergent politically and religiously, and especially by their clear-headed and tireless struggle against the growing danger of fas-

[1] Labor Research Association, *Labor Fact Book 3*, p. 70.

cism and war. Enemies of the A.Y.C.—Socialists and others—shouted that the Communists were in complete control of the youth movement. Gilbert Green was the chief Communist youth leader.

The Socialists, Lovestoneites, and Trotskyites, while maintaining a precarious affiliation with the A.Y.C., generally took such a sabotaging position toward the movement, in their hatred of the Communists, that they could only stagnate in their political degeneration. The Young Communist League, however, flourished as a result of its sound policies. Its active participation in the broad mass youth movement largely broke down its long-time sectarianism. The League grew in numbers, influence, and experience, and it acquired a more solid base among the young workers. At its ninth convention in 1939, it reported a membership of 22,000, as compared with 11,000 in 1936 and 3,000 in 1933. In Green, Winston, Thompson, Weiss, Gates, Strack, Ross, and others, the League was building a strong Marxist-Leninist youth leadership.

THE WOMEN'S MOVEMENT

Women, who form one-half of the American electorate and about one-third of all wage workers, also took a prominent part in the broad mass upsurge that developed among all the democratic strata of the population during the early years of the New Deal. The women, however, did not create a strong and well-defined national organization such as those we have been describing in this and the previous chapter. They rather constituted a basic and very active part of all these mass movements. During the period we are dealing with, the most generalized form of the women's movement was that around the Women's Charter.

The Women's Charter was written in 1936 by a group of liberal and labor women.[1] It had the support of a vast range of organizations, including, with qualifications, the Communist Party. It was supported, among others, by such government officials as Mary Anderson, head of the Women's Bureau of the Department of Labor. This signified that it had the backing of the Roosevelt regime. Eventually, in the ensuing few years the Charter was endorsed by organizations totaling several million women. It was incorporated in the Resolution on Equal Rights for Women adopted at the International Labor Conference in Geneva in 1937.

The Women's Charter was an assertion of the rights of women to full equality in all spheres of social activity. Mother Bloor welcomed it[2] also on the grounds that "it may be a great unifying force for peace—

[1] Mary Van Kleeck in *The Woman Worker*, Feb. 1937.
[2] *The Woman Today*, Feb. 1937.

and the struggle against reaction and fascism." Ann Rivington says of it that it was for women the "high point of the united front during this decade."[1] Margaret Cowl Krumbein, head of the Party's Women's Commission during this period, gave the Charter active support.

Women wage workers made up a large part of the masses of newly organized workers in various industries—needle, textile, electrical, and others—and the Party paid its main attention to them. They constituted a vital force with the big network of women's trade union auxiliaries that grew up largely under Communist stimulation in the C.I.O. unions in steel, auto, and various other industries. The Party women workers also greatly concerned themselves with strengthening the activities of the Women's Trade Union League.

Communist women were always the Party leaders in the people's health movement. They organized the Workers Health Bureau of America in New York, and in June 1927, they held a national trade union health conference in Cleveland. Official delegates were present from the A.F. of L. state federations of Ohio, Illinois, Pennsylvania, Michigan, Washington, and Rhode Island, and from many city central bodies and local unions. This pioneer conference concerned itself mainly with occupational hazards and diseases, and it worked out a program of extensive educational work, health protection, prevention of accidents, and workmen's compensation. In the later stages of the New Deal, the Party women were also most active in the big mass movement for federal health insurance and a broad national health program.

Besides fighting for their own specific demands, and especially for maternity insurance, protection in industry, and child care, the women advanced the whole program of the Party. They were particularly effective in fighting against the high cost of living and cuts in W.P.A. relief, and in supporting all the current strikes for better wage and working conditions. They devoted special attention to the needs and demands of Negro women. They also fought tirelessly against the reactionary Equal Rights Amendment, which was sponsored by the Women's Rights Party and endorsed by both the Democratic and Republican parties. They made the recurring International Women's Day, on March 8th, the occasion of big demonstrations. Women were especially effective in the fight for peace, and they formed the backbone of the American League Against War and Fascism.

The development of international fascism lent new fire to the struggles of the women, for as Dimitrov said at the Seventh C.I. Congress, "Fascism enslaves women with particular ruthlessness and cynicism, playing on the most painful feelings of the mother, the housewife, and the single

---

[1] Ann Rivington, unpublished manuscript.

working woman." The Communist women made effective propaganda use of the superior economic, political, and social status of women in the Soviet Union over that of women generally in all the capitalist countries.[1] The Party during these years was building up a strong group of women Marxist-Leninist leaders. The attraction of the Party for women fighters was exemplified by the fact that in the big recruiting drive of 1937 over 30 percent of the new members were women.

THE "PANACEA" MASS MOVEMENTS

Striking manifestations of the broad democratic upsurge of the masses during the early New Deal period were the many "panacea" mass agitations. These were wide movements of farmers, city middle classes, and proletarian elements, sometimes running into the millions. Generally it was the workers who gave vitality to these movements. Shaken by the deep economic crisis, these masses struck out blindly against capitalism, desperately striving for some remedy. Usually their programs were fantastically utopian, and the demagogic leaders were frequently fascist-minded, but the masses were full of democratic fighting spirit. That such confused movements could spring up testified to the ideological backwardness of the American workers and their lack of a broad political party with progressive working class leadership.

1. *Technocracy*: Fathered by Howard Scott and based upon a mishmash of the ideas of the I.W.W. and Thorstein Veblen, this movement developed during the deepest phases of the economic crisis and ran like wildfire throughout the country in 1932-33, the entire capitalist press being agog with it. Technocracy was based on the fallacy that the evils of capitalism originated not primarily in its production relations, but simply in its "distributive system." Its cure-all was to substitute a system of "ergs," or energy units, in place of the current "price system." Technocracy denied that the workers were exploited, repudiated the class struggle, and rejected the revolutionary role of the workers. In substance, it advocated a ruling aristocracy of engineers. For a while it had a big vogue among the intellectuals, making a special appeal to engineers and technicians. It declined as swiftly as it arose, but some remnants still linger.

2. *End-Poverty-in-California (Epic)*: This movement grew up rapidly in California and neighboring states following the publication, in October 1933, of Upton Sinclair's book, *I, Governor of California*. Epic was based upon the idea of self-help among the unemployed. It proposed that idle factories be turned over to the unemployed workers, who would operate them and develop a system of barter. It held to the utopian belief

[1] Margaret Cowl Krumbein in *The Communist*, June 1937, Jan. 1938.

that a separate system of non-profit-making production and exchange could exist independently within the framework of the capitalist system, which is based upon private ownership and distribution. On the Epic ticket Upton Sinclair, Democratic candidate for governor of California in 1934, polled 879,000 votes against 1,138,000 for Merriam, after which the Epic movement gradually faded out.[1]

3. *The Utopian Society*: This organization, launched by E. J. Reed, in the fall of 1933, soon grew to claim a million adherents in southern California. The Utopians, declaring for the "Brotherhood of Man" and "Plenty for All," hoped to achieve general prosperity through government ownership. Largely middle class, the movement rejected the class struggle and had no day-to-day demands. Its life span was short.

4. *The Townsend National Recovery Plan*: Animated by a fanatical enthusiasm and eventually claiming several millions of adherents, this huge mass movement was launched, in April 1934, by Dr. F. E. Townsend in Long Beach, California. It was basically a movement of the elderly and middle-aged. Its panacea was to establish maximum pensions of $200 per month for the aged, to be financed chiefly by a national two percent transactions tax. The $20 billion thus raised yearly, it was hoped, would not only provide for the aged but, keeping the industries in active operation, would provide a general and lasting prosperity for the whole population. The Townsend Plan failed to realize, however, that the basis of the crisis and destitution was the private ownership of the industries, and that only when this was abolished and socialism established could economic crises be averted and prosperity and full employment be assured. The Townsend movement was a considerable pension force for many years and still exists.[2]

5. *The "Ham and Eggs" Movement*: This was another mass panacea movement having a special appeal to the aged. It, too, originated in southern California, where old people doubly abound. Formally known as the Retirement Life Payments Association, it was founded during the 1930's by L. W. Allen of Hollywood. In 1938 and 1939 the movement succeeded in placing on the referendum ballot a constitutional amendment providing that the state of California would pay $30 per week (every Thursday) for life to every unemployed or retired California citizen 50 years old or over. The move was defeated both times at the polls. The official weekly organ was called *National Ham and Eggs*.

6. *The National Union for Social Justice*: This movement, in organized form, was launched in November 1934, in Detroit, by Rev. Charles E. Coughlin, Catholic priest. *Fortune*, at the time, estimated

[1] Robert Minor in *The Communist*, Dec. 1934.
[2] Alexander Bittelman, *The Townsend Plan*, N. Y., 1936.

that this demagogue had ten million listeners to his weekly radio broadcasts. An expression of this movement was the notorious Christian Front, with its organized groups of hoodlums and storm troopers. Coughlin's utopia was built upon the traditional American illusion that prosperity could be achieved by issuing huge quantities of paper currency. His following was especially strong among Middle West farmers, city middle class elements, and Catholic industrial workers. Coughlin himself, a silver speculator and associate of big bankers, was a violent critic of everything democratic, and he undoubtedly aimed at establishing a fascist America—presumably with himself as the dictator. He was finally "silenced" by the Catholic Church, which apparently did not yet want to be so completely identified with fascism in the United States. The Communist Party conducted a most active struggle against this dangerous movement.[1]

7. *Share-the-Wealth*: This mass movement sprang up in 1934 and spread with the rapidity characteristic of the "panacea" agitations generally. Its founder was Senator Huey P. Long of Louisiana. Long, the "kingfish," had as his main slogans, "Share the Wealth" and "Every Man a King." He proposed to take away most of the capitalists' wealth by a gigantic capital levy. The resulting $165 billion in the hands of the government he would distribute among the people, each family getting $5,000 down and each worker also being assured a yearly income of $2,500. The Share-the-Wealth movement was the most fantastic of all the panaceas and Long the most effective fascist demagogue the United States had yet seen. He set up a virtual dictatorship in Louisiana and also had a wide following among the poor farmers and workers all over the South. He was assassinated in September 1935, by a man whom he had victimized, after which his movement, fallen into the less capable hands of Gerald L. K. Smith and others, gradually disintegrated.[2]

The Communist Party paid close attention to the "panacea" movements. Although often led by dangerous demagogues, these movements were not wholly in vain. They dramatized the plight of the workers, the unemployed, the aged, the farmers, and the impoverished petty bourgeoisie. They also evidenced the determination of the people to fight against the outrageous conditions which engulfed them. The development of the reform aspects of Roosevelt's New Deal program was a fundamental factor in undermining and preventing the further development of such movements. That the "panacea" movements did not become perverted into a real base for American fascism was also due in no small measure to the activities of the Communist Party in exposing their economic

[1] A. B. Magil, *The Truth About Father Coughlin*, N. Y., 1935.
[2] Alexander Bittelman, *How Can We Share the Wealth?* N. Y., 1935.

fallacies, in combating their reactionary leaders, and in directing their masses into more practical channels of political struggle.

THE CULTURAL UPSURGE

From its inception, the Communist Party has challenged the domination of the capitalists in the cultural field. It has striven for the development of the arts and sciences in the interest of the people, not of the ruling exploiters. Over the years, despite its small size, the Party has exercised a powerful influence in this vital field. Its efforts, constantly improving in effectiveness, began to be especially felt during and after the great economic crisis years.

During the Coolidge boom of the 1920's monopoly capital greatly strengthened its control over the main media of mass cultural expression—the newspapers and magazines, the school system, the church, the motion picture, and the young radio industry. This resulted not only in an unparalleled standardization of the people's intellectual fare, but also in turning capitalism's cultural workers into a force to glorify the current "prosperity," the blessings of Fordism, and the wonders of the "new capitalism." It was consequently a period of unprecedented degeneration of bourgeois art and literature. Anti-Semitism and white chauvinism ran wild in every capitalist cultural area. The blatant and cynical Mencken was the most authentic bourgeois literary spokesman of the period. James-Dewey pragmatism, the hard-boiled philosophy which says that whatever the capitalists are and do is right, flourished and spread in bourgeois circles. Pragmatism's great value to the capitalists is that it robs the working class of a theory of society. It undertakes to substitute an idealist, rule-of-thumb practice for a scientific Marxian analysis of the laws of social development. This cynical philosophy permeates not only capitalist ranks, but also the ranks of the bosses' labor lieutenants, and it contaminates the entire fabric of the educational system of this country.

Democratic forces, mostly in the "little theater" and "little magazine" movements, fought an uphill struggle against the current overwhelming flood of standardized capitalist trash and reaction. But the most clearheaded and energetic in the fight for a real people's culture were the Communists and other lefts, including Art Young, Robert Minor, Michael Gold, William Gropper, Fred Ellis, and Moissaye J. Olgin, who were mainly associated with *The Liberator* and its successor, *New Masses*.[1] In October 1929, the first John Reed Club, a left-wing literary organization, was formed in New York. Three years later there were a score of such clubs in all parts of the country.

[1] *Proletarian Literature in the United States, an Anthology*, N. Y., 1935.

The Communist Party during the 1920's, as part of its struggle against the deluge of reactionary capitalist cultural slush and for the beginnings of a democratic people's culture, also began to appreciate and evaluate the democratic, artistic, literary, and scientific elements that have been expressed historically within the framework of American bourgeois culture as a whole. This was the start of the breakaway from the traditional sectarian attitudes of American Marxists toward culture. It was an essential part of the maturing of Marxism-Leninism in this country.

The great economic crisis dealt a shattering blow to the whole dizzy capitalist economic propaganda structure of the Coolidge prosperity period. Exploded overnight were the complacency, conceit, and rosy dreams of the "new capitalism." Stark hunger preyed upon the country. The bourgeois intellectuals and artists, singers of the glories of capitalist "prosperity," also felt the blasts of the economic hurricane. They were thrown into ideological confusion and their economic position was undermined. Their incomes were slashed, almost as much as were those of the workers and farmers; about 30 percent of them were unemployed, and in May 1934, some 91,000 professionals were on the W.P.A. relief rolls.[1] They began to listen to the Communists.

The big mass democratic upheaval, which brought Roosevelt to the presidency and was responsible for the building of the new trade unions, the "panacea movements," and the reforms of the New Deal, was also shared in by the artists and professionals generally. Overcoming their traditional bourgeois aloofness, large numbers of them made common cause with the workers and other democratic elements fighting against reaction. From bitter experience they had sensed that their previous individualistic attitude of each fending for himself was disastrous and that they had to make an organized struggle to protect their interests. Consequently, during these years nearly all the organizations of professionals, both of a technical and trade union character, experienced the greatest growth in their history. Teachers, actors, engineers, artists, lawyers, and newspaper workers shared in the movement, and "white collar" workers of all kinds for the first time became an important factor in the labor movement. These elements forced the Roosevelt regime to give them some consideration in the Federal Arts Projects for writers, musicians, and actors.

There was not only an economic but also an ideological content to this upsurge of the intellectuals during the New Deal years. They wanted to know the cause of the great economic crisis, of the decay of culture, of the threat of another great imperialist war. They attacked

[1] Labor Research Association, *Labor Fact Book 3*, p. 109.

the bourgeois theories of "art for art's sake" and of the artist standing above the class struggle. The teacher, as well as looking out for her wages, began to have something to say about what she was teaching. The writers and actors of Hollywood and Broadway started to raise their voices against the mass of capitalistic swill which the movie moguls and theatrical producers were inflicting upon the American people under the guise of entertainment. With the great Theodore Dreiser at their head, the novelists struck a new note of revolt against outrageous social conditions. Dreiser himself became an ardent member of the Communist Party. The newspapermen, through their new national Guild, became a force for democracy in journalism. And the lawyers began to come forward with new and democratic concepts of what the law and court practice should be. The inspiring development of Soviet art, notably in the films, stimulated the whole cultural awakening.

The reactionaries looked with grave alarm upon this upsurge among the intellectuals and artists, upon whom they counted to drive their propaganda into the heads of the workers. But in the existing political situation, they were unable to stifle it.

This democratic movement among the professionals and cultural workers was given added strength by the shocking events under the barbaric policies of German fascism. What fascism held in store for the cultural workers was made quite clear by the dictum of the Nazi youth leader who declared, "When I hear the word culture, I cock my revolver," by the savage book burnings of May 1933, by the general strangling of art under Hitler, and by fascism's total subjugation of cultural workers of all kinds to the propagation of anti-Semitism and similar barbarities—excesses which, obviously, incipient American fascism would be only too eager to duplicate.[1]

The most general expression of the upsurge of the cultural workers was the formation of the American Writers Congress in New York on April 26, 1935. Present were 216 delegates from 26 states, with 150 writers attending as guests. There was a public attendance of 4,000, "the largest audience that ever participated in a literary event in this country."[2] Thirty papers were read at the Congress, dealing with many aspects of the writer's craft and social role. In accordance with the united front spirit of the times, the Congress was much broader in scope than the earlier John Reed clubs, which had pioneered the movement. For the next few years the Congress was a powerful force in cultural circles, not the least in Hollywood. The Communists were most active in this

[1] Sidney Finkelstein, *Art and Society*, N. Y., 1947; Louis Harap, *Social Roots of the Arts*, N. Y., 1949.
[2] Michael Gold, *The Hollow Men*, p. 37, N. Y., 1941.

development, as in nearly every other phase of the cultural movement of the period. The Communist Party was officially represented at the founding convention of this very important writers' united front movement.[1] Another significant organization was the American Artists Congress, founded in 1936.

The greatest and most lasting achievement of the cultural renaissance of the New Deal period, however, was the real stress it laid upon Negro culture. This movement was many-sided. Its most important aspect was the crushing attack it delivered through the distinguished anthropologist Franz Boas, many other scientists, and a whole group of Communist writers, against every attempt of the racists and white supremacists in science, in industry, in politics, on the stage, and everywhere else, to picture the Negro people as inferior beings. The movement also made real progress toward developing an understanding of the profound contributions that the Negro people have made to the best in American culture. The movement also began to develop an appreciation of the splendid body of artists and cultural workers that the Negro people had been developing in the face of a world of difficulties—Paul Robeson, Langston Hughes, Marian Anderson, Sterling Brown, and many others. Especially important was the beginning made at revaluating the history of the Negro people—by James W. Ford, Harry Haywood, Doxey Wilkerson, James Jackson, Herbert Aptheker, Philip S. Foner, James S. Allen, Robert Minor, John Howard Lawson, and others—to free this persecuted people from the mountains of slanders and belittlement built up by generations of white chauvinist historians.[2] In this vital struggle with and for the Negro people in their fight for cultural recognition and development, it is hardly necessary to state, the Communists were the most devoted and tireless fighters, and their influence was far-reaching.

THE SEVENTH COMINTERN CONGRESS AND THE ROOSEVELT COALITION

The great mass struggles of workers, unemployed, farmers, Negroes, youth, women and intellectuals in the early New Deal years in the United States were directly related to the developing struggle against world fascism. Only in this sense can they be fully understood. The fight against fascism was clarified and organized on an international scale at the

---

[1] *American Writers Congress* (reports), N. Y., 1935.
[2] Important new works are *The Hidden Heritage* by John Howard Lawson, and *A Documentary History of the Negro People in the United States* by Herbert Aptheker.

Seventh Congress of the Communist International, held in Moscow, from July 25 to August 21, 1935. At this historic congress, in which a strong delegation from the C.P.U.S.A. participated, Georgi Dimitrov, head of the Comintern and hero of the Reichstag fire trial, swept aside the current liberal-Social-Democratic nonsense to the effect that "fascism is a revolt of the middle class" and exposed it in its full nakedness as "the open terrorist dictatorship of the most reactionary, most chauvinistic and most imperialist elements of finance capital." "Fascism," said he, "is a most ferocious attack by capital on the toiling masses; fascism is unbridled chauvinism and annexationist war; fascism is rabid reaction and counter-revolution; fascism is the most vicious enemy of the working class and of all toilers."[1]

Dimitrov proposed, and this became the political line of the congress, that to fight fascism a great anti-fascist people's front of workers, farmers, intellectuals, and all other toiling, democratic sections of the population must be built up. The purpose of this broad united front, said Dimitrov, is that "in countries of bourgeois democracy, we want to bar the road to reaction and the offensive of capital and fascism, prevent the abrogation of bourgeois-democratic liberties, forestall fascism's terrorist vengeance upon the proletariat, the revolutionary section of the peasantry and the intellectuals, save the young generation from physical and spiritual degeneracy. We are ready to do all this because in the fascist countries we want to prepare and hasten the overthrow of the fascist dictatorship. We are ready to do all this because we want to save the world from fascist barbarity and the horrors of imperialist war."[2]

Speaking of the United States, Dimitrov pointed out that "millions of people have been brought into motion by the crisis." He signalized the menacing fascist danger in this country and warned of its insidious approach. "It is a peculiarity of the development of American fascism," said he, "that at the present time it appears principally in the guise of an opposition to fascism, which it accuses of being an un-American tendency imported from abroad." He indicated the need for a people's front in the United States and stated that "A Workers and Farmers Party might serve as such a suitable form. Such a party would be a specific form of the mass people's front in America."

The people's front was the application of the historic united front policy to the conditions of the struggle against fascism and war. The Communists have long advocated and carried out the principle of the united front. In *The Communist Manifesto,* written over a century ago, Marx stated that the Communists fight for immediate demands in

[1] Georgi Dimitrov, *The United Front,* N. Y., 1938.
[2] Stalin was active in this famous congress.

alliance with groups, classes, and parties which do not accept the long-range goal of socialism.

Dimitrov's statement on the workers and farmers party, which the American Communists had long advocated, as the form of the people's front in the United States, fitted right in with the traditions and conditions of the American class struggle. For a long time, even as far back as President Jackson's era, as we have noted in previous chapters, there has always existed a strong tendency for the workers and farmers to join forces together in united front political struggle against the common enemy, the capitalists. This trend was evidenced with especial sharpness during the important political fights of the Greenbackers, the Populists, and the LaFollettites. Indeed, the characteristic united front alliance of workers and small farmers has more of a background of political history in the United States than it has in industrial Europe, where Social-Democracy, ignoring the political potentialities of the peasantry, traditionally concerned itself almost exclusively with the fight of the proletariat and the middle class.

During the general period under consideration, 1933-38, the Communist Party greatly improved the character of its united front work. It broke more and more with the sectarian leftism which it had manifested to some extent in the depth of the great crisis. This was shown by its effective work among the trade unions, in the struggles of the unemployed, the Negro people, the youth, and in many other fields. The Party was playing a very important part in the ever-increasing fight against fascism and war.

The growth and activities of the C.I.O., the Unemployed Councils, the National Negro Congress, the American Youth Congress, the women's movement, the upsurge of the intellectuals, and the broad "panacea" organizations during these years were not isolated phenomena. They sprang from the same basic cause—the ravages of the great economic crisis; they had many direct ties and much spirit of solidarity with each other; they headed toward the same goal, the defeat of threatening reaction; and they tended naturally to coalesce in a general movement of struggle. The united front policies of the Communist Party greatly aided this unification. In the period of imperialism and the struggle against fascism and war, the historic American practice of the toiling democratic masses to fight side by side moved toward the creation of a people's front.

However, the incipient people's front movement of those years, a blood brother to the great people's front movements of Europe, never reached the stage of becoming a full-fledged mass "Workers and Farmers Party" as described by Dimitrov. This was partly because of Roosevelt's skillful maneuvering to keep the workers tied to the Democratic Party, and partly because of the timidity and treachery of the workers' own union leaders, who refused to break with the two-party system. Consequently, the movement never rose to a higher level than that of an unco-ordinated popular coalition around Roosevelt, a loose "democratic front"; but it nevertheless proved powerful enough to halt, at least temporarily, the advance of fascism in the United States.

THE COMMUNIST PARTY AND THE NATION

A fundamental implication of the anti-fascist people's front developed by the Seventh Congress of the Comintern, in line with American tradition and political conditions, was the great stress it laid upon the reality that the Communist parties, besides being the leading parties of the proletariat, were by the same token also the basic parties of their respective nations. Marx and Engels had long before taught—and Marxists generally understood—that in defending the interests of the working class and other toilers, the Marxist party is thereby defending the interests of the overwhelming majority of the people. It is functioning in the interest of the nation against a reactionary bourgeois nationalism, against an exploiting capitalist class which always advances its own class interests at the expense of the people in general. The classic example of the Marxist party as the party of the nation was seen in the Bolshevik Party in Russia which led the people of that country, who had faced ruin and slaughter at the hands of their treasonable ruling class, in overthrowing tsarism-capitalism and building socialism.

In the situation confronting the peoples of the world with the rise of fascism during the 1930's, there was a supreme need for the Communist parties, with greater clarity and consciousness on the national question than ever before, to come forward as the defenders and champions of their respective nations against their treacherous bourgeoisie, and this they did. The big capitalists, frightened at the great cyclical economic crisis, at the deepening general crisis of the capitalist system, and at the revolutionary mood of the workers, were trying to betray and force their respective nations into the fateful traps of fascist tyranny and an imperialist world war.

It was to unite the respective peoples against this murderous treason by the ruling bourgeoisie that the Seventh Congress of the Comintern enunciated its famous call for an anti-fascist people's front. The new tactical orientation—namely, the creation of a broad alliance of all the democratic strata and the agreement for participation by the Communists in the people's front governments—was, in fact, the organization of the nation to save itself from disastrous betrayal by the capitalist class. "The socialist revolution will signify the *salvation of the nation*,"[1] said Dimitrov; and as he also indicated, here was a situation, under capitalism, where the workers, following the leadership of the Communist Party, had to save the nation from disaster.

There was a time, before the imperialist era, when the interests of the developing national capitalist class, in a measure at least, coincided with those of the nation. But that time is now forever past. The people, led by the workers, at the head of which stands the Communist Party, must take their fate into their own hands, in opposition to the treasonable capitalist class. "We Communists," says Dimitrov, "are the irreconcilable opponents, on principle, of bourgeois nationalism of every variety. But we are not supporters of national nihilism."[2] The capitalists' pretense of leading the nation is a monstrous lie and betrayal. This historic fact was dramatically signalized by the anti-fascist people's front policy of the Seventh Congress of the Communist International. And it is now being further demonstrated by the peace fight of the Communist Party against the war-mongering, pro-fascist monopolists, who, for the sake of their own profits, are driving the people toward the national disaster of war.

[1] Dimitrov, *The United Front*, p. 80.
[2] Dimitrov, *The United Front*, p. 79.

23. Roosevelt and Wall Street
(1933-1936)

When President Roosevelt began to put his New Deal into effect early in 1933, he had, as we have noted, the support of the bulk of big business. Frightened and demoralized, the capitalists grasped at his program in the hope that it could pull them out of the deadly crisis. Indeed, it might even take them along the road to the fascism which so many of them wanted. In the meantime they grudgingly agreed to make some small concessions to the workers, with the objective of holding them back from taking more drastic political action. But it was not long before the big capitalists began to break with Roosevelt and to attack his program. Eventually their opposition grew so fierce that he became perhaps more hated and denounced by them than any other man ever to occupy the White House.

This big business opposition to Roosevelt started to develop within a year after he took office. Economic conditions had begun to improve, chiefly through the normal tendency of capitalism eventually to work its way temporarily out of its cyclical crisis and a little as a result of the government subsidies to industry and agriculture under the New Deal. By January 1, 1934, industrial production stood at 73.1, as against 58.5 in March 1933, and 116.7 in October 1929. In 1932, 1,435 big corporations suffered a deficit of $97 million, but in 1933 the same concerns reaped profits of $661 million. Prices rose sharply and unemployment decreased somewhat from the unprecedented figure of 17 million a year before. The Democrats, with redoubled energy, sang "Happy Days Are Here Again"; big business, feeling that "prosperity" was about at hand and relieved of its fears of collapse and revolution, believed that it could dispense with even Roosevelt's niggardly relief to the unemployed, his equivocal concession to the workers of the right to organize, and his skimpy subsidies to the farmers.

It was a "false dawn," however, so far as the economic situation was concerned, for industry had by no means escaped from the slump. Stalin, at the Seventeenth Congress of the Communist Party of the Soviet Union (in January 1934), gave a clear picture of what was happening in the major capitalist countries. He summed up his analysis with the statement:

"Evidently what we are witnessing is a transition from the lowest point of the industrial crisis to a depression—not an ordinary depression, but a depression of a special kind which does not lead to a new upward trend and industrial boom, but which, on the other hand, does not force industry back to the lowest point of decline."[1] Stalin's profound Marxist analysis was proved brilliantly correct during the ensuing years. World capitalism, and particularly capitalism in the United States, could not and did not overcome its "depression of a special kind," but continued with under-average production and huge unemployment, meanwhile plunging into the economic crisis of 1937, until the outbreak of World War II in the fall of 1939 put the wheels of industry once more into full operation. It took a huge blood transfusion from slaughtered millions to revive even temporarily the hopelessly sick capitalist system.

WALL STREET'S ATTACK UPON THE NEW DEAL

The big capitalists of Wall Street, alarmed at the workers' militant strikes and organizing campaigns of the first years of the New Deal, demanded that the government take drastic action to curb the rebellious workers. Nor did their demands go unheeded. Troops were used freely by governors in many states against strikers; 88 workers and farmers were killed in 1933-34, with the murderers going unpunished; 18,000 strikers and demonstrators were arrested in 1935; scores of drastic injunctions were directed against striking unions; lynchings mounted in the South; and the K.K.K., vigilantes, and other terroristic organizations ran riot. Nor did the supposedly pro-labor federal government stir a finger to halt this mounting wave of employer-provoked violence.

But the great mass movements of the period which we have described in the two previous chapters—the big strikes, organizing drives, unemployment demonstrations, Negro and youth organizations, and the confused "panacea" movements—were not to be halted by this violence. The workers and other toilers were in a fighting mood, with prices soaring and wages lagging, with up to 13 million jobless, with a total of 24 million dependent upon government aid (the average family receiving only $19 monthly in relief), and with the employers once again piling up huge profits. The workers were insisting militantly that the promise of a "new deal" for them should be realized.

The basic "crime" that big business held against Roosevelt was that his policies were leading to the unionization of the basic industries. This fact underlay every charge of "red" and "Socialist" that they made against him. The tycoons of Wall Street regarded with the gravest alarm

[1] Joseph Stalin, *Selected Writings*, p. 303, N. Y., 1942.

the militant movements of the workers during 1933-34, in which the Communist Party played such a vital part. These movements, they realized, signified that their main industrial fortress—the "open shop" in the trustified industries, the pride and hope of every reactionary—was crumbling into collapse. The workers were finally breaking through this barrier which, with its network of company unionism, spy systems, gunman control, and violent anti-unionism, had long balked every forward move of the trade unions. This was a political defeat of major proportions for big business, and the latter blamed Roosevelt for the disaster.

THE AMERICAN LIBERTY LEAGUE

After incubating for several months, the American Liberty League was formally incorporated on August 15, 1934. Its chief sponsors were the du Ponts, and on its list of supporters were many of the largest capitalist concerns in the United States. These included representatives of the Morgans, Rockefellers, Mellons, and numerous other leading Wall Street corporations, such as United States Steel, General Motors, Bethlehem Steel, Pennsylvania Railroad, Baltimore & Ohio Railroad, Reading Railroad, Bankers Trust, Montgomery Ward, General Foods, Armour & Co., Guaranty Trust, United States Rubber, American Telephone & Telegraph, International Harvester, and a host of similar firms. The organizer of this big capitalist political outfit was John J. Raskob, a du Pont "angel" of the Democratic Party. Its chief front man was Alfred E. Smith, Democratic candidate for president in 1928. Smith, a boy from New York's slums who had "made good," was counted on to give a democratic flavor to the reactionary enterprise. In addition to its general anti-Roosevelt agitation, the Liberty League directed heavy blows against Roosevelt's control of the Democratic Party, the president's chief political stronghold. The Communist Party, from the outset, exposed and fought this vicious organization.[1]

The Liberty League quickly attracted to itself all the outstanding fascist demagogues of the country. Hearst backed it and gave it endless publicity; Huey Long and Father Coughlin also lent it their considerable support. The two latter had originally given Roosevelt their backing, when they believed that his program was leading toward fascism; but they quickly became his enemies when they perceived the progressive mass movements that were developing under his regime. The Liberty League worked hand in glove with the Republican Party, and their combined forces violently combated Roosevelt, opposed the advance

[1] Grace Hutchins, *The Truth About the Liberty League*, N. Y., 1936.

of the trade unions, and gave open or covert support to anti-Semitism, Negro discrimination and every other reactionary and fascist-like political current. They demanded a return to Hooverism, so despised by the masses.

ROOSEVELT FIGHTS BACK

This developing attack of big capital put Roosevelt between two fires. On the one hand, there was the pressure of the great mass movements of the people, resolved upon winning drastic economic and political reforms; and on the other hand, there was the increasingly violent opposition of big business, which wanted to put a quick end to every democratic reform. Roosevelt himself was a liberal who had taken office as the representative of what was virtually a national front including most of big business. He vacillated under these two heavy pressures, striving to reconcile the irreconcilable. But he was finally compelled to take a more definite stand against the section of finance capital which wanted to force the country along the Hitler road toward fascism, and to support of that section of the capitalists which favored a policy of mild reform and minimum concessions to the working class. Roosevelt still steered a middle course, but now, as he called it, "a little to the left of center."

Lenin long ago pointed out that the bourgeoisie, in its need to hold the workers in subjection, uses alternately, as the situation demands, two general methods of control: "They are, firstly, the method of force, the method which rejects all concessions to the labor movement, the method of supporting all the old and obsolete institutions, the method of irreconcilably rejecting reforms. . . . The second method is the method of 'liberalism' which takes steps toward the development of political rights, toward reforms, concessions and so forth."[1] Under the growing pressure of the masses, Roosevelt took this second course. His section of the bourgeoisie believed that a policy of limited reforms was both possible and indispensable. It was on the basis of these reforms, particularly facilitating the growth of trade unionism, that the strong "Roosevelt tradition" was built up among the workers. Under the given conditions, the other way—stark repression—would have been the road toward fascism, leading to eventual defeat of the capitalists at the hands of the awakening workers.

The first major political clash between the Roosevelt forces and the Liberty League-Republican Party combination came in the mid-term fall elections of 1934. It was a hot battle, and Roosevelt emerged from it vic-

[1] Lenin, *Selected Works*, Vol. 11, p. 741.

torious, substantially strengthening his hold upon Congress and in many states. But this victory was by no means a decisive one. Undeterred by their defeat at the hands of the people, the anti-New Deal forces of big business called upon their faithful ally, the Supreme Court, to help them. This body promptly responded, declaring unconstitutional, early in 1935, the National Industrial Recovery Act, the Railroad Retirement Act, the Frazier-Lemke Act (which gave partial relief on farm mortgages), and the Agricultural Adjustment Act. These were all key New Deal laws. At the outset of the New Deal, big businessmen had pinned their hopes upon N.I.R.A., as we have seen, depending upon it to give them solid control of the industries and to build up a system of fascist-like company unions; but it backfired and they had the Supreme Court get rid of it, dealing Roosevelt a sharp blow.

Roosevelt, heavily pressed by the workers, retaliated against this attack from the Supreme Court by having the Democratic Congress adopt several new laws in 1935. Chief of these were, as enacted in April, the Works Progress Administration (W.P.A.); in July, the National Labor Relations (Wagner) Act; and in August, the Social Security Act. The Guffey Coal Act was also passed.

The W.P.A. was the work relief project, however skinflint the relief rates and wages. The Wagner Act, more clearly than Section 7 (a) of the N.I.R.A., granted the workers the right to organize and set up certain restraints against employer interference with the workers using this right. At once it became a great bogey to the capitalists and a major issue in their "Hate Roosevelt" campaign. The Wagner Act legally abolished the employers' spy and gunman system. Under Section 7 (a) of the N.I.R.A., company unionism had made the biggest strides in its career. The La-Follette Commission, authorized by the Senate on June 6, 1936, exposed the fact that in their union-wrecking schemes the employers spent $80 million per year for their espionage-terrorist system. There were 230 agencies (Burns, Pinkerton, Sherman, etc.) engaged in this nefarious work. It was estimated that the employers had 100,000 spies, with at least one in each of the 48,000 local unions of the labor movement.[1] The Social Security Act established small federal benefits for the aged and unemployed. The Guffey Act, in certain features, favored the United Mine Workers. All of these laws were literally written by the workers themselves by their great industrial and political struggles of the period. The president also set out, in the midst of wild opposition, to alter the composition of the Supreme Court accordingly. This brought down upon his head violent charges that he was packing the high court.

Roosevelt confined himself to the foregoing relatively modest re-

[1] Labor Research Association, *Labor Fact Book 4*, p. 108, N. Y., 1938.

forms, most of which were already in effect in various European countries. He carefully opposed any and all measures that could directly weaken the capitalist system or that might worsen the basic position of the monopolists—such as democratic nationalization of the banks and railroads, a capital levy to procure government relief, a stated limitation upon capitalist profits, or the establishment of a farmer-labor party. Roosevelt, in his New Deal program, remained at all times the champion and defender of capitalism, which meant, of course, monopoly capitalism. Under his presidency big business made much of the most rapid and substantial economic progress in its entire history.

The Communist Party actively supported Roosevelt in his fight against the most reactionary sections of big business. Its general line, while combating bourgeois-democratic illusions among the workers about Roosevelt and his New Deal, was to support his reform measures and to get from them the maximum possible benefit for the working class. It was a policy of support with active criticism.

THE ELECTIONS OF 1936

The Presidential elections of 1936 were among the hardest-fought in the life of this country. Never were class lines more sharply drawn, and never was the partisan strife more bitter. The biggest and most fascist-minded reactionaries of Wall Street were resolved to get rid of Roosevelt at any price and to put into the White House a more pliable figure, one who would further their ultra-reactionary policies. The men they chose for their standard bearers were Alfred M. Landon, governor of Kansas, and Colonel Frank Knox, owner of the *Chicago Daily News*. Landon, known as the "Kansas Coolidge," was an ultra-reactionary, and the substance of his program was to undo all the work of the New Deal and to return to the policies of Herbert Hoover. As for Roosevelt himself, he promised, if re-elected, a continuation and development of the New Deal program. He demanded the defeat of the Wall Street "economic royalists."

The election was fought out against a background of mounting political struggle, not only on the domestic, but also on the international scene. The Hitler-Mussolini-Hirohito axis by now had its drive for world conquest under way. The Japanese were overrunning North China, the Italians had invaded Ethiopia, Hitler was blazing ahead in Germany, and the Germans and Italians had provoked the Spanish Civil War. World fascism was on the march, and it was in this spirit that the most reactionary sections of Wall Street finance capital fought Roosevelt. Their first attempt to shove the country toward fascism under the National Industrial Recovery Act had failed, but perhaps they would have better success in 1936. Many undoubtedly calculated that a defeat of the Roosevelt forces in the election would clear the way for the beginnings of fascism in the United States.

The big reactionaries rallied their forces to defeat Roosevelt and to elect the Landon ticket. The National Association of Manufacturers, the United States Chamber of Commerce, and other big combinations of capital used all their strength. The Republican Party spent money like water, and so did the American Liberty League and other Wall Street groups. The press was lined up at least 85 percent for Landon, who was the special darling of William Randolph Hearst.

A cunning election device of the Republicans was the setting up of the so-called Union Party. The agents of big business who did this job were the fascists Father Coughlin and Gerald L. K. Smith. Coughlin and Smith were assisted by Dr. Townsend, of old age pension fame. These elements chose as their presidential candidate Congressman William Lemke, an old time Non-Partisan Leaguer. The purpose of the Union Party maneuver was to play upon the third party sentiment among the workers and also upon the radicalism of the masses in the confused "panacea" movements, and thus to win these elements away from the Roosevelt camp.

The election struggle had not progressed far, however, before it became clear that big capital, lined up strongly against Roosevelt, was meeting determined resistance among the masses of workers and farmers. Especially significant was the pro-Roosevelt attitude of the Negroes in the North, who possessed votes. Ever since the Civil War the Negro people, in the main, had supported the Republican Party, the party of Abraham Lincoln and Negro emancipation. But great masses among them broke with this strong tradition in 1936. It was mainly a rank-and-file revolt, the old-line Negro politicians trying to keep the Negro masses in the Landon column. *The Defender* and other prominent Negro journals followed this course. But the Negro masses nevertheless voted for Roosevelt: four to one in Harlem, two to one in Brooklyn, with similar majorities in Chicago, Detroit, and other strong northern Negro centers. James W. Ford said of the election, "The Roosevelt landslide saw twenty-five Negroes elected to the state legislatures and one to the Congress of the United States. The majority were Democrats. In several instances Negro Republicans were succeeded by Negro Democrats. No Negro legislative candidate running on the Democratic ticket was defeated."[1] This break of the Negro masses from Republican tutelage was of his-

[1] James W. Ford in *The Communist*, Jan. 1937.

toric importance. Never since then have they gone back to their old-time allegiance. Instead, with a strongly marked political progressivism, they occupy a highly strategic political position in several key northern states, especially New York, Pennsylvania, and Illinois.

LABOR IN THE ELECTIONS

Organized labor went heavily for Roosevelt. This was particularly the case with the newly-established C.I.O. Whereas William Green and his A.F. of L. cronies still maintained the form of the old Gompers policy of rewarding labor's friends and punishing its enemies, John L. Lewis and Sidney Hillman, the leaders of the C.I.O., came out strongly for Roosevelt. In April 1936, they induced George L. Berry, president of the International Pressmen's Union (A.F. of L.) to work with them in setting up Labor's Non-Partisan League, of which Berry became the first president. The League, a step forward from the old Gompers policy, not only followed the practice of working within the Democratic Party (and also the Republican Party), but it likewise co-operated with such independent farmer and labor parties as existed at the time. Organized before the C.I.O.'s final suspension by the A.F. of L. convention in November, 1936, and before the League was condemned as "dual" to the A.F. of L., the League quickly won a wide support in official A.F. of L. ranks. It assembled 35,000 national and local union leaders as active workers in its cause. It was a power in the elections, carrying on agitational and organizational work upon a far broader scale than anything yet seen in the American labor movement.

The situation presented a splendid opportunity to launch a farmer-labor party, a more favorable moment even than during the LaFollette campaign of 1924. The workers were on the march politically, even as they were advancing in the industrial field. They gave every indication that they would have supported an independent party movement under the leadership of organized labor. Their militant spirit was indicated by the foundation and rapid growth during this period of the American Labor Party of New York, the Washington Commonwealth Federation, a similar federation in Oregon, the Minnesota Farmer-Labor Party, the Progressive Party of Wisconsin, the Epic movement in California, and various other such organizations in a number of states. Communists played a very important part in all these state movements.

The strength of the workers' political movement was further indicated by the fact that at the second national convention of Labor's Non-Partisan League (held in Washington, March 1937), there were present 600 delegates, representing 3,500,000 workers in the A.F. of L.,

C.I.O., and Railroad Brotherhoods. But the top union leaders, true to form, did not rise to the situation. Despite the broad demand of the rank and file and the energetic agitation of the Communists, they refused to establish an independent party of the toiling masses, even though this would have strengthened, not weakened, the mass support for Roosevelt. So this golden opportunity to launch the working class on the path of independent political action was lost.

The position of the Communist Party in the 1936 elections, in line with its general attitude toward the New Deal, was one of objective, but not official support for Roosevelt. At its ninth convention (in New York, June 24-28, 1936), the Party took the stand that the central issue of the campaign was "democracy versus fascism," and it pointed out that the major forces of reaction and fascism were ganged up behind Landon. It called for "the concentration of all forces of the working class and its allies in the fight against the Republican-Liberty League-Hearst combination and for the defeat of its plans in the elections of 1936." The Party directed its main fire against Landon. As for Roosevelt, while the Party realized that he had made certain concessions to the toilers, it correctly asserted that he had made bigger "concessions to Hearst, to Wall Street, to the reactionaries."[1] It declared that Roosevelt's "middle course" was "not a barrier to reaction and fascism,"[2] and that the Party could not therefore give him a full endorsement. Consequently, the Party put up its own national ticket, Earl Browder and James W. Ford. It was on the ballot in 34 states. The type of campaign which the Party carried on, however, calling for the defeat of Landon at all costs, militated against the Party polling its own full potential vote in the elections—hence its ticket received only 80,181 votes.

The Socialist Party, which at that time was displaying some activity, particularly in the unemployed field, and was passing through its phony "left" orientation mentioned in a previous chapter, took an ultra-left stand in the elections. Norman Thomas, in an absurd burst of radicalism for this opportunistic mountebank, stated that the issue in the elections was socialism versus capitalism and that the only immediate demand of the Socialists was for socialism. The S.P. declared that it was of no interest to the workers whether Landon or Roosevelt were elected, and it condemned the Communist Party for giving even conditional support to Roosevelt.

The elections were fought with extreme vigor and bitterness. Roosevelt was attacked as a near-Communist, and every device was used by the reactionaries to delude or scare the masses into voting the Republican

[1] *Communist Party Election Platform*, 1936.
[2] Resolution, Ninth Convention, C.P.U.S.A., Apr. 1936.

ticket. But these efforts were quite in vain, the wild redbaiting failing of its purpose. Roosevelt's victory was of spectacular proportions. He carried every state in the Union, except Maine and Vermont. His popular vote was 27,750,000, over 11 million votes more than Landon's total—the largest election plurality in American political history. Both houses of Congress went solidly Democratic, and the Rooseveltites controlled the governorships of all the states except seven. The fascist tool Lemke, on the Union Party slate, polled only 891,858 votes, carrying not a single state. The Socialist Party, which for many years had polled a large "protest vote," got only 187,342 votes in 1936, or less than one-fourth of its vote in 1932.[1] The attempt of the Wall Street reactionaries to push the country in the direction of fascism had failed, wrecked upon the rocks of the democratic will of the American people.

THE POLITICAL LINE OF THE COMMUNIST PARTY

During the early New Deal years here under consideration, from the beginning of 1933 to the end of 1936, the general policy of the Communist Party was sound, although a number of weaknesses and some outright mistakes developed in its application. The basic correctness of the Communist political line was reflected in a wide increase in the Party's mass influence and in a steady growth in the number of its members throughout this period.

The Party was essentially correct in its attitude toward Roosevelt, its sharp opposition to the strong fascist influences in the early phases of the New Deal, and its later limited and critical support of Roosevelt and a number of his reforms. As early as 1936, however, Browder was slackening in necessary criticism of Roosevelt, an opportunism that was later to have disastrous consequences.

The Party was correct in the major stress which it laid upon stimulating the struggles of the masses for their immediate demands, more and more on a united front basis—for wages, unemployment relief, Negro rights, the youth, and trade union organization. It was quite right, too, in warning the masses that they would secure consideration for their demands only to the extent that they fought for them. This militant stand of the Party against all trimmers and compromisers was a major factor in the workers winning such concessions as they did during these years. Although the Party still tended to put somewhat too much stress upon the "revolutionary way out of the crisis," this did not prevent it from making an aggressive and successful fight for the everyday demands of the toiling masses.

[1] The S.P. split and its membership fell to but 6,194 dues-payers in 1937, as against 16,656 in 1936.

In particular, the Communist Party was a highly constructive force in the persistent and intelligent fight it made to strengthen the trade union movement. Of course, the Party, as the vanguard party of the working class, was intensely interested in every trade union question; however, it did not itself intervene in the life of the trade unions. The Communists worked energetically to have the unions adopt progressive policies; nevertheless, in the highest sense of discipline and solidarity, they faithfully carried out the union's decisions, even when they might not fully agree with them. Communists were in the forefront of every organizing campaign, strike, and other union activity. They were also militant champions of labor unity. And they tirelessly worked to prevent the A. F. of L. and C.I.O. from splitting, and also to reunite the two organizations after the split had become a reality.

In its endless fight for labor unity, the Party made a united front proposal, in March 1933, to the A.F. of L. and S.P. to work together jointly on the basis of a common program of struggle.[1] This proposal was in line with the realities of the American political situation and also with the fight that the Communists everywhere, in the face of the growing fascist menace, were making for world labor unity. The top leadership of both the A.F. of L. and S.P., however, were unresponsive to the C.P.'s unity proposals, but many of the lower organizations were not. During these years hundreds of A.F. of L. local unions and many local branches of the S.P., against the will of their main leaders, participated in such progressive united front organizations as the National Negro Congress, the American Youth Congress, the American League Against War and Fascism, the Workers Alliance, the League of American Writers, and the Councils for the Foreign-Born. In the 1936 campaign the C.P., following its correct united front policy, also proposed a joint election slate with the S.P. (which had grown considerably since 1933 and was then showing "left" tendencies), but this proposal was ignored by the Thomas leaders. In January 1936, the Y.C.L. proposed ineffectually to the Y.P.S.L. to form a united youth organization.

The Party correctly took a stand for the stronger political crystallization of the loose democratic mass coalition that was backing Roosevelt. It particularly stressed the necessity for establishing a definite people's front, in its American form of the farmer-labor party. In all the state parties and political federations of the period the Communists were active and effective workers, and in Labor's Non-Partisan League, the Communists and other lefts were also the most dynamic elements. The Party was quite aware of the historic opportunity which the early New Deal years presented for the working class to break with the poison-

[1] Alexander Bittelman, Introduction to *The Advance of the United Front*, N. Y., 1934.

ous capitalistic two-party system and to embark upon a course of independent political action.

In this general matter, however, the Party narrowly escaped making a serious blunder. After the C.I.O., the A.F. of L., and the various existing state labor and farmer parties had clearly indicated, early in 1936,[1] that they were not going to launch an independent party for the presidential elections of that fall, Earl Browder, general secretary of the C.P., nevertheless insisted in our Party that it put a labor party ticket in the field. If this had been done, it would have meant another Federated Farmer Labor Party (1923), but upon a still narrower basis. Browder sought to justify this impractical, right-sectarian proposition, which would have disastrously isolated our Party, on the absurd grounds that such a party would draw votes from Landon's column rather than from Roosevelt's. Only after he was defeated did Browder withdraw his proposal and accept the policy of a qualified endorsement of Roosevelt, which the Party successfully followed in the 1936 elections.

The Party, too, was essentially correct in its sharp opposition to Roosevelt in the initial three years or so of his regime. Fascism was a burning menace throughout the capitalist world and there were many pronounced fascist trends in the Roosevelt program, especially in the N.I.R.A. However, when Roosevelt, under the pressure of the big mass struggles and the attacks of the extreme right, began to take a more definite stand against militant reaction, then the Party changed its attitude toward him. At the ninth convention of the Communist Party, in June 1936, it was decided, in substance, to give Roosevelt indirect support by directing the Party's main fire against Landon. This correct policy, however, as later events were to show, was eventually to be distorted by Browder into an impermissible subordination of the Communist Party to the bourgeois Roosevelt program in general.

BROWDER AND AMERICAN DEMOCRATIC TRADITIONS

The most serious theoretical error made by the Communist Party during the early Roosevelt period was its erroneous handling of the question of the American national democratic traditions. The matter of national traditions, long neglected by many Communist parties, became of imperative importance with the rise of world fascism and the attempt of the fascists to rewrite their peoples' history to suit their own reactionary purposes. The Communist Party, leader of the powerful People's Front movement in France, in accordance with the facts in France and on the

---

[1] Chicago Conference, in May 1936, at which all the farmer-labor party forces, including the Communist Party, were present.

basis of principles established long before by Lenin and Stalin, greatly stressed the question from 1933 on. It demonstrated effectively to the masses that the Marxist-Leninists, in fighting against fascism and war and for socialism, were not only acting as the immediate leaders of the nation, but at the same time were carrying forward the revolutionary and democratic traditions of the French people. This correct policy blasted the fascists' historical pretensions and greatly strengthened the whole fight of the People's Front. Georgi Dimitrov, at the Seventh Congress of the Comintern, emphasized the importance of this task, pointing out that "The fascists are rummaging through the entire history of every nation so as to be able to pose as the heirs and continuers of all that was exalted and heroic in its past."[1]

Earl Browder, distorting the sound example of the French Communists, undertook after 1934 to analyze the relationship of American communism to American democratic and revolutionary traditions. In doing this he fell into the grossest opportunistic errors. Browder's central mistake in this general respect was his failure to distinguish between bourgeois democracy and proletarian democracy. He ignored the basic facts that bourgeois democracy is the rule of the bourgeoisie and proletarian democracy the rule of the working class, and also that between the two lies the establishment of socialism. In applying his opportunist theories to American history, Browder did not differentiate fundamentally between the narrow, restricted type of democracy conceived by the bourgeoisie and the broad popular democracy fought for by the proletariat.[2] He obscured the reality that the bourgeoisie systematically limits, thwarts, and distorts the democratic institutions under capitalism in its own class interest, and that the working class historically fights to expand the bourgeois democracy. The workers, as Lenin points out, develop bourgeois democracy to the utmost, and then *make the leap* to Socialist democracy. The fight for socialism is a struggle, by democratic means, for the highest form of democracy, which is completely unachievable under capitalism.

Browder, with his un-Marxist, undifferentiated concept of "American democracy," stood for bourgeois democracy in itself, and he was already, at this early date, putting forward the perspective of its constant, evolutionary growth. This implied the abandonment of socialism and the indefinite continuation of the capitalist system. Browder summed up his opportunist conceptions of American revolutionary and democratic traditions in the slogan, "Communism Is Twentieth Century Americanism," which he introduced at the eighth convention of the Party in

[1] Dimitrov, *The United Front*, p. 77.
[2] See Betty Gannett in *Political Affairs*, Apr. 1951.

Cleveland in 1934. As H. Jennings points out, the meaning of this slogan was that "what passes for the American tradition, with all its vague classless connotations and its illusion of an abstract and timeless democracy standing above class antagonisms, is acceptable as a definition of Communism."[1] Browder's slogan was criticized, and he later made a public restatement of it, supposedly self-critical.[2] He continued to advocate the slogan; but it soon fell into disuse.

After 1934 Browder's writings were saturated with his "all-class" conceptions of "American democracy." He developed his idea that Marxism-Leninism was only a sort of expanded, unbroken continuation of bourgeois democracy. At the tenth convention of the Party, held in New York, beginning on May 27, 1938, Browder stated that "A full and complete application of Jefferson's principles, the consistent application of democratic ideas to the conditions of today, will lead naturally and inevitably to the full program of the Communist Party, to the socialist reorganization of the United States, to the common ownership and operation of our economy for the benefit of all."[3] In accordance with this revisionist conception, Browder was instrumental in having the convention write into the Preamble of the C.P. Constitution his false notion of the gradual evolution of Jeffersonianism into Marxism-Leninism. The Preamble, as amended, read that the C.P. simply "carried forward the traditions of Washington, Jefferson, Paine, Jackson, and Lincoln under the changed conditions of today." This was a complete denial of the class content of bourgeois democracy.

Browder's opportunist conception of bourgeois democracy not only eliminated the fight for socialism, but also ignored the democratic role of the working class in American history. Washington, Jefferson, Paine, Jackson, and Lincoln, it is true, fought for certain restricted democratic freedoms, needful to the ruling classes of a country emerging from a bourgeois agrarianism and slave economy into industrial capitalism, including limited rights of free speech, assembly, worship, trial by jury, and the like. These democratic freedoms the working class also struggled to establish, defend, and expand; but it fought, too, for its own specific democratic demands—higher wages, shorter hours, popular education, Negro people's rights, the right to organize and strike, social insurance, protection of women and children in industry, etc., to all of which, historically, the ruling class has been opposed. These working class demands, fundamentally different in substance from the limited democracy of all American bourgeois leaders, past and present, are the roots, within

[1] H. Jennings in *Political Affairs*, Aug. 1945.
[2] *The Communist*, Dec. 1938.
[3] *Report to the Tenth National Convention of the C.P.U.S.A.*, p. 93, N. Y., 1938.

the framework of capitalism, of what will eventually mature under socialism as proletarian democracy.

The working class has played a most vital part in establishing such democracy as there is in the United States. And now the workers and their democratic allies, here as in all other capitalist lands, have become the sole protectors and developers of democracy. Without the workers' democratic fight, the fascist-minded monopoly capitalists would soon destroy every democratic institution in this country. Browder undertook to ignore or deny all these realities. Despite the gross opportunism of Browder's formulations, they nevertheless remained in the Preamble of the Party Constitution until the emergency convention of July 1945, when the present sound Marxist-Leninist clauses were substituted.

Browder's identification of proletarian democracy with bourgeois democracy signified his acceptance historically of the capitalist class as the democratic leader of the American people. It was a specific repudiation of the role of the working class, especially when headed by the Communist Party, as the leader of the nation. Uncorrected, this false idea was to cause Browder, several years later, also to accept the leadership of American imperialism in the realm of practical politics. This he did in January 1944, in his notorious Teheran thesis, which extolled "progressive capitalism." At its conventions of 1934, 1936, and 1938 the Party was not yet keen enough in its Marxist-Leninist clarity to grasp the significance of Browder's developing opportunistic interpretations of American democratic history, and thereby to kill this particularly venomous political snake in the egg. For this political shortcoming the Party was to pay dearly in subsequent years.

24. The Communists in the Building of the C.I.O.
(1936-1940)

The building of the C.I.O. unions was the greatest stride forward ever made by the American labor movement. It changed the whole situation of the trade unions and brought the working class to new high levels of industrial and political strength and maturity. In this historic movement the Communist Party played a vital and indispensable role. It acted truly as the vanguard party of the working class.

As we have seen in Chapter 21, the Committee for Industrial Organization was established late in 1935 under the leadership of John L. Lewis. Its first main concentration was upon steel. In June 1936, the Steel Workers Organizing Committee, led by Philip Murray, was formed; district headquarters were set up in Pittsburgh, Chicago, and Birmingham, and some 200 full-time organizers were put into the field. The eight associated C.I.O. unions, especially the miners, were prepared to spend millions in the work.

The steel workers were ripe for organization. Many were paid as little as $560 per year, as against a $1,500 standard cost-of-living budget; and long hours and tyranny prevailed in the shops. The workers were inspired by the world-wide proletarian fighting spirit of the period. So the organizing work was immediately successful. By the end of 1936 the S.W.O.C., which had virtually swallowed the old, fossilized Amalgamated Association of Iron, Steel and Tin Workers, had 150 local unions with 100,000 members.

Meanwhile, dramatic and decisive events were also happening in the automobile industry. The United Automobile Workers, which had been formed by the A.F. of L. but later joined the C.I.O., succeeded in building, by December 1936, an organization of about 30,000 members. Demanding an agreement with the General Motors Corp. and being refused, the workers, whose earnings then averaged but $20 per week, began to strike—in Atlanta and Cleveland. Finally, by January 1937, 51,000 were on strike, and they tied up 60 G.M. plants in 14 states, employing some 140,000 workers.

The center and decisive point of the strike was in the major G.M.

plants in Flint, Michigan, the heart of this great industrial empire. There the workers, patterning their actions after a strike of rubber workers in Akron a few months earlier, and in line with workers' experience in France and Italy, occupied the plants. It was a "sit-down strike." The workers barricaded themselves in the workshops, set up a military-like discipline, beat off all armed attempts of company gunmen and police to recapture the plants, and threatened to resist with every means any attempt of the state militia to dislodge them, as the company was demanding from the governor. The solidarity of the workers was unbreakable, and after 44 days of struggle the great $1.5 billion General Motors Corp. capitulated, recognizing the union and granting substantial improvements in wages, hours, and working conditions.[1]

The G.M. strike, particularly in its key Flint section, was one of the most strategically decisive strikes in American labor history. It made the first real breakthrough for the C.I.O. into territory of open shop monopoly capital, and its effective sit-down tactics were a tremendous inspiration to the entire working class. The other C.I.O. campaigns thereafter went like wildfire, with the sit-down tactic being used successfully in many places. On March 8th, some 63,000 workers of the big Chrysler Corp. also went on strike (about two-thirds of them sit-downers), and they won a victory after a short struggle. Then, indeed, the unionization of the auto industry proceeded with great strides.

In steel also, dramatic success was being achieved. On March 2, 1937, the country was amazed by the announcement of an agreement between the S.W.O.C. and the United States Steel Corp., covering some 240,000 workers in its basic plants. The agreement established the eight-hour day and 40-hour week, provided for a 10-cent hourly wage increase, and for grievance committees, seniority, and other improvements. At long last, after nearly half a century of struggle, the unions had finally blasted their way solidly into the greatest open shop fortress of them all, Big Steel.

These decisive successes in steel and auto, the heart of basic industry, did not, however, complete the organization of these two great industries. "Little Steel"—the Bethlehem, Inland, Republic, and Youngstown companies—held out and with traditional violence, in May 1937, smashed the strike of 75,000 of their workers. In the infamous Memorial Day massacre in Chicago 10 picketing workers were killed and over 100 wounded by the police. In auto also, the great Ford empire managed to resist the current ground swell of unionization. But both Ford and Little Steel, within the next four years, finally had to submit to the organization of their workers.

[1] William W. Weinstone, *The Great Sit-Down Strike*, N. Y., 1937.

In the meantime, militant and successful organizing campaigns were proceeding in various other industries—radio and electrical, maritime, metal mining, textile, lumber, transport, shoe, meat-packing, leather, rubber, aluminum, and glass, among white collar workers, etc.—but a description of all these campaigns would pass beyond the scope of this outline. Suffice it to say that by the end of 1940 the C.I.O. unions encompassed some four million workers, a growth of over three million in four years. By the time World War II began to engulf the world, the organizing drive of the C.I.O. had proved to be an unqualified success; the heart of trustified industry was unionized.

THE A.F. OF L. LEADERS SABOTAGE THE CAMPAIGN

As the demand for industrial unionization began to grow during the early thirties in the A.F. of L., Daniel J. Tobin, head of the Teamsters Union, "scornfully characterized the unskilled workers in mass production industry as 'rubbish.'"[1] This was a true, if unusually frank, expression of the real attitude of the top leaders of the A.F. of L. toward the problem of organizing the basic industries. Give them the skilled workers, and the fate of the rest did not concern them. With this attitude, Green and Co. tried to stifle the current big spontaneous upheavals of the masses. They refused to grant the workers industrial charters; they expelled the C.I.O. unions in an attempt to break up the organizing drive at its inception; they condemned the sit-down strike as illegal and a harm to organized labor; they repeatedly had their craft unions play strikebreaking roles; they seconded every employer condemnation of the C.I.O. as "red." But the workers, with their wonderful fighting spirit and solidarity, and especially under Communist influence, smashed through this A.F. of L. sabotage (which had been so fatal in past union drives) and carried their organizing campaigns and strikes through to success.

By a historical irony, however, the A.F. of L. unions also profited hugely from the great mass organizing movement which their top leaders were doing so much to scuttle. Several of the more alert unions—machinists, teamsters, electrical, boilermakers, hotel and restaurant, etc.,—took advantage of the favorable situation and organized workers on all sides, paying little attention to jurisdictional lines. They became mass, semi-industrial unions, all increasing heavily in membership. Communists were active in all of these campaigns. By 1940 the A.F. of L., in spite of losing several unions to the C.I.O., numbered about as many members as the C.I.O. did. At no time, however, did the A.F. of L. top leadership

[1] F. R. Dulles, *Labor in America*, p. 294, N. Y., 1949.

put on a general systematic campaign to organize the awakening workers.

It was one of the more significant aspects of the labor situation that the growth of the C.I.O. and the influx of large numbers of unskilled workers into the craft unions had a restraining effect upon the reactionary course of the leaders in the A.F. of L. There was a noticeable relaxation of gangster control and of the crass corruption that had so long been such a disgrace to the A.F. of L. leadership. The Federation also began to take a little more interest in progressive political programs, to be achieved through legislation. The old apoliticalism of Gompers, which opposed legislation on wages, hours, and working conditions as tending to liquidate the trade unions, was now a thing of the past. There was even a substantial decline in redbaiting in A.F. of L. unions.[1]

At their 1940 conventions the C.I.O. and A.F. of L. represented 3,810,318 and 4,247,443 members respectively. The total for the whole labor movement, including the independents, was about ten million. During the great organizing campaign of the late thirties the C.I.O. directly added to itself some three million members, and the A.F. of L., as compared with 1935, grew by 1,750,000. The railroad unions had practically overcome the disastrous losses of the 1922 strike, and the original eight C.I.O. unions increased by some 800,000. The C.I.O. principal unions at this time were the miners with 600,000 members, steel workers 535,109, auto workers 206,824, packinghouse workers 90,000, and transport workers 90,000. Up to 1940, the total gain to the trade union movement in the broad campaign initiated by the C.I.O. was about seven million members.

Although at this time the C.I.O. and A.F. of L. were about the same size numerically, the former was the most basic and promising section of the labor movement. This was because it was founded principally upon the heavy industries, and because of its more advanced policies, its more progressive leadership, and the greater influence of the Communists in its ranks.

LABOR'S SOLIDARITY OVERCOMES ALL OBSTACLES

The key to the great success in building the C.I.O. during these years was the high solidarity and fighting spirit of the workers, which was assiduously cultivated by the Communists. This spirit was bred of long years of tyranny under the open shop, of the bitter destitution during the great economic crisis, of the feeling of economic and political power that the workers had gained through the successful strikes since 1933, and of their realization that they had beaten the Republican Party in the

[1] Jack Stachel in *The Communist*, Nov. 1936.

elections of 1932 and 1936. The high morale was all-pervasive, running through the ranks of the workers, the unemployed, the Negroes, the foreign-born, the women, and the youth. Its central symbol was the sit-down strike and its highest expression the unbreakable unity between the employed and the unemployed. Although there were never less than ten million unemployed throughout this whole period, and there was also a developing economic crisis in 1937, the strikes were extremely solid, it being very difficult to recruit strikebreakers to take the place of strikers. It was this unparalleled proletarian solidarity and militancy that—apparently with ease—defeated the employers and forced open the way for the unionization of the trustified industries.

A factor highly favorable to the organization of the workers was the deep split in the ranks of the top bureaucracy of the trade unions—as distinguished from the split in the labor movement itself. Previously, attempts at mass organization had to face the united and usually fatal opposition of the upper leadership, who based themselves primarily upon the skilled. Hence, organizing campaigns in the basic industries had to be undertaken by the rank and file or by independent unions, with all the money, organizers, and prestige of the conservative union leadership arrayed against them. Except for this top opposition, the mass production industries could have been organized long before—certainly during World War I or during the Coolidge years. But now, with the Green-Lewis split in the bureaucracy and with Lewis pushing for organization, it became possible to tackle the job seriously for the first time with the real power and prestige of solid trade unions behind the campaign. Success was thus assured from the outset.

The hard-boiled employers—in steel and auto, for example—caved in with surprising ease before the advance of the C.I.O. Even the Girdlers and Fords could not long resist the organizing movement. Their "Mohawk formula" and all other approved and tested strikebreaking methods had lost their potency. This was primarily because the intense fighting spirit of the workers destroyed ruthlessly the company unions, spy systems, gunman control, and the rest of the open shop demagogy and terrorism which the employers had been building up for a generation, and which had hitherto been so drastically effective in preventing unionization. The leaders of U.S. Steel, General Motors, and other trusts, facing an aroused working class, feared that an open struggle would bring about even more radical labor organization than what they finally got. The Communist Party, dynamic force in the whole movement, was at the time advocating a joint strike movement in steel, auto, and coal mining; and such a broad strike was definitely a practical perspective. So the big magnates of industry made the best of a bad situation, and they set out to try to control the new unions that they could no longer forestall. After all, "labor lieutenants" like Green, Woll, Frey, and Co. were not very terrifying people to contemplate dealing with, and such figures, they apparently hoped, would also come to lead the C.I.O.

In fighting against the formation of the C.I.O. unions, the employers were hampered because the current Federal Administration was not the facile and effective strikebreaking machine that it had been in the past. Roosevelt was not a Grover Cleveland smashing the 1894 American Railway Union strike, a Woodrow Wilson giving the green light to Gary and his steel union-crushers in 1919, nor a Warren G. Harding tearing to pieces the 1922 strike of the railroad shopmen. Instead, Roosevelt, a liberal, favored unions in a moderate way, more especially in view of his need for their support against the violent attacks that extreme reaction was making upon him. He recognized that the days of the old-time open shop were over. But without the great militancy of the masses little union-building would have taken place under his regime. Indeed, in co-operation with William Green, Roosevelt had "compromised" out of existence the strong union drives in steel and auto in 1934, by referring their demands to labor boards which knifed them. The Administration also condemned the vitally important sit-down strike tactic. And Roosevelt's Wagner Act, although a real improvement over Section 7 (a) of the N.I.R.A., was anything but the all-decisive "Magna Carta of Labor" that union officials called it. While it recognized the right of the workers to organize, the latter had to fight to make that right real. The Wagner Act was a reflection of the great contemporaneous advance of the workers, not the cause of it. Minus the aggressive spirit of the workers, this act would have remained only a paper declaration without real substance, had it ever been written at all.

THE ROLE OF THE COMMUNIST PARTY

The Communist Party fully supported the C.I.O. program of establishing new industrial unions in the basic, unorganized industries. Although the C.I.O. was split off from the A.F. of L., the Party in no sense identified this broad independent mass movement with the narrow left-wing dual unionism which the Party had long opposed—despite certain deviations of its own during the T.U.U.L. period. The traditional left dual unionism had the effect of withdrawing the militant elements from the unions and isolating them from the general labor movement in small unions, but nothing like this took place with the founding of the C.I.O. On the contrary, the C.I.O. was in every sense a broad mass movement.

The Communists played a decisive part in the great strikes and organizing drives that established the C.I.O. This was evident on the very face of things. It was to be seen in the highly militant character, as remarked in Chapter 21, of the methods and spirit of the general movement. The new unions certainly did not learn their militant organizing spirit, intensified political activity, internationalism, more enlightened Negro policy, shop steward system, rank-and-file democracy, anti-racketeer fight, mass picketing, union singing, sit-down strikes, slow-down strikes, and sound fighting policies from the old-line trade union leaders who officially headed the historic movement. Nor did they get them from the Trotskyites or Socialists, who took very little part in these struggles. And the I.W.W. tradition was long since inactive. Stolberg, a redbaiter who hated the Communist Party and loved its enemies, in 1938 said of the Trotskyites as participants in these struggles: "The Trotskyites in the C.I.O. we may dismiss." And of the Socialists, who were not much more of a factor than the Trotskyites on the fighting-organizing line, Stolberg also stated: "The Socialist Party has no clear trade union policy in the C.I.O. or elsewhere."[1] Significantly, almost the whole of his book is devoted to describing Communist influence in the C.I.O. The plain fact is that the ideological spirit of the great union-building movement and its militant tactics were chiefly a direct reflection of the big mass influence of the Communists, who were everywhere active in the work of organization and struggle. The C.I.O. took over the bulk of the immediate program of the Trade Union Unity League.

Actually, the "Old Guard" Socialists opposed the C.I.O. and its program. At the Tampa convention of the A.F. of L. they voted to expel the C.I.O. unions. And it was under "Old Guard" pressure that Dubinsky got cold feet, withdrew the I.L.G.W.U. from the C.I.O. and brought it back into the A.F. of L.

The Communists were well fitted to play their vital part in the C.I.O. drive. For years they had paid major attention to the question of organizing the basic industries, and they had assembled vast practical experience, as well as many mass contacts. They had conducted innumerable T.U.E.L. and T.U.U.L. strikes and Unemployed Council and Workers Alliance activities in many heavy and trustified industrial centers. The Communist Party, with its system of shop groups and shop papers, also had valuable connections among the most militant workers in many open shop industries. The left wing had hosts of other such contacts in these plants through the various Negro, foreign-born, and other mass organizations in which it had an important influence. All of these connections the Party set in motion when the great organizing drive got

[1] B. Stolberg, *The Story of the C.I.O.*, N. Y., 1938.

under way. The 15-year struggle of the Party in the basic industries trained thousands of fighters, who later formed the very foundations of the C.I.O.

These basic contributions of the Communists to the building of the C.I.O. are now conveniently ignored or denied by the present right-wing leadership. But occasionally some credit is given our Party. Thus, Alinsky, in his "unauthorized" biography of John L. Lewis, which was written in close collaboration with the latter, says of the role of the Communists in building the C.I.O.: "Then, as is now commonly known, the Communists worked indefatigably, with no job being too menial or unimportant. They literally poured themselves completely into their assignments. The Communist Party gave its complete support to the C.I.O. . . . The fact is that the Communist Party made a major contribution in the organization of the unorganized for the C.I.O."[1]

As the general C.I.O. movement developed the Party published a series of pamphlets, outlining in detail the ideological case for industrial unionism, effective methods of organizational work in mass production industries, the elements of strike strategy, and the principles of the construction and operation of democratic industrial unions. These pamphlets summarized the constructive experience of the I.W.W., the T.U.E.L., the T.U.U.L., and the independent industrial unions over the past generation, and also that of the organizing campaigns in the A.F. of L., such as those in meat-packing and steel in 1917-19. They were given a wide circulation, and in many instances were to be found in local C.I.O. headquarters, serving as handbooks on organization for those doing the field work.[2]

In discussing necessary conditions for the success of the general organizing campaign then getting under way, the Party laid down as the most fundamental of all, as condition number one, that there be developed free working relations between the progressives and Communists in the movement. This was in accord historically with the best experience of the labor movement, in all phases of its growth. As the Party put the matter: "The organization work must be done by a working co-ordination of the progressive and left-wing forces in the labor movement. It is only these elements that have the necessary vision, flexibility, and courage to go forward with such an important project as the organization of the 500,000 steel workers in the face of the powerful opposition of the Steel Trust and its capitalist allies."[3]

[1] Saul Alinsky, *John L. Lewis*, p. 153, N. Y., 1949.
[2] Several of these pamphlets were later combined into a book, *Organizing the Mass Production Industries*, N. Y., 1937.
[3] William Z. Foster, *Organizing Methods in the Steel Industry*, N. Y., 1936.

A handicap to the maximum work and growth of the Communist Party during this general period was the developing opportunism of Earl Browder, its general secretary. Browder, with no mass union organizing experience and no talent for or appreciation of such work, preferred to maneuver opportunistically with top union and political leaders. He constantly sought to dampen the insistent working and fighting spirit of the Party. Especially he shied away from actively recruiting Party members in the basic industries, for fear that this would antagonize the top C.I.O. leaders. Such opportunist tendencies, which a few years later were to mature as a full-fledged system of revisionism and liquidationism, caused much friction in the top leadership of the Party and they worked against the organizational growth of the Party and the broadening of its influence among the masses of workers.

There was another very harmful tendency at the time—to overestimate the progressive character of the top leaders of the C.I.O. This wrong tendency was exemplified by Browder's extravagant adulation of Lewis and Murray, in turn, as the super-greatest of American labor leaders. Not enough attention was given to the fact that the "progressive" role being played by these leaders at the time was essentially opportunistic and that, when opportunity beckoned to them from another quarter, they would quickly drop their "progressivism," as they eventually did. At most, it was only skin deep.

John L. Lewis, Sidney Hillman, and their co-workers were apparently convinced of the value of Communist co-operation, because from the outset the organizing work and the leading of innumerable victorious strikes were done by a combination of the left-center forces—that is, Lewis, Hillman, the Communists, and other progressives. This working combination, although largely informal while Lewis remained president of the C.I.O. (up to the end of 1940), was a matter of common knowledge. As F. R. Dulles says, "Lewis did not hesitate to draw upon their [the Communists'] experience and skill in building up the C.I.O."[1] Practically everywhere, therefore, Communists became active and effective members of the big organizing crews. With the accession of Philip Murray to the presidency of the C.I.O., the left-center bloc was, for some years, even more definitely consolidated, and it became virtually a working alliance. The C.I.O. could not have succeeded upon any other basis.

The Communists worked very diligently to build and strengthen the left-center bloc. They refrained from grabbing for office in the new unions, and they gave unselfishly of themselves to the organizing work. As an example of the Party's co-operative spirit, in 1939 it liquidated its system of trade union fractions and shop papers. The Party's trade union

[1] Dulles, *Labor in America*, p. 317.

fractions—educational groups of Communists in the local unions—were dissolved to end all fears that they were formed for the purpose of controlling the unions. The Party's shop papers, which had performed invaluable services in the initial stages of the C.I.O. campaigns, were also given up for the same general reasons.

It was this left-center bloc, the working combination of progressives and left-wingers (mainly Communists), that carried through successfully the great organizing campaigns and strikes which unionized the basic industries and established the C.I.O. It was also this combination, throughout the ten years it lasted, that made the C.I.O. the leading section of the American trade union movement and a constructive force among the organized labor unions of the world. Mr. Murray and his friends, however, in the post-World War II years, have seen fit to break their connection with this left-center bloc, which has been of such vital importance in the life of the C.I.O.—but of all this more later.

THE COMMUNISTS IN THE STEEL INDUSTRY

In 1936, when the campaign began, the Communists had many valuable contacts with which to help organize the steel industry. The Party had branches in the main steel towns and mills, and it also had many scattered individual steel worker members. There were also a large number of left-wing members in the political and fraternal organizations of Negro and foreign-born workers in these areas. The T.U.U.L. had conducted several strikes and led many unemployed movements among steel workers over the years, and the Communists were very active in the steel organizing campaign of 1933-34. Besides, the national chairman of the Party, William Z. Foster, had led the great steel strike of 17 years before and was well known throughout the industry.

Co-operative relations, an informal united front, existed between the Communists and Philip Murray, head of the S.W.O.C., in carrying on the steel campaign. Of the approximately 200 full-time organizers put into the steel areas on the payroll of S.W.O.C., some 60 were Party members, as Murray well knew. The Party gave many of its best workers to the campaign, including a number of Negro organizers. Among them were Gus Hall, Ben Carreathers, John Steuben, and Pat Cush. All its local units and contacts were stimulated to work; for the Party the organization of the steel workers became the first order of business. W. Gebert was the Party's liaison with the S.W.O.C., and he held many conferences with the heads of that organization.

One example of the effectiveness of the Communists' organizing work was the national conference of Negro organizations held in Pittsburgh,

Pennsylvania, on February 6, 1937, to help organize steel. There were 186 delegates, representing 110 organizations with a total membership of 100,000. The conference was brought together by Benjamin L. Carreathers, a leading Negro Communist of Pittsburgh and full-time organizer for the S.W.O.C. The Party rallied all its Negro worker contacts to make this basic organizing conference the success that it was. The great importance of the conference may be grasped when it is realized that there were then about 100,000 Negroes working in the steel mills.[1] The intense activity of the Communists on the Negro question was a basic reason why the Negro workers joined all the C.I.O. unions in such numbers and also why the C.I.O. took its generally advanced position regarding the Negro people.

Another example of the systematic Communist organizing work in the steel campaign was the national conference of the organizations of the foreign-born. This was the work of W. Gebert, Party organizer in the steel industry, and it had the endorsement of Philip Murray and Clinton Golden. The conference, held in Pittsburgh on October 25, 1936, brought together 447 delegates, officially representing 459,000 members of many Lithuanian, Polish, Croatian, Serbian, Slovenian, Ukrainian, Russian, and other groups,[2] including several important Catholic organizations. Gebert was chairman, and Murray and Golden spoke. In view of the huge number of foreign-born workers in the steel industry, this conference was obviously of basic importance in the organization work.

The Young Communist League was also responsible for the holding of numerous broad conferences in various steel centers, to win the support of the young workers for the drive. Communist women took similar measures. In the steel areas the entire Party was active in the work of organization, and its influence in bringing the masses into the union was undoubtedly very great.

The Communists and other lefts, although becoming influential in the steel union in many localities, never got a corresponding position in the top leadership. This was partly because the C.I.O. leaders, realizing that steel was the key to the general organization they were building up, took elaborate precautions to keep tight control of the new steel workers' union. They manned all the key official union posts with coal miners, from Philip Murray on down, and to this day an authentic steel worker leadership of the union has not developed. Indeed, not until six years after signing of the agreement with Big Steel did Philip Murray even permit the closely-controlled S.W.O.C. to become reorganized into the supposedly democratic United Steelworkers of America.

[1] B. L. Carreathers, unpublished manuscript.
[2] *Laisve*, N. Y., Oct. 27, 1936.

More basic, however, in the failure of the left to consolidate its forces in steel were its own errors and shortcomings, typical of the Browder period. These included inadequate criticism of the Murray leadership, failure to build the Party and its press in the shops and mills, failure to develop independent union election activities, and the like. Devoting themselves whole-heartedly to the building of the union, as in the case of other industries, the Communists did not pay enough attention to the question of developing a progressive union leadership. The Communists and lefts in the steel industry were in a strong enough position locally at the time to have insisted that representative steel workers be brought into the top leadership; but they failed to do so. So the miners union functionaries, many of whom were mere chair-warmers and time-worn bureaucrats, retained full control of all decisive top positions.

THE COMMUNISTS IN THE AUTO INDUSTRY

When the A.F. of L., in 1935, was compelled by the demand of the automobile workers to charter an international union, the United Automobile Workers, the Communists already had a long record of activity in that industry. Raymond, McKie, Schmies, and others were well known as loyal fighters. There were many C.P. shop units and individual members in the plants. The T.U.U.L. had also conducted several local strikes, the Unemployed Councils had organized scores of demonstrations of the unemployed, and for 15 years the Party in its general political agitation had laid constant stress upon union organization. So that when the U.A.W., late in 1935, quit the A.F. of L. and became part of the C.I.O., the left wing was a central factor in the young union. Says Alinsky: "When Lewis turned to help the auto workers, he saw that they were being organized and led by the leftists. The leaders and organizers of the U.A.W. group in General Motors were the left wingers Wyndham Mortimer and Robert Travis. These two built the union inside the great General Motors empire. If Lewis wanted to take the auto workers into the C.I.O. he had to take their left-wing leadership."[1]

The main stroke in organizing the auto industry nationally, as we have seen previously, was the big G.M. sit-down strike of January 1937. After this resounding victory, it was only a question of gathering in the mass of auto workers now thoroughly ready for organization. It is no exaggeration to say that the G.M. strike organized the United Auto Workers. Indeed, this may also be said, within limits, of the whole C.I.O.; for this strategic strike produced such a tremendous wave of enthusiasm and fighting spirit among the workers throughout the basic

[1] Alinsky, *John L. Lewis*, p. 153.

industries that their organization into the C.I.O. unions became largely routine.

It was the left wing—Communists and their close progressive co-workers—that led the historic G.M. strike to this brilliant victory. The heart of the great strike was in Flint, Michigan. There, as Alinsky says, the union was built and led by the broad left wing, with Mortimer and Travis at the head. The center of the Flint strike was Fisher Body Plant No. 1. There the great sit-down strike began in the Michigan area, from there it spread, and there too it was won. Travis was the union organizer in Flint, where the whole strike found its decisive bulwark and organization. As the national strike progressed, the decisive question was whether or not the strikers, under the heavy pressure of the employers and the city, state, and federal governments, would abandon their sit-down and quit the plants. Had they done so, the strike would have been lost. But due primarily to the unshakable stand of the workers in Fisher Body No. 1, and the backing of the local Communist forces, the sit-down was maintained, and eventually the great strike was won. John L. Lewis and Wyndham Mortimer were the main negotiators and signers of the decisive G.M. agreement.

Nearly all of the seven members of the strike committee in the key Fisher Body No. 1 plant were Communists, and their leader, Walter Moore, was the Party section organizer in Flint. The Communist Party in Michigan, of which W. W. Weinstone was the district organizer, gave everything it had to the strike, and not without success. In the later successful general Chrysler strike and other work in further building the union, the Communists were no less active.

The auto workers, unlike the steel workers, developed their own top leadership. This was accompanied by many internal struggles and much factionalism. The auto manufacturers, resolved upon controlling the new union, took a hand in this internal strife. Consequently, at the 1936 South Bend convention, when the Dillon A.F. of L. reactionaries were cleaned out by the rank and file, the employers managed to wangle their new man, Homer Martin, into the presidency of the union. A number of left-wingers and progressives, however, were elected to the top leadership, including Mortimer, Travis, Hall, Anderson, and others. In the winter of 1938-39, Homer Martin (whose chief advisor was Jay Lovestone, a renegade from Communism), fearing he was going to be displaced by the rank and file, expelled the left-wing majority of the executive board, and with the help of a gang of thugs, took over control of the international office by force.[1] Dubinsky was a backer of Martin.

At the Cleveland convention, in April 1939, where Martin was

[1] Wyndham Mortimer in *March of Labor*, July 1951.

exposed and expelled as an agent of Ford, the left-progressives — the "Unity Caucus"—controlled three-fourths of the delegates. Murray and Hillman insisted that R. J. Thomas, whom Lewis later called a "dunder-headed blabbermouth," be elected president. This proposition, the left-progressives mistakenly agreed to accept, instead of electing a progressive to head the union, as they could have done. Murray and Hillman at the same time abolished all vice-presidencies, thus further weakening the position of the left. The main weakness of the Communists and the real progressives in this struggle was that they did not develop a sufficiently independent line, as against that of Addes and Thomas, and Murray and Hillman as well, in the general struggle against the right.

The conservative and incompetent President Thomas, with his persistent knifing of the left-progressive bloc, prepared the way for the rise of Walter Reuther to the presidency several years later. In the 1936-38 formative years of the auto union Reuther was a relatively minor figure. He had just returned from a year's visit to Soviet Russia, where, he said, he had been favorably impressed by what he saw of socialism. For a while he even pretended to be a Communist. It was with the support of the Communists that he managed to locate a job in the shops and eventually become president of the West Side local in Detroit—his main base in his later successful fight for national leadership. Reuther's inordinate ambitions and crass opportunism, however, soon led him in directions other than communism.

THE COMMUNISTS AND PROGRESSIVES IN OTHER INDUSTRIES

The broad progressive forces also displayed high initiative in the organizing work of practically all the other C.I.O. unions. In the maritime industry, on the Atlantic, Gulf, and Pacific coasts, they built the International Longshoremen's and Warehousemen's Union and the National Maritime Union, in a whole series of successful strikes from 1934 on. Harry Bridges, the outstanding figure in this situation, became C.I.O. director on the Pacific Coast. The Atlantic Coast N.M.U. leader, Joseph Curran, now a fevered redbaiter, worked closely with the Communists. The majority of the N.M.U. board were Party members. Altogether, the several new unions in the maritime industry numbered about 125,000 members by 1940.

In the textile industry the Party, as a result of its many earlier strikes and unemployed campaigns, also had many members and contacts, and they all went to work vigorously building the new United Textile Workers of America. This project was under the direct leadership of

Sidney Hillman. While quite willing to make a united front with the Communists and other progressives, Hillman always maneuvered to balk their efforts to build up a truly representative leadership.

In the radio and electrical industry the left-progressive group was the decisive organizing force that established the big United Electrical, Radio, and Machine Workers of America, now headed by Albert J. Fitzgerald, Julius Emspak, and James Matles. The first president of this union, the notorious James Carey, lost his post at the 1940 convention of the organization because he attempted to push through a resolution aimed at barring Communists and other left-wingers from holding union office. It was a mistake of the progressive forces not to have insisted then that this later-to-be extreme reactionary, who had been repudiated by his own union, be replaced as national secretary of the C.I.O. With vigorous insistence this could have been readily accomplished.

In the woods and sawmills of the Northwest, where the I.W.W. tradition was still strong, the left wing was responsible for building the C.I.O. union, the International Woodworkers of America, whose first president was Harold Pritchett, a Canadian Communist. This union was the result of a breakaway from the United Brotherhood of Carpenters.

The International Fur and Leather Workers Union, the most militant and progressive union in the needle industry, was brought into the C.I.O. when the Communists and the progressives won the leadership of the union at its convention in Chicago in 1937, and withdrew it from the A.F. of L. Organizing the fur industry completely and branching out into the unorganized leather industry, it then quickly tripled its membership. Its leader then and now is Ben Gold, brilliant veteran fighter. Irving Potash is a mainstay in this union.

The Transport Workers Union was organized mainly by the Communists. The president of this union, the redbaiting Michael Quill, at that time proclaimed himself as a leftist among the lefts. He was a pseudo-Communist. The International Union of Mine, Mill, and Smelter Workers, an organization with a great fighting tradition (dating back to the old Western Federation of Miners) and one of the most important basic unions in the United States, was also built by the broad left wing-progressive combination. And so, mainly, were the Packinghouse and Cannery Workers, the Farm Equipment and Metal Workers, the American Communications Association, United Office and Professional Workers, State, County and Municipal Workers, and the American Newspaper Guild. In the building of the other new C.I.O. unions, such as Shoe, Rubber, Aluminum, Flat Glass, etc., the Communists also did their part.

Communists were likewise pioneers, along with other progressive elements, in building many C.I.O. city and state industrial councils. Consequently the councils in nearly all the big cities—New York, Chicago, Los Angeles, Philadelphia, Milwaukee, Seattle, San Francisco, Buffalo, and elsewhere—were led by left-progressive forces, as also were a number of the state bodies—Illinois, California, Wisconsin, Indiana, Washington, and others.

By 1940 the Communists were a strong influence in the leadership of the C.I.O. This position of influence they had won, in spite of many mistakes, by clear-thinking, successful organizing work, militant fighting on picket lines, and all-around devoted service to the working class. The Communists were everywhere identified in the minds of the workers with the big organizing campaigns of these foundation years of the C.I.O. and with such hard-fought strikes as those of San Francisco, Flint, Ford, Little Steel, and the Atlantic and Pacific coast waterfronts. In the A.F. of L. unions the Communists were less strong, although about one-third of all Communist trade unionists belonged to these organizations. Main Communist positions in the A.F. of L. were in the food, painters, and machinists unions. This comparative weakness in the A.F. of L. was due to neglect of Communist work in that organization and to the concentration upon work in the C.I.O.

Communist influence in the C.I.O. ran far beyond the degree of formal leadership exercised by Party members. As we have indicated earlier, it was to be seen in the comparatively advanced political program of the C.I.O., in its progressive attitude toward the Negro workers, in the up-to-date organizational methods used in building the unions, and in the militant fighting spirit with which strikes were carried through. The Communist Party may well be proud of the role it played in the building of the C.I.O. and the unionization of the trustified industries. In view of this splendid record, charges by A.F. of L. and C.I.O. top leaders that the Communists are trying to "dominate the trade union movement," or even "to break it up," are simply ridiculous.

25. The Good Neighbor Policy
(1933-1941)

The "good neighbor" policy, Roosevelt's program toward Latin America, was a cornerstone of the New Deal. In his Inaugural Address of March 4, 1933, the president introduced this program, stating that "In the field of world policy, I would dedicate this nation to the policy of the good neighbor—the neighbor who resolutely respects himself, and, because he does so, respects the rights of others." This doctrine the president also enunciated shortly afterward in Montevideo, Uruguay, at a meeting of the American states. Thenceforth, until his death, the good neighbor policy, so far as Latin America was concerned, remained a definite part of the general Roosevelt program.[1]

Roosevelt followed up his professions of inter-American friendship and equality at Montevideo by introducing a minimum of liberalism into United States-Latin American relations. He proceeded to abolish the Platt Amendment in Cuba, which gave the United States the right to intervene in that country; he abrogated the U.S. treaty right to send troops into Mexico; he withdrew American troops from Haiti and other Caribbean countries; and he abandoned the "right" of the United States to interfere in Panama and the Dominican Republic.

These steps were widely hailed in Latin America and the United States as signifying the end of Yankee imperialism in Latin America and the beginning of a system of fraternal equality among the nations of the western hemisphere. But this, of course, was incorrect. The same fundamental imperialist-colonial relations remained between the United States and the other countries of the Americas. The "Colossus of the North" continued, under even more favorable circumstances, to dominate the economic and political life of its Latin American and Canadian neighbors. This was the net effect of the good neighbor policy. American investment remained and continued to draw huge profits, and Yankee political intervention went right on in more subtle forms, as illustrated by U.S. opposition to the overthrow of Machado in Cuba, its interference in the Gran Chaco War in South America, its support to the fascist opposition to Cardenas in Mexico, its interference in Argentina, and the like.

[1] Foster, *Outline Political History of the Americas*, pp. 430-33.

Roosevelt with his New Deal did not abolish monopoly capitalism in the United States; nor did he, with his good neighbor policy, do away with Yankee imperialism in the rest of the hemisphere. In both instances, with his liberalism, Roosevelt simply adopted a few badly-needed reforms in order to make this system of exploitation more workable. The fact is, the good neighbor policy operated so advantageously for American imperialist interests that it soon came to be endorsed by the big American monopolists as an effective imperialist policy, and their political leaders vied with Roosevelt in claiming its authorship.

The good neighbor policy was not officially designed to apply to highly industrialized Canada, although Wall Street definitely considers that country to be part of its all-American hinterland and accordingly carries on an active economic and political penetration of it. American investments in Canada now total over $6 billion and are rapidly increasing; whereas those of Great Britain are only about one-fourth as much and are steadily diminishing. American political influence is correspondingly growing in Canada, and British influence is in decline. The United States, with its many bases, has now established virtual military control over Canada, and it has the further imperialist advantage in the fact that the labor union movement of Canada is dominated by Americans, through the A.F. of L. and Railroad Brotherhoods, to which it is mainly affiliated. The C.P.U.S.A. has always co-operated closely with the Communist Party of Canada in its fight for the national independence of its country against the encroachments of Wall Street.

THE YANKEE RECORD OF EXPLOITATION AND TYRANNY

When President Monroe proclaimed on December 2, 1823, the doctrine which came to bear his name, it was primarily an attempt to prevent the newly-freed colonies of North, Central, and South America from becoming re-enslaved by the Holy Alliance (Russia, Prussia, and Austria) or by Great Britain. But even in those early years there were many American landgrabbers and expansionists who looked forward to a time when the United States would dominate the whole western hemisphere. As early as 1786 the liberal Jefferson declared, "Our confederacy must be viewed as the nest from which all of America, north and south, is to be peopled."[1] And in 1820, Henry Clay, expressing similar widely-held expansionist ideas, proposed a Yankee-run league of "all the nations from Hudson Bay to Cape Horn."[2]

1 Cited by J. F. Rippy, *Latin America in World Politics*, p. 14, N. Y., 1928.
2 Cited by A. C. Wilgus, *The Development of Hispanic America*, p. 743. N. Y., 1941.

With the growth of the United States, and especially with the development of American imperialism in the period of 1880-1900, Yankee interventionist tendencies in Latin America grew much more pronounced. The Monroe Doctrine became transformed into an instrument to lend a legal coloring to American domination of the hemisphere. The Pan American Union, a U.S.-inspired association of Latin American states under American hegemony, was organized in 1889. It was from the outset a weapon of Yankee imperialism with which to combat the British imperialists and to exploit the Latin American peoples.

As a result of the Spanish-American War of 1898 the United States seized Cuba, Puerto Rico, and the Philippines and other strategic islands in the Pacific. It was the beginning of the establishment of an American colonial empire. Then followed a whole series of gross imperialist military and political aggressions, some of the more important of which were the seizure of Panama, interference in Venezuela, occupation of Haiti, the Dominican Republic, and other Caribbean countries, invasion of Nicaragua, intervention in the Mexican Revolution, and the making and unmaking of various Latin American governments. The symbol of all this ruthless Yankee imperialism was President Theodore Roosevelt, with his "dollar diplomacy" and his "big stick," arrogantly asserting the right of the United States to police the whole western hemisphere.

Behind this extreme political and military aggression by the United States was a no less active drive for the imperialist economic penetration of Latin America. In 1900 American investments in Latin America were very small, but by 1913 they reached $173 million, and by 1930 they had skyrocketed to almost $5 billion. United States-Latin American trade developed correspondingly; by 1938 the United States was selling Latin America 39.8 percent of its imports and buying 32.8 percent of its exports.[1] These economic activities were highly advantageous to the United States, profits ranging from 10 to 50 percent. Rippy says that by the end of 1930 the bulk of the mineral resources of Latin America was owned by United States capitalists.[2] It was estimated that the United States in 1934 controlled in Latin America, "all the bauxite, a considerable part of the coal, about 90 percent of the copper, one-third of the gold, practically all of the iron ore, more than one-third of the lead, one-half of the manganese, over one-half of the petroleum, approximately one-half of the platinum, 70 percent of the silver, only one-tenth of the tin, all of the tungsten and vanadium, and two-thirds of the zinc."[3] The economic and political domination of the United States was particularly

1 S. G. Hanson, *Economic Development in Latin America*, p. 424, N. Y., 1951.
2 J. F. Rippy, *Latin America and the Industrial Age*, p. 194, N. Y., 1945.
3 Cited by Hanson, *Economic Development in Latin America*, p. 239.

marked in the Central American countries of the Caribbean area.[1]

The United States has long reaped super-profits from its big investments in Latin America. In 1951, the rich United Fruit Co. alone pulled out profits, after taxes, of $66,159,375. American concerns are now milking Latin America of at least half a billion dollars yearly. Lazaro Pena, Cuban labor leader, states that between 1913 and 1939, the imperialists (mostly the Americans) drew $6.5 billion out of Latin America and reinvested there less than $2 billion.[2]

AMERICAN IMPERIALISM GETS A "NEW LOOK"

By the time Franklin D. Roosevelt came to the presidency in March 1933, the—to Wall Street—hitherto very favorable situation in Latin America had fallen into sad disarray. The great cyclical crisis had played havoc with economic conditions. Latin America, like the United States, was flattened by the industrial holocaust; so that United States-Latin American trade fell off from $686 million in 1930 to but $96 million in 1932, and American yearly investment in the Latin American countries, which amounted to $175 million in 1929, was nothing at all during the years 1931-35.

To make matters worse, new and dangerous competitors were appearing on the horizon to contest the Latin American markets and political controls with the Yankee businessmen. These rivals were Germany, Italy, and Japan. The history of Latin America had been one long record of a developing struggle, chiefly between British and American imperialism, for economic and political supremacy, with the British slowly getting the worst of it. But especially with the rise of fascism and in view of the intense importance the fascists placed upon conquering Latin America, the Germans, Italians, and Japanese constituted an additional set of militant imperialist enemies who were a real menace to Yankee imperialism and the Latin American peoples.

Moreover, the workers and peasants of Latin America, like the toiling masses in the United States, were beginning to organize politically and in unions and to go on the march against their exploiters after the terrible years of the great economic crisis. Much of their resentment was directed against the Yankee capitalists, who everywhere were allied with the domestic big landlords and employers. The peoples were very bitter against Wall Street imperialism, which for so many years had inflicted upon them the grossest indignities and injuries.

It was to improve the position of American imperialism in this most

[1] See Victor Perlo, *American Imperialism*, Chapter 5, N. Y., 1951.
[2] Conference, World Federation of Trade Unions, Havana, June 1949.

unfavorable situation that the good neighbor policy was formulated, carrying as it did some recognition of the national independence of the Latin American states. The good neighbor policy, particularly in the latter 1930's, had some stimulating effect upon the peoples' defeat of the fascist attempts to seize the governments of Brazil and other countries, and also was a factor in uniting the Latin American peoples for the international struggle against fascism during World War II.

THE STUNTED ECONOMY OF LATIN AMERICA

Latin America is very much less developed industrially than the United States. Although that great area has adequate material resources and a population just about as large as that in the United States, nevertheless its industrial output is hardly more than 10 percent of that of the latter country. In the United States only 20 percent of the population are actual farmers, whereas throughout Latin America the average runs to about 70 percent. There are in the United States six times as many miles of highway, four times as much railway mileage, 20 times as many telephones, and 30 times as many automobiles as in all of Latin America. The production capacity of the steel industry of the United States (about 105,000,000 tons annually) is about 70 times that of the whole of Latin America (1,500,000 tons).

The economic underdevelopment of Latin America generally (some countries, such as Argentina, are more advanced, and others, like Paraguay, more backward) stems primarily from the relative incompleteness of the bourgeois revolution in these countries. The hemisphere-wide bourgeois (*i.e.* capitalist) revolution through the years 1776-1837 shattered the colonial systems of Spain, Portugal, France, and Great Britain in America. It made the American peoples politically independent; it set up a score of new states, and it gave a tremendous impulse to the development of capitalism throughout the western hemisphere.

In Latin America, however, the revolution was incomplete, in that it did not result in breaking the power of the big feudal land-owners. Consequently, down to the present time the latifundia system of immense landholdings prevails over almost all of Latin America. Small farmers hardly own more than 10 percent of the land in the aggregate, and the vast bulk of the land workers own no land at all. The big landowners, besides using incredibly backward techniques in agriculture, have deliberately checked the growth of industry. Their domination of the national governments and of the national economies has thereby restricted the growth of the characteristic capitalist, middle, and working classes. The landowners are the chief source of the many tyrannies and dictatorships that have plagued the Latin American peoples for generations. The Catholic Church, with its powerful economic, political, and ideological controls, is tied in with this reactionary big landowning system, which is the basic curse of Latin America.

Imperialist economic and political penetration of Latin America, which became an important factor from about 1880, has operated even more powerfully to hinder the growth of Latin American industry. This is because the imperialists develop only such enterprises—usually mining, transportation, and certain plantations—as serve their exploitative purposes. They pump huge profits out of the countries and rob them of their natural resources. They especially prevent the development of all industries which would produce the means of production and thus bring about an industrialization competitive with the imperialists. They also contribute to maintaining the latifundia system, both by political alliances with the landowners and by grabbing great stretches of land for themselves—examples being the vast holdings of the United Fruit Co. in Central America, the gigantic American sugar and coffee plantations in Cuba and Brazil, Ford's big plantation in Brazil, and the huge copper, coal, oil, and other mineral lands owned by United States capitalists in Chile, Peru, Brazil, and elsewhere. The American holdings in Venezuelan oil and iron are fabulously rich.

One of the worst features developed by this big landowner-imperialist system is so-called monoculture. This is the production of but one or two commodities for export by a given country, whether coffee, sugar, bananas, copper, oil, or whatnot. Thus, in five republics more than two-thirds of the total value of their exports comes from one product, in six from two products, and in five from three. The most deadly effect of monoculture is that this system prevents the development of an efficient agriculture and a rounded-out industrial economy, making the given country dependent upon the foreign imperialists for all sorts of manufactured goods; and it also leaves the various countries totally exposed to the disastrous fluctuations of world market prices for their export commodities.

Another very detrimental feature of the Latin American economy, bred of imperialist dictation, is the dependence of its foreign and domestic trade upon the interests of the dominating foreign capitalists, principally Americans. By controlling the main market for a country's given product—say Cuban sugar, Brazilian coffee, or Caribbean bananas —the United States is able to establish arbitrarily the price of these commodities, to restrict the respective countries from trading with each other or with rival imperialist competitors, and to dump its own goods upon their domestic markets at extravagant prices.

What the United States has done in the Philippines and Latin America (including Puerto Rico, an outright colony) is to build up a vast system of puppet governments more or less completely under its control. It is a lie to say that this country is opposed to colonialism. Wall Street's specific type of colonialism, in which the colonialized lands are given a shadow of political independence, is merely a more up-to-date brand, designed to confuse the people's demand for national liberation.

THE EXPLOITED AND FAMISHED PEOPLES OF LATIN AMERICA

As the result of the ferocious oppression and robbery which they have experienced for so long from landowners, local capitalists, and foreign imperialists, the peoples of Latin America have been pushed down to extremes of poverty and destitution. Wages for workers in industry average from one-tenth to one-third of what they are in the United States, while the great masses of agricultural workers in the *haciendas, estancias,* and *fazendas*—mostly Indians, Negroes, Mulattoes, and Mestizos[1]—live in a state of virtual peonage, overwhelmed with debt to the landowners.

Conditions of semi-starvation are widespread in many of the Latin American countries. "Two-thirds, if not more, of the Latin American population are physically undernourished, to the point of actual starvation in some regions," say George Soule and his associates.[2] Illness and early death are the inevitable consequences of such extreme poverty. The toiling masses are saturated with sickness, including tuberculosis, malaria, syphilis, gonorrhea, dysentery, trachoma, typhoid, hookworm, jungle fever, and many other diseases. Miguel Pereira, a Brazilian scientist, recently remarked that "Brazil is an immense hospital," and the same could be said with equal truth of many other Latin American countries. "One-half of the Latin American population," say Soule and his co-writers, "are suffering from infectious or deficiency diseases." The annual death rate in Latin America is over twice as high as it is in the United States. Mass illiteracy naturally accompanies this dreadful poverty and sickness. There are 70 million illiterates in Latin America and 50 million more who have had only one or two years of schooling.

American imperialists, because of the exploitation they practice, are largely responsible for these horrible conditions in Latin America. But, characteristically, they shrug off this responsibility, attributing Latin American poverty to what they slanderously call the shiftlessness and

---

[1] About two-thirds of the population of Latin America as a whole is non-white, and about one-half of this total is either wholly or partially of Indian descent.
[2] Soule, Efron, and Ness, *Latin America in the Future World,* p. 4, N. Y., 1945.

incompetence of these peoples. They cannot, however, evade their responsibility for the miserable conditions prevailing in Puerto Rico, which for over half a century has been completely under American domination.

When it was taken over by General Miles' forces during the Spanish-American war in 1898, Puerto Rico was promised early freedom. But this promise has been flagrantly violated and Puerto Rico has ever since remained a colony, a United States military base guarding the Panama Canal. It suffers all the typical economic ills of colonialism, as well as all its political tyranny. The island has a monoculture—sugar, and it has been prevented from developing substantial manufactures. Its trade, both foreign and domestic, is controlled and dominated by the United States. Wages are about one-third as high as they are in the United States, although the cost of living is about the same in both countries. Sickness is rampant, and the huge slums in San Juan and other Puerto Rican cities are among the worst in the world. The whole situation is a burning crime against the Puerto Rican people and a disgrace to the United States. Similar conditions prevail in the Virgin Islands, owned by the United States since 1917.

THE LATIN AMERICAN PEOPLES FIGHT AGAINST FASCISM

During the great 1929-33 economic crisis in Latin America, when unemployment ran as high as 50 to 75 percent in the various countries, the workers and peasants conducted many hard fights in order to live. After 1933, with the rise of world fascism, and particularly in view of the determined efforts of domestic reactionaries and Hitler-Mussolini agents to set up fascist governments in Latin America, these struggles of the democratic peoples took on a broader scope, a deeper intensity, and reached higher political levels. The Seventh Congress of the Comintern, with its slogan of the people's front, gave a clear political direction to this mass fight.

Among the most significant of the mass struggles in Latin America during this pre-war period was the revolutionary overthrow in 1933 of the bloody Machado tyranny in Cuba, an action which brought about many vital democratic reforms in that country. In Chile also, after long and bitter struggles, a people's front government—the first in the western hemisphere—was elected in 1938. In Brazil it was the embattled people's democratic forces that prevented the seizure of the government, during 1935-37, by the Hitler-inspired Integralistas. In Mexico, during the Cardenas regime of 1934-40, the bourgeois-democratic revolution in that country took on a new and greater vigor under the pressure of the masses. There were similar people's struggles in Argentina, Colombia, Peru,

Venezuela, and various other countries. The general result of these mass struggles was that the peoples of Latin America smashed the attempt of Hitler and Mussolini, in collusion with the local reactionaries, to seize South America.

The Communist and trade union movements were the backbone of these militant struggles. In the face of the most brutal opposition, the labor organizations had built up their strength in most of the countries. They came together in Mexico City in September 1938, and formed the Latin American Confederation of Labor (C.T.A.L.), with some four million members. This was a labor event of world-wide importance. The president of the new organization was Vicente Lombardo Toledano, who designates himself as an "independent Marxist." Among the labor notables from various countries present at the founding convention was John L. Lewis, then head of the C.I.O. The advent of the C.T.A.L. marked a deep intensification of the struggle of the workers and a general raising of their fight to a higher level.

The political leaders of the broad people's front, anti-fascist struggle throughout Latin America were the Communist parties. These parties, led by such men as Victorio Codovilla, Luis Carlos Prestes, Blas Roca, Dionisio Encina, Juan Marinello, Louis Recabarren, Rodolfo Ghioldi, Gustavo Machado, and Eugenio Gomez, began to be organized shortly after the outset of the Russian Revolution. They had been building and developing themselves mostly under conditions of sheer terrorism and illegality. They were everywhere the leaders and inspirers of the people's front and the general struggle against fascist reaction. In these countries the Social-Democrats were a negligible force, save in a few places, chiefly Argentina and Chile; also the syndicalists, once a powerful element throughout Latin America, were decidedly in decline, and the counter-revolutionary Trotskyites had but tiny grouplets here and there.

Roosevelt's pronouncement of his good neighbor policy in 1933 had a stimulating effect upon the growing democratic struggles throughout Latin America. The peoples, while antagonistic to the "Colossus of the North" as a result of much bitter experience, welcomed Roosevelt's democratic utterances, his promises of fraternal relations among all the nations of the Americas, his assurance of an end to the long-continued and barbarous intervention of the United States in the lives of its Latin American neighbors. The masses also sympathized fully with Roosevelt's developing opposition to world fascism. Roosevelt's reputation as a liberal soared all over Latin America.

On the basis of the good neighbor policy, which was replete with glowing (but mostly unfulfilled) democratic promises, Roosevelt established friendly working relations with most of the governments and with the democratic forces throughout Latin America. The latter began to interest themselves in the doings of the Pan American Union, which hitherto had been "a hissing and a by-word" throughout Latin America. There was also a new all-American co-operation of democratic elements as, for example, in the International Congress of the Democracies of America, held in Montevideo in March 1939. The general outcome of all this democratic friendliness was that when the great clash came with the fascist Axis in World War II, all the countries of Latin America, with the exception of Argentina (which finally was forced to break relations with Germany) were in the same anti-fascist war alliance with the United States.

THE COMMUNIST PARTY AND LATIN AMERICA

Lenin was a great champion of the colonial and semi-colonial peoples. Once, in 1920 he suggested a modification of Marx's famous slogan, "Workers of the World, Unite!" to "Proletarians of All Countries and Oppressed Peoples, Unite!"[1] As a Leninist organization, therefore, the Communist Party of the United States has always interested itself deeply in the struggles of the peoples suffering under the heel of the imperialist aggressor. This has been particularly true in connection with Latin America, and above all, regarding Puerto Rico and Cuba. The Party has also always supported the struggle in the Philippines. For all this is the hinterland of Yankee imperialism, and these are the direct colonies of Wall Street. This area is definitely heading toward a great anti-imperialist, national liberation revolution, much on the broad lines of the great movements now stirring other parts of the colonial and semi-colonial world. It is the proletarian duty of the Communist Party of the United States to give these peoples its untiring support in their fight.

The Communist Party of the United States, from its inception, took a firm stand against all the manifestations of American imperialism in Latin America. It worked in close cooperation with all the Communist parties in these countries. It was active in organizing the All-American Anti-Imperialist League in Mexico City in 1924, a body which fought Yankee imperialism throughout the Hemisphere. The Party especially gave vigorous support to August Cesar Sandino, the brave Nicaraguan patriot, who for five years fought off the invading U.S. Marines, only to die in 1934 at the hands of an American-trained assassin, after peace had been established.

[1] Cited in *The Communist*, Jan. 1931.

One of the major means of Wall Street's penetration into Latin America during the "twenties" was the Pan-American Federation of Labor, organized in November 1918 by the leaders of the A.F. of L. These labor imperialists used the P.A.F.L. to support every incursion of Wall Street against the peoples of Latin America. The Communists of the United States, along with those of Latin America, vigorously fought this treacherous organization. Consequently, badly discredited, the influence of the P.A.F.L. waned and after 1930 it existed (for several years longer) only on paper.

The C.P.U.S.A., throughout the years, has constantly kept the Latin American question before the American working class. It participated in many inter-American conferences with the Latin American Communist parties. It attended their conventions and welcomed their delegates to its own conventions. In New York, in June 1939, six American Communist parties held a conference and issued a statement calling upon the peoples to rally to defeat fascism.[1] The Communists were chiefly responsible for the friendly attitude taken by the C.I.O. toward the Confederation of Latin American Workers (C.T.A.L.). The question of Latin America has always been on the order of business in the journals and meetings of the Communist Party of the United States but the Party has never done enough on the question.

The general line of the various Communist parties during the Roosevelt era was to fight for "A democratic application" of the good neighbor policy in Latin America. In this pre-war period, however, certain wrong attitudes were beginning to develop on the question of Roosevelt's Latin American policy. A marked tendency grew up both in the U.S. Party and in the parties of other countries in the western hemisphere, to look away from the fact that Roosevelt, together with his liberalism, was an imperialist, and that the good neighbor policy, for all its democratic trappings, was a policy of Yankee imperialism, designed to meet a given different situation. Earl Browder, as usual, encouraged this serious right deviation. In 1942, when the false trend had become quite definite, he expressed it thus:

"There is still much to be done to dissipate the fear and suspicion of Yankee imperialism in order to create confidence throughout Latin America in the role of the United States as a leader of the United Nations. Memories of the past, however bitter they may be, of broken promises and violent intervention, of economic pressures, sharp diplomatic practices and financial exploitation, all could be removed to the archives of history and no longer play a damaging role in the present, once the peoples of Latin America felt an assurance that the 'good

[1] *The Communist*, July 1939.

neighbor' policy was something deeper than the expediency of the historical moment."[1]

The essence of this Browder statement was that the good neighbor policy was not imperialist in character and that, therefore, the peoples of Latin America should put their trust in Roosevelt. This was a dangerous position, a surrender to bourgeois-inspired illusions. While the main enemy in those years was Hitler fascism, nevertheless the policy advocated by Browder would have made the Latin American peoples put down their guard before an aggressive power, Wall Street imperialism. The United States, under the banner of the good neighbor policy, was rapidly strengthening its position in Latin America and infringing upon the rights and welfare of the peoples in that vast area. In the long run it was to prove, in the post-war period, even more menacing to the Latin American peoples than Hitlerism itself.

[1] Earl Browder, *Victory—and After*, p. 217, N. Y., 1942.

26. The Fight Against Fascism and War (1935-1939)

Immediately after Hitler took over power in Germany, one month and four days before Roosevelt was inaugurated President of the United States in March 1933, the Nazis, the agents of German big capital, launched their program of ruthless imperialist expansion. To solidify their home front, they banned the Communist and Socialist parties, seized and reorganized the trade unions and co-operatives, wiped out the rival bourgeois parties, abolished the Weimar Republic, and set up a fascist regime.

Declaring their determination to destroy the Versailles Treaty by force, the Nazis at once embarked upon a vigorous foreign policy of conquest. Rapidly they quit the League of Nations in order to have a free hand; began to rearm Germany in violation of the treaty; signed an anti-Soviet pact with Poland; engineered a fascist putsch in Austria; regained control of the Saar basin by a terroristic plebiscite; and forcibly reoccupied the Rhineland. Meanwhile, Germany's fascist allies, Italy and Japan, were busy with similar aggressions. In 1935 Italy invaded Ethiopia and subjugated that country, and Japan had been actively overrunning North China since 1931. In November 1936, Germany and Japan signed their anti-Comintern pact, "to fight communism," which Italy joined a year later.

The League of Nations stood impotent in the face of all these violent aggressions. This was because of three basic considerations: First, the ruling big capitalists of Great Britain, France, and other European countries were themselves saturated with fascist ideas, believing that Hitler, in Nazism, had found the means for finally disposing of the labor movement and for averting the danger of socialism. Second, they were sure that the war which the German fascists were obviously preparing would be directed against the U.S.S.R., and that in such a war both belligerents would about destroy each other. The big capitalists in the United States had essentially the same ideas. So they all "appeased" Hitler and his fascist allies; that is, they gave him active economic and political support. Third, the Social-Democrats reflected the moods and policies of their capitalist governments and made no fight against the advance of Hitlerism.

THE SOVIETS FOR COLLECTIVE SECURITY

The violent aggressions of Germany, Italy, Japan, and the group of satellite countries which they quickly gathered about them in Eastern Europe, manifestly threatened mankind with another world conflagration. The Hitler-Mussolini-Hirohito gang of imperialists were going to try to cut their way out of the general crisis of the world capitalist system by ruthless war and an attempt to bring the whole world under their sway. Humanity faced the most terrible threat of butchery and enslavement in its entire history.

In this grave crisis it was the Communists who came forward with the basic preventive means. True to its nature, the Socialist peace-loving country, the Soviet Union, presented the historic policy to check and defeat fascism. In the League of Nations, which the U.S.S.R. had joined toward the end of 1934 after the three major fascist aggressors had quit it, Maxim Litvinov, on behalf of the Soviet government, repeatedly proposed that the peace-loving countries get together in an international peace front and restrain the fascist aggressors. "Collective security," he called the policy.[1] This peace proposal, had it been adopted, could have nipped world fascism in the bud and prevented World War II; for at that time the fascist powers were still weak and the United States, Great Britain, France, the Soviet Union, and their friends had an overwhelming superiority in armed forces, industrial productive capacity, and natural resources.

But the capitalist powers of the West were not interested in halting Hitler and fascism, for the reasons stated. As for international Social-Democracy, true to its nature as a prop of capitalism, it followed its capitalist masters and also rejected collective security. Roosevelt, who had recognized the Soviet government in November 1933, under broad mass pressure, made a couple of gestures toward collective security. He weakly moved to support oil sanctions against Italy for invading Ethiopia, and on October 5, 1937, in Chicago, he proposed to "quarantine the aggressors." But nothing came of all this. Even these mild moves toward checking the fascist Axis met with powerful capitalist resistance in the United States. Roosevelt, therefore, refused to back the Soviet Union's peace proposal, the only practical way to achieve collective security. He let Germany and Italy run their aggressive course without challenge, and he permitted a great flood of scrap iron and other war materials to flow to Japan, at that time engaged in overrunning huge sections of

[1] Labor Research Association, *Labor Fact Book 4*, p. 215.

China. The fascist powers pushed the world toward war, and the capitalist "democratic" powers refused to halt them.

THE PEOPLE'S FRONT

Meanwhile, the Communists, who were the outstanding fighters for peace on the world scale, also took the lead in combating the fascist menace in their respective countries. This they did through the famous policy of the anti-fascist people's front. In Chapter 22 we have shown how this policy was developed at the Seventh World Congress of the Comintern in Moscow in 1935. The policy called for a united front of all those democratic elements—workers, peasants, intellectuals, small business people, Communists, Socialists, Catholics, and others—who were willing to make a common fight against fascism and war. These masses had to fight for their unions, their living standards, their democratic liberties, their very lives, and the Communists led the way in this. The Communists were giving another basic illustration of the truth that they were the leaders of the nation, as well as of the working class, in this time of dire national and international peril.

In the face of the malignant fascist-war menace, the people's front policy almost immediately scored important victories. In February 1936, the workers of France led an offensive of the broad democratic forces that smashed the domestic drive of the French fascists for power, launched a vast sit-down strike movement, increased the membership of the General Confederation of Labor (C.G.T.) from 900,000 to four million members, and that of the Communist Party from 40,000 to 270,000. They elected a modified form of people's front government in France. Simultaneously, the workers of Spain made a similar, but broader movement. On February 16, 1936, the people's front won an election victory in Spain, which raised the number of the left's seats in the parliament to 268 members, as against 205 for the reactionaries. In various other countries the people's front became a powerful force.

The Communist parties gave all possible assistance to the embattled people's front in France and Spain. But in each case a right-wing Social-Democrat became the prime minister—Leon Blum in France and Largo Caballero in Spain. From 1934 to 1939 the Second International refused ten different proposals from the Comintern for a general united front opposition to fascism, each time referring the matter to the national parties.[1] In the countries where the people's front was strong the right-wing Social-Democrats, who still held the decisive posts in the labor movement all over Western Europe, would head such movements in order to

[1] D. Z. Manuilsky, *The World Communist Movement*, N. Y., 1939.

decapitate them. The influence of Blum in France and Caballero in Spain was disastrous. The right-wing Social-Democrats everywhere added to the fascist-war menace by carrying on a poisonous campaign of Soviet-baiting.

THE SPANISH CIVIL WAR

Hitler and Mussolini, emboldened by the success of their aggressions (due to the pro-fascist policies of Britain, France, and the United States), at once set out to overthrow the People's Front Spanish Republic. On July 17, 1936, their stooge, General Franco, led a revolt in Morocco. Had the Republican government, headed then by Caballero, acted promptly, the uprising could have been speedily stamped out, but it was paralyzed by the usual Social-Democratic conservatism, so the fascist revolt gained headway. Hitler and Mussolini supplied large numbers of troops, guns, tanks, and planes to the Franco counter-revolutionaries, and soon the latter were knocking at the gates of Madrid.

In the League of Nations the U.S.S.R. repeatedly demanded collective action to halt the fascist aggression in Spain. But this was refused, and instead a policy of "non-intervention" was adopted. That is to say, while Hitler and Mussolini poured a flood of men and munitions into Spain, the various capitalist democratic countries, Great Britain, France, and the United States, obviously hostile to the Spanish Republic, assumed a hypocritical "neutral" attitude, refusing to sell war supplies to either side. Roosevelt followed this policy under the Neutrality Act of January 8, 1937, and the Embargo Act of May First of the same year. Thus the legally elected People's Front Republican Government of Spain, which under international law had every right to buy munitions anywhere with which to defend itself, was placed at a disadvantage to the fascist bandits who freely got arms from Germany and Italy. This betrayal was another gross "appeasement" of Hitler. It doomed the Spanish Republic to defeat and opened the road for World War II. The right-wing Social-Democrats of the world supported the outrageous "non-intervention" policy, while the Communists everywhere denounced it.

The Communist parties gave all possible assistance to the embattled Spanish Republic. Most important of this help, they organized the International Brigades, which were made up of Communists and other anti-fascist fighters from all over Europe—France, Poland, Italy, Germany, Bulgaria, Great Britain, and elsewhere, and also from many countries of the Americas. Fifty-four nations were represented. All told, the International Brigades were estimated to number up to about 30,000 men. Their political leader was the well-known French Communist, André

Marty. The International Brigades constituted a tower of strength in the long and heroic struggle of the Spanish people.

The C.P.U.S.A. and the Y.C.L. organized the sending of some 3,000 soldiers, many of them non-Party, to the Loyalist forces in Spain. This was a tremendous job under the circumstances. On January 6, 1937, the Abraham Lincoln Battalion was formed, and shortly afterward, the George Washington Battalion. Later they were merged into the Lincoln-Washington Battalion. The American forces, together with the British, Canadians, Irish, and other English-speaking groups, belonged to the 15th Brigade. Officers and leaders of the American volunteers included I. A. Valledor, R. H. Merriman, Hans Amlie, Leonard Lamb, Milton Wolff, Dave Doran, John Gates, Robert Thompson, Steve Nelson, Joseph Dallett, George Watt, Bill Lawrence, Saul Wellman, Joe Brandt, and others. American medical units were headed by Dr. E. K. Barsky.

Among the 3,000 Americans there were several hundred Negroes who displayed characteristic heroism throughout the bitter war. Unlike the U.S. army, which is saturated with Jim Crow and discrimination, in the International Brigades Negroes came forward as officers and in skilled military fashion led their men, both Negro and white, in battle. Many gave their lives in the gallant effort to wipe out fascism, with its hideous racism and human slavery.

The American brigade fought in the Brunete offensive, at Jarama, Quinto, Belchite, Fuentes de Ebro, Teruel, Aragon, in the Ebro offensive, and in many other battles. They gave a splendid account of themselves, and their military achievements were noted far and wide in the American press, and among the great masses of the pople, who were sympathetic to Loyalist Spain. The medical units, working under the most primitive and dangerous conditions, rendered an heroic service. Along with the soldiers from the United States there fought some 500 from Mexico, Cuba, Puerto Rico, Argentina, and the Philippines.[1] The Canadians were mainly members of the Mackenzie-Papineau Battalion, the "MacPaps." They numbered 1,300. Dr. Norman Bethune of Canada, who later served with the Chinese People's Armies, introduced the first large-scale use of the blood bank under battle conditions.

The fight of the Spanish Republic was one of the most heroic in history, but the odds against it were too great. Betrayed, outnumbered, and outgunned, the brave Loyalist fighters were gradually defeated. Madrid fell on March 28, 1939, after almost three years of desperate struggle. Four days later the Roosevelt government rushed indecently to recognize the regime of the butcher Franco and to lift the arms embargo.

[1] *The Book of the XV Brigade,* Madrid, 1938; Edwin Rolfe, *The Lincoln Battalion,* N. Y., 1939.

The casualties in the Civil War were frightfully heavy, not only from the fighting but also from the post-war massacres by the fascists. All told, Spain probably lost at least two million people killed. In Seville after the war 50,000 were shot; in Navarre, 20,000; and there were similar butcheries elsewhere.[1] Of the American volunteers, some 1,500, or about 50 percent never returned, and in the Canadian, British, and other battalions the casualties were equally heavy. Among our heroic dead were such well-known fighters as Dave Doran, Joseph Dallet, R. H. Merriman, and the young Negro leaders, Milton Herndon, Oliver Law, and Alonzo Watson.

The Communists of the United States may well be proud of the active part they took in the gallant defense of the Spanish Republic. It constituted the most glorious event in the entire life of the Party. The volunteers fought in the resolute spirit that Communists invariably have shown on the battlefields of Russia, China, and in many other parts of the world. The fight to save Spain was the fight to save the world from fascism and a second world war. It was a fight, therefore, in the interest of the American people. That fight was lost, owing to betrayal of the Spanish Republic by the western capitalist governments and by world Social-Democracy. In consequence, scores of millions of people had to die in World War II.

MUNICH AND WAR

The fascist would-be world conquerors redoubled their aggressions after the successes in the Saar, Ethiopia, China, and Spain. In February 1938, Hitler sent his *Wehrmacht* into Austria, occupying that country. At the same time he cooked up a big crisis with Czechoslovakia over alleged injustices to the German minority there. President Roosevelt suggested that an effort be made on a general scale to adjust the critical European situation, whereupon Hitler organized the notorious Munich conference of May 1938. The heads of the governments of Germany, Italy, Great Britain, and France—Hitler, Mussolini, Chamberlain, and Daladier—got together and agreed that Germany should take over the Sudetenland, which meant eventually all of Czechoslovakia. This outrageous appeasement of the fascists, the latest in a long series of similar betrayals, was hailed all over the world by bourgeois and Social-Democratic statesmen and spokesmen as establishing "peace in our time." The Communists, virtually alone in so doing, condemned Munich as a criminal sell-out and war provocation. The objective of the fascist-minded ruling classes of Britain and France at Munich was not to establish

[1] *New Republic*, July 13, 1939.

peace, but to turn Hitler's guns eastward against the Soviet Union.

During this period, on March 10, 1939, Stalin stated the peace policy of the U.S.S.R. as follows: "We stand for peace and the strengthening of business relations with all countries. . . . We stand for peaceful, close, and friendly relations with all neighboring countries which have common frontiers with the U.S.S.R. . . . We stand for the support of nations which are the victims of aggressors and are fighting for the independence of their country. . . . We are not afraid of the threats of aggressors, and are ready to deal two blows for every blow delivered by instigators of war who attempt to violate the Soviet borders."[1]

In line with this policy, the Soviet government persisted in its efforts to organize an international peace front against the fascist bandits. Time and again it proposed joint action with the western democracies to save Ethiopia, to save China, to save Spain, to save Austria, to save Czechoslovakia. But the capitalist governments of Western Europe, and the United States as well, were not interested in any such peace front and joint action. The Soviet Union therefore agreed to put into effect its mutual defense pact and to defend Czechoslovakia, with the help of France; but France demurred. The U.S.S.R. similarly offered to defend Poland when Hitler was about to attack it, but Poland refused to allow Russian troops to cross its soil. Meanwhile, the efforts of the U.S.S.R. to negotiate a mutual assistance treaty with Great Britain during early 1939 failed—the Soviets already having made similar pacts with France, China, and a dozen other countries. Tory Britain, deliberately seeking to create a German-Russian war, wanted no such pact, and its negotiations with the Russians were a swindle. The delegation that it sent to Moscow had no mandate to make a pact; it was headed by a third-line hack diplomat, and it merely stalled along for the sake of appearance.

The Soviet government repeatedly warned Great Britain that its treacherous course was impermissible. Stalin on March 10 declared that the Soviet Union was not going to be a cat's-paw to pull British chestnuts out of the fire. Similar warnings came almost weekly from Litvinov, Zhdanov, and other Soviet leaders—all of which were ignored by the British government.

Finally, seeing that it was being flagrantly betrayed by Great Britain and France (as well as by the United States), the Soviet Union moved for peace on its own account by signing on August 24, 1939, a 10-year pact of non-aggression with Germany. Molotov said of this agreement: "The decision to conclude a non-aggression pact between the U.S.S.R. and Germany was adopted after military negotiations with France and Great Britain had reached an impasse . . . the conclusion of a pact of mutual

[1] Joseph Stalin, *From Socialism to Communism in the Soviet Union*, p. 7, N. Y., 1939.

assistance could not be expected [and] we could not but explore other possibilities for insuring peace and eliminating the danger of war between Germany and the U.S.S.R."[1] The Soviet Union was criticized by its enemies for this action. Later events showed, however, that the 22 months of breathing space gained by the U.S.S.R. through the pact, by enabling it to arm itself effectively, were a decisive factor in winning the eventual world war. The charge that during the pact the Soviets helped Hitler is a lie. The latter found the pact a hindrance to his plans—hence his invasion of the U.S.S.R.

Meanwhile, Hitler, who had been boiling up a big crisis with Poland, undertook to solve it by marching into that country on September 1, 1939. World War II, which had its beginnings in the invasions of China, Ethiopa, Spain, Austria, and Czechoslovakia, was now a reality.

THE UNITED STATES AND THE WAR

With the development of the aggressive fascist expansionist drive of German, Japanese, and Italian imperialism, during the immediate pre-war years, the general policy of American imperialism (with certain differences within the capitalist ranks) was to direct the coming war blow against the U.S.S.R. This explains the American government's "appeasement" of Hitler, and also its endorsement of the Munich sell-out. When the war against the West actually began, however, the split in the American bourgeoisie, which had been more or less in evidence all through the great economic crisis (see Chapter 23) and in the pre-war years, became more pronounced. The Roosevelt group took a line of co-operation with Britain, while the Republicans and Tory Democrats gave indirect support to Hitler. Beneath these differences, however, American imperialism was basically aiming at securing the world predominance of the United States through the weakening of the U.S.S.R., Germany, and Japan, and the accentuated break-up of the British empire as a result of the war.

When Roosevelt brought about the long-delayed recognition of the Soviet Union on November 16, 1933, he was probably motivated chiefly by the need, in fighting the economic crisis, to develop an extensive trade with that country. But all through the pre-war crisis years he steadily refused to join in the repeated proposals of the Soviet Union to establish a system of international collective security—to save China, Ethiopia, Spain, Austria, and Czechoslovakia from the maw of advancing fascist powers and to avert a world war. Obviously, he, too, was not anxious

[1] V. M. Molotov, *The Meaning of the Soviet-German Non-Aggression Pact*, pp. 6-7, N. Y., 1939.

to divert Hitler's preparations and threats of war from the East.

When war in Europe began, the Roosevelt Administration adopted the line of an informal alliance with Great Britain (a combination which it figured on controlling). This pro-British policy was largely explainable by the fact that of the total of almost $12 billion U.S. foreign investments at the time no less than 42 percent were inside the British Empire. Besides this big stake in the British Empire, Roosevelt also considered that the rise of militant German-Italian-Japanese fascist imperialism was a menacing threat to the position of American imperialism in Europe, the Far East, and Latin America. To avert this threat, he pushed aggressively the arming of the United States. He adopted a policy of active co-operation with Britain and France, which went through advancing stages from "aid to Britain" and "the arsenal of democracy," to "all means short of war," and finally to war itself.

The Republican-Tory Democrat opposition to Roosevelt, which had the support of the bulk of big capital, repudiated his pro-British policy and followed what amounted to a line of pro-German support. This was because this opposition, saturated with fascist ideas, favored a partial victory or a stalemate in Europe, believing that the United States was powerful enough to take care of itself in a fascist world. Its planned-for objective was a debilitating war between Germany and the Soviet Union, with the capitalist countries more or less supporting the former. It also looked for a growing break-up of the British Empire. The anti-Roosevelt forces were alarmed, however, by the advance of Japanese imperialism in China, which was imperiling their chosen field for imperialist expansion in the Far East, and they therefore favored an all-out war against Japan. In view of the strong anti-fascist and peace sentiments among the masses, even limited open support of the Axis powers was impossible; hence, the anti-Roosevelt opposition followed a policy of "isolationism" toward Europe. This, in fact, consisted of giving covert support to Hitler, and of opposing every form of aid to Great Britain and of collaboration with the Soviet Union.

All the fascist forces of the country rallied to this opposition as to a magnet. The Hearsts, Coughlins, Winrods, Smiths, Ku Klux Klanners, the men of Wall Street who had tried to get General Smedley D. Butler to organize an army of 500,000 veterans to march on Washington, the German-American Bund, the fascist groups among the national minorities —they were all there. "Dr. Birkhead counted 119 pro-fascist organizations in the United States in 1936 and estimated that there were probably more than 250 of such organizations, having connections with at least 5,000,000 people."[1] In June 1938, the so-called House Committee on Un-

---

[1] A. B. Magil and Henry Stevens, *The Peril of Fascism*, p. 280. N. Y., 1938.

American Activities, headed by Martin Dies, was set up and began its pro-fascist campaign of thought control. The fascist danger in the United States reached the highest level it had yet achieved in the immediate pre-war years.

The Communist Party collided head on with the pseudo-"isolationism" of the pro-Hitler Republican-Tory Democrat opposition. It also opposed the pro-British line of the Roosevelt Administration, while actively supporting its domestic reforms. The Party fought for world peace, and it insisted that the only way this could be assured was on the basis of international collective security, as proposed by the Soviet Union. Its main slogans were against fascism and imperialist war. It declared, "Keep America out of war by keeping war out of the world!" The Socialists and Trotskyites, buried in deep hatred of the U.S.S.R., found themselves virtually in the camp of the reactionary "isolationists."

THE AMERICAN PEOPLE—ANTI-FASCIST AND ANTI-WAR

During these crucial pre-war years the workers and other democratic strata of the American people were overwhelmingly opposed to fascism, particularly in its more obvious European types. But as for the trickier American varieties, hiding under pretenses of democracy and peace, their judgment was not always infallible. They wanted to aid those peoples who were being assailed and conquered by the fascist states, but generally in their organizations they did not rise to the heights of demanding a system of world collective security to restrain and defeat the aggressors. They were largely isolationist. Above all, they were flatly opposed to war.

At its 1938 convention, the A.F. of L., always cultivating the conservative bourgeois currents among the workers, condemned Hitler and Mussolini fascism, but decided to give the infamous Dies Committee "all possible assistance." It did, however, vote down the attempt of Matthew Woll and John P. Frey to have the New Deal condemned as "socialistic." But it rejected the O'Connell Peace Act and the "policy of 'quarantining the aggressors.'" It favored a boycott against Germany and Japan. Under the leadership of John L. Lewis, and especially the influence of the Communists, the C.I.O., at its first constitutional convention in Pittsburgh, in November 1938, gave a ringing endorsement to the New Deal and also to the policy of collective security.[1]

The Negro people were in the forefront of the forces fighting against fascism and imperialist war. The National Negro Congress held its

[1] Labor Research Association, *Labor Fact Book 5*, p. 134, N. Y., 1941.

second general convention in Philadelphia in May 1937. It was a broad united front movement of 1,200 delegates, with figures such as Walter White (N.A.A.C.P.), Philip Murray, Norman Thomas, and T. J. Kennedy (U.M.W.A.) speaking there. Its mainspring was the Communist Party. The organization was a power in every anti-fascist, peace-striving movement, as well as in the fight for the special economic and political demands of the Negro people. The Southern Negro Youth Congress, an offshoot of the N.N.C., exercised considerable influence among the Negro people in the South, taking a strong position against fascism and for collective security.

A development of major importance in the life of the Negro people and the fight against fascism during this period was the formation of the Southern Conference for Human Welfare in Birmingham, Alabama, in November 1938. This organization had the backing of the Roosevelt Administration, which had called the South "the nation's economic problem number one." Its founding convention attracted 1,250 delegates, among them many of the most outstanding liberals and labor men in the South. The Communist Party was officially represented and exercised much influence in the organization. Dr. Frank Graham was chairman, and John P. Davis, of the National Negro Congress, was a member of the council of 15 chosen to head the organization. The convention laid down a program calling for jobs, civil rights, and federal education for Negroes, also taking a sharp stand against lynching and other persecutions of the Negro people. For the next several years the S.C.H.W. was a considerable force against the hidebound tories of the South.[1]

The American Youth Congress, representing the bulk of the organized young people of the United States, held yearly conventions during the pre-war period. It took generally an advanced stand against fascism and for collective security. This, despite the disruptive efforts of Catholics, Social-Democrats, and Trotskyites, whose sole objective in the organization was to weaken the Communists' influence even if they had to wreck the Congress in the attempt. At the fifth convention of the A.Y.C. in July 1939, in an ill-advised attempt to fend off the charge of communism being directed against the organization, a resolution was adopted opposing dictatorship "whether Communist, fascist, Nazi, etc." Among its many mass activities, the Congress organized a pilgrimage to Washington of 35 national youth organizations and youth-serving agencies "for jobs, health, and education." In August 1938, the Second World Youth Congress was held in Poughkeepsie, New York, with delegates from 53 countries, representing 40 million young people. In all these activities

[1] Robert W. Hall in *The Communist*, Jan. 1939.

the Young Communist League took a very energetic leading part.

One of the most important united front organizations of this period in the fight against the rising menace to democracy and peace, was the American League Against War and Fascism, of which Dr. Harry F. Ward was the national chairman. It was established on September 29, 1933, in New York. After its convention of November 1937, in Pittsburgh, the organization was known as the American League for Peace and Democracy. The Communist Party was affiliated with the former but not with the latter. In both it had much influence. This was a large united front organization, carrying on a general struggle for economic and political demands, for the rights of the Negro people, for democracy, and for collective security. Women were very active in the organization, as in all others fighting the fascist-war danger. The League held big annual congresses, with 2,000 to 3,500 delegates, representing as many as four million people. At these gatherings there were large delegations of Negroes, youth, and trade unionists. At its 1937 convention, for example, about 30 percent of the entire labor movement was represented, either by endorsements or by direct delegates. The League was a major influence in the fight for peace and democracy.

THE ELECTIONS OF 1938

The mid-term elections of 1938 were fought out in an atmosphere of intense class struggle. The economic situation was bad, the cyclical crisis of 1937 having again knocked the bottom out of industry. There was wide discontent at the inadequacy of the New Deal reforms. At least ten million workers walked the streets idle, while capitalist profits soared. Obviously, the Keynesian "pump-priming" policy had failed. Although Roosevelt's huge subsidies to industry and to "strengthen the purchasing power of the workers" had added $16 billion to the national debt, they could not liquidate the "depression of a special kind." Only the approach of war, causing an enormous output of munitions, did that.

The big employers, violently antagonized by the organizing campaigns and strikes of the C.I.O., viciously attacked Roosevelt and the New Deal. At the same time, they demagogically promised a whole row of reforms to offset those of Roosevelt. Organized labor was badly divided in the elections. The A.F. of L. reactionaries were doing their best to kill off the C.I.O., and they also condemned Labor's Non-Partisan League, to which many A.F. of L. elements were affiliated, as being "as dual to the non-partisan political policy of the A.F. of L., as the C.I.O. is to the A.F. of L. itself."

The Communist Party put on an energetic campaign. It fought for a democratic front of all progressive elements. It concentrated its fire against the reactionaries, while criticizing the Roosevelt policies, although inadequately. While putting up candidates of its own in various localities, it also supported "progressives" upon the Democratic and other tickets, including a few Republicans. It actively advanced the O'Connell Peace Bill (H.R. 527), designed to implement Roosevelt's "quarantine the aggressors" speech. Its central slogan was, "For Jobs, Security, Democracy, and Peace."

The Republicans had the best of it in the elections. They won 79 new seats in the House and eight in the Senate, as well as numerous governorships. Although both houses of Congress remained nominally Democratic, the Republican-Tory Democrat alliance dominated them. In the 1939 session, therefore, reaction proceeded to slash into the New Deal, reducing W.P.A. wages, cutting taxes of the well-to-do, lavishly financing the Dies Committee, supporting various anti-sedition and anti-foreign-born measures, and refusing to amend the Neutrality Act and thus to allow the United States to join in a concerted effort with other countries to prevent war.

A favorable by-product of this generally reactionary election, however, was the release in California by the newly-elected New Deal Governor Olson of Tom Mooney (on January 7, 1939) and Warren K. Billings (in October 1939). Mooney, his health ruined by 22 years in prison, did not long survive; he died on March 6, 1942. He was a warm sympathizer of the Communist Party. Matt Schmidt (of the McNamara case) was also paroled (in August 1939) but the heroic J. B. McNamara was left to perish in jail. He died on March 8, 1941, in Folsom prison, a member of the Communist Party, after serving 29 years. Four of the Scottsboro Boys were also released on January 24, 1937, leaving five still in jail. Ray Becker, the last of the I.W.W. Centralia prisoners of 1919, was also set free in September 1939.[1]

THE GROWTH OF THE COMMUNIST PARTY

During the pre-war years here under consideration, years of rapid organization of the working class, the Communist Party made substantial progress. And this in the face of the growing Browder neglect of opportunities for Party building and even opposition to such work, as we have seen. The tenth Party convention in New York, in May 1938, registered 75,000 members for the Party and 20,000 for the Y.C.L. This was an increase in two years of 35,000 for the former and 10,000 for the latter. An

[1] Labor Research Association, *Labor Fact Book 5*, p. 212.

important occasion at the convention was the announcement of the establishment of the *People's World* on January 1, 1938, in San Francisco, and of the *Midwest Daily Record*,[1] on February 12, 1938, in Chicago.

The Party's progress was based upon an essentially sound political policy, although it made numerous individual errors, some of the most important of which we have indicated in passing. The Party conducted a militant fight for the workers' economic interests, for their organization into trade unions, for the rights of the Negro people, for the demands of the youth and women, and especially against the growing menace of fascism and war. In all these spheres the Party displayed initiative and leadership. It was greatly helped in developing the generally correct political line because of its active participation in the Communist International, where it had the benefit of the counsels of the leading Marxists of the world. Particularly helpful to the Party during these years were the books, *Foundations of Leninism* and *History of the Communist Party of the Soviet Union*, by Joseph Stalin, and also the writings of Georgi Dimitrov. The *History* especially is an encyclopedia of Marxism-Leninism and a work of immense educational value. It gives not only a history of the great Russian Revolution, but also of the developing theoretical work of Lenin. It contains a fine exposition of Marxist dialectical materialism.

An important element in the Party's expanding influence during these years—an influence which ran far beyond the scope of its membership totals and its votes in elections—was its united front policy. The Party was learning how to unite and lead the masses in their everyday struggles over burning issues. An important feature of this policy, stressed at the tenth Party convention, was the "outstretched hand" to the Catholic workers. This was in line with the Communist challenge all over the world to the attempt of the Catholic hierarchy, on the basis of their religious controls, to mobilize their huge following into the camp of reaction.

Communists, of course, have the same basic economic and political interests as Catholic workers. That friendly co-operation between the two groups is possible has been amply demonstrated by the fact that literally tens of millions of Catholics, in the post-World War II period, have joined the Communist Parties and Communist-led trade unions in France, Italy, Poland, Czechoslovakia, East Germany, Latin America, and elsewhere. American Communists have also always worked in a most co-operative spirit with Catholic workers in the C.I.O. and other labor unions.

A very important development at the tenth convention also was the

[1] *Midwest Daily Record* was discontinued as a daily on Nov. 13, 1939, and ran as a weekly until March 2, 1940.

enunciation of the policy of the "democratic front." Previously, since 1935, the Party had held the position that the farmer-labor party was the specific American form of the people's front. With the development of strong left trends in the Roosevelt wing of the Democratic Party, however, the conception of the people's front was broadened to include this Democratic element, along with such bodies as the American Labor Party, Minnesota Farmer Labor Party, Washington Commonwealth Federation, the trade unions, the National Negro Congress, the American Youth Congress, and so on. This "democratic front," says the main resolution of the convention, "under the conditions prevailing in our country, represents the beginning of the development of a real people's front against reaction and fascism." This was essentially what later became known as the "Roosevelt coalition."

The democratic front was undoubtedly a correct policy, and only by the grossest distortion of it was Browder able, a few years later, to arrive at his monstrous revisionist policy. He did this by rejecting an independent line for labor and following the lead of Roosevelt; by subordinating the class struggle to Roosevelt's policies; by refusing to build solidly the alliance of workers, Negro people, working farmers, and poor city middle classes; by failing to promote labor's influence and eventual leadership in the coalition; by repudiating the independent policy and vanguard role of the Communist Party; by failing to build the Party; and by the gradual watering down and elimination of Marxist ideology from the Party's mass work.

27. World War II: The Early War Phases (1939-1941)

World War II, like the first world war and the great economic crisis of 1929-33, was a manifestation of the deepening general crisis of world capitalism. It was a great explosion of imperialist contradictions, within the framework of the rapidly decaying capitalist system. The war was precipitated as a murderous struggle among the big capitalist powers for control of world markets, resources, territory, and populations—for a political redistribution of the world. In its largest aspect, the war was also an attempt by reactionary big capital in the major countries to destroy democracy and socialism and to establish a fascist world in which the workers would be merely so many robots. The chief aggressors were the German, Japanese, and Italian imperialists who, after wiping out democracy in their own countries, directly initiated the conflict by brazenly setting out to conquer the world. But the imperialists of Great Britain, France, and the United States, through their governmental appeasement of the fascist powers, also bore a large share of the war guilt. Before the war was finished, the capitalist war criminals were responsible for the deaths of at least 50 million people, for a vast ocean of mass suffering, and for the destruction of $4,000 billion in wealth.[1]

From the outset the war also had a deep people's content. This was the struggle of the democratic masses, battling in self-defense against enslavement by the fascist imperialists of the Axis powers. It was this growing struggle of the peoples against slavery that finally put the stamp of a people's war, a just war, upon World War II as a whole. Stalin, after showing that the hostilities had originated in the irreconcilable antagonisms between the two camps of big imperialist powers, thus characterized the war: "Unlike the first world war, the second world war against the Axis states from the very outset assumed the character of an anti-fascist war, a war of liberation, one of the aims of which was also the restoration of democratic liberties. The entry of the Soviet Union into the war against the Axis states could only enhance and did enhance, the anti-fascist and liberation character of the second world war."[2] As the great war developed, the peoples fought with desperation against

[1] Labor Research Association, *Economic Notes*, Oct. 1951.
[2] Joseph Stalin, *For Peaceful Coexistence*, p. 8, N. Y., 1951.

the most bloody and menacing tyranny the world had ever known. They fought for their civil rights, their living standards, their labor unions, their national independence, their very lives.

In the early, imperialist-dominated stages of the war, Communist policy called for defense of the invaded peoples (in China, Spain, Ethiopia, Poland, Czechoslovakia and elsewhere), prevention of the spread of the war, and for a democratic peace. After the involvement of the Soviet Union, which drastically changed the character, scope, and perspectives of the war in a democratic direction, the Communists militantly supported the prosecution of the war, to the overwhelming defeat of the fascist enemy.

THE "PHONY" WAR

World War II proper began with Hitler's attack upon Poland, on September 1, 1939. The war was led on both sides by imperialist governments. Hitler's powerful, highly mechanized army shattered the Polish resistance in three weeks, and the fascist Polish government, cowardly taking to its heels, fled across the border, leaving the country to its fate. Hitler, therefore, speedily fanned out his forces all over western Poland. Meanwhile, the U.S.S.R., in self-defense in the face of the advancing Nazi troops, took over eastern Poland, essentially up to the so-called Curzon Line, which many years before had been designated by a League of Nations commission as the proper demarcation point in the Soviet-Polish border dispute. The revolutionary peoples of Lithuania, Latvia, and Esthonia, who had been torn away from Russia twenty years before by the Versailles Treaty, proceeded to rid themselves of their pro-Nazi governments and voted to resume their affiliation with the U.S.S.R.

After the fall of Poland the so-called "phony war" set in. Great Britain and France, which were both pledged to defend Poland, never stirred to help that assailed country. Obviously these two great powers were utterly dumbfounded by the unwanted situation confronting them. Through several years they had systematically "appeased" and built up Hitler's Germany and its armed forces, in the full expectation that this great might would be used to destroy the hated Soviet Union. But now, by the unexpected turn of events, these very forces were being turned into a destructive drive against themselves, while the Soviet Union stood unscathed. The British-French-American imperialists had been hoist by their own petard. They had developed a "wrong war"; now they must needs transform it into the "right war" against the Soviet Union. This murderous scheme was their goal during the next six months, during the "phony war" period, when neither side in the conflict made a military move against the other.

Hitler had his own strategy for world conquest. He would have gladly united with the western powers for an all-out attack against the U.S.S.R., could he have made a satisfactory bargain with them—this was the motive of the Hess flight to England, and Goebbels hammered on it all through the war. There were two great obstacles which prevented such an agreement, however; namely, the antagonistic imperialist ambitions of the western powers and the powerful anti-fascist spirit of their working class, led or heavily influenced by the Communist parties. Moreover, the arrogant Hitler believed Germany was strong enough to defeat all its imperialist rivals, plus the Soviet Union. His war plans, therefore, conflicted directly with those of his western capitalist rivals. His strategic objectives were first to knock out Britain and France and their satellites as the easiest marks, and then later to defeat the Soviet Union. Thus, he hoped to kill two birds with one stone; he would gain the productive capacity of western Europe and he would not have to share with Britain and France his anticipated rich plunder of the Soviet Union. As for the task of beating the Soviet Red Army, Hitler had no doubt that this would be a small chore for his powerful *Wehrmacht*.

While the western imperialists, after the collapse of Poland, were trying desperately to shift the war away from themselves and against the U.S.S.R., the Finnish-Soviet war broke out on November 30, 1939. The war was immediately caused by Finnish incursions across the Soviet borders, but at bottom it was a British-French provocation, an attempt to unite the armed capitalist world against the U.S.S.R. in a frenzied anti-Communist war crusade. Finland had been armed by Great Britain, and its famous fortifications on the Soviet frontier were built by British engineers. The Finnish government was run by the typically fascist clique of the ex-tsarist general, "Butcher" Mannerheim, with the help of a particularly degenerated group of Social-Democratic leaders, all of whom were also tied in with Hitler.

The Finnish-Soviet war lasted until March 12, 1940. Upon that date the U.S.S.R., after smashing the "impregnable" Mannerheim Line, made a fair and democratic peace with Finland. During the war period the wildest agitation against the Soviet Union was carried on in Great Britain, France, Scandinavia, and the United States. Fascist Finland was pictured as an abused democratic country, and the U.S.S.R. was expelled from the League of Nations as an "aggressor." Fantastic stories were broadcast about Finnish military exploits in the war. Volunteer anti-Soviet armed forces were raised in Britain, France, and elsewhere. In the United States, where a frenzied pro-Finland incitement raged,

President Roosevelt denounced Russia and granted Finland a $10 million loan, while reactionaries and confused liberals cried out for general war against the U.S.S.R. But later on, to the embarrassment of all its friends in the western world, the government of "democratic" Finland clearly displayed its true fascist colors by fighting on the side of the Axis powers in World War II.

Hitler, as remarked earlier, had his own war plan, and it was not based upon co-operation with the western capitalist nations. When he was all prepared, he launched his crushing attack upon the western countries. His armies invaded Denmark and Norway on April 9, 1940, and finished off those countries in a few days. By May 28th of the same year, *Der Fuehrer's* forces had smashed the "invincible" French army, forced the Low Countries out of the war, and driven the British army into the sea at Dunkirk, France. The capitalist governments of western Europe, with their ruling classes and army officers corps saturated with fascism, callously betrayed their peoples and crumbled before the attack of Nazi Germany.

AMERICAN REACTIONS TO THE WAR

While highly sympathetic to the peoples attacked by the fascist aggressors, the American people were sharply opposed to the United States entering the war. Several Gallup polls, between September 1939 and May 1940, indicated that over 96 percent of the American people opposed American participation in the war.[1] All the mass organizations reflected this general anti-war sentiment. At its 1939 convention, in October, the A.F. of L. declared, "As for our own country, we demand that it stay out of the European conflict, maintaining neutrality in spirit and act." The C.I.O. convention, meeting at the same time, took a similar stand, stating that "Labor wants no war nor any part of war."[2]

The three major farm organizations—the American Farm Bureau Federation, the National Grange, and the National Farmers Union—assembled in their conventions during November 1939, protested against the current high military expenditures and opposed the United States entering the war. Such united front organizations as the American League for Peace and Democracy, National Negro Congress, American Youth Congress, League of American Writers, Southern Congress for Human Welfare, and the like, also went on record against United States participation in the war. When President Roosevelt, therefore, two days after

[1] Labor Research Association, *Labor Fact Book 5*, p. 57.
[2] Congress of Industrial Organizations, *The C.I.O. and the War*, Washington, D. C., 1939.

THE "PHONY WAR" PHASE   387

the invasion of Poland, declared that the attitude of the American government toward the war would be one of neutrality, he was undoubtedly supported by the great masses of the people.

The powerful pro-fascist elements in the United States took a position of so-called neutrality toward the war. But this was of a very thin variety. Actually their line was to prevent the American people from aiding in any way the invaded nations of Europe and Asia, and at the same time themselves to give all possible assistance to the fascist aggressors. To this end they systematically cultivated and exploited the strong and traditional isolationist sentiments among the people.

THE COMMUNIST POSITION ON THE WAR

On the day Hitler attacked Poland, thus precipitating World War II, the National Committee of the Communist Party was holding an enlarged session in Chicago in honor of the twentieth anniversary of the founding of the Party in that city. Regarding the war, the National Committee declared, through the general secretary's report, that "The American government cannot take sides in the imperialist rivalries which directly led up to the invasion of Poland. But it can, and must, intervene jointly with the Soviet Union on behalf of peace, on behalf of the national independence of Poland, on behalf of a peace policy which would prevent the realization of new Munich betrayals."[1] This was an unclear position.

On September 19, 1939, the National Committee of the Communist Party issued a formal statement on the war.[2] It said, "The war that has broken out in Europe is the Second Imperialist War. The ruling capitalist and landlord classes of all the belligerent countries are equally guilty for this war. This war, therefore, cannot be supported by the workers. It is not a war against fascism, not a war to protect small nations from aggression, not a war with any of the character of a just war, not a war that workers can or should support. It is a war between rival imperialisms for world domination." The Party called for "maximum support to China and to all oppressed peoples in their struggle against fascism, for freedom and national independence." It urged the forging of "the Democratic Alliance of the workers, toiling farmers, and middle classes against the economic royalists and imperialist warmakers." It would fight to "protect and improve living standards, democratic liberties, and the right to organize and strike." It called for support of "the peace policy of the Soviet Union—the land of Socialist democracy,

[1] Earl Browder, *Unity for Peace and Democracy*, p. 20, N. Y., 1939.
[2] *The Communist*, Oct. 1939.

progress, peace, and national liberation." The central slogan was, "Keep America Out of the Imperialist War."

This attitude of opposition to the war in its early stages, when the imperialists dominated it, was in accord with the position of the Communists all over the world. On November 7th, the twenty-second anniversary of the Russian Revolution, when the political leadership of the western allies' war forces was still in the hands of the British and French imperialists, the Communist International issued a manifesto on the war, entitled *Peace to the People*. The Comintern characterized the war as "an unjust, reactionary, imperialist war, which the ruling circles of Britain, France, and Germany are waging for world supremacy." It stated, "The bourgeoisie began this war, because they became entangled in the insurmountable contradictions of the capitalist system and are trying to solve these contradictions by means of new wars." This war, the bourgeoisie would not have begun or waged, "had it not been aided by the treacherous top leaders of the Social-Democratic parties. . . . The working class cannot support such a war." The statement declared, "Down with the imperialist war," and it called upon the proletariat, while defending its living standards, organizations, and liberties, to "demand the immediate cessation of the predatory, unjust, imperialist war."[1]

The Communist policy was not one of isolationism or neutrality, but of dynamic struggle to defend the rights of the conquered peoples, to prevent the spread of the war, and to bring the war to the quickest possible democratic conclusion. It was along this general line that the C.P.U.S.A. conducted its fight in the first phase of the war, between September 1939 and June 1941.

During this period, among the many peace activities backed by the Communist Party was the American Peace Mobilization. This organization was formed in Chicago, on August 31, 1940, at a great united front convention of trade unions, youth organizations, Negro groups, women's clubs, fraternal societies, etc. There were present some 6,000 delegates from 39 states, representing a total membership of about 12 million. Along with defending the economic and political rights of the American toiling masses, this big movement fought against the further extension of the war and "For a People's Peace. For a peace without indemnities, without annexations, based upon the right of all people in subjugated or colonial countries to determine their own destinies."[2]

[1] *The Communist*, Dec. 1939.
[2] Labor Research Association, *Labor Fact Book 5*, p. 58.

ROOSEVELT HEADS TOWARD WAR

Although President Roosevelt at the war's beginning had pledged the country to a policy of neutrality, he at once began to orientate toward supporting the western powers against the Berlin-Rome-Tokyo Axis. A whole body of legislative and executive orders started to take shape, designed to recruit large armed forces, to mobilize industry and the workers for war production, to finance the military effort, to give aid to the western powers, and to curb all opposition to the war. This war program became much more definite when in the spring of 1940 Hitler's *Wehrmacht* began to overturn and break up the rotten governments and fascist-saturated armies of Britain, France, and their allies.

On November 4, 1939, Congress amended the Neutrality Act of 1937, and the eventual great flood of munitions to Great Britain began. At first this operated according to the so-called cash-and-carry-plan, whereby the western allies could get whatever supplies they could pay for. Fifteen months later, however, beginning on March 11, 1941, this was followed by the Lend-Lease Act, which conferred upon the president dictatorial power with regard to the disposition of American war materials. According to this law, the president was authorized to transfer the whole or any part of U.S. naval and army equipment to other countries and to place new defense production at their disposal, upon such financial terms as the president saw fit to impose. This direct aid to the Allies was supplemented by such measures as the defense pacts with Canada, on August 18, 1940, and with Great Britain, on September 2, 1940, by which that country was given fifty destroyers in return for granting the United States 99-year leases on bases in her colonies all the way from Newfoundland to Guiana. In March 1941, a $7 billion aid-to-Britain bill was passed.[1]

Industrial mobilization was also pushed energetically. The United States was now becoming "the arsenal of democracy." To bring some faint traces of order into the characteristic capitalist production chaos, the government set up the National Defense Advisory Commission, headed by William S. Knudsen, president of General Motors. When this failed, the president established the Office of Production Management on January 7, 1941, with Knudsen and Sidney Hillman as co-chairmen. On May 27th, Roosevelt declared an unlimited national emergency. Intense propaganda was also instituted to speed up the workers. The general result of these combined efforts was that production began to climb. Unemployment largely subsided. War put into operation the industries which capitalism otherwise could not get under way. Whereas in 1939 the gross national product was $88.6 billion, by 1941 it had

[1] Labor Research Association, *Labor Fact Book* 5, p. 24.

reached $120.5 billion. Congress poured out huge appropriations to finance the mounting production and the other war expenses. These soared from $931.5 million in 1938 to $8.2 billion in 1941.

The traditional volunteer system for recruiting manpower for the armed services was quickly superseded by the principle of compulsion, for the first time in American peacetime history. On September 16, 1940, therefore, the president signed the Selective Training and Service Act, submitting some 16,500,000 men, aged from 21 to 35, to conscription. Most of the war measures in Congress had been adopted with top-heavy majorities, but this one, confronting widespread popular resistance, faced a one-third opposition vote in Congress.

THE 1940 ELECTIONS

In the midst of these far-reaching preparations for war the presidential elections of 1940 took place. The Democrats nominated Roosevelt, with Henry A. Wallace, Secretary of Agriculture, for vice-president. The Republicans picked out for their candidates Wendell L. Willkie and Senator Charles L. McNary. Willkie, formerly a Democrat, was a Morgan man and previously the head of a monopoly, the Commonwealth and Southern Corp. A "Wall Street liberal," he saw eye to eye with Roosevelt on many phases of domestic and foreign policy. That this type of liberal was able to win the Republican nomination (against Senator Taft) signified that the "isolationist," pro-Hitler leaders of the Republican Party had passed into a temporary eclipse because of the powerful mass alarm at the startling victories which Hitler's armies were then winning in Europe.

Although the Republican Party platform assailed the New Deal, Willkie's attitude was, in substance, that he would, if elected, out-New-Deal Roosevelt. In a speech at Elwood, Indiana, Willkie quoted the precise words of President Roosevelt as expressing their common stand on domestic and foreign policy. As the election approached, however, Willkie realized that he could not be elected with any such me-too stand. So he demagogically appealed to reactionary anti-red prejudices by declaring that Roosevelt had "Communistic tendencies," and he also tried to misuse the peace sentiments of the masses by stating that Roosevelt was forcing the country into the war. In addition, he made a big fight against Roosevelt's breaking of the two-term tradition.

Roosevelt, who assured the people that he would not lead their sons into war, was duly elected for his third term. He carried 38 states with 449 electoral votes, while Willkie won in only 10 states with 82 electoral votes. Roosevelt's plurality in 1940, however, was much reduced from that of the elections of 1936, dropping from 10,797,090 to 4,938,711.

The Communist Party, at its eleventh convention held in New York City, beginning on May 30, 1940, put up as its presidential candidates Earl Browder and James W. Ford. Meeting much local resistance, however, from the American Legion and other reactionary organizations, the Party succeeded in getting on the ballot in only 23 states, being barred by one device or another in New York, Illinois, Ohio, Indiana, Missouri, and other important states. This accounted for the Party's low election vote of 46,251. The Party centered its main fight around the slogans, "Keep the United States out of the imperialist war" and "For a people's peace." It also made a vigorous fight for the demands of the Negro people and the youth, for the preservation of democratic rights, and especially in defense of the living standards of the working class, which were being undermined by the insatiable demands of the growing war machine.

An important by-product of the 1940 election was the resignation of John L. Lewis as president of the C.I.O. Lewis, who had fallen out with Roosevelt, claimed that the latter was not giving sufficient concern to the needs of the workers and called upon the people to elect Willkie. He declared, "I think the re-election of President Roosevelt for a third term would be a national evil of the first magnitude."[1] Therewith, Lewis promised to resign if Willkie were not elected, a pledge which he duly carried out by quitting at the Atlantic City convention, on November 18, 1940, as head of the C.I.O. Thus Lewis, instead of taking the line of independent political action, had tried to lead the workers deeper into the two-party trap. Philip Murray was elected as the new president of the C.I.O.

John L. Lewis did a real service for the working class in leading the great organizing drive of the C.I.O. which resulted in the unionization of the basic and trustified industries of this country. His most glaring contradiction as a labor leader, however, was that while making an economic fight for the workers, at the same time he gave his support to the ultra-reactionary Republican Party. Only during Roosevelt's first two terms did he waver in this life-long Republican affiliation. At the time of Lewis' resignation his popularity in the C.I.O. and far and wide among A.F. of L. workers was immense.

PERSECUTION OF THE PARTY

In the pre-Pearl Harbor period militant reaction, under cover of the proclaimed "national emergency," developed a sharp attack against the Communist Party. Roosevelt obviously gave his sanction to this. Among

[1] Dulles, *Labor in America*, p. 322.

these attacks, during October-November 1939, Earl Browder, general secretary of the C.P., William Weiner, I.W.O. leader, and Harry Gannes, foreign editor of the *Daily Worker*, were arrested charged with passport violations. Browder was sent to Atlanta prison in March 1941, and served one year of a four-year sentence, when he was released by Roosevelt under heavy mass pressure. Weiner and Gannes were not tried, on account of grave illness.

William Schneiderman, Secretary of the C.P. in California, a naturalized citizen living in this country since the age of two, had his citizenship revoked in June 1940, on grounds of membership in the Y.C.L. and C.P. before his naturalization. The U.S. Supreme Court in October 1942, however, during the war situation, reversed the lower court's ruling, stating that it was a tenable conclusion that the "Party in 1927 desired to achieve its purpose by peaceful and democratic means."[1] Wendell Willkie was Schneiderman's attorney. Judge Murphy wrote the Court's opinion.

A number of other prosecutions were directed against Party leaders. Several were condemned by the Dies Committee for contempt for refusing to turn over Party membership lists. Also, in West Virginia the C.P. candidate for governor, Oscar Wheeler, in August 1940, was sentenced to 15 years in jail for collecting signatures on a Party election petition. During the same month 18 workers carrying on routine election activities were arrested in Oklahoma, charged with violating the state anti-syndicalism law, and held in $100,000 bail each. R. Wood and A. Shaw were sentenced to 10 years apiece, but were shortly released.

Among the many vicious laws passed during this period was the notorious Smith Act, of June 22, 1940. This law, under which the Party is now, in 1952, being prosecuted, provides ferocious sentences for the alleged crime of "teaching and advocating the overthrow of the United States government by force and violence," and for conspiring to do this. Its chief significance in 1940, however, was that, as a repressive measure, it forced the Hitler-like finger-printing and registration of 3,600,000 non-citizen foreign-born.

Another vicious piece of legislation was the Voorhis Act, fathered by Congressman Voorhis, a member of the Dies Committee. It was signed by the president in October 1940. This reactionary law deprived the Communist Party of the right of international affiliation, a right enjoyed for generations by a host of organizations—economic, political, scientific, industrial, educational, and religious. To meet this attack, the Party held a special convention in New York, November 16-17, 1940. This

---

[1] American Committee for the Protection of Foreign Born, *The Schneiderman Case*, p. 26, N. Y., 1943.

convention, while reaffirming the "unshakable adherence of our Party to the principles of proletarian internationalism," and resolving to fight for the abolition of the Voorhis Act, declared, "That the Communist Party of the U.S.A., in convention assembled, does hereby cancel and dissolve its organizational affiliation to the Communist International, as well as any and all other bodies of any kind outside the boundaries of the United States of America, for the specific purpose of removing itself from the terms of the so-called Voorhis Act." This act of disaffiliation killed the contemplated prosecution of the Party by the Department of Justice, which was designed to illegalize and break up the Party and to jail its leaders. The Party did not abandon its internationalist position.

As a result of the newly-passed Smith Act, the Party at the 1940 convention, upon Browder's proposal, incorrectly adopted a clause in its constitution restricting the Party's membership to United States citizens. This cost the Party about 4,000 members and substantially weakened its influence among the foreign-born. The clause was removed at the 1944 convention. At the latter convention, also, the admission age for Party membership was reduced from 21 to 18 years.

THE AMERICA FIRST COMMITTEE

The sinister movement comprising the America First Committee was the nearest thing to a general fascist party that the United States has yet had. Its line was the familiar "isolationism." Under cover of elaborate peace demagogy it cultivated every form of reaction in the United States and gave all possible assistance to the fascist Axis powers. The America First Committee was much more definitely fascist than its predecessor, the American Liberty League of the 1936 presidential campaign.

The America First Committee was launched on the campus of Yale University, initiated by R. Douglas Stuart, a 24-year-old law student, in the spring of 1940. It spread rapidly, being taken over by General Robert E. Wood, head of Sears, Roebuck and a member of the *Chicago Tribune* gang. The movement was lavishly financed, having among its many backers Henry Ford, L. J. Rosenwald, E. P. Weir, Robert M. McCormick, T. N. McCarter, and others. Among the large number of public figures associated with it were Senators Wheeler, Nye, and Lodge, Hugh S. Johnson, Amos Pinchot, Philip LaFollette, Edward Rickenbacker, John T. Flynn, Kathryn Lewis, and others. It attracted many muddle-headed liberals, including Chester Bowles, later the head of Americans for Democratic Action. William H. Hutcheson, first vice-president of the A.F. of L., was a member, and Norman Thomas spoke from its platform at a mass meeting in New York, in March 1941.[1] The influence of the Catholic hierarchy was also much in evidence. Every fascist organization in the country was directly or indirectly connected with the Committee. Charles A. Lindbergh, the noted aviator whom Roosevelt called a "copperhead," was its principal spokesman. Headquarters were in Chicago.

A subsidiary of the America First Committee was the No Foreign Wars Committee. This outfit was run by such notorious fascist-like elements as Merwin K. Hart, Vern Marshall, and G. T. Eggleston. Its special task, in the broad America First movement, was to propagate a virulent anti-Semitism. The Communist Party made an all-out campaign against the America First Committee and all its works.

The America First Committee, playing upon the intense peace sentiments of the people, mushroomed into a national organization claiming 15 million adherents.[2] It had a tremendous propaganda organization, large numbers of neighborhood public headquarters being established in all parts of the country. The aim of the backers of the movement was to crystallize it into a political organization, as a reinforcement for the Republican Party. But the whole vast agitation met a sudden shipwreck after the Japanese attack upon Pearl Harbor, on December 7, 1941. In the face of the surging war spirit of the people, the America First Committee was immediately dissolved.

HITLER MARCHES TOWARD DISASTER

Now let us turn back to the war proper. After Hitler had driven the British into the sea at Dunkirk, obviously the next strategic step was to overrun the British Isles. They were largely defenseless. Hanson W. Baldwin states that "the British in the summer of 1940 had less than one fully equipped division able to meet German invaders."[3] The British air force and navy were similarly weak, and could not have repelled an invasion. Nevertheless Hitler did not venture to seize the great prize lying so temptingly before him. This was primarily because of his fear of a two-front war, his dread of the Red Army in his rear in the East. The fact is that up to this time, so great was this fear, Hitler kept three-fourths of his army in Eastern Europe, on guard against the Russians. It is a fiction that the Royal Air Force, in the "Battle of Britain," saved that country from invasion.

Instead of grabbing Britain when he could, in 1940, Hitler had to turn his urgent attention to the Balkans, particularly as the Red Army

1 Oneal and Werner, *American Communism*, p. 292.
2 John Roy Carlson in *American Mercury*, January 1942.
3 *New York Times*, May 14, 1945.

had just occupied the former Russian province of Bessarabia. For the next few months, therefore, Hitler devoted his main efforts to the East, pulling Bulgaria into the war, militarily crushing Yugoslavia, Greece, and Albania, and otherwise getting the Balkan situation under control. Then, considering that Great Britain could be no danger in his rear for the next period, he delivered his major blow—against the U.S.S.R. Hitler felt it was indispensable to smash the Soviet Union in order to subjugate Europe and to break his way through to the lush perspectives of conquest in Asia and Africa. Therefore, on June 22, 1941, cynically violating his non-aggression treaty with that country, he suddenly sent his armies storming across the borders of the Soviet Union. This was Hitler's fatal step. It changed the whole course of the war, and it marked the beginning of the end for Nazi Germany and its pirate allies.

28. World II: The Peoples' Anti-Fascist War (1941-1945)

Hitler assumed that it would be a relatively easy task to whip the U.S.S.R., and almost unanimously the bourgeois military experts of the world agreed with him.[1] A few weeks at most would do the job. These elements were drugged by their own lying propaganda against the Soviet Union. They believed that the Russian economic system was weak and rotten, that the Soviet people were discontented slaves and would revolt if given arms, and that the Red Army, with its best officers purged, was a third-class military organization. So they all waited for Hitler quickly to chop up the supposedly decrepit Soviet Union. The Communist Party of the United States, however, never wavered in its firm conviction that the powerful and healthy young Socialist Republic could withstand every force that decadent capitalism could throw against it.

Realities in the U.S.S.R. were fundamentally different from the fantastic lies that had long been spread over the capitalist world by the professional Soviet haters. Economically the country had been growing at a stupendous rate for fifteen years past, and it had become the leading industrial land in Europe. Also the Red Army, in anticipation of the attacks that were sure to be made by imperialist capitalists against the Soviets, had been built up to a high level of strength and efficiency. Indeed, events were to show that in discipline and fighting spirit it was far and away the most effective army in the world. As for the morale of the people, that was superb. They were proud of their new Socialist system and willing to defend it with their lives. The great state trials during the 1930's, of the Trotsky-Zinoviev-Tukhachevsky-Bukharin wreckers and counter-revolutionaries, instead of weakening the country as capitalist leaders believed, had enormously strengthened it. The trials destroyed the sprouting fifth column root and branch and had deprived Hitler of a most powerful weapon, one that he had counted upon heavily.

[1] Of all the military experts in the United States, only Max Werner stated that the U.S.S.R. had a fighting chance, and only Captain Sergei Kournakoff predicted the victory of the Red Army.

THE GREAT GERMAN OFFENSIVE

When the German armies crossed the frontiers of the Soviet Union on June 22, 1941, Hitler threw a mighty power against the great Socialist Republic. He had behind him not only the vast armies and industries of Germany and Italy, but also the factories and manpower of a host of satellite countries and conquered nations, comprising virtually all of Europe—France, Belgium, Holland, Norway, Denmark, Spain, Austria, Poland, Hungary, Romania, Bulgaria, Finland, Luxemburg, Greece, Yugoslavia, and Czechoslovakia. He also dominated the production powers of the "neutral" nations, Sweden and Switzerland. Hitler's forces enormously outnumbered those of the Soviet Union in manpower and industrial production—in everything except the main things, revolutionary fighting spirit and Socialist organization.

Hitler's great "blitz" blow carried him far and fast into the Soviet Union. His "irresistible" *Wehrmacht* marched to the tune of the most fantastic stories of Russian defeats and the destruction and capture of millions of Red Army soldiers. These lying tales, sent out by the Nazi propaganda agencies, were readily believed by the gullible in all the capitalist countries, who daily expected the complete collapse of the Soviet government. But again the realities of the situation were far different from the picture painted for the capitalist world by Goebbels. The German army was advancing at frightful cost, the Red Army taking a ghastly toll as it backed up against the main Soviet bases. Already, by August 11th, only six weeks after the great offensive began, General Halder was warning Hitler that they had fatally "underestimated the Russian Colossus," and was saying that "Germany's last reserves were committed in a last desperate effort to keep the line from becoming frozen in position warfare."[1]

How much of the great Russian withdrawal was a question of calculated strategy and how much of it a matter of compulsion, remains to be told by Soviet military historians. The bourgeois military writers' insistence that the Soviet government had been "surprised" strategically by the Nazi invasion is obviously incorrect; if that had been true, the Red Army would have been destroyed before it could mobilize its real strength.

The German army besieged Leningrad on September 8th, and on October 3rd the vainglorious Hitler shouted to the world that Russia was defeated and "will never rise again." On November 12th the Germans reached the gates of Moscow, but Hitler's forces, held at both Moscow and Leningrad, were forced into the dreadful winter struggle of 1941-42. Hitler's army then got a triple taste of what Napoleon's legions, over a century before, had experienced from the indomitable Russian people.

[1] *New York Times*, Dec. 14, 1948.

THE JAPANESE ATTACK UPON PEARL HARBOR

Meanwhile the Japanese imperialists, encouraged by Hitler's conquests in Europe, decided that the time had come for them also to deliver their major blow against their traditional enemy, United States imperialism. So they struck at Pearl Harbor. Early on December 7, 1941—one of the most tragic days in American history—the Japanese sent 105 planes over the sleeping, unsuspecting garrison. "So great was the surprise that most American aircraft were destroyed on the ground, leaving the American fleet at the mercy of the treacherous foe. Nineteen of the eighty-six American ships in the harbor were seriously hit, five great capital ships were either sunk or otherwise put out of action, and casualties to personnel reached 4,575 killed, wounded, or missing. . . . Had the Japanese brought with them troops to effect a landing, they might with ease have taken the whole of the Hawaiian Islands."[1]

This monstrous crime, made all the more outrageous because it was committed during the course of U.S.-Japanese peace negotiations, utterly shocked and enraged the American people. The next day Congress recognized a state of war with Japan. On December 11th, Germany and Italy, in common action with Japan, declared war against this country. The United States was now in World War II, with its navy badly crippled. The American officers responsible for permitting the barbarous assault upon Pearl Harbor were never punished for their criminal negligence. Indeed, the two ranking men, General W. C. Short and Admiral H. E. Kimmel, were allowed to resign on full retirement pay, and the whole disgraceful matter was eventually hushed up. The "great" General Douglas MacArthur was equally guilty, his planes being all destroyed on the ground in Manila by the Japanese at the same time, despite repeated warnings from Washington beforehand.

After Pearl Harbor, Japan launched an aggressive expansionist offensive. Within the next five months its forces conquered the Philippines, Wake, Guam, Hong Kong, Singapore, Thailand, Burma, British Malaya, the Dutch East Indies, much of China, and they were threatening India. Almost overnight the Japanese had built up one of the hugest empires in history and had come into possession of enormous quantities of manpower and natural resources.

THE SOVIETS MARCH TO VICTORY

The winter of 1941-42 was a disastrous one for the Germans, at the gates of Leningrad and Moscow. In the spring of 1942, however, Hitler

[1] John D. Hicks, *A Short History of American Democracy*, p. 581, Boston, 1943.

managed to organize another offensive, aimed against industrial Stalingrad and the Caucasus oil fields, with the end in view of eventually encircling Moscow and finally defeating the U.S.S.R. But with this vast plan Hitler broke his neck. He tried in vain to capture Stalingrad. His troops arrived before that city in August 1942, and for five months nearly a million men were locked in desperate struggle. On January 31, 1943, the Nazi Marshal Von Paulus, defeated, encircled and isolated, surrendered with 200,000 men and 16 generals to the Red Army. This was all that was left of the 400,000 men in the German Sixth Army. The heroic defense of Stalingrad was the most decisive battle in world history. It ruined the German *Wehrmacht* and wrote finis to Hitler's dreams of world conquest.

The world rang with praise of the Russians for their great fight. Long before the battle of Stalingrad, even reactionary General Douglas MacArthur was constrained to declare, "The world situation at the present time indicates that the hopes of civilization rest upon the worthy banners of the courageous Russian Army. During my lifetime I have participated in a number of wars and have witnessed others, as well as studying in great detail the campaigns of outstanding leaders of the past. In none of these have I observed such effective resistance to the heaviest blows of a hitherto undefeated enemy, followed by a smashing counter-attack which is driving that enemy back into his own land. The scale and grandeur of this effort marks it as the greatest military achievement of all time."[1]

After Stalingrad the Red Army, in a never-ending offensive, proceeded to drive the German-Italian-Romanian-Hungarian-Finnish-Spanish armies out of Russia, inflicting catastrophic losses on them. For the next two years, almost daily, the world's press heralded great victories of the advancing Red Army. On February 16, 1943, Kharkov was recaptured; on November 6th, Kiev was retaken; and on November 26th the Russians liberated Gomel. On April 10, 1944, the Red Army retook Odessa; on May 9th it captured Sevastopol; and on June 4th, it crossed the Polish border. Since Stalingrad, the "invincible" Nazi *Wehrmacht* had been driven back halfway across Europe by the "defeated" Red Army. With boundless joy the peoples of the world, including those in the United States, hailed the victorious advance of the Soviet forces.

On June 6, 1944, the United States and Great Britain opened up the long-promised western front in France and the death agony of the Nazi regime was on. On August 25th Paris was liberated, and on September 11th, the Anglo-American-Canadian forces crossed the German border. On January 17, 1945, the Russians captured Warsaw, and on February

[1] Associated Press Dispatch, Feb. 23, 1942.

7th, they reached the defenses of Berlin. On April 25th the American and Soviet forces met on the Elbe; on May 2nd, the Russians captured Berlin; and on May 7th, Germany surrendered unconditionally. President Roosevelt died on April 12th, less than a month before the victory was won.

The great offensive of the Soviet people and their Red Army against the Nazi hordes was guided daily by Stalin, a highly experienced soldier from the time of the Russian revolutionary wars. This brilliant war achievement greatly enhanced Stalin's already tremendous prestige among the Soviet people, won by his vital services, side by side with Lenin, in founding and defending the Soviet Republic, his magnificent leadership in the building of Soviet socialism, his epic defeat of Trotsky, Zinoviev, Bukharin, and the rest of the wrecker opposition in what were perhaps the most complex political debates and struggles ever to take place, his outstanding theoretical work as the greatest living Marxist, and his brilliant diplomacy as far and away the outstanding statesman of our times. Now Stalin faces the most difficult task in his entire career of leading the Soviet People—to fend off the malignant and aggressive offensive of the Anglo-American imperialists, to preserve world peace against their war policy, and to protect Soviet socialism, the bulwark of world democracy and social progress.[1]

THE QUESTION OF THE WESTERN FRONT

No sooner had the U.S.S.R. become involved in the war than Great Britain and the United States, which in the pre-war years had so stubbornly rejected Soviet anti-fascist co-operation, pronounced the Soviet Union their ally. Churchill promptly declared that "any man or state who fights against Nazism will have our aid," and a couple of days later Roosevelt announced that Russia would be given military help under the lend-lease plan. On January 1, 1942, also, 26 anti-Hitler nations, laying the foundation of the United Nations war alliance, endorsed the Roosevelt-Churchill Atlantic Charter of August 14, 1941, pledged each other all-out mutual aid, and agreed not to make any separate peace with the fascist powers.[2]

On the surface, therefore, the U.S.S.R. was considered a full-fledged ally by the western powers, but the truth was quite otherwise. The big imperialist powers did not lay aside their anti-Soviet hatred and fear so easily. In reality Anglo-American war policy was based throughout upon the old pre-war Munich project of letting the Soviet Union and Germany fight out the war together in the hope that they would undermine

---

[1] Joseph Stalin, *The Great Patriotic War of the Soviet Union*, N. Y., 1945.
[2] L. P. Todd and Merle Curti, *America's History*, p. 798, N. Y., 1950.

or destroy each other in the process. Neither before, during, nor after the war was the U.S.S.R. either accepted or treated honorably as an ally by the United States or Great Britain.

With the fate of the world at stake, many bourgeois statesmen even openly proclaimed the let-Germany-and-Russia-fight-it-out treachery. Thus, President—then Senator—Truman, declared on June 23, 1941, "If we see that Germany is winning we ought to help Russia, and if Russia is winning, we ought to help Germany."[1] Ex-President Hoover, in the same outrageous and reactionary vein, declared that when "Stalin and Hitler were locked in deadly combat . . statesmanship required the United States to stand aside in watchful waiting, armed to the teeth."[2] This was also Churchill's line. The Truman-Hoover-Churchill conception was in fact the decisive opinion of the American and British bourgeoisie and it provided the basis for the policy of their two governments. If President Roosevelt thought otherwise, he certainly was not able basically to change American-British war policy. The attitude of betrayal toward the U.S.S.R., however, was buried under a mountain of hypocritical expressions of co-operation—to avoid alienating the Soviet Union and in order to satisfy the strong pro-Soviet sentiment among the American masses.

The purpose of the Anglo-American imperialist advocates of the let-Germany-and-Russia-butcher-each-other policy was easy to understand. They figured cold-bloodedly that in the post-war period, with both Russia and Germany knocked out, they would be able to reorganize and dominate the world to suit themselves, with the United States playing the decisive role. Already in 1941, Henry Luce, the big magazine publisher, was filling the air with his shrill cries that "The twentieth century is the American century."[3]

The great test of Anglo-American policy toward the U.S.S.R. came on the question of the western front. Obviously a sound allied military strategy demanded that a front in western Europe should be established at the earliest possible date, to catch Hitler in the vise of a two-front war and to relieve the heavy pressure against the U.S.S.R. A prompt establishment of the western front could have ended the war at least a full year earlier. The Soviet government demanded this second front, and the masses all over the world clamored for it. The Communist Party of the United States made this fight its major campaign, and undoubtedly the bulk of the American people agreed with its general contention. But the United States and British governments stubbornly refused to set up

[1] *New York Times*, June 24, 1941.
[2] Cited boastingly by Herbert Hoover, *New York Times*, Feb. 10, 1951.
[3] Henry R. Luce, *The American Century*, N. Y., 1941.

the badly-needed western front, although military means were undoubtedly at hand in Great Britain to have invaded Europe by the fall of 1942. The American and British forces refused to stir, however, and they went on piling up military supplies in the British Isles until, as the current saying had it, they were in danger of sinking the country into the sea.

Meanwhile, lend-lease supplies were being forwarded by the United States to the embattled Soviet Union. But here, too, the strong anti-Soviet bias of Anglo-American policy was in evidence. That is, the Russians, who were doing practically all the fighting in Europe, were given only about one-fourth as much lend-lease war materials as Great Britain, which was doing hardly any fighting at all.

Finally, in November 1942, in the face of a widespread demand for the western front, the western allies got into motion—but by invading Africa, not Europe. The African-Italian invasion was in no sense the second front needed. First, it involved relatively few divisions, and second, it was essentially political, not military, in character. The basic purpose of this Churchill-inspired invasion against "the soft underbelly of Europe" was not to relieve the pressure upon the Soviet Red Army, but to occupy Italy and if possible the Balkans with Anglo-American troops in order to forestall expected post-war revolutions in these areas.

It was not until June 6, 1944, nineteen months later, that the American-British-Canadian forces finally crossed the English Channel, established themselves in France, and began their push into Germany. The invasion could not have been postponed any longer. Not only was the mass demand for the second front imperative, but—what was even more urgent—the Russians had decisively licked the Germans and were triumphantly advancing across enslaved Europe. The Red Army, as we have noted, had smashed the backbone of the *Wehrmacht*, driven it back 1,300 miles, and crossed the border of Poland on June 4th, two days before "D-Day" in France. It was only then that the gigantic forces of Great Britain and the United States were activized and the long-delayed western front opened. It was a matter of comment among the newspaper columnists at the time that if Eisenhower did not hurry up and get his troops across to France it would be too late, as the Red Army would march across the whole continent in its fight to destroy the Nazi forces.

THE WAR AGAINST JAPAN

The main enemy and by far the most powerful fascist power in World War II was Nazi Germany, controlling as it did nearly all of Europe. It was against Hitler, therefore, that the decisive blow had to be struck.

Japan, as it turned out, proved to be only a second-rate power so far as fighting capacity was concerned. The Roosevelt Administration was aware of the primacy of Germany as the major enemy and the need of making the heaviest concentration against it. Secretary of the Navy Knox declared, "We know who our great enemy is, the enemy who before all others must be defeated first. It is not Japan, it is not Italy. It is Hitler and Hitler's Nazis, Hitler's Germany."[1]

This remained ostensibly the American as well as the United Nations policy throughout the war. Actually, however, the United States struck its hardest blows against Japan, leaving the main enemy, Germany, as we have seen, primarily for the U.S.S.R. to dispose of. This course was partly due to heavy pressure from those reactionary elements who wanted to let Russia and Germany fight each other to death, but it was especially due to the fact that American imperialism felt itself much more affected by the far-flung conquests of Japan in the Pacific and the Far East, areas which American imperialism had staked out for itself.

It was not long after the disaster of Pearl Harbor, therefore, that the tremendously superior production and manpower of the United States began to make itself felt in the Pacific phase of the world war. The naval Battle of Midway, fought June 3-6, 1942, was an American victory and it marked the end of Japan's advance toward Australia. Then came Guadalcanal—in August-November 1942—which was another major defeat for Japan. After this the "island-hopping" got under way, with the American and allied forces gradually pushing north, capturing during 1942-43 the Solomons, New Guinea, Tarawa, and other key islands. The 1944-45 campaign found the Japanese everywhere on the retreat and the (chiefly) American forces taking one island stronghold after another—the Dutch East Indies, Kwajalein, Saipan, the Philippines, Iwo Jima, Okinawa, etc. Then came the fire-bombing of Tokyo and other Japanese cities, and on August 6th and 9th the horrifying and needless atom-bombing of Hiroshima and Nagasaki.

The war in the Pacific has been falsely portrayed to our people as almost exclusively an American affair; but it was in reality a coalition war, far more so, in fact, than the war in Europe. Indispensable factors in defeating Japan were the great armies of Russia and People's China. All through the war the Soviet Red Army, although locked in a death struggle against Hitler's powerful armies in Europe, kept Japan's finest land force, the Kwantung army of one million men, tied up along the Siberian frontiers. This enormously weakened Japan's armed strength available to extend and defend its conquests against American and other

[1] Associated Press Dispatch, Jan. 13, 1942.

allied troops. Without this fact, the American advance would have been vastly more difficult, if not impossible. The U.S.S.R. also gave powerful aid to the Chinese People's Army in the field in the early stages, at a time when the United States was still sending scrap iron and other war materials to Japan. And when the U.S.S.R., in accordance with the agreement with its allies, entered the war against Japan on August 8th, it speedily wiped out the crack Kwantung army. This was another body blow against Japan.

The forces of Free China, led by the Communists, also were a most vital factor in winning the war in the Pacific. For several years they kept over a million Japanese soldiers fully occupied in the field, inflicting upon them gigantic losses in manpower and war material. "In the eight years of the War of Resistance, they [the Eighth and Fourth People's Armies] engaged 64 percent of the Japanese troops in China and 95 percent of the puppet troops."[1] Japan was greatly weakened by the war in China and was hamstrung in its fight against the American and Soviet forces. As for Chiang Kai-shek's national armies, however, they directed their main attacks, not against Japan but against the Chinese people's armies.

Japan surrendered on August 14, 1945, thoroughly beaten by the combined American, Russian, and People's Chinese forces. The British had little to do with Japan's defeat.

AN ESTIMATE OF WORLD WAR II

The U.S.S.R. was the decisive force in the coalition which won the general victory over fascism in World War II. Its entry into the hostilities changed the character of the war in that it greatly strengthened the democratic element in the struggle, making it basically a peoples' war. This was a qualitative as well as a quantitative strengthening of the fight of the peoples. With its enormous political, economic, and military strength, the Soviet Union contributed to the war its perspective and final realization of victory. When the U.S.S.R. entered the war, the struggle was a lost cause so far as the western allies were concerned. They were virtually defeated, politically as well as militarily, and their prospect for victory was just about hopeless. From the time of its entry into the hostilities the Soviet Union became the peoples' leader of the war. This was the basic reason why the war was won.

The Soviet Union gave the cause of the allies democratic political strength, stability, and direction. As a great Socialist country, the very

[1] Hsiao Hua in *People's China*, Aug. 1, 1951.

antithesis to fascism, the Soviet Union, a land without imperialists, was squarely and irrevocably anti-fascist in its whole war drive. Its interest in utterly destroying fascism was identical with that of the democratic masses of the world. In the war the U.S.S.R. gave a smashing demonstration of the political idiocy of those who shout that "fascism and Soviet socialism are the same."

The capitalist governments of the United States and Great Britain, controlled by reactionary ruling classes tainted heavily with fascism and having in mind only one objective—the making of billions for themselves, could not possibly rise above the sordid level of their own imperialist interests during the war. They could not represent the anti-fascist spirit of the American, British, and world masses, nor could they have led a people's democratic anti-fascist war. Their imperialist interests in pulling such territorial and other conquests as they could out of the war, had nothing in common with the aims of the peoples, who were fighting desperately for their freedom and their very lives. The imperialists constantly betrayed the democratic war aims of the allied coalition. The only consistently anti-imperialist and anti-fascist force among the big powers in the war alliance was the U.S.S.R.

The imperialists of the United States and Great Britain showed their unwillingness and inability to fight fascism by their active support of Hitler before the war and by their constant pressure for a negotiated peace during the war. Without the anti-fascist influence of the Soviet Union, they would have arrived at a settlement with Hitler, far more definitely than they did with Hirohito. Significantly, in the present postwar years of "cold war," when the Anglo-American imperialists are trying desperately to organize an all-out capitalist war against the U.S.S.R., they are complaining that the biggest mistake they ever made was to yield to the mass pressure and to smash the Hitler regime so completely in World War II. The only way that the war could have the degree of anti-fascist content that it did attain, and the "unconditional surrender" slogan be carried through, was by the predominant democratic influence of the Soviet Union. In this respect, the Soviets were in harmony with the democratic masses everywhere, including those of the United States. The political leader of World War II in the fight against Hitlerism was the U.S.S.R., and it could not have been otherwise.

The Soviet Union also, naturally enough, contributed the basic political-military strategy to the democratic side of the war. That is, the policy of an all-out international alliance of the democratic powers, and of national, anti-fascist unity in the various countries, was simply the wartime expression of the line developed by the Seventh Congress of the Communist International in 1935; namely, that of an international peace front to halt the fascist aggressor states and of a people's front to defeat fascism in the individual countries. Great Britain and the United States (and their Social-Democratic stooges) rejected this anti-fascist co-operation with the Communists in the pre-war years, and if they accepted it in the war situation (to the limited degree we have indicated), it was only because of the desperate debacle into which they had plunged themselves through their "appeasement" policies. In this grave crisis their need for Communist help was imperative.

In addition to being the political leader of the war and giving it its main political-military strategy, as we have remarked, the U.S.S.R. also did the bulk of the fighting to win the war. This is obvious at once from a comparison of the list of killed, wounded, and missing of the respective big powers on the democratic side—Britain, 755,257; the United States 994,893; the U.S.S.R. 23,417,000.[1] In soldier deaths, the Russian losses, 6,115,000, were almost eleven times as great as those of the United States (325,464) and Britain (244,723) combined.

As we have seen earlier, it fell to the lot of the Soviet Union, virtually single-handed, to defeat the main enemy, Nazi Germany. Hence the gigantic Russian losses in manpower and territorial devastation. Of course, the U.S.S.R. got some help from the Anglo-American bombing of German cities and through American lend-lease military supplies. But this help was more than offset by the fact that the U.S.S.R., all through the war, was subjected to the tremendous strain of keeping over a million of its best troops on the Siberian borders to hold the Japanese in check. Moreover, the crippling effect of the air-bombing of German industry upon the Nazi war effort has been greatly overestimated. The fact is that German production of war materials went on increasing right up to within two months of the end of the war.

As for lend-lease help, which some people, anxious to rob the Soviet people of their due war credit, claim saved the Russians from being defeated—this help was relatively small in amount and late in arriving. The $10 billion worth of munitions sent to the U.S.S.R. from the U.S.A. (large amounts of which never arrived) was less than five percent of our total of $210 billion of wartime munitions production. Moreover, this assistance began to arrive on the eastern front only after the Russians had done the main job of defeating Germany. We have this fact from no less an authority than the Soviet-hating Herbert Hoover, who has said that "she [the U.S.S.R.] had stopped the Germans even before Lend-Lease had reached her."[2]

1 *Information Please Almanac*, pp. 220-21, N. Y., 1951.
2 *New York Times*, Feb. 10, 1951.

A basic lesson to be drawn from all these facts is that in World War II the Soviet Union saved the world from fascist enslavement. This was a fitting role for the U.S.S.R. as the great champion of democracy. The capitalist governments of Great Britain and the United States neither could nor would have saved even their own limited democracy from fascism. This was so because they lacked the military strength to do so and, more important, because they did not have the necessary democratic political compulsion (despite the democratic urge of their peoples), these governments having been soaked with fascism and imperialist reaction. Had Hitler been able to demolish the Red Army that would have been the end of world democracy for an indefinite period. The United States, although not falling an immediate victim, could not have long withstood the tremendous power Hitler would then have had at his disposal. These are important facts to bear in mind during the present years of the "cold war," when Anglo-American imperialism, more reactionary and more expansionist than ever, is violently on the offensive, under the false pretense that it is striving to preserve world democracy from attacks by the Soviet Union.

29. The Communists in the War (1941-1945)

Throughout the early stages of the war, as we have seen, the American people were overwhelmingly—at least 90 per cent—opposed to the United States entering the war. This, too, in general, was the basic position of the Communist Party of the United States.

When Hitler, on June 22, 1941, attacked the Soviet Union, however, the Party realized that all possibility of limiting the war had vanished and that now there was a world people's war. The Party therefore shifted its political position to one of military participation in what had now become a full-fledged people's anti-fascist war. In its statement of June 22nd, condemning the Nazi invasion of the U.S.S.R., the Party called for "full support and co-operation with the Soviet Union in its struggle against Hitlerism."[1] Six days later the National Committee elaborated its position to "Defend America by giving full aid to the Soviet Union, Great Britain, and all nations who fight against Hitler," and "For full and unlimited collaboration of the United States, Great Britain, and the Soviet Union to bring about the military defeat of Hitler."[2]

The Party called upon the workers at home to be especially alert to defend their living standards, to protect the rights of the Negro people, to fight against anti-Semitism, and to establish national and international trade union unity. It especially warned against the danger of a new Munich, aimed at transforming the war into a struggle of the capitalist world against the Soviet Union. For the reactionaries felt that at last, in the struggle between Germany and Russia, they had the "right war." Another Munich sell-out was the aim of Hess's fantastic flight to England at this time, even as it was that of Hoover in his N.B.C. radio broadcast of June 29, 1941, when he declared that there would be "no possibility of bringing the war to conclusion except by a compromise peace" with Hitler against the U.S.S.R. Calling for an organized fight against reaction abroad and at home, the Communist Party conducted an active struggle during the next six critical months in the midst of a rising war spirit among the American people.

[1] *The Communist*, July 1941.
[2] *The Communist*, Aug. 1941.

THE COMMUNISTS IN THE WAR

The Japanese attack upon the United States forces at Pearl Harbor, Hawaii, on December 7, 1941, radically changed the sentiment of the American people. Their hopes of staying out of the war, which had persisted even after the Nazi invasion of the Soviet Union, now disappeared overnight. The American masses girded themselves for war.

The Communist Party, on the day of the attack, denounced the attack on Pearl Harbor as "the culminating outrage of Axis aggression aimed at the domination of the entire world. The fate of every nation and every people has been thrown into the arena for determination by military means." The Party declared, "The Communist Party pledges its loyalty, its devoted labor and the last drop of its blood in support of our country in this greatest of all crises that ever threatened its existence." The Party called for "Everything for National Unity!" "Everything for victory over world-wide fascist slavery!"[1]

During the ensuing years of hard-fought war the Communists loyally lived up to these patriotic pledges. No organization in the country made a better record in the people's war than did the Communist Party and the Young Communist League. They gave 15,000 of their men and women members to the armed services. On the battle fronts the fighters conducted themselves with characteristic Communist courage and devotion. Many became officers and many others were decorated for personal bravery, notable among these being Robert Thompson, Alexander Suer, and Herman Boettcher, all of whom received the Distinguished Service Cross.[2] Suer and Boettcher, both captains, were killed in action. There were many others, too, who never returned, among the numerous Communist casualties being Hank Forbes, district secretary in Pittsburgh.

On the home front the Communists were in the forefront of all work calculated to strengthen the national war effort. They were outstanding fighters for a strong anti-fascist war policy by the government; they stood second to nobody in rallying the workers for all-out production; they were militant participants in all phases of civilian defense work; and they carried on a ceaseless battle against all "isolationists" and other reactionary compromisers and saboteurs of the war effort.

Through the war the women comrades in the Party especially distinguished themselves; during the absence of so many men leaders at the front, they came forward and took over a very large share of leadership

[1] *The Communist*, Dec. 1941.
[2] Among the 414 delegates at a national encampment of Communist veterans in Washington, D. C., held in May 1947, there were holders of the following decorations: 1,019 Battle Stars, 44 Purple Hearts, 21 Bronze Stars, 6 Silver Stars, 107 Air Medals, 9 Distinguished Flying Crosses, 44 Presidential Unit Citations, 2 Legion of Merit, and 1 Distinguished Service Cross.

in the Party. Four women were members of the National Committee —Mother Bloor, Anita Whitney, Elizabeth Gurley Flynn, and Alice Burke. Five were members on the editorial staff of the *Daily Worker*. Hundreds of women comrades fulfilled leading functions in state, county, and branch organizations all over the country. Similarly the left and progressive unions drew heavily upon their women members to fill leading posts during the war.

THE BATTLE FOR PRODUCTION

The most important contribution of the United States toward winning the war was in the field of producing war munitions. Production in general went up almost 100 percent over pre-war times.[1] This production included 297,000 military planes, 86,388 tanks, 16,438 armored cars, 2,434,535 trucks, 123,707 tractors, 2,700,000 machine guns, 17,400,000 rifles, 315,000 pieces of field artillery, 71,060 naval vessels, 45 million tons of merchant shipping, etc.[2] This tremendous output was achieved by lengthening the work-day, speeding up the workers, and expanding American industrial capacity to the extent of $25 billion in new plants. To accomplish all this a veritable battle for production was organized.

The Communist Party, recognizing the immense importance of production in winning the war, threw its whole force into this phase of the struggle. With its characteristic vigor, it activated all its members in the unions, in its press, and elsewhere to speed the wheels of industry. None served with better results in this general sphere than did the Communists.

The workers, who had displayed little or no interest in increasing munitions production during the imperialist World War I, made big efforts to turn out the maximum output during the anti-fascist World War II. Nearly all the trade unions shared in this effort, with the C.I.O. in the lead, under the heavy influence of the left. Among the more important means used to increase production were the union-management production committees, of which by 1945 there were 5,000 in leading industrial plants. Another vital production factor was labor's no-strike pledge. It was adopted by both C.I.O. and A.F. of L. at their 1941 conventions. This action cut the number of strikers in 1942 to one-third of what it had been in 1941. Organized labor in the main lived up to this pledge, and during the war there were no authorized strikes. John L. Lewis managed, however, to conduct several big mine strikes, and the

[1] Labor Research Association, *Labor Fact Book* 7, p. 9, N. Y., 1945.
[2] Todd and Curti, *America's History*, p. 776.

Walter Reuther faction in the United Auto Workers, while publicly proclaiming support for the no-strike pledge, surreptitiously promoted many local walkouts in the plants. As for the Communist Party and the left-led unions, they insistently enforced the pledge—even too rigidly where shop grievance stoppages were concerned. They also actively supported the plant production committees.

During the war years, although prices were supposedly frozen, there was a steady rise in the cost of living. The employers, as always, put their profits before the national interest and wrung out of the lush war production all possible financial benefits for themselves. They reaped even greater profits than they did in World War I, and monopoly domination of the country was enormously strengthened during the war. At the outset of the war the capitalists conducted their notorious "sit-down strike of capital" until they secured from the government such profit rates as they demanded.[1] Besides, seeing that the workers had their wages frozen and that the unions had pledged themselves not to strike, the employers maneuvered on all government levels to keep wage rates down. This necessitated an energetic fight by the unions to have wages at least keep pace with soaring prices. In this broad fight to maintain living standards, the Communists were naturally in the front line.

Late in 1942, however, Earl Browder introduced into the Party a proposition that threatened to compromise the Party's struggle to protect the workers' living standards. This was his so-called "incentive wage." Browder proposed, in substance, that henceforth wages should be tied to production. That is, the workers would be paid in accordance with their output. It was correct that the workers, in the war against fascism, should turn out maximum production; it was correct also that, because of their greater productivity, they should get higher wages; but Browder applied all this wrongly in both theory and practice. He drew fantastic pictures of the beneficial results to be achieved by his payment-by-results system, declaring that "we could have a general increase in productivity that would give us in the course of six months or a year twice as much war production as we have today. For the workers that would mean, under this principle, at least twice as much wages."[2] Browder's plan, supposedly able to reap such great advances for the workers, placed no stress, however, upon the improvement of existing hourly, daily, and weekly wage rates, which he considered an obsolete system. This was

---

[1] The supposedly high wartime wages were a fiction. In 1944, the average weekly wage of all workers in manufacturing industries was $47.45, whereas the generally recognized Heller Cost-of-Living Budget then called for a weekly wage of $54.00.

[2] Earl Browder, *Wage Policy in War Production*, p. 8, N. Y., 1943.

an error. The scheme, which had been adopted by the Party after considerable opposition, was not widely advocated in the unions.

THE FIGHT FOR THE SECOND FRONT

The struggle to induce, or rather to compel, the United States and British governments to open up the western front in France, occupied the center of attention of the Communist Party during the 1941-44 period. The Red Army was bearing the whole burden of the war against the main fascist fortress, Nazi Germany, and its two big "allies" in the West were calmly standing aside allowing it to do so, under the obviously false pretext that they as yet lacked sufficient forces to carry through a successful invasion of France. It was imperatively in the interest of the whole allied forces, including the United States, that the second front be opened as soon as possible. The Communist Party utilized all of its strength and influence in a prolonged and persistent agitational struggle to bring about the long and deliberately delayed attack upon Hitler from the West. The Party stood out in the whole country, for its clarity and militancy on this decisive question.

The American people, in general, were full of admiration for the Red Army's magnificent struggle and undoubtedly favored the opening of the second front at the very earliest opportunity, even though they realized what the cost would be to them in casualties. But they were constantly deluged by the flood of propaganda from the let-Germany-and-Russia-fight-it-out reactionaries, in the government and outside, to the effect that we were "not yet ready." The A.F. of L. top leaders—Soviet-haters and reactionaries—also displayed no haste about the second front, and they were willing to leave the matter to the anti-Soviet military experts to decide. Large numbers of their international, state, city, and local affiliates, however, joined in the popular demand for the early invasion of France. The C.I.O., with its then characteristic left orientation, took a forthright position for the second front. Thus, at its 1943 convention it declared that "coalition warfare of the United Nations is the key to our victory," and that "the issue before the United Nations is the decisive, full-scale invasion of Europe."

As remarked earlier, it was only when the Anglo-American reactionaries could no longer delay the opening of the western front without imperiling their imperialist interests, that they finally agreed with the Russians upon the long-delayed date for the beginning of the invasion. This was done at the famous conference of Roosevelt, Churchill, and Stalin at Teheran, Iran, in December 1943.

Browder made two grossly opportunist errors on the general question of the second front. When Hitler attacked the Soviet Union, in view of the fact that Great Britain and the United States had agreed to help the U.S.S.R., Browder hopped to the conclusion that henceforth they would be trustworthy allies. "They have crossed the Rubicon," he sent word from the Atlanta jail to the National Committee. "Munichism is now at an end. We have nothing further to fear on that score." This belief, that there had been a solid merger of the war effort simply because the U.S.S.R. and the western powers were in the war together on the same side, contained the embryo of Browder's later Teheran revisionism. The Party rejected Browder's opportunist estimate of the type of the war alliance, and the correctness of its action was evidenced by the fact that almost immediately afterward the Party had to begin the two-and-a-half-year struggle against the reluctant British and American governments to have the second front established.

Browder's second error on the western front question came at the very conclusion of that historic struggle, after he had been released from jail. It was based on an enormous overestimation of the significance of the Teheran agreement to open the second front. It was a great irony that the Party should conclude its otherwise splendid struggle for the second front by making in this connection, upon Browder's initiative, by far the most serious political mistake in its career. This error will be discussed in full in the next chapter.

THE FAIR EMPLOYMENT PRACTICES COMMISSION

During the war the employers put a halt to Roosevelt's social security program on the basis of economy, although they themselves were making two to three times as much profit as they had immediately before the war. One of the major casualties in this respect was the Wagner-Dingell Bill for compulsory health insurance. In the same vein, Congress passed the notorious Smith-Connally Act in 1943, which outlawed strikes in defense plants and restricted the political activities of trade unions. Nevertheless, the workers in the democratic spirit of the people's war, did manage to secure some concessions, following the Fair Labor Standards Act (1938), and buttressed the 40-hour week. Also in 1944 Roosevelt enunciated the Economic Bill of Rights.[1] But the most important advance was the setting up of the Fair Employment Practices Commission, devised to break down some of the discrimination against Negro workers in industry.

On June 25, 1941, the president, in his Executive Order 8802, declared that it shall be the "policy of the United States that there shall be

[1] Labor Research Association, *Labor Fact Book* 7, p. 22.

no discrimination in the employment of workers in defense industries or government because of race, creed, color, or national origin." On July 18th Roosevelt established the Fair Employment Practices Committee to enforce this directive.

Previously the president, although assuming a friendly attitude toward the Negro people, had done practically nothing to mitigate the outrageous discrimination practiced against them. With his heavy support in the South, he had never made a real attack upon Jim Crow there. Also throughout the war the 920,000 Negro men and women in the armed forces suffered the indignities of segregation, when Roosevelt by a word could have abolished it. Nor did the president actively support the anti-poll tax and anti-lynching bills, so valorously championed for years by Vito Marcantonio, House member from the 18th Congressional District of New York City, and which almost became law. If the F.E.P.C. was set up it was due primarily to the need for workers in the war emergency, to the pressure of the mass of Negro trade unionists, to the fighting spirit of the Negro people, and to the growing unity in struggle between Negro and white progressives. The Communist Party, by its never-ending fight for and with the Negro people, also deserved no little of the credit for the measure.[1]

The F.E.P.C., while relieving somewhat the conditions of Negro workers during the war and establishing in principle their rights in industry, never became federal law. Roosevelt did not support the Marcantonio bill, H.R. 1732, designed to put teeth into his Executive Order. When the reactionary Truman became president he managed to slough off the F.E.P.C. altogether, under cover of his usual cloud of demagogy, as we shall see later. The A.F. of L. and Railroad Brotherhoods, with the aim of preserving their Jim Crow restrictions, also opposed the F.E.P.C. practices and legislation as "an infringement upon the trade unions' right to regulate their own internal affairs."

THE DISSOLUTION OF THE COMMUNIST INTERNATIONAL

On June 10, 1943, the Communist International was dissolved by the unanimous action of all its affiliated parties. On May 15th a motion to this effect had been submitted to the various parties.[2] Thus came to a conclusion the great world organization of Communists founded by Lenin in March 1919.

This serious action was taken as a war measure, as a means to fur-

[1] Benjamin J. Davis, Jr., in *The Communist*, Aug. 1942.
[2] *The Communist*, July 1943.

ther strengthen the unity of the peoples fighting against fascist aggression. Stalin, in an interview with Harold King, Reuters correspondent, stated that "The dissolution of the Communist International . . . facilitates the organization of the common onslaught of all freedom-loving nations against the common enemy—Hitlerism. It exposes the lie of the Hitlerites to the effect that 'Moscow' allegedly intends to intervene in the life of other nations and to 'Bolshevize' them." Stalin also showed concretely that the action would aid in organizing the progressive forces in the various countries, and would also help to "unite all the freedom-loving peoples into a single international camp for the fight against the menace of world domination by Hitlerism."[1]

The dissolution of the Comintern was a heavy sacrifice by the Communists for the common cause of victory. From the days of its foundation the C.I. was the indomitable leader of the world forces for freedom, national independence, and socialism. It was an invaluable body, where working class leaders of all countries could discuss the situation facing the workers everywhere, thus helping in the formation of programs for advancing the welfare of the working people of each country, based on their real needs and their real situation. It was also the means of educating, in the fire of actual struggle, tens of thousands of militant Communist fighters, many of whom are now the leaders of the governments of their respective countries. The Communist International represented the world Socialist movement at a vastly higher level than was the case with either the First or Second International.

The Communist Party of the United States, as we have seen in the course of this history, owes a great debt to the Comintern for its own Marxist-Leninist development. In meeting the difficult post-war problems it has seriously felt the loss of its one-time direct contact with the world's best Marxists through that organization.

OPPORTUNIST CONCEPTION OF NATIONAL UNITY

Above we have dealt in passing with some of Browder's developing deviations. But these were only the beginning of a veritable system of distorting Marxism-Leninism. While Browder was in prison, the Communist Party correctly called for national unity of the anti-Hitler forces to prosecute the war. But Browder later proceeded to give this sound policy a highly opportunistic orientation. He interpreted national unity as "uniting the entire nation, including the biggest capitalists, for a complete and all-out drive for victory."[2] This all-inclusive conception

[1] *The Communist*, Nov. 1943.
[2] Browder, *Victory—and After*, p. 112.

of national unity attempted to ignore the basic fact that the "biggest capitalists," following a course dictated by their own imperialist interests, had nothing politically in common with the masses of the American people, who were fighting to destroy Hitlerism. Instead of uniting with such reactionaries in order to have a sound war policy, it was necessary for the great masses of the people to organize and fight against them.

Browder's conception of national unity, which was essentially of a Social-Democratic character, also subordinated the political role of the working class to bourgeois dictation. During the war situation organized labor, with a membership which advanced from 11 million to 14 million in the war years, should have united its forces politically, however loosely. Inasmuch as labor was fully supporting the war, it should also have demanded that its relation to the Roosevelt government be placed on a coalition basis. There ought to have been several labor members in a joint cabinet, instead of none at all. But Roosevelt naturally was opposed to such a project, and so, too, were the top leaders of organized labor, who wanted to do nothing that could even remotely threaten their beloved two (bourgeois) party system.

In the Commmunist Party demands were raised that organized labor fight for a coalition status and for members in the Roosevelt Cabinet, but Browder defeated this proposition. He tailed right along with Roosevelt, Lewis, Murray, and Green, taking the two-party system for granted and discarding for good the perspective for a third, or labor party. Said he, "We have rejected as impractical for the war period any general readjustment or regrouping of the party structure in our national political life."[1] The result of labor's refusal to demand its rights was that the workers were denied the greatly enhanced political power which they could have gained through a coalition status. Browder's idea was not that labor should "co-operate" with Roosevelt in the war, but that it must simply "support" him. The workers went through the war with insignificant, third-line representation in the many national war committees and agencies. One of Roosevelt's most marked efforts was to prevent independent working class political action, and during the war period, with Browder's blessing, he carried out this labor-crippling line very effectively.

To appease the widespread demand for more worker leadership in the war, Roosevelt finally set up the Combined Labor Victory Committee, consisting of three representatives each from the C.I.O. and A.F. of L. and one from the Railroad Brotherhoods. This Committee, which occasionally met with the president, had no real power of decision. Browder, in chorus with the labor bureaucrats, hailed this makeshift

[1] Browder, *Victory—and After*, p. 140.

formation as adequate labor representation and a big accomplishment for organized labor.

Browder's false conception of national unity deeply cut down the leading political role of the Communist Party. It would have been of great advantage to our Party, as well as to the labor movement in general, had the Communists more clearly exposed the imperialist policy of big capital during the war, in contrast to the democratic line of the workers, and also had the Party made a real fight for effective political recognition of the workers in the conduct of the war. Browder's opportunism denied the Party both of these vital war-time issues.

BROWDER'S PLAN FOR ORGANIZED CAPITALISM

Many right-wing Social-Democrats and pseudo-Communists—Bernstein, Kautsky, Bukharin, and others—following the lead of "progressive" bourgeois economists, have from time to time developed theories of "organized capitalism"; that is, of a capitalist system which, overcoming its inner contradictions and inescapable chaos, would carry on production in a planned and systematic way, nationally and internationally. Browder tried his hand at this opportunist game, as a wartime policy, in 1942. He got the idea from Congressman Tolan who, in a report to Congress, proposed that "every phase" of the national economy must be "planned, must be guided, must be brought under administration control." This was a futile bourgeois attempt to parody the planned, Socialist production of the U.S.S.R. Browder called his own scheme of organized capitalism a "centralized war economy." There was opposition in the Party to Browder's scheme, but not enough to prevent its being at least formally adopted.

According to Browder, "Maximum war production requires a central administration which will plan, direct, guide, and control the entire economy of the nation."[1] The whole economic machine would be operated by the government, with labor (also according to Browder's policies) occupying only third-line advisory posts. How far-reaching Browder considered his project is evidenced by a few further quotations from his book *Victory—And After*. "In a centralized war economy, prices lose their former significance as a registration of market relationships and become a convenience of bookkeeping and accounting" . . . "profits lose their former significance as a source of unlimited personal consumption" and . . . "although private ownership remains intact, private capital loses its significance as the pre-condition to production"

[1] Browder, *Victory—and After*, p. 228.

... "wages tend to lose their significance as a market relationship" ... and "there is no necessity for the government to 'take over' the plants except to the degree that Congress had already provided for in the federal statute authorizing plant seizures when such steps are made necessary, by resistance to public policy by the present individual owners."[1] Browder saw the virtual disappearance of the wages system altogether under his "organized capitalism." He says, "Wages expressed in money no longer represent a standard of life; wages must now, therefore, be expressed in a guaranteed supply of the workers' needs as a producer."[2]

As Lenin and Stalin have repeatedly pointed out, capitalism cannot carry on planned production either in war or in peace. This conclusion applies not only to Bukharin's brand of organized capitalism, but also to Browder's "centralized war economy" and the Truman "managed economy" scheme. The capitalist system's domination by monopoly capital, its violent competition between hundreds of thousands of capitalist firms producing blindly for the market, its bitter struggle between the ruling and exploited classes over the question of wages, etc., its ruthless fight among the imperialist powers over the markets of the world, its sharp collision of the capitalist world against the socialist world—all make the world capitalist system hopelessly chaotic and unorganizable.

Lenin, in his famous Introduction in 1915 to Bukharin's book, *Imperialism and World Economy,* had the following to say on this general question: "There is no doubt that the development is going *in the direction* of a single world trust that will swallow up all enterprises and all states without exception. But the development in this direction is proceeding under such stress, with such a tempo, with such contradictions, conflicts and convulsions—not only economic, but also political, national, etc., etc.—that *before* a single world trust will be reached, before the respective national finance capitalists will have formed a world union of 'ultra-imperialism,' imperialism will inevitably explode, capitalism will turn into its opposite."

In the given war circumstances, Browder's "organized capitalism" dreams served to sow illusions among the workers about the ability of capitalism to carry on planned production, and they also tended to cut down the political initiative of the proletariat and to subordinate it to the leadership of the bourgeoisie. In an immediate sense Browder's utopian scheme weakened the fight for President Roosevelt's more practical seven-point program (taxes, price controls, materials allocation, profits limitations, etc.), which was designed to establish some faint

[1] Browder, *Victory—and After,* pp. 245-49.
[2] Browder, *Victory—and After,* p. 238.

traces of order in the inevitable jungle of capitalist productive and distributive relationships.

BROWDER'S OPPORTUNISM AND THE CHINESE REVOLUTION

Wall Street imperialism has a long record of aggression and exploitation in China.[1] The Communist Party, usually under the slogan of "Hands Off China," almost from its inception fought against this imperialist penetration of China and gave the Chinese Revolution such help as it could. In particular, it vigorously opposed the Roosevelt policy of shipping scrap iron and other war munitions to Japan during the thirties when that country was invading and overrunning China. In appreciation of this support, in 1937, Mao Tse-tung, Chou En-lai, and Chu Teh, the chief Chinese Communist leaders, sent separate letters of thanks to the Communist Party of the United States.[2]

During World War II, however, as part of his developing revisionism, Browder departed fundamentally from the Party's correct line toward the Chinese Revolution. His opportunism became marked after his interview with Assistant Secretary of State Sumner Welles in October 1942. Browder had previously made a statement criticizing sharply the anti-Communist policy of the Roosevelt Administration in China. Welles summoned Browder to Washington for this and gave him a statement, denying Browder's allegations and asserting that the United States aimed at unifying the forces of Chiang Kai-shek and the Communists in China. This "unity" policy amounted to no more than a wartime effort to turn all Chinese guns against the Japanese, but Browder interpreted it as a genuine, long-term desire to establish a democratic Chinese national unity. He swallowed Welles's proposition whole, apologized publicly for his previous statement attacking the State Department's China policy,[3] and thenceforth became a supporter of the reactionary line of American imperialism in China.

Thus, typically, in a speech on March 13, 1945, Browder stated that "The United States finds the Yenan [Communist] policies closer to our understanding of the two nations than are the policies of Chungking [Chiang Kai-shek]"; that "The economic policies of the Communist-led area are much more closely related to the American 'free enterprise' methods than are those of Chungking"; and that "The Chinese Communists trust America."[4] He climaxed his endorsement of Wall Street

1 Frederick V. Field in *Political Affairs*, Jan. 1946.
2 Text in Earl Browder, *The People's Front*, pp. 316-18, N. Y., 1938.
3 See Earl Browder, *Policy of Victory*, pp. 20-22, N. Y., 1943.
4 Earl Browder, *Why America Is Interested in the Chinese Communists*, N. Y., 1945.

policy in China by declaring at the Party's emergency convention, in July 1945, that "Official American policy, whatever temporary vacillations may appear, is pressing toward the unity and democratization of China."[1] Browder even tried to create the false impression that the State Department was backing the Communists against Chiang.

How completely wrong Browder was in his sizing up of the Chinese situation is demonstrated by present State Department policy in China, with its seizure of Taiwan (Formosa), attempted conquest of Korea, proposed A-bombing of Chinese cities, economic boycott against China, armed support of Chiang Kai-shek against People's China, and blocking of the seating of the Chinese People's Republic in the United Nations. This is the logical fruition of the traditional aggressive policy of American imperialism toward China. As Marxist-Leninists, the Chinese Communists followed a totally different line from Browder's, a line of anti-imperialist struggle which was foreseen 25 years ago by the great Marxist, Stalin, and it brought them to complete victory.

THE PARTY AND THE MASSES

The combination of lefts and progressives, which had built the C.I.O. and made it the leading section of the trade union movement on questions of the war, the organization of the unorganized, the Negro people, the women, the youth, and so on, continued right on through the war years. This was due chiefly to a general agreement on the aims and tasks of the war, and also partly to Philip Murray's acute need for Communist help in his struggles against John L. Lewis and the Green clique in the A.F. of L. The effectiveness of the left-center bloc during this period was lessened greatly, however, by the various Browder mistakes which we have indicated—especially by his tailing after Murray on such questions as those of organized capitalism and of no working class independent political action.

The several broad united front movements of left and progressive elements that had played such a prominent role in the immediate prewar years, mostly either died out or became skeletonized with the development of the war. This was basically because the new situation changed the issues confronting these organizations and rendered them largely obsolete. Quarrels between right and left over such questions as the Soviet-German pact, the Finnish War, and the "phony" war generally, hastened their disintegration. The American League for Peace and Democracy was dissolved in 1940, and the American Peace Mobilization in 1941. The American Youth Congress died out in 1942, and

[1] *Daily Worker*, July 28, 1945.

the League of American Writers dissolved in 1941. The Workers Alliance, with unemployment no longer an issue, also perished as the war began. The National Negro Congress, Southern Negro Youth Congress, and Southern Conference for Human Welfare went on into the post-war period, but in skeleton form. The American Committee for Protection of Foreign Born, with a continuing vital task, lived on. So did the united front defense organizations, in the shape of the Civil Rights Congress.

During the war period the Party membership grew only slowly. At the beginning of 1944 it reached its maximum of some 80,000 members, including the 15,000 whose membership had been discontinued while they were in the armed services. This was only 5,000 more than the Party reported at its 1938 convention. Large numbers of workers joined the Party; the recruiting campaign of early 1944, for example, brought in 24,000 new members, about 30 percent of whom were Negroes; but the membership turnover was very heavy. At that time 33,000 members had been in the Party less than one year.[1] About 14 percent of the Party members in 1944 were Negroes, 46 percent industrial workers, 46 percent women, and 25 percent professional and white collar workers.

The Party's growing strength among the masses was evidenced in the New York municipal elections of 1943, when Peter V. Cacchione (first elected in 1941) was re-elected to the City Council as a Communist by the biggest first-choice vote of any candidate in the city. Of historical importance was the election, at the same time, of the first Negro Communist to public office, Benjamin J. Davis, Jr. Both Cacchione and Davis made excellent records in the City Council.

Opportunities for Party building were exceptionally good during the war, and the Party should have come into the post-war period with at least 150,000 solidly organized members. If it failed to do so, it was principally due to the opportunist Browder policies, which, by blunting the Party's initiative and distorting its program, made the Party far less attractive to the workers. In the Party there was considerable opposition to Browder's errors, his twisted use of American democratic traditions, his compromising Latin American policy, his "incentive wage" theory, his opportunist concept of national unity, and his theory of a centralized war economy. But this opposition was neither clear nor strong enough as yet to expose thoroughly and to defeat the revisionist system that Browder was rapidly building up. This was to come later.

[1] John Williamson in *Proceedings of the Constitutional Convention of the Communist Political Association*, May 20-22, p. 51, N. Y., 1944.

30. The Communist Political Association (1944-1945)

The Teheran agreement of Roosevelt, Churchill, and Stalin, in December 1943, was basically a military one, setting the date, place, and strategy for the opening, on June 6, 1944, of the long-delayed western front in France. The three war leaders also took occasion to express the hope diplomatically that this wartime unity could be carried over into the post-war period and would result in peace "for many generations." On the basis of the Leninist policy of the possibility of the peaceful co-existence of the capitalist and Socialist powers, Stalin definitely planned for such a peace. But aggressive Anglo-American imperialism, which was already aiming at world conquest, and of which Churchill and Roosevelt were the representatives, had no such peaceful purpose in mind, as later events soon demonstrated.

Earl Browder, general secretary of the Communist Party, immediately jumped to the conclusion that the post-war unity that the "Big Three" expressed in wishes at Teheran was, in fact, an actual agreement and that post-war peace and co-operation were therefore guaranteed. He assumed that the dominant circles of United States monopoly capital were interested in and favored a peaceful coexistence and friendly competition with the U.S.S.R. With the glib assurance of a utopian and an opportunist, Browder undertook to state all the essentials of this imagined agreement at Teheran. This he did at the January 1944 meeting in New York, of the National Committee of the Communist Party. Later, in his book, *Teheran: Our Path in Peace and War,* he developed his thesis at length. In the face of much doubt and some opposition among the membership, Browder managed to get the Party to endorse his policy, if not to accept it wholeheartedly.

"Capitalism and socialism," said Browder, "have begun to find the way to peaceful coexistence and collaboration in the same world." Post-war unity of the "Big Three," he argued, was based upon assurances by Churchill and Roosevelt to Stalin that the Soviet Union would be left to develop in peace, and promises by Stalin to Churchill and Roosevelt "that a victorious Red Army would not carry the Soviet system and socialism on its bayonets to the rest of Europe." Thus old "fears and suspicions" had been liquidated and genuine world co-operation virtually established.

The expected revolutionary upheavals in Europe after the war need not, according to Browder, disrupt the new international unity; for, said he, "It is the most stupid mistake to suppose that any American interest, even that of American monopoly capital, is incompatible with the necessary people's revolution in Europe." The developing colonial revolutions were disposed of by Browder with equal ease. Obviously, American capitalism had a compelling profit interest, he argued, to create broad markets in the colonial and semi-colonial lands. Hence, highly practical (nay, inevitable) would be an agreement between the United States and Great Britain to liberate, industrialize, and democratize these areas. This was Truman's "Point Four," originated by Roosevelt and theorized about by Browder. Trade conflicts between the two powers could (would) also be worked out in friendly agreement.

Thus, in Browder's assumed "Teheran" post-war world the imperialists would abandon their innate hostility to the Soviet Union, liquidate their own trade rivalries, tolerate people's revolutions in Europe, and collaborate with the independence movements of the colonial peoples. Consequently, peace would be assured for many generations.

This idyllic international unity of Browder's also presupposed an equally idyllic national unity in the capitalist countries. In the United States the main consideration for such unity was economic. This involved, said Browder, disposing of $80 billion yearly in surplus commodities that would develop once the war industries returned to civilian production. This problem he prepared to solve, first, by increasing American foreign trade by $40 billion annually; that is, by upping United States exports to Latin America by $6 billion, to Africa $6 billion, to Asia $20 billion, to Europe $6 billion, and to the U.S.S.R. $2 billion. "I am quite willing," said Browder, " to help the free private enterprisers to realize the forty-billion dollar market that is required entirely and completely by their own methods." This was a suggestion to Wall Street to grab the trade of the world with the help of the working class.

In order to dispose of the $40 billion of American overproduction that would be left even after this vast extension of foreign trade, Browder expected that the employers would voluntarily double the real wages of the workers. "There seems to be no other way," said Browder, "but to double the buying power of the individual consumer. How that shall be done we will not suggest at this time. We look forward to practical suggestions from the capitalists who must find the solution in order to keep their plants in operation."

Browder declared that the "intelligent" capitalists would establish national unity on the basis of all his projects—acceptance of the European and colonial revolutions, doubling the workers' wages, abolition of anti-Semitism and Negro persecution—in accordance with their "true class interests." In his enthusiasm for a class collaborationist national unity he declared in a speech at Bridgeport, Connecticut, on December 12, 1943, "If J. P. Morgan supports this [pro-Teheran] coalition and goes down the line for it, I as a Communist am prepared to clasp his hand on that and join with him to realize it."[1]

On such a basis Browder foresaw national unity in the United States. There would be, he said, "very little discontent in labor's ranks and very little strained relations between labor, government, and management." The trade unions would have few problems. Working under an incentive wage and a no-strike pledge, which he wanted carried over into the post-war period, Browder expected that the unions would surely arrive at "an agreed practical program, which grants to the capitalists the maximum initiative in working out the problems of distribution in their own way."

One of the worst elements in Browder's so-called national unity was his abandonment of the fight of the Negro people for self-determination. His theory was that the Negro people, by their attitude at the close of the Civil War, had exercised their right of self-determination and given up all perspectives of being a distinct nation. This was a repudiation of the national character of the Negro question. The political substance of this was that the Negro masses, like the workers, had no real need for further struggle against the supposedly benevolent ruling class, but would automatically achieve their rights. The ultimate results of this conception were a grave weakening of the Party's fight among the Negro people and a virtual liquidation of the Communist Party in the South.[2]

Browder's national unity also presupposed the workers' acceptance indefinitely of the two-party electoral system. He said, "The working class shares very largely the general national opinion that this 'two-party system' provides adequate channels for the basic preservation of democratic rights." He defended this system and said, "The political aims which we hold with the majority of Americans we will attempt to advance through the existing party structure of our country, which in the main is that of the peculiarly American two-party system."

On the basis of his acceptance of capitalism, class collaboration, the two-party system, and the elimination of the Negro people's struggle for national liberation, logically enough Browder also saw no need for the Communist Party. So he proposed its dissolution and the reorganization

[1] *The Communist*, Jan. 1943.
[2] Resolution, Emergency Convention, C.P.U.S.A., July 28, 1945.

of the Communists into an educational institution. This body should put up no election candidates of its own and would "be *non-partisan* in character." It would carry on "Marxist" work among the masses. As for Leninism, the Marxism of the present period, that was out entirely; Lenin's name was not even mentioned by Browder in the whole presentation of his Teheran thesis.

THE ESSENCE OF BROWDER'S OPPORTUNISM

The heart of Browder's opportunist ideas was the traditional "American exceptionalism," the illusion that the capitalist system in this country is basically different in that it is not subject to the laws of growth and decay that govern capitalism in other countries. Because of the relatively favorable conditions of its development—the absence of a feudal political past, the control of tremendous natural resources, a vast unified land area, and, in late years, its ability, because of its strategic situation, to profit from the world wars that were destroying other capitalist countries, capitalism in the United States has retained the appearance of great strength in a world of developing capitalist weakness. Lenin long ago explained this phenomenon by his law of the uneven development of capitalism; but opportunists such as Lovestone and Browder, in full harmony with the bourgeois economists, considered that the superficial, specific features of American capitalism set it apart basically from capitalism in general. This "American exceptionalism" saturated Browder's entire political outlook.

Browder's opportunist plan, as is customary with "American exceptionalists," contained an enormous overestimation of the power of American capitalism. His Teheran thesis virtually showed the American monopolists running the entire world, and conceded Wall Street imperialist world hegemony. Henry Luce never portrayed "the American century" so vividly as Earl Browder did.

Another major element in Browder's opportunism was its Keynesism. That is, he undertook to show that by government planning the United States could overcome its crises of overproduction. The false implication of this was that capitalism could thereby vanquish its general crisis. Browder's utopia was the characteristic Keynesian illusion of a "progressive capitalism," moving ahead in an ever-rising spiral. The picture he painted was one of the evolutionary advance of an all-satisfying capitalism, not of militant struggles to socialism.

Browder's opportunism also had in it the typical right Social-Democratic policy of class collaboration, which means the subordination of the working class to the dictation of the capitalist class. He put the whole control of society in the hands of "intelligent capitalists." The working class had no revolutionary role, nor had the Communist Party.

Browder's scheme was a crass revision of Marxism-Leninism. In his Teheran thesis he obliterated the class struggle, overcame the basic contradictions of capitalism, eliminated the conception of imperialism (the very word "imperialism" became taboo to him), and he did away with the perspective of socialism. For, if the capitalists should voluntarily double the wages of their workers, industrialize and democratize the undeveloped areas of the world, abolish war, and establish rising living standards all over the world, as Browder maintained they would, where would be the grounds for the proletarian revolution and socialism? Browder was even more ambitious than all this in his revisionism. He was insolently striving to rewrite the whole body of Marxist-Leninist-Stalinist principles and program.

Browder's opportunist Teheran policy was the climax of his several years of wrong attitudes toward the Roosevelt coalition and the national unity of the pre-war and war years. This systematic misinterpretation produced a whole series of developing errors, from the time the Party began to support Roosevelt in 1936. Among these errors, as we have remarked in passing, were Browder's failure to criticize Roosevelt and his dictum of "follow Roosevelt and subordinate everything to his policies" (as early as 1937, a prominent European Marxist said that Browder was "bedazzled by Roosevelt"), his betrayal of the national liberation movements in Asia and Latin America, his "crossed-the-Rubicon" theory of Anglo-American imperialism in the war, his wrong conception of the national liberation struggle in China, his refusal to insist upon a wartime coalition government, his incentive wage, his centralized war economy, his ousting of 4,000 foreign-born from the Communist Party, his abolition of shop groups, his growing assumption in practice that the class struggle had disappeared, his underplaying of the leading and independent role of the working class and the Communist Party, and, all along, his opportunistic interpretation of American history. The Teheran policy was only the final maturing of Browder's ever-more-marked orientation to the right.

In his Teheran policy, Browder was a voice of American imperialism. He glorified the "progressive" role of American monopoly capitalism; he sowed imperialist illusions among the workers; he sought to demobilize the labor movement and the colonial peoples in the face of aggressive imperialism, and he tried to wipe out the greatest of all enemies of American imperialism, the Communist Party. The Teheran policy was an attempt to write an effective program in the interest of the

American big bourgeoisie, not of the working class. It was designed to further Wall Street's post-war drive to master the world and to get the working class to support it.

HOW BROWDER'S REVISIONISM ORIGINATED

In the present period of sharp domestic class struggles, international war danger, and the Leninist position of the Communist Party, it seems almost incredible that the Party could ever have made the fundamental error of accepting Browder's impossible Teheran scheme. The basic reason for this error was the inadequate Marxist-Leninist development of the Party and its leaders. The mistake was a mistake of the Party, not merely of its then leader, Browder. He merely capitalized upon the weak Marxist-Leninist development of the Party. He was the theoretician, spokesman, and originator of the deviation.

The Party at the time was part of a national unity made up of all classes, and it was supporting a bourgeois government allied with the U.S.S.R. in a great war against fascism. This was basically a correct line. But the Party had been so conditioned in the complex situation by the development of Browder's opportunism over the previous several years as to exaggerate grossly the progressive significance of the existing national and international unity. Browder, a cunning sophist, was able to give a sinister plausibility to his Teheran project. Hence, the Party was deceived into believing, or at least partially believing, that the wartime national and international unity would be continued and greatly developed in the post-war period. Other Communist parties at the time, especially in the western hemisphere, made similar mistakes, endorsing either Browder's line or variations of it.

Browder's revisionism had deep roots in the inadequate social composition of the Party. The Party's strength was relatively weak among the workers in the basic industries, and this weakness was accentuated by the Browder-inspired liquidations of the shop units in this period. There had also been a large influx of ideologically undeveloped white collar workers and professionals into the Party. Many, if not most, of these elements eventually developed into sound Communists, but Browder, himself a white collar worker, an accountant, systematically allied himself with the right-wing currents among them. He also had close ties with those opportunist (later renegade) Communist trade union leaders, who had become corrupted by the high wages and political opportunism prevalent in the C.I.O. official circles. Browder cultivated all these right tendencies, based himself upon them, and directed his inner Party fire solely against the real Marxists in the Party. All this was akin to the petty-bourgeois opportunism which historically had ruined the Socialist Party.

Browderism was also enabled to flourish through the lack of democratic centralism in the Party. Under a correct Leninist system of democratic centralism, there must be within the Party full political discussion, penetrating self-criticism, sound discipline, a vigorous fight against both right and "left" deviations, and an energetic application of Party decisions. These are the conditions for a strong Party and correct policies. An approximation to this regime has normally been the life of our Party, but not always. During the long factional fight of 1923-29, for example, the Party's democratic centralism was stifled by the prevailing captious criticism, factional attitudes, lack of discipline, and the placing of group interests before those of the Party. Then again, under the Browder regime, the violation of democratic centralism went to the opposite, but related extreme, in the drastic curtailment of real political discussion, the virtual abolition of self-criticism, the cultivation of bureaucratic methods of work, the general development of a super-centralization, and the almost complete abandonment of the fight against right tendencies in the Party. Browder, to stifle political discussion, harped demagogically upon the dangers of factionalism, vivid memories being still prevalent in the Party of the great harm done by the long factional fight of 1923-29. It was under such artificial conditions, alien to Marxist-Leninist Party life, that Browder's revisionist Teheran thesis, without adequate discussion, was foisted temporarily upon the Party.

The Teheran deviation of our Party was essentially of a Social-Democratic character. The right Social-Democracy, as its settled policy, always tails after the bourgeoisie. This policy, as we have seen, has, among other treacheries, brought it to the point of supporting the program of American imperialism for world conquest through a major war. Browder's policies would have led our Party in this same general direction. The Party, however, proved its Communist quality by recognizing its serious error and drastically correcting it. This is something which the right Social-Democracy cannot possibly do. Marxist-Leninists are not infallible. They, too, occasionally make mistakes. What characterizes them, however, is that they make fewer mistakes than any other Party and then, on the basis of penetrating self-criticism, they openly correct these mistakes and learn the lessons from them.

FOSTER OPPOSES BROWDER'S LINE

Browder made his report on Teheran, on January 7, 1944, to the National Committee and other leading Party workers, about 500 in all.

William Z. Foster, national chairman of the Party, presided over the meeting. As soon as Browder had concluded, Foster put his name on the speakers' list and notified the Political Committee that he was going to speak against Browder's report. Several members of the Committee strongly urged him not to do this, on the ground that it would throw the Party into grave confusion in the midst of the war. They also assured him that Browder had spoken without a previous review of his speech and that the whole matter would be taken up shortly for reconsideration by the Political Committee.

With this understanding Foster withdrew his name from the speakers' list. But as no Political Committee discussion of Browder's report took place, on January 20th he addressed a letter to the National Committee expressing his views.[1] In this letter Foster challenged the whole line of Browder's report. In the sphere of foreign policy, he attacked Browder's underestimation of the general crisis of capitalism, his illusions about the liquidation of imperialism and his "progressive" role of American capitalism, his belief that the big capitalists in Great Britain and the United States would no longer assail the Soviet Union. He pointed out that Roosevelt was an imperialist, and he warned of the post-war drive for world domination that would come from American imperialism.

In the domestic sphere Foster showed the fallacy of proposing a post-war national unity that would include the "biggest capitalists," assailed the Browder-Morgan symbol of national unity, foresaw a post-war perspective of class struggle instead of class peace, opposed Browder's acceptance of the two-party system, attacked the post-war no-strike policy, condemned the discarding of socialism, and warned the Party of the danger of falling into the right Social-Democratic error of tailing after the bourgeoisie. As for the dissolution of the Party, Foster and other comrades had opposed this ever since it had been proposed some weeks before. Obviously, however, he should have again pressed this question in his letter to the National Committee. On Browder's thesis as a whole, Foster's letter said: "In this picture, American imperialism virtually disappears, there remains hardly a trace of the class struggle, and socialism plays practically no role whatever."

Foster demanded that a new meeting of the National Committee be called to discuss his letter. This was refused, but instead an "enlarged meeting" of the Political Committee, of some 80 leading Party workers was held on February 8, 1944. Foster's letter was read and overwhelmingly rejected, only one of those present voting with him. Browder then

---

[1] Full text in *Political Affairs*, July 1945. Beginning with the issue of Jan. 1945, *The Communist* was renamed *Political Affairs*.

served notice upon Foster that if he carried his position to the membership, this action would be met by his expulsion. Foster's letter was suppressed by Browder and kept from the Party as a whole.

Convinced that any attempt to raise the issue broadly among the membership would result in a fruitless Party split, Foster decided, for the time being at least, to confine his opposition to the National Committee—"a course which," he said, "I followed for the next year and a half by means of innumerable criticisms, policy proposals, articles,[1] etc., all going in the direction of eliminating Browder's opportunistic errors. I was convinced that the course of political events and the Communist training of our leadership would eventually cause our Party to return to a sound line of policy."[2] And so matters turned out in reality.

DISSOLUTION OF THE COMMUNIST PARTY

Browder, in the earliest discussions of his general Teheran thesis, proposed the liquidation of the Communist Party. Among other arguments, he cited the dissolution of the Communist International in May 1943, which, however, had taken place, as we have seen, for reasons completely different from Browder's opportunist purposes. He encountered much opposition in the Political Committee, but eventually won his point.

Consequently, the National Committee of the Communist Party, on January 11, 1944, sent out a letter to the Party districts recommending that the Party as such be dissolved and reorganized into a "political-educational association." This was endorsed practically unanimously by all the districts. During May 20-22, 1944, therefore, the plan was carried out at the regular twelfth convention of the Party held in New York City.

The Communist Party convention proper lasted only a few minutes. Browder made the proposition to dissolve the Party, stating, "I hereby move that the Communist Party of America be and hereby is dissolved and that a committee of three consisting of the Chairman, General Secretary, and Assistant Secretary of the Party, be authorized to take all necessary steps to liquidate its affairs and that such committee be further authorized to dispose of all its property and to turn over any surplus that may remain to any organization or organizations that in their opinion are devoted to our country's winning of the war in which it is presently engaged and in the achieving of a durable peace." The motion

[1] William Z. Foster in *Political Affairs*, June 1945.
[2] William Z. Foster in *On the Struggle against Revisionism*, p. 18, N. Y., 1945.

was adopted without discussion, whereupon the C.P. convention adjourned.

The delegation then immediately reconvened and proceeded to organize itself into the Communist Political Association. Browder made the main political report, along the lines of his by then well-known Teheran thesis. This was adopted as the general program of the C.P.A. The old structure of the C.P., with considerable changes, was taken over by the new organization, and so, too, were its journals, properties, and funds, the special committee placed in charge of this matter at the C.P. convention so deciding. The leadership, district and national, remained substantially the same, except that Foster, because of his opposition stand, was dropped as national chairman, Browder taking over this position with the title of president. Eleven vice-presidents were also elected, thus centralizing more power in Browder's hands. The heads of the state organizations were called presidents.

The Preamble to the Constitution was drastically modified in line with the new political orientation. The C.P.A. dubbed itself "a nonpartisan association of Americans," which "adheres to the principles of scientific socialism, Marxism" [not Marxism-Leninism]. The Preamble said nothing of the class struggle, of imperialism, of the revolutionary role of the working class, of the establishment of socialism. Instead, "it looks to the family of free nations, led by the great coalition of democratic capitalist and socialist states, to inaugurate an era of world peace, expanding production and economic well-being, and the liberation and equality of all peoples regardless of race, creed or color." Some months later Browder proposed dropping the word Communist from the title of the C.P.A., but was defeated by one vote in the Political Committee.

Thus Browder's system of revisionism had reached its ultimate expression. It had gone to its last extreme in the liquidation of the Party. Browder had not only revised the principles and policies of the Party, he had also dissolved the Party itself. He did this under the pretext that the C.P.A. was a better instrument to work with. This was an abandonment and betrayal of the most fundamental concepts of Marxism-Leninism. It was a surrender to the Social-Democratic and bourgeois demand that the C.P. be abolished, an attempt to deprive the working class of its indispensable leading political party. In its convention of May 1944, the Communist Party of the United States made the greatest political mistake in all its history.[1]

[1] See *Proceedings of the Constitutional Convention of the Communist Political Association*, New York, 1944.

EFFECTS UPON THE MASS WORK

Browder's revisionism promptly had weakening effects upon all branches of Communist mass work. In the trade unions attempts to develop a post-war no-strike outlook along the lines of the Teheran thesis badly misfired, and the right-wing opposition correspondingly prospered. In the work among the Negro masses Browder's theory that the Negro people, having abandoned (satisfied) their national aspirations, were now integrated into the white population, threw confusion into the ranks of the Communists and their sympathizers and undermined their fight for the rights of the Negro people. In the field of women's work, Browder's reliance upon the progressive role of the bourgeoisie tended to liquidate all conceptions that the women would actually have to fight for their rights in order to get them. In the national group work similar opportunist conceptions took root, and for the first time in American Communist history bourgeois nationalism became an acute problem among the left forces in this sphere. In cultural work, Browder's bourgeois catering to "big names" was a debilitating influence. And in the South, where the Communists had carried on so heroically for so long, work was practically abandoned.

The Young Communist League suffered early and heavily from Browder's revisionism and liquidationism. On October 16, 1943, the Y.C.L. in convention dissolved and then reorganized its forces into the American Youth for Democracy. This was not an effort to find the basis for a broader Marxist organization—the traditional Y.C.L. objective—but an attempt to wipe out Marxism-Leninism in youth work. Says Betty Gannett, "The new organization was conceived as educating the youth not in socialism, but in the traditions of the best in bourgeois democracy. It was to be a non-partisan organization, with free discussion of the policies and theories proposed by *all* political parties.... Fraternal ties with the Communist Party were dissolved.... Emphasis was laid on the service character of the organization, thus differentiating it but little from other youth service organizations. And Marxism was to be studied on a voluntary basis, as one of the important 'currents of democratic thought.' This opportunist trend was intensified as Browderism grew. The effects of revisionism negated every basic principle of Marxist-Leninist work among the youth."[1] Corrections were made in this line in 1945 after Browder's defeat, and these were amplified at the formation of the Labor Youth League in May 1948.

In the 1944 presidential elections, with the sick Roosevelt leading the Democratic ticket together with Harry S. Truman, Browder, in line

---

[1] Betty Gannett in *Political Affairs*, Sept. 1948.

with his Teheran program, tried to make a grandiose maneuver. In a speech in Cleveland he proposed that the heads of the Republican and Democratic parties should come together and agree upon a single win-the-war ticket. This step was logical from Browder's revisionist position. He was contending that the bulk of finance capital was supporting the Teheran policy, therefore to him it made small difference whether the Republicans or Democrats won, both parties being controlled by "progressive" finance capital. The election, consequently, had little real significance to him, and all the election fury was mere narrow partisanship without real political content. Therefore, the two parties should pick a common ticket. This scheme obviously would imply the ditching of Roosevelt; for, of course, the Republicans would never agree upon him. But Browder quickly backed away from his hare-brained project, owing to vigorous opposition in the Political Committee and also to clear indications that his proposal would have been almost unanimously condemned by the strong Roosevelt forces among the broad masses. So the C.P.A. continued its endorsement of Roosevelt and helped elect him to his fourth term.

GROWING OPPOSITION IN THE C.P.A.

The Party membership from the outset accepted Browder's revisionist Teheran policy without firm conviction. Before long this uncertainty began to develop into doubt and opposition. This changing attitude was primarily due to the fact that the course of American and world events was swiftly exposing the fallacy of Browder's whole line. Obviously, in the field of labor what the post-war period was bringing would not be Browder's long period of peaceful class collaboration, but many hard-fought strikes. And in the realm of foreign policy, although the war was not yet over, American imperialism (with its new political chieftain, Truman) was clearly preparing to grab what it could of the war-stricken world. This became especially evident with the opening of the United Nations founding conference in San Francisco on April 25, 1945. "All the great struggles of the conference," says Frederick V. Field, "revolved around the effort of imperialism to reassert itself against the forces of democracy to which the war had given such impetus."[1] Particularly sinister signs of this basic fact were the admission of Peron's Argentina to the U.N. and the exclusion of democratic Poland.

The threatening domestic and international situation produced increasing doubts in the C.P.A. about its political line. These were reflected in the Political Committee. Eugene Dennis began to develop

[1] Frederick V. Field in *Political Affairs*, Aug. 1945.

a perspective of active struggle, instead of class peace, in the post-war United States; Gilbert Green proposed that a National Committee meeting be held to review the post-war situation (to which Browder's thesis was supposed to be the basic answer); Benjamin J. Davis, Jr., warned of the evil effects that the present policies were having in Negro work; Jack Stachel spoke of American imperialism (which supposedly Browder had liquidated); Robert Thompson expressed growing doubt on various aspects of the Browder line; John Williamson complained of the lethargy in the C.P.A. and the big loss of members. Foster cultivated all these doubts about the correctness of the Party line and lost no occasion of criticizing the Browder policy and exposing its fallacies. Browder, therefore, had all plans laid for Foster's expulsion in the near future.

THE DUCLOS ARTICLE

In the midst of this rapidly developing internal situation, Jacques Duclos, secretary of the Communist Party of France, published in the French journal, *Cahiers du Communisme*, in April 1945, an article colliding head on with the Browder policies.[1] Duclos was motivated to write his article primarily because, some time before, an article had appeared in *France Nouvelle*, a Communist paper, lauding Browderism, and also because Browder's dissolution of the Communist Party in the United States was encouraging liquidationist tendencies in the French Communist Party.

In his article, Duclos made a long statement of Browder's policy, counterposing to it copious quotations from Foster's letter to the National Committee. In drawing his own conclusions, Duclos declared that "one is witnessing a notorious revision of Marxism on the part of Browder and his followers, a revisionism which is expressed in the concept of a long-term class peace in the United States, of the possibility of the suppression of the class struggle in the post-war period and the establishment of harmony between labor and capital." He condemned Browder's distortion of the Teheran diplomatic declaration "into a political platform of class peace," and he excoriated the liquidation of the Communist Party. He declared that "nothing justifies the dissolution of the American Communist Party." Instead, the situation "presupposes the existence of a powerful Communist Party."

The Duclos article had an electrifying effect upon the C.P.A. It speedily matured the already developing opposition to the Browder policies. Within a matter of weeks the whole Party, from the local clubs to the Political Committee, almost unanimously rejected the Teheran oppor-

[1] *Political Affairs*, July 1945.

tunism. Undoubtedly, with events at home and abroad daily showing the stupidity of Browder's revisionism, the American Communists, without Duclos' intervention, would eventually have cleared the Party of this political poison. But it would have been a difficult process, probably involving a serious Party split. As it was, his famous article greatly facilitated the smashing of Browder's opportunist system; for which the Communist Party of the United States remains deeply indebted to Jacques Duclos and the French Communist Party.

THE EMERGENCY CONVENTION

The C.P.A. received a copy of Duclos' article on May 20, 1945.[1] It was immediately discussed in the Political Committee. The whole policy of the C.P.A. quickly came under survey, with the result that Browder's line was rejected by a two-thirds majority of the Committee, which soon became unanimous, except for Browder. The latter, packed with conceit and arrogance and devoid of any trace of self-criticism, clung to his position, despite its obvious bankruptcy. Consequently, a few days later he was suspended as general secretary, and a secretariat of three—William Z. Foster, Eugene Dennis, and John Williamson—was chosen in his stead.

On June 18-20, a meeting of the National Committee was held. The Committee, reflecting the virtually solid sentiment of the membership, unanimously condemned Browder's line, agreed with the Duclos article, fully endorsed Foster's earlier letter to the National Committee, and adopted the draft of a new policy resolution. It also supported the removal of Browder as general secretary, making this permanent, and it called a special convention for July 26-28, in New York City.

The Emergency (thirteenth) Convention unanimously endorsed the actions taken by the Political Committee and the National Committee. It was a convention of deep self-criticism for the great mistake that had been made in the Party's falling victim to Browder's revisionism. In this respect the convention declared, "The source of our past revisionist errors must be traced to the ever active pressure of bourgeois ideology and influence upon the working class."

The convention set about thoroughly cleansing the Party of Browderism and putting it once more upon a solid Marxist-Leninist basis. The C.P.A. was liquidated and the Communist Party reconstituted. The Party Constitution was correspondingly rewritten. A secretariat was chosen to head the Party, consisting of William Z. Foster, Eugene Dennis, and Robert Thompson. Foster was reinstated as national chairman. Numerous changes were made in the composition of the National

[1] *Daily Worker,* May 27, 1945.

Committee and, later by local action, also in the state and local committees.

The Preamble of the Party Constitution was also rewritten and given substantially its present text. It broke with Browder's adulation of bourgeois democracy and struck a clear note of proletarian democracy and socialism. It declared that "The Communist Party of the United States is the political party of the working class, basing itself upon the principles of scientific socialism, Marxism-Leninism." While defending the achievements of American democracy, it pledged an uncompromising fight "against imperialism and colonial oppression, against racial, national and religious discrimination, against Jim Crowism, anti-Semitism and all forms of chauvinism," and for socialism. It was sharply and clearly based upon the class struggle.

The main resolution[1] made a realistic survey of the world situation—the war with Japan being not yet concluded at the time. It repudiated all the Browder nonsense about the "progressive" role of American imperialism and pointed out the sinister dangers in the international policies being followed by Wall Street and the Truman government. The resolution declared that "the most aggressive circles of American imperialism are endeavoring to secure for themselves political and economic domination of the world." It also stated that "if the reactionary policies and forces of monopoly capital are not checked and defeated, America and the world will be confronted with new aggressions and war and the growth of reaction and fascism in the United States." This incisive Marxist-Leninist analysis gave a clear picture of the international situation and made a forecast of the course of events which remains completely valid today.

In the domestic sphere the resolution broke completely with Browder's class collaborationism. It rejected the post-war no-strike line, incentive wage, subservience to the two-party system, and "organized capitalism" of Browder, and it wrote a program of class struggle. It outlined a militant win-the-war program; urged the workers to prepare for the difficult struggles of the post-war period; retained the sound Communist policy of building the Roosevelt coalition and set out to strengthen it in a Leninist sense. The resolution sharply criticized Truman, who had been president for only a few months, and declared, "It is of central importance to build systematically the political strength of labor, the Negro people, and all true democratic forces within the general coalition for the struggle against imperialist reaction, for combating and checking all tendencies and groupings in the coalition willing to make concessions to reaction. The camp of reaction must not be appeased. It must be

[1] *Political Affairs*, Sept. 1945.

isolated and routed." The resolution restated a correct policy on the Negro question. The Party had reasserted its Communist quality.

The convention, in short, made a clean sweep of the reformist trappings of Browderism. But it took the work of the next few years to eliminate from the Party the many revisionist moods and practices that had been growing for so long under Browder's cultivation. After the Emergency Convention a great surge of joy and enthusiasm went through the ranks of the Communist Party. But the adventure into revisionism of the C.P.A. had been a costly one, the Party losing some 15,000 members, who were repelled by Browder's opportunism. This had been evident earlier when large numbers of Party members had refused to register in the C.P.A. A report by Betty Gannett in mid-1944 stated that but 63,044 members, or 88 percent of those on the rolls of the C.P. (not counting 15,000 in the armed services) joined the C.P.A., a loss of 9,000 at this point. The Party registration of January 1946 showed but 52,824 members, a figure which was raised to 59,172 in the registration of 1947.

An aftermath of Browder's revisionism was the organized defection of a few dozen disgruntled sectarians in New York, Philadelphia, San Francisco, and elsewhere. These included Sam Darcy, William F. Dunne, Harrison George, Vern Smith, and others. They developed a leftist line of criticism, charging that the new Party leadership was centrist. This was their way of retreating from the increasingly difficult class struggle under cover of revolutionary phraseology.

THE EXPULSION OF BROWDER

Browder promised the Party to obey the convention decisions, and the Party leadership offered to give him minor Party work. He refused this, however, as he had obviously decided upon breaking with the Party. Soon he began a factional correspondence inside the Party, and toward the latter part of 1945 he started publishing a sheet called *Distributors Guide*. This paper propagated Browder's revisionist line and made sneaking attacks on the Party. He also tried to build a factional grouping.

Although repeatedly warned, Browder continued his unprincipled maneuvering. He challenged the authority of the Political Committee and the secretariat to examine his political activities. Therefore, at a meeting of the National Committee, on February 12-15, 1946, upon the report of Robert Thompson,[1] he was unanimously expelled from the Communist Party. A mere handful—his wife, his brother, his financial "angel," and a few others—departed with him as his following.

Once outside of the Party, Browder intensified his anti-Party activi-

[1] Robert Thompson, *The Path of a Renegade*, N. Y., 1946.

ties. But he could never assemble more than a baker's dozen in his group. With the whole world situation daily giving the lie to his absurd Teheran thesis, Browder went right on reiterating it to "fit" the completely contradictory political conditions. He disintegrated into an open enemy of the Communist Party, a shameless mouthpiece for American imperialism, and a snide vilifier of the Soviet Union.[1]

[1] For the later political decay of Browder, see articles by Gilbert Green in *Political Affairs*, Oct., Nov., 1949, and March 1950.

31. The Revolutionary Aftermath of the War (1945-1951)

World War II, with its wholesale slaughter of human beings and gigantic destruction of property, had far-reaching revolutionary consequences. The great democratic masses of workers and farmers, the victims of this monstrous devastation, widely realized that the basic cause of the war was capitalism itself, and they struck back as best they could at that outworn and murderous social system. This post-war upheaval was a natural extension of the great war against fascism. With varying degrees of intensity, it affected all parts of the world. Like the two world wars, the Russian Revolution, the growth of fascism, and the great economic crisis of the 1920's, all of them products of the deepening crisis of world capitalism, the revolutionary movement following World War II dealt a further shattering blow to that already sick system.

The post-war upsurge also affected the United States, the stronghold of world capitalism. This was expressed by developing anti-fascist, anti-monopoly moods among the people, by many big strike movements, by the forward surge of the Negro people, by the powerful demonstrations of soldiers for demobilization, and by other mass manifestations of growing resistance in the United States to the rule of monopoly capital.

THE ADVANCE OF THE SOVIET UNION

Outstanding in the world revolutionary development following the recent war was the tremendous growth in strength and political prestige of the U.S.S.R. This was all the more marked because of the profound weakening of many capitalist countries during the war. Not only absolutely, but also relatively, the position of the Soviet Union was strengthened. Prior to the war the capitalists considered the U.S.S.R. as a secondary influence among the states; after the war it is universally recognized as one of the two great and decisive powers of the world. The war showed the Soviet system to be the most powerful in the world.

The tremendous advance of the Soviet Union, with its 200 million people, was all the more striking in view of the enormous losses suffered by that nation during the war—over 23 million human casualties, property losses of $128 billion, not to mention the huge cost of waging the war and the vast areas and industries of the country overrun and wantonly devastated. No capitalist state could possibly have suffered such terrific destruction without being defeated in the war. The capitalists, in fact, particularly the big monopolists of Wall Street, thought they had really accomplished their objective of "letting Germany and Russia shoot each other to pieces," and that the U.S.S.R. would not be able to rise again for a long period, if ever. To make the recovery of the U.S.S.R. all the more difficult, they, through their obedient Truman government, not only refused to grant post-war loans to this ally who had suffered so much in the war, but they have actually persisted in trying to compel the U.S.S.R. to pay the United States for the lend-lease supplies it was furnished during the war. This pinch-penny attitude of the government was a shameful disgrace to the generous-minded American people.

But, with the huge, powerful strength innate in its Socialist system, the U.S.S.R., led by its great Communist Party, headed by Stalin, confounded its capitalist enemies by making a very swift recovery from its stupendous wartime property losses. It has far outpaced economically all other countries in Europe, despite the latter's immense subsidies from the United States and their far lesser war destruction. So speedy was its recovery that, by November 1951, industrial production had doubled that of 1940[1] and was still rapidly rising. In its great industrial vigor, moreover, the Soviet government was already outlining a whole series of monster new developments—including great new power plants, a further big expansion of industry, vast irrigation projects, and the huge enterprise of changing the climate of arid areas in the country through forestation belts.

Along with its vast post-war increase of industrial strength, the Soviet Union has also acquired huge new political prestige. With its sane industrial system and its resolute stand for world peace, it has won the confidence of the many new people's governments born since the end of World War II, and also of great toiling masses in all capitalist countries. The U.S.S.R. is the leader of the world camp of peace, democracy, and socialism.

The Communist Party of the U.S.A. has never slackened in its tireless efforts to demonstrate to the American people the peace role of the U.S.S.R. and also the indispensability, for the welfare of the world, of the peaceful collaboration of the American and Soviet peoples. This is in line with the C.P.'s role as the Party most loyally defending the true interests of the American people.

[1] L. P. Beria, *The Soviet Union Builds for Peace*, N. Y., 1952.

THE RISE OF THE EUROPEAN PEOPLE'S DEMOCRACIES

Another basic revolutionary development following World War II was the foundation of the new People's Democracies in Eastern and Central Europe, comprising about 100 million people. These include Poland, Czechoslovakia, Romania, Hungary, Bulgaria, and Albania. The progressive Democratic Republic of Eastern Germany grew from the same great movement. Yugoslavia was also in this group of advanced democracies until the renegade Tito treacherously sold it out to Wall Street for a share of the Marshall Plan slush funds, made it a war vassal of American imperialism, and headed it into reaction. Tito's name, along with that of Trotsky and Quisling, has become a very symbol of treason to the international working class.

The People's Democracies of Europe took shape at the end of the war. The Red Army of the Soviet Union smashed the armies and puppet governments of Hitler in their respective countries, and all the anti-fascist parties, particularly those that had fought in the underground, were thereby assisted in taking over and forming coalition governments. This policy was a continuation and development into the post-war period of the program of all-out anti-fascist unity initiated by the Seventh Congress of the Comintern in 1935. These coalition governments were all democratically elected, usually in the face of violence, potential or real. All of this reactionary resistance was encouraged, if not financed and organized, by United States reactionaries. The Soviet Union's proximity shielded the young governments of the People's Democracies from actual armed attacks by the capitalist imperialists of the West.

The People's Democracies constitute a new form of the dictatorship of the proletariat. They are led by the Communist parties, the strongest parties as well as the most valiant fighters during the period of the Nazi occupation. The military defeat of Hitler by the Red Army was the precondition for the establishment of these democracies. The progress of the new democratic states has been marked internally by a growing consolidation of working class power, by the amalgamation of the Communist parties and the best elements of the Socialist parties, and by the strengthening of the leading political role of the Communist parties.

Led by the working class with the Communists at its head, the tremendous anti-fascist upsurge and the elemental swing of the European masses toward socialism at the end of the war resulted also in the creation of coalition governments in France, Italy, and other West European countries. Here, too, the Communist parties were the strongest and most clear-sighted parties in the new governments. But unlike Eastern and

Central Europe, these countries did not produce People's Democracies. This was primarily due to the fact that they were occupied by the armies of the United States and Britain, which balked the democratic will of these peoples. Vital, too, in this respect was the continued reactionary, capitalist pressure of Social-Democracy, the Catholic hierarchy, and the financial intimidation of the United States government.

The general post-war upheaval in Europe also produced the Labor Government in Great Britain. It was elected on the slogan of socialism, but its Social-Democratic leadership held the government tightly to a capitalist basis. The capitalists made bigger profits than ever before. The Labor Government served as the ruling agent for British imperialism until it was defeated by the big-business Tory, Churchill, in the election of October 1951. So careful was it of capitalist interests that the Churchill Government now finds that business tax rates, inherited from the Labor Government, are too low, and it proposes, in the country's desperate financial straits, to increase them.[1] Fittingly enough, after the election, the king gave the ousted Attlee the Order of Merit for his distinguished services to British capitalism and the monarchy.[2]

THE PEOPLE'S REVOLUTION IN CHINA

One of the most basic indications of the deepening general crisis of capitalism, in the aftermath of World War II, is the growing collapse of imperialist controls in colonial and semi-colonial countries all over the world. Formerly the main struggle there was among the various imperialist powers for the profit and pleasure of exploiting the peoples in these areas; but now this has been superseded by a great revolutionary struggle of these peoples, comprising half the population of the earth, to drive out all the imperialist robbers. Thus one of the pillars of world capitalism, its colonial system, is being rapidly destroyed. Asia, Africa, Latin America are all affected to various extents by this vast movement for human freedom and prosperity.

The outstanding leader in the colonial liberation revolution is the People's Republic of China, embracing 475 million people. It is the trail blazer and standard bearer of the whole gigantic movement. The Chinese Revolution is the classic type of colonial revolution of this period of the general crisis of capitalism. It points the way in which the revolution, at varying tempos, is going in all the colonial and semi-colonial lands—India, Burma, Malaya, Indo-China, Pakistan, Indonesia, Africa,

[1] *U.S. News and World Report*, Nov. 9, 1951.
[2] *New York Post*, Nov. 6, 1951.

Latin America, and the many countries of the Moslem world all the way from Pakistan to Morocco.

The heart and brain of the Chinese people's revolution is the Communist Party, which is inspired by the teachings of Marx, Engels, Lenin, and Stalin, and directly headed by the brilliant Marxist writer and fighter, Mao Tse-tung. The Chinese Communist Party, organized in 1921, has led the democratic masses through 25 years of warfare against the invading imperialists and their big landlord allies. This struggle includes the First Revolutionary Civil War (1925-27), the Second Revolutionary Civil War (1927-36), the War of Resistance to Japanese Aggression (1937-45) and the Third Revolutionary Civil War, beginning in 1946.[1] In July of the latter year the reactionary Chiang Kai-shek, "running dog" of American imperialism and of the Chinese landlords and usurers, launched an all-out armed attack to destroy the People's Liberation Army and the Communist Party. But at the end of December 1949, after a series of spectacular defeats, Chiang's American-equipped army was smashed and the remnants of his forces were driven from the mainland of China. During this fierce struggle the People's Liberation Army destroyed or captured 8,700,000 of Chiang's troops, won over 1,700,000 more, and seized from Chiang 50,000 pieces of artillery, 300,000 machine guns, 1,000 tanks, 20,000 motor vehicles, and many other kinds of miltary equipment, nearly all American-made.[2]

The Chinese People's Government is a new form of people's democracy—a government of the proletariat and peasantry, but without Soviets. Mao Tse-tung describes it as "a dictatorship of the people's democracy based on an alliance of the workers and peasants led by the working class (through the Communist Party). This dictatorship must be in agreement with the international revolutionary forces."[3] The writings of Mao Tse-tung are classical analyses of the colonial revolution and how to win it, in the period of the general crisis of world capitalism.

Lenin and Stalin long ago demonstrated the basic kinship of the Russian and Chinese Revolutions. And Sun Yat-sen, leader of the Chinese Revolution of 1911, on his deathbed in 1925, wrote the following message to the government of the Soviet Union: "You head a union of free republics—that tangible heritage which the immortal Lenin has bequeathed to the oppressed peoples of the world. By virtue of this heritage the victims of imperialism will inevitably achieve freedom and emancipation from

---

[1] Frederick V. Field in *Political Affairs*, Jan. 1949; Hsiao Hua in *People's China*, Aug. 1, 1951.
[2] Chu Teh in *For a Lasting Peace* . . . , June 29, 1951.
[3] Mao Tse-tung in *For a Lasting Peace* . . . , June 29, 1951 (from "The Dictatorship of the People's Democracy").

that entrenched system which, from time immemorial, has been based upon slavery, wars, and injustice."[1] And Chu Teh, great Chinese military leader, says, "Under the influence of the October Socialist Revolution [in Russia] the Chinese working class and the Chinese people learned the invincible revolutionary theory of Marxism-Leninism, and created a revolutionary political party of the proletariat along the lines indicated by Lenin and Stalin, namely, the Communist Party of China."[2]

American imperialism, eager to seize the great natural riches of China and to exploit its myriads of toilers, has traditionally been the enemy of the Chinese people and its national liberation revolution. This it has demonstrated time and again—by its participation in the all-power invasion of China in the Boxer uprising in 1900; by its attempt to strangle the Revolution of 1911 led by Sun Yat-sen; by its hypocritical Open Door policy, which was but a cloak for American imperialist penetration; by its furnishing of scrap iron and other war materials to the Japanese aggressors right up to World War II; by its subsidizing of the ultra-reactionary Chiang Kai-shek with $5 billion to put down the people's colonial revolution; and by its present attempt to defeat China and to steal Taiwan (Formosa) from that country.[3]

The Communist Party of the United States has always fought against American imperialist aggression in China, for many years under the slogan of "Hands Off China." But its Chinese policy weakened (as we have seen on page 419) during the period of the Teheran revisionism. In ridding itself of Browderism in general, the Party also did away with this opportunist policy. Thus, in keeping with the Party's re-established Marxist-Leninist line, Eugene Dennis, at the National Committee meeting of November 1945, called for 500 public meetings (which were held) to protest against American imperialist intervention in China against the people's revolutionary forces led by the Communists. And Foster declared that "The war in China is the key to all problems on the international front and it is here, above all else, where we have to deal the hardest blows against reaction."

THE ADVANCE OF THE AMERICAN NEGRO PEOPLE

A strong echo of the big national liberation revolutions in the colonial lands is found in the intensified struggle of the oppressed Negro people in the United States. This has become especially marked since the end of World War II. The Negro people in this country are greatly stimulated in their struggle by the big victories now being won by the dark-skinned

---

[1] Cited in *People's China*, Nov. 1, 1950.
[2] *People's China*, Nov. 16, 1950.
[3] Henry Newman in *Political Affairs*, Aug. 1949.

peoples in the colonial areas against the imperialist oppressors. By the same token, the awakening colonial peoples, joining with the peoples of the Soviet Union and the People's Democracies, are acutely aware of the anti-democratic significance of Negro oppression in the United States and are alert to protest against it upon all occasions. They have become powerful allies of the American Negro people. During the past ten years, the Negro question in this country has become a world issue in a real sense. The Wall Street imperialists are finding that on the international scene their cherished Jim Crow system is a real obstacle in their path of world conquest.

According to the 1950 federal census, Negro migration from the South to the North has continued during 1940-50. In this period the Negro population increased by only 55,637 persons in the thirteen southern states, whereas it went up from 2,808,549 to 4,364,000, a gain of 1,555,451, in the industrial states of California, Illinois, Michigan, New Jersey, New York, Ohio, and Pennsylvania.[1] This means more working class leadership in the fight of the Negro people.

In recent years, especially since the end of the war, the American Negro people have dealt many heavy blows against Jim Crow—by their own militant efforts, with the tireless help of the Communists and of their other domestic allies, and with the powerful assistance of their friends abroad. They have built up a splendid army of a million Negro trade unionists; they have slowed down the murderous lynch gangs; they have become recognized as a force in science—there are 20 Negro names in the latest edition of *American Men of Science;* they have forced their way into the first ranks of literature and the theater; they have cracked the color bar and distinguished themselves in many sports—baseball, boxing, bowling, tennis, track and field, etc.; they are generally battering their way into Jim Crow southern universities; and they are increasingly winning the right to vote in the reactionary South.[2] But this progress barely touches the fringes of the monstrous Jim Crow system, and it is all threatened by the sinister growth of reaction in this country. The Negro people are still the target of every reactionary force in the United States and they remain outrageously discriminated against in industry, politics, and social life. "Phrases about the progressive integration of the Negroes in the total life of the United States are meaningless," says Gus Hall, "when the Negro people comprise 9.8 percent of the population but receive less than three percent of the national income."[3] And as Pettis Perry

1 *New York Times,* Oct. 31, 1951.
2 For details on the recent advances of the Negro people see *Progress in Negro Status and Race Relations, 1911-1946,* Phelps-Stokes Fund, N. Y., 1946.
3 Gus Hall, *Marxism and Negro Liberation,* N. Y., 1951.

states, "Not since the Reconstruction period has there been a single Negro elected to the Senate of the United States, nor has there been a Negro elected to Congress from any Southern state since George H. White, of North Carolina, left Congress fifty years ago. Yet, the South is the area where over 10,000,000 Negroes live."[1]

American imperialism is gravely worried over the relentless criticism of Jim Crow that it is now encountering in this country from the Communist Party, and abroad from the Soviet Union and the other democratic countries of the world. Jim Crow is a dead giveaway of all of Wall Street's pretenses of being the world champion of democracy. One of the many means the imperialists are now adopting to try to stifle this just criticism is to inveigle outstanding Negro leaders in various spheres into glossing over and minimizing Negro discriminaton in the United States. Among those who have allowed themselves to be thus used against their own people are Ralph J. Bunche, Mrs. Edith Sampson, Jackie Robinson, Sugar Ray Robinson, Roy Wilkins, and Dr. Channing Tobias. The conservative Negro press is also contaminated with such apologist attitudes for white chauvinism. It is a deplorable spectacle to all friends of the Negro people when Negro spokesmen level their attacks against the great Paul Robeson and, addressing themselves to the world, tell the darker-skinned peoples that it is all a tissue of lies—the report that the Negro people are shamefully abused and discriminated against in the United States.

THE WORLD FEDERATION OF TRADE UNIONS

One of the most basic aspects of the great democratic-revolutionary mass upheaval during and following World War II was the enormous growth of the trade unions all over the world (except in the U.S.S.R., which was already completely unionized). This expansion of labor unionism affected not only the industrial countries, but also, to a huge extent, the colonial and semi-colonial lands. The United States was not exempt from this world-wide wave of organization, the total number of trade unionists in this country—A.F. of L., C.I.O. and independent—going up from about 10 million in 1940 to well on to 16 million at the end of 1948. In this country about one-third of the broad working class is now unionized. On the basis of government calculations, of the present 62 million "gainfully employed" in the United States some 46,500,000 are wage earners. Of these 10,500,000 are "clerks and kindred workers"; seven million are "skilled workers and foremen"; 13 million are "semi-skilled workers"; and 16 million are "unskilled workers." The remaining

[1] Pettis Perry in *Political Affairs*, Dec. 1951.

15,500,000 of "gainfully employed" are professionals, managers, officials, farmers, tradesmen, etc.[1]

Along with the tremendous world-wide growth of the trade unions went a powerful urge for their unification, on both a national and an international scale. This culminated in the formation of the World Federation of Trade Unions in Paris, on October 3, 1945, after several preliminary conferences in London, Paris, Washington, and San Francisco. The W.F.T.U. at its foundation had a membership of 64 million workers in 52 countries. It has since, by 1951, despite a world split-off by the reactionaries, grown to 78 million workers in 65 countries.[2]

Already at its foundation the W.F.T.U. was far and away larger than any previous trade union international, and it extended into many more countries, particularly the colonial and semi-colonial lands. In its elemental sweep of organization it drew into its fold hitherto irreconcilable Communist, Social-Democratic, syndicalist, Catholic, and non-party trade unionists. In the face of the W.F.T.U. the old International Federation of Trade Unions, dominated by the Social-Democrats, folded up and formally dissolved. Every important labor organization in the world, except the A.F. of L., joined the new world federation of labor.

The powerful unifying tendency of the W.F.T.U. was also felt in the United States, the C.I.O. taking an active part, especially under the leadership of Sidney Hillman, in the formation of the new international. The progressive position of the C.I.O. during those years on the question of world labor unity, like its advanced stand on various other issues, was primarily due to the influence of its powerful minority of Communists and progressives. The Communists were long the outstanding champions of national and international trade union unity. The A.F. of L., however, true to the Wall Street spirit of its top leadership, refused to join the W.F.T.U. and from the very outset laid a course designed to split that organization.

WORLD ORGANIZATIONS OF WOMEN AND YOUTH

The toiling women of the world also responded to the great democratic upheaval following World War II. They had learned a bitter lesson from the barbarities of fascism, the legitimate offspring of capitalism. Enormous post-war organizations of women developed in many countries. These came together in Paris on November 26, 1945, and founded a great organization to fight for a democratic and lasting peace —the Women's International Democratic Federation. Some 900 dele-

---

[1] Based on U.S. Census Bureau, *Statistical Abstract*, 1947, p. 100.
[2] Labor Research Association, *Labor Fact Book 10*, p. 145, N. Y., 1951.

gates were present from 42 countries. A couple of years later the organization had 81 million women members, or co-operators, of many religious and democratic political groupings.

American women sent 13 delegates to the initial congress, including prominent women leaders. In the spring of 1946 the returning delegation launched the Congress of American Women. This body developed many activities in the fields of peace, prices, civil liberties, health, child care, etc. It sharply opposed the Truman war policy and attracted the affiliation of a number of women's organizations. But its greatest weakness was a failure to establish a firm base among working class and Negro women. Because of its affiliation with the W.I.D.F., the C.A.W. was condemned as a subversive body by Attorney General Clark and ordered to register as a foreign agent—which it refused to do. Late in 1950 the organization, lacking a solid mass foundation, dissolved.

The youth of the world were no less responsive to the great democratic urge brought about by fascism and the war. Progressive young men and women were determined that these monstrous outrages should never happen again. The World Federation of Democratic Youth was organized in London in October 1945, with its headquarters in Paris. It was an outgrowth of the World Youth Council, set up in London during the war. Two years after its formation, the W.F.D.Y. reported a membership of 46 million young people in 64 countries. These included youth organizations of workers, peasants, Catholics, Social-Democrats, Communists, etc. The W.F.D.Y. in 1951 numbered 70 million members. It is a militant fighter for world peace.

An American delegation attended the founding congress of the W.F.D.Y. It included representatives from the Y.W.C.A., Jewish Welfare Board, N.A.A.C.P. Youth Councils, and other organizations. Mollie Lieber West, a Communist youth leader, was on the delegation. The returning delegates set up the American Youth for a Free World, but with the outbreak of the Korean war the bourgeois organizations retreated, and the A.Y.F.W. disbanded in 1951.

THE POST-WAR UPSURGE AMONG CULTURAL WORKERS

One of the most striking aspects of the world upheaval among the masses during and after World War II was its profound effects among intellectuals of all crafts and callings. This was marked throughout Europe, particularly in the countries of the new People's Democracies. It was even more pronounced in the Far East—in China, India, Pakistan, Burma, Malaya, and Indo-China. Trained intellectuals, scientists, writers, engineers, artists, and the like turned en masse against capitalism and toward socialism. This was one of the most significant aspects of the rapidly growing anti-capitalist sentiment among the masses of the peoples all over the world.

The United States, too, felt this world cultural movement, but not to the extent it was felt in those countries that were more overwhelmed by the general crisis of capitalism, where the war damage was greatest, and where the revolutionary movements were stronger. Following the war, a number of significant books, plays, and motion pictures appeared in this country, written by progressive democratic authors. The Communist Party, keenly appreciating the struggle on the cultural front, strongly encouraged such writings. These works, following the antifascist impetus given by the war, dealt primarily with anti-Semitism, white chauvinism, and similar themes. But the crop was meager. In 1947, V. J. Jerome said, "Apart from the fight against racism, it is difficult to point to actual trends of democratic content in creative work of the postwar period."[1] Most of the erstwhile progressive bourgeois writers were even then hearkening to the call of American imperialism and were busy confusing the masses ideologically, in Wall Street's drive for world conquest.

The only real cultural vigor shown in this period was on the left, among the Communists and others influenced by Marxism-Leninism. Philip Foner's *History of the Labor Movement in the United States*, Howard Fast's *The American*, Herbert Aptheker's *The Negro People in America* and his *Documentary History of the Negro People in the United States*, W. E. B. DuBois' *The World and Africa*, John Howard Lawson's *The Hidden Heritage*, Meridel Le Sueur's *North Star Country*, Albert Maltz's *The Journey of Simon McKeever*, Barbara Giles's *The Gentle Bush*, and Richard Boyer's *The Dark Ship* were only a few of the more notable works turned out by this group. In the field of the theater, the cultural-political leader Paul Robeson loomed as a towering giant. The Party, although a considerable force in the cultural field, has by no means developed its democratic possibilities.

THE GROWTH OF THE COMMUNIST PARTIES

A dynamic feature of the post-war period was the rapid expansion of the Communist parties in the countries that had felt the weight of the war. This was a result, on the one hand, of the brave leadership of the Communists during the fascist occupation and the war and, on the other, of the fact that only the Communists came out of the war with an intelligent program with mass appeal. They were the leaders in

[1] V. J. Jerome, *Culture in a Changing World*, p. 55, N. Y., 1947.

organizing all the great mass movements and struggles mentioned above in this chapter. As a result, the small pre-war and wartime Communist parties expanded prodigiously, producing by 1947 such big European mass parties as that in France with 1,000,000 members; in Italy with 2,100,000; in Czechoslovakia with 1,700,000; in Poland with 700,000; in Bulgaria with 450,000; in Hungary with 600,000; in Rumania with 500,000; in Eastern Germany (U.S.P.) with 1,700,000, etc. Since 1947 nearly all of them have grown very rapidly. The same tendency was manifested in the Far East, in many colonial lands, with the enormous Chinese Communist Party, then with 3,000,000 members (and now with twice as many) taking the lead. In Latin America, the same trend developed, the Communist parties as a whole increasing their membership from 100,000 in 1940 to 500,000 in 1949. The C.P. of Brazil, the outstanding example, grew from 4,000 in 1945 to 150,000 in 1948. In the United States, primarily (but not exclusively) because of objective national conditions, no such gigantic expansion of the Communist Party took place.

The great growth of mass democratic organizations immediately after the war was accompanied by strong tendencies toward solidarity, all actively cultivated by the Communists. There were new get-together movements between the workers and peasants, between Catholic and Marxist workers, between the workers and all other democratic strata. One of the most significant of these trends was the movement, initiated by the Communists, to bring about co-operation and eventual party unity between the Communist and Social-Democratic parties. In the People's Democracies of Eastern and Central Europe actual unity between these parties was achieved (save for small right-wing split-offs); but in Western Europe—France, England, etc.—the right-wing Social-Democrats were still strong enough to prevent united front action and two-party unity from being achieved. In Italy the S.P., led by Pietro Nenni, supported the united front.

Basically, the extensive growth of the Communist forces during and after World War II—in governments, parliaments, trade unions, and democratic movements of all sorts—signifies that the predominant leadership of the world proletariat has passed from the hands of the right-wing Social-Democrats into those of the Communists and their allies. For the previous two generations the right-wing Social-Democrats dominated the leadership of the political and economic movement of the working class on a world scale. But now all this is changing swiftly, with the leadership going into the hands of the Communists. This development is not uniform, of course. It has not yet taken place in the United States, Canada, Great Britain, and a number of other countries, but it is already a fact in France, Italy, and most of Eastern and Central Europe, and in the Far East and Latin America. It signifies a reorientation of the main battalions of the international labor movement away from capitalism and war to peace, national liberation, and socialism.

THE CAPITALIST AND SOCIALIST WORLDS

Capitalism's murderous folly of World War I precipitated the loss of a nation of 200 million people and one-sixth of the earth—the Soviet Union—from the orbit of its control. The even more dreadful World War II, also a lethal product of the insane workings of the capitalist system, cost that system another 600 million people. So that now no less than 800 million people, one-third of all humanity, are either living under Socialist governments or under regimes that are definitely heading toward socialism. And many scores of millions more, at present living under the capitalist system in various parts of the earth, are also turning their hearts and minds toward socialism. All these vast forces comprise the backbone of the still broader world camp of democracy and peace.

These enormous masses are determined to fight their way out of the welter of exploitation, hunger, poverty, ignorance, sickness, tyranny, and war that is the capitalist system. They are on the way to a new system of society in which they will enjoy freedom, peace, and general well-being. The supreme idiocy of our times is that the ruling classes of the world, viewing this great emancipation movement—the most immense in the history of the world, are trying to condemn it as a subversive plot of a minority of Communists and are seeking to crush it by violence.

Humanity, especially since World War II, literally comprises two worlds. The one is the old, outworn, historically obsolete capitalist world—the world of exploitation, hunger, imperialism, fascism and war, full of confusion, hopelessness, and despair. The other is the great new world of socialism—alive, vibrant, healthy, bearing the mandate of history, and with it a message of hope and security to the oppressed of the earth. The very existence of the Soviet Union is an inspiration and a powerful protection to the awakening peoples of Europe, Asia, Africa, and America. Every Marxist-Leninist agrees that these two worlds, the obsolete and the oncoming, can and should live and develop within a framework of world peace; but the ruling classes of capitalism, particularly in the United States, think and act otherwise. Theirs is a program of atomic war for world conquest. But this violent imperialist orientation can only turn out eventually to be their death warrant. The basic development of our times is that the world is advancing from capitalism to socialism, a forward movement which is both irresistible and inevitable. As Molotov has said, "All roads lead to Communism."

32. American Imperialism Drives for World Mastery (1948-1951)

One of the major consequences of World War II, and thereby also of the general crisis of the world capitalist system, has been the establishment of the hegemony, or domination, of the United States over the rest of the capitalist world. This is a further working out of Lenin's law of the uneven development of capitalism, whereby the respective capitalist economies grow at different speeds. In this extreme case one capitalist power, the United States, has acquired such a lopsided superiority over the other capitalist countries that it has come to be relatively the boss over the rest of the capitalist world. This development, unique in capitalist history, is striking evidence of the grave sickness of the capitalist system on a world scale. For only because the other powers are basically weak do they knuckle under to the Wall Street masters. The most generalized form of this hegemony is the practical dictation of United Nations policy by the United States. However, because of its destructive effects, American hegemony still further deepens the general crisis, and it may well be the thing to provoke the death of the capitalist system through another world war.

AMERICAN CAPITALIST HEGEMONY

American capitalist predominance has been brought about, first, by the serious weakening economically and politically of the other great powers during the war—Great Britain, Germany, Japan, France, and Italy—and, secondly, by the enormous growth of American productivity during the war and post-war periods—an increase of about 75 percent. The United States, unduly bloated economically, now possesses about two-thirds of the industrial capacity of the capitalist world, it has some three-fourths of the world's gold reserves, and its foreign investments far exceed "the combined investment total of all the other imperialist powers."[1] Therefore, this country has become relatively the boss of the capitalist world. But it is a very shaky rule, and the ramshackle edifice is constantly threatened with collapse.

American hegemony over the capitalist world deepens the general

[1] Perlo, *American Imperialism*, pp. 27-28.

crisis of the capitalist system, because it greatly sharpens all the inner contradictions of that system, as well as those between the capitalist and socialist worlds. For example, a severe strain has been placed upon the whole world by the precipitation of the Korean War by the United States, which literally had to slug other capitalist states in order to get them to send even token bodies of troops to the Korean slaughterhouse. Also, the United States, as the capitalist boss, has put Britain, Italy, Belgium, and others under such economic pressure in its arms race against the U.S.S.R. that they are bankrupt. The United States is likewise weakening the general fabric of capitalism by its ruthless penetration of the domestic and foreign markets of the other imperialist powers. It also antagonizes the British, French, Dutch, and Belgian empires by setting up economic and political controls over their colonies and dominions, under a cloud of propaganda to the effect that the former powers use "obsolete" colonial methods. Arrogant Wall Street pressure upon the national independence of other countries, too, is creating a violent anti-American spirit all over the world, which is being reflected in a growing opposition to the United States in the United Nations. But most important of all, the United States, through its dominant position, is pushing the other capitalist countries toward a war which, if it takes place, will very probably destroy world capitalism altogether.

Within the general scope of Wall Street's mad project of trying to conquer the world, a particularly insane policy is the Truman Government's arrogant insistence that all capitalist countries cease trading with the U.S.S.R. and the People's Democracies of Europe and Asia. This boycott policy cannot hurt the latter countries seriously, because among themselves they possess all the raw materials they require. Moreover, their collectivist regimes make it relatively easy for them to do without trade with capitalist countries. The policy can, however, be disastrous for world capitalism. For Great Britain, France, Germany, Japan, and others, not to mention the United States, have an increasingly urgent need for the great potential markets in the boycotted countries. To cut them off from these markets can well generate an economic explosion from overproduction and mass unemployment, which will blow the whole capitalist war alliance to smithereens, and with it American world capitalist hegemony.

One of the most explosive pressures now being generated by U.S. capitalist hegemony is Wall Street's arrogant attempt to deny the peoples of the world their right to set up progressive governments in France and Italy, the establishment of national independence in the Middle East, and the carrying through of the great colonial revolution in Asia. All such people's movements are condemned and combated as Russian "plots" and Communist "infiltration." The ultimate consequences of such a policy will definitely prove disastrous for capitalism.

Within the framework of its world capitalist hegemony the United States maintains a sort of alliance with its major imperialist rival, Great Britain, which it treats as a minor partner. For all its arrogance, the United States has to make some small concessions to the subordinate capitalist powers, for it could not possibly drive through with its warlike policies, even in the United States itself, without their support. Nevertheless the growing British-American antagonism is the most basic within the capitalist world, and it is now deepening. A split with Great Britain would be disastrous for Wall Street. This fact emphasizes the big role the European countries could play in the peace movement to restrain warlike American imperialism, if pressed by their peoples to do so.

FORCES BEHIND WALL STREET'S WAR DRIVE

The United States, ruled by great monopoly capitalists, cannot rest content even with its present leading position among the capitalist nations. It must also push on for complete mastery of the world; for domination over the world's great socialist sector, as well as its capitalist sector. Wall Street is determined to rule the whole world, cost what it may. It knows very well that to drive ahead for that mastery would involve another great war, and such a war it is cold-bloodedly preparing. This ruthless course is in the very nature of imperialism. The American bourgeoisie is motivated to make this relentless drive for imperialist expansion and universal power by four major pressures, underlying all of which is the insatiable capitalist urge for more and more profits.

First, as a great capitalist, imperialist power, in its determined search for markets, raw materials, strategic military positions, and peoples to exploit, the United States is irresistibly impelled into a policy of aggression, limited only by the opposition it encounters. Such imperialism, most Americans will readily agree, is characteristic of all the other big capitalist countries — Great Britain, Germany, Japan, France, Italy, and others—but however much this thought is disliked by Americans, it is even more true of the United States. For this country, far more powerful economically and more completely dominated by monopolies than any other, is also more aggressive politically. Inevitably it sets a more grandiose imperialist goal for itself than any capitalist power has ever done before—namely, the complete domination of the world.

Second, the United States is also impelled into its aggressive policy of universal domination out of the capitalist fear that the rest of world capitalism is falling to pieces and that it can be saved only if the American capitalists, with their wealth and "know how," take it all over. These capitalists may deny the Marxist-Leninist theory of the general crisis of the capitalist system, but they nevertheless realize that international capitalism is in desperate straits and that drastic measures must be taken if there is to be any real chance to preserve it even temporarily.

Third, the Wall Street capitalists who own and run the United States[1] are frightened in their very bones at the rise of world socialism. Not for a moment do they believe their own lying propaganda, prepared for mass consumption, that socialism is impractical and that the U.S.S.R. is about to collapse. They fear that they see the handwriting on the wall in the historic fact that within a generation 800 million people have broken their capitalist shackles and are now either already living under socialism or on the way to building it. Hence, at any cost, they are resolved to try to crush the U.S.S.R., the European People's Democracies, the great Chinese People's Republic, and all other people's states and movements heading toward socialism.

Fourth, and very important in causing the drive of American imperialism toward war and world conquest, is the central fact that United States industry, on its present capitalist course, needs war in order to remain even temporarily in substantial operation. As we have seen in previous pages of this history, American industry has reached its present enormous development primarily because of the artificial markets created by two world wars—that is, by producing munitions to carry on these wars and by post-war production to make up the commodity shortages and the property destruction wrought by the two wars. And American industries are still being rapidly overextended on the basis of another war.

As the Communist Party has constantly pointed out, there is no ground in the normal national and international capitalist markets for the present high development of the industries. Leon Keyserling, prominent American economist, says that during the next decade we must find new markets at home and abroad for $400 billion worth of commodities or face economic collapse.[2] So the capitalists set out to create markets for these enormous surpluses by extensive war preparations, and finally by war itself. This Keynesian policy makes the war drive doubly dangerous. As we will show in Chapter 36, the belief that inflated American industry can be kept in full operation by arms

[1] Rochester, *Rulers of America;* Allen, *World Monopoly and Peace.*
[2] Jefferson School of Social Science, *The Economic Crisis and the Cold War,* p. 18, N. Y., 1949.

production is a great illusion. This is the road to economic smash-up, as well as to military disaster. But momentarily it is a very profitable one for the big capitalists. "In the pre-war years, 1936-39, the annual net profit of U.S. corporations was $3.4 billions; in 1940-45 it was $8.7 billions; in 1946-50 (cold war and Korea), it was $18.5 billions; in 1951 it is at least $30 billions. From 1940 through 1950, corporations in the United States *reported a total net* profit of $145 billions."[1] Even more blood money is in store for the exploiters, with the current enormous increase in war preparations. Hence the push toward war and ultimate ruin.

The Communist Party, while warning that crises are inevitable under capitalism, urges the workers, who have created the wealth of America, to seek to absorb much of the present great surpluses of production by raising living standards of the masses, expanding social security, developing education, and giving the people decent housing. The vast productive power of American industry, properly distributed, could enormously improve living conditions in this country. But this course would slash the profits of the employers; hence they resist every effort to absorb the surplus production by improving the conditions of the people. The ruling capitalists prostitute the huge American industrial machine to the destructive purposes of war.

Wall Street's war drive for world conquest is at the same time a drive to establish world fascism—a gigantic effort to strangle the liberties of the peoples, both in the United States and on a world scale. For only by drastic repressive measures could the peace will of the masses possibly be broken and the big capitalists of the United States succeed in precipitating their projected anti-Soviet war and driving toward their contemplated system of American world rule.

The program of world war and fascism, of United States world mastery, is the policy of American monopoly—finance capital—, of its Truman government, and of its two major political parties. There is, however, much hesitation regarding this imperialist war-fascist line in capitalist ranks in this country. Many businessmen are afraid of national bankruptcy from the big munitions expenditures. Other capitalist elements fear disaster in another war and in the drive toward fascism. Especially are these capitalist moods of hesitation and resistance to the war drive to be found in the countries of western Europe.

Such hesitation trends may increase in the United States, and develop into real opposition. But the present noisy pre-election quarrels between Republicans and Democrats in this country are primarily

[1] Herbert Aptheker in *Masses and Mainstream*, May 1951.

disputes over political-military war strategy and tactics, and sharp rivalries among cliques of capitalists and their political agents as to who shall control the rich prize of the United States government, which is now spending over $70 billions yearly. They are mainly partisan janglings within the main framework of Wall Street's imperialist policy of world domination. Truman, Taft, Eisenhower, Warren, Stassen, et al, are all warmongers, cut from the same cloth. The democratic masses fighting for peace, while taking advantage of every split in the ranks of the capitalists nationally and internationally, must always realize that the maintenance of world peace depends upon their own mighty action, not upon opposition groups among the capitalists.

THE PEACE WILL OF THE PEOPLES

The drive of Wall Street capital toward war and fascism flagrantly violates the interests and desires of the great democratic people in this country, of our nation. The workers, farmers, Negro people, intellectuals, and others of the toiling masses in this country are democratic and peace-minded. They wish to live in harmony with the peoples of the rest of the world. They have no desire for the imperialist loot, bloody war adventures, and eventual national catastrophe inherent in the expansionist policies of Wall Street. But unfortunately they are not controlling the government nor determining its policies. The big capitalists dominate the United States government and use it to further their own sinister class interests, to the detriment of the interests of the nation.

The democratic masses of the American and world's peoples have repeatedly shown that they are deeply opposed to war—to the war that Wall Street is organizing. This they have done by their support of the vast Stockholm Peace Pledge, with half a billion signatures, by the campaign for a Five-Power Peace Pact, with some 600 million names on it; by the marked anti-militarist spirit among the peoples of Europe (including Germany), Asia (including Japan), Latin America, Africa, and Australia, and of the United States and Canada; by the catastrophic fall in American democratic prestige all over the world as Wall Street's program of imperialist aggression becomes better understood; and by the great peace demonstrations in many parts of the world. In the United States the peace will of the people has been shown by the remarkable demonstrations of the soldiers and the people at the end of the war, which forced a huge slash in the armed forces; by the stubborn popular resistance to military control of the atom-bomb, to the institution of conscription and universal military training, to the sending of a large American army to post-war Europe, and to the threat of employing the atom-bomb in Korea; and by the striking lack of enthusiasm generally for the Korean war. The Gallup poll, in November 1951, reported that 56 per cent of the American people agreed that the Korean war was "utterly useless," and in December it reported 70 per cent of the people as favoring a big power peace conference, although Truman sharply opposed this.

The strong center of the international peace movement of the peoples, now, as before World War II, is the Soviet Union. Today, in the United Nations, Vishinsky fights against the war danger, as Litvinov did in the previous League of Nations, and as Lenin did before the outbreak of the first World War. The great Soviet Union —without capitalists, hence without imperialists—ardently needs and works for peace as an indispensable condition for carrying out the enormous tasks of internal development which it now has under way. It is the strong buttress of peace and democracy all over the world, the real protection for such rebellious but weak countries as Iran, Egypt, Iraq, Burma, etc., etc. The U.S.S.R. has no exploiters, who get rich from the production of munitions and the waging of war, and, besides, its healthy socialist industries need no deadly stimulant of war production to keep them in operation. In the U.S.S.R. the advocacy of war, such as rages feverishly in the American press and radio, has been made a criminal offense. The very social structure of the Soviet Union commits it to peace and against aggression, and its entire foreign and domestic policy structure is built upon this anti-imperialist foundation. During World War II the U.S.S.R. saved world democracy from being destroyed by fascism, and now it is the main force in fighting to preserve world peace.

The Wall Street imperialists, however, in their urgent need for a pretext to justify the contemplated war, picture the peace-loving Soviet Union as a great imperialist menace. They thus stand reality on its head. Their pen-pushers and windjammers are carrying on an immense campaign designed to prove that the peaceful policies of the U.S.S.R. are warlike; that the spontaneous democratic revolutions in Czechoslovakia, Poland, China, and elsewhere are belligerent instigations by the Soviet Union; and that the United States' gigantic war preparations are only defensive.

The Wall Street warmongers have upped the military budget in 1951 by 500 percent over 1950, in the face of Soviet proposals to ban the atomic bomb and to reduce armaments drastically. Yet the instigators of war cry out that the latter is the aggressor. They have surrounded the U.S.S.R. with a world-wide ring of air bases[1]—it is as though the Soviets had great bases in Canada, Mexico, and the West Indies—and still the warmongers declare that all this aggression is merely defensive. They are openly arming the whole capitalist world for an all-out attack against the Soviet Union. But they shout that the Russians are about to overwhelm the world with their Red Army. The Wall Street-Truman policy is the pre-war and wartime Munich policy all over again—that is, the development of a general capitalist attack to demolish the U.S.S.R. And all this is being done under the heavy cloak of deceit and hypocrisy that it is only a program of peace and democracy.

THE U.S. PUSHES TOWARD WAR

The American capitalist drive toward a third world war, a war which was already implicit in Wall Street's anti-Soviet policy during World War II, began to take shape immediately in the post-war period. This is the meaning of the "get-tough-with-Russia" policy and of "atom-bomb diplomacy." From the first there was a general brandishing of the bomb, and soon the atom-bomb fanatics began openly to advocate a "preventive war" against the Soviet Union. In the United Nations the U.S.S.R. early confronted a hard-boiled Anglo-American majority, which followed an anti-Soviet policy. The Baruch plan of atomic control, which was designed to keep the bomb in American and out of Russian hands, was presented to the U.S.S.R. on a take-it-or-leave-it basis. All Russian peace proposals were voted down on principle. The influence of the generals in the making of American foreign policy became decisive.

Early in 1947, as the war policy was developing, President Truman enunciated the so-called Truman Doctrine. That is, the United States took over the job of shooting to pieces the Greek revolution, a task which the British announced they were unable to accomplish. This unilateral interference in the affairs of Greece, by-passing the U.N. as it did, was an outgrowth of earlier Anglo-American attempts to defeat the People's Democracies of Czechoslovakia, Poland, Hungary, and elsewhere by promoting civil war. As a result, with the help of Tito's treachery, the Greek People's Democracy was defeated and United States capitalism got a powerful foothold on the Adriatic, to the dismay of its ally, Great Britain. In the same aggressive spirit, at about this time, the United States government ordered the French

[1] George Marion, *Bases and Empire*, N. Y., 1948.

and Italian governments, on pain of being cut off the American dole, to oust the Communist parties, the strongest parties in these countries. Try to imagine any socialist government daring to thus interfere in the internal affairs of the United States! All this was in violent contradiction to American democratic traditions.

Another big step in the developing imperialist program of American big business came with the Marshall Plan, announced in June 1947. This proposition called for a Congressional appropriation of $17 billion, presumably to bring about European economic recovery, but actually to facilitate Wall Street's economic and political penetration of the European Continent and to organize the capitalist countries there to wage war against the U.S.S.R. and its democratic neighbors. The toilers had to pay for these imperialist adventures. The Marshall Plan, which expired December 30, 1951, was superseded by the Mutual Security Act of October 1951. This measure, financing the North Atlantic Treaty Organization, has already cost the American people $7 billion, and President Truman proposed that the outlay for it in this fiscal year should be $10 billions. The heart of the entire Truman European policy is an armed and Nazified Germany as the basis for an aggressive war against the Soviet Union and the People's Democracies of Central Europe.

Meanwhile, the United States kept paying close attention to its planned conquest of the Far East. Lined up with the other imperialist countries—Great Britain, France, and Holland—and cynically violating the revolutionary traditions of the American people, the Truman Administration strives to stamp out the revolutionary liberation movements in China, Indo-China, Burma, Indonesia, Malaya, and the Philippines, furnishing vast quantities of war materials to the reactionary forces who are trying to keep intact the threatened colonial system. A crowning infamy in this imperialist program is the setting up of a militarist Japan, a course which violates the wartime agreements of the allied powers. This is the significance of the reactionary Japanese treaty of September 1951.

The general regional political framework within which United States big business plans to rule the world is taking shape in such combinations as the Organization of American States (United States and Latin America), the North Atlantic Pact (the capitalist countries of Europe), the Pacific Security Pact (capitalist and colonial countries of the Pacific), and the projected Mediterranean Pact. Presumably these regional groupings are within the scope and control of the United Nations, but in reality they are all completely dominated by the United States. This domination is also true of the United Nations itself, although recently the

AMERICAN DRIVE FOR WORLD MASTERY 461

United States' grip on that organization has been somewhat weakened.

On June 25, 1950, the Korean war began with an invasion of North Korea by the troops of the American puppet government of Syngman Rhee. The Wall Street warmongers behind that aggression believed that it would be a simple matter for Rhee's troops to overrun North Korea and open up the way for a big attack against People's China. It was to be the opening wedge for a vast extension of Wall Street influence in Asia. But the story turned out quite differently. All the American military experts were shocked and amazed at the magnificent fighting qualities shown by the North Koreans and later by the Chinese volunteers. Immediately the United States had to run to the aid of its collapsed puppet state. Without consulting Congress, and even before he took the matter up with the United Nations, President Truman rushed the United States into a war which has already cost three million lives of soldiers and civilians and which might easily have provoked a third world war.

What Truman contemptuously called a "police action," turned out to be a full-scale war, and a lost one. The successful stand of the North Korean and Chinese forces against the highly mechanized western armies is of historic significance. These peoples, just emerging from colonialism, have successfully held off the armed capitalist world—a far cry indeed from fifty years ago when, in the Boxer rebellion of 1900, the capitalist powers marched easily and arrogantly to Peking. President Truman and General MacArthur, in their desperation, were ready to use the atom-bomb and to blast Chinese cities, had it not been for the world-wide outcry of protest at the mere announcement of such a possibility and the fear of the world capitalists that it would get them into an even worse mess. The stalemating of the war, almost along the line of the old 38th parallel, constitutes a major defeat for Wall Street's aggressive plans.

Keeping pace with Wall Street's military aggression abroad, there is a feverish campaign at home to militarize the American people. There is a sadistic glorification of the war in Korea, with its brutal "Operation Killer," "Operation Strangler," and the like. Peacetime conscription has been established, the building of a four million-man army is under way, the navy and air force are being enormously expanded, and the traditionally anti-militarist American masses are being regimented. The United States also adds endlessly to its immense string of air bases—it now has about 150 of them in England, France, Greenland, Iceland, Denmark, Norway, Greece, Western Germany, Italy, Turkey, Spain, Yugoslavia, Canada, Latin America, South Africa, Algeria, Morocco, Lybia, Thailand, the Philippines, Japan, Hawaii, Alaska, Pakistan, Saudi Arabia, Australia, etc., etc. A frantic campaign is also being carried on to frighten and confuse the masses into believing that war is inevitable, because of

"Russian aggression." Already during the six years since the end of the war against Japan, over $100 billion have been spent in waging the "cold war"; in 1951 alone the military expenditures ran to $50 billion, and in the fiscal year beginning on July 1, 1952, they may mount to over $65 billion. In his budget message of January 21, 1952, President Truman called for the fabulous sum of $85.4 billion, 85 percent of which is for war—past, present, and future. This general arms race is a confession of the strategical failure of the atom-bomb, which was originally believed sufficient to assure world domination for Wall Street.

These aggressive foreign policies and huge military expenditures, coupled with the mass indoctrination of the people by the Truman Administration, constitute imperialist war preparations on a gigantic scale. Only the politically naive can believe them to be defensive measures. What else can possibly be the calculated purpose of the United States in building a ring of air bases around the U.S.S.R. at a cost of many billions? The Wall Street magnates, for whom the government is an obedient instrument, are resolved upon war. Only through war against the U.S.S.R., they are convinced, can they assure the full operation of their industries, perpetuate huge profits for themselves, save the tottering capitalist system, wipe out the threat of socialism, and make themselves the overlords of mankind.

As the United States builds its enormous military establishment—a great army, huge air force, expanded navy, big supply of atom-bombs, and air-naval bases all around the world—the militaristic arrogance of its capitalist leaders grows accordingly. Thus Congress passes the Mutual Security Act, brazenly appropriating $100 million to develop civil wars in the U.S.S.R. and the People's Democracies. President Truman recklessly declares that agreements with Russia are not worth the paper they are written on, and he demands "the unconditional surrender of Russia as the price of peace."[1] The gangsters of the press increasingly cry out for a "preventive war" against the U.S.S.R.—*Collier's* (of October 27, 1951) outdoing itself in this shouting for a blood bath, devotes its entire issue to a lurid description of how the United States won the hoped-for-war against the Soviet Union. It is quite clear that the warmongers, unless restrained by the American people, will, when they deem the moment ripe, deliberately create an "incident" and plunge the world into a third great conflagration, under the pretext of waging what they call a preventive or defensive war. They are consciously trying to develop the present tense world situation as the opening phases of a third world war.

At any time during the several tense years of the "cold war" the

[1] *Daily Compass*, Oct. 26, 1951.

United States could have had a democratic peace with the U.S.S.R. had it so desired. But peace is the last thing the Wall Street monopolists want. Every prospect of international understanding creates a "peace scare" and sends stocks tobogganing. So the warmongers reject with insults the Soviet Union's rational proposals to establish peaceful international relationships, and they seize upon every pretext to intensify their war preparations. They want war, and only the peace will of the American and other peoples, resolutely expressed by organized resistance, can balk Wall Street's murderous imperialist designs. Popular resistance was decisive in stalling the Korean war, it can also avert the planned third world war.

THE TREND TOWARD FASCISM

American imperialism's program of conquest also implies a drive toward reaction and fascism, because only by means of intense demagogy and terrorism, the characteristic methods of fascism, can the peoples of the United States and the world possibly be compelled to accept the drastic cuts in living standards and civil liberties, and finally the wholesale death, bound up in Wall Street's fight for world domination. Victory for the American capitalist warmongers and imperialists would probably imply a fascist world.

Naturally enough, the United States, in its campaign for war, has as its allies the most reactionary forces throughout the world. Practically everywhere, the more conservative the group, the more ardently it supports Wall Street's anti-Soviet drive. The big capitalists everywhere in the world are the basic allies of the United States, and so are their many subsidized fascist groupings and parties. Then there is the Catholic Church hierarchy which, now in the deepest religious, political, and financial crisis of its history, has committed itself heartily to Wall Street's anti-Soviet crusade, despite its assertions of pacifism and neutrality. What type of society the Vatican would like to establish has been made quite clear by its previous or present aggressive support of the fascist-clerical regimes of Mussolini in Italy, Dollfuss in Austria, Franco in Spain, Pétain in France, Perón in Argentina. To sum up its alliance with this reactionary force, the Truman Administration, in October 1951, decided to send an ambassador to the Vatican, thereby crassly violating the basic American policy of the separation of Church and State. More and more aggressively, the top American Catholic churchmen are trying to dictate Vatican policy. American imperialism would also take control over the Church.

Another loyal ally of Wall Street is right-wing Social-Democracy, both here and abroad. The Social-Democratic leaders, long since fully committed to the maintenance of the capitalist system whatever the cost to the workers, are thoroughly decayed politically and are willing to follow the heads of world capitalism, the Wall Street capitalists, wherever they decide—to fascism and war. In Europe and Asia the Social-Democratic leaders lined up with domestic reaction and foreign imperialism in order to block the establishment of people's democratic governments on the road to socialism, in the big post-war revolutionary upheaval. A particularly crass example of their betrayal of socialism was the work of the Labor Government in Great Britain in the post-World War II years. The right-wing Social-Democratic leaders of that government, Attlee, Morrison, Strachey, *et al.*, did not protect the workers' living standards, defend world peace, or work to make Britain a Socialist land. Instead, they supported the entire war aims of American imperialism—the Truman doctrine, Marshall Plan, North Atlantic Pact, Greek and Korean wars, arming of Germany and Japan, and all the rest of it. The opportunist right-wing Socialists are everywhere a ready force for war and fascism.

The essentially fascist content of the foreign policies of Wall Street and its allies is unmistakable. In Great Britain, the United States, while using the late Labor Government as its tool, placed its real reliance upon the ultra-reactionary Winston Churchill and maneuvered for the re-election of his government. In France, to be utilized when the situation warrants, is the notoriously fascist General de Gaulle. In Western Germany, American policy is re-creating the Nazi movement, and avowed followers of Hitler, daily growing bolder, are to be found by the thousands in all kinds of key economic and political positions, with American consent and support. In Italy, the same thing is happening with regard to the old Mussolini gang, which is gradually preparing to try to take over when the reactionary de Gasperi government collapses. All through Eastern Europe the fascist movement—its seedlings and remnants—is rallying instinctively around Wall Street's anti-Soviet drive. The United States itself welcomes reactionaries from these countries, all of them militant supporters of Wall Street's projected anti-Soviet war. To put its further stamp of approval upon fascism, the United States has also sewed up a war alliance with the butcher Franco, who not only murdered the Spanish Republic but was openly a Hitler-Mussolini ally during the war. Under U.S. pressure the post-war governments of Great Britain, France, Italy, and Germany have all been pushed steadily to the right.

In the Far East, the allies and policies of the United States have the same reactionary core. Chiang Kai-shek, the very symbol of reaction throughout the colonial world, is Wall Street's chosen agent wherewith to re-establish a reactionary regime in China. In Indo-China, it is the ultra-reactionary French puppet, Bao Dai, whom Wall Street is supporting. In Malaya and Indonesia, the U.S. is going along hand in hand with the reactionary British and Dutch imperialists and their puppets. In the Philippines, the puppet republic, the State Department's policy sustains the worst enemies of the people. In Pakistan, the deepest reactionaries are the best friends of Wall Street. And the same is true in Japan, where American imperialism's warmest co-operators are Emperor Hirohito and the gang of big industrialists and landlords behind him. In India, the ultra-reactionary internal opposition to Premier Nehru, a Social-Democrat who himself has outlawed the Communists and arrested masses of militant workers, is being cultivated by American influences, because Nehru has not sufficiently supported Wall Street's warlike and grasping policy toward rebellious Asia.

In Latin America, a similar situation prevails. The many dictators who infest that great area are all either outright puppets of the United States or are fully committed to its war-against-Russia policies. In these countries to the south of the Rio Grande, American policy is uniformly against the democratic demands and organizations of the people and in support of the local domination of the landowners, the big capitalists, the Church hierarchy, and other ultra-conservative groupings.

All these reactionary and fascist allies of Wall Street—in Europe, Asia, and Latin America—with Social-Democracy performing the special task of hamstringing the opposition struggle of the workers—are going along with the Wall Street program of eventual fascism and all-out war against the U.S.S.R., under hypocritical slogans of the defense of world peace and democracy. Everywhere Wall Street's real line is the same—to beat down the people's living standards, to strip the masses of their democratic liberties, to remilitarize the capitalist countries, and to deprive them of their national independence. This is the path to fascism as well as to war.

BUILDING A POLICE STATE IN THE UNITED STATES

In the United States proper, the fascist element in Wall Street's war policy is also alarmingly evident. The American people, in their great numbers, are democratic and peace-loving, and they can be dragooned into another world war only by being deceived and terrorized. This pressure is being applied to them now on a scale altogether unique in American history. It is being done mainly under the pretext of fighting communism. Never was the danger of fascism in the United States more acute and menacing than it is at the present time.

The people's democratic rights are being slashed. Wholesale arrests of Communists, smelling of the Palmer raids of 1920, follow one another in rapid succession. Hundreds of foreign-born are picked up for deportation, in order to terrorize the millions of others. The government service is plagued by loyalty tests, and everyone is suspect who has ever publicly supported Franklin D. Roosevelt or read *The Nation*. The trade unions under the Taft-Hartley Act are systematically being denied rights which they have enjoyed for a hundred years. The war industries are infested by an army of stoolpigeons, hysterically seeking out "reds." The advocacy of socialism, which American left-wingers have practiced freely for a century, has now become a crime. And to advocate peace negotiations is to subject oneself to charges of being a "foreign agent."

Redbaiting has developed into one of the most flourishing and lucrative callings. Subtle, and not so subtle, moods of anti-Semitism, Negro discrimination and Anglo-Saxon superiority are cultivated all over. Senator McCarthy, who has far-reaching capitalist support and is the most dangerous demagogue since Huey Long, denounces and threatens everybody of even a mildly liberal tinge of opinion. And General MacArthur boldly comes out, fascist fashion, with a glorification of war and American world conquest. The Ku Klux Klan takes on a new lease of life in the South. Westbrook Pegler, an authentic bellwether of fascism, demands the arrest of "thousands of New Dealers,"[1] and the F.B.I., fingerprinting tens of millions and holding files on vast numbers of people, snoops everywhere and spreads like a poison weed. Thought control laws—Smith, Voorhis, McCarran, and a host more—follow each other in rapid succession into federal, state, and local statute books. Vigilanteism is rampant in many communities. The reactionaries are even trying to condemn as traitors, dupes, and foreign agents all those government figures—Truman, Acheson, Marshall, Jessup, Service, Lattimore, and so on—who co-operated with the U.S.S.R. and People's China, in however niggardly a fashion, when these were military allies of the United States during World War II.

The people are also being frightened with a sensational "spy scare," which has resulted in several convictions, including the savage death sentences against the two Rosenbergs. This hysteria is being fomented by the fantastic cloak-and-dagger tales of Whittaker Chambers, Elizabeth Bentley, Louis Budenz, and other renegades and stoolpigeons, now being played up by the gutter press and radio. The attempt to involve the Communist Party in this manufactured "plot" is an absurd frame-up,

---

[1] *New York Journal-American*, June 27, 1951.

which has already been completely exposed. The current artificial "spy scare" is a calculated part of the warmongers' systematic campaign to terrorize the American people into submitting to their reactionary program.

Every semblance of opposition to the reactionaries, in whatever sphere of our national life, is denounced as Communist. Never in its entire history was the country so browbeaten and mentally strait-jacketed as now. Intimidated citizens have repeatedly refused to sign excerpts from the Declaration of Independence, when presented to them in petition form. The number of liberal dailies can now be counted on one hand, and liberal radio commentators are now a thing of the past. Reactionary political illiterates, like Winchell, Kaltenborn, and Lewis, blather to audiences of millions at fabulous salaries. The movies and television are unblushing propagandists of reaction, and the daily press serves up as news a mess of jingoistic war propaganda, anti-Russian lies, and journalistic filth, sinking more and more into the Pegler level.

The universities and schools are being stripped of all vestiges of liberalism, and the teachers and students, fearful of being labeled as "reds" and fired, are shying away from every controversial question. Justice Douglas, in dissenting from the Supreme Court decision on the notorious Feinberg law of New York, thus describes the deplorable situation created by this law: "Regular loyalty reports on the teachers must be made out. The principals become detectives; the students, the parents, the community become informers." The High Court decision establishes the infamous principle of "guilt by association."

This is fascism in the making, the building of a police state in the United States. Malignant and impetuous forces in its creation are such political ultra-reactionaries as MacArthur, McCarran, and McCarthy. But the main drive toward fascism and war during the post-war period has come from the present Administration, with Truman's get-tough-with-Russia policies, his Korean war, his fake national emergency and frantic war preparations, his loyalty tests and cynical persecution of the Communists, his ditching of the civil rights program for the Negro people, his deliberate sacrifice of the people's living standards through an inflation which he does nothing to curb, his phony peace demagogy, and his snide cultivation of every reactionary tendency in the country.

Between the two big capitalist parties there is a sort of division of labor. The Republican Party serves as the more open champion of reaction, while the Democratic Party, no less reactionary in practice, does its job for the bosses by crippling the natural opposition of labor through dousing it with hypocritical demagogy about peace and democracy. They are twin parties of reaction. Both are controlled by finance capital, and both are applying Wall Street's policies of war and fascism. Neither is a "lesser evil" than the other. When one set of capitalist demagogues—Truman, Taft, etc.—discredit themselves, capitalism knows how to raise up another set—Eisenhower, Kefauver, etc.—to keep bourgeois illusions alive among the toiling masses.

Hardly less responsibility for the present dangerous situation in the United States rests at the doors of those cowardly liberals, Social-Democrats, and top labor leaders who put their tails between their legs and fly before the increasing fascist storm. Besides supporting the war program, the basis of the current reaction, these elements systematically demoralize and undercut the democratic resistance of the masses. All the more credit then to the valiant Communist Party, to the progressive unions, and to those intellectuals who dare to face up to the threatening reaction.

Bearing in mind the democratic traditions and peace will of the American people, American fascism cloaks itself with an elaborate pretense of liberalism and national defense. Unlike the cruder and more outspoken Hitlerism, it masks its doctrines of the "superiority" of the Anglo-American peoples; it hides its growing glorification of war under deep pretenses of peace; and it calls its imperialism "world moral leadership."[1] As Georgi Dimitrov pointed out many years ago, American fascism comes forth hypocritically as the pretended champion of democracy, of equality among nations, of freedom, peace, and independence for all peoples. It makes the most outrageous attacks against the workers' and the Negro people's rights under cover of supporting popular liberties. Wall Street reaction's glittering democratic generalities are only a demagogic façade; they are but so many hypocritical pretensions designed to mislead, confuse, and intimidate the masses. Underlying the thick layer of misrepresentation is the stern reality of American imperialism's march toward war and fascism. This democratic false face of Wall Street reaction makes it all the more difficult for the masses to understand and combat Wall Street.

All this, of course, is only one side of the story. The great working class will be effectively heard from in the growing struggle to save the United States from fascism and war. Although at present traitorously misled by their top union leaders, the workers will find the way to wreck all the reactionary plans of Wall Street. But of this, more in later chapters.

[1] Herbert Aptheker, *America's Racist Laws*, N. Y., 1951.

33. The Communist Party and the "Cold War" (1945-1951)

After the Communist Party broke the backbone of Browder revisionism, it took and maintained a sharp and clear position against the Wall Street-Truman war-fascist program of world conquest. As we have remarked earlier, the aggressive implications of the United States government's line were already obvious to Marxists during the war, in the hostile attitude toward our ally, the U.S.S.R. At its Emergency (thirteenth) Convention, on July 28, 1945, therefore, the Party warned that if the imperialist policies of American monopoly capital were not checked, there would be "new aggressions and wars and the growth of reaction and fascism in the United States."[1] In the same vein, at its fourteenth convention, on August 2, 1948, the Party issued an even sharper warning against the war danger. The election platform then formulated stated the central issue in the coming elections to be "Shall America follow the path of peace or war, democracy or fascism?"[2] And at its fifteenth convention, beginning on December 28, 1950, the Party declared that "The frenzied imperialist drive toward war and fascism has now entered a new stage,"[3] that of actual armed agression in the Far East.

During the post-war period the Party's main political line has been in favor of building a united front anti-fascist peace coalition, led by labor. All its individual policies have been based upon and interlocked with the people's general struggle against fascism and war. This policy has been founded on the conviction that the masses do not want war and can prevent it if they will but make their will felt. In this fight the Party has had to be constantly alert to combat remnants of Browderism among its leaders and membership and in its general ideological and political mass work.

As against the war policy of the Truman government, the Communist Party has militantly counterposed the peace policy of U.S.A.-U.S.S.R. collaboration. The Party has tirelessly pointed out to the workers and the masses of the American people that American-Soviet co-operation is the supreme political necessity of our times. It is the central means of

---

1 *Political Affairs*, Sept. 1945.
2 *Political Affairs*, Sept. 1948.
3 *Political Affairs*, Jan. 1951.

preventing war, preserving and extending democracy, and opening the way to prosperity for the toiling masses. This policy would make the United Nations into what the peoples intended it to be, a body willing and capable of maintaining world peace, instead of the instrument for war that it has become under the domination of the United States. American-Soviet collaboration is the mutual desire of both the American and Soviet peoples, and it is also the settled policy of the Soviet government. The great obstacle to the two big nations living in amity is the policy of the monopoly capitalists of the United States, whose entire plan for world control rests upon the hope of a successful war against the U.S.S.R.

The Party has exposed and combated the individual phases of the Wall Street program of world conquest as they have developed in the post-war period. It immediately condemned the Truman Doctrine as a fomenter of reactionary civil wars, directed toward the overthrow of the governments of peoples striving for democracy and socialism; it promptly stigmatized the Marshall Plan as cut from the same cloth as the Truman Doctrine and as a gigantic attempt to chain Europe to the war chariot of American imperialism; and it showed that President Truman's "Point Four" proposals were nothing but a plan to further Wall Street's imperialist economic and political penetration of the industrially less developed areas of the world, and it also opposed the North Atlantic Pact and the Japanese treaty.

The Party vigorously opposed United States intervention in Greece; its interference in the national elections in France and Italy; its building of the North Atlantic war alliance; its armed support to Chiang Kai-shek in China; its shipping of munitions to the imperialist armies in Indonesia, Indo-China, Burma, Malaya, and the Philippines, with which to shoot down the rebellious peoples; its attempts to fascize Germany, Italy, and Japan, its ruthless oppression and exploitation of the peoples of Latin America; and its casting of the burden of war preparations upon the workers through inflation, high taxes, and so on. The Party has especially exposed the hypocrisy of the government's propaganda to the effect that the huge military preparations in the United States are "defensive." In its fight for peace the Party has shown real initiative and vigor.

THE NINE-PARTY COMMUNIST CONFERENCE

The world struggle for peace and democracy, against the Wall Street aggressors, was given a powerful impetus by the conference in Warsaw, in September 1947, of the nine leading Communist parties in Europe;

namely, those of the Soviet Union, Poland, Czechoslovakia, France, Italy, Romania, Hungary, Bulgaria, and Yugoslavia.[1] This historic conference pointed out sharply the growing fascist-war danger, due to the aggressive policies of American imperialism. It stated that the world had therefore become divided into two camps: "the imperialistic and anti-democratic camp, which has as a main aim the establishment of world domination of American imperialism and the smashing of democracy; and the anti-imperialist and democratic camp, which has as a main aim the undermining of imperialism and the strengthening of democracy and the liquidation of the remnants of fascism." The conference called upon the peoples of Europe to defend world peace and their national independence against the imperialist aggressions of the United States, aided by its servile allies, the right Social-Democrats. The conference set up an Information Bureau to facilitate co-operation among the nine Communist parties.[2]

The policy of the nine-party Communist conference confirmed the anti-war line that the C.P.U.S.A. had been developing independently since its convention of 1945. The U.S. Party hailed the establishment of the Information Bureau as a much-needed center of co-operation. In view of the Voorhis law and other reactionary legislation in the United States prohibiting international connections, however, the Party decided not to seek affiliation with the new Bureau.[3]

THE 1948 ELECTIONS

The Communist Party made the fight for peace the center of its work in the 1948 presidential elections. It supported the candidates of the Progressive Party, former vice-president Henry A. Wallace and Glen Taylor, Senator from Idaho. The new Progressive Party was organized as a national body early in 1948. At its Philadelphia convention of July 23-25, 3,240 delegates and alternates were present. The Progressive Party had a program calling for "peace, freedom, and abundance," but it put its main stress upon the question of peace. The new organization, due chiefly to the efforts of the progressive unions and the Communists, got on the ballot in 45 states, thus refuting the stubborn illusion that the third party could not get its candidates before the national electorate.

The Progressive ticket, although heavily opposed by the top A.F. of L. and C.I.O. leaders, nevertheless won considerable labor support. By

---

[1] This was before it was evident that Tito had turned traitor to socialism.
[2] See Resolutions of the Nine-Party Communist Conference, in *Political Affairs*, Nov. 1947.
[3] Statement of National Board, C.P.U.S.A., in *Political Affairs*, Dec. 1947.

July 1948, seven national unions, with a total membership of 549,000 were announced as officially backing the new party, while five others, with a membership of 873,000, were listed as active supporters.[1] This endorsement came in the greatest part from C.I.O. unions.

Wallace at this time was advocating a peaceful collaboration between the U.S.A. and the U.S.S.R. But the opposition was powerful, and the ticket polled only 1,158,000 votes. Many workers, although anxious for peace and sympathetic to the ticket, were caught in the "lesser evil" trap of the two-party system and were not ready to support a third-party movement. The relatively small vote greatly discouraged Wallace, and he later displayed less and less interest in the fight for peace. When the Korean war broke out he collapsed altogether and, swallowing everything he had said before, he gave his blessing to Wall Street's attempt to subjugate Korea and China. Later, he undertook to atone for his "sin" of formerly opposing militant American imperialism by redbaiting the U.S.S.R., the People's Republic of China, and the Communist Party in this country. Wallace's course, ranging from a show of radicalism to an abject surrender to the war program of big business, expressed the characteristic vacillating position of the petty bourgeoisie.

President Truman, to the surprise of nearly everyone, carried the 1948 election over the cocksure Dewey. What gave him victory was his elaborate pretense of being an advocate of world peace, which appealed to the peace-loving masses. No sooner was he re-elected, however, than he jettisoned his peace promises and redoubled his drive for a war against the Soviet Union. Into the discard, as useless baggage, also went his pre-election pledges for rent ceilings, civil rights of Negroes, price controls, repeal of the Taft-Hartley law, federal aid to education, slum clearance, low-cost housing, and the expansion of social security. To the reactionary Truman these reforms never had any validity, except to serve as demagogic bait to trap unwary voters.

The C.P. was historically correct in making peace its key issue in the elections, but in doing so it suffered from some errors and shortcomings, of both a right and a left sectarian character. There was a too uncritical support of Wallace, not enough exposure of the "lesser evil" danger, and an unskillful handling of the united front election fight. In particular the left-wingers in the unions fought inadequately against the Marshall plan, for peace, for friendly relations with the U.S.S.R., for independent political action. These weaknesses cut into the Wallace vote.

During the post-war period the Communist Party also carried on many important local election struggles. Thus, in Cleveland, Ohio, in

[1] Labor Research Association, *Labor Fact Book 9*, p. 153, N. Y., 1949.

COMMUNISTS AND THE "COLD WAR" 473

March 1947, A. Krchmarek, Communist candidate for the school board, received 64,213 votes, and in California, in June 1950, the well-known Communist, Bernadette Doyle, polled the big total of 613,670 votes on a non-partisan ticket as candidate for Superintendent of Public Schools. In New York City, in the 1950 councilmanic elections the reactionaries, in order to defeat the Negro Communist councilman Benjamin J. Davis, Jr., had to abolish the city's system of proportional representation and also to rig up a Republican-Democratic-Liberal candidate against him.

An especially vital election battle of this period and one full of significance in the fight to preserve world peace was that, in November 1951, of Vito Marcantonio, American Labor Party member in the House of Representatives from the 18th District in New York City. Marcantonio, the most outstanding labor member in the whole history of the American Congress, had won himself the violent hatred of all reactionaries. during his seven terms in the House. So they ganged up against him with a joint candidate on the Republican, Democratic, and Liberal tickets. The fight was an extremely bitter one. Marcantonio increased his vote from 38 percent in 1948 to 42 percent in 1950, but it was not enough to save him from defeat.

THE PARTY AND THE KOREAN WAR

As the warmongering of reaction increased, the Communist Party initiated and supported many mass peace activities. It based its defense of the workers' living standards and democratic liberties (of which more in succeeding chapters) upon the general struggle to maintain world peace. These activities were greatly increased with the outbreak of the Korean war in June, 1950.

In the face of bitter government persecution, the Party took a forthright stand of opposition to this war of aggression against the Korean and Chinese peoples. This was in line with the fights made in our national history against other unjust wars. The Party declared on June 27th, the day when Truman, acting like a dictator, personally ordered the air force and navy (and later, the army) to attack the North Koreans, that the purpose of the war was "to conquer the peoples of Asia, to rob them of their natural resources, to multiply Big Business' profits from a subjugated world." The Party warned of the danger of a third world war and declared, "Hands Off Korea! Demand the immediate withdrawal of the United States warships and air force and an end to the shipment of arms to the puppet Rhee government!" "Not a cent, not a gun, not a plane for Wall Street's puppet regimes in Korea, Formosa, Viet Nam!" It called for "full support to the peoples of Korea, China, Formosa, the

Philippines, Indonesia, Indo-China, Malaya, in their brave struggle for unity, for independence, for liberation." The Party demanded the seating of People's China in the United Nations and its recognition by the United States, and it proposed direct negotiations between the United States, the Soviet Union, and China for peace.[1]

In taking this forthright stand against the reactionary Korean war, despite harsh government persecution, the Communist Party has acted truly as the Party of the working class and of the American people, bravely expressing their true anti-war sentiments and interests. The masses have hated this war from the outset, nor could all the intensive propaganda of the warmongers induce them to support it wholeheartedly.

ANTI-WAR ACTIVITIES OF THE PARTY

As the Party reiterated several months later, the fight for peace is "the central, all-embracing task for the whole present historic period. The future of our nation, the welfare of our people depends on the outcome of this struggle." The Party followed a broad united front policy, stating, "We declare our readiness to work together with anyone, regardless of his political views, so long as he truly desires peace."[2] The Party demanded the withdrawal of American troops from Korea, hands off China, and the banning of the atom-bomb, and opposed the fascization and rearming of Germany and Japan.[3]

On an international scale the great progressive mass organizations, which grew so rapidly at the close of the war, have been taking an active part in the fight against war. These organizations include the World Federation of Trade Unions, the Women's International Democratic Federation, and the World Federation of Democratic Youth. The general organized world peace movement is the World Congress of the Defenders of Peace. The widespread peace activities of these world-wide mass movements have had considerable repercussions and support in the United States. The Party has actively supported them.

The American workers and the democratic masses generally were greatly shocked by the outbreak of the Korean war. Many anti-war activities have grown up among them. The C.P. has supported these vigorously, but without the co-operation of the Social-Democrats, who are eagerly following the war lead of Wall Street. The women and youth are particularly active in the general struggle against war and fascism.

Among the more outstanding of the American peace movements and

---

[1] *Daily Worker*, June 28, 1950.
[2] *Daily Worker*, June 28, 1950.
[3] Main Resolution, Fifteenth Convention, C.P.U.S.A., in *Political Affairs*, Jan. 1951.

organizations, after 1948, were the American Cultural and Scientific Conference for World Peace in New York, on March 25, 1949, and the National Labor Conference for Peace, held in October 1949, in Chicago, of some 1,200 delegates, mostly rank-and-filers. The latter organization carried on considerable activity, forming local councils in numerous cities. Another big demonstration was that near Peekskill, New York, on September 4, 1949, of 15,000 people, at which Paul Robeson spoke and sang and which was attacked by fascist-like hooligans. Then there was the organized circulation of the great Stockholm Peace Pledge, put out by the first World Peace Congress, held in Stockholm, March 15-19, 1950. Of the half billion signatures on this pledge, some 2,500,000 were gathered in the United States, despite arrests, beatings, and loss of jobs for signature gatherers. Shortly afterward came the even greater signature campaign for the Five-Power Peace Pact, which now has 600 million names.

One of the most significant of the many mass protest meetings against the Korean war was that on August 2, 1950, in Union Square, New York, which was brutally dispersed by police violence. To the Second World Peace Conference, in Warsaw, November 16-22, 1950, was sent a delegation of 52 Americans, with 13 observers, including many outstanding liberals, trade unionists, and left-wingers. Among the groups represented at the Warsaw Congress was the American Women for Peace. This organization has carried on many anti-war activities, including the sending of a delegation of 1,000 women on October 24, 1950, to the United Nations to demand the ending of the Korean conflict. A further important domestic peace organization was the Peace Information Center. The head of this organization, the world-renowned Negro scholar and fighter, Dr. W. E. B. DuBois, 83 years old, was arrested as a foreign agent for circulating the World Peace Appeal.[1]

The most important concentration of peace forces, up to this writing, however, was the American People's Congress for Peace, held in Chicago, June 29-July 1, 1951, under the auspices of the American Peace Crusade. This vital gathering, held in an atmosphere of raids upon the Communist Party and of growing terrorism, drew together some 5,000 delegates —workers, farmers, small businessmen, clergymen, scientists, artists, and active political figures. Among them there were 1,500 Negroes and 1,000 young people, and over one-third of the Congress were women. C.I.O. unions sent 229 delegates and A.F. of L. unions 68. The Declaration of Principles of the Congress demanded the cessation of the war in Korea, an immediate conference of the great powers, and controlled disarmament and destruction of weapons of mass annihilation. The congress proposed to hold 100,000 peace meetings within the following few

[1] Labor Research Association, *Labor Fact Book 10*, pp. 27-30.

months and to send a petition of one million signatures to President Truman. A National Committee to direct the movement was elected, including such noted peace fighters as Paul Robeson, Rockwell Kent, and others; its chairmen were Dr. DuBois, Professor A. J. Carlson of the University of Chicago, and Professor Robert Morss Lovett, former governor of the Virgin Islands.

A significant event during this post-war period was the holding of the big civil rights congress in Washington, on January 15, 1950. The congress, assembling some 5,000 delegates, was initiated by the N.A.A.C.P. and endorsed by the A.F. of L., the C.I.O., and a host of churches and other economic, political, and civic organizations. The purpose of this conference was to support the civil rights program of President Truman, which the latter had cynically abandoned. A very significant post-war movement, too, among the Negro people is the National Negro Labor Council, formed in Cincinnati, October 27-28, 1951, at a convention of 1,052 delegates, speaking in the name of one million Negro trade unionists. Its general purpose is to break down Jim Crow, both inside and outside the unions, and to bring about a better working solidarity among the Negro and white members of the whole trade union movement. Along with its program of defense of the economic and political rights of the Negro toilers, the new Council also denounced the Truman war policy. William R. Hood is the Council's president.

Another important development during this period was the presentation to the United Nations in December 1951, by the Civil Rights Congress, of a protest petition in defense of the American Negro people. It was presented simultaneously, in New York by Paul Robeson, and in Paris by William L. Patterson. The document, entitled *We Charge Genocide*, is a powerful exposure of Jim Crow in the United States. A demand was made for U.N. intervention and relief.

All these pro-peace anti-fascist activities, which the C.P.U.S.A. has supported, have not been able to force the government to drop its general war policy, but they have nevertheless been of real service in shaping American public opinion, in halting the use of the A-bomb in Korea, and in letting in some rays of truth and humanity through the thick fog of imperialist war propaganda and brutality which now envelop this country. Their greatest weakness is that they have not yet secured solid mass trade union support.

THE COMMUNISTS AND THE NEGRO PEOPLE

In the growing atmosphere of terrorism, as the government's war program has developed through the post-war years, the Negro people have been a particular object of attack by organized reaction. This is because, in addition to their great militancy in all spheres of the people's struggles, Negroes especially have no liking for the war that American imperialism is now carrying on against the darker-skinned peoples of Asia. They largely recognize and speak out against the imperialist-white chauvinist content of this war. Hence, they have been subjected to many injuries and indignities. A characteristic example was the "race riot" of Cicero, Illinois, in July 1951, over an attempt by a Negro family merely to live in this "lily-white" town, famous for its bootleggers, prostitutes, gamblers, and open shop industries. Another example was the brutal bomb murder of H. T. Moore, N.A.A.C.P. Negro leader in Florida, and his wife in December 1951.

Since the end of the war the Negro people have been the target, among other outrages, of a number of particularly atrocious frame-up cases, on the usual fake charge of "rape." Where the lynch gangs used to hang or burn offhand Negroes whom they chose to accuse of crime, they now proceed to lynch them legally. A monstrously outrageous example of this was the electrocution in 1951 of the "Martinsville Seven"—J. Hampton, F. Hairston, B. T. Millner, H. L. Hairston, F. Grayson, J. C. Taylor, and J. T. Hairston—for a "rape" which never occurred. No white man in Virginia's history has ever been executed for rape; but not even a powerful mass movement of international protest could save these innocent Negroes from the hands of the legal lynchers. The execution of Willie McGee shortly afterward in Mississippi, also on a trumped-up rape charge, was a similar legal lynching. And at the present writing the country is being afflicted with the further shameful spectacle of the ruthless attempt to execute the "Trenton Six" Negroes—C. English, McK. Forrest, H. Wilson, R. Cooper, J. Thorpe, and J. MacKenzie—on the lying charge that they murdered a man. After a nationwide struggle four were freed, but two were given life sentences.

The Communist Party rallied to the defense of the Negro people in all these outrageous attacks, making several of the cases into causes of national and international attention. The Party worked on a united front basis with the Civil Rights Congress and other defense organizations.

During the post-war years the Communist Party, in line with its keen appreciation of the profound political importance of the Negro question, has conducted a number of far-reaching theoretical discussions of this issue. One of these, in late 1946 and early 1947, was a self-critical survey of the Party's whole policy and activities in the Negro people's fight for economic, political, and social equality, and especially of the matter of their demand for self-determination in the South. The result was a clarification and general reaffirmation of the Party's line. On the complex question of self-determination the resulting resolution says: "In fighting for their equal rights the Negro people are becoming more unified as a people. Their fight for liberation from oppression in the Black Belt—the area of Negro majority population—is a struggle for full nationhood, for their rightful position of full equality as a nation."[1] An important contribution to these discussions was Harry Haywood's book, *Negro Liberation*.

The Negro people are obviously developing a national consciousness under especially difficult circumstances. This consciousness is evidenced, among other things, by the former growth of the nationalist Garvey movement, by the huge expansion of Negro organizations, by the growing use of the term "people" instead of "race" by Negroes, and by many other manifestations. If the Negro people have not yet widely adopted the slogan of self-determination, this is fundamentally because they are a young, developing nation, in the midst of strongly repressive conditions. This slogan is violently opposed by every brand of reactionary and reformist, Negro and white. Besides, the Negro people are still heavily afflicted with bourgeois-democratic illusions, even as, for similar but not identical reasons, the great mass of the working class has not yet accepted the slogan of socialism.

Another vital theoretical discussion of the Negro question by the Party related primarily to the important matter of white chauvinism. The discussion took place around the report of Pettis Perry to the National Committee on April 24, 1949. This penetrating and frank discussion brought to light many of the subtle manifestations of the systematic ideological and physical persecution of the Negro people. It restressed the fact that the white workers are often deeply penetrated with the poisonous white chauvinism, and even the Communist Party itself has to be on constant guard against its infection. This was one of the most important discussions in the entire life of the Party, and the reports of it occupy the full June 1949 issue of *Political Affairs*. The general result is a much greater alertness on the part of the Party's leadership and membership to the major danger of white chauvinism within the Party, the labor movement, and society generally.

In the debates the Party laid great stress upon the fact that the leadership by the Negro proletariat is indispensable in the fight for emancipation of the Negro people as a whole. This especially requires the building of strong organizations, such as the Negro Labor Councils, and the development of thorough-going co-operation with progressive white workers. It necessitates, too, a persistent fight against petty-bourgeois na-

[1] *The Communist Position on the Negro Question*, p. 11, N. Y., 1947.

tionalist influence in Negro ranks. But, above all, it implies a powerful Communist Party.

In these summations of its Negro policy the Communist Party, despite many shortcomings in its work, registered justifiable pride in its prestige among the Negro people and in the splendid body of Negro Marxist-Leninist leaders that it has succeeded in building up during its many years of devoted struggle around this question. The percentage of Negro members in the Party during the post-war years was as follows: 1946—14 percent; 1947—17 percent; 1948—17 percent; 1949—14 percent; 1950—15 percent.

THE FORMATION OF THE LABOR YOUTH LEAGUE

On May 28, 1949, in Chicago, the left-wing youth of the United States organized the Labor Youth League. The L.Y.L., which continues the traditions of the Y.C.L. and the Marxist youth movement generally, educates the young men and women of the working class in the spirit of socialism. The L.Y.L. has a fundamental role to play in the decisive "battle for the youth," advancing the unity of young people to prevent their regimentation and slaughter on the altar of Wall Street's imperialist ambitions. The most important publications of the Marxist youth in the United States are *New Challenge* and *New Foundations,* a student publication. The national chairman of the L.Y.L. is Leon Wofsy.

In the stormy years since its foundation, the L.Y.L. has taken an important part in the great struggle for peace, particularly in relation to the Korean war and the fight to prevent the militarization of America's young people. The League has conducted various demonstrations, and it collected half a million signatures for the Stockholm Peace Pledge. On November 24, 1950, it rallied 5,000 youth in an anti-war demonstration in New York. It has sent delegations to the great world youth festival of the W.F.D.Y. Roosevelt Ward, Negro youth and leader of the L.Y.L., was arrested in the summer of 1951 on a trumped-up draft charge and sentenced to three years in jail.

THE COMMUNISTS AND THE REPUBLIC OF ISRAEL

The conditions and struggles of the national groups and minorities in the United States have always been a subject of close concern to the Communist Party. This has been even more the case since World War II, when these sections of the population have been under heavy fire from the forces of reaction. The Party devoted much attention to the malignant attempts to deport non-citizen, foreign-born workers, many of them in this country for up to half a century. It also started to defend the cause of Mexican-Americans in the Southwest, who number some three million and suffer from Jim Crow-like persecution.[1] It began, too, to interest itself in the bitter plight of the American Indians, who have been practically ignored by the labor movement throughout its more than a century of existence.[2] The Party has also been on the alert to combat every manifestation of anti-Semitism. Its most important struggle on the Jewish question, during the post-war years, turned around the issue of the foundation of the state of Israel.[3]

Prior to World War II there was a considerable movement among the world's 16,600,000 Jews, launched by Theodor Herzl in 1897, for the creation of a Jewish homeland in Palestine. The brutal slaughter of about six million Jews by Hitler before and during the war stimulated this movement. It became very powerful and developed into an acute international issue. The Arab governments of the Near and Middle East, controlled by reactionary landlords and dominated by British imperialism, violently opposed the creation of a Jewish state in Palestine. Great Britain, eager to keep its grip on the whole area, also opposed such a state. American imperialism, seeking to control the British as well as the Arabs and Jews, blew hot and cold on the issue. The only true friend of the Jewish people in their fight for national freedom was the Soviet Union, which steadfastly supported the setting-up of the longed-for homeland of the Jews. The United Nations, torn by conflicting imperialist interests, backed and filled on the question. Eventually, the Jewish masses themselves virtually settled the matter by establishing the Republic of Israel, in May 1948. They then defended their government, arms in hand, against the British-inspired attacks from the neighboring Arab governments. Zionism, which dominates this situation and pretends to speak in the name of the Jewish people, expresses a bourgeois-nationalist ideology. In the past it collaborated chiefly with British imperialism; now it works with American imperialism, and the latter has finally come practically to dominate the new state of Israel.

Within the United States, which has approximately five million Jews, the question of Palestine became an important political matter, with the Truman Administration, tongue-in-cheek, endorsing the proposed Jewish state. Rich Jews—Zionists—in alliance with right Social-Democrats, controlled the pro-Israel movement in the United States, and both groups played the game of American imperialism. The Communist Party took a very active part in the whole struggle. In general it fought for the creation of the new state, for an understanding be-

---

1 *Political Affairs*, May 1949.
2 Foster, *Outline Political History of the Americas*.
3 A. B. Magil, *Israel in Crisis*, N. Y., 1950.

tween the Jewish and Arab peoples, and for co-operation between Israel and the U.S.S.R. and generally with the peace forces of the world. The Party laid emphasis upon the leadership of the Jewish workers in the movement, both in Palestine and abroad. The Party militantly opposed the violence of British imperialism against the Jewish people, and it especially combatted the trickeries of American imperialism and of its Zionist and Social-Democratic allies. The American Communists and other left forces were a constructive force in the long, bitter, and complicated struggle,[1] despite some failure to fight aggressively to preserve Israel from imperialist domination, particularly domination by American imperialism. In this work some sectarian mistakes also were made and some traces of bourgeois nationalism crept in.

THE QUESTION OF KEYNESISM

During the post-war period a major phase of the work of the Communist Party, through its press, schools, and so on, has been to expose and combat the complex and hypocritical demagogy by which the big capitalists, through their government, press, radio, church, labor bureaucracy, etc., are pushing the nation toward war. This poisonous war propaganda has undoubtedly confused vast masses of the people, including large sections of the working class. The Party's educational campaign involved fighting such "big lies" as that the United States is a non-imperialist country; that its foreign policies are based on the defense of democracy; that its economic system is "exceptional" and does not suffer from the decay common to capitalism in other countries; that the U.S.S.R. is "red imperialism," and the like. In this ideological work the Party also made an extended theoretical analysis of Keynesism, which forms the economic basis of American government policy in this period.

The late Sir John Maynard Keynes, noted British bourgeois economist (see Chapter 21), took issue with the current capitalist economic dogmas to the effect that the capitalist system was a self-regulating mechanism that automatically overcame its own internal crises. Keynes argued that with the development of the productive forces into modern monopoly the economic system at the same time produced a tendency to restrict capital investment and therewith had exposed itself to profound economic crises and huge chronic mass unemployment. This situation, if uncorrected, he said, could lead to revolution and socialism.

---

[1] See Alexander Bittelman in *Political Affairs*, July 1945; July 1947; Jan., Feb., Aug. 1948; A. B. Magil in *Political Affairs*, March 1949; John Williamson in *Political Affairs*, July 1950; Resolution, C.P.U.S.A., in *Political Affairs*, Nov. 1946.

Keynes therefore proposed that capitalism could overcome this basic flaw, achieve full employment of the workers, and proceed on an upward spiral of development, if the government stimulated capital investment in various ways, principally by subsidizing industry. This, in brief, was his theory of "progressive capitalism." Keynes, in seeking to avert the cyclical crises of capitalism, also undertook therewith to cure the general crisis of the whole capitalist system.[1]

Keynesism is the bourgeois economics of the period of the general decline of world capitalism. It forms the basis of the economic policies of all the leading capitalist countries, including the United States. It is also reflected in the United Nations. Recently, a committee of U.N. experts, charged in 1949 with bringing in measures to enable affiliated states to assure full employment of their workers, submitted a typical Keynesian program. The committee consisted of leading capitalist economists from Great Britain, France, Australia, and the United States, and its report was unanimous.[2] This ambitious report proposed nothing less than the "management" of the economies of the various capitalist countries and of the world as a whole, so as to avert cyclical crises—a project wholly unrealizable under capitalism.

Keynesism has come to be widely, if not generally, accepted in American bourgeois circles—among liberals, labor leaders, Social-Democrats, and also big capitalists. It has also deeply penetrated working class ranks, which is its greatest menace. Varying interpretations have been placed upon Keynesism by different groups. Wallace, Browder, Murray, Reuther, Green, and such liberal and labor advocates of "progressive capitalism," argue in theory, if they do not apply it in practice, that capitalism can and must save itself through an expansion of the market for commodities by various reforms supposedly designed to increase somewhat the purchasing power of the masses. They swallow whole Keynesism as bourgeois reformism. But the big capitalists, although they may even sneer at the very name of Keynes, nevertheless express their own Keynesian conceptions through the huge armaments program. Their theory and practice of how to keep sick capitalism going is by producing gigantic quantities of munitions at government expense and by eventually precipitating war. This Keynesian conception is extremely profitable to the capitalists at present, and it fits right in with their program of imperialist expansion. In practice the "liberal" Keynesians go along with this armaments program.

Keynesism fails to prevent periodic capitalist economic breakdowns

---

[1] For discussion, see *Political Affairs* from Jan. 1948 through Feb. 1949, and Jefferson School of Social Science, *The Economic Crisis and the Cold War*.

[2] O. Nathan in *Science and Society*, Summer 1951.

because it leaves unchanged the basic cause which brings about these crises. This is the private ownership of industry, with its inevitable exploitation of the workers, anarchic character of production, monopoly practices of the trusts, imperialist robbery of the colonial peoples, and violent trade rivalries among the capitalist powers. Keynesism, with its government subsidizing of industry, dabbling with the tax structure, etc., leaves all the basic capitalist weaknesses uncured. Hence, the cyclical crises remain unconquered. Only socialism, with its social ownership, planned economy, and production for social use instead of private profit, can finally abolish economic breakdowns and insure permanent full employment.

The Roosevelt "New Deal" was Keynesism, with American adaptations. It did not, however, as we have seen, bring about industrial recovery. This recovery took place in its sick and distorted form, only with the outbreak of war in Europe and the growth of huge munitions production in the United States. The Truman "Fair Deal," or "managed economy," or "welfare state," which is essentially an application of Keynesism, was, despite the expenditure of immense amounts of government funds here and abroad, heading straight into a profound economic crisis before the present arms race began. This is giving industry a shot in the arm, but is only postponing briefly the inevitable economic smashup.

American Keynesism, whether known as the "New Deal," "Fair Deal," "managed economy," "progressive capitalism," the "welfare state," or just the arms program of big capital, is an instigator of gigantic munitions production, and it gives a new and more sinister impulse to war itself. It is no accident that Truman, Wallace, Green, Murray, *et al.*, the so-called liberal advocates of Keynesism, however they may name it, are at the same time militant warmongers. President Truman threw the reforms proposed by his "welfare state" into the wastebasket when Wall Street called for war production. Fundamentally reactionary, Keynesism dovetails with the drive of American imperialism for world conquest. It is the path to war, the way to mass slaughter and economic disaster.

As against reactionary Keynesism, the Communist Party stresses its constructive economic and political program. It points out that the way the workers of America can secure the maximum employment and generally conserve their economic interests to the greatest extent possible under the capitalist system, is not along the fatal Keynesian path of munitions production, but by developing a solid mass struggle for the increase of real wages, the shortening of working hours, the development of social security, the carrying out of needed public works, and the achievement of various other economic reforms. But so long as capitalism lasts, the Party warns, the workers will be plagued by economic crises, mass unemployment, and low living standards. The only way these deadly evils can be finally done away with is by the abolition of the capitalist system. The power of monopoly capital, the breeder of destitution, fascism, and war, must be curbed and finally broken. To carry through this program requires a great strengthening of the working class and its allies economically and politically, the progressive nationalization of the main industries, and eventually the establishment of socialism. Not Keynes, but Marx, points the way to prosperity and peace.

THE PARTY MEETS THE TEST

The Party, with its new leadership, established at the Emergency Convention in 1945, has met successfully the hard tasks placed upon it by the complex problems of the post-war years. In addition to the daily struggles in defense of the interests of the workers and the Negro people, it has had to deal with three big overriding tasks characteristic of this post-war period.

The first of these, chronologically speaking, was the elimination of the opportunist poison of Browderism. This disease, continued over several years, had seriously infected the Party. But the new leadership resolutely attacked the problem and has definitely established the Party on Marxist-Leninist principles. An active two-front fight was conducted against right and "left" opportunism in all their forms, including various brands of renegades.

The second and most decisive of all tasks of the post-war period has been the fight against the world war that Wall Street is attempting to organize, and specifically the war in Korea. This fundamental responsibility, too, the Communist Party has met in a Leninist manner, displaying real political initiative in its fight for peace.

The third task confronting the Party in the post-war years has been the defense of its own organization and rights, and therewith the whole body of democratic rights, against the attacks of reaction, which would destroy the Communist Party and force the United States into fascism. But more about this key struggle in Chapter 35.

These are most crucial years in the history of our country and the world. The Communist Party of the United States, although still limited in strength and resources, is meeting this situation in a genuine Leninist manner, as the vanguard party of the working class. This is why the Party is under such fierce attacks and why Eugene Dennis and so many others of the Party's leaders and members are being railroaded to jail.

34. American Imperialism Hobbles the Trade Union Movement (1945-1951)

One of the major problems confronting Wall Street in the development of its war program of world imperialist conquest, upon emerging from World War II, was to avert and break up the broad and powerful opposition of the working class—for, obviously, monopoly capital could not make any serious headway toward world mastery if it had to confront a rebellious proletariat. Regarding the workers, it was imperative, if they were to be drawn into the war program or at least not successfully to oppose it, that their heads be stuffed full of war propaganda, that they be made to bear the lion's share of the economic burdens, that they be crippled in their right to strike, and, above all, that the left wing among them be crushed.

The most effective ones to tackle these tasks for the Wall Street capitalist warmongers were, of course, the conservative trade union leaders—the characteristic American brand of Social-Democrats. They had always served the bosses well in the past, as we have pointed out—during World War I, during the following post-war capitalist offensive, during the Coolidge prosperity years, during the great economic crisis, and on many other occasions, and they would not fail them this time. Nor did they. This was because they are, indeed, "labor lieutenants of capital in the ranks of the working class."

It was not much of a problem for the bosses to get a man such as William Green, A.F. of L. president (and those around him) to take up the job of dragooning the working class into the war program. For Green talks and feels and lives like a capitalist, and he is ever on guard to defend the capitalist system. Recently he declared: "The American Federation of Labor supports our American capitalist system and free enterprise . . . just as vigorously as we support trade unionism and the right to organize and bargain collectively."[1]

Philip Murray (and his associates), for all his posing as a progressive, might well have said these very words himself, because they express his sentiments precisely. Not long since he also stated his opinion of

[1] William Green at the A.F. of L. Convention, New Orleans, Nov. 1940.

the capitalist system as follows: "We have no classes in this country; that's why the Marxist theory of the class struggle has gained so few adherents. We are *all* workers here. And in the final analysis the interests of farmers, factory hands, business and professional people, and white collar workers prove to be the same."[1]

The history of the American trade union movement during the post-World War II years, in one sense, is the story of the systematic demobilizing of the workers' opposition to the war program of Wall Street imperialism by the top leaders of the A.F. of L., C.I.O., and Railroad Brotherhoods. These people do not, of course, do this reactionary work for nothing. They reap a variety of rewards, all very valuable to them. For one thing, and the most important, the employers have tacitly agreed not to try to destroy the unions outright by an open shop drive, as they did after World War I. This gives the union leaders a semblance of guarantee that they can maintain intact their huge body of dues-payers, from whom they milk their enormous salaries.[2] Besides, as never before, the Greens, Murrays, Reuthers, Harrisons, *et al.* are being played up in the public eye and heroized as great "labor statesmen." Also, more than ever, the labor bureaucrats are being given sinecure jobs in the government apparatus, even though as yet only in third-line capacities—as advisers to the war economic committees, as "labor attachés" to the various U.S. embassies, and the like. The time is not yet here, however, when the American capitalists, in seeking to control the masses of workers, will corrupt their Social-Democratic leaders by giving them posts in the Cabinet, ambassadorships, or even by making them the heads of the government, as their likes in Europe have done.

The major reward, however, which the top American trade union leaders hope to gain by supporting imperialism's drive for world conquest, is to secure a big share in the latter's loot. Their aim, in tune with that of Wall Street, is to establish control over the labor movement of the entire world. This is the first time in labor history that any national trade union movement has set such an imperialistic goal for itself, but it is precisely what the A.F. of L.-C.I.O. leaders are trying to do. They are indeed labor imperialists, with their "foreign departments" and roving agents in Europe and Asia. With millions of dollars, their attitude is arrogant toward all other countries' union leaders. Such elements, as the Communist Party declares, are most dangerous enemies of the working class.

---

[1] Philip Murray in *American Magazine,* June 1948.
[2] These salaries are double to 15 times what the officials could earn as workers, G.M. Harrison of the A.F. of L. Railway Clerks getting as high as $76,000 per year.

THE TAFT-HARTLEY LAW

As they came out of World War II, the workers were in a militant, fighting mood. Having just participated in the winning of the great anti-fascist war, they had absorbed much of its aggressive democratic spirit. They also suffered under many economic grievances. During the war they had been held to 15 percent wage increases above 1941 rates under the "Little Steel" formula, while the cost of living advanced about 35 percent. Moreover, with the cutting off of munitions production and the elimination of overtime work at the end of the war, the workers' "take-home pay" was deeply slashed. So they demanded wage increases up to 35 cents per hour. And they struck to enforce their demands—over 4,500,000 of them in 1946, the first post-war year. This was the biggest strike year in American history. Miners, steel workers, auto workers, electrical and radio workers, maritime workers, railroaders, packinghouse workers, and many other groups participated in the strikes. Nearly all the strikes were victorious. The fight of the workers was facilitated because big foreign loans, huge domestic commodity shortages, a wartime piling up of purchasing power, and the beginning of armament preparations for a new world war had prevented a deep post-war economic crisis.[1] Naturally, the progressive unions and the Communist Party did all they could to strengthen the great strike movement and to give it clear political direction.

All this made, indeed, a pretty kettle of fish for the ruling class. With the workers so very militant, the prospects of the American drive for world conquest through war were not too brilliant. The employers and their Truman government were gravely alarmed, as were the top union leaders, at the aggressive spirit of the workers (which, incidentally, knocked into a cocked hat Browder's theory of a post-war class peace). Something had to be done to control the situation, and the employers undertook it in the Republican 80th Congress, in June 1947, by the passage of the Taft-Hartley Act, with the help of many Democrats in both houses. In 1947, also, 30 states passed "little Taft-Hartley" laws.

The federal Taft-Hartley law was neatly designed to weaken the trade union movement. Among its many reactionary provisions, it abolishes the closed shop, establishes a 60-day "cooling-off" period before strikes may be declared, outlaws mass picketing, authorizes employer interference to prevent the unionization of their plants, condemns secondary boycotts, re-establishes the use of injunctions in labor disputes, enables unions to be sued for "unfair labor practices," denies the unions the right to use their funds for political purposes, grants decisive powers

[1] John Steuben, *Strike Strategy*, N. Y., 1950.

to the National Labor Relations Board, and compels union officials to sign affidavits to the effect that they are not Communists.

The Taft-Hartley law drastically robs the trade unions of their customary independence and freedom of action by subordinating them to control by the capitalist government, as never before in their history. This was dramatized by repeated huge fines against the United Mine Workers for striking, and also by the Supreme Court's fine of $750,000 against Bridges' longshoremen's union for "boycotting" and for refusing to cross the picket lines of a striking trade union. The law constitutes a long move toward transforming the unions into state-dominated labor bodies on the Hitler-Mussolini model. The harmful nature of this legislation is shown by the fact that the trade union movement, although previously expanding rapidly, has made no substantial numerical growth since its passage, although the economic situation has been highly favorable. Also company unionism has been given a new lease on life, and the whole wage fight has been slowed up.

President Truman, with his eye on fooling the labor voters, formally vetoed the Taft-Hartley bill, but he made no effort whatever to rally his party members in Congress to fight it—about one-half of them supported the measure in the first place and also voted to override his veto. Indeed, Mr. Truman's drastic action in breaking the national strike of the 280,000 railroad engineers and trainmen in May 1946, and his subsequent proposal to Congress to force the railroad workers into the army as strikebreakers, demonstrated that he, like the employers, was quite in accord with the basic principles of the new law.

The Communist Party conducted an energetic nation-wide struggle against this fascist-like law, before, during, and after its passage. The Party warned the working class that this attempt to put the unions under government control and domination would not only injure the workers' living standards but would facilitate Wall Street's drive toward fascism and war.

The top leaders of the A.F. of L. and C.I.O. made a big to-do of opposition to the Taft-Hartley Act, but their resistance to it was without solid substance. Green denounced the law as "a slave measure, un-American, vicious, and destructive of labor's constitutional rights," and Murray declared it to be part of "a co-ordinated program to destroy the living standards of our people." The law could have been defeated by a bold refusal of the trade union leadership to sign up under it. John L. Lewis, many progressive leaders, and the Communists proposed just this; but the top A.F. of L.-C.I.O. leadership would have none of it. The 1947 convention of the A.F. of L. voted compliance with the law, "under protest," which traitorous action caused the U.M.W.A. to quit the Federation. The C.I.O., at its convention in the same year, left it up to its affiliates "to decide upon a course of action."

Gradually the Steelworkers, Auto Workers, and other conservative-controlled C.I.O. unions, like the A.F. of L. unions, accepted the law. Only the United Mine Workers, the Typographical Union, and the dozen broadly progressive unions in the C.I.O., along with the Communist Party, made a real fight against the infamous act. What has actually happened regarding the Taft-Hartley legislation is that the employers, with the indirect help of the Truman Administration, and with the connivance of the top A.F. of L., C.I.O. and Railroad Brotherhood leadership, have hobbled the labor movement—a major necessity for the carrying out of Wall Street's plans of world conquest and war.

LABOR AND THE MARSHALL PLAN

The next big war job the employers had for their imperialistic labor lieutenants was to have the latter help them put across the Marshall Plan among the workers of the United States and Europe. The Marshall Plan, launched in mid-1947, was the heart, at that stage, of Wall Street's developing war plan. As the Communist Party pointed out, it was the main means to achieve American political and economic penetration of the European countries and also to arm them for an eventual anti-Soviet war. The Party showed tirelessly the folly of liberals and labor leaders in supporting this key imperialist war measure. In order to jam the plan through, the whole current imperialist propaganda about economic recovery and the defense of world democracy, coupled with violent Soviet-baiting, was greatly stepped up. In appreciation of the role of the labor bureaucrats in all this, Secretary of Labor Maurice Tobin declared that they were worth to the government "a hundred divisions or all the striped pants diplomats that are to be found in the State Department."[1]

The A.F. of L. leaders were easy game for the State Department to enlist in this war campaign. At their 1946 convention they violently attacked Soviet foreign policy and indulged in their usual orgy of red-baiting. In their 1947 convention, likewise, they gave full endorsement to current State Department policy. They backed the Truman Doctrine and the Marshall Plan, supported the government's developing economic attack upon the U.S.S.R., endorsed the plan for a Western European pact, poured out limitless hatred upon the Soviet Union, and repeated to the workers all of Wall Street's tricky imperialist propaganda for war.

With the C.I.O., however, things were a bit more difficult for the

[1] *New York Times*, May 4, 1950.

warmongers. The group of progressive-led unions, counting well onto a million members, were very influential and had kept the organization on a relatively progressive course. Thus, at its 1946 convention the C.I.O. actively opposed the tendencies toward Soviet-baiting, militarization, and war. Its resolution declared that "We reject all proposals for American participation in any bloc or alliance which would destroy the unity of the Big Three."[1] This resolution, inspired by the left, was adopted in spite of strong inner-committee opposition from Reuther, Rieve, and other right-wing elements.

The 1947 convention of the C.I.O. in Boston faced a greatly intensified national propaganda for war. Nevertheless it was impossible for the right-wing elements, as they tried to do in committee, to make the convention endorse either the Truman Doctrine or the Marshall Plan. The resolution which was finally unanimously adopted was a compromise, vaguely worded. It endorsed American help to foreign countries in need; but it qualified this endorsement by stating that "under no circumstances should food or other aid given to any country be used as a means of coercing free but needy people in the exercise of their rights of independence and self-government or to fan the flames of civil warfare." The resolution also demanded disarmament and condemned the prevailing war propaganda. It called for "the fulfillment of the basic policy of our late President Roosevelt for unity of purpose and action among the three great wartime allies—the United States, Great Britain, and the Soviet Union within the United Nations." The left and progressive group stated its opposition to the Marshall Plan during the discussion on the resolution.

The situation in the C.I.O. was very disconcerting to the warmongers; so Secretary of State Marshall was sent to address the convention and to push its political line to the right. This gave Philip Murray the opportunity he had been waiting for—to wangle through an endorsement of the government's war program. What he could not do through the regular action of the convention he accomplished indirectly, by stating personally, after Marshall's speech, that the convention resolution on foreign policy really signified an endorsement of the Marshall Plan. It was a mistake that the progressive delegates did not challenge this interpretation on the spot. Murray's statement was wired all over Europe, with the lying comment that the C.I.O., the progressive wing of the American trade union movement, had, with the agreement of the Communists, unanimously endorsed the Marshall Plan.

During the subsequent months Murray came out fully for the government's war program, with some criticism designed to soften the dis-

[1] Cited by John Williamson in *Political Affairs*, Jan. 1949.

content in the C.I.O. Soon, however, he took his place among the most bitter denouncers of the Soviet Union and the Communist Party. This general pro-war line prevailed at the 1948 C.I.O. convention in Portland, Oregon. Besides endorsing the basic war policies of the State Department in the face of the left-wing opposition, the convention developed an orgy of redbaiting, in some respects even more virulent than that customary in A.F. of L. conventions. The C.I.O. leadership was now well on its way to supporting the American-sponsored civil wars, first in Greece and later in Korea, the gigantic militarization plans of the United States, the reduction of the workers' living standards, and all the rest of the preparations for war. Like the heads of the A.F. of L., the C.I.O. leadership thenceforth became a labor branch of the State Department.

THE SPLIT IN THE C.I.O.

The most imperative task confronting the warmongering American employers in the capitalist countries, if they were to break up the elementary working class opposition to their war program, was to isolate the Communists and other left-wingers and progressives from the trade union masses. If successful, this would deprive the labor movement of its clearest thinkers and best fighters for peace. This attack upon the left wing in the trade unions, world-wide in scope, would imply, among other anti-labor operations, a split in the C.I.O. in the United States. To this latter crime against the workers the Murray-Reuther leadership, at the behest of the government, gave a willing hand.

The alliance between the progressive left wing and the center forces, as against the Reuther-Rieve-Green right wing, had lasted and led the C.I.O. for a full decade. From 1936 to 1941, as we have seen, the main basis of this alliance was the organization of the workers in the great trustified industries; from 1941 to 1945 the left-center bloc worked for the winning of the war; and from 1945 on, as the left proposed, its task should have been to fight for the realization of the kind of democratic peace for which the war had been fought and won. But now the Murray group, swallowing whole the Reuther right-wing program and doing the bidding of the Truman war makers, decided to destroy the progressive bloc, which had built the C.I.O. and made it into the most advanced labor federation this country had yet known.

After the Boston convention, where Murray had sneaked through his snide endorsement of the Marshall Plan, the tension between right and left in the C.I.O. sharpened rapidly. At the January 1948 meeting of the C.I.O. Executive Board an open rift occurred between the broad progressive wing and the Murray forces. It developed when Murray demanded that the Board endorse the Marshall Plan outright and also commit itself to the candidates of the Democratic Party in the coming presidential elections. The broad progressive bloc opposed both of these propositions, which were carried nevertheless. Murray then insisted that all affiliated unions must support these decisions, under an implied threat of expulsion. The eleven attacked and progressive-led unions, however, in line with a century of American trade union experience, claimed the autonomous right to take such positions as they saw fit on political questions.[1]

The following eighteen months were marked by hundreds of membership raids by the right-wing against progressive unions, by the reorganization of the New York City Industrial Union Council and other local and state councils headed by left-wingers and progressives, and by intense quarrels within the C.I.O. over the Wallace election campaign. The attacks upon the Communists and the progressive unions were all supported by Murray.

Meanwhile, the progressive unions, facing an increasingly severe war hysteria, suffered some losses through renegade leaders. That is, in the auto industry the Addes-Thomas group folded up in the face of the war fever, and union control went into the hands of Reuther. Joseph Curran, president of the National Maritime Union, who formerly had worked freely with the Communists, also went over to the right. Most of the board members of the N.M.U. and the Transport Workers Union, seeing the tremendous prestige of the Party won by the good work of the Communists in the union struggles, had previously taken out cards in the C.P. Among them were many who were mere opportunists, and as soon as the government put pressure upon the unions to support the war program, they promptly collapsed. These defections were due to a mixture of sell-out, ideological confusion, and just plain "cold feet."

One of the more notorious of the turncoats was Michael Quill, president of the Transport Workers Union, a close crony of Browder. A combination of Browderism, war hysteria, and bureaucracy and extravagant expense accounts in the C.I.O. caused him to abandon his left pretenses. The first outright sign of his renegacy came early in 1946, when he voted in the New York City Council to give an official reception to Cardinal Spellman upon the latter's return from hobnobbing with dictator Franco—whereas Benjamin J. Davis, Jr., and Peter V. Cacchione, Communist Councilmen, voted against this reactionary proposition. The final break came in New York in 1948 over the matter of subway fares,

[1] John Williamson in *The Worker*, Sept. 25, 1949.

when Quill took the bosses' line and supported the ten-cent fare, while the Party, in harmony with the people's interests, backed the five-cent fare.

An important element in cultivating the split in the C.I.O. was the Association of Catholic Trade Unionists (A.C.T.U.). This body, organized in 1937 by the hierarchy of the Catholic Church, has as its aim typical, but thinly disguised, clerical fascism. Frantically anti-Communist, it bases itself upon the labor encyclical issued by Pope Leo XIII in 1891, and it aims at controlling the labor movement. With local groups and its own press, plus active support from the hierarchy, the A.C.T.U. is a major reactionary force, dividing the workers along religious lines. Its militants were fanatically active in splitting the C.I.O., and Murray, Carey, Brophy, Haywood, and other top C.I.O. leaders actively supported the A.C.T.U.[1] When Murray worked with the progressives, he opposed the A.C.T.U., but later he gave up this opposition, along with the rest of his thin veneer of "progressivism."

The developing split situation came to a head at the C.I.O. convention in Cleveland, Ohio, in October 1949. Murray and Reuther were resolved at all costs to expel the progressive unions. The latter, on the other hand, fought for the unity of the C.I.O., declaring that trade unions necessarily had to include all the workers, of whatever political opinions. The broad, progressive-led forces controlled 71 of the 308 delegates, representing over 900,000 members, without counting the large progressive minorities in the right-led unions. The convention was a swamp of redbaiting.

The central attack by the right wing at the convention was made against the big United Electrical, Radio, and Machine Workers. This progressive union, the U.E., was charged mainly with opposing the Marshall Plan and the Atlantic Pact, refusing to support Truman, the Democratic party presidential candidate, and criticizing the C.I.O. leadership for not fighting aggressively against the Taft-Hartley Act and the wage-paring policies of the government—all of which actions, even if true, the union had a perfect right to carry on, both under the C.I.O. constitution and in accordance with long-established American democratic trade union practice.

In this convention, which was loaded with redbaiting and war hysteria, the U.E. was ruthlessly expelled and its charter turned over to the fascist-minded national secretary of the C.I.O., James B. Carey, who not long before had declared at a public meeting in the Hotel Astor in New York: "In the last war, we joined with the Communists to fight the fascists. In another war, we will join with the fascists to defeat

[1] George Morris in *Political Affairs*, June 1950.

the Communists." So the splendid U.E. union was split, about half of its members eventually going to either side. The convention also decided to bring to trial, later on, all the other progressive unions.

During the next few months, therefore, the C.I.O. Executive Board expelled one union after another, giving them mock trials. Finally, including the U.E. (450,000), eleven unions were ousted—the United Farm Equipment Workers (40,000); International Union of Mine, Mill and Smelter Workers (85,000); Food, Tobacco and Agricultural Workers (36,000); United Office and Professional Workers (25,000); United Public Workers (60,000); American Communications Association (15,000); International Union of Fur and Leather Workers (100,000); International Longshoremen's and Warehousemen's Union (85,000); National Union of Marine Cooks and Stewards (6,000); and the International Fishermen and Allied Workers (20,000). At the 1950 convention of the C.I.O. in Chicago there was not one left-wing delegate in attendance; the process of transforming the C.I.O. top bureaucratic machine into a tool of the State Department was complete.

Thus was perpetrated one of the worst crimes in the whole history of the American labor movement. The C.I.O. right-wing leaders, by ousting the entire eleven progressive unions, had deliberately stripped the C.I.O. of the principal dynamic force that had built the organization and made it into the advance guard of the American trade union movement.

The group of eleven expelled unions not only gave the progressive political lead to the C.I.O., but the strongest among them, such as the U.E., Longshoremen, Fur Workers, and Metal Miners, have won much better working conditions and far higher wages for their members than the right-wing C.I.O. and A.F. of L. unions. They are pace-setters for the whole labor movement. In particular, these unions are alert to improve the Negro workers' conditions in the industries, and also to open the door to their advance to official positions in the labor movement.

The criminal splitting action was finally to produce disastrous consequences for the C.I.O., as we shall see later. Murray, Reuther, and company, who engineered this outrage against the working class, did it with the acclaim and assistance of the capitalist press, the employers, and the government. Wall Street could well rejoice over the services of its labor lackeys heading the C.I.O. The progressive unions made a hard fight to save the unity of the C.I.O.; but in this fight they often lacked united action. At the beginning, too, some of their leaders were unable to realize the depths of treachery to which the Murray group, with whom they had worked for so long, was sinking in order to further Wall Street's war program.

THE A.F. OF L.-C.I.O. ATTACK UPON THE C.T.A.L.

The Latin American Confederation of Labor (C.T.A.L.) has long been a thorn in the side of American imperialism throughout the latter's great hinterland in the countries south of the Rio Grande. Communists and other progressives of Latin America were decisive in founding this most important body. Organized in 1938 and headed by the independent Marxist, Vicente Lombardo Toledano, the C.T.A.L. immensely strengthened trade unionism in Latin America. It has given real power to the people's fight against landlordism, capitalism, clerical reaction, and American imperialism. It has vigorously opposed Wall Street's war program. Hence, it had to be destroyed, and monopoly capital set its "labor lieutenants" in the A.F. of L. and C.I.O. top leadership to the task.

The A.F. of L. leaders are old-time tools, sort of third-line partners of American imperialism in Latin America. From 1918 to 1930 they operated with the so-called Pan-American Federation of Labor, through which the Gompers A.F. of L. clique shamelessly supported the policies of American imperialism. The Pan-American Federation of Labor finally became such a stench in the nostrils of the Latin American workers that it had to be abandoned. Nothing abashed, however, the A.F. of L. leaders—Green, Woll, Dubinsky, *et al.*—responding to State Department orders for the post World War II period, proceeded to organize the Inter-American Confederation of Workers (C.I.T.) in 1948, in Lima, Peru. It was founded as a hostile body to the C.T.A.L., a second edition of the Pan-American Federation of Labor.

The C.I.O. leaders, however, were in a more difficult position where wrecking the C.T.A.L. was concerned. In the years when the C.I.O. was hearkening to the left and following a progressive course, they had hailed the founding of the C.T.A.L., entered into close co-operative relations with it, and condemned as treason to labor the attacks already being made upon it by the A.F. of L. But when the orders went out from the State Department that the C.T.A.L. had to be split, Philip Murray, swallowing his erstwhile principles, joined hands with the A.F. of L. in the attempted union-smashing. All of a sudden he discovered that the splendid Communist fighters in Latin America were a "menace."

The joint disruptive activities of the A.F. of L. and C.I.O. resulted in holding a labor conference in January 1951, in Mexico City, at which the C.I.T. already discredited, was reorganized into the Inter-American Regional Workers Organization (O.I.R.T.).[1] This body is a direct rival of the Latin American Confederation of Labor. Although making the usual extravagant membership claims, its founding conference in reality

[1] George Morris in *The Worker*, Feb. 4, 1951.

consisted of a collection of decayed Social-Democrats, Trotskyites, and representatives of government-controlled unions of Latin America. It has no solid working class backing in these countries.

The O.I.R.T. conference was a twin to the meeting of foreign ministers of all the American states (O.A.S.), held in Washington, in March 1951.[1] They were related parts of the same imperialist machinery. The O.I.R.T. undertook to break the resistance of the Latin American workers and peoples to Wall Street's war program, and the O.A.S. sought to push the governments, armies, raw materials, and manpower of Latin America even more completely under the control of the United States government. The programs of both conferences were dictated completely by the respective American delegations, acting in the interest of American monopoly capital.

The C.T.A.L. is withstanding the Wall Street-inspired attack by the A.F. of L. and C.I.O. leadership; but trade unionism in Latin America has nevertheless been seriously injured. The American leaders, who are insolently trying to break up the labor movement of the neighboring countries to the south, bear a direct responsibility for the reign of terror which, under State Department stimulation, has raged throughout a large part of Latin America since the end of the war. This has resulted in several reactionary governmental coups d'état and in the shooting and jailing of hundreds of trade union militants and other left-wing fighters for the peace, material welfare, and national independence of their peoples and countries.

THE ATTEMPT TO WRECK THE W.F.T.U.

To destroy the strong and united trade union movement that developed after World War II in Europe, which is a powerful factor for peace and democracy, was also a "must" for the Wall Street warmongers, if they were to make any headway with their program of world conquest. Nothing loath, therefore, their faithful cliques of imperialist-minded strikebreakers and union-wreckers, the top leaders of the A.F. of L. and C.I.O., set actively about the task of splitting the trade union movements in France, Italy, Germany, and other countries. They were animated by the Hitlerite slogan of the crusade against communism. This work was handled on the spot by such men as Irving Brown (A.F. of L.) and James B. Carey (C.I.O.). Millions of dollars were spent lavishly under State Department direction. From 1948 on there was to be seen throughout Europe the shameful spectacle of American labor leaders

[1] Robert F. Hall in *Political Affairs*, June 1951.

working hand in hand with reactionary Social-Democrats, governments, and employers to break the hard-pressed workers' strikes and to split their unions. Later on this disruptive campaign was extended to the Far East, where big trade union movements had also sprung up after the war.

The American and European Social-Democratic forces, unable to win the democratic leadership of the great post-war labor movements, which more and more looked to the Communists for guidance, characteristically set out to wreck them. Their meager results in France and Italy, their main points of concentration, are the measure, however, of their union-wrecking failure in general. Says the official organ of the World Federation of Trade Unions (September 1951): "The C.G.T. unites more than 80 percent of all French union members. Actually, the C.G.T. has many more Catholic members than the Catholic unions, and many more Socialists than the Jouhaux outfit." And in Italy, reports a trade union delegation from the United States, the "C.G.I.L. has a great majority of the workers in its ranks. It has a membership of 5,000,000, while the Christian Democratic Union has 500,000 and the Social-Democratic Union—150,000."[1]

The international union-wrecking campaign, engineered by the U.S. State Department, reached its greatest intensity, however, in the organized drive to split and break up the World Federation of Trade Unions itself. This powerful body (see page 446), founded as the war was nearing its end, is at the heart of the great post-war democratic-socialist movement that has swept through Europe. It represents an altogether higher level of international labor union organization than had ever before been achieved. It stands as a tremendous force squarely in the path of American imperialism, and as such it has been fiercely attacked by all the latter's labor agents and stooges.

The C.I.O., affiliated to the W.F.T.U., opened up the latest organized attack. On April 30, 1948, through its fascist-minded agent, James B. Carey, it demanded that the W.F.T.U., whose Executive Committee was then meeting in Rome, come out in support of the Marshall Plan. The British and Dutch unions, controlled by reactionary Social-Democrats, backed up this demand. The proposal was rejected, the W.F.T.U. majority supporting the position that in order to preserve world labor unity each affiliated national trade union center should take such position as it desired on the Marshall Plan. This sane proposition, of course, did not satisfy the agents of the State Department; so on January 1, 1949, at the W.F.T.U. Executive Bureau meeting in Paris, Carey and his pals proposed to suspend the activities of the organization for a year—an obvious way of getting rid of the W.F.T.U. altogether. When this out-

[1] *News*, Moscow, Aug. 31, 1951.

rageous proposal was voted down, the C.I.O., British and Dutch union leaders walked out.[1] The world labor movement was split, and the capitalist press everywhere emitted a howl of joy.

Meanwhile, the A.F. of L. leaders, long-time enemies of effective international labor organization, were also up to their necks in this union-wrecking business. Teaming up with the C.I.O. and the other splitters, they called a general congress in London in November 1949, and formed the International Confederation of Free Trade Unions (I.C.F.T.U.). The United States and Canada had 21 delegates there from A.F. of L., C.I.O., U.M.W.A., and Christian unions. Needless to say, the Americans ran the whole show as dictatorially as their capitalist bosses were running the United Nations. This was bureaucratic labor imperialism at work.

The I.C.F.T.U., ever since its foundation, has continued its union-smashing, strikebreaking course. It has not been successful, despite its heavy backing from the American, British, and French governments, as well as from employers all over the world. It now claims some 50 million members, but actually it has (principally in the British and American unions) about 30 million. On the other hand, the W.F.T.U., due chiefly to the huge growth of its affiliates, reported 78 million members in 65 countries at the end of 1950. The W.F.T.U. continues with its progressive program of helping the workers in all countries to build their labor movements, of fighting against fascism, and of bringing forward the interests of labor in all international spheres for maintaining world peace. The W.F.T.U. has proposed a united front with the I.C.F.T.U. to fight to maintain peace, but this was rejected.

The C.I.O. leaders, aping the reactionaries in the A.F. of L. top circles, are seeking to justify their crime of splitting the W.F.T.U. by howling the usual litany of anti-Soviet charges—that the Soviet trade unions are not real labor organizations, that the Russian Communists dominate the W.F.T.U. autocratically, and the like. But these redbaiting charges fit ill indeed with what the C.I.O. said and did in the years when it was still following a progressive policy. Thus, in 1945, the C.I.O. sent a labor delegation to the U.S.S.R., including the present-day redbaiters, James Carey and Joseph Curran. This delegation upon its return submitted a unanimous report lauding the Russian unions. "Our observations," says the report, "have increased our pride in being associated with such a great trade union movement through the World Federation of Trade Unions." The delegation also declared that "It has greatly strengthened our own determination as C.I.O. representatives to do everything within our power to cement cordial relations with the Soviet trade unions and to establish even closer unity between our two

[1] *World Trade Union Movement*, Paris, Oct. 5, 1950.

great countries for the maintenance of lasting peace and for growing prosperity and democratic progress."[1]

Repudiating the then current charges of A.F. of L. leaders that the W.F.T.U. was Communist-dominated, the C.I.O. convention of 1947 in Boston declared: "This organization [the W.F.T.U.] has demonstrated that the representatives of the labor movements of all the world can meet, work together, and co-operate in complete agreement toward solution of the problems which vex the world." The convention decided that "the C.I.O. pledges its continuing support to the strengthening of the W.F.T.U. and to the decisions and policies of the W.F.T.U."[2]

But needs must when the devil drives. So when Wall Street decided that the W.F.T.U. had to be split as a basic obstacle to its program of expansion, fascism, and war, Murray, Carey, Curran, Green, Rieve, and other C.I.O. leaders, plus the A.F. of L. upper clique, loyal to the maintenance of capitalism, leaped to do their masters' bidding, with all the fixings of anti-Communist, anti-Soviet slander. It mattered little to them that in doing so they not only had to fly in the face of all the facts and to betray the interests of the world's workers, but they also had to turn tail upon everything they had previously said and done regarding the W.F.T.U.

Business Week (July 21, 1951) openly boasts of the U.S. State Department control of the new, scab international. It says, "Though disguised, lest it give Communist propaganda a further opportunity to charge American domination of non-communist unions abroad, U.S. influence was almost unchallenged at the international labor meeting that ended its sessions in Milan, Italy, this week. It was exerted through American union delegates who came from the A.F. of L., C.I.O., and independent unions."[3]

But the imperialist A.F. of L.-C.I.O. leaders are having serious difficulties in establishing their hegemony over the conservative wing of the world trade union movement, just as their imperialist capitalist masters are meeting great obstacles in consolidating their hegemony over the capitalist world. At the November 1951 meeting of the I.C.F.T.U. in Brussels two major A.F. of L. proposals were rejected. Now A.F. of L. leaders are petulantly threatening to cut off their big subsidy to the I.C.F.T.U., and some are even talking of withdrawing from that body altogether.[4]

---

1 *Report of the C.I.O. Delegation to the Soviet Union*, pp. 24-25, N. Y., 1945.
2 Cited by George Morris in *Daily Worker*, Jan. 24, 1949.
3 Cited in *March of Labor*, Sept. 1951.
4 *New York Times*, Feb. 2, 1952.

THE CRISIS OF THE AMERICAN LABOR MOVEMENT

The alliance (subordination) of the A.F. of L. and C.I.O. leadership with Wall Street imperialism in its expansionist drive is having destructive effects upon the American trade union movement. It is sapping the basic vitality of organized labor. This bastard hook-up with big capital is, in sum, pushing the labor movement into a crisis, despite its outward appearance of wealth, strength, and prosperity.

The top union leaders, tied up with the bosses on the war program, are failing to maintain the workers' living standards. This is because, like President Truman, they are in tacit agreement with the exploiters that the workers must bear the lion's share of the cost of the preparations for war. Inflation is a definitely planned part of the war program, agreed upon by these misleaders of labor. Between 1944 and the end of 1950, consumers' prices went up 40.3 percent, while wages advanced only 25 percent. Meanwhile, the bosses' profits soared by 97.5 percent. The workers' taxes have gone sky-high. Real wages in the United States are now at least 25 percent below pre-war, and capitalist profits are about six times higher. President Truman, in San Francisco, even boasted that 1951 profits will reach the enormous total of $46 billion.[1] Yet the union leaders do everything possible to check the workers' fighting spirit. Indeed, sitting on the Wage Stabilization Board, they are helping to enforce the wage freeze. The only way they will take action is when forced to do so by the rebellious workers.

The union leaders also are making only a token, for-the-record opposition to the deadly menace of fascism which is steadily creeping upon the country. Their "struggle" to repeal the Taft-Hartley law is only a sham battle, and they will accept minor amendments. They make even less resistance to such deadly measures as the McCarran Act, the loyalty tests and job screenings, the persecution of the Communist Party, and the many invasions of the rights of the Negro people. At its 1951 convention, however, the C.I.O., under mass pressure, did condemn the Smith Act and the prosecutions under it. The failure of the A.F. of L. and C.I.O. leaders to act vigorously against the growing fascist menace is due to the fact that, inasmuch as the bosses know that only by curtailing the people's democratic liberties can they put across their war program, their labor lieutenants inevitably reflect the same attitude. These misleaders are trying to ignore the major lesson, so brutally taught by Hitler and Mussolini, that the attack upon the Communists is but the opening phase of a general assault upon the entire labor and progressive movement.

The top union leaders are likewise, at the behest of the bosses, fasten-

[1] *New York Times*, Sept. 5, 1951.

ing a new and more deadly system of class collaboration (working class subordination) upon the unions in the industries. This course, typified by the current General Motors contract with the U.A.W.-C.I.O., is expressed by five-year agreements, escalator clauses which tie wage rates to lying government statistics on living costs, no-strike pledges, speed-up, and an all-out reliance upon biased government wage boards. *Fortune* says that the Reuther-G.M. agreement "goes further in its affirmation of free enterprise and of the workers' stake in it than any other major labor contract ever signed in this country."[1] The results of all this class collaborationism are to hamstring the militancy and fighting capacity of the unions, to undermine and destroy collective bargaining, to force the workers into declining living standards, and to guarantee limitless profits to the employers. Before the Korean war only 500,000 workers had such boss-inspired agreements, but by the middle of 1951 the number had reached five million and was rapidly increasing.

The deepening crisis of the trade union movement, due to the leaders' support for the war program of Wall Street imperialism, is most clearly seen in the political degeneration which has overtaken the C.I.O. leadership since its expulsion of the progressive unions. The organization has lost its fighting spirit, its policies now being dictated mainly by the cunning opportunist, Walter Reuther. Once the C.I.O. was the dynamo of labor unionism, but no longer can the C.I.O. claim to be the progressive, leading section of the trade union movement. E. A. Lahey remarks correctly that since the split, the C.I.O. "and the traditionally more conservative A.F. of L. have been much more alike in their ways of thinking."[2] Indeed, in some respects, in its slavish subordination to the Truman government (which only a few years ago Murray denounced as "reactionary" and "cowardly"), in its violent redbaiting and warmongering, in its suppression of trade union democracy, in its surrender to the new escalator type of union agreement, and in its cultivation of the sinister A.C.T.U., the C.I.O. top leadership has become even more conservative than the heads of the A.F. of L. About the only difference is that the C.I.O. top leadership still clings to a few progressive phrases in its resolutions, remnants of the time when the C.I.O. followed a real progressive course.

The political degeneration of the C.I.O. leadership has also resulted in numerically weakening the organization. In 1947 the C.I.O. could justly claim its often stated figure of six million members, but now it numbers hardly more than four million.[3] Actually, the A.F. of L., which

---

[1] The editors of *Fortune, U.S.A.: The Permanent Revolution*, N. Y., 1951.
[2] *Collier's*, Sept. 1, 1951.
[3] *New York Times*, Dec. 23, 1951.

during the war had fewer members than the C.I.O., now has nearly twice as many. The C.I.O.'s old-time vigor in organizing the unorganized—due to the influence of the left wing—is now a thing of the past. The C.I.O. drive to organize the South—"without participation of the Reds" —was a flat failure. The C.I.O. is also torn with jurisdictional fights, bred of the earlier raids upon the now-expelled progressive unions.

The Green-Woll-Meany-Hutcheson clique of reactionaries controlling the A.F. of L.—long-time enemies of industrial unionism—have perceived the internal crisis of the C.I.O. and are now proposing to try to tear that organization to pieces. This is the meaning of their slogan of "organic unity," and of their break-up, in August 1951, of the United Labor Policy Committee of the A.F. of L., C.I.O. and independents.[1] The real head of the C.I.O., Walter Reuther, who aspires to be grand chief of the whole labor movement, and who wants a broader field than the C.I.O., would not hesitate to scuttle that organization if he saw the chance of coming to terms with the A.F. of L. leaders on the basis of their phony "organic unity" proposals.

In the present great international crisis, with American imperialism making a ruthless fascist-war drive for world domination, it is the imperative task of the trade union movement, particularly in the absence of a mass workers' political party, to take an active lead in fighting this imperialist program. It needs to make a resolute struggle to protect the workers' living standards, to preserve democratic rights, and to save the world from another terrible war. But the reactionary leaders of the A.F. of L., C.I.O. and conservative independent unions, themselves rabid imperialists, have completely betrayed this responsibility and have identified the labor movement with the aggressive aspirations of Wall Street. Such a betrayal cannot take place without most serious consequences to the labor movement, and if uncorrected by the mass of workers, it will lead eventually to a major disaster.

Never was the gap so great between the policies of the trade union leaders and the interests of the rank-and-file membership. The leaders are following a course which leads toward worsened living conditions for the workers, a drastic curtailment of their democratic rights, and the precipitation of an aggressive imperialist war; whereas the workers, although in many cases confused by Wall Street's tricky war propaganda, are opposed to all of these things. A sharpening collision between the war-bound top labor leaders and the militant masses of workers is clearly on the political agenda in the U.S.

In the face of this situation Communist policy is essentially that of the

[1] Organized in Dec. 1950, to bind the workers more effectively to the war program.

united front from below, with the rebellious masses of the workers. The Party is alert, however, to work freely with such honest officials, low or high, who want to conduct a real struggle to protect the economic and political rights of the workers and the Negro people.

THE INDEPENDENT UNIONS

The progressive independent unions, expelled by the C.I.O., and numbering some 600,000 members, have a heavy responsibility in continuing and developing outside of the C.I.O. the role they played inside of that body—that of the standard bearers of the whole trade union movement. Under the combined pressures of the employers, the government, the A.F. of L., and the C.I.O., and in the face of the current war hysteria, they have no small task in doing their progressive work. At present writing, they are all being viciously attacked by the McCarran Internal Security Committee of the Senate, the House Un-American Activities Committee, and the Humphrey subcommittee of the Senate Labor Committee. All of these committees are arbitrarily interfering in the internal affairs of the independent unions, presumably to purge them and the industries of progressive leaders and members—"reds," they call them—but in reality to break up these unions. All this constitutes an attack upon the trade union movement as a whole.

The expelled independent unions have performed a historic service in their opposition to the Marshall Plan and the rest of the war program of the Truman Administration. Above all, this fight for peace must be intensified, and all tendencies rejected which would reduce the present-day union struggles simply to questions of "pork chops." It is to the great credit of these unions that they have never allowed themselves to fall victims to the wild redbaiting and warmongering which are having such destructive effects upon A.F. of L. and C.I.O. unions. The defense by these unions of the interests of the workers and of the Negro people generally is also of great importance. And so is their fight against the Murray-Reuther-Green-supported treacheries of wage freezes, high taxes, increasing prices, and no-strike policies. Experience has already shown (and it has been voiced even by leaders like McGowan, head of the Boilermakers, and Potofsky, head of the men's clothing workers), that Wall Street's war program has been a great detriment to European as well as American workers. And Truman's "friendship" for labor, upon which Murray based his treason to a progressive labor policy, has now worn utterly threadbare.

The top trade union leaders' assumption that mass production of war materials is the way for the workers to keep their jobs is a monstrous illusion that could lead organized labor to disaster. Against this deadly folly the independent unions must militantly counterpose their practical program of maintaining worker employment through greatly increased wages and shortened hours, wide extension of social insurance, broad development of many-sided public works, systematic cultivation of trade with the U.S.S.R., China, Poland, Czechoslovakia, etc. To fight for this alternative program is a task of the greatest importance.

To combat all the trends leading toward the development of a police state in the United States is also a major responsibility of the independent unions. Not the smallest part of this danger is the increased role of the generals in shaping national policy and the tendency of the president to assume more and more arbitrary powers. This bipartisan trend reflects the fascist-like war program of the big capitalists, who would be only too glad to establish a military dictatorship in this country.

The independent unions, however, manifestly need strengthening in various respects. They should sharpen their fight against the white chauvinism which still operates in their ranks (although it is in no way as serious as the situation in the A.F. of L. and C.I.O. unions) and serves to prejudice the working conditions and union status of Negro workers. The unions, too, must beware of all tendencies toward a "non-partisan" political stand, which could smack of "economism" and Gompersism. They need to make a positive fight for a broad, independent coalition of labor and its allies to fight reaction and its two-party system. There should also be revived the propagation of socialism among the members, something which, since the days of Browder, has been almost completely abandoned. The fight for peace is now the heart of any progressive trade union policy, and it should involve close co-operation with such progressive international labor movements as the Latin American Confederation of Labor and the World Federation of Trade Unions.

The progressive unions have need also to pay attention to the important task of winning the huge numbers of proletarian war veterans to a progressive program and organization. It was one of the worst treasons of the conservative union leadership in the post-war period to surrender the demobilized veterans to such reactionary organizations as the American Legion and the Veterans of Foreign Wars. It was an error that the left in the C.I.O. and A.F. of L., after the end of the war, did not fight for the creation of a broad organization of labor's war veterans, which could have easily been achieved at the time.

There is a great need, too, for the independent unions to lead the fight for a general unity of the whole labor movement. The only unity that Green and Murray could have in mind is one whereby the workers would be controlled in the interest of the warmongers and the domination of the conservative labor bureaucrats assured. Real trade union unity, however, must be based upon a fundamental labor program for peace and the workers' well-being and must rest upon a genuine trade union democracy.

Along with the fighting for general trade union unity, there is an obvious need, likewise, for closer co-operation among the independent unions, as they now stand pretty much apart from each other. The same holds true for a fraternal collaboration on urgent issues between the independent unions and the progressive minorities in the right-led C.I.O., A.F. of L., Miners, and Railroad unions. An expression of this co-operation of the left trade union and progressive forces throughout the labor movement was the appearance in August 1950 of *March of Labor*, a monthly progressive trade union organ, edited by John Steuben. The workers look to the independent progressive unions to give a strong lead to the whole trade union movement.

The foregoing criticisms and evaluations of the policies of the independent unions are, in the main, valid also for the unions of the A.F. of L., C.I.O., United Mine Workers, Railroad Brotherhoods, etc. They represent the general course which organized labor as a whole should take, in order to develop to the utmost the tremendous progressive power of the great labor movement.

35. Persecution of the Communist Party (1948-1951)

To outlaw and destroy the Communist Party is another imperative necessity for the capitalists in their attempt to break down working class opposition to their drive for imperialist mastery of the world. For these rulers understand very well, even if many workers and their friends do not, that the Communist Party is indeed the vanguard of the working class, the true party of the people. They realize that the Communist Party has the only basically anti-fascist, anti-war program, and that it is the key fighter for democracy and peace. They have found out in this era of imperialism that only to the extent that there is a strong Communist Party, do the workers and the broad democratic masses have effective leadership. The ruling classes have learned this, on the positive side, from the many solid people's struggles led by the Communist Party and, on the negative side, from the collapse of the trade union leaders, the Socialists, and the liberals (such as Wallace, the *New Republic*, etc.) in the face of Wall Street's war drive. The monopolists know that the Communist Party is their most fundamental enemy; hence they are trying to wipe it out at any price. All of which is a testimonial to the Communist Party, its clear-sighted program, and its fighting spirit.

The capitalists understand very well that the Communist Party is the greatest defender of democratic rights. That is, if the Party's democratic rights can be abolished, then the whole structure of the people's liberties is undermined. This is a dangerous lesson which American reactionaries learned from Hitler, Mussolini, Franco, and other fascist dictators. The Taft-Hartley law, the Smith, Voorhis and McCarran Acts, the Magnusson Act, the loyalty oaths, the attacks upon the Negro people and the foreign-born, are all blood kin to each other. Under cover of the pretended Communist menace, trade unionism, social democracy, academic freedom, and liberalism, are all being assailed. The fight to destroy the Communist Party is the attempt of the warmongers to cut the heart out of trade unionism, to eliminate the Bill of Rights, to advance toward fascism in the United States, and to clear the way for war.

THE SHARPENING ATTACK AGAINST THE LEFT

Ever since it was organized in 1919, the Communist Party, as we have seen earlier in these pages, has always been under attack from the government. During World War II, with the Communists militantly supporting the war, this persecution subsided somewhat, but as soon as the war was over the anti-Communist drive was resumed with intensity. Wall Street, launched for world conquest, was doubly resolved to get rid of its most hated enemy, the Communist Party. The main official instruments used for this purpose and for the attack upon all other activities of the progressive forces by the Truman government were the Federal Bureau of Investigation, headed by J. Edgar Hoover, the McCarran Committee in the Senate, and the House Committee on Un-American Activities (the chief of the latter, J. Parnell Thomas, was indicted in November 1948, and later convicted as a common thief).

Among the many arrests in the growing post-war terrorism have been those of the leaders of the Joint Anti-Fascist Refugee Committee, including Dr. Edward K. Barsky, chairman, and a dozen members of the board—Howard Fast, Prof. Lyman Bradley, Dr. Joseph Auslander, Dr. Louis Miller, H. M. Justiz, Mrs. Ruth Leider, James Lustig, M. Magana, Mrs. Marjorie Chodorov, Mrs. Charlotte Stern, and later Mrs. E. G. Fleischman and Helen R. Bryan. They were charged with contempt of Congress and convicted, on June 27, 1947, for refusing to turn over to the reactionary Un-American Committee the names of their contributors and also those of Spanish Republican refugees. They got sentences up to six months in jail and fines of $500.

Another famous contempt-of-Congress case was that of the "Hollywood Ten"—Alvah Bessie, Herbert Biberman, Lester Cole, Edward Dmytryk,[1] Ring Lardner, Jr., John Howard Lawson, Albert Maltz, Samuel Ornitz, Adrian Scott and Dalton Trumbo. On December 5, 1947, these men, noted progressive motion picture writers and directors, were indicted. They were eventually sentenced to jail sentences of up to a year, with fines up to $1,000, for refusing to tell the Un-American Committee their political beliefs and affiliations. This outrageous case caused world-wide protest.

Other court cases piled up, too numerous to mention. Among them were those of Gerhart Eisler, Leon Josephson, Carl Marzani, Richard Morford, and George Marshall, charged variously with perjury, contempt, etc. William L. Patterson, noted Negro leader, was charged with contempt of Congress after being called a "black son of a bitch" and threatened with violence at a House committee hearing. Some defendants were sentenced to as much as three years, with heavy fines. In Los Angeles and Denver there were cases of some sixteen and seven men and women respectively, charged with contempt before federal

[1] Dmytryk later became a turncoat.

grand juries for refusing to disclose their political affiliations and opinions.

Eugene Dennis, general secretary of the Communist Party, was enmeshed in the net of contempt persecutions spread by the government in an effort to still all opposition to its developing war program. Dennis, formerly a seaman, teamster, and worker in various callings on the Pacific Coast, has always been a militant fighter in the class struggle. Belonging to the Communist Party since 1926 and long a member of its leading district and national committees, he was elected general secretary of the Party on July 17, 1946.[1] The government was especially determined to "get" Dennis. He was summoned to testify before the Un-American Committee on April 9, 1947, but he boldly refused to do so on the ground that the committee was illegal, because it contained the notorious Rankin of Mississippi who was elected in an election in which Negroes were not allowed to vote. Dennis declared that the hearing would constitute an infringement upon his constitutional rights. He was convicted of "contempt of Congress" in June 1947, in the Federal District Court in Washington, D. C., and was sent to jail in New York, on May 12, 1950, to serve a sentence of one year, with a fine of $1,000.[2]

On the eve of Dennis' imprisonment Gus Hall, outstanding member of the National Board and chairman of the Ohio State Committee, was elected to head the Party in Dennis' stead, with the title of national secretary.

To intensify the witch-hunting drive against the Communists and other progressive forces, government agencies, without any legal justification or precedents whatever, outrageously began to publish a blacklist of organizations designated as "subversive." The condemned groups were given no previous hearings or trials whatsoever. A few fascist organizations were included among the proscribed bodies for form's sake, but the bulk of the list was on the left. The blacklisted organizations included every conceivable type, and many of them were long since defunct. Relief, defense, fraternal, trade union, educational, veteran, Negro, women's, and youth organizations—all were blasted. Attorney General Tom Clark listed some 160 of such groups during 1947-48, and the Un-American Committee had no less than 608 organizations on its rolls as subversive. This arbitrary proceeding was an attempt to terrorize the left, particularly the foreign-born workers.

One of the more outrageous aspects of this general attempt to deny the workers the right to organize is the government's effort to destroy

---

[1] *Political Affairs*, Sept. 1946.
[2] See Labor Research Association, *Labor Fact Books 9* and *10*, for details on labor defense cases.

the International Workers Order. This broadly progressive fraternal body, with a present membership of about 165,000, of varied political opinions, was founded in 1930 by 5,000 workers who had split from the Social-Democratic Workmen's Circle. The I.W.O. has strictly adhered to the state insurance laws, under which it is incorporated, and it has been of great economic value to its members, but it is nevertheless attacked as subversive.

The major united front organizations defending the people's democratic rights during this period were the Civil Rights Congress, with William L. Patterson as secretary, and the American Committee for Protection of Foreign Born, with Abner Green as secretary. Among these defense cases were hundreds of workers arbitrarily threatened with deportation.

THE INDICTMENT OF THE COMMUNIST PARTY

On July 20, 1948, twelve members of the National Board of the Communist Party were arrested and indicted for violation of the Alien Registration law of 1940, the Smith Act. They were William Z. Foster, national chairman; Eugene Dennis, general secretary; Henry Winston, organization secretary; John B. Williamson, labor secretary; Jacob Stachel, education secretary; Robert G. Thompson, chairman of the New York District; Benjamin J. Davis, Jr., New York City Councilman; John Gates, editor of the *Daily Worker;* Irving Potash, manager of the Joint Council, Fur Workers Union; Gilbert Green, chairman of the Illinois District; Carl Winter, chairman of the Michigan District; and Gus Hall, chairman of the Ohio District. Foster's case was later separated from the others because of a heart ailment; four leading New York physicians, appointed by the court, affirming that to submit him to a long trial would hazard his life.

The Board members were charged by the Federal Grand Jury: "That from on or about April 1, 1945, and continuously thereafter up to and including the date of the filing of this indictment, in the Southern District of New York, and elsewhere [names of 12 defendants], the defendants herein, unlawfully, willfully, and knowingly, did conspire with each other, and with divers other persons to the Grand Jurors unknown, to organize as the Communist Party of the United States of America, a society, group, and assembly of persons who teach and advocate the overthrow and destruction of the Government of the United States by force and violence, and knowingly and willfully to advocate and teach the duty and necessity of overthrowing and destroying the Government of the United States by force and violence, which said acts are prohibited by Section 2 of the Act of June 28, 1940 (Section 10, Title 18, United States Code), commonly known as the Smith Act." They were also charged with liquidating the Communist Political Association on or about June 2, 1945, and of "organizing as the Communist Party of the United States." There were second indictments, charging the defendants with membership in the Communist Party.

The trial of these leading Communists took place in the Foley Square Federal Courthouse, before Federal Judge Harold R. Medina. The chief prosecutor was John F. X. McGohey, and the attorneys for the defense were George Crockett, a Negro attorney from Michigan; Abraham J. Isserman of New York; Louis McCabe of Pennsylvania; Richard Gladstein of California, and Harry Sacher of New York. Eugene Dennis acted as his own counsel. The trial began on January 17, 1949, and lasted until October 14th of the same year, the longest "criminal" trial in American history.

A POLITICAL PERSECUTION

The trial of the eleven Communist leaders was not a trial in a civil or criminal sense. It was a political attack by the government upon the Communist Party, aided by the Court. The whole proceeding was organized upon this basis. There was neither law nor justice in it, in the accepted meaning of these terms. The affair had the form of a trial, but this was only a thin façade to provide a sort of democratic cover to facilitate the railroading of the Communist leaders to jail and the breaking up of their Party. It was only a mockery of a trial. It was another flagrant example in the long list of labor frame-ups, of capitalist "class justice" meted out to the working class. All the trappings of the trial fitted into this general picture of the arbitrary political condemnation of a Party, under the mask of democratically "trying" its leaders.

The Smith Act, under which the defendants were tried, clearly violates the Constitution of the United States by abolishing the rights of free speech, free press, and free assembly. It is fascist thought-control legislation. The law is also unconstitutional in that it is a bill of attainder, which is legislation directed against a specified group of persons, in this case the Communist Party.[1] Its like has not been seen in the United States since the hated Alien and Sedition Laws of 1798. But then, any stick would do to beat the Communist Party.[2]

[1] This law was first used to prosecute the Trotskyites during the war. They were charged with overt acts. For the Party's stand against the Smith Act in this case see Milton Howard in *Daily Worker*, Aug. 16, 1941.
[2] For briefs on the unconstitutionality of the Smith Act, see *Political Affairs*, Sept. 1948.

The court proceedings were also flagrantly unconstitutional in that they denied the defendants the right of trial by jury. The twelve men and women who acted as jurors in the Communist case were a group of hand-picked middle and upper class citizens, a so-called "blue ribbon" jury. Although New York is largely a proletarian city, not one manual worker managed to get on the Grand Jury which indicted the Communist leaders, nor on the jury which tried them. Besides the hostile class composition of the jury, one juror even publicly stated his prejudice against the defendants, an action which should have resulted in a mistrial, but did not.

Judge Medina, himself a millionaire landlord and corporation lawyer, as well as a violent redbaiter, was an organic part of the government's trial-offensive against the Communist Party. Violating his judicial role, Medina worked hand in glove with the prosecution and lost no opportunity to help the government put in its case and to cripple that of the defense. Then he hypocritically cried out endlessly through the newspapers that he was being abused by the defendants and their attorneys.[1]

The capitalist press also did its share to further the political persecution of the Communist defendants. It totally distorted the facts of the trial and used every means to inflame the public against the defendants and to intimidate the jury. Among the results of the widespread redbaiting at the time was the infamous Peekskill, New York, riot of September 4, 1949, in which gangs of fascist-minded ruffians attacked a Paul Robeson concert meeting of 15,000 people.

Significantly, the indictments of the eleven leaders were initiated at the beginning of the 1948 presidential election campaign. This special timing was caused by the need of President Truman, the Democratic candidate, to have as an election issue the fact that he was prosecuting the Communist Party.

Under these circumstances of an organized government frame-up, a verdict of guilty was a foregone conclusion. The government's anti-Communist offensive could have been forestalled only by a broad mass democratic counteroffensive, which could have brought the true issues of the trial to the public and thus protected the legal rights of the defendants. This democratic offensive, however, in the prevailing conditions of "cold war" and redbaiting hysteria, did not emerge in sufficient strength.

THE GOVERNMENT'S CASE

The trial began on January 17, 1949, and the first two months of it consisted of a determined effort by the defense, with Doxey Wilkerson

[1] Joseph North, *Verdict Against Freedom*, N. Y., 1949.

many days on the stand, to knock out the discriminatory jury system. Some time previously, while practicing before the bar as a lawyer, Judge Medina had attacked this "blue ribbon" type of jury. But when the issue was placed squarely before him in the trial of the eleven Communists, he promptly swallowed all his former arguments and declared the system to be fully just and legal.[1]

The government began putting in its case on March 21st. The indictment did not charge the defendants with committing overt acts, or with conspiring to commit any such. They were accused of "conspiring to teach and advocate" the violent overthrow of the government. The issue, therefore, was one of speech and thought-control. Under this indictment, which Judge Medina, as a definite part of the prosecution, duly held to be constitutional, Jefferson, Paine, and Lincoln all could have been jailed for their revolutionary utterances, not to speak of their deeds. The American capitalist class, having come to power by its own revolutions, very violent ones, would bar the revolutionary path of the proletariat and make its own social system sacrosanct, above all basic criticism.

The prosecution could produce no examples of the advocacy of force and violence by American Communist leaders, except for the obviously lying statements of its stoolpigeons; so to "prove" its case it read lengthy extracts from *The Communist Manifesto, State and Revolution, Problems of Leninism, History of the Communist Party of the Soviet Union,* and other Marxist classics dealing with the Socialist revolution. The trial was an American version of the Nazi book burning. All these works, as every serious student knows, put the question of violence in the class struggle in the true sense that it is the bourgeoisie that originates this violence. That is, in the face of a working class backed by the majority of the nation and resolved upon establishing socialism, the ruling capitalists always undertake to crush the movement by armed force, to which the revolutionary workers necessarily reply in self-defense, no matter how peaceful their intentions are. This is what Marx, Lenin, and other Communist theoreticians have in mind when they speak of the workers' overthrow of the capitalist state. The substance of what Marxist writers and speakers have to say on the matter of violence is to point out what history teaches regarding violence and to warn the workers what to expect when the class struggle finally comes to its crisis.

This scientific analysis the prosecution tried to torture into an advocacy of force and violence. The small Communist Party was pictured as a "clear and present danger" to American imperialism. To put in its manu-

[1] Civil Rights Congress, *Censored,* pp. 8-14, N. Y., 1950.

factured case, the government called to the stand, not a number of "experts" who might have built up a complex theoretical sophistry, but a collection of renegade Communists, labor detectives, strikebreakers, professional informers, and outright criminals. These witnesses included such as L. Budenz, J. V. Blanc, W. Cummings, W. O. Nowell, C. Nicodemus, H. Philbrick, G. Herron, and others.[1] They knew nothing of Marxism-Leninism. Nor did they have to. All that was required of them was to declare, without proof or analysis, that the works of Marx, Engels, Lenin, and Stalin constitute an advocacy of force and violence. What the state's witnesses lacked in theoretical knowledge, they made up by perjury.

All this trash was quite sufficient for Judge Medina, who carefully shielded the state's witnesses from embarrassing cross-examination, and who also used every device to enable the government to wangle in its distorted picture of Communist policy.[2] The prosecutor, judge, and state's witnesses were also unsparing in their praise of Browder and Browderism, as representing the type of "communism" with which they could agree.

The renegade Budenz was the star government stoolpigeon. This man, formerly known in the Communist Party for his blistering articles against the Vatican,[3] posed on the stand as a devout Catholic (strictly of the rice variety). He insolently tried to sweep away all the Party's militant defense of democracy in theory and practice as only so much pretense, as mere "Aesopian language." According to Budenz, when Communists say "peace" they mean "war," when they say "democracy" they mean "tyranny," etc. He also had the gall to state that the very term "Marxism-Leninism" in itself constituted a secret advocacy of force and violence. The cynicism of all this is emphasized when it is realized that no political movement in the world is even remotely as careful as the Communist Party to state precisely what its analysis and policy mean in all its theoretical documents and public statements. Budenz's mumbo-jumbo was followed by endless perjury from other state witnesses, who lyingly declared that they had heard Party leaders, in conspiratorial meetings, declare that Marxism-Leninism consists of an advocacy of force and violence and that they were only awaiting "the day" in order to put this into effect.[4]

Thus the American government, producing as witnesses at its trial politically illiterate and corrupted stoolpigeons, spies, renegades, and other nondescripts, put in its case against the Communist Party. Its whole presentation was strictly on a gutter level. But the bourgeois press,

[1] Civil Rights Congress, *Censored*, pp. 8-14.
[2] George Marion, *The Communist Trial*, N. Y., 1950.
[3] Louis Budenz in *The Communist*, May 1940.
[4] Elizabeth Gurley Flynn, *The Plot to Gag America*, N. Y., 1950.

reveling in redbaiting, hailed the whole sorry mess of brazen perjury, political imbecility, and factual distortion as a masterful defense of the "American way of life." The government rested its case on May 18th.

THE PARTY FIGHTS BACK

The Party replied to this barrage of slander, misrepresentation, and redbaiting by making an offensive against the government and its contemptible frame-up. The main line of the Party's case is to be found in the opening and closing statements of Eugene Dennis,[1] in the testimony of Gates, Green, Davis, Thompson, Winter, and Winston, and in the deposition of Foster.[2] Paul Robeson, Simon Gerson, Alan Max, Joseph Starobin, Abner W. Berry, A. Krchmarek, and several others also testified.

The Party put in its case in the face of constant opposition by Judge Medina, who tried by every device to prevent the Party from making a rounded-out presentation of its policy and activities. Medina constantly badgered the Party witnesses, actually jailing Gates, Green, Winston, Hall, and Winter for terms up to six months during the trial, for alleged contempt of court. He also bullied the defense attorneys and wound up at the end of the trial by sentencing all of them to jail for from one to six months apiece for contempt, and also moving against them for their disbarment and the loss of their profession. Georgi Dimitrov had a much fairer trial before the Nazi tribunal at Leipzig, not to speak of getting an acquittal.

The Party's spokesmen in court explained, in the face of strong resistance from both judge and prosecutor, the war and fascist content of the trial. They showed that the whole process was part and parcel of the drive to get the United States into war and to force it more completely under the domination of big business. They demonstrated, too, that if it were possible to condemn as criminal the Communist Party, the most resolute fighter for world peace, then the way would be open to silence the whole labor and liberal movement. The Communists were being attacked first; the other democratic organizations would follow in turn.

The Party witnesses developed, as best they could in the face of the judge's opposition, the day-to-day policies of the Party. They traced the generation-long fight of the Communists for improved wage and living conditions for the workers, for the rights of the Negro people, for protection of the foreign-born, for the rights of women and youth, for the adoption of progressive legislation of all sorts, and against fascism and war. Medina ceaselessly hammered his gavel at all this, being particularly

[1] Eugene Dennis, *Ideas They Cannot Jail*, N. Y., 1950.
[2] William Z. Foster, *In Defense of the Communist Party and Its Leaders*.

anxious to prevent the real nature of the Communist Party and its program from being brought out before the jury and the public. About half of the defense's time was consumed in fights to get into evidence vital phases of the Party's program.

The Party made a militant defense of the democratic rights of the people, so gravely threatened in this fascist-like trial. Its witnesses defended the Bill of Rights and demonstrated that the attack of the government upon the Party, if successful, would undermine all guarantee of popular rights. In this broad democratic sphere the Party also defended the people's right of revolution, twice practiced by the American people —in 1776 and 1861—and long advocated unchallenged on the public forum and in the press.

The Party's witnesses also shattered the government's contention that the Communists teach and advocate the violent overthrow of the United States Government. They made a theoretical review of everything that leading Communist writers have said on the question of force and violence, and they also analyzed the experience of the workers in all countries where proletarian-led revolutions have taken place. They showed that the sources of violence in the class struggle are the big monopolists, even as these elements are the instigators and organizers of imperialist war. In doing this, the Party's witnesses demonstrated clearly that the Communists, far from being the teachers and advocates of violence, are precisely the greatest champions of peace and democracy. They are the historical leaders of the masses in restraining and defeating capitalist violence and in putting an end, once and forever, to the centuries-long stream of capitalist civil and international wars.

As to the immediate attitude of the Party toward the American Government, the Communist witnesses cited, as a typical example, the Party's policy in the recent presidential elections. Eugene Dennis said in his summary speech to the jury: "We did *not* advocate the forcible overthrow of the United States Government headed by President Truman. We *did* advocate its defeat at the polls in 1948." Foster and others outlined the course of the workers' struggle for socialism, through a people's front government and a people's democracy.

The Party's witnesses competely demolished, in the field of theory and practice, the absurd contention of the government prosecution that, because of the similarity of the American Communist Party's policies for international peace with those of the Soviet Union, it therefore takes orders from the latter. They showed by innumerable examples how the Party formulates its own policies on the basis of developing events. There was nothing unusual in the fact, they contended, that Communists in all countries, having a common theoretical background of Marxism-Leninism, should arrive at similar or identical analyses. This trend is true, they showed, not only of Communists, but of all other international ideological groups. Another major factor making for the unity of Communist policy, they pointed out, is that the various parties naturally learn from each other's experience. Thus the American Communist Party learned immensely from the historic Russian Revolution, from the pre-war people's fronts in France and Spain, from the Spanish Civil War, from the People's Democracies in Eastern Europe, from the great Chinese Revolution, from all the daily and revolutionary struggles of the masses everywhere. The significance of the capitalists' attempt to characterize all Communist parties and revolutionary mass movements as Russian "plots" and "fifth columns," it was made clear, is that the former dare not look in the face the basic modern reality of their dying capitalist system and the rising new socialism.

The Party's shattering refutation of the government's indictment, however, was altogether unavailing. The hand-picked, rubber-stamp jury did what it was organized to do, and on October 14th, after only a brief deliberation, it brought in a verdict of guilty against all the defendants. Thereupon Judge Medina, in his savage hatred of the Communist Party, sentenced the eleven defendants, save Robert Thompson, to terms of five years in the penitentiary and fines of $10,000 each. Thompson, a holder of the Distinguished Service Cross for bravery in the Pacific area during World War II, was condemned to three years. The United States had taken another long stride toward fascism and war.

THE SUPREME COURT SUSTAINS THE FRAME-UP

On August 1, 1950, the verdict and sentences against the eleven Communist leaders were upheld in the Second Federal Circuit Court of Appeals. And on June 4, 1951, they were affirmed by the United States Supreme Court, by a vote of six to two. Chief Justice Vinson headed the majority, Justices Black and Douglas dissented, and Justice Clark disqualified himself. In October 1951, the Supreme Court refused to reconsider its decision.

During World War II, under the pressure of the people's fight against fascism, and at a time when the ruling class felt it necessary to make at least a show of protecting civil liberties, the Supreme Court had ruled rationally regarding the Communist Party. Thus, in the Schneiderman case of 1942 (see Chapter 27), the Supreme Court correctly said that it was a tenable conclusion that the Party "desired to achieve its purpose by peaceful and democratic means, and as a theoretical matter justified the use of force and violence only as a method of preventing an attempted forcible counter-overthrow once the Party had obtained control in a peaceful manner, or as a method of last resort to enforce the majority will if at some indefinite future time because of peculiar circumstances constitutional or peaceful channels were no longer open." And in the Bridges case in 1945, the Supreme Court similarly ruled that "not the slightest evidence was introduced to show that . . . the Communist Party seriously and imminently threatens to uproot the Government by force or violence"—although the prosecution had brought in bushels of the usual "proofs" of such a threat.

But in these present days of feverish war preparations the Supreme Court, discarding its erstwhile "liberal" sentiments and abandoning its elaborate pose of being "above the battle," came a-running, like every other capitalist institution in the country, to do the bidding of the fascist-minded Wall Street warmongers by condemning the Communists. Its decision was political, not juridical, even as were those of the lower courts. The high court's ruling was a triple-phased lie: first, that the Communist defendants "had conspired to teach and advocate the overthrow of the United States Government by force and violence"; second, that the "petitioners intended to overthrow the Government of the United States as speedily as the circumstances would permit"; and third, that "their conspiracy to organize the Communist Party and to teach and advocate the overthrow of the Government of the United States by force and violence created 'a clear and present danger' of an attempt to overthrow the Government by force and violence."

The Supreme Court arrived at this outrageous decision by refusing even to consider the perjured testimony of the prosecution's witnesses, the rigged jury system, and the prejudiced rulings of Judge Medina, by disemboweling the First Amendment to the U.S. Constitution, and by torturing, twisting, and virtually annulling Justice Holmes's doctrine of "a clear and present danger." It simply assumed that the Communist Party advocated force and violence, without weighing the evidence one way or the other. On this arbitrary basis the Supreme Court declared the Smith Act constitutional and affirmed the conviction of the eleven Communist leaders.

This reactionary nonsense was too much for Supreme Court Justices Black and Douglas. Justice Black declared that the decision had so watered down the First Amendment, "the keystone of our government," "that it amounts to little more than an admonition to Congress." And Justice Douglas, pointing out that the decision crippled free speech, scoffed at the silly conclusion of the august Supreme Court that the propaganda of the comparatively small Communist Party constitutes "a clear and present danger" of a violent revolution in the United States.

Undermining the Bill of Rights, the Supreme Court decision dealt a body blow to popular liberty in this country. It evoked widespread popular resentment; newspapers, trade unions, Negro organizations, women's clubs, educators, lawyers, and others speaking out in condemnation. Notably silent in this democratic protest, however, were the top leaders of organized labor, who should have led the fight. These elements, themselves rabidly imperialist, look upon the government's attacks upon democracy much as the capitalists do, as necessary for carrying through the war program. At most they content themselves with a few futile grumbles, "for the record," and then let the infamous measures go into effect without a real fight.

On July 2, 1951, the Communist leaders started serving their sentence; that is, all except Thompson, Hall, Winston, and Green, who did not show up in court when called to go to jail. In October, Hall was arrested in Mexico, kidnaped back across the border without any legal formality, and was given an additional sentence of three years in jail. The prisoners were scattered in various penitentiaries—Atlanta, Lewisburg, Leavenworth, Terre Haute, Danbury—"to keep them from conspiring together." Following this raw undermining of American democracy, Judge Medina and Prosecutor McGohey were both promoted to higher posts in the federal judicial hierarchy. Meanwhile, as "democratic" America was being discredited by these disgraceful proceedings, the people of Australia, in September 1951, defeated by national referendum a law aimed at outlawing the Communist Party.

MULTIPLYING RAIDS AND PERSECUTIONS

The final conviction of the eleven top Communist Party leaders was immediately followed by further arrests: on June 20, 1951, in New York —Elizabeth Gurley Flynn, Claudia Jones, Pettis Perry, Israel Amter, Betty Gannett, Alexander Bittelman, Alexander Trachtenberg, Simon W. Gerson, V. J. Jerome, Albert Lannon, William Weinstone, Marion Bachrach, Louis Weinstock, George B. Charney, Isidore Begun, Jacob Mindel, and Arnold Johnson (four others were indicted with this group, —who did not appear in court—Fred Fine, Sid Stein, James Jackson and William Norman); on July 26th, in California—Al Richmond, P. M. Connelly, William Schneiderman, Rose Chernin, Dorothy R. Healey, H. Steinberg, E. O. Fox, R. Lambert, A. J. Lima, Oleta O'Connor Yates, Loretta S. Stack, and Bernadette Doyle; on August 8th in Maryland— R. Wood, G. Meyers, Maurice Braverman, Philip Frankfeld, Dorothy M. Blumberg, and Regina Frankfeld; on August 17th, in Western Pennsylvania—Andrew Onda, James H. Dolsen, Benjamin Carreathers, Steve Nelson, William Albertson, and I. Weissman; on August 28th in Hawaii —J. W. Hall, C. K. Fugimoto, Eileen T. Fugimoto, K. Oryoshi, D. J. Freeman, J. D. Kimoto, and Dr. J. E. Reinecki; on August 31st, in California—F. Carlson, B. Dobbs, and Frank Spector. Meanwhile, Frederick V. Fields, Dashiell Hammett, Alphaeus Hunton, and Abner Green, trustees of the bail fund of the Civil Rights Congress, were thrown into jail for contempt of court because they refused to furnish names of contributors to the bail fund to federal inquisitors. In November 1951 came the trial of Dr. W. E. B. DuBois, the noted, 83-year-old scholar, Kyrle Elkin, Abbott Simon, Sylvia Soloff, and Elizabeth Moos, charged with failing to register as "foreign agents" because, in the Peace Information Center, they had circulated pledges for peace. It was so outrageous that the trial judge threw the case out of court. The F.B.I. announced that all these arrests were only the beginning, as it had 43,000 Communists under surveillance for early arrest, and also that half a million Party supporters would be thrown into concentration camps in case of war.

As this book goes to press Comrades Onda, Nelson, and Dolsen have been convicted of sedition in Pittsburgh, and trials under the Smith Act are either going on or immediately scheduled in New York, California, Maryland, and Hawaii.

THE McCARRAN ACT

Another line of attack on the Communist Party, under the growing police state, is through the infamous McCarran Act. This law was enacted by Congress on September 23, 1950. The demagogue Truman, tongue in cheek, vetoed the bill, but made no fight to have it defeated in Congress. Akin to the Alien and Sedition Acts of a century and a half ago, the McCarran Act condemns communism as an international conspiracy and Communists as foreign agents, and it also establishes the reactionary principle of "guilt by association." The law requires the registration of the officers and members of all "Communist Action" organizations, *i.e.*, the Communist Party, under the control of the new Subversive Activities Control Board. Such registration, amounting to an admission of criminal guilt, would immediately expose the registrees to prosecution under the Smith Act, which has virtually made Communist belief a crime punishable by ferocious penalties. The McCarran Act also permits the Department of Justice to dominate the activities of non-citizens and arbitrarily to deport them. To climax its many ultra-reactionary features, this law also provides that in case of "a declaration of war," of "invasions," or of "insurrections," the authorities may throw into concentration camps, without previous trials, all those whom they may deem "subversives"; that is, the Communists and other protestors against war. For this purpose the government is now busily constructing concentration camps.[1]

The McCarran Act also requires registration of the officers of what it designates as "Communist Front" organizations. These are progressive mass organizations of various types. For over a century the workers and other progressives have followed the practice of setting up united front committees and mass organizations for supporting or fighting against various causes, such as Negro emancipation, Negro civil liberties, women's suffrage, anti-labor injunctions, child labor, lynching, poll tax, fascism, peace, strike relief, labor defense, etc. The Communists, with their united front policy, support and participate in all such movements. But now the government cracks down upon all these movements displaying a militant spirit, denounces them as especially sinister, bans them as subversive organizations, and, under the McCarran Act, provides that their officials, under pain of long jail sentences, shall register as criminals and traitors.

The Communist Party and individual Communists all over the country have refused to register under the McCarran Act, as have the officers of various united front organizations, on the ground that the law does not apply to them. Under the terms of this law Attorney General J. Howard McGrath on November 22, 1950, therefore, called upon the Control Board to force the Party and its members to register. As things stand at present writing, the Communist Party has been hailed before this inquisitorial board, and since April 23, 1951, it has been fighting there against registration and the other barbarous features of this law. Its attorneys are Vito Marcantonio and John Abt. To rig up the hearings, the government has as witnesses Gitlow, Zack, and the usual string of professional stoolpigeons. The McCarran police-state law has been condemned by virtually the entire labor movement, as well as by a myriad of liberal groups and individuals. As usual, however, the protests of the top union leaders are little more than formal, without any real weight in them.

Pro-war liberals and Social-Democrats, however, share a large part of the responsibility for the adoption of these infamous fascist-like laws and practices. Morris L. Ernst ardently pioneered for registration of Communists by the government; Norman Thomas publicly supported the proposal of concentration camps for Communists; and Senator Humphrey, with a special Senate subcommittee, is setting out in Dies-Rankin fashion to purge the progressive independent unions of left wingers or to break them up.

[1] *New York Herald Tribune,* Jan. 2, 1952.

THE SITUATION OF THE COMMUNIST PARTY

The purpose of such barbarous legislation as the Smith and McCarran Acts is to illegalize the Communist Party and to destroy it, as part of the broader plot to destroy democracy in general. These laws are the culmination of a long series of assaults upon the Communist Party and its individual members by the government. This general and developing attack has come to a climax as American imperialism steps up its fascist-war drive for world conquest.

For many years past Communists have been treated as second-class citizens and denied fundamental rights of citizenship because of their political opinions. Now this trend has become even more intensified. Many A.F. of L. unions, since far back in the 1920's, have denied Communists the basic right to hold membership in them, and some C.I.O. unions also have the same undemocratic regulations. According to the Taft-Hartley law, Communists, in effect, are also denied the right to hold office in trade unions. Under various thought-control loyalty tests Communists are prohibited, with savage penalties, from working in government employ or in "defense" plants, which means practically all important industry. Such legislation as the Feinberg law of New York State bars Communists from the teaching profession. Communists are also often denied the right to place their names on the ballot during election times, and are notoriously discriminated against in securing living quarters, in hiring meeting halls, and the like. They are also being treated with prejudice in the armed services, and the government denies them passports with which to travel. And now under the existing legislation, Communists are classed as criminals, kangarooed into jail, and may be arbitrarily thrown wholesale into concentration camps. In the face of this sinister development, the Party is resolute in its efforts to maintain a legal existence.

The government's attack against the Communist Party confronts it with many urgent tasks. It must learn how, under increasingly difficult conditions, to develop its united front policy in the broad peace movement, in the economic struggle, in the fight of the Negro people, and in the growing mass movement against the Smith Act and other phases of fascist development. Especially the Party will have to become skilled in defending its members and organizations, and it must intensify its vigilance to protect itself from provocateurs and stoolpigeons.[1] As never before, the Party must vigorously practice self-criticism and fight every manifestation of bureaucracy. The Party must also be keenly aware of

---

[1] Gilbert Green in *Political Affairs*, May 1950; John Gates, Report to Fifteenth Convention, C.P.U.S.A., Dec. 1950.

liquidationist dangers, from both right and left. Above all, the Party must strengthen its grasp of Marxism-Leninism. And whatever the difficulties, the Party must persevere in its tireless efforts to win and maintain a completely open existence.

Those who think the Communist Party will fold up or perish under the present government persecution would do well to reread their American history. In colonial days, the Quakers, Catholics, and other sects defied the attempts of bigots to destroy them. The patriotic Committees of Correspondence, prior to and during the American Revolution of 1776, were declared illegal by the tory British, but they nevertheless carried their just cause to ultimate victory. The pre-Civil War Abolition movement, too, fighting in the great cause of Negro emancipation, carried on its agitation and its heroic Underground Railroad in the face of violent legal and extra-legal persecution—until its struggle triumphed. The trade union movement also fought for a century, courageously and eventually successfully, to establish itself, notwithstanding endlessly hostile employers, courts, and government. In the early years of the Republic strikes were outlawed, the labor unions were condemned in the courts as "conspiracies," and their members were thrown into jail.[1] Even as late as the advent of the C.I.O., in many open shop industries in this country the trade unions functioned virtually as an underground movement.

The Communist Party represents an even greater cause than any of the foregoing—namely, its defense of world peace, democracy, the people's well-being, and, eventually, socialism. And if it should be forced underground, it will be worthy of these American democratic traditions. But it will never abandon its fight for the fullest democratic rights for itself and the masses. The present government attacks cannot destroy the Communist Party. The Party represents far too fundamental a movement and program to be disposed of by this brutality. The need for Communist leadership in the workers' daily struggles is imperative, and socialism, which is historically destined to supersede capitalism, is inevitable. Indestructible, too, is the political organization of socialism, the Communist Party.

It is not at all new in Communist world experience for the Communist Party to be forced underground through the desperation tactics of dying capitalism, which systematically denies to Communists all constitutional guarantees of speech, press, assembly, political action, and even liberty. The Communist parties in tsarist Russia, China, France, Italy, Poland, Czechoslovakia, Germany, Japan, Hungary, Bulgaria, Brazil, Cuba, Canada, Venezuela, Chile, the Philippines, and

---

[1] Foner, *History of the Labor Movement in the U.S.*, p. 73.

many other countries, have all had this experience. The C.P.U.S.A. also had its "underground" period during its founding years, 1919-21. Everywhere, however, the general result has been the same: The hardships of such an existence have steeled the parties and cleansed them of opportunists and fair-weather sailors. The consequence has been that, finally emerging from underground, they were more powerful than ever. The Communist Party's present experience in the United States will not result differently, if in spite of its battle for an open existence, it should be driven "underground."

36. Victory Ahead For the People

With the war danger hanging over the world like a great storm cloud, humanity is now in gravest peril of being plunged, by the machinations of the Wall Street monopolists and profiteers, into the most terrible man-made disaster in all its history. Despite the threatening aspect of things, however, war is not inevitable; nor is fascism. Notwithstanding all the lying bourgeois propaganda to the contrary, there is no reason why the American, Soviet, and other peoples should butcher each other. Instead, there are the most fundamental reasons why they should and can live and work in harmony together, as they have done ever since the foundation of this Republic. Tirelessly, the Communist Party presses these great facts upon the people's minds.

Lenin pointed out long ago that by its very nature imperialism is inevitably and incurably warlike. This does not mean, however, that war under present conditions is unavoidable. The peace-loving workers of the world have now become so strong—through the U.S.S.R., the People's Democracies, the great colonial liberation movements, the vast trade union movement, and the powerful Communist parties—that they have the power, if they and their democratic allies will but use it, to block the imperialists' drive toward war. It is this superior strength of the peace-loving democratic masses which makes increasingly possible the peaceful co-existence of capitalism and socialism.

Ever since the Russian Revolution took place in 1917, Marxist-Leninists have always held the view that, although socialism is a basically different system from capitalism, the two regimes can exist in the world together, in competition with each other but without making war upon each other. The foreign policy of the Soviet government has always been based upon this assumption. Stalin has stated and restated this policy time and again.

In his interview with the American newspaperman, Roy Howard, fifteen years ago, Stalin said: "American democracy and the Soviet system may peacefully exist side by side and compete with each other." Replying to the allegation that the Soviet government is making revolutions in other countries, Stalin also stated the basic Leninist concept

VICTORY AHEAD FOR THE PEOPLE 525

that "The export of revolution is nonsense. Every country will make its own revolution if it wants to, and if it does not want to there will be no revolution."[1] Only a few years ago, Stalin told Harold Stassen the following: "The systems in Germany and the United States are the same but war broke out between them. The U.S. and U.S.S.R. systems are different but we didn't wage war against each other and the U.S.S.R. does not propose to. If during the war they could co-operate, why can't they today in peace, given the wish to co-operate?"[2] And in May 1948, Stalin replied to Henry Wallace on this question as follows: "The government of the U.S.S.R. believes that in spite of differences in economic systems and ideologies, the coexistence of these systems and the peaceful settlement of differences between the U.S.S.R. and the U.S.A. are not only possible, but absolutely necessary in the interest of universal peace."[3]

Wall Street monopoly capital, however, has a totally different idea. It denies the possibility of the peaceful coexistence of capitalism and socialism, and it proceeds on the premise that capitalism can, must, and will wipe out socialism with fire and sword. This fact is proved beyond question by capitalism's constant anti-Soviet policies, which we have discussed earlier in these pages. No sooner had the Soviet government been established than the big capitalists of the world, including those of the United States, tried to overthrow it by violence. They undertook this unsuccessfully during 1918-21; they made similar attempt in their efforts to turn Hitler's aggression against the U.S.S.R. in the 1930's; and now they are boiling up again for an even more desperate assault upon the great Socialist Republic.

As we pointed out in Chapter 32, Wall Street imperialism, boss of the capitalist world, is deliberately preparing a third world war. Wall Street is systematically organizing the United States and the capitalist world for an aggressive war against the Soviet Union and the People's Democracies. But even though the warmongers control the big capitalist governments, including most of all that of the United States, this fact still does not make war inevitable. The American people still have the power to balk and defeat the war makers if they will but realize the true source of the war danger—their own monopoly capitalists—and take the necessary steps to bridle them and eventually break their power. The greatest obstacle to the workers and other democratic strata taking this action, as we have also seen, is the treacherous policies of their own trade union leaders, who have signed up and become recruiting sergeants and strikebreakers for Wall Street's war.

1 *The Stalin-Howard Interview*, p. 13, N. Y., 1936.
2 Stalin, *For Peaceful Coexistence*, p. 32.
3 Stalin, *For Peaceful Coexistence*, p. 2.

WHAT IF WAR COMES?

The peoples of this country and the world are fighting to preserve world peace (see Chapters 32 and 33); but what if their efforts should fail, the worst should happen, and Wall Street should precipitate its projected anti-Soviet war? The warmongers, to grease the skids towards war, long tried to make it appear that it would be a relatively easy job to defeat the Soviets and their allies. They declared, as Hitler did, that the Soviet government is incapable of making a real fight, that its people are disloyal, its industries weak and decrepit, and the like. So long as the United States had a monopoly of the atom-bomb this "picnic" theory of an anti-Soviet war seemed very plausible to the unthinking; but now, with the Soviets also possessing this fearsome weapon, even the most fevered warmongers have to warn the American people that an anti-Soviet war would be a very serious matter.

But the fact is that the United States and its allies could not win such a war at all. Instead, they would be certain to go down to catastrophic defeat, with fatal effects upon the world capitalist system. That is the only way in which another wholesale murder of the peoples, an aggressive war led by Wall Street imperialism, could possibly end.

The western warmongers—so open have become their preparations for aggression—are now busily counting up their war strength in industries, materials, and manpower, as against those of the U.S.S.R. They are trying to convince the peoples everywhere that in the event of a war this country and its allies would have an enormous preponderance of strength in all these spheres and therefore would win the victory. But they forget that battles are not won according to arithmetic, nor are wars decided by political-minded statisticians.

Most of the countries teamed up with the United States in its war alliance are undermined by incurable economic and political crises, and they are torn by trade and political rivalries with each other. They cannot be welded together into a solid fighting force. Their weakness is being glaringly demonstrated by the heavy difficulties now being encountered in the attempt of the U.S. government to organize and arm capitalist Europe for an anti-Soviet war. Especially significant since the arms race began is the revival of the historic antagonism between France and Germany.

Eisenhower's sinister European military plans are in serious crisis, for a variety of related reasons. The United States is proving such an arrogant boss that it is rapidly alienating the peoples and states of Europe. Great Britain is refusing to become part of the unified European army or to support the Schuman plan for industrial unity of France and

Germany, and it will not join the so-called United States of Europe scheme. Like France, Germany, and Italy, Great Britain is also being bankrupted by excessive armaments. The colonial and semi-colonial countries of the Middle and Far East have no taste whatever for the projected war, but instead are moving to break completely with all imperialist controls. And the refusal of Mexico (in February, 1952) to make a joint military pact with the United States, dramatically illustrated the anti-war spirit of the peoples of Latin America.

The lost war in Korea demonstrates glaringly the weakness of the capitalist countries, and another world war would make this decisive reality catastrophically clear. The plain sense of the situation is that if a new world war should begin—and the only way this could happen would be through Wall Street's instigation—the rotten international capitalist system would prove no match for rugged young world socialism.

Among the basic handicaps that the capitalist powers would face in such a struggle would be the unwillingness of their great masses to defend a system that is now bringing them not only reduced living standards, but also fascism and one world war after another. Instead, these masses would increasingly strive to put an end to this deadly system and establish socialism. On the other hand, the capitalist powers would have to face the fierce loyalty of the masses in the Socialist lands to their new and developing system. In the long run the superior ideological strength of the Socialist peoples and those on the way to socialism would more than make up for the illusory statistical advantages now apparently on the side of capitalism. The Socialist economic and political system would prove much the stronger and more able to stand the great blow.

Germany and Japan, which Wall Street is now so feverishly rearming, cannot possibly be reconstructed into the powerful fighting machines that they were in World War II. France and Italy, also, with decayed economic systems and with one-third at least of their people Communists or Communist sympathizers, will turn out to be military liabilities rather than assets for Wall Street. Great Britain, too, with its empire in the process of disintegration, will prove but another weak and unwilling ally. And as for such feeble and reactionary states as Spain, Turkey, Greece, and Yugoslavia, they will be only inferior military allies for the capitalists. The United Nations military alliance is creaking at every joint and is threatened with collapse.

The strong anti-war and largely anti-capitalist spirit in all the capitalist countries will especially hinder their becoming militarily powerful. Their growing hatred and fear of American imperialism will prevent their fighting effectively for Wall Street. This explains the vast mass neutral sentiment now prevailing all over capitalist Europe. It is because of this profound anti-war, anti-American sentiment among the world's masses that Wall Street is being compelled, as in the sessions of the General Assembly of the United Nations in Paris early in 1952, to camouflage its aggressive war preparations heavily with hypocritical pretensions of acting for world peace, disarmament, and national defense.

President Truman, at this writing, has declared that the United States has developed "fantastic weapons"—atomic, chemical, bacteriological—for the proposed world war. Such propaganda is designed to reassure the American people and to frighten the Russians, but it fails in both respects. For, obviously, the United States would have no monopoly of such "fantastic weapons." The Russians would be sure to have them also, even as they now have the atomic bomb and, as recent events have shown, they also have jet planes which American experts have admitted are superior to anything the United States possesses. Mr. Truman's propaganda about "fantastic weapons" only means that the war would be all the more terrible, not that the United States would win it.

A third world war, if it should come, would have to be fought mainly with the manpower and resources of the United States, and to a devastating extent upon this country's territory. The Korean war, in which the United States furnishes 90 percent of the armed forces, is a picture in miniature of what could be expected, on an aggravated scale, in case of a general war. In World Wars I and II the United States came out the victor after other peoples had done the main fighting, and in its projected world war Wall Street is trying to duplicate this profitable experience by building up big armies in Europe and Asia. But it can achieve no real success in this rearmament. In another world war the peoples of the world would display even less enthusiasm for being butchered in the services of American imperialism than they are now doing in Korea. The opposition of the American people to a third great war would also astonish the warmongers. Only political and military fools or fanatics can believe that the United States could win a third world war under such conditions.

A SUICIDAL WAR FOR CAPITALISM

World War I cost the capitalist system the loss of one-sixth of the earth—Russia—to socialism, a disaster to capitalism from which it has never recovered. World War II resulted in further enormous land and population losses to world capitalism—China, Poland, Czechoslovakia, Hungary, Romania, Bulgaria, Albania, Lithuania, Latvia, and Estonia—as well as in a profound weakening of its basic economic, political, and colonial systems. A third world war would deal the capitalist system a further deadly blow, one that it could not possibly withstand. Such a war would probably bring about the end of capitalism as a world system. Socialism would become far and away the predominant world social order. This perspective puts fear in the hearts of the capitalists. It is a nightmare which haunts their otherwise rosy dreams of imperialist conquest.

The Communist Party of the United States has stated its position, in the event of the threatened world war, as follows: "If, despite the efforts of the peace forces of America and the world, Wall Street should succeed in plunging the world into war, we would oppose it as an unjust, aggressive, imperialist war, as an undemocratic and an anti-Socialist war, destructive of the deepest interests of the American people and humanity. Even as Lincoln while a Congressman opposed the unjust annexationist Mexican War and demanded its termination, so would we Communists co-operate with all democratic forces to defeat the predatory war aims of American imperialism and bring such a war to a speedy conclusion on the basis of a democratic peace."[1]

Present-day Western Europe is a revolutionary tinder box; so are Asia and, although less obviously so, Latin America and Africa. The peoples of the various countries in these areas would never passively allow themselves to be butchered in another imperialist war. In the event of a world war, many if not most of them would surely abolish the collapsing capitalist system in their countries and begin their orientation toward socialism. There would be a basic difference between the case of a third world war and the conditions prevailing at the time of World Wars I and II; whereas in the latter situations the revolutions came toward the end (World War I) and after the war (World War II), this time they would begin in the earliest stages of the war. Great masses of the world's peoples would take up the democratic march that would eventually bring them to socialism.

Socialism, organized and led by the Communists and supported by the workers and the broad democratic masses, is the great peace force of history. It is destined to put an end finally to the centuries-long plague of war. The proletariat, with its basic program of economic prosperity, political freedom, and world peace, represents the interests of the overwhelming masses of the entire nation. It has no need for war to achieve its great social objectives. Indeed, it is the most basic of all the enemies of war, and it always seeks to achieve its program by peaceful means. But if world capitalism, dominated by Wall Street, has recourse to war in its greed and desperation, then this will be its funeral. The masters of the present social system will learn to their irretrievable disaster that

[1] Statement by William Z. Foster and Eugene Dennis in *Political Affairs*, Apr. 1949.

socialism is vastly superior to capitalism not only economically, politically, and culturally, but also on the field of war.

THE DECAY OF WORLD CAPITALISM

The capitalist system, as pointed out long ago by Lenin, has become obsolete and is in decline.[1] It is a prey to its own general crisis. Consequently, this is the period of great wars and proletarian revolutions. This is the era of the transformation of society from a capitalist to a socialist basis.

The general crisis of capitalism has been brought about by a sharpening of all the internal and external contradictions inherent in capitalism, to the point where they increasingly undermine and destroy that system. The driving force behind the development of the general crisis is the growth of predatory monopoly capital, or imperialism, with all its profound ramifications, which began before the turn of the twentieth century. Thus, the conflict between workers and capitalists over wages, hours, and so on, which in earlier periods produced numerous smaller strikes, now, with the development of monopoly and imperialism, creates enormous national class struggles which shake the very state itself. The contradiction between the producing power of the workers and the ability of the capitalist markets to absorb their products currently results in world-shattering economic crises. The antagonisms between the monopolies and the rest of society at home and abroad have expanded so greatly during the past half century that the Wall Street monopolists are now brazenly seeking to subjugate the entire world. The contradictions between the colonies and the imperialist countries, which the latter could once easily resolve in their own favor by shooting down the ill-armed "natives," have at present expanded into great, irresistible colonial revolutions which are tearing the foundations from underneath the world capitalist system. Likewise, the rivalries among the capitalist countries themselves have now intensified to such an extent that they produce ever more devastating world wars, one after the other. And finally, and most decisive of all, the conflict between capitalism and socialism, which was only a minor situation half a century ago, has in our times reached the point where literally two great worlds, the capitalist and socialist, stand arrayed against each other.

All this adds up to a profound and ever-deepening general crisis of the world capitalist system. Fifty years ago, at the dawn of imperialism, things looked rosy for capitalist society. As an economic system it held unchallenged supremacy throughout the world. While it had many in-

[1] Lenin, *Imperialism, the Highest Stage of Capitalism.*

ternal difficulties—cyclical economic crises, strikes, chaotic competition between rival capitalist concerns, minor colonial wars, and occasional wars between the capitalist countries—nevertheless capitalism could and did advance and spread rapidly in spite of all these drawbacks. Today, however, the situation is fundamentally changed. The internal contradictions of capitalism, once manageable, have now reached catastrophic proportions. And the whole system is challenged by the growth in the world of the new system of socialism, which at present embraces about a third of the earth and its inhabitants.

The capitalists, particularly of Wall Street, are making desperate efforts to repair world capitalism again after its latest huge internal explosion—World War II. But without success, as even capitalist writers cannot deny. In September 1951, *U.S. News and World Report* commented, "U.S. billions thus far have not been able to put Western Europe back on its feet for keeps. New economic troubles are piling up . . . more U.S. aid, not less, will be asked."[1] In Great Britain the gap between income and expenditure in 1951 will reach almost $3.5 billion, the worst in post-war history.[2] Italy now has four million unemployed, and in France, one government after the other collapses, unable to cope with the huge problems of inflation and rearmament. West Germany suffers the general capitalist disease. There are two kinds of capitalist countries in Europe—the sick and the sicker. Meanwhile American monopolists, with their mad scheme of a new war to kill socialism, arrogantly drive these weak countries deeper into economic crisis and closer to political revolution.

The Wall Street-inspired scheme for a united capitalist (anti-Soviet) Europe, with its industrial amalgamation (Schuman plan), general European Army (Eisenhower), West-European Parliament, and so on, is foredoomed to failure. It will be wrecked upon the incurable European imperialist rivalries and the disintegrating effects of American domination, as well upon the widespread mass opposition.

The ravages of the general crisis among the European capitalist countries is dramatically illustrated by the rapid decline of the British Empire, especially marked since the war's end. The British colonial system in the Far East is collapsing—in India, Burma, Malaya, Ceylon, etc.—and so are its holdings and spheres of influence in the Middle East—in Iran, Iraq, Egypt, Turkey, Greece, etc. Its African colonies, too, are in a growing state of ferment and are gradually taking the liberation path of those in the Far East. Besides, Britain's dominions—South Africa, Canada, Australia, and New Zealand—are more and more falling under the domination of the United States. And Great Britain herself is in chronic crisis.

1 *U.S News and World Report*, Sept. 14, 1951.
2 *New York Daily News*, Sept. 14, 1951.

Nor can the Churchill government, with all its imperialist bluster, halt the disintegration of the empire; it can only hasten it. The French and Dutch empires are similarly crumbling under the blows of the awakening colonial peoples.

In Asia generally, things are no less threatening for capitalism than among the capitalist countries of Europe. China, in full revolution, is on the way to socialism, and Communist strength among India's peoples is swiftly on the increase. Bourgeois economists are speculating that there will be a "Communist India by 1960."[1] Governor Dewey, returned recently from Asia, was alarmed at four revolutionary struggles which he found then going on—in the Philippines, Indonesia, Burma, and Indo-China, with more in prospect. In the Middle East, and all along the 4,000 miles from Pakistan to Morocco, the Arab powers are stirring with anti-imperialist spirit. This Britain is now learning to its consternation, by the loss of its billion-dollar oil refinery in Iran and the threatened loss of its control over the Suez Canal in Egypt. In Africa also, powerful colonial liberation movements are getting under way. For the time being the United States is able to keep the lid on in Latin America, but it will be a matter of only a short while until this also blows off, as this whole area is increasingly restive under United States domination. The *New York Times* of February 14, 1952, reported that 30,000 political prisoners are now languishing in Latin American prisons.

The many new states coming into being in Asia and Africa, as a result of the growing colonial liberation revolution, will not develop into capitalist nations, despite the hopes (and fears) of the capitalist world that they will do so. On the contrary, the rebellious colonial peoples must take the road forward to rising socialism, not backward to bankrupt capitalism. The capitalist system, dying in the West, will never be rejuvenated in the East.

The general crisis of capitalism is bound to get worse. It is impossible for the capitalists to reverse the irresistible historic trends of economic and political evolution which have produced two world wars, fascism, the great world economic crisis of the 1930's, and especially the revolutions in Russia, China, and various parts of Europe and Asia. All of these are developments which are gradually wiping out world capitalism. The very difficulty of the situation of capitalism is in itself increasing the war danger by developing a mood of desperation among the imperialists. For the capitalists may rush into a war in trying to find a way out of their multiplying problems. But if the world monopoly capitalists, dominated by Wall Street, insanely try to re-establish their system by an all-out war against the U.S.S.R. and the People's Democracies of

[1] *U.S. News and World Report*, Aug. 17, 1951.

Europe and Asia, this will only speed up the natural course of events by wrecking capitalism altogether and giving an enormous stimulus to the growth of socialism in many countries.

THE UNITED STATES AND THE GENERAL CRISIS

For all its apparent strength, the United States is involved in the general crisis of world capitalism and is subject to that system's basic course of decay and decline. Contrary to all the "American exceptionalists," from Truman to Browder, capitalism in the United States is fundamentally the same as capitalism in all other countries. Its specific features, greatly magnified by the exceptionalists as constituting great health and power, are only secondary and temporary in character. They are due to this country's special position and historical development and do not set the United States apart from the fate of the world capitalist system in general.

Just now American capitalist spokesmen are characteristically drunk on the "prosperity wine" of the upward swing of the capitalist economic cycle and dizzy with the alluring prospect of early world domination; they are luridly lyrical in describing the strength and glories of American imperialism. "Prosperity is moving in for an extended stay. . . . There will be plenty of everything. This includes jobs, spending money and things to buy," cries Wall Street.[1] And President Truman shouts, "There never was a time like this in the history of the world. . . . Since 1933, national income has gone up from $40 billion a year to $278 billion a year. . . . More people are at work right now on good jobs and good wages than ever before in the history of the country, or the history of the world by any country. Our economy is stronger than it has ever been."[2]

This is simply demagogic deceit. It is a matter of common knowledge to every serious economist that the recent extensive growth of American output has been based primarily upon the bloody stimulant of war: in preparing for war, in carrying on war, and in repairing war's damages. This was made clear when, as we have pointed out in Chapter 23, President Roosevelt, with his New Deal, poured billions in subsidies into industry, but could not revive the sick economic system, whose industries were paralyzed by the great economic crisis of 1929-33. The slowly improving situation was worsened by the crisis of 1937, so that in 1939 there were still some 10 million unemployed. It was primarily the huge war orders of World War II, from 1939 on, that brought "pros-

[1] *U.S. News and World Report*, Aug. 31, 1951.
[2] *New York Times*, Sept. 5, 1951.

perity" to capitalist America. After the end of the war in 1945, the brief period of industrial activity which then set in was also based on war, on making up the domestic shortages of commodities caused by the war and repairing the huge property damage caused by the war in Europe and elsewhere. Despite these war stimulants, however, by 1949 this country was fast sinking into another deep economic crisis, which caused a drop of nearly 20 percent in production. It was "miraculously" spared from a crash by the outbreak of the Korean war, which was opportunely launched by the Wall Street puppet Syngman Rhee government of South Korea. So the present "prosperity," over which Mr. Truman becomes so enthusiastic, is based upon the quicksand of war. And now, notwithstanding the huge current government expenditures for armaments, there are multiplying signs of a developing crisis of overproduction in the civilian sectors of the nation's economy.

The American economic system is incurably sick—it is rotten at the heart. Its dependence upon arms production to keep going exposes its basic weakness. No country, however rich, can prosper upon war and munitions-making. The present arms race, while producing fabulous profits for the capitalists, is having disastrous effects upon the living standards of the workers. For the latter it means soaring prices and taxes, lagging wages, increased speed-up, and creeping unemployment. The continuation of the arms economy can only result in a further gigantic increase in the national debt, the exhaustion of available capital for civilian production, further inflation, impoverishment of the people, mass unemployment, and an eventual undermining of the whole economy.[1] Besides its ultimate ruinous economic effects, the worst aspect of the arms economy is that its logical end is war, with universal slaughter and overwhelming economic disaster to all the peoples of the world who still live under capitalism. The plan of the Trumanites and other Keynesians to keep American industry in operation by arms production is a fatal mirage. Such artificial production can only disastrously worsen the nation's economy in the long run and still further deepen the general crisis of world capitalism as a whole, of which the American economy is an organic part.

The political situation of the United States, both nationally and internationally, as well as its economic position, also show that this country is caught inextricably in the world capitalist crisis. The rapid growth of fascist trends in the United States constitutes one of the characterisic weaknesses of monopoly capitalism. For everywhere, as it sinks into its international crisis, monopoly capitalism feels the need to suppress democracy in order to force the workers and lower middle class to accept their worsening

---

[1] Eugene Varga, *Two Systems*, p. 137.

economic conditions and to support capitalism's wars. The supposedly strong international position of the United States—that is, one of hegemony, or predominance, over the rest of the capitalist world—is but a product of the general crisis of world capitalism. It constitutes a sort of imperialist cannibalism, in which the United States exploits not only the peoples of the colonial lands but also those of the imperialist countries. Such a condition, where one capitalist power dominates and exploits all the others, could not possibly exist were not the capitalist system in a serious state of weakness. This very hegemony of American capitalism, precisely deepens the general crisis of the whole world capitalist system disastrously because it intensifies all the capitalist contradictions and pushes all the capitalist countries toward war.

BOURGEOIS CULTURE AND THE CRISIS

The world capitalist crisis manifests itself also in our cultural life. What is called American culture is in fact bourgeois ideology. It cultivates the interests of the capitalists and is expressed through various art forms, which are opposed to the national interests and democratic cultural strivings of the working class and the masses of the American people. This bourgeois cultural life exhibits to the highest degree the characteristic features of capitalism in decay, of imperialism heading into fatal war. The capitalist class has enlisted the paid services of the Pounds, Eliots, Joyces, Faulkners, Hemingways, Dos Passoses, Mumfords, Hickses, Eastmans, and the like, and with their aid, it is filling the country with a stifling miasma of intellectual chaos, obscurantism, and hopelessness, designed to bewilder the people and to disarm them before the reactionary policies of American imperialism.

Every modern school of cultural decay finds a ready backing in the capitalist United States. Pragmatism, the cynical doctrine of full justification of every capitalist outrage, is accepted as a great contribution to human knowledge. Freudianism, which insolently attempts to explain all economics, politics, and social phenomena on the basis of disordered mentality, has just about conquered the field of decadent American bourgeois culture. The apostles of confusion and social reaction who find even these doctrines inadequate have imported the putrid theories of Sartre, Heidegger, Kierkegaard and other devotees of cosmopolitanism, fascism, demoralization, and death. The capitalist-minded scientists are engaged in the reactionary and impossible task of harmonizing science with religion. The priests and preachers, supposedly men of peace, are busy in the front ranks of the warmongers. In no great nation does bourgeois cultural life show such marked evidence of decay—in science, music, literature, art, sports, theater, radio, television—as in the United States.¹ Bourgeois culture rots as the capitalist system dies.

A boycott is established against left and progressive cultural workers. They are denied the right to express their talents in the press, radio, and all other cultural mediums. This outrageous situation is dramatized by the ban on the great artist, Paul Robeson, including a refusal to grant him a passport, although many European countries are clamoring for him to appear before their people. As usual, the Negro people are the keenest sufferers from cultural discrimination. The largest union in the motion picture industry—I.A.T.S.E.—has no Negro members. Of the 43,000 members of the American Bar Association only six are Negroes, and only 25 of the 7,000 attorneys employed by the federal government are Negroes. Negroes are systematically excluded from the editorial and business departments of the big newspapers, etc., etc.²

This current cultural degeneration, bred of the structural breakdown of the capitalist system, is matched by a related decay in many other phases of American bourgeois social life. Never was corruption in local and national official circles so rampant. The mink-coaters, five-percenters, tax grafters, and deep-freezers, plus the police-underworld hook-ups exposed by Senator Kefauver, are only small surface indications of the great mass of rottenness saturating the whole fiber of American capitalist political life. The capitalist rulers are keen to see to it, however, that no modern Steffenses, Sinclairs, Tarbells, or other real "muckrakers" are given an opportunity really to uncover this stinking decay.

The recent enormous spread of gambling of all kinds, which has become a big American industry, is an indication of the fascist-like rot affecting capitalist society in the United States in the period of its imperalist ascendency and its drive for world supremacy. Sport has become corrupted to the core, the press carrying one lurid story after another about the trafficking in athletic contests—in basketball, football, boxing, wrestling, and what not. And this type of corruption is even outdone by the shocking plague of juvenile delinquency that is developing all over the country. For the youth of the nation cannot remain uncorrupted in sports, student life, and otherwise, when it has before its eyes the ever-present example of the leading industrialists and politicians who, in the normal workings of the capitalist system, grab all they can get by every means possible, just so they manage to keep out of the penitentiary.

[1] See Sidney Finkelstein in *Masses and Mainstream*, Aug. 1951; George Siskind and Harry Martel in *Political Affairs*, Dec. 1950; articles on psychoanalysis by Milton Howard in *The Worker* during 1948-51; V. J. Jerome in *Political Affairs*, Feb. 1951; Lloyd Brown in *Masses and Mainstream*, Oct. 1951.
[2] *Daily Worker*, Nov. 14, 1951.

Crime has also become a major American industry. The F.B.I. reported on April 12, 1951, that during the previous year 1,790,030 major offenses were committed in the United States—or one every 18 seconds.[1] Radio, television, and the publishing business would go bankrupt without their flood of crime stories. This development is directly related to the decay of capitalism. The spread in the use of narcotics, even among school children, is no less spectacular and shocking, the trade in this poison having also become another large-scale business. In the hectic life of capitalist America, full of robbery, corruption, and deceit, it is small wonder that insanity is also rapidly on the increase. Capitalism in its degeneration is becoming neurotic and psychotic.

Such phenomena—the corruption of sport, the wide extension of gambling and crime, and the growing decay in bourgeois political and cultural life generally—are but so many examples of the development of fascist trends in the United States. This, in turn, is but an expression of the general crisis of the capitalist system, and of the desperate determination of American imperialism to cut its way out of its multiplying difficulties by means of another still more terrible world war.

SOCIALISM, THE BASIC ANSWER

Innumerable sober-minded American citizens, men and women, fearful of disaster to our nation and to civilization itself, have gravely warned of the terrible dangers, inherent in another world war. The Communist Party heartily seconds these patriotic warnings against war. It urgently calls upon the American people not to be misled into a needless and monstrous mass slaughter, in order to further the imperialist aims of the greedy monopolists who now dominate this country economically and politically. Our Party, instead, urges the people to bridle the Wall Street war mongers and to orient this country peacefully along the road of democratic progress and toward eventual socialism.

The peoples of the capitalist world are fighting resolutely against the specific evils of the decaying capitalist system—its deepening economic crisis and spreading mass impoverishment, its growing spirit of reaction and fascism, its relentless colonial oppression, its recurrent world wars. The masses, led and aided by the struggles of the C.P. on immediate issues, are trying to protect themselves as best they can under the existing decadent social order; but in the long run they must and do turn toward socialism. For that is the only final answer to the many basic contradictions which produce the terrors and hardships of rotting capitalism. One-third of the people of the earth have already adopted

[1] Max Gordon in *Political Affairs*, June 1951.

the logic of this great alternative, and the rest, including the people of the United States, will eventually follow suit.

The vanguard of the world movement toward socialism is the U.S.S.R., led by the Communist Party. Palmiro Togliatti, leader of the Communist Party of Italy, says: "In order to create such a powerful country and to secure for it such prestige, this Party and these people passed through the most trying ordeals: three revolutions, two world wars, two foreign invasions. They triumphed because they possess the correct teaching—Marxism—which was developed and applied by Lenin and Stalin in the new conditions of imperialism, in the conditions of victorious revolution and construction of socialist society."[1]

As we have seen earlier, the peoples are either building socialism or approaching it under considerably differing forms in the Soviet Union, the European People's Democracies, and People's China. But the fundamentals of socialism are everywhere the same. Founded upon the people's ownership of the social means of production (industries, banks, railroads, land, etc.), the abolition of the exploitation of man by man, and the establishment of the political rule of the working class, socialism represents the next higher stage in the course of social evolution. Based on the principle of "From each according to his ability, to each according to his work," socialism constitutes the preliminary stage of communism, the underlying principle of which is "From each according to his ability, to each according to his need."

Socialism abolishes capitalists and landlords, and therewith also does away with exploitation of the producing masses. It leads to a rapid growth of production and to a continuous rise in the well-being of the working people of field, factory, and office. This has been demonstrated in practice by the tremendous improvement in the mass living standards of the Soviet people since the great Revolution, despite enormous handicaps in the shape of ten years of devastating imperialist and civil war, and the need to build and rebuild the industries from the ground up. Meanwhile, the working class throughout the capitalist world has suffered a steady deterioration of its living standards, a decline which in many capitalist countries has been catastrophic.

Socialism removes the fetters from industry fastened there by the private ownership of the industries and the limitations of the capitalist markets, and it tremendously speeds up industrialization. This was dramatically illustrated by the fact that from 1929 to 1949, when the production index for steel advanced only from 100 to 111 in the capitalist world, it climbed from 100 to 582 in the socialist Soviet Union. In the fifteen years before World War II, the U.S.S.R. achieved as much industrial

[1] *For a Lasting Peace...*, Dec. 21, 1951.

growth as the major capitalist powers had done in eighty years. This swift industrialization is especially to be noted in the undeveloped areas of the Soviet Union. Thus, in Soviet Central Asia, during the years 1927-37, industrial output went up by 950 percent, while industry stagnated in the capitalist-dominated backward areas of Asia, Africa, and Latin America. Under the Socialist system also, those great plagues of capitalism—economic crises and mass unemployment—are completely eliminated.

Socialism alone will be able to utilize constructively the great new discovery of atomic energy. Capitalism has been able to spread the benefits of steam and electricity to only a fraction of the world's population; it will be even less capable of giving atomic energy a world-wide application. Characteristically, its major use for this great new power is for war purposes. Only the Socialist system can make use of the vast potentialities of atomic energy, even as it can of all other great inventions, by bringing them everywhere to the masses.[1] Socialism, too, will conserve the world's store of natural resources, now being recklessly squandered under capitalism.

Under Socialism, by establishing the leadership of the working class, which is called the dictatorship of the proletariat, human society for the first time establishes real democracy in the world. The arbitrary, needless, and parasitic rule of the wealthy capitalists and landlords is done away with completely. Fascism, which is such a deadly danger at present, is utterly liquidated. White chauvinism becomes a crime, and peoples of many nationalities, colors, and creeds live together harmoniously. These democratic principles have been basically established in the Soviet Union and the People's Democracies, despite the oceans of capitalist lies to the contrary.

By creating a classless society without exploitation and tyranny, socialism gives mankind and womankind their first real opportunity to develop as individuals. Slavery in every form comes to an end under socialism. Higher education is general. Woman is truly free for the first time, and the door of opportunity is flung wide open for the youth. The aged, neglected and kicked about under capitalism, enjoy a position of dignity and security under socialism. The robot-like culture of capitalism, whose decay now stinks to the high heavens, is succeeded by a true Socialist culture, worthy of the highest aspirations of mankind. Socialism is producing a new and higher type of man and woman, physically, mentally, socially. Socialist society is guided by science for the benefit of all, and not, as under capitalism, by the dictation of the ruling classes in the interest of the wealthy few. All these constructive

---

[1] See James S. Allen, *Atomic Energy and Society*, N. Y., 1949, and *Atomic Imperialism: The State, Monopoly, and the Bomb*, N. Y., 1952.

principles constitute the warp and woof of the new Socialist societies now establishing themselves in various parts of the world.

What is vitally important in this period of menacing war danger, socialism puts a final end to armed conflict among nations. Socialist countries, such as the U.S.S.R. and the People's Democracies, have no capitalists, and hence no imperialist warmakers. Whereas capitalism—and above all American capitalism—lives on war (and is also dying on it), socialism, in its whole economic and political structure, is fundamentally committed to a policy of peace.

The defenders of capitalism assume that the people can successfully carry on their industries and government only if these are owned and controlled by a relative handful of capitalists, who thereby become the wealthy and arbitrary rulers of society. But this whole conception is not only an empty defense of brutal and needless exploitation, but also an insult to the people's intelligence. The workers of the U.S.S.R. and of the People's Democracies are demonstrating in practice, as Marx did long ago in theory, that the people need no parasitic masters but can run society infinitely better without them. The abolition of capitalism and the establishment of socialism will end forever the tragic exploitation and slavery which man has endured for many centuries.

The foregoing are the basic reasons why the toiling masses of the world are turning so rapidly toward socialism. The motive power behind the vast international Socialist movement is the imperative demand of the workers for greater freedom and well-being. Capitalism, rotting away in its general crisis, cannot satisfy these needs of the masses. All it can give the peoples is increasing economic destitution, fascism, and war.

Hence, in their own ways and at their own tempo, the workers and other toilers in all capitalist countries are becoming more and more Socialist in their strivings and outlook. Nor will the United States prove exempt from this general rule. The Communist parties in all countries are the leaders and guides of the awakening toiling masses. Capitalism in its earlier stages was progressive, inasmuch as it overthrew feudalism, founded the present industries, and gave rise to the industrial proletariat; but now the system has become hopelessly obsolete and reactionary. It must be replaced by socialism.

37. The American Working Class and Socialism

Spokesmen of American capitalism, both inside and outside the labor movement, shout tirelessly that there is no basis for socialism in the United States. They maintain that ours is a special type of economy, not really capitalism at all, and that it progresses in an endless upward spiral of development. This is "American exceptionalism." Such reactionaries declare, with a voice of dogmatic finality, that the American working class, as well as the rest of the nation, neither needs nor wants socialism; that the workers have the highest wage standards in the world; that they elect capitalist-minded officials to head their trade unions; that they have no mass labor party, that they are not class-conscious, that they have no revolutionary perspective. From all of which the capitalist spokesmen conclude that the American workers, living in a basically different economy from the workers of other lands, are immune to Marxism-Leninism and are permanently dedicated to the capitalist system.

All this is nothing more than whistling in the dark on the part of the ruling class in a capitalist world that is decaying. In reality, American capitalism is fundamentally the same as the system in every capitalist country, although, as we have seen in earlier chapters, certain historical factors have favored its greater growth and strength. In the United States, as everywhere else under capitalism, the industries and the land are privately owned and are operated for the profit of their owners. Production, based upon competition at home and abroad, is carried on chaotically, without plan. Through the wage system, the workers are systematically exploited and robbed by their employers. Consequently, this country also suffers from overproduction and cyclical economic crises. The United States too, possesses the same classes—capitalists, middle classes, and workers—that are characteristic of capitalist economies generally. And, as elsewhere, among these rival classes, the class struggle has raged with greater or less intensity ever since the foundation of the Republic. The American economy has typically produced monopoly and imperialism and, as we remarked previously, like all other capitalist countries, the United States is definitely involved in the general crisis of the world capitalist system.

FACTORS RETARDING THE IDEOLOGICAL DEVELOPMENT OF THE WORKERS

Although the great bulk of the American working class has long lacked a Socialist ideology, this condition is only temporary. The workers in this country have an extensive and militant record of class struggle. During their struggle against the employers for over a century, they have built up a vast trade union movement, they have carried on many huge and bitter strikes and political fights, and they have evolved an ever-stronger class spirit. Although, in the main, they have not yet developed the degree of class consciousness and Socialist perspective common to the workers in Europe and elsewhere, they are on the way to doing so.

The ideological development of the American working class has been retarded by the effects, over a long period, of a number of important, but secondary, features in the development of capitalism in this country. These factors have tended to cultivate petty-bourgeois illusions among the workers and to lead them to believe that they can solve their economic and political problems within the framework of the capitalist system. These specific American economic and political characteristics are the fruitful soil out of which grows "American exceptionalism" in its various forms of Gompersism, Hillquitism, Lovestoneism, Browderism, Wallaceism, and the like. Chief among these characteristics are the following:

First: Owing to the lack of feudal political hangovers and to the more thorough-going bourgeois revolutions of 1776 and 1861, the workers in this country, but not the Negro people, won broader civil liberties than existed in Continental Europe. Particularly important in this respect was the more extensive right to vote. This situation tended to cultivate among workers in the United States widespread and deep-seated illusions about the possibilities of bourgeois democracy in this country, despite their long struggle for the right to organize unions, for woman suffrage, for popular education, for social security, and for other popular liberties. By contrast to the situation in the United States, in many European countries franchise rights of the workers were severely limited by the so-called class system of voting, right up to the revolutionary aftermath of World War I. Hence, they built their big Social-Democratic parties primarily by two generations of struggle for "equal, direct, secret, and general" manhood suffrage, acquiring a high degree of class consciousness in the process. The American working class in general, during these decades, did not have to make such an elementary fight for the vote.

Second: The long-continued lack of uniformity in the composition of the American working class has been, historically, another important factor militating against the growth of proletarian class consciousness and a Socialist outlook in this country. For generations huge masses of the workers were immigrants, of two score or more nationalities and possessing widely varying languages, religions, cultures, and historical backgrounds. These factors obviously made it more difficult for them to organize economically and politically, and to develop ideologically.

Third: For the first century of the Republic's life there existed immense tracts of government-owned land, small parcels of which could be had without great difficulty, especially after the passage of the Homestead Act of 1862. This free land served for decades as a sort of safety valve for the class struggle and a deterrent to the growth of class consciousness. It gave the workers the goal of a farm, and all the early trade unions interested themselves keenly in the land question. As we have seen, this "free land" even gave birth to special forms of "American exceptionalism." In actual fact, however, comparatively few workers ever got "free land," most of it being grabbed by the railroads, coal companies, lumber and cattle kings, and big farmers and planters.[1]

Fourth: Another long-term deterrent to the growth of class-consciousness in the American working class was the fact that, in the vast and swift growth of industry and agriculture, numbers of workers were able to acquire property and to pass into the ranks of the middle class. Not a few even became big capitalists. The expectation of one day establishing little businesses of their own was common among the workers, and it operated to keep them thinking in terms of capitalism.

Fifth: The most powerful element, tending traditionally to slow down the development of a Socialist ideology among the workers in this country, has been the big shortage of labor power, due to the unusually favorable conditions under which American capitalism has developed. This enabled the workers, especially the skilled among them, to achieve wage rates considerably higher than those prevailing in other major capitalist countries. These "high" wages were offset, however, by such factors as a greater intensification of labor, more danger of unemployment, far more hazardous working conditions, a total lack of social insurance, and so on. While the central fact of the higher money wages in this country did not prevent the workers from forming trade unions and waging bitter strikes to defend and improve their living conditions, it nevertheless militated against their becoming fully class-conscious and revolutionary-minded.

Sixth: There grew a very big labor aristocracy, those workers whom Engels called "bourgeoisified," to whom the employers conceded relatively high wages at the expense of the unskilled, the Negro toilers, and the people of colonial lands. Especially with the development of

[1] Kuczynski, *Labor Conditions in the U.S.*

imperialism, a corrupt labor bureaucracy grew up on the basis of this labor aristocracy. This reactionary officialdom, the characteristic American counterpart of European Social-Democracy, repeated the slogans of the employers and dominated the economic and political activities of the workers. Historically, it has been a potent weapon in retarding the ideological development of the working class. The employers have always helped this bureaucracy to gain and hold power in the trade unions.

FACTORS MAKING FOR CLASS CONSCIOUSNESS

Today, however, the foregoing factors, hindering the development of class-consciousness and a Socialist perspective among the workers, have either wholly disappeared or are on the eve of so doing. First, the United States, with the growth of monopoly and imperialism, has long since lost its democratic leadership among the nations and is now veering toward fascism—a degeneration of capitalist democracy which is fast undermining bourgeois illusions among the workers. Second, the working class is swiftly becoming more homogeneous. The immigrant masses have largely learned the English language and domestic customs; the second and third generations of their descendants, while not ignoring their national backgrounds, are quite American; and the Negro and white workers are developing a real solidarity in organization and action. Third, the free land has been gone now for at least sixty years, and the prospect of getting a real farm has been practically forgotten by the working class. Fourth, with the growth of the trusts, the traditional hope of the workers eventually to become small tradesmen or industrialists has steadily faded, until now, among the bulk of the working class, little remains of this expectation except illusory speculation here and there about one day "opening up a gas station." Today the great mass of actual workers, although hoping "to do better for their children," themselves expect to live and die as workers—which is obviously a long stride toward developing class consciousness. Fifth, the wages of American workers, while still generally above those in Europe, are now resting precariously upon a very treacherous quicksand, and this chief barrier to the development of a Socialist perspective among the workers is steadily being undermined. The imperiling of American wage rates threatens the privileged position of the labor aristocracy and also that of the reactionary labor bureaucracy, which bases itself upon this aristocracy.

THE IMPOVERISHMENT OF THE WORKERS

The primary factor undermining the traditionally higher American wage standards is what Marx called the *relative* impoverishment of the workers. This is taking place to an ever-increasing degree in this country, as in all capitalist economies. That is, taking all elements together—wages, prices, and productivity—American workers are more deeply exploited and are getting a smaller proportion of what they produce than they did half a century ago. "By 1939," says Perlo, "the employers were not only getting twice as much production from each worker as forty years earlier, but they were keeping a much larger share of the production for themselves; their real profits had increased by much more than 100 percent."[1] The Labor Research Association states, too, that "the 'relative position' of the worker in manufacturing in 1949 was 34 percent below the level of the last century. . . . The index fell from 100 in 1899 to 66 in 1948, even on the basis of inadequate government statistics."[2] And the U.S. Department of Labor, in trying to make a favorable case for American capitalism, unwittingly substantiates the above conclusions of Perlo and the L.R.A. by stating that whereas real wages in the United States have about doubled since 1900 (a gross misstatement), the productivity of the workers has increased four to five times during the same period.[3] Kuczynski says, "The relative position of the American industrial worker has deteriorated very considerably during the last seventy years."[4]

In fact, in no other country in the world is the *relative* impoverishment of the workers so pronounced as it is in the United States. Nowhere are the workers so heavily exploited, for all their alleged "high wages," as they are in this country. And from this deep exploitation and *relative* impoverishment inevitably grow the roots of overproduction, cyclical economic crises, mass unemployment, lowered living standards, class consciousness, and the eventual breakdown of the capitalist system.

The second factor to consider regarding the decline of the traditionally higher real wages of the workers in the United States is that the *relative* impoverishment under capitalism inexorably brings about *absolute* impoverishment of the workers. This is clearly to be seen all over the rest of the capitalist world, where the workings of the capitalist system—its exploitation, economic crises, and wars—have plunged

---

1 Perlo, *American Imperialism*, p. 223.
2 Labor Research Association, *Economic Notes*, Apr. 1951.
3 *Monthly Labor Review*, July 1951.
4 Kuczynski, *Labor Conditions in the U.S.*, p. 183.

the toiling masses into deepest poverty. The workings of this economic law are also very much in evidence in the United States, where huge masses of the workers, despite recent enormous increases in production, are living in a state of destitution.

Only a few years ago, Roosevelt spoke of "one-third of a nation ill-housed, ill-clad, ill-nourished"—in a country with the greatest productive capacity in the world. The widely accepted Heller Budget, in 1948, called for a weekly wage of $79.04, in order to provide an average-sized worker's family with a decent living. However, only 67 percent of the people were actually getting an income equal to this budget, the average wage in manufacturing being but $54.48. In 1939 the top one percent of the population received 12 percent of the national income.[1] The widespread poverty now existing in the United States was dramatically indicated recently by a Congressional report which showed that 10,500,000 famiiles—about one-fourth of all families—are now living upon incomes of $2,000 a year or less; that is to say, at poverty levels.[2] At present, of 17 million women employed in industry, 50 percent are married, which means that in the greater part of these cases at least two persons must work in order to support the family adequately.

The worst sufferers in the widespread *absolute* impoverishment are the Negro people and the great armies of unskilled workers, whose plight is obscured by the government's generalized statistics and Pollyanna interpretations. This widespread poverty among the masses is accentuated by new insecurities and difficulties from the industrial speed-up, disruption of normal family life, early obsolescence of workers, fears of economic crises and wars, loss of popular freedoms, and so on.[3]

The U.S. Census Bureau recently reported on wealth ownership in the United States. It stated that the top one-fifth of the population now owns 47 percent of the wealth and the lower one-fifth only 3 percent.[4] Of the total national savings (banks, insurance, etc.) the lower 40 percent of American families owns nothing at all, whereas the upper 10 percent owns 65 percent. Actually, 200 super-wealthy families dominate the industries and organized wealth of the United States. Such polarization of great wealth and deep poverty is characteristic of capitalism the world over.

With the continuation of capitalism and the deepening of its general crisis the perspective is one of great intensification and extension of mass

---

1 Labor Research Association, *Trends in American Capitalism*, p. 92, N. Y., 1948.
2 *Report of National Social Welfare Council to a Joint Committee of Congress*, Aug. 1951.
3 Alexander Bittelman in *Political Affairs*, Oct. 1951.
4 *New York Herald Tribune*, Dec. 2, 1951.

absolute impoverishment in the United States. Although the wages of American workers are on the average higher than those prevalent in Europe, they now rest upon a most insecure basis. Today they are dependent on a feverish arms economy, instead of, as in former years, on the normal growth of the industries. Present-day American "prosperity" is artificial, drawing its sustenance from munitions production and war, and from imperialist exploitation of peoples all over the world. The present American gross national output of $324 billion ($180 billion in 1939 dollars) is tremendously overswollen from war production. Those sections of the American people, including many top labor leaders, who believe that "full" employment and "high" wages can be continued on this basis are living in a fool's paradise and are due for a sad awakening.

Already the huge armaments program, with its inflation, high taxes, gigantic profits, and wage freeze, is sending American living standards tobogganing. The continuation of this program will eventually climax in either a deep economic breakdown or a catastrophic war, either of which will spread *absolute* mass impoverishment over the country like a plague. The great economic crisis of 1929-33, when living standards were cut in half, millions of jobless walked the streets, and mass starvation stalked the country, was the result of the normal workings of the American capitalist economy. The present arms production cannot possibly avert a similar disaster in the near future; but instead, it will produce an even greater economic smash-up. The existing mass destitution in capitalist Europe is only a foretaste of what is eventually in store for American workers, if they do not succeed in putting a halt to Wall Street's war-fascism plans and adopting the fundamental programs, making toward socialism, necessary to conserve their own well-being and to create a healthy economic system.

The condition of the American working class fully confirms the correctness of the general law of capitalist accumulation, discovered by Marx; namely, "that in proportion as capital accumulates, the lot of the laborer, be his payment high or low, must grow worse. . . . It establishes an accumulation of misery, corresponding with accumulation of capital. Accumulation of wealth at one pole is, therefore, at the same time, accumulation of misery, agony of toil, slavery, ignorance, brutality, mental degradation at the opposite pole."[1]

THE WORKERS WILL TURN TO SOCIALISM

Achieved at the expense of the unskilled, the Negro people, and the exploited of other lands, the relatively higher American living standards,

[1] Marx, *Capital*, Vol. 1, p. 661.

especially among the skilled workers, are a phenomenon of the upswing of American imperialism. Capitalism here will no longer be able to furnish these wages when it goes into decline, as it surely will through the workings of its own internal contradictions and of the general crisis of the world capitalist system. When in its prime and on the upgrade, British imperialism could and did corrupt the labor aristocracy with relatively high wages, at the expense of the colonial peoples and the unskilled at home, as Marx and Engels pointed out. At that time the British workers as a class, bemused by this hollow imperialist "prosperity," were also not interested in socialism. The British capitalists boasted that even though workers on the Continent might be Marxist, this could never be in Britain.

But with British imperialism now far on the downgrade, those times are gone forever. Consequently, the British working class, with lowered living standards, is now irresistibly heading toward socialism, despite its opportunist Social-Democratic leadership. The general political development in the United States, although not so far advanced as in Great Britain, is going inevitably in the same direction. The American working class is facing a situation in which, in developing crisis and destitution, it will also surely learn that the only way it can protect and improve its living standards is by taking the road that eventually leads to socialism.

Because of the relatively strong position of American imperialism there is at present comparatively little demand for socialism among the broad working class. The specific type of bourgeois illusions now predominant among the bulk of American workers and their conservative leaders amounts to Rooseveltism, or Keynesism (see Chapter 33). This is the false theory that a "progressive capitalism," capable of full employment, can be created by government subsidies to industry and agriculture, plus doles to the workers. Keynesism in the United States plays approximately the political role of right-wing Social-Democracy in Europe in keeping the workers tied to the capitalist system. Although the European right-wing Social-Democrats, who deal with more radical workers, pepper their reformist dish with pseudo-nationalization of industry, seeming independent political action, and much talk about socialism, actually they, too, base their economic and political programs upon a framework of Keynesian "progressive capitalism."

American Social-Democracy has surrendered outright to bourgeois reformism, of which Keynesism is the latest expression, and it has abandoned completely the propaganda for socialism that it once carried on. This surrender was marked by the gradual acceptance of the succeeding forms of so-called progressive capitalism—Theodore Roosevelt's "Square

THE WORKING CLASS AND SOCIALISM 549

Deal" (1912), Woodrow Wilson's "New Freedom" (1916), and Franklin D. Roosevelt's "New Deal" (1932), and during the current period, Truman's demagogic "Fair Deal." Nowadays such "Socialists" as Dubinsky and Reuther are practically indistinguishable from Green and Murray in their general political outlook. The fighters for socialism are the Communists.

The capitalist system in this country is a colossus with feet of clay. American imperialism will lose ideological and organizational control of the workers as its dominant world position weakens. And because of the inevitable deepening of the general crisis of capitalism, this decline is bound to come. The political advance of the working class will then become very rapid, as Engels remarked long ago. The workers will speedily throw off their bourgeois illusions and reactionary leaders, as they have already done in many countries.

During the past twenty years the workers in this country, despite lingering capitalist "prosperity" illusions among them, have made real progress in political understanding and organization. This was evidenced by the great mass unemployed struggles, the building of the C.I.O. and the independent unions, the organization of the large body of Negro workers, the development of the program for social insurance, the increasing movements for independent political action, and the continued struggle against fascism and war. These major political developments, in which the Communist Party played a very important part, are so many sure signs of developing class-consciousness among the workers of the United States.

With the deepening general crisis of capitalism and its involvement of American imperialism in growing economic difficulties, the near future will produce an ever swifter political development of the working class. More advanced economic and political demands, a great independent party with labor as its base, a broad people's front movement, a progressive trade union leadership, and the growth of a Socialist ideology and a mass Communist Party—these developments are also inevitable for the American working class, even as they have been for the workers in other capitalist countries. They will arrive upon the political scene in this country far sooner than the power-drunk capitalist ruling class now even dreams. In these vital developments, the Communist Party, in the very nature of things, will be more and more of a leading factor.

THE AMERICAN ROAD TO SOCIALISM

The transition from capitalism to socialism involves a fundamental reorganization of the nation's economy, from one based on the private ownership of industry for private profit to one of collective ownership for social use, and also a basic political shift from the tyrannical rule of a small group of monopolists to the democratic regime of the broad working class and its allies, which leads to the abolition of class society. Therefore, it is a revolution. Capitalism established itself in all the major countries by revolutions. These revolutions, accomplished in the youth and progressive period of capitalism, were constructive. In the United States there have been two such bourgeois revolutions: that which achieved national independence in 1776-83, and that which abolished Negro slavery in 1861-65. The workers' advance to socialism will be infinitely more progressive than the bourgeois revolutions, because it not only promises but realizes democracy and well-being for the broadest masses of the people.

Socialism is not an invention of the Communists, as reactionaries assert. Nor is the abolition of capitalism the fruition of a Communist conspiracy. On the contrary, socialism grows out of the long-continued everyday struggles of the workers, enlightened and organized by Marxist theory and guidance. It is the ultimate expression and climax of these struggles. The working class and its allies—the Negro people, small farmers, professionals, and others—making up a vast majority of the people, are oppressed by ever greater economic and political hardships under capitalism. They are especially menaced by war and fascism. These evils are greatly accentuated because the capitalist system is sinking deeper and deeper into general crisis. Inexorably the masses must unite ever more strongly and fight with increasing vigor to combat the growing disasters of economic breakdown, destitution, fascism, and world war. The daily struggles around broader and ever more urgent demands, led increasingly by the Communist Party, finally culminate in a mighty movement to abolish the capitalist system itself, as the source of the intolerable evils from which the people suffer. The struggles of the workers for immediate demands, in which they create the necessary economic organizations, build the Communist Party, acquire class-consciousness, develop a program, and win democratic rights for themselves, are an organic part of the historic struggle for socialism. This has been basically the course of political development in all those countries where socialism has been, or is now being established. The breakdown of the capitalist system makes socialism both indispensable and inevitable all over the world, including the United States.

The central task of the Communist Party, with its Marxist-Leninist training and in its role as the vanguard of the working class and the nation, is to give the elemental mass anti-capitalist movement the necessary understanding, organization, and leadership. Without this the workers and their allies could never arrive at their historic goal of socialism. The Communist Party is not an intruder among the toiling masses, as the Department of Justice alleges, seeking to thrust an alien program upon them. Instead, the Party is flesh and bone of the working class. It always marches in the forefront of that class, expresses most clearly its interests, and finally leads it and its allies in realizing the great objective of socialism, which is the culmination of the entire historic experience of the working class.

The Communist Party projects and works for a democratic conduct of the daily class struggle and also of the advance to socialism. The Preamble to the Constitution of the Party states this policy as follows: "The Communist Party upholds the achievements of American democracy and defends the United States Constitution and its Bill of Rights against its reactionary enemies who would destroy democracy and popular liberties. It seeks to safeguard the welfare of the people and the nation, recognizing that the working class, through its trade unions and by its independent political action, is the most consistent fighter for democracy, national freedom, and social progress."

Communists are the chief fighters against the two major threats of violence in modern society—imperialist international war and fascist civil war—both of which emanate from the capitalists. The Communist Party's democratic aims are in line with the writings of Marx, Engels, Lenin, and Stalin, with the course of the everyday struggles of the workers and their allies, and with their world experience in establishing socialism. The danger of violence in the daily class struggle and in the inevitable and indispensable advance of the workers and the nation to socialism could come only from the capitalist class, which, seeing its profits threatened and itself being deposed from its rich dictatorship, then uses every means possible to thwart the democratic socialist will of the people. For as the great Marx has truly said, there is no case in history where a ruling class has yielded up its domination without making a desperate struggle.

Marxist theoreticians, while warning the workers against capitalist violence, have always pointed out possibilities for the peaceful establishment of socialism in countries where the democratic elements are strong. Thus, Karl Marx, three generations ago, before the advent of imperialism, with its highly centralized, heavily armed, and bureaucratic state, said that "If, for example, the working class in England and the United States should win a majority in Parliament, in Congress, it could legally abolish those laws and institutions which obstruct its development."[1] Lenin also, in mid-1917, outlined a peaceful perspective

[1] Cited by Foster, *In Defense of the Communist Party and Its Leaders*, p. 22.

for the Russian Revolution. And Stalin, writing in 1928, while pointing out the danger of capitalist violence at that time, also said that with the strong growth of world socialism, "a peaceful path of development is quite possible for certain capitalist countries."[1] The C.P.U.S.A. proceeds upon the basis that such a possibility exists in the United States.

The Communist Party's orientation for a possible peaceful transition to socialism in the United States is based upon four elementary considerations: first, the fight of the working class for its immediate demands is the very substance of democracy, it strengthens basically the democratic forces in our country, and by the eventual establishment of socialism it raises democracy qualitatively to a new high level; second, the working class, led by the Communist Party, harmonizes its methods with its ends by fighting for both its immediate and ultimate objectives with the most peaceful and democratic means possible; third, the workers and their allies, constituting the vast majority of the people and possessing immense organizations, now have the potential power to curb, restrain, and make ineffective whatever violence the capitalists may undertake in their attempt to balk the will of the people and to prevent the establishment of socialism; and fourth, in recent years, on the international scale, there has been an enormous growth of power in the camp of democracy and socialism.

The fundamental difference between the Communist Party and right-wing Social Democracy (and its Browderite variant) is not that the Social-Democrats want to establish socialism by peaceful means and the Communists want to achieve it by violence. Instead, the difference is that the Social-Democrats everywhere have abandoned socialism altogether and are committed to an indefinite perpetuation of the capitalist system; whereas, the Communists have shown conclusively that, in line with the democratic will and interests of the workers, they are the ones that are resolutely leading the peoples of the world to socialism.

The Communist Party, although it does not advocate violence in the workers' struggles, cannot, however, declare that there will be no violence in the establishment of socialism in this country. This is because of the certainty of reactionary attacks from the capitalists. The latter might even be able, in case of inadequate resistance by the masses, to destroy democracy outright and to establish an American type of fascist-like regime. In such event there would result an entirely new political situation, where the masses would be faced with the need of militant struggle for the most elementary economic needs and democratic rights. In the United States there is a grave danger of such fascism.

The Communist Party holds the view that socialism in the United

---

[1] Cited by Foster, *In Defense of the Communist Party and Its Leaders*, p. 22.

States, although inevitable in the future, is not now on the immediate political agenda. Therefore, the Party never has, and does not now, venture to predict the precise time, forms, and methods of the eventual establishment of socialism in this country. Those who state that the C.P.U.S.A. has a blueprint of some kind, or is organizing a conspiratorial "plot" for achieving socialism, are deliberate liars and perjurors. Any consideration that the Party, therefore, gives to this whole question at the present time, to refute the government's indictment leveled against it, can be only on the basis of an estimate of the eventual working out of general Communist principles in this country, in the light of world experience and American political conditions.

There is no timetable nor blueprinted route to socialism. The American people, led by the working class, will embark upon the road to socialism, all in their own good time and with their own specific methods. As Lenin says, "All nations will come to socialism, this is inevitable, but they will come to it in not quite the same way, each will contribute original features to this or that form of democracy, to this or that variant of the proletarian dictatorship, to this or that tempo of the socialist transformation of the various aspects of social life."[1] The experience of the workers in Russia, China, Poland, Czechoslovakia, and other countries, in their advance to socialism, has borne out this statement by Lenin, and the ultimate course of events in the United States will doubtless give it further confirmation.

American conditions and world socialist experience make it realistic, however, to suppose that, in their march to socialism, the American people, as many others are doing, will take their path through the successive phases of the people's front and the people's democracy. But in so doing, they will doubtless reflect specific American conditions. That is, just as there have been in this country special adaptations of the people's front slogan (examples, the farmer-labor party, the democratic front, the Roosevelt coalition, and now the peace coalition), so there will also almost certainly develop special American forms and applications of the people's democracy and its slogans.

The basic difference between these two state forms is that whereas the people's front government still operates within the framework of the capitalist system, the people's democracy is a form of the dictatorship of the proletariat. In both of these types of government, judging from experience elsewhere, there would be several parties represented. In view of the basic tasks confronting the democratic masses, the influence of the Communist Party (or a broad Workers Party based on a consolidation of the most advanced elements among the workers, farmers, Negro

[1] *Bolshevik*, Moscow, Nov. 19, 1951.

people, etc.) would necessarily be of decisive importance, especially in the people's democracy. For only Marxist-Leninists can lead the nation to socialism.

Soviets are the highest form of the dictatorship of the proletariat, but they are not the only form. The people's democracy represents a new and distinct type of proletarian rule. It has arisen particularly as a result of the radicalization of vast masses of the people, the great growth of the camp of world socialism, and the continued decline of world capitalism.

It is in line with the foregoing general principles and perspectives that the Communist Party has long proposed the regular election, under the United States Constitution, of a broad coalition government, an American variant of the people's front, made up of the representatives of the political and economic organizations of the workers, the Negro people, small farmers, intellectuals, and other democratic strata, who constitute the great bulk of the American people. In the 1948 election campaign the Communist Party, through its general secretary, Eugene Dennis, stated this political policy as follows: "For a people's government that will advance the cause of peace, security and democracy! For an anti-imperialist, anti-monopoly government! What is projected in this slogan, it should be made clear, is a political objective that reflects the united front program which is bringing into a broad coalition all the democratic and anti-imperialist forces including the third party movement."[1] Despite the dangerous threat of fascism in this country, the Communist Party holds that the workers and their allies could elect such a people's front government under the Constitution by vigorous action.

Beyond this point, in practical policy, the Communist Party has not planned. But it is clear that such a people's front government would be elected, probably, when the great masses of the people, facing conditions of a serious political crisis, would feel the urgent need of it in order to protect their most vital interests. Such a situation is definitely in the political perspective for the United States, resulting from the deepening of the general crisis of world capitalism, intensified by Wall Street's aggressive drive towards war.

A people's front government in this country would have as its great task to preserve the workers and the masses of the people from devastating crisis, from the consequences of the breaking down of capitalism and the reactionary policies of big capital. Its program, therefore, would necessarily involve vigorous measures to maintain or restore world peace, to preserve and extend popular democratic liberties, to keep the industries in operation, to improve radically the living standards of the peo-

---

[1] Eugene Dennis in *Political Affairs*, March 1948.

ple, and to realize the economic, political, and social equality of the Negro people, and their right to self-determination in the "Black Belt" of the South.

However, standing athwart the war and fascist policies of monopoly capital, such a democratic people's government, both in its election and in its functioning, would have to face a most determined opposition from the monopolists and their Social-Democratic tools. No one who knows the American capitalist class, with its long record of war aggression, brutality in strikes, slaughter of workers in industry, persecution against the Negro people, etc., can doubt but that the reactionaries would use every available means of Social-Democratic treachery and of outright violence to prevent or destroy any government that cut into their rule and into their robbery of the people. Consequently, the only way the people's government could be elected in the first place and could be enabled to live and to carry out its progressive program would be by defeating this Social-Democratic treachery and capitalist violence. This would also require weakening the economic and political power of the monopolists by the nationalization of the banks, the basic industries, the press, radio, television, etc., and eventually by the reorganization of the army, police, etc., and by beginning to lay the basis for a planned economy. All of which measures the legally elected people's coalition government would have the full authority and national mandate to carry out. This course would be the path to a people's democracy.

Failure of a people's government to take such necessary measures would surely result in its downfall and probably bring about the victory of fascism in the United States. It was, for example, the fatal mistake of the pre-war people's government in Spain that it did not, from the outset, proceed to weaken the capitalists basically, as indicated, and did not nip in the bud the potential military rebellion which finally destroyed it. On the other hand, the fulfillment of the above historic tasks by an American people's government would so strengthen the working class and all the forces of socialism, while weakening those of reaction, that a peaceful transition from capitalism to socialism would become possible through a people's democracy, in its American forms.

The establishment of a people's democracy in the United States would signify that the coalition of workers and their allies had won a decisive political victory over monopoly capital and that a government had come into power, committed to the abolition of capitalism and the establishment of socialism. Such a government, made indispensable under the severe pressure of the capitalist crisis, might evolve either from a people's front coalition government through an internal regrouping of forces, or it might be elected by the masses of the American people after the people's front government had served its historic function. In either event the working class and its allies, with the potential power to do so, would carry through their democratic program, curbing all violent and illegal efforts of monopolist reaction to defeat it and to set up a fascist state.

With the establishment of a Socialist government on the basis of a people's democracy, the American people would logically and necessarily proceed to re-organize and democratize the state. They would make such constitutional changes as the majority would decide. They would learn from Marx and from their own experience that the workers cannot simply take over the bourgeois state machinery and use it to build socialism. Within the framework of the people's democracy, the American people would gradually construct a higher type of democracy and democratic state, in order to build a socialized economy and to make the people the real rulers of the land. With the workers in power, the path from socialism to the higher stage of communism would be one of gradual and peaceful evolution.

This, very briefly, is "the American road to socialism," on the basis of our country's conditions and of the socialist experience of the workers of the world. But this tentative outline is by no means a blueprint. When the American working class actually starts out to establish socialism, as an imperative necessity under the deepening crisis of capitalism, it will adopt the best, shortest, most fitting routes and forms for the American people. What stands out clearly in this analysis, however, is that, in its perspective for ultimate socialism in the United States, the Communist Party, as the Supreme Court, with a rare exhibition of objectivity, clearly stated in the Schneiderman case of 1942, always strives for a peaceful and democratic course to socialism, supported at all times by a huge majority of the American people. The great toiling masses of our country, as of all others, are fundamentally the builders and defenders of peace and democracy, and this elementary course they will strive to follow in their eventual advance to socialism.

Communist Parties in other industrial countries, facing conditions basically similar to those in the United States, generally have a comparable conception of the manner of democratically establishing socialism. Thus, the Communist Party of Great Britain, in its program entitled *The British Road to Socialism*, calls for the election of "a People's Parliament and Government which draws its strength from a united movement of the people, with the working class as its core." On the question of eventual capitalist violence, the program states that "The great broad popular alliance, led by the working class, firmly based on the factories, which has democratically placed the People's Government in power, will have the strength to deal with the attacks of the capitalist warmongers and their agents."

LESSONS OF COMMUNIST WORLD EXPERIENCE

In a capitalist world which is sinking deeper into general crisis, and in which the capitalists, as a matter of course, turn toward world war and fascist civil war in their desperate efforts to solve their insoluble problems, the great defenders of national and international peace and democracy, and the forces that make for the defeat of capitalist violence, are the workers and their allies, led by the Communist Party. The fundamentally peaceful and democratic policy of the Communists is now being dramatically expressed by their present fight all over the world to prevent the re-birth of fascism and the outbreak of a third world war.

This general policy of curbing capitalist national and international violence was well illustrated by the worldwide struggle of the Communists to defeat fascism and prevent war in the 1930's. During these years the big monopoly capitalists in many countries, under the pressure of the general crisis of capitalism and of their own ruthless imperialist drive for power, were pushing relentlessly towards the fierce violence of fascism and war. To combat these twin dangers, the Communists fought for the building of broad people's front governments in the respective countries, in order to strengthen democracy and to avert fascist civil war; and on the international scale the Communists worked tirelessly for the creation of a great world front of all the democratic powers, in order to restrain the fascist Axis aggressor states and to avert a world war.

This Communist course constituted basically a policy of striving to prevent both civil and international war, of holding intact and strengthening the democratic institutions in the respective capitalist countries, of compelling the wolf-like capitalist states to live together without devouring one another, and of assuring the peaceful co-existence of socialism and capitalism in the world. They were the basic democratic tasks of the time, in the workers' historic march towards socialism.

In those years the Communists and their allies were able to prevent civil war and fascism in many countries, and if they were unable to avert World War II, this was primarily because Social-Democratic treachery disunited and weakened the workers' forces of peace and democracy. But at the present time, vastly increased in strength over that period of the 1930's, the workers and other democratic masses, in harmony with basic Communist policy, are in a much better position to push forward with their program of social progress and at the same time to prevent monopoly capital, which grows more desperate with the breaking down of the capitalist system and from the enormous worldwide strengthening of the democratic forces, from plunging the various individual capitalist countries into fascist civil war and from catapulting the world into a devastating atomic war.

The history of the various proletarian and people's revolutions since World War I also proves conclusively that the Communists in other countries, as well as in the United States, seek to accomplish by the most peaceful means possible the inevitable transition of society from capitalism to the higher stage of socialism. Thus, during the great Russian Revolution of 1917, Lenin called for the winning of the leadership in the Soviets, which were not yet led by the Bolsheviks, by a patient, systematic, and persistent explanation. On this matter Stalin said: "This meant that Lenin was not calling for a revolt against the Provisional Government, which at that moment enjoyed the confidence of the Soviets, that he was not demanding its overthrow, but that he wanted, by means of explanatory and recruiting work, to win a majority of the Soviets . . . to alter the composition and policy of the Government. This was a line envisaging a peaceful development of the revolution in Russia."[1] But Kerensky, like so many other capitalist agents, believed he could stamp out the Revolution by violence. The world knows the results of his folly. Lenin was the greatest of all champions of peace and democracy.

The establishment of the People's Democracies of Eastern Europe—in Poland, Czechoslovakia, Romania, Bulgaria, Hungary, and Albania—demonstrated the basic Communist policy for a peaceful advance toward socialism. The puppet Hitler governments in these countries were overthrown in the war by the Red Army and these peoples. On the conclusion of peace, democratic governments based on coalitions of all the anti-fascist parties, including petty bourgeois, peasant, socialist, and other parties, were duly and constitutionally elected. These democratic elements put down such violence as the reactionaries were able to organize. By a democratic and peaceful process, these regimes became the People's Democracies, which then, with their peoples' national democratic mandate and with the Communist Parties in the lead, proceeded on their advance toward socialism.

In China, too, the responsibility for the civil war in the great people's liberation revolution, rests squarely upon the shoulders of the reactionary Chiang Kai-shek and the gang of foreign imperialists behind him. During the early 1920's, the Communists, seeking the peaceful and democratic development of China, made a united front with Chiang's Kuomintang Party; but Chiang in 1927, after he had gained political

[1] *History of the Communist Party of the Soviet Union*, p. 186.

power, violently disrupted this united front and tried in vain to drown the Communist Party in blood. Again, during World War II, the Chinese Communists, led by the brilliant Mao Tse-tung, developed a national united front with Chiang to fight the Japanese. This broad coalition the Communists persistently tried to extend over into the post-war period. But Chiang, in obedience to Wall Street, deliberately broke up the united front with the Communists and in 1946 he launched the civil war to destroy the Communist Party and to disperse its gigantic mass following. But having rejected the Communist path of peace and chosen that of civil war, Chiang, like Kerensky before him, wound up by having his own regime annihilated. Others who may try to block by violence the people's democratic advance to socialism will not fare any better than did Kerensky or Chiang Kai-shek.

The attempt of the Truman government to destroy the Communist Party, on the pretext that it advocates the forceful overthrow of the United States Government, is a lie and a political frame-up. There is no basis for such an accusation—in Marxist-Leninist theory, in the program and activities of the C.P.U.S.A., or in the world experience of the Communist movement. It is an irony of history that the Communists, who throughout the world are the great defenders of peace and democracy, should be condemned in the United States for advocating force and violence, and this by a capitalist class which helped bring about two world wars and is now trying to organize a third mass slaughter. The political purpose of the government's red-baiting attack upon the Communist Party is to cripple this valiant leader of the democratic masses and thereby to demoralize the people and to break down their opposition to Wall Street's ill-omened drive toward fascism and war.

38. The Party of the Working Class and the Nation

Standing out clearly in the history of the Communist Party of the United States is the basic fact that the Party, throughout its entire existence, has been the most devoted and resolute figher for the interests of the working class and of the whole American people. On every field of the class struggle it has proved itself in this respect by its active initiative, its political integrity, and its fighting qualities. Despite many errors in practice, it has worthily carried on the best traditions of the Marxists in the organizations which preceded the Communist Party—the Socialist Party, the Socialist Labor Party, the International Workingmen's Association, and the Communist Club—as well as the traditional class struggle spirit of the American trade union movement. The history of the Communist Party makes ridiculous the charges of redbaiters that it is "the agent of a foreign power," and that it "exploits for selfish purposes the grievances of the workers." The life of the C.P.U.S.A. is a living demonstration of the truth of the statement, made by Marx and Engels in *The Communist Manifesto,* that the Communists "have no interests separate and apart from those of the proletariat as a whole." To satisfy the needs of the working class and of the nation has always constituted the basic program of the Communist Party.

THE COMMUNIST PARTY AS WORKING CLASS LEADER

As the vanguard of the proletariat, the Communist Party has played a leading role in the building and functioning of the trade union movement, ever since it became an active factor in the American class struggle. Every struggle of the workers for higher wages, shorter hours, or improved working conditions has found the Communists in the front battle line. The employers and the government understand this fact very well and they have made innumerable Communist pickets and strike leaders pay dearly in jail terms, injuries, and death for their militancy. None are more effective strikers than the Communists.

In the organization of the unorganized, which was for many years the greatest immediate problem of the workers in this country, the Communists, more than any other group, were pioneer leaders and tireless workers. They fought for industrial unionism and against the treacheries and stupidities of craft unionism; they introduced new strike strategy and tactics into the workers' struggles, as against the asinine methods used by the old-line conservative trade union leaders. The Party, therefore, can well claim a large share of the credit for the building of the C.I.O. and the organization of the basic industries.

To develop working class independent political action, to liberate the workers from the employers' political domination through their two-party system, and to build an alliance between them and their natural political allies, has always been a central endeavor of the Communists. Neither a labor party, nor a farmer-labor party, nor a democratic coalition has yet been realized in strength, but this will take place in due time. The Party has always fought also for working class leadership in the political movements of the masses.

The Communists also have always been indefatigable workers for trade union unity. They were militant opponents of left dual unionism when this was a real problem; they have fought against the C.I.O.-A.F. of L. split, and they have ever since striven to achieve united action and organic unity between these two national centers. In the international sphere, the Communists have been no less ardent supporters of unity and opponents of Gompersite American trade union isolationism and disruption. They have ever sought to link up the labor movement of the United States with that of other countries. In late years this has meant active backing of such organizations as the Latin American Confederation of Labor and the World Federation of Trade Unions.

Trade union democracy is another issue which has always had strong Communist support. The Communists have steadily fought against excessive initiation fees, against overpaid officials, and especially against gangster and dictatorial reactionary control of the unions. They struggled courageously during the 1920's against the entrenched Gompers and Social-Democratic thugs, and later on they were largely responsible for the democracy that prevailed in the C.I.O. during its early years. The left and progressive unions, now independent, possess the highest types of trade union democracy ever achieved by the American working class.

The Communists also led in the workers' fight for social security in all its forms. Their fight for unemployment insurance during the great economic crisis was one of the classic struggles of American labor history. The workers' growing struggle for old age pensions and other forms of state insurance, which is a sure sign of their diminishing faith in the ability of the capitalist system to furnish them a decent living, has the most active Communist backing.

The Communists have especially championed a fighting policy for the working class. They have always been inveterate enemies of the poisonous class collaboration (working class surrender) policies of the Gompers-Green-Murray-Reuther-Dubinsky leadership, whether this was aimed at speeding up the workers, as in the 1920's, or dragging them into fascism and war in the 1950's. The Communists have fought continuously for a strong, unified trade union movement and a labor party, both operating with a fighting policy. They have also sought tirelessly to imbue the workers with a Socialist perspective. In battling for these objectives, the Communists have faced many persecutions, both inside and outside the trade unions. They have pioneered every forward movement to strengthen the working class, without counting the cost to themselves. In all these activities the Party has played a truly vanguard role.

THE COMMUNIST PARTY AND THE NEGRO PEOPLE

In the pre-Civil War days the Marxists, led by Marx and Engels themselves, laid great stress upon the Negro question. During the period of the predominance in the left of the opportunist-led S.L.P. and S.P., from 1876 to 1919, this issue was greatly neglected. With the foundation of the Communist Party and under the influence of the teachings of Lenin and Stalin on the national question, the Negro question was restressed and raised to the highest significance. The C.P. has always considered the defense of the most abused and exploited section of the American people to be a very vital matter. Consequently, for a generation past, the Party has devoted its most determined efforts to strengthening the fight of the Negro people for jobs, union membership, union leadership, and union protection, and against lynching and the whole monstrous system of Jim Crow. Not the least of the Party's work in this general respect has been its fight to abolish the rank discrimination against Negroes in sports, the theater, and literature. The Communist Party has unquestionably been a powerful factor in the political advance made by the Negro people during the past thirty years. It is especially proud of its work in this field.

The Communist Party has contributed a number of new and vital features to the struggle of the Negro people: (a) It has elevated this question to its proper high political status, in the realization that the oppressed Negro people are the greatest of all allies of the workers in the class struggle; (b) It has expressed boundless confidence in the feasibility of mass Negro-white co-operation, finding many forms and issues for bringing this about; (c) It has raised the theoretical level of the Negro question to that of a national question, thereby providing the Negro people with their true perspective as an oppressed nation; (d) It has singled out the insidious danger of white chauvinism in the broad working class and in its own ranks and has fought against it as no other organization has even begun to do; (e) It has considered the Negro question as a key question by which to measure the class integrity and understanding of every individual and organization in the broad labor movement.

The Communist Party, by the same token, is a tireless enemy of every form of anti-Semitism. It was only with the rise of world communism that the struggles against white chauvinism, anti-Semitism, and similar forms of national and racial discrimination became powerful political factors. International Social-Democracy, in its heyday, never even raised these vital issues.

THE COMMUNIST PARTY AND OTHER DEMOCRATIC STRATA

The Communist Party, as the Party of all the oppressed and exploited, has always devoted major attention to the struggle of the women against the load of restrictions and prejudices from which they suffer under capitalism. As we have seen during the course of this history of the Party, the Communists have supported every attack—economic, political, and social—upon the vast network of discrimination against women. One of the very greatest achievements of socialism, as the Soviet Union and the People's Democracies are daily demonstrating, is the creation of a new regime of freedom and opportunity for women. The Communist Party has always had a keen appreciation of the question. During its long struggle over this issue, the Communist Party has built up what is by far the finest corps of women political leaders possessed by any organization in the United States.

Communism, representing the society of the future, naturally makes a powerful appeal to the youth. The C.P.U.S.A., in the spirit of all Communist parties, therefore, has always made the question of the youth a central object of its attention. The Communist level of political activity in behalf of this huge category of the population is immeasurably above that of any other political party, trade union, or youth organization. The greatest achievements of the Communists in this field were made during the big youth movement of the 1930's, the period of the American Youth Congress. It is not claiming too much to state that the Young Communist League was the principal political leader in this historic struggle of the young people, the most significant of its kind that the United States has ever known.

The Communist Party has also paid major attention to the needs of the millions of foreign-born in our country. Reaction, with its never-ending plots to split the working class, is quick to direct its attack against those workers who have not been born in the United States. The harsh weapon of deportation, a splitter of families, has been used ruthlessly against them. The trade unions and the Socialist Party have grossly neglected the rights of the foreign-born, but the Communist Party has ever had this question in the center of its program.

The farmers are a vital segment of American political life and upon many occasions and over many years the poorer sections of them in the various mass organizations—the Grange, Greenback, Populist, Non-Partisan League, and Farmer-Labor Party movements—have shown that they are powerful and dependable allies of the proletariat. Lenin, above all others, demonstrated the enormous political significance of the worker-farmer alliance. But the American Communist Party, while appreciating the great political importance of the farmers as working class allies, nevertheless has not succeeded in establishing a strong base among them. This is one of the gravest weaknesses of the Party. During the 1920's, as we have seen in the chapters covering that period, the Communists were very active, and effectively so, among the farmer movements of the Middle and Far West. But of recent years, as the sparse consideration of the agrarian question in the later pages of this book shows, Communist work in this major field has been negligible, save to a certain extent among the Negro sharecroppers in the South.

THE COMMUNIST PARTY, THE PARTY OF THE NATION

The Communist Party is *the* party of the working class. This it has demonstrated beyond question throughout its entire history. The Party has always been in the vanguard, fighting along with other progressive forces for every measure in the economic, political, and social interests of the workers. The time was, before World War I, when the Socialist Party, despite all the wrong policies of its opportunist leaders, could claim to be the party of the proletariat, but that time has long since passed. The S.P. both here and abroad, as this history makes clear, has identified itself with the interests of capitalism and is going down with that doomed system. The S.L.P. and the Trotskyites, following basically the same opportunist line, are scheduled for the same fate. All over the world, including the United States, the Communist Party is the basic political organization of the toiling masses.

The Communist Party is not only *the* Party of the working class, but also *the* party representing the true interests of the nation. By fighting loyally and intelligently, as it has always done, for the interests of the workers, the Negro people, women, youth, farmers, veterans, and foreign-born, the Communist Party is in actuality defending the best interests of the American people in general—minus, of course, the 10 percent or so of capitalist parasites and their hangers-on. The Socialist Party, like its Trotskyite and S.L.P. auxiliaries, has no right to speak authoritatively in the interest of the American people as a whole because of its subservience to the exploitation and war plans of Wall Street.

In addition to defending the specific interests of the workers and other broad democratic strata who make up the vast bulk of the American nation, the Communist Party always supports vigorously every general measure and cause directly beneficial to the great mass of the people of this country. The Communist Party is to be found on the progressive side of every political struggle. Thus, in the domestic sphere, the Party supports now, and always has supported, every piece of state or federal legislation of a progressive character. It militantly defends the Bill of Rights and American democratic traditions; it is the most resolute enemy of the present fascist-like attacks upon the people's democratic liberties; it opposes the current military domination of the government, the industries, and the schools; it proposes a people's peace coalition against the Wall Street warmongers; it fights against inflation and every attempt of the government, the employers, and their labor leader allies to throw the burden of the war preparations upon the workers and lower middle class; it opposes with concrete measures the present degeneration of American culture that is being fostered by the fascists and war makers. In all these general respects Communist policy is obviously in the interests of the American people as a nation.

In the international sphere, the Communist Party, in opposition to the imperialists, has always stood on the Marxist-Leninist position that the national welfare is best served by a policy of friendly co-operation with other peoples. In this sense, the very cornerstone of Communist policy has always been to establish good working relations between the U.S.A. and the U.S.S.R. This policy is the key to world peace, and certainly it is in the most profound interest of our whole people. The Party opposed the imperialist World War I, supported the democratic World War II, and it fights against the precipitation of an imperialist third world war—policies which were and are in the true interests of our people. Before the recent World War the Party urged a strong policy of collective security to halt and defeat fascism, and now only fools dare to assert that this historic policy was not in the American national interest. The Party, too, strives to make the United Nations into a genuine instrument of peace, which the American people certainly desire, instead of the aggressive war alliance into which Wall Street is trying to make it.

In view of the constant fight for the best interests of the nation by the Communist Party, in both its domestic and foreign policies, charges that it "takes orders from Moscow" come with very bad grace, particularly from capitalist sources which, as a matter of fundamental action, always put their class interests before the welfare of the nation. Today, as always, the true capitalist motto is Vanderbilt's "the public be damned."

SOCIALISM IN THE NATIONAL INTEREST

The eventual establishment of socialism in the United States by the working class and its democratic allies will also be supremely in the interest of the overwhelming majority of the American people. As matters now stand, the country is owned and run primarily in the interest of a group of capitalistic parasites who comprise only a very small segment of the population. The 200 major monopolies now possess 65 percent of all American non-financial corporate wealth, as against 50 percent in 1929.[1] The capitalist propaganda to the effect that the people own the industries is sheer nonsense—about one percent of all stockholders own about 60 percent of all stock, with dividends in proportion.[2] Big capital owns outright the press, radio, television, and motion pictures, as well as all the industries, and its agents occupy the leading posts in the decisive boards of the government, churches, colleges, fraternal and veterans' organizations. They even control the top trade union leadership. The whole vast social organization operates to funnel the products of the workers away from them and into the hands of the minority of drones who own the industries. This is how the latter are enabled to grab for themselves scores of billions of dollars yearly in profits, interest, rent, and in various other schemes for robbing the toilers.

The United States Government is what Karl Marx and Frederick Engels long ago described as "the executive committee of the capitalist class." It is the dictatorship of the bourgeoisie, a tiny minority of the population. President Truman represents Wall Street, not the American people. The key government posts are held or controlled by men such as Dulles, Acheson, Lovett, Harriman, Wiggins, Wilson, Johnston, Symington, Brown—wealthy capitalists and corporation lawyers, who are tied in with big monopoly capital and are loyally serving its interests. The workers, Negroes, poor farmers, women, and youth, who make up the overwhelming mass of the American people, are virtually unrepresented in all the branches of the government—legislative, executive, or ju-

[1] Jefferson School of Social Science, *The Economic Crisis and the Cold War*, p. 40.
[2] U.S. government figures cited in Labor Research Association, *Trends in American Capitalism*, p. 14.

dicial. The pretenses of Truman and others that the present Administration is a "welfare state" devoted to improving the lot of the American people, is just so much demagogic nonsense. The Administration is entirely under the control of big capital, and it has no other purposes than to swell the already fabulous profits of Wall Street and to further big capital's insane fascist-war drive to dominate the world.

Socialism will drastically change this whole situation in the United States. It will put the ownership and control of the industries, the government, the press, and all other vital institutions into the hands of the overwhelming majority of the people, to serve their interest and not the greed of the profit-grabbers. It will rapidly raise the living standards of the toiling masses by reserving to the workers the many billions in interest, rent, and profits now going to the useless owning parasites; by abolishing the activities of millions of people engaged in the numberless quackeries, fakeries, and useless occupations of capitalism; by applying the newest techniques to industry and agriculture; and by doing away with the tremendous losses caused by economic crises, military armaments, and war.

Socialism in the United States will wipe out the monstrous Jim Crow system. The Negro people, for the first time, will enjoy the dignity and happiness of full equality in every sense of the word: economic, political, social. Socialism, too, will put an end forever to the dread insecurity about the morrow which now haunts the lives of the toiling masses in this country. The masses, at last, will have won their way to a situation where they can have perfect confidence that society will always provide them with a secure means for winning a good livelihood for themselves and their families. And old age will be entirely free of the economic anguish which it now holds for the vast bulk of the American people. American socialism will also develop a culture based upon science and the welfare of the people as a whole, in place of the capitalist-inspired drivel, superstition, and intellectual obscurantism of today.

By the establishment of socialism, the American people will put a final end to the war-fascist policies of Wall Street and will truly open up the way to peace, democracy and well-being on an altogether higher level than is possible under capitalism. There can be no higher national interest than all this.[1]

THE PARTY'S IMMEDIATE DEMANDS

The Communist Party fights for a series of immediate demands, based upon the urgent needs of the workers, the Negro people, and the

[1] See A. B. Magil, *Socialism: What's in It for You*, N. Y., 1946, and James S. Allen, *Who Owns America*, N. Y., 1946.

mass of the people. As formulated at the Party's Fifteenth Convention (1950) and in later decisions, the chief among these demands are the following.

To guard against war, the Party demands: a five-power peace conference; the banning of the A-bomb; the end of the Korean war; liquidation of the trade embargo against the U.S.S.R., China, and the European People's Democracies; the seating of People's China in the Security Council of the United Nations and its recognition by the United States; the return of Taiwan (Formosa) to China; the withdrawal of all American armed forces stationed in foreign countries; a U.S. hands-off policy toward the peoples' struggles in Indo-China, Malaya, the Philippines, and in the Middle East, Africa, Latin America, etc.; national independence for Puerto Rico; severance of all diplomatic relations with Franco Spain and the Vatican; the slashing of U.S. military appropriations to the bone; active support of world disarmament; abandonment of the policy of arming western Europe, West Germany, and Japan for an anti-Soviet war; support for the development of the United Nations into a genuine peace body instead of a U.S.-dominated anti-Soviet war alliance.

To develop safeguards against economic crisis and mass unemployment, the Party demands that America's tremendous producing power—now worse than wasted in the frantic production of war munitions—be applied to furthering the welfare of the American people. It therefore fights for radically higher wages and decreased working hours for the workers, price and profit controls, fundamental improvement of the national system of social insurance (unemployment, sickness, accident, maternity, old age, death), real protection against accidents in industry, construction of all necessary public works (slum clearance, flood control, reforestation, soil conservation, road-building, park and playground construction, etc.), extensive federal aid for the public school system, a national housing program which will provide homes for all, abolition of all taxes upon low incomes, protection for the poorer farmers on prices, credits, mortages, and co-operatives, adequate safeguards for women and youth in industry.

To combat the increasing trends towards a police state in the United States, the Party's main demands are as follows: repeal the Taft-Hartley, Smith, McCarran, Voorhis, and Feinberg laws, together with all similar national, state, and local legislation; establish the right of the workers to strike in all industries without government interference; abolish all loyalty tests and other systems of thought control in the government services, schools, arts, and industries; liquidate the House Committee on Un-American Activities, together with the McCarran and Humphrey sub-committees of the Senate and all other witch-hunting bodies; grant full citizenship rights for Indians, Chinese, Japanese, Mexicans, and other persecuted minorities; restore the right of passports and foreign travel; relieve foreign-born citizens of the fear of deportation hung over their heads by reactionary legislation; make warmongering a crime punishable by imprisonment; punish anti-Semitism, white chauvinism, and similar anti-democratic practices; halt the attempt to outlaw and destroy the Communist Party; release the Communists and other political prisoners.

To check and defeat the attacks of the white supremacists upon the Negro people, the Party makes these principal demands: complete economic, political, and social equality for the Negro people; the full right of Negroes to employment, seniority, promotion, and trade union conditions in all industries; the enactment of federal and state F.E.P.C. legislation; the passage of a national anti-lynching bill providing the death penalty for this crime; abolition of the poll tax by a federal law; liquidation of the Ku Klux Klan and all such lynch gangs; repeal of all laws against racial intermarriage; the complete wiping out of all Jim Crow legislation, as well as such discrimination on railroads, in schools, hotels, sports, the theater, the armed forces, etc.; the opening up of the highest offices in government, industry, trade unions, and all other organizations and occupations to Negroes and other persecuted minorities; work toward the right of self-determination for the Negro nation in the Black Belt of the South.

In accordance with the needs of the given situation, the Communist Party fights militantly for the achievement of these demands—in legislative bodies, trade unions, factories, and everywhere else. The Party co-operates actively with all democratic forces supporting these or other progressive measures. The heart of its immediate program is the struggle against the war danger. To this end, it works for the formation of a broad peace coalition of the organizations of the workers, the Negro people, the poorer farmers, intellectuals, and all other democratic strata, constituting the vast majority of the American people.

These major points of Communist immediate policy, outlined above, comprise a sane, practical, and constructive alternative to the present reactionary policies of the employers and the government, which are pushing the country down the chute to war, fascism, mass impoverishment, and national ruin. The Communist program, harmonizing with the best interests of the working class, the Negro people, and the great bulk of our nation, constitutes the road to peace, democracy, and the people's economic well-being.

THE PROGRESS OF THE COMMUNIST PARTY

The Communist Party is the party of socialism. The Communist parties have demonstrated this in practice in various parts of the world. The Socialist parties are parties of capitalism and are doomed with that system. This, too, as we have seen, has been clearly proved in many countries. With the general crisis of world capitalism more completely involving the capitalist system of the United States, the toiling masses—the workers, the Negro people, the farmers, intellectuals, and others—will strengthen enormously their economic and political organizations, and they will build themselves a great anti-monopoly coalition. The political leaders of this mass movement, if it is to fight effectively and eventually to challenge capitalism, must be the Marxist-Leninists, the Communist Party. Stalin was right when he said, on May 6, 1929, "The American Communist Party is one of those very few Communist parties of the world that are entrusted by history with tasks of decisive importance from the point of view of the revolutionary movement."[1]

It is no simple task to build a mass Communist Party in the heartland of world capitalism, the United States. During its lifetime the Communist Party of the United States has had to meet and master many difficult questions of theory and practice. The toughest and most complex of all these problems have been related to the characteristic illusion of "American exceptionalism." According to this stubborn and insidious notion, as we have remarked earlier, American capitalism is progressive in character, and is fundamentally distinct from capitalism in all other countries. This gross misconception, which has persisted for generations, falsely magnifies the secondary, specifically national features of American capitalism into qualities which supposedly make it basically different from capitalism in the rest of the world. It is in this spirit that the defenders of the current American regime proclaim that American capitalism is not imperialist; that it has no ruling class nor class struggle; that it does not exploit the workers; and that, in fact, it is not really capitalism at all. This song is sung with variations by reactionaries, liberals, and Social-Democrats. Never was this typical "American exceptionalism" more virulent and dangerous than it is at the present time. Thus aggressive American imperialism is pictured to the masses here and throughout the world not only as totally exempt from the general crisis of capitalism, but also as an all-powerful and beneficent people's regime altruistically resolved upon saving the world for democracy and peace.[2] In

[1] *The Communist*, June 1930.
[2] A recent flamboyant statement of this demagogy is *U.S.A.: The Permanent Revolution* by the editors of *Fortune*.

its long struggle against the illusion of "American exceptionalism," the Communist Party has rendered one of its greatest services to the working class.

During its generation of struggle, naturally the Communist Party has made many errors, for Marxism-Leninism is not a blueprint that can be mechanically applied, but a guide to action that must be skillfully used. Most of the Party's more serious mistakes, which we have reviewed in passing, have been in the direction of yielding to "American exceptionalism." The consequences of this error have been to overestimate the power of American imperialism and to underestimate its reactionary character. By the same token, it underestimates the power of the working class and its allies. Sometimes this characteristic American deviation has manifested itself in the Party as "left" sectarianism and sometimes as right opportunism. The worst political mistake ever made by the Communist Party—its temporary toleration of Browder's revisionism—was precisely an error of "American exceptionalism." Browder carried this theoretical weakness, which saturates American Social-Democrats as well as bourgeois elements, to the last extreme of accepting American monopoly capital as progressive and democratic.

As we have seen, the traditional weakness of our Party and of preceding Marxist groups has been the stubborn trend toward "left" sectarianism. Historically, this sectarian tendency to use Marxism as a dogma instead of a guide has been largely an immature political reaction against right opportunism in the labor movemnt. It has militated very greatly against the development of sound political policies and the working out of broad united front movements with potential allies: the more conservative workers, the Negro people, the Catholic masses, the farmers, the progressive intellectuals, and others. The basic cure for both the right and left dangers in the Party is to raise the Marxist-Leninist theoretical level of the Party membership and leadership.

The strength of the Party, however, is that in the spirit of the great Lenin it admits its errors and learns from them. No other party does this. In this respect Lenin says: "The attitude a political party adopts toward its own mistakes is one of the most important and surest criteria of the seriousness of the party and of how it *in practice* fulfills its obligations toward its *class* and the toiling *masses*. Frankly admitting a mistake, disclosing the reasons for it, analyzing the conditions which led to it, and carefully discussing the means of correcting it—this is the sign of a serious party; this is the way it performs its duties, this is the way it educates and trains the *class*, and then the *masses*."[1]

Another strength of the Communist Party is that it builds itself out of

---

[1] Lenin, *"Left-Wing" Communism, an Infantile Disorder*, p. 41.

the best fighters of the working class. It ruthlessly cleanses its ranks of the opportunists, cowards, weaklings, confusionists, turncoats, renegades, and stoolpigeons who, from time to time and for their own peculiar purposes, have infested its ranks, as they do those of all working class fighting organizations. In this respect the Communist Party differs fundamentally from the Socialist Party, which is a nesting ground for every kind of anti-working class element. Thus, in the course of its growth, our Party has eliminated the Cannons, Lovestones, Browders, and their like. The ouster of such people has meant not losses to the Party, but gains. The Communist Party of the United States, like the Communist parties of all other countries, has developed and increased in strength by its struggles against such agents of the capitalist class.

After a generation of hard struggle, the Communist Party has laid the foundation for what will eventually be a powerful mass party in the United States. It has created a solid, indestructible core of trained Marxist-Leninists. This is its most vital achievement of all. The Party, it is true, is still relatively small, but like all other Communist parties it has the capacity for swift growth when the political situation demands it. Today in many countries—in the Soviet Union, China, Czechoslovakia, Poland, and elsewhere—Communist parties stand at the head of their peoples; and in other countries like Italy and France, they are the biggest of all political parties. But the time was when these parties, too, were all very small, condemned, persecuted, and faced what superficially seemed like an invincible opposition. The Communist Party of the United States works and grows in the spirit of these Communist parties. It knows that, living up to the principles of Marxism-Leninism, it will one day lead the American working class and the nation, even as it is now the best representative of their interests. Nor can all the powers of arrogant capitalist reaction balk the C.P.U.S.A. from fulfilling this historic role.

Appendix

CONVENTIONS OF THE COMMUNIST PARTY OF THE U.S.A.

This list gives the date, the place, and—in parenthesis—the number of each convention. However, the regular conventions of the Party were numbered only after the formation of the Workers Party in December 1921, although certain exceptions were made later for special conventions.

Communist Labor Party of America—August 31, 1919, Chicago
Communist Party of America—September 1, 1919, Chicago
United Communist Party of America—May 15, 1920, Bridgman, Mich.
Communist Party of America—July 1920, New York
United Communist Party of America—January 1921, Kingston, N. Y.
Communist Party of America—February 1921, Brooklyn, N. Y.
Communist Party of America (unified)—May 15, 1921, Woodstock, N. Y.
American Labor Alliance—July 1921, New York
Workers Party of America—December 24, 1921, New York (First)
Communist Party of America—August 17, 1922, Bridgman, Mich.
Workers Party of America—December 24, 1922, New York (Second)
Communist Party-Workers Party (merger)—April 7, 1923, New York
Workers Party of America—December 30, 1923, Chicago (Third)
Workers Party of America—July 10, 1924, Chicago (Nominating)
Workers (Communist) Party of America—August 21, 1925, Chicago (Fourth)
Workers (Communist) Party of America—August 31, 1927, New York (Fifth)
Workers (Communist) Party of America—May 25, 1928, New York (Nominating)
Workers (Communist) Party of America—March 1, 1929, New York (Sixth)
Communist Party of the U.S.A.—June 20, 1930, New York (Seventh)
Communist Party of the U.S.A.—May 29, 1932, Chicago (Nominating)
Communist Party of the U.S.A.—April 2, 1934, Cleveland (Eighth)
Communist Party of the U.S.A.—June 24, 1936, New York (Ninth)
Communist Party of the U.S.A.—May 27, 1938, New York (Tenth)
Communist Party of the U.S.A.—May 30, 1940, New York (Eleventh)

Communist Party of the U.S.A.—November 16, 1940, New York (Special)
Communist Political Association—May 20, 1944, New York (Twelfth)
Communist Party of the U.S.A.—July 26, 1945, New York (Thirteenth)
Communist Party of the U.S.A.—August 2, 1948, New York (Fourteenth)
Communist Party of the U.S.A.—December 28, 1950, New York (Fifteenth)

CONGRESSES OF THE COMMUNIST INTERNATIONAL

First Congress, March 2-6, 1919
Second Congress, July 17-August 7, 1920
Third Congress, June 22-July 12, 1921
Fourth Congress, November 5-December 5, 1922
Fifth Congress, June 17-July 8, 1924
Sixth Congress, July 17-September 1, 1928
Seventh Congress, July 25-August 21, 1935

The Communist International was dissolved on June 10, 1943.

INDEX

Abolitionists, anti-labor tendencies of, 38; and Brown, John, 37; and Douglass, Frederick, 37; and early Marxists, 39; as fighters against slavery, 35; and Garrison, William Lloyd, 37; and Negro slave revolts, 37; and Truth, Sojourner, 38; and Tubman, Harriet, 38; and Underground Railroad, 522
"Aesopian language," 513
Africa, 227, 395, 442, 451, 457; liberation movement in, 531; new states in, 532
African Blood Brotherhood, 268
Agrarian question, and American Revolution, 16; and Black Belt, 267, 291, 478, 555; Communist Party on, 267, 291; and free land, 543; in Latin America, 360-62; Left Wing Manifesto on, 168; and Marx on Kriege, 28; and monoculture, 361; in U.S., 29. *See also* Farmers
Agriculture, and cotton, plowing under of, 280; and free land, 23; international crisis of, 276, 278; Lenin on, in U.S., 18; and public lands in U.S., 17; U.S. (1900), 91. *See also* Agrarian Question
Alien and Sedition Laws, 510, 519
All-American Anti-Imperialist League (1924), 365
Allen, James S., 320; editor of *Southern Worker*, 286; on Negro nation, 267
Altgeld, John, 67. *See also* Haymarket Case
Amalgamated Clothing Workers of America, 240, 254-55
Amalgamation of trade unions, 207-08; and Chicago Federation of Labor, 205-06; and T.U.E.L., 203; and Workers Party, 205
American Alliance for Labor and Democracy (1917), 133
American Artists Congress, 320
American Committee for Protection of Foreign Born, 421

American Cultural and Scientific Conference for World Peace, 475
Americans for Democratic Action, 393
"American exceptionalism," 28, 34, 533, 541, 568; attack upon (1923-29), 247; and Browder, 425-28; and economic crisis of 1929, 275; forms of, 542; and Kriege, 28, 34; and Lovestone, 270-74. *See also* Opportunism; Revisionism
American Farm Bureau Federation, 386
American Federation of Labor, and American Alliance for Labor and Democracy, 133; anti-Negro policies of, 70, 229; and "boring from within," 82; and British Trades Union Congress constitution, 70; class collaboration policies of, 238-40, 242-46; and Communists, 521; and Conference for Progressive Political Action 218; conventions of, (1923) 208, (1935) 306; corruption in, 92-93, 243-44; and craft organization, 70, 72; and decentralization, 72; degeneration of labor bureaucracy in, 243-45; and economic crisis of 1929, 280; expulsion of militants in (1923-29), 248; on F.E.P.C., 414; and general strike of 1886, 72; growth of, after World War II, 446; and "the higher strategy of labor," 242-43; and industrial unionization drive, 342; on intervention in Mexican Revolution, 110; and Knights of Labor, 71-72; and labor aristocracy, 70, 73, 99; and labor banking, 243; labor bureaucracy, split in, 305; and Latin American Confederation of Labor, 495-96; leaders, and development of imperialism, 73; leaders, rewards of, 486; and limited industrial charters, 306; on Marshall Plan, 489; misleaders of labor in, 201-02; Negro question, resolution on (1893), 85; and no-strike pledge, 410; predecessors of, 57; program of, during forma-

576 INDEX

tive years, 70-71; and Progressive Party, 471; and Purcell, A. A., 259; and San Francisco general strike, 302; and "Sanial case," 83; on second front, 412; and skilled workers, 73; and Socialist Party, 92, 98-99, 113, 248-49; and socialist perspective, 73; on speed-up, 239; splitting unions in Europe, 496; and strikes, (pre-World War I) 109, (1915-16) 130; on Taft-Hartley Act, 488-89; and "trade union capitalism," 243, 246; T.U.U.L. merges with, 303-04; on war (1939), 386; and white chauvinism, 73; and World Federation of Trade Unions, 447
A. F. of L. Committee for Unemployment Insurance and Relief, 283
America First Committee, 393-94
American Labor Alliance (1921), 187-90. *See also* Communist Party of the U.S.
American Labor Alliance for Trade Relations with Russia (1919), 207
American Labor Party, 332
American Labor Union (1857), 31
American League for Peace and Democracy, 379, 420
American League Against War and Fascism, 379
American Liberty League, 327-28
American Negro Labor Congress (1925), 268
American Peace Crusade, 475
American People's Congress for Peace, 475-76
American Railway Union, 103, 154; dissolved, 94; strike of, 78
American Revolution, 522; and abolition of slavery, 17; leadership of, 16; Lenin on, 16; and national market, 16
American Scottsboro Committee, 287
American Student Union, 311
American Women for Peace, 475
American Workers League, and Weydemeyer, 40
American Writers Congress, 319
American Youth Congress, 563; dissolved, 420; on fascism, 378; and Roosevelt Administration, 310
Amter, Israel, 282, 518
Anarcho-syndicalism, and Goldman-Berkman group, 117; influence of, in U.S., 66-67
Ancient Society by Lewis Henry Morgan, 64
Anderson, Mary, 312

Anglo-Russian Committee, 259
Anti-Imperialist League (1898), 96
Anti-Semitism, 449, 480, 563
Aptheker, Herbert, 320, 449
Arab states, 480-81, 532, 544
Arbeiterbund, 41
Aristocracy of labor. *See* Labor Aristocracy
Aronberg, Phil, 255
Asia, 395, 451, 457, 473; revolutionary struggles in, 532. *See also* China
Association of Catholic Trade Unionists, 493
Atlantic Charter, 400
Atom bomb, 528; and Baruch Plan, 459; and war, 451
Atomic energy, and socialism, 539

Bakunin, Michael, 60
Ballam, John, 165, 250
Baltimore and Ohio plan, 200, 239
Baron, Rose, 184, 209
Baruch Plan, 459. *See also* Atom Bomb
Basle Conference (1912), 128
Batt, Dennis E., 164
Battle for production, during World War II, 410-11
Bayles, J. C., 197
Bebel, August, 106
Bellamy, Edward Lawrence, and *Looking Backward*, 75
Berger, Victor L., and Debs, 94; and revisionism, 106; as Socialist congressman, 113; white chauvinism of, 104
Bernstein, Eduard, 106. *See also* Revisionism; Social-Democracy
Berry, Abner W., 514
Berry, George L., 244
Bill of Rights, 17, 512, 518, 551, 565
Billings, Warren K., 131, 380
Biscay, Joseph S., 121-22
Bittelman, Alexander, 180, 221-23, 518; on Hillquit leadership, 164; on left wing (1918-19), 156
Black Belt, 267, 291, 478, 555. *See also* Negro People
"Black International," 60
"Black Republicanism," 42
Bloor, Ella Reeve ("Mother"), 125, 184, 312-13, 410
Boas, Franz, 320
Bohn, Frank, 125

Bouck, William, 218
Bourgeois-democratic revolutions, 550; and Civil War in U.S., 45, 52; in Mexico, 363; and socialism, 149
Bourgeois nationalism, 323, 432, 478, 479; Dimitrov on, 324; and Garvey, 228. *See also* National and Colonial Question
Bovay, Alvin E., 40
Boyce, William, 257
Bridges, Harry, and C.I.O., 353; and longshoremen's union, 301-03, 488; and San Francisco general strike, 301-02; Supreme Court on case of, 517
Briggs, Cyril, 183, 268
Briggs, Sam, 31
Brisbane, Albert, 23
British Trades Union Congress constitution, 70
Brodsky, Joseph, 286
Brook Farm, 23
Brophy, John, 256, 259
Browder, Earl, and American democratic traditions, 337-39; and "American exceptionalism," 425, 569; on "centralized war economy," 417; on Chinese Revolution, 419-20; and democratic centralism, 428; on "democratic front," 382; on dissolution of Communist Party, 424-25, 430-31; on doubling wages, 426; and Duclos article, 434-35; on elections of 1944, 433; expulsion of, 437; on "good neighbor policy," 367; imprisoned, 392; and "incentive wage," 411; and "intelligent capitalists," 422-23, 426; on labor party ticket (1936), 336; on Negro question, 432; opportunism of, 425-26; opportunism of, on national unity, 415-17, 424; opportunism of, on trade union question, 348; origin of revisionism of, 427-28; as presidential candidate, 333, 391; and "progressive capitalism," 339; on real wages, 423; on Roosevelt, 426; on second front, 413; and seventh Communist Party Convention, 292; Teheran thesis of, 339, 422-23, 426, 428; and slogan, "Communism Is Twentieth Century Americanism," 337-38; on two-party system, 416, 424; and work in the South, 424
Brown, Irving, 496
Brown, J. G., 204
Brown, John, 37, 39
Bruce, Blanche K., 51
Bryan, William Jennings, 86, 91, 96

Buck, Tim, 204, 206
Budenz, Louis F., 466, 513
Bukharin, Nikolai, 272, 418
Butler, Smedley D., 376

Cabet, Etienne, 23
Cacchione, Peter V., 289, 421
Cadden, Joseph, 311
Cameron, A. C., 52
Canada, 70, 172, 204, 206, 212, 354, 357
Cannon, James P., 269
Capitalism, and atomic energy, 539; contradictions of, 548; contrasted with socialism, 451, 530; general crisis of, 530-32; and revolution, 550; socialism as an answer to, 537-40; transition from, to socialism, 80, 549-50; and war, 526-29. *See also* Capitalism, U.S.
Capitalism, U.S., and monopolists' need of war, 455; effects of slavery upon, 45; hegemony of, 452-53; weakness of, 549. *See also* Capitalism
Capitalist accumulation, Marx on, 547
Carey, James B., and delegation to Soviet Union, 498; and splitting of European unions, 496; and U.E. convention of 1940, 354; on unity with fascists, 493
Carnegie, Andrew, 96
Carreathers, Ben, 349-50, 519
Carter, R. A., 309
Catholic hierarchy, 463
Centrists, 106, 148; and Hillquit, 135; in Socialist Party, 120, 158
Chambers, Whittaker, 466
Chiang Kai-shek, 470; and civil war in China, 558-59; subsidized by U.S., 444; and Wall Street, 465; in World War II, 404
Chicago Federation of Labor, and Chicago militants, 138; and union organizing during World War I, 138-40
China, 265, 273, 291, 374, 376, 384, 426, 470, 473, 538; and Korea, 461; as leader of colonial liberation movement, 442; letters of leaders of, to Communist Party of U.S., 419; "open door" policy in, 237; People's Army of, fights Japan, 403, 404; as a People's Democracy, 443; revolution in, 442-44; and Soviet Union, 443-44; struggle of, against imperialism, 443
"Chinese exclusion" debate in Socialist Party, 116

Christensen, Parley Parker, 214
Chu Teh, on Lenin and Stalin, 444
Churchill, Winston, and African-Italian campaign, 402; and Labor Government, 442; and Nazi attack on Soviet Union, 400; U.S. reliance on, 464
Cincinnati Social Workingmen's Association, 39
Civil Rights Congress, 475, 477; defense activities, 509; and genocide petition, 476
Civil War, a bourgeois-democratic revolution, 45; and class tensions, 37; Communists in, 47; and Davis, Jefferson, 43; and eight-hour-day movement, 71; and Lee's surrender, 45; and Lincoln, 44; Marx on, 48-49; and McClellan, 44; and Negroes in Northern army, 44; and Negro revolts, 37; and secession, 43; and slavery, 45
"Class Against Class," 257, 266
Class collaboration, 100, 109, 208, 242, 252-53, 258; and Browder, 424, 436; and Communist Party, 562; during Coolidge period, 245-46; and Gompers, 93; from 1900 to World War I, 93; and U.A.W.-C.I.O., 501. See also Opportunism
Class consciousness, 46, 99, 541, 549; in 1850's, 33-34; factors making for, in U.S., 544; factors retarding, in U.S., 542-44; and free land, 33. See also Working Class
Class struggle, 260, 271; and A.F. of L. constitution, 70; after Civil War, 71; and early Socialist Party, 169; Lenin on, 149; and Murray, Philip, 485-86; pre-Marxist theories of, 24-25; in U.S., 541; Workingmen's Political Association on, 22. See also Class Consciousness
Classes, 18; pre-Civil War conflicts of, 36; and socialism, 538-39. See also Negro Working Class; Working Class
"Clear and present danger" doctrine, 512, 517-18
Cluss, Adolph, 31
Codovilla, Victorio, 364
Coexistence of capitalism and socialism, 440, 469-70; Browder on, 422; Stalin on, 524-25
Collective security, 369, 378
Colonial question, and capitalist decay, 530; Lenin on, 266; and new states in Asia and Africa, 532. See also National and Colonial Question
Committee of Forty-Eight (1918), 213-14

Committee for the Third International, 188-89
Communism, 538
Communist Club of New York, and International Workingmen's Association, 50; as national leader, 32
Communist Information Bureau, 470
Communist International, dissolved, 414; and factional fight in U.S. Communist Party, 223; and labor party slogan, 223; and imperialist war, 130; letter of, to I.W.W., 182; on international situation after World War I, 265; organization of, 159; role of, 178-80, 415; Seventh Congress of, and call for people's front, 321, 323; Seventh Congress of, on nations, 323-24; Seventh Congress of, and Roosevelt coalition, 320, 323; Sixth Congress of, 265-66; and "21 points," 179
Communist Labor Party, 171-74. See also Communist Party of the U.S.
Communist Manifesto, The, on bourgeois rule, 566; on dictatorship of proletariat, 79; as guide to early American Marxists, 30; as guide to early trade unions, 35; on immediate demands, 321; on relation of Communists to working class, 560; teachings of, 26, 30; on united front with bourgeoisie, 41
Communist movement, expansion of, after World War II, 449-51
Communist Party of Canada, 357
Communist Party of China, 176, 522
Communist Party of Czechoslovakia, 450
Communist Party of France, 337, 450, 522
Communist Party of Italy, 450
Communist Party of Poland, 450, 522
Communist Party of the Soviet Union, and Lenin, 151; as party of nation, 323
Communist Party of the United States, Address to, from C.I., 274; agrarian program of, 267, 287, 291, 554; on American bourgeois culture, 318; and "American exceptionalism," 568-69; on A.F. of L.-C.I.O. leaders, 486; on A.F. of L.-C.I.O. split, 307; and American Youth Congress, 311-12; on anti-Semitism, 563; anti-war activities of, 474-76; arrest of leaders of, 518-19; and attacks on Negro people, 477; and Axis aggression, 409; and Browder, 421, 424-25, 437, 484; and China, 387, 419, 444, 474; and class struggle, 16; cleansings of, 569-70; on collective security, 565; on Communist

INDEX 579

Information Bureau, 471; and Comintern, 178-80, 273-75, 415; and Communist Party of Canada, 357; concentration policy of, 262-63; and conference of six American Communist parties (1939), 366; and C.I.O., 345-49; on Constitution of U.S., 551; conventions of, 171-74, 177-78, 186-87, 194-95, 212-13, 215, 223, 261, 292, 307, 333, 380-81, 391-93, 430, 435-37, 469; on crises, 456; and cultural upsurge, 449; on defense of nation, 323; and democratic centralism, 428; on "democratic front," 382; and democratic traditions, 17, 336-39; and Duclos article, 435; and elections, (1924) 219, (1928) 263, (1932) 291-92, (1936) 333, (1938) 379-80, (1940) 391, (1944) 433, (1948) 471-73; and expulsion of Trotskyites, 269-70; Extraordinary Conference of, 298; fight of, for open existence, 523; forerunners of, 27; formation of 170, 172; growth of (1933-36), 307; and industrial unionism, 305, 561; on Keynesism, 483-84; and Korea, 473; and Landon, 336; and Latin America, 365-67; as leader of unemployed, 281-82; letters from Chinese leaders to, 419; in local elections, 472-73; main tasks of, in postwar period, 484; on Marshall Plan, 489; Marxist-Leninist development of, 381, 427; as mass party, 570; and McCarran Act, 520; membership, 171, 292, 307, 380, 393, 421, 437, 469; and *"Messenger* group," 232; and Mexican-Americans, 480; on N.I.R.A., 298; and national Negro conference on steel, 350; on national unity, 415, 427; on Nazi invasion of Soviet Union, 408; Negro leaders in, 479; Negro members of, 269, 479; on Negro nation, 478; and Negro people, 562-63; on Negro question, 232-35, 266-67, 477-78; and Negro-white co-operation, 232-35, 562; and New Deal, 294, 330 334-35; and New York City elections 421, 473; on North Atlantic Alliance, 470; on no-strike pledge, 411; and organization of auto workers, 351-53; and "outstretched hand" policy, 381; on Palestine, 481; on "panacea" movements, 316-17; as party of the nation, 564-65; as party of a new type, 260-63; as party of socialism, 568; as party of the working class, 564; and peace, 440, 515; and peaceful transition to socialism, 551-52; on Pearl Harbor, 409; and People's Front government, 554-55; persecution of, 391-92, 506-09; and pioneer Communist women, 184; reconstitution of, 435; on right of self-determination, 266-67, 478; and Roosevelt, 330, 333-36; on Roosevelt cabinet, 416; and Scottsboro case, 286-87; on second front, 401, 412; and shop papers, 349; and slogan, "For an Independent Federation of Labor," 303-04; social composition of, 427; and Social-Democracy, 552; and Socialist goal, 537, 552-53; and Socialist Party, 124, 157, 188, 212, 214, 252, 333, 335, 378; and South, 285-88; and Spanish Republic, 371-73; in steel organizing campaign, 349-51; on Taft-Hartley law, 488-89; and trade union unity, 304, 335, 561; and Truman, 436-37; "underground" period of, 195; unification of, 180-82, 274-75; and U.S. aggression, 469; on U.S.A.-U.S.S.R. relations, 469, 565; as vanguard party, 15, 308, 335, 340, 484, 550, 552, 560-62; on violence, 551-52, 557; and war, 529; warning of, on new Munich, 408; and women in health movement, 313; work among unemployed, 299-300; work among women and youth, 263-64; and World War II, 387-88, 409-10; and Yokinen trial, 288. *See also*, American Labor Alliance, Communist Labor Party, Communist Political Association, Left Wing (of Socialist Party), United Communist Party, Workers (Communist) Party, Workers Party

Communist Party, Trial of Eleven Leaders, and book burning, 512; charge by Federal Grand Jury before, 509; conviction of defendants in, 516-18; defense lawyers at, 510; defense of principles at, 514-16; indictment preceding, 509-10; role of Judge Medina in, 511

Communist Political Association, and Browder, 433-34; and elections of 1944, 433; and Duclos article, 434-35; emergency convention of, 435-37; organization of, 431; preamble to constitution of, 431, 436. *See also* Communist Party of the U.S.

Communists, aims of, in 1850's, 32; arrests of, 466; and C.I.O., 345-49; employers' attempt to isolate, 491; and European coalition governments, 441; expulsion of, from unions (1923-29), 248; fight against

wage cuts, 284-85; and international labor unity, 259; and Latin-American liberation struggles, 364; and peaceful transition to socialism, 558; struggle of, against fascism, 557
Company unions, 197, 329
Confederate States of America, 43
Conference for Progressive Political Action (C.P.P.A.), 218-21; organizations represented in, 214; presidential nominees (1924), 218; program of, 249. *See also* LaFollette Movement
Congress of American Women, 448
Congress of Industrial Organizations (C.I.O.), building of, 340-55; and Communists, 345-49; convention of 1947, 490; decline in membership of, 501; expulsion of progressive unions from, 494; on F.E.P.C., 414; formation of, 304-07; growth of, after World War II, 446; labor delegation to Soviet Union, 498; and Latin American Confederation of Labor, 495-96; left-center coalition in, 420, 491; on Marshall Plan, 490; and national conference of Negro organizations, 350; and National Negro Congress, 309; and Negro organizers, 349; and no-strike pledge, 410; political degeneration of, 501; and Progressive Party, 471; and reorganization of N. Y. C. Industrial Union Council, 492; rewards of leaders of, 486; on second front, 412; and South, 502; split in, 491-94; and splitting of European unions, 496; on Taft-Hartley law, 488-89; and U.E., 493; and World Federation of Trade Unions, 447, 498-99; on World War II, 388
Constitution of the U.S., and Bill of Rights, 17; as compromise, 36; and Fourteenth Amendment, 51; on Negro slavery, 36; as originally formulated, 17; and Thirteenth Amendment, 51
Contradictions of capitalism, and general crisis, 128, 530; and theories of "organized capitalism," 417-18; U.S. overcoming of, 241. *See also* Capitalism; Capitalism, U.S.; General Crisis
Coolidge "prosperity" period, Ford versus Marx during, 240-42; speed-up during, 237-38; worsening of labor's conditions during, 245-46
Copenhagen Congress (1910), 128
Corruption, in A.F. of L., 343; and cabinet posts to Social-Democrats, 486; of labor aristocracy, 99; of labor bureaucracy, 92, 109, 201, 243-44; in trade unions, 244; in U.S. today, 536-37
Cosmopolitanism, 535
Coughlin, Rev. Charles E., and N.I.R.A., 297; and National Union for Social Justice, 315-16; and Union Party, 331
Coxey, Jacob S., 79
Craft unions, 69, 257; and A.F. of L., 70, 72, 305; Debs's attack on, 118; and Communist Party, 561; and Knights of Labor, 68
Crime, in U.S. today, 537
Crises, economic, 274, 284, 534; of 1819, 19; of 1837, 19; of 1857, 31; in 1880's and 1890's, 77; in 1914, 130; of 1929, 275-76, 547; and capitalism, 456; Communist Party on, 456; and "depression of special kind," 325-26; Marxists on, 27, 34; and "new capitalism," 247; and U.S. recognition of U.S.S.R., 375; Stalin on, 273; and strikes (1920-21), 199; and trade unions (1879), 68. *See also* Capitalism; Capitalism, U.S.
Crisis, general. *See* General Crisis
Crockett, George, 510
Crosswaith, J. H., 249
Cuba, 77, 356, 358, 365
Culture, and "art for art's sake," 319; during Coolidge era, 317; decay of, 535-36; Negro contribution to, in U.S., 320; and reactionary propagandists, 467; upsurge of, in New Deal period, 318-20; after World War II, 448-49
Curran, Joseph, break with left by, 492; and delegation to Soviet Union, 498; and Communists, 353
Cush, Pat, 349
Czolgosz, Leon F., 91

D-Day, 402
Daily Tribune, New York, and Karl Marx, 48
Damon, Anna, 209
Davis, Benjamin J., Jr., in elections, (1943) 421, (1950) 473; and Herndon case, 288; indictment of, 509; on work among Negro people (1945), 434
Davis, Jefferson, 43
Davis, John P., 309
Debs, Eugene V., and American Railway Union strike, 78, 83-84; anti-war stand

INDEX 581

of, 161; arrest of, 141; in campaign of 1904, 101; and craft unions, 118; and dual unionism, 97; and founding of Socialist Party, 94; and left wing, 124; on Russian Revolution, 161, 189; on Spanish-American War, 95, and Social Democracy of America, 94; on T.U.E.L., 204
Declaration of Independence, 16, 21, 467
De Leon, Daniel, and "boring from within," 82; on dual unionism, 80; on farmer-labor movements, 212; on Gompers bureaucracy, 82; on immediate demands, 81; and "left" sectarianism, 79; on "locking out the capitalists," 81, 152; on Negro question, 81, 87; as revisionist, 76, 79; role of, 79-82; on role of Party, 81; on socialism, 81; on Spanish-American War, 95; on strategy and tactics, 81; and syndicalism, 79; on trusts, 81; and *Weekly People*, 76
Democratic centralism, 428
Democratic front. See People's Front
Democratic Party, 86, 91, 382; current policies of, 467; in elections of 1932, 290-91; and slavery, 37; split of (1856), 41. See also Roosevelt, Franklin D.; Truman, Harry S.
Dennis, Eugene, activities of, 508; on elections of 1948, 515; indictment of, 509; on intervention in China, 444; jailed, 484; on People's Front, 554; on post-war perspectives, 433-34
De Priest, Oscar, 309
Dewey, Thomas E., 472
Dictatorship of proletariat, 79, 153, 167, 172, 189, 223, 539; Communist Party on, 553-54; Lenin on, 149; and People's Democracies, 441; and Soviets, 554
Dies Committee. See House Committee on Un-American Activities
Dimitrov, George, on bourgeois nationalism, 324; on democratic traditions, 337; on fascism in U.S., 321, 468; on People's Front, 321; on salvation of nation, 324; on women and fascism, 313-14; on workers' and farmers' party, 321-22
Dolsen, James H., 519
Doran, Dave, 373
Douai, Adolph, 29, 39
Douglass, Frederick, 15; as Abolitionist, 37; on Civil War tactics of North, 44; on Negroes in civil war, 44
Doyle, Bernadette, 473, 518

Dreiser, Theodore, 319
Dual unionism, attacked by Lenin, 154-55; and Debs, 97, 118; and De Leon, 82; and I.W.W., 100; effects of, on left wing, 103; Workers Party on, 192
Dubinsky, David, 275, 346, 495
Du Bois, W. E. B., arrest of, 475; and National Negro Congress, 309; and Niagara movement, 115; trial of, 518
Duclos article, 434-35

Eight-hour day, 64; Marx on, 71; movement for, 71-72; and National Labor Union, 53. See also Haymarket Case
Eighteenth Brumaire of Louis Bonaparte, 30
Eisenhower, Dwight D., 402, 468, 526, 531; and "bonus marchers," 290
Elections, of 1856, 41; of 1860, 41; of 1904, and Socialist Party campaign, 101; of 1936, 330-34; of 1938, 379-80; of 1940, 390-91; of 1944, and Browder, 433; of 1948, 471-73; Cacchione-Davis victories in, 421; and Henry George campaign, 73; and "lesser-evil" theory, 472; of Negroes since Reconstruction, 446
Ellis, Fred, 317
Emancipation Proclamation, 44
Emerson, Ralph Waldo, 22
Emspak, Julius, 354
Encina, Dionisio, 364
End-Poverty-in-California (Epic), 314-15
Engdahl, J. Louis, 287
Engels, Frederick, on labor aristocracy, 543, 548; on military strategy in Civil War, 48; on Morgan, Lewis Henry, 64; on "Sanial case," 83; on S.L.P., 75-76; on tactics, 82-83; on U.S. working class, 34; on utopian socialists, 24; on a workingmen's party, 85. See also Marx, Karl, and Engels, Frederick
England, America's liberation from, 15; and "Battle of Britain," 394; and Civil War in U.S., 49; collapse of colonial system of, 531; decline of, 548; as junior partner of U.S., 454; Labor Government in, after World War II, 442; Marx and Engels on labor aristocracy in, 548; Marx on peaceful transition to socialism in, 551; and negotiated peace, 405; and *Road to Socialism*, 556-57; and sec-

ond front, 402; World War II losses of, 406
Equal Rights Amendment, 313
Ethiopia, 374
Ettor, Joe, 118
Evans, George Henry, 22, 28, 38

Factionalism, in Communist Party, 194, 221-23, 263-64, 273-75
"Fair Deal," 483, 549. *See also* Truman, Harry S.
Fair Employment Practices Commission (F.E.P.C.), 413-14
Farmer-labor alliance, 20, 85
Farmer-labor movements, De Leon on, 212; and National Greenback Labor Party, 65; after World War I, 211. *See also* La Follette Movement; Populist Movement
Farmer-Labor Party, convention of (1923), 215; and "democratic front," 382; in elections of 1920, 214; and Clarence Hathaway, 218; situation favorable for (1936), 332
Farmers, and Communist Party program, 267, 287, 291, 554; De Leon on, 85; and economic crisis of 1929, 288-89; and elections of 1860, 41; and free land, 543; grievances of, in 1890's, 85; Lenin on role of, 153; and Lincoln, 42; and National Relief Conference (1932), 289; and New Deal, 293-94; number in Latin America and U.S., 360; and plantation system, 267; in political life, 564; and program of National Committee of Action (1932), 289; and Republican Party in 1854, 40; revolt of (1929-33), 288-89. *See also* Agrarian Question
Fascism, Dimitrov on women and, 313-14; Dimitrov on development of, in U.S., 321; and German bourgeoisie, 295; and monopoly capital, 295; and People's Front, 555; trend toward, in U.S. today, 465-68; and Wall Street's war drive, 456; world trends toward, 463-65
Fast, Howard, 449, 507
Federal Bureau of Investigation, 194, 507, 519
Federated Farmer-Labor Party, 216-17
Feinberg Law, 467, 521
First International. *See* International Workingmen's Association

Fish Committee, 285
Fitzgerald, Albert J., 354
Fitzpatrick-Nockels group, in Chicago labor movement, 138
Five-Power Peace Pact, 475
Flynn, Elizabeth Gurley, 182, 518; and International Labor Defense, 209; and I.W.W., 125; on National Committee of Communist Party, 410; and Passaic textile strike, 250
Foner, Philip S., 320, 449
Ford, Henry, 241, 361, 393
Ford, James W., and "bonus march," 289; as vice-presidential candidate, (1932) 291, (1936) 333, (1940) 39
"Forgotten man," 291
Fort-Whiteman, Lovett, 268
Foster, William Z., activities of, at time of 1912 Socialist Party split, 124; arrest of (March 6, 1930), 282; and Conference for Progressive Political Action, 214; and I.T.U.E.L., 137; joining Communist Party, 185; kidnaped, 205; on Negro question (1924), 233; opposing Browder, 429-31; and organization of meat-packing industry, 139; on Party dissolution, 429; as presidential candidate, (1924) 219, (1928) 263, (1932) 291; and Seattle Socialist Party split, 121; as secretary of T.U.U.L., 257; and steel organizing campaign, 139-40; and Syndicalist League of North America, 117
Fourier, Charles, 23
Fourteenth Amendment, 51
Fourth International, 270
France, feudal tyranny in, 16; People's Front government in, 370
Franco, Francisco, 371, 463, 560
Fremont, John C., 41
Freudianism, 535
Fugitive Slave Act, 37
Fuller, Margaret, 23

Gabriel, A., 62
Gannes, Harry, 184, 392
Gannett, Betty, 437, 518
Garrison, William Lloyd, 37
Garvey movement, 226, 234; "Back to Africa" slogan of, 227; national content of, 228; and Negro-white co-operation, 234; and Workers Party, 228
Gates, John, 372, 509

General Association of German Workers, 58
General Confederation of Labor (C.G.T.), 370
General crisis of capitalism, 16, 265, 295, 425, 540, 546, 549, 557, 568; causes of, 530; and Russian Revolution, 143; and U.S., 533-35, 541; and U.S. capitalist hegemony, 452-53; and World War I, 128; and World War II, 383, 442. See also Capitalism; Capitalism, U.S.
George, Henry, 73
Gerber, Julius, 162
Ghioldi, Rodolfo, 364
"Gilded Age," 52
Gitlow, Benjamin, 275
Gladstein, Richard, 510
Gold, Ben, 253-54, 354
Gold, discovery of, in California, 26
Gold, Michael, 317
Gomez, Eugenio, 364
Gompers, Samuel, and class collaboration, 93; indictment of, 109; and International Workingmen's Association, 53, 70; leadership discredited, 213; and Marx's Capital, 70; and National Civic Federation, 93; and Pan-American Federation of Labor, 495; and "Sanial case," 83; and steel strike (1919), 140; and World War I, 132-33
Good Neighbor Policy, 360, 364; Browder on, 367; and Roosevelt, 356-57. See also Latin America
Gray, Ralph, 287
Greeley, Horace, 23
Green, Gilbert, and American Youth Congress, 310-11; indictment of, 509; on post-war situation, 434
Green, William, 281, 345; on capitalist system, 485; and needle trades strike (1926), 253; on organization of General Motors, 238-39; on San Francisco General Strike, 302; on Taft-Hartley Law, 488
"Greenbackism," 57, 64-65
Grönlund, Lawrence, 75
Gropper, William, 317
Guffey Act, 329

Hall, Gus, arrest of, in Mexico, 518; elected national secretary of Communist Party, 508; indictment of, 509; on integration of Negro people, 445; in steel campaign (C.I.O.), 349
"Ham and Eggs" movement, 315
Hanford, Ben, 101
Hathaway, Clarence A., 218
Hawthorne, Nathaniel, 23
Hayes, Max S., 90, 113, 210
Haymarket case, 67
Haywood, Harry, 268, 320; and Negro Liberation, 478; on Negro nation, 267
Haywood, William D. ("Big Bill"), 101, 141; attitude of, to A.F. of L., 118; and formation of I.W.W., 100; joining Communist Party, 182; and left wing, 124; and Rocky Mountain states strikes, 78
Health, during Hoover period, 279-80; in Latin America, 362; movement for, 313; of workers in early America, 18
Herndon, Angelo, 288
Hilferding, Rudolph, 241-42
Hill, Joe, 112
Hillman, Sidney, 353; and Communists, 348, 354; on elections of 1936, 332; and launching of C.I.O., 305
Hillquit, Morris, and "neutrality" toward unions, 99; "pink terror" of, 163; and resolution on war at Socialist Party convention (1917), 134-35; and Russian Revolution, 148; and Socialist Party referendum (1919), 162; and Volkszeitung, 89
Hinckley, William, 311
History of the Communist Party of the Soviet Union, 381
Hitler, Adolph, and attack upon Soviet Union, 395, 397; and Dunkirk, 394; and invasion of Poland, 375; and occupation of Austria, 373; on Red Army, 396-97; and Stalingrad defeat, 399; and strategy for world conquest, 385; taking power in Germany, 295, 368
"Hollywood Ten," 507
Homestead Act (1862), 543
Hood, William R., 476
Hoover, Herbert, and "bonus marchers," 290; on "compromise peace," 408; and "Hoovervilles," 279; on lend-lease to Soviet Union, 406; and living standards, 279-80; on Nazi attack on Soviet Union, 401
Hoover, J. Edgar, 175, 507
Hopkins, J. A. H., 213
House Committee on Un-American Activities, 337, 376-77, 380, 503, 507-08

Howat, Alex, 204
Hunger marches, 283-84
Hutcheson, William H., 306, 393

Ideological questions, and confusion of workers after 1857 crisis, 33; and cultural upsurge in New Deal years, 318-20; and divisions among German immigrants, 28; and early labor movement, 21; and early Marxists, 32-34; and First International, 60-61; and free land, 18; and immaturity of working class in U.S., 211-12, 542-44; and Keynesism, 481-82; and LaFollettism, 220; and S.L.P., 75-76; and Socialist Party, 169-70; and white chauvinism, 87. *See also* Marxism; Marxism-Leninism
Immediate demands, 63, 153, 180-81; of Communist Party today, 567-69; and De Leon, 88, 90; and De Leon on Negro question, 87-88; in first American Marxist program, 31; and Left Wing Manifesto (1919), 168; and Lenin, 150; and socialism, 550; and Workers Party, 193
Immigration, 18, 26, 544; shut off, 198; and Lincoln, 42
Imperialism, Browder on, 426; and class struggle, 530; on downgrade in England, 548; De Leon on, 96; and labor bureaucracy, 544; Lenin on, 150; as political framework of U.S. rule, 460; and position of U.S. today, 548; and Spanish-American War, 77; struggle of China against, 443; and U.S. bid for world domination, 16; and U.S. drive toward fascism, 463-65; U.S., and monoculture, 361; and U.S. monopolists' war aims, 454-57; U.S., "New Look" of, 359-60; and U.S. People's Front government, 555; and U.S. stand at founding of United Nations, 433
"Impossibilists," 96, 102
Impoverishment of working class, 58, 106, 534; absolute, 545-46; during Hoover period, 279-80; Marx on, and relation to capitalist accumulation, 547; relative, in U.S., 545
Independent political action, 20-21, 54, 74, 92, 212, 332, 472; and A. F. of L., 73; and Browder, 416, 424; *Communist Manifesto* on, 30; and Workers Party on LaFollette movement, 219-21

Independent unions, expelled from C.I.O., 503-05
Indians, 16, 64, 362, 480; pioneer Marxists' neglect of, 35
Industrial production, in Latin America, 360
Industrial production, U.S., 52, 62, 73, 77; in 1900, 91; 1923-29, 236; in 1932, 293; in 1934, 325; capacity of, 452; compared with Latin America, 360; rapid growth of, 26; before World War I, 107; during World War I, 141; during World War II, 410
Industrial unionism, 79-80, 92, 117, 125, 154, 172, 257, 304-05; and Communist Party, 561; and C.I.O., 345; De Leon on, 81; Left Wing Manifesto on, 167; and Socialist Party convention of 1912, 122-23; and Workers Party, 205
Industrial Workers of the World (I.W.W.), anarcho-syndicalism of, 110-11; anti-political orientation of, 110-11; attack on, after World War I, 198; and Debs, 100-01; and "direct actionists," 111; and dual unionism, 100; endorsing Communist International, 182; formation of, 100-01; government terror against, 140-42; and Haywood, 100-01; membership of (1918), 137; preamble to constitution of, 80; on religious question, 112; and Socialist Party left wing, 101; and strikes before World War I, 111; and strikes during World War I, 136-37; weaknesses of, 112; and World War I, 136
Inter-American Confederation of Workers (C.I.T.), 495
Inter-American Regional Workers Organization (O.I.R.T.), 495-96
Intercollegiate Socialist Society, 113
International Confederation of Free Trade Unions (I.C.F.T.U.), 498
International Congress of the Democracies of America (1939), 365
International Fur and Leather Workers Union, 354, 494
International Labor Defense, and Bridgman defense, 210; formation of, 209; and Herndon case, 288; and Scottsboro case, 286-87
International labor solidarity, 32, 49, 56, 61; and Communists, 259
International Ladies Garment Workers Union, 248, 253-54
International Longshoremen's and Ware-

INDEX

housemen's Union, 353, 494
International Socialist Review, 125, 141
International Trade Union Educational League (I.T.U.E.L.), 137-40
International Women's Day, 113
International Woodworkers of America, 354
International Workers Order, 509
International Workingmen's Association (I.W.A.), and Communist Club of New York, 50; dissolution of, 60; foundation of, 50; groundwork laid for, 32; headquarters in U.S., 60; Lenin on, 61; and Marx, 50; national and international contributions of, 60-61; and National Labor Union, 56; and Negro people, 55; and Social Party of New York, 50; and support to North in Civil War, 48-49; and United Irish Workers, 54
Israel, 480-81
Isserman, Abraham J., 511

Jackson, Andrew, 322
Jackson, Harry, 301
Jackson, James, 311, 320
Jacobi, Fritz, 29, 32, 47
Japan, attack on Pearl Harbor by, 398; and Chinese People's Army, 404; and U.S., in World War II, 403
Jefferson, Thomas, 338; and Declaration of Independence, 16; and Locke, John, 21; and Negro people, 17; as president, 17
Jerome, V. J., 449, 518
Jessup, W. J., 56
Jim Crow, 115, 226, 229-30, 309, 414; and A.F. of L., 231, 288, 414; blows against, 445; Communist Party fight against, 562; and genocide petition to United Nations, 476; I.W.W. on, 116; and National Labor Union, 55; and socialism, 567; world criticism of, 446. *See also* White Chauvinism
Johnston, William H., 213
Johnstone, Jack, 185, 230; and Chicago "race riots" (1919), 231; in meat-packing organizing campaign, 139
Joint Anti-Fascist Refugee Committee, 507
Jones, Claudia, 518
Jones, Mary ("Mother"), 124-25

Kamm, Friedrich, 32
Katovis, Steve, 281
Kautsky, Karl, 106, 146, 152, 157-58, 242, 417
Keany, Frank, 256
Kearney, Denis, 65
Kefauver, Estes, 536
Keynesism, and Browder, 425; essence of, 481-84; forerunners of, 241; and New Deal, 294; and "progressive capitalism," 482, 548; in ranks of workers, 482; and U.S. government policy, 481-82. *See also* "American Exceptionalism"
Kienthal Conference (1916), 129
Kinkel, Gottfried, 29, 31
Kjar, Nels, 204
Knights of Labor, Noble and Holy Order of the, and A.F. of L., 71-72; and craft unions, 69; growth of, 68; high point of, 71; and Negro workers, 69; organization of, 68; predecessor of, 57; program of, 70; and S.L.P., 69
"Know-nothing" movements, 42
Korean war, 473-75, 484, 491, 527-28, 534; beginning of, 461; popular resistance to, 463; and protest against atom-bomb threat, 461; role of U.S. in, 453, 461
Krchmarek, A., 473, 514
Kriege, Hermann, and "American exceptionalism," 28-29, 34
Krumbein, Charles, activities of, in T.U.E.L., 204; on Hillquit leadership, 164; and Passaic strike (1926), 250
Krumbein, Margaret Cowl, 205, 313
Kruse, William F., 184
Ku Klux Klan, and enforced peonage, 52; membership claims of, 186; revival of, 466
Kuhn, Henry, 89

Labor aristocracy, 70, 73, 99, 105, 155, 543-45, 548
Labor banks, 28, 243, 246
Labor frameup, Haymarket, 67; McNamara brothers, 110; Mooney-Billings, 131, 209; Moyer-Haywood-Pettibone, 110; Sacco-Vanzetti, 209
Labor movement, and achievements of National Labor Union, 57; and amalgamation campaign, 205-06; and contrast of A.F. of L. and C.I.O. (1940), 343; crisis in, 500-02; and Espionage Act

(1917), 140; impact of Russian Revolution on, 147-48; and Jeffersonian ideology, 21; key issues before (1922-23), 205; and Marshall Plan, 489-90; misleaders in, 229; and National Colored Labor Union, 55; and Socialist Party "neutrality," 99; solidarity of, in building C.I.O., 343-44; and union organizing during World War I, 138-40; use of troops against (1933-34), 326. *See also* Strikes; Trade Unions

Labor party movements, 64-65; and Communist International (1925), 223; disappearance of, in early years, 21; S.L.P. on, 103. *See also* Farmer-Labor Movements; Farmer-Labor Party; Progressive Party

Labor-Progressive Party of Canada, 172

Labor Reform Party, 54

Labor unity, 504; and Communist Party, 304, 335, 561; and World Federation of Trade Unions, 447; on world scale, 447

Labor Youth League, 479

Labor's Non-Partisan League, 332-33

LaFollette movement, 119, 213-14, 218, 220

Landon, Alfred M., 330, 333-34

"Language federations." *See* National Federations

Lassalle, Ferdinand, 58

Lassalleans, attitude of, toward unionism, 57-58; and founding of S.L.P., 62; and Karl Klinge, 58; opportunism of, 65; Sorge's struggle against, 58; struggle of, with Marxists, 58-60

Latin America, agrarian question in, 362; and American Revolution, 16; economy of, 360-62; and fight against fascism, 363-65; illiteracy in, 362; people's living standards in, 362-63; post-war expansion of Communist parties in, 450-51; U.S. puppets in, 465. *See also* Good Neighbor Policy

Latin American Confederation of Labor (C.T.A.L.), 495-96

Lawson, John Howard, 320, 507

League of American Writers, 421

League of Nations, 227, 368-69, 371, 385

League of Struggle for Negro Rights, 268

Left wing (of Socialist Party), on affiliation to Communist International, 159; and call for Communist Party convention (1919), 166; development of, before World War I, 158; and formation of Communist Party, 182; government terror against, during World War I, 140-42; and *Industrial Socialism* by Haywood and Bohn, 125; "leftist" revisionism of, 126; Manifesto of (1919), 166-67; national conference of (1919), 163-65; in New York, 162; press of, 160-61, 165; and referendum of 1919, 162; and relation of forces in Socialist Party, 119-23, 160-62; and Russian Revolution, 148; sectarianism of, 155; status of (1914), 123-25; and World War I, 129, 131. *See also* Communist Party; Socialist Party

Legien, Karl, 122

Lend-lease, 389, 406

Lenin, V. I., on American Revolution, 16; analysis of imperialism by, 152; on bourgeois and socialist democracy, 153, 337; on capitalism as obsolete, 530; as champion of colonial peoples, 365; on class consciousness, 120; colonial thesis of (at Second Congress of C.I.), 266; contributions of, to Marxism, 149-56; on correcting party errors, 571; death of, 223-24; on dual unionism, 103, 180; influence of writings by, on American left wing, 160; on imperialism and war, 524; on International Workingmen's Association, 61; on law of unequal development of capitalism, 127, 425; letter to Socialist Propaganda League of America, 131; on methods of bourgeois control, 328; and organization of Communist International, 159; on "organized capitalism," 418; on overthrow of capitalism, 512; as peace champion, 129-30; on possibility of peaceful coexistence, 150; on religion, 153-54; on revolutionary wars, 49; on sectarianism, 211-12; and slogan on attitude to imperialist war, 129-30; on state, 80, 149; at Stuttgart Conference (1907), 128; on syndicalism, 152; on transition to socialism, 551, 553; on U.S. agriculture, 18; on U.S. capitalist development, 18; on U.S. elections of 1912, 119; on U.S. industrial development, 77; on U.S. intervention during Russian Revolution, 145; on winning Soviets, 558; on worker-farmer alliance, 564

"Lesser evil" theories, 295, 468, 472

INDEX

Levin, Emanuel, 289
Lewis, John L., and Communists, 348; on elections of 1936, 332; and elections of 1940, 391; expulsion policy of, during 1920's, 255; and industrial union organization, 306; and launching of C.I.O., 305; and mine strikes during World War II, 410; and organization of C.I.O., 306-07; on Taft-Hartley Law, 488
Liebknecht, Karl, 129
Lincoln, Abraham, address to Manchester textile workers, 49; assassination of, 51; and elections, (1856) 41, (1860) 43; and Emancipation Proclamation, 44; and German immigrants, 42; and McClellan, 44; on Mexican War, 36, 529; and middle class, 43; and slogan, "Save the Union," 44; supported by organized labor, 46; thanking First International, 49; views of (1860), 42
Lindbergh, Charles A., 394
Little, Frank H., 137
Litvinov, Maxim, and collective security, 369
Locke, John, 21, 27
London, Jack, and *The Iron Heel*, 121
Long, Huey P., 316
Lovestone, Jay, and "American exceptionalism," 270-74; attempt of, to split Communist Party, 223; group expelled, 270, 274; and Martin, Homer, 352; and policy of T.U.U.L., 258; revisionism of, and its effect on Party work, 247, 272-73
Lowell, James Russell, 23
Luxemburg, Rosa, 128
Lynching, during crisis of 1929, 280; extent of, 225-26; resistance to, 226; Socialist Party position on, 116

MacArthur, Douglas, and atom bomb, 461; and "bonus marchers," 290; on Red Army, 399
Machado, Gustavo, 364
Maloney, James T., 90
Managed economy, and Keynesism, 483
Manley, Joseph, 205, 217
Mann, Tom, 117
Mao Tse-tung, and Chiang Kai-shek, 559; and Communist Party of China, 443; on People's Democracy, 443

Marcantonio, Vito, 520; bills introduced in Congress by, 414; in elections of 1950, 473
Marine Workers Industrial Union, 301
Marinello, Juan, 364
Marshall Plan, 470, 491-92; aims of, 460; and labor movement, 489-90; and split in World Federation of Trade Unions, 497; and Tito, 441
Martin, Homer, 352-53
"Martinsville Seven," 477
Marx, Karl, address to American people (1865), 51-52; appeals to European workers during Civil War, 48-49; on bourgeois state machinery, 556; on British labor aristocracy, 548; on capitalist accumulation, 547; on Civil War in U.S., 48; on eight-hour-day movement in U.S., 71; and First International support to North, 48-49; on immediate demands, 321; and importance to U.S. of *Value, Price and Profit*, 58; and International Workingmen's Association, 50; on Kriege, 28; on labor and the Negro people, 38; on name Communist, 26 fn.; and *New York Daily Tribune*, 48; on overthrow of capitalism, 512; on peaceful transition to socialism, 551; on relative impoverishment of working class, 545; on role of English workers in U.S. Civil War, 49; on sectarianism in U.S., 59; on slave territory, 43; on southern slaveholders, 37; on Sylvis, 56; on transition to socialism in U.S. and England, 80; on united front with bourgeoisie, 41; on utopian socialism, 24
Marx, Karl, and Engels, Frederick, on bourgeois democracy in U.S., 34; and struggle against "lefts" and "rights" in U.S., 34
Marxism, application of, to American conditions, 33; and class consciousness in 1850's, 33-34; and Communist Party, 15; and defense of nation, 323; and De Leon, 80; and early American working class, 27; earlier works of, 33; and first struggle for national Marxist political party, 33; and German immigrants, 27-29; roots of, in U.S., 27; and Socialist Party attitude to theory, 102; theoretical foundations of, in U.S., 32-35. *See also* Ideological Questions
Marxism-Leninism, application of, 151; not a blueprint, 569; and Browder re-

visionism, 426; and Communist International, 415; and cultural upsurge, after World War II, 449; impact of, on left wing in U.S., 152; Lenin's contributions to, 149-56; and Russian Revolution, 148-49; and self-criticism, 428; Stalin on, 149; and U.S. workers, 541. *See also* Ideological Questions

Marxists, and Abolitionist movement, 35, 39; anticipation of 1929 economic crisis by, 277-78; on Brown, John, 39; Civil War record of, 47; and Communist Club of Cleveland, 39; on co-operating with bourgeoisie, 47; and *Deutsches Haus* conference (1860), 43; and early labor press, 35; and early unemployed struggles, 31-32; on economic and political struggles, 35; in elections, (1856) 41, (1860) 42; on Greenback Party, 65; on Indian tribes, 35; on land distribution in Civil War, 47; and Lassalleans, 58-60; and National Labor Union, 53-54, 57; on native and immigrant workers, 35; on Negro question, 562; and Negro slavery, 36-49; as pioneer trade union builders, 35; and S.L.P., 62; and Stuttgart Conference (1907), 128; winning foreign-born to Lincoln, 42; and works of Marx and Engels in U.S., 35

Masses, The, 141
Matchett, Charles, 86
Matles, James, 354
May Day, and A.F. of L., 72
McBride, John, 84
McCabe, Louis, 510
McCarran Act, 467, 506; and "guilt by association," 519; provisions of, 519-20; and union leaders, 500
McCarran Internal Security Committee, 503, 507
McCarthy, Joseph, 467
McDonald, Duncan, 218
McDonnell, J. P., 54, 63, 66, 68, 82
McGee, Willie, 477
McGuire, P. J., 62
McKie, William, 351
McNamara brothers, 110, 380
McNutt, Waldo, 311
Medina, Harold R., 510-12, 516, 518
Memorial Day massacre (1937), 341
Mexican Revolution (1910), 107, 110, 358, 363
Mexican War, 36
Mexico, 36, 107, 110, 209, 356, 363-64, 366

Meyer, Hermann, 39
Meyer, Siegfried, 29
Midwest Daily Record, 381
Minor, Robert, 274, 320; arrest of (March 6, 1930), 282; and fight for people's culture, 317
Mitchell, John, 93
"Molly Maguires," 63
Molotov, V. M., 374-75, 451
Monoculture, and American imperialism, 361, 363
Monroe Doctrine, 77, 358
Mooney-Billings case, 209
Mooney, Tom, 131, 380
Morgan, Lewis Henry, 64
Morgan, Thomas J., 84
Mortimer, Wyndham, 351
Most, Johann, 66
Moyer-Haywood-Pettibone case, 110, 112
Mullaney, Kate, 54
Munich, 373, 408
Murray, Philip, 348, 350, 353, 378; Browder revisionism and, 420; on classes, 485-86; and Communists, 349, 420; and C.I.O., 305; on Marshall Plan, 490-91; and Steel Workers Organizing Committee, 340; on Taft-Hartley Law, 488
Mussolini, Benito, 371, 463-64
Muste, A. J., 249
Mutual Security Act (1951), 460
Mutual Security Pact, 462
Myers, Isaac, 54

National Association for the Advancement of Colored People (N.A.A.C.P.), 286; and attack on Harry T. Moore, 477; and congress on civil rights, 476; organization of, 115; on trade unions, 229
National Association of Manufacturers, 97, 331
National Civic Federation, 93
National and colonial question, 180, 266, 269, 562; Lenin on, 150, 153, 179-80; and Negro national consciousness, 228; and Negro people, 86, 88, 234-35, 267, 478; and Socialist Party, 103; Stalin on, 150, 267. *See also* Bourgeois Nationalism; Colonial Question
National Colored Labor Union, 55
National Farmers Union, 386
National federations, 102, 114, 171; at Communist Party convention (1919), 78;

expulsion of, from Socialist Party, 163; and factional fight, 222; and Socialist Party, 114, 189; on the United Communist Party, 177
National Grange, 386
National Greenback-Labor Party, 65
National Industrial Conference (1919), 197
National Industrial Recovery Act (N.I.R.A.), 329. *See also* Roosevelt, Franklin D.
National Labor Conference for Peace, 475
National Labor Party (1919), 213-14
National Labor Relations (Wagner) Act, 329
National Labor Union (N.L.U.), campaigns of, 53-54; and International Workingmen's Association, 56; and Marxists, 54, 57; on Negro question, 54-55; and working women, 54
National Maritime Union, 353, 492
National Miners Union, 257, 286
National Negro Congress, and C.I.O., 309; influence of Communists in, 309; leaders at second convention of, 378; organization of, 308; and political advance of Negro people, 308-09; program of, 309; second convention of, 377-78; after World War II, 421
National Negro Labor Council, 476, 478
National Open Shop Association, 197
National Student Union, 311
National Textile Workers Union, 251
National Trade Union (1834), 19, 57
National Unemployed Council, activities of, 282-84; and hunger marchers, 283; organization of, 282; and strike movements, 299
National Union for Social Justice (1934), 315-16
National Urban League, 115
National Youth Act, 310-11
National Youth Administration, 310
Needle Trades Workers Industrial Union, 254
Negro culture, 320, 445, 449; and discrimination, 536, 562
Negro liberation movement, and Abolitionists, 37; and Browder, 424; and Communist Party, 233, 267, 476-79; and Negro proletariat, 234-35; and Niagara movement, 115; role of Negro slaves in, 37; and Workers Party, 192-93. *See also* Negro People

Negro people, absolute impoverishment of, 546; in Alabama sharecroppers' struggle (1931), 287; and A.F. of L. convention (1893), 85; and American Negro Labor Congress, 268; bias against, in A.F. of L., 70; breaking with Republican Party, 331-32; and Brotherhood of Timber Workers (I.W.W.), 116; in Civil War, 45; and Communist program, 233, 476-79; cultural discrimination against, 536; and early national movement, 234-35; and election of Benjamin J. Davis, Jr., 421; and elections (1870-81), 51; and F.E.P.C., 413-14; and Federated Farmer Labor Party, 217; as force in Abolitionist movement, 37; and integration, 445; and International Workingmen's Association, 55; and Knights of Labor, 69; leaders' attitude to trade unions, 229-31; leaders used against, 446; and Loyalist Spain, 372; and lynchings, 225-26; as members of Communist Party (1944), 421; as members of unions, 445; and *The Messenger* group, 183, 231-32; migration North, (1910-20) 225, (1940-50) 445; and National Colored Labor Union, 55; and national conference of Negro organizations (1937), 350; national consciousness of, 478; and National Labor Union, 54-55; and National Negro Congress, 308-09; and National Negro Labor Council, 476, 478; and national question, 266-67; and Negro proletariat, 198, 445; and Negro-white solidarity, 230-32; and packinghouse organizing campaign (1917-18), 139, 230; and People's Conventions, 51; pre-Civil War struggles of, 37-38; and "race riots" of 1919, 231; recent advances made by, 445; and renaissance of Negro liberation movement (1905-14), 114-16; and right of self-determination, 267, 478; role of middle class among (1905-14), 115; and Skidmore guards, 55; stimulated by victories in colonial countries, 444-45; struggle of, against petty-bourgeois nationalism, 478-79; as target for reaction, 477; and T.U.E.L., 233; troops in Civil War, 45-46; and white chauvinism in Socialist Party, 103-05, 116; on winning Civil War, 44; Workers Party on, 192-93; writers revaluating history of, 320. *See also* Black Belt; Garvey Movement.

Negro question, Browder on self-determination, 424; Communist position on, 233, 476-79; De Leon on, 81; discussion on, in Communist International, 266; and national consciousness, 478; and national question, 266-67; and right of self-determination, 267, 478; S.L.P. position on, 86-87. *See also* National and Colonial Question; Self-Determination
Negro senators, 51
Negro-white unity, 55, 230-33, 544
Negro women, 38, 45, 268, 320; and Communist Party, 313
Negro working class, 108, 309, 350, 414, 445; and A.F. of L., 73; and attitude of Negro petty-bourgeois leaders to trade unions, 229-30; and Communist Party, 193; growth of, in North, 225; launching own organizations, 54-55; and meatpacking organization drive, 230; and Socialist Party, 104
Nelson, Steve, 372, 519
New Deal, 293-94, 533, 549; and Keynesism, 483; and "panacea" mass movements, 314-17; Wall Street attack on, 326-27. *See also* Roosevelt, Franklin D.
"New Freedom," 118, 549
New National Era, 55
Niagara movement, 115
Nine-Party Communist Conference, 470; on two camps, 471
Nockels, Ed, 204
Nonpartisan League, 213
North Atlantic Pact, 460, 464

Olgin, Moissaye J., 188, 317
Onda, Andrew, 519
Opportunism, 121, 337-39; of Bernstein, 120; of Browder, 419-20, 425-26; of "Chicago militants," 138; and De Leon, 79; and immediate demands, 102; and imperialism, 105; of the Lassalleans, 65; of Lovestone, 271; of Social-Democracy in U.S., 105, 147; and "social fascists," 266; of S.L.P., 66; of Socialist Party, 159; Stalin on, in U.S., 273. *See also* "American Exceptionalism"; Class Collaboration; Social-Democracy
"Organized capitalism," Browder on, 417-18, 436; Lenin on, 418
Owen, Robert, 23

Palmer raids, 174-75; effects of, on Communist organization, 176; and Workers Party convention (1922), 194-95
"Panacea" mass movements, in New Deal period, 314-17
Pan-American Federation of Labor, 366, 495
Parsons, Albert R., 64, 66-67, 71
Partial demands. *See* Immediate Demands
"Party of a new type," 97, 169, 223, 260-61, 275
Patterson, William L., 507
Peace, 391, 440, 519; and coexistence of capitalism and socialism, 524-25; Communist Party's activities in behalf of, 474-76; desire for, in U.S., 457-58; and elections of 1948, 471-72; and Five-Power Pact, 457; and Nine-Party Communist Conference, 471; organizations for, 475-76; sentiment for, in capitalist countries, 527-28; Soviet Union's struggle for, 458, 463; and Stockholm Pledge, 457
Peekskill riot, 475, 511
Pepper, John, 220, 272, 274
People's Democracies, 462, 524-25, 538-40, 558; and dictatorship of proletariat, 441; and People's Front, 553; rise of, 441-42
People's Front, 321-23, 364, 382, 516; in Chile, 363; in France, 370; and People's Democracy, 553; in Spain, 371; in U.S., 554-55
People's Party, 86. *See also* Populist Movement
People's World, 381
Perry, Pettis, 445-46, 518
Philadelphia, as early center of labor organization, 20
Philippines, 77, 95-96, 358
Plumb Plan, 213-14
"Point Four," 423, 470
Police state, and U.S. today, 465-68
Populist movement, 85-86
"Possibilists," 96
Potash, Irving, 354, 509
Powderly, Terence V., 46, 68
Pragmatism, 317, 535
Prestes, Luis Carlos, 364
Prevey, Margaret, 124, 184
Pritchett, Harold, 354
"Progressive capitalism," 482, 548-49
Progressive Party (1948), 471-72
Progressive Party ("Bull Moose"), 119

Proletarian League (1852), 29-30
Proletarian Party, 191
Puerto Rico, 77, 107, 362, 365; monoculture in, 363; promises of freedom for, 363
Purcell, A. A., 259
"Pure and simple" trade unionism, 68

Quill, Michael, 354, 492

Racial theories, 104; Boas on, 320; Communist Club on (1858), 32; in Communist Labor Party, 173; in Socialist Party, 116
Radical Republicans, 43, 51
Railroad brotherhoods, 63, 200, 333
Rand School, 113
Randolph, A. Philip, 183, 309
Recabarren, Louis E., 364
Reconstruction Acts, 51
Red Army, carrying burden of World War II, 412; defense of Stalingrad by, 399; "experts'" opinions of, 396; and General Halder, 397; Hitler's fear of, 394; and Pacific war, 403; smashing of Wehrmacht by, 402; strategy of, 397
Red International of Labor Unions (R.I.L.U.), 182, 254, 257-59
"Red Republicanism," 42
Reed, E. J., 315
Reed, John, 161-62, 164, 166, 170
Reform, Die, 30
Republican Party, 91, 119; and early banking interests, 40; in elections, (1856) 41, (1860) 43, (1932) 290, (1936) 334, (1938) 380, (1940) 390-91, (1948) 471-72; formation of, 40; and new coalition in 1860, 41; as party of free labor, 41; policies of, today, 467; and Reconstruction, 51; and Roosevelt, Theodore, 118-19; and Stevens, Thaddeus, 43
Reuther, Walter, 486, 490, 501, 503, 549, 562; and Addes-Thomas group, 492; aims of, in C.I.O., 502; return of, from Soviet Union, 353; and walkouts during World War II, 410
Revels, R. H., 51
Revisionism, 272-73; and "American exceptionalism," 569; of Bernstein, 106; of Browder, 427-28, 432-33; of De Leon, 79; Lenin's fight against, 149; in Second International, 105-06. *See also* Opportunism
Revolution, definition of, 549-50
Revolution, Die, 30
Revolutionary Socialist Labor Party (1881), 66
Rhee, Syngman, 534
Right of self-determination. *See* Self-Determination
Robeson, Paul, ban on, 536; and cultural upsurge after World War II, 449; Negro spokesmen's attack on, 446; and Peekskill riot, 475; and trial of eleven Communist leaders, 514
Roca, Blas, 364
Roosevelt, Eleanor, 310
Roosevelt, Franklin D., and "brain trust," 293; Browder on, 426; and Communist Party, 330, 333-36; death of, 400; and "democratic front," 323; and Economic Bill of Rights, 413; in elections, (1932) 290-91, (1936) 334; on F.E.P.C., 414; and "forgotten man," 291; on Germany as main enemy, 403; and "good neighbor" policy, 356-57, 364; heading toward war, 389; and informal British alliance, 376; labor vote for (1936), 332; and lend-lease to Soviet Union, 400; and N.I.R.A., 296-97; and Negro vote, 331-32; and New Deal, 293-94; new legislation under (1935), 329; on "one-third of nation," 546; political coalition around, 308; and "pump priming," 379; and "quarantine the aggressors" slogan, 369; and recognition of Soviet Union, 369; seven-point program of, 418-19; and Supreme Court, 329; and Wall Street, 325, 328-29, 339. *See also* New Deal
Roosevelt, Theodore, 73, 118-19
Rosa, Robert, 29, 47
Russian Revolution, 143-56, 170; and call for world peace, 143; Debs on, 161, 189; and De Leon, 80; and development of Marxism-Leninism, 148-49; and European workers, 145-46; Hillquit's stand on, 159; impact of, on American labor movement, 147-48; and left wing of Socialist Party, 148; and Lenin on peaceful transition to socialism, 551-52; marking new era of world history, 143; S.L.P. on, 183; U.S. inter-

vention in, 144-45. See also Soviet Union
Ruthenberg, Charles E., arrest of, 141; on Communist Party in 1919, 202; and Conference for Progressive Political Action, 214; death of, 264; on European Communist parties, 168; on Hillquit leadership, 164; at Socialist Party conventions, (1912) 123-24, (1917) 135
Ryan, Joseph, 301-02

Sacco-Vanzetti case, 209
Sacher, Harry, 510
St. John, Vincent, 78, 111
Sandino, August Cesar, 365
Schmidt, Matt, 380
Schneiderman, William, 392, 516-18, 556
Schuman Plan, 526-27, 531
Scottsboro case, 286
Secession of southern states, 43
Second front, in World War II, 412-13
Second International, influence of, on Socialist Party in U.S., 105-06; reformist illusions in, 105-06; and Stuttgart Conference (1907), 128
Second World Peace Conference, 475
Sectarianism, 64, 69, 264, 569; and Communist Party in early years, 186-87; and De Leon, 79, 97; of early German Marxists, 35; in elections of 1932, 292; in International Workingmen's Association, 59; and left wing, 155; Lenin on, 211-12; and Proletarian Party, 191
Seidel, Emil, 113
Self-criticism, 151, 260, 428, 435, 477, 521
Self-determination, 266-67, 291; Browder on, 424; and Communist Party, 266-67, 478; and Garvey movement, 227; Negro people on, 478. See also National and Colonial Question; Negro Question
Share-Croppers Union (Camp Hill, Ala.), 287-88
"Share the Wealth" movement, 316
Sinclair, Upton, and Epic movement, 314-15
Skidmore guards, 55
Slavery, effect of, on trade unions in North, 38; fight of Marxists against, 41; and northern industrialists, 36; and socialism, 539; and U.S. Constitution, 36
Slobodin, Henry L., 89
Smith Act, passage of, 392; and restricting Party membership, 393; and Supreme Court, 517; and trials of Communist leaders, 510, 518-19
Smith, Gerald L. K., 316, 331
Social-Democracy, betrayal of Socialist principles by, 128-29; and bourgeois reformism in U.S., 548-49; and Browder's Teheran thesis, 428; and "collective security," 369; European, and American Keynesism, 548; European, and class consciousness, 542; European, stand of, on World War I, 131; European, after World War I, 146; European, after World War II, 464; as force for war and fascism, 464; fundamental difference between, and Communists, 552; and Hitler, 295; and Marshall Plan, 497; and McCarran Act, 520; and "organized capitalism," 241-42; post-war influence of, in Western Europe, 450; and Russian Revolution, 147-48, 183-84; U.S. form of, 485. See also Opportunism; Revisionism
Social Democracy of America (1897), and Debs, 94
Social Party of New York (1867), 50
Social Reform Association (1845), 28
Social security, 329, 561
Socialism, as answer to capitalism, 537-40; no blueprint for, 553; and classes, 538-39; conflict of, with capitalism, 530; contrasted with capitalism, 451; definition of, 550; doctrines of, introduced in U.S., 26; and immediate demands, 550; and Jim Crow, 567; and markets, 538; in national interest, 566-67; as peace force, 529; and post-World War II governments, 451; principle of, 538; and slavery, 539; transition to, from capitalism, 549-50; and U.S., 567; and war, 540
Socialist Labor Party, and Busche-Rosenberg leadership, 76; composition of membership of, 88; declaration of principles of, 62-63; decline of, 88; and De Leon, 76; founding of, 62, 64; and George, Henry, 73; and Greenback-Labor Party, 65; and Knights of Labor, 69; on Negro question, 86-87, 562; opportunism of leadership of, 65-66; on People's Party, 86; and railroad strike of 1877, 63; on Russian Revolution, 183; and "Sanial case," 83; and Schewitsch-Jonas group, 76; sectarian trends in, 81; split in, 89-90; status of (1890), 74-75, 79; and trade unions, 82-85; and Volks-

zeitung revolt, 76; and Workingmen's Party, 62
Socialist Party, activities of, in trade unions, 98-99; alliance of, with A.F. of L. bureaucracy, 249; "Article II, Section 6" amendment to constitution of, 122; and bourgeois culture, 121; causes of split in (1919), 158-60; and "centrists," 120; "Chinese exclusion" debate within, 116; and Communist Party, 94, 124, 157-58, 188, 212, 214, 252-53, 333, 335, 378; decentralization of, 102; decline of, 169-70, 189; in elections, (1900) 96, (1936) 334; and European Social-Democrats on World War I, 131; expulsions from, 163; formation of, 62, 91, 94-95; high point of, 113; indictment of national officers of, 141; and "language federations," 114; left-right struggle in, 119-23; and Marxist theory, 102; members of, at A.F. of L. convention (1902), 98-99; and middle class intellectuals, 99, 120; on national question, 103; neglect of Negro question by, 562; "Old Guard," on C.I.O., 346; open split in, 171; opportunism in, 102, 120, 157-58; policy during economic crisis of 1929, 281; "possibilists" and "impossibilists" in, 96; press of, 113-14; program of, 95-97; and "progressive capitalism," 119; prosecution of publications of, 141; raids on, during World War I, 141; on Russian Revolution, 147-48; St. Louis convention of (1917), 134-35; and Seattle split, 158; splits in, (1912) 122-23, (1919) 160-62; struggle against opportunist leadership in, 159; struggles of, in pre-World War I decade, 112-13; theoretical writings of, 121; and white chauvinism, 103-04, 116, 288; on work among women, 113; on World War I, 130-31, 134-35. *See also* Left Wing (of Socialist Party)
Socialist Propaganda League of America, 131, 158
Socialist Trades and Labor Alliance (S.T.L.A.), 83-84, 89, 100
Sorge, F. A., 29, 50, 57
South, and Browder, 424; Communist Party activities in, 267, 285-88, 291; Socialist Party activities in, 288. *See also* Black Belt, Farmers
South Africa, 212, 531
Southern Conference for Human Welfare, 378; influence of, 311; after World War II, 421
Southern Negro Youth Congress, organization of, 311; on fascism, 378; after World War II, 421
Southern Worker, 286
Sovereign, J. R., 68
Soviet Union, anti-fascist influence of, 405; attacked by Hitler, 395, 397; and Baruch Plan, 459; and capitalist economic crisis of 1929, 277; on collective security, 369; *Collier's* article on war with, 462; conditions of people in, 538; criticism of Jim Crow by, 446; and defense of Stalingrad, 399; entry of, into World War II, 383; and Finnish-Soviet war, 385-86; industrial growth in, 538-39; inspiration of, 451; and lend-lease, 402, 406; losses of, in World War II, 406, 439; and non-aggression pact with Germany, 374-75; and Pacific war, 403; political-military strategy of, in World War II, 405-06; production increase in, after World War II, 439; recognition of, by U.S., 369; role of, in World War II, 404-05; on second front, 401; as Socialist vanguard, 538; and Stalin on peace, 374; strength of (1941), 396; struggle for peace by, 458; trade union delegations to, 259; and U.S. air bases, 459, 462; Wall Street's fear of, 455; women in, 563. *See also* Red Army; Russian Revolution
Soziale Republik, Die, 41
Spain, 360; Civil War in, 371-73; People's Front government in, 370-71
Speed-up, 236-37, 239-40, 247-48, 252, 255
Spies, August, 66
"Square Deal," 548-49
Stachel, Jack, 269; indictment of, 509; and T.U.U.L. strikes (1933), 298
Stalin, Joseph, on building socialism in one country, 269; on Communist Party of U.S., 274, 570; definition of nation by, 267; on "depression of special kind," 325-26; on dissolution of Communist International, 415; on Leninism, 149; on national and colonial revolutions, 150; on party of a new type, 260; on peace policy of U.S.S.R., 374; on role of labor party, 212; on transition to socialism, 552; as war leader, 400; on winning Soviets, 558; on World War II, 383
State, Left Wing Manifesto on, 167; Lenin

on, 149, 154; strengthening of, in U.S., 107
Steel production, in capitalist world and U.S.S.R. (1929-49), 538
Steel Workers Organizing Committee (1936), 340-41, 349-50
Stephens, Uriah S., 68
Steuben, John, 349
Stevens, Thaddeus, on crushing southern rebellion, 43; on Reconstruction, 51; on slavery, 43; and Thirteenth Amendment, 51
Steward, Ira, 53
Stockholm Pledge, 475
Stokes, Rose Pastor, 141, 162, 184
Stone, Warren S., 213
Strasser, Adolph, 62
Strikes, of agricultural workers, 136; of American Railway Union, 78; in early labor movement, 19; in 1833-37, 19; and economic crisis of 1921, 199; of farmers, 289; Gastonia textile (1929), 251-52; general, (eight-hour day) 71-72, (San Francisco) 300-03, (Seattle, 1919) 160, (Winnipeg) 160; Homestead (1892), 78; of I.W.W., before World War I, 111; and "Molly Maguires," 63; and National Industrial Conference (1919), 197; needle trades (1926), 252-55; New Bedford textile (1928), 251-52; in 1910-14, 109; in 1917, 133; in 1919-22, 199-201; in 1933-36, 298-303; in 1946, 487; and no-strike pledge, 410-11; Passaic textile (1926), 250, 252; railroad (1877), 63-64; in Rocky Mountain states, 78; "sit-down," in auto (1937), 341; steel, (1901) 97, (1919) 140; under T.U.U.L. leadership in Hoover period, 284-85
Strong, Edward, 311
Student League for Industrial Democracy (1905), 311
Stuttgart Congress (1907), anti-war resolution of, 128
Sun Yat-sen, on Soviet Union, 443-44
Supreme Court, 210; Dred Scott decision of, 37; on Feinberg law, 467; fining of trade unions by, 488; and First Amendment, 517; and Herndon case, 288; on New Deal laws, 329; and Smith Act, 517; and trial of eleven Communist leaders, 516-18
Sylvis, Williams, activities of, in Civil War, 46; death of, 56; on international solidarity of workers, 56; and International Workingmen's Association, 53
Syndicalist League of North America, and "boring from within," 118; and Foster, William Z., 117; program of, 117-18

Taft-Hartley Act, 489, 521; effect of, on labor movement, 466; provisions of, 487-88; and Truman, 488; and union leaders, 500
Technocracy, 314
Teheran Conference, 412; Browder on, 422-23, 426, 428; overestimation of, 413
Third party movements. See Labor Party Movements
"Third period," discussion on, 265-66, 271
Thirteenth Amendment, 51
Thomas, Norman, 281, 333, 378, 393
Thompson, Robert, 372, 435, 437; on Browder, 434; decorated for bravery, 409; indictment of, 509
Thoreau, Henry David, 22-23
Tillman, Ben, 115
Tito, Joseph Broz, 441
Titus, Herman, 112, 121
Togliatti, Palmiro, 538
Toledano, Vicente Lombardo, 364, 495
Toohey, Pat, 255, 257
Townley, A. P., 213
Townsend, F. E., and Townsend National Recovery Plan, 315
Trachtenberg, Alexander, 188, 518
Trade Union Educational League (T.U.E.L.), and amalgamation, 203, 205; and carpenters union, 249; and coal strike (1922), 204; and Communist Party, 185, 203-05, 249-54; early activities of, 202-05; and independent political action, 203-05; and industrial unionism, 203-04; and *Labor Herald*, 203; mass campaigns of, 205-07; in mining industry, 255-56; program of, 184-85; on Russian Revolution, 184
Trade union unity. See Labor Unity
Trade Union Unity League (T.U.U.L.), Communists in, 258, 298; dissolved, 303; formation of, 257; and Marine Workers Industrial Union, 301; merging with A.F. of L., 303-04; and organization of unorganized, 257-58; program of, 257-59; in strikes (1933), 298; and unemployed demonstration (March 6, 1930), 281-82

Trade unions, in auto, 351-53; and battle for production in World War II, 410; Browder on post-war problems of, 424; bureaucracy in, 243-45; C.I.O. drives to organize, 353-55; and C.T.A.L., 495-96; Communists in drives to organize, during 1930's, 349-55; and company unions, 197; condemned as "conspiracies," 522; craft, 68-70, 72, 118, 257, 561; drive against, after World War I, 198-201; early organization of, 19; and fight for trade union democracy, 561; industrial, 79-80, 92, 117, 125, 154, 167, 205, 257, 561; and International Confederation of Free Trade Unions, 498; and labor banking, 243, 246; and labor unity, 561; Lenin on, 154-55; in meat-packing, 139; and National Association of Manufacturers, 97; Negro membership in, 445; and "new wage policy" of A.F. of L. (1925), 239; in steel, (1919) 139-40, (1937) 349-51; and World Federation of Trade Unions, 447. See also A.F. of L.; C.I.O.; I.T.U.E.L.; I.W.W.; Knights of Labor; Labor Movement; National Labor Union; Strikes; T.U.E.L.; T.U.U.L.
Transport Workers Union, 354, 492
Travis, Robert, 351
"Trenton Six," 477
Trotsky, Leon, 269-70
Trotskyites, 275, 307, 346, 377-78, 565; expulsion of, 269-70
Truman Doctrine, 459, 470, 489
Truman, Harry S., Communist Party criticism of (1945), 436-37; in elections of 1948, 472; and Keynesism, 483; and Korean "police action," 461; and "managed economy," 418; on Nazi attack on Soviet Union, 401; and "Point Four," 470; on profits, 500; on prosperity in U.S., 533; and Taft-Hartley Bill, 488
Truth, Sojourner, 38
Tubman, Harriet, 38, 45
Turner, Nat, 38
Turnverein, 29
Twain, Mark, and Anti-Imperialist League, 96
"Twenty-one points," 179-80

Un-American Activities Committee. *See* House Committee on Un-American Activities

Unemployed Councils. *See* National Unemployed Council
Uneven development of capitalism, 271; Lenin on, 127, 150, 425; and U.S. capitalist hegemony, 452; and World War I, 127, 142
Union Party (1936), 331, 334
United Automobile Workers of America, 340, 351-53, 411, 489
United Communist Party, 177-78, 180-81. *See also* Communist Party of the U.S.
United Electrical, Radio, and Machine Workers of America, 354, 493-94
United Mine Workers of America, 132, 199-201, 329, 488
United Nations, 433, 461, 470, 565; dictation by U.S. in, 452; foundations laid for, 400; and genocide petition, 476; growing opposition to U.S. in, 453; and Keynesism, 482; policy of, during World War II, 403
United States, and accession of Oregon, 36; agriculture in (1900), 91; air bases, 461; and "American tradition," 338-39; army today, 461; "atom-bomb diplomacy," 459; and atomic war, 451; and attack on Pearl Harbor, 398, 409; attitude toward Red Army, 412; battle for production in World War II, 410-11; and bourgeois revolutions, 550; bourgeoisie and Hitler, 375-76; Browder on surplus production in, 423; building a police state, 465-68; capitalism in, 541; and Chiang Kai-shek, 444; and Chinese Revolution, 419-20; Communists as second class citizens of, 521; conditions in South of (1930), 286; conquest of Latin America by, 107; Constitution as originally formulated, 17; corruption in, 536; cost of living in, during World War I, 130; culture in, 449, 535-36; and Dawes and Young Plans, 196; delegates to Second World Peace Conference, 475; and democratic leadership, 544; and "depression of special kind," 326; dictation by, in United Nations, 452; drive toward war, 454-57, 461-62, 525-29; economic development of, 18, (1880-1900) 77, (1923-29) 236-37, (1929-33) 293, (1940-50) 452; effects of gold discovery on, 26; employment in, 446-47; endorsement of Munich by, 375; entry into World War I, 132-33; entry into World War II, 398; exploitation of Latin America by, 358-59; and

fascist danger (1929-33), 296; fascist trends in, 464-65, 534, 544; seizure of Florida by, 36; frame-up of Communist Party in, 550; and free land, 543-44; and general crisis of capitalism, 452-53, 533-35, 541; and Germany's unconditional surrender, 400; as headquarters of First International, 60; immigrants in, 18; imperialism, 77, 91, 460, 535; impoverishment of workers in, 545-47; intervention in Russian Revolution, 144-45; invasion of Africa in World War II, 402; Jewish population of, 480; lend-lease to Soviet Union, 406; living standards in, 279-80, 547-48; losses in World War II, 406; and Louisiana Purchase, 36; Marx on transition to socialism in, 80, 551; military budget of (1951), 458; monopolies (1900), 77; monopolists' aims, 454; and negotiated peace, 405; Negro people in, as target of reactionaries, 445; neutrality of, early in World War I, 130; and peaceful coexistence, 525; and People's Democracy, 555-56; and People's Front government, 554-55; progressive legislation in, 413-14; real wages in, since 1900, 500, 544-45; repressive legislation in, during World War I, 140; rejection of Soviet peace offers by, 463; and second front, 399, 402; seizure of Mexican territory by, 36; and socialism, 540; and surrender of Japan, 404; terrorism in, after World War I, 507-08; and trade boycott of Socialist countries, 453; treaty with Japan (1951), 460; trial of eleven Communist leaders in, 511-13; and Truman Doctrine, 459, 470, 489; Wall Street in government of, 566; and war in Pacific, 403; and war production, 534, 547; wealth concentration in, 546, 566. *See also* Capitalism, U.S.; Industrial Production, U.S.

United Textile Workers Union, 300

United Toilers of America (1922), 194

Universal Negro Improvement Association. *See* Garvey Movement

Urban League, 229

Utopian Society (1933), 315

Utopians, 22-23

"Vanguardism," 264
Van Patten, Philip, 62

Vanzetti, Bartolomeo. *See* Sacco-Vanzetti case

Varga, Eugene, on aims of New Deal, 294

Veblen, Thorstein, 241

Vesey, Denmark, 38

Violence, 195, 513, 517; and American Revolution, 512; and Bakunin, Michael, 60; Communist Party on, 552; and Gastonia strike (1929), 251; against I.W.W., 198; Marx on, 80, 149; Marxists on, 512; in strikes (1934-36), 299, 301; and "open shop" movement, 250

Virgin Islands, 363

Voorhis Act, 392-93, 471, 506

Voyzey, George, 255

Wage Workers Party (1910), 121-22

Wagenknecht, Alfred, arrest of, 141; on Hillquit leadership, 164; and Passaic textile strike, 250; and Seattle Socialist split, 121

Wages, 19, 250, 533, 560; Browder on, 418, 426; in early years of U.S., 18; on eve of World War I, 108; and Heller budget, 546; in Hoover period, 279; in 1923-29, 246; in 1944-50, 500; and U.S. living standards, 73; after World War II, 487

Wagner Act. *See* National Labor Relations Act

Wallace, Henry A., 390, 472

War of 1812, 18

Ward, Harry F., 379

Warren, Fred O., 114

Washington, Booker T., on trade union movement, 229; and Tuskegee movement, 115

Watson, Tom, 115

Watt, John, 257

Wayland, J. A., 114

Weiner, William, 392

Weinstone, William W., 274, 292, 518; on Hillquit leadership, 164; and organization of auto, 352; and Passaic textile strike, 250

Weitling, Wilhelm, 24, 28

"Welfare state," 483

Western Federation of Miners, 78, 100-01

Weydemeyer, Joseph, as commander in Civil War, 47; defense of Marxist principles by, 29; fighting sectarianism, 39-40; and National Labor Union, 53; on struggle against slavery, 40

INDEX 597

Whig Party, 41
White chauvinism, 103, 539; and A.F. of L., 73; and Berger, Victor, 104; a bourgeois ideology, 87; Communist Party struggle against, 233-34, 478, 563; and conservative Negro press, 446; and S.L.P., 87; and Socialist Party, 103-05, 116; among white workers, 229; and Yokinen trial, 288. *See also* Racial Theories
Whitney, Anita, 124, 184, 410
Wiggin, Ella May, 251
Wilkerson, Doxey A., 320, 511-12
Williamson, John B., 184, 435; on Browder line, 434; indictment of, 509
Willich, August, 29, 47
Willkie, Wendell L., 390-91
Wilson, Woodrow, in elections of 1912, 119; and "New Freedom," 118; re-election of, 132
Wing, Simon, 86
Winston, Henry, 514, 518; indictment of, 509; and Southern Negro Youth Congress, 311
Winter, Carl, 509, 514
Woll, Matthew, 242, 275, 281, 284
Women, among Abolitionists, 37-38; active in labor movement, before World War I, 124-25; and Browder revisionism, 432; Communist, and World War II, 409-10; conditions of, before World War I, 108; and Congress of American Women, 448; Dimitrov on fascism and, 313-14; and Equal Rights Amendment, 313; and International Women's Day, 113; and National Labor Union, 54, 57; and National Women's Commission of the Communist Party, 263; Negro, 37-38; and socialism, 539; and Socialist Party, 113; and Soviet Union, 563; in trade unions, 313; and Women's Charter, 312; and Women's Councils, 263; and Women's International Democratic Federation, 447-48; in women's movement of 1930's, 312-14; Workers Party on, 193
Women's Councils, 263
Women's Rights Party, 313
Women's Trade Union League, 313
Workers Alliance, 299, 421
Workers (Communist) Party, class struggle policy of (1925), 247; in elections of 1928, 263. *See also* Communist Party of the U.S.
Workers Council, call for a new party by, 190; on Communist International, 188; press of, 176; quitting Socialist Party, 189; and Trachtenberg, Alexander, 188. *See also* Workers Party
Workers Defense League (1922), 194
Workers Ex-Servicemen's League, 289-90
Workers International Relief, 252
Workers Party, and campaign for recognition of Soviet Union, 205, 207; conventions of, (Bridgman) 194, (Fourth) 223; and defense of class war prisoners, 208-10; on dual unionism, 192; factionalism in, 221-23; and Farmer-Labor Party, 215-16; formation of, 190-91; Foster presidential candidate of (1924), 219; and Garvey movement, 228; on labor party, 212-13, 219-21; name changed to Workers (Communist) Party, 247; on Negro question, 192-93; and Palmer raids, 194-95; on parliamentary action, 193; program of, 191-93, 205; on Russian Revolution, 192; and Sacco-Vanzetti case, 209; split with Fitzpatrick group, 221. *See also* Communist Party of the U.S.; Workers (Communist) Party; Workers Council
Workers Party of Canada (1922), 172
Working class, and "American exceptionalism," 541; and Civil War, 38, 46; class consciousness of, in U.S., 543; and class struggles under imperialism, 530; composition of, in U.S., 542-44; conditions of, in early America, 18; contradictions within, in U.S., 33; early outlook of, 22; and early strikes in U.S., 19; effects of slavery on, 38; on eve of World War I, 108; ideological development of, in U.S., 542-43; illusions of, 544; immediate demands of, and socialism, 550; impoverishment of, 545-47; and independent political action, 561; and Keynesism, 482; learning to organize, 20; militant record of, in U.S., 542; and Negro people as allies, 562; political movement of, under New Deal, 332; after World War II, 487: *See also* Class Consciousness; Classes; Negro Working Class
Workingmen's Party (1876), 62-64
World Federation of Democratic Youth, 448
World Federation of Trade Unions, 447, 498-99, 561
World War I, and eight-hour day, 196; and general crisis of capitalism, 128; and Lenin slogan on imperialist war,

129-30; and living costs, 130, 133; and Russian Bolsheviks, 129; Social-Democratic betrayal during, 128-29; and Soviet Union, 451, 528; and uneven development of capitalism, 127, 142

World War II, American reactions to (1939-40), 386-87; battle for production during, 410-11; Communist position on, 387-88; and Dunkirk, 394; effects of, on colonial world, 442; estimate of, 404-06; and expansion of Communist influence, 449-51; and fascist enslavement, 407; and general crisis of capitalism, 383, 442; and Hitler attack on Soviet Union, 397; and "Little Steel" formula, 487; and living costs, 411; losses to capitalist system, 451, 529; and Pacific war, 403-04; "phony war" phase of, 384-85; Red Army strategy in, 397; revolutionary consequences of, 439; trade union growth after, 439; and Trotskyite trials, 396; and unconditional surrender, 400; U.S. entry into, 398; women during, 447-48

Young, Art, 317

Young Communist League (Y.C.L.), and Browder revisionism, 432; formation of, 184; growth of (1933-36), 307; and Loyalist Spain, 372; and Marxist-Leninist youth leadership, 312; proposal to Y.P.S.L., 335; and steel organizing campaign, 350; strength of (1939), 312; and "vanguardism," 264; war record of, 409; and Young Workers League, 184

Young People's Socialist League (Y.P.S.L.), 113, 183, 335

Young Workers League, 184, 222

Youth, and American Youth Congress, 310-12; communism's appeal to, 563; and juvenile delinquency, 537; and Labor Youth League, 479; Workers Party on, 193; and World Federation of Democratic Youth, 448: *See also* Y.C.L., Y.P.S.L.

Zimmerwald Conference (1915), 129
Zionism, 480-81

PARTIAL BIBLIOGRAPHY

(Below is a list of the books and pamphlets cited in this work which were published by International Publishers, New York.)

James S. Allen, *Atomic Energy and Society*, 1949
James S. Allen, *Atomic Imperialism: The State, Monopoly, and the Bomb*, 1952
James S. Allen, *Negro Liberation*, 1938
James S. Allen, *Reconstruction, the Battle for Democracy*, 1937
James S. Allen, *World Monopoly and Peace*, 1946
American Writers Congress (reports), 1935
Herbert Aptheker, *To Be Free: Studies in American Negro History*, 1948
Anthony Bimba, *History of the American Working Class*, 1927
Ella Reeve Bloor, *We Are Many*, 1940
Eugene Dennis, *Ideas They Cannot Jail*, 1950
George Dimitrov, *The United Front*, 1938
Robert W. Dunn, ed., *The Palmer Raids*, 1948
Frederick Engels, *The Origin of the Family, Private Property, and the State*, 1942
Frederick Engels, *The Peasant War in Germany*, 1926
Sidney Finkelstein, *Art and Society*, 1947
Philip S. Foner, ed., *Frederick Douglass: Selections From His Writings*, 1945
Philip S. Foner, *History of the Labor Movement in the United States*, 1947
William Z. Foster, *From Bryan to Stalin*, 1937
William Z. Foster, *Outline Political History of the Americas*, 1951
Michael Gold, *The Hollow Men*, 1941
Louis Harap, *Social Roots of the Arts*, 1949
Harry Haywood, *Negro Liberation*, 1948
William D. Haywood, *Bill Haywood's Book*, 1929
History of the Communist Party of the Soviet Union, 1939
Labor Research Association, *Labor Fact Books 2-10*, 1934-51
Labor Research Association, *Trends in American Capitalism*, 1948
Elizabeth Lawson, *Lincoln's Third Party*, 1948
Elizabeth Lawson, *Thaddeus Stevens*, 1942
V. I. Lenin, *A Letter to American Workers*, 1934
V. I. Lenin, *Capitalism and Agriculture in the United States*, 1946

V. I. Lenin, *Collected Works*, Vol. 18, *The Imperialist War*, 1930
V. I. Lenin, *Imperialism, the Highest Stage of Capitalism*, 1939
V. I. Lenin, *"Left Wing" Communism, an Infantile Disorder*, 1934
V. I. Lenin, *Marx, Engels, Marxism*, 1933
V. I. Lenin, *Materialism and Empirio-Criticism* (in *Selected Works*, Vol. 11), 1943
V. I. Lenin, *Religion*, 1933
V. I. Lenin, *Selected Works*, Vols. 1-12, 1943
V. I. Lenin, *State and Revolution*, 1932
V. I. Lenin, *What Is to Be Done*, 1929
V. I. Lenin and Joseph Stalin, *Marxism and Revisionism*, 1946
A. B. Magil, *Israel in Crisis*, 1950
A. B. Magil and Henry Stevens, *The Peril of Fascism*, 1938
Karl Marx, *Capital*, Vol. 1, 1947
Karl Marx, *Critique of the Gotha Programme*, 1938
Karl Marx, *The Eighteenth Brumaire of Louis Bonaparte*
Karl Marx, *Founding of the First International*, 1937
Karl Marx, *Value, Price and Profit*, 1935
Karl Marx and Frederick Engels, *The Civil War in the United States*, 1937
Karl Marx and Frederick Engels, *The Communist Manifesto*, 1948
Karl Marx and Frederick Engels, *Letters to Americans*, 1952
Karl Marx and Frederick Engels, *Selected Correspondence*, 1942
Herbert M. Morais, *The Struggle For American Freedom: The First Two Hundred Years*, 1944
Karl Obermann, *Joseph Weydemeyer, Pioneer of American Socialism*, 1947
Victor Perlo, *American Imperialism*, 1951
Proletarian Literature in the United States, an Anthology, 1935
Anna Rochester, *The Populist Movement in the United States*, 1943
Anna Rochester, *Rulers of America*, 1936
David J. Saposs, *Left Wing Unionism*, 1926
Frederick L. Schuman, *American Policy Towards Russia Since 1917*, 1928
Joseph Stalin, *Dialectical and Historical Materialism*, 1940
Joseph Stalin, *Foundations of Leninism*, 1939
Joseph Stalin, *The Great Patriotic War of the Soviet Union*, 1945
Joseph Stalin, *Marxism and the National Question*, 1942
Joseph Stalin, *For Peaceful Coexistence*, 1951
Joseph Stalin, *Problems of Leninism*, 1934
Joseph Stalin, *Selected Writings*, 1942
John Steuben, *Labor in Wartime*, 1940
Charlotte Todes, *William H. Sylvis and the National Labor Union*, 1942
Alexander Trachtenberg, *History of May Day*, 1947
Eugene Varga, *Two Systems*, 1939

www.ingramcontent.com/pod-product-compliance
Lightning Source LLC
Chambersburg PA
CBHW020629230426
43665CB00008B/99